Hegel's Quest for Certainty

SUNY Series in Hegelian Studies
Quentin Lauer, S.J., Editor

Hegel's Quest for Certainty

Joseph C. Flay

State University of New York
Press • Albany

Published by
State University of New York Press, Albany

© 1984 State University of New York

All rights reserved

Printed in the United States of America

No part of this book may be used or reproduced
in any manner whatsoever without written permission
except in the case of brief quotations embodied in
critical articles and reviews.

For information, address State University of New York
Press, State University Plaza, Albany, N.Y., 12246

Library of Congress Cataloging in Publication Data

Flay, Joseph C., 1932–
   Hegel's quest for certainty.

   (SUNY series in Hegelian studies)
   Bibliography: p.
   1. Hegel, Georg Wilhelm Friedrich, 1770–1831.
2. Certainty—History—19th century. I. Title.
II. Series.
B2948.F54   1984   193   83-18139
ISBN 0-87395-877-2
ISBN 0-87395-878-0 (pbk.)

10 9 8 7 6 5 4 3 2 1

To Bonnie

CONTENTS

Preface .... (vii)
I   The *Phenomenology* and the Quest for Certainty 1
II   Sense-certainty and Philosophy 29
III Interest as Intentionality 51
IV Interest as Desire 81
V   Interest as Purpose: Observation 113
VI Interest as Purpose: Action 137
VII Interest as Reflection: True Spirit 163
VIII Interest as Reflection: Culture 183
IX Interest as Reflection: Morality 207
X   Interest as Reflection: Absolute Spirit 227
XI The Absolute Standpoint: A Critique 249
Notes 269
Bibliography 413
Indexes 441

PREFACE

ALTHOUGH THE MAJOR PORTION of the present work contains analysis and interpretation of Hegel's *Phenomenology of Spirit*, its concern is with the whole of his philosophical system. As the title states, I am concerned with Hegel's quest for certainty, i.e., with his attempt to show warranty for his claims to have access to the truth about reality. In what follows in this brief preface, I will first explain what I mean by this quest for certainty and how it is related to the general philosophical project of our western tradition. Then I shall offer a brief outline of my view of Hegel and his quest.

The project of a quest for certainty is not the invention or discovery of Hegel. From the pre-Socratics to Hegel's own time, the question of justifying one's right to make and defend claims of access to ultimate truth was distinguished from the question of articulating and defending that truth. The task of philosophy, accordingly, could be divided into at least two projects: the first was to prove or establish the degree to which 1) one can have access to the unconditioned and to ultimate truth about reality; the second was to articulate, on the grounds of the warranty already established, the truth so far as it is accessible to us. In other 2) words, the pursuit of philosophy involves within itself a preparation for that pursuit. And although attention is often paid mainly to the second task—that of articulating systematic truth in so far as it can be articulated—in order to understand the philosophy of the thinker in question, the first or preliminary project is not to be ignored; for it is through the initial quest for certainty of access to truth that the foundation for the systematic presentation is laid. Thus, Parmenides in the Proem to his poem offers an allegory which presents us with a journey undertaken in order to leave "the paths of men" and to come into the presence of a goddess who gives us the truth; Socrates in the Platonic dialogues constantly challenges the professed certainty of his interlocutors in order to come to some understanding of even the possibility of claims to truth; in various ways, *credo ut intelligam* served to satisfy the demands of this quest for medieval philosophy and, of course, modern rationalism and empiricism were centrally concerned with the quest. The modern tradition which led to Hume's treatise and inquiry and thence to Kant's *Critique of Pure Reason* establishes the proximate tradition in which Hegel's *Phenomenology of Spirit* of 1807 stands, a tradition which goes back to the beginnings of western philosophy. The system proper which Hegel then articulated constituted the second task of philosophy; the sciences of logic, nature, and spirit focus on the "complete speech," a speech based on the legitimacy established in the *Phenomenology*.

The general argument of my present work depends upon the relationship between these two tasks of philosophy. The general relationship is such that the outcome of the quest for certainty establishes the degree to which one has a *right* to claim *access* to ultimate truth. If one finds that access is limited in specific ways or because of specific problems involved in cognition, then only those truth claims are to be taken seriously which do not violate these limits. If, on the other hand, the outcome of the quest is the establishment of absolute or unconditioned access to ultimate reality, then all claims to truth, made on the basis of the successful quest for certainty, are to be entertained and examined. Hegel's claim is the latter. Therefore, if it can be shown that Hegel indeed establishes through the *Phenomenology* the absolute warranty he professes to have acquired, one must then turn to the system itself and examine the detailed working out of absolute or unconditioned truth. If, on the other hand, the *Phenomenology* can be shown to fail in its attempt to establish warranty for claims to an absolute standpoint, the whole of the system which follows is thrown into question and must be held in suspension until the standpoint can be established in some other way. Furthermore, if it can be shown not only that Hegel does not establish the sought-after warranty, but also that there is something in his quest which shows that one cannot *in principle* reach such an absolute standpoint, then one is forced either to reject Hegel's system or to rethink the problems of philosophy by taking into consideration the critique which the examination of the *Phenomenology* has established. This last alternative is the outcome of the present work.

I am attempting here to offer a criticism of Hegel's system, not by opposing him in some external way, but by taking seriously his quest for certainty. I do not think that this way through Hegel has yet been accomplished; and in an age in which we are told by some not only that Hegel finished philosophy, but that philosophy is itself at an end, it is important to accurately understand what this pivotal thinker did or did not do. I shall attempt to show, by means of a sympathetic interpretation and reconstruction of the *Phenomenology*, that by Hegel's own standards the outcome of his quest for certainty of access to reality is flawed. Mine is certainly not the first critique of Hegel's claims to absoluteness, but as I shall try to establish both in the text itself and in the notes, it is the first extended critique which criticizes Hegel in a strictly dialogical-dialectical form, and thus the first extended critique from within the Hegelian position itself.

In Chapters One and Two, I analyse the general nature of Hegel's quest for certainty and show how it differed radically from the quest as previously undertaken in the tradition. In Chapter One it is shown that

Hegel neither pitted philosophy against the natural, everyday attitude as various forms of rationalism traditionally had done in order to establish the privileged position of philosophy, nor limited philosophy to conditions immediately laid down by that natural attitude, as had the various forms of empiricism. Rather, he undertook to show in his quest for certainty that the standpoint of philosophy as absolute access to ultimate reality is to be found within the everyday natural attitude itself. The progress through the *Phenomenology* is thus not so much the transformation of the natural attitude as it is an exploration of the depths of the natural attitude. In what may be called Hegel's "archeology," he thus putatively overcame the distinction between empiricism and rationalism by working within the natural attitude itself and by finding there the absolute standpoint which would give warranty for the claims of absolute idealism.

It is for the purpose of accomplishing this task that a unique epistemic dialectic is developed in the *Phenomenology*. This dialectic involves a dialogue of sorts between the philosophical and the natural attitude. Chapter One ends with a discussion of this method as I have attempted to reconstruct it within the framework of the logic of presuppositions uncovered by British and American philosophers in recent years.

In Chapter Two I take a closer look at the relationship between the natural and philosophical attitudes by discussing the first section of the *Phenomenology*, the section titled "Sense-certainty." It will be seen there that the discussion of sense-certainty is not a discussion of perception or of sense-perception in particular, or even of our faculty of sensibility as such, but rather a discussion of the certainty which putatively belongs to common-sense, i.e., to a natural attitude which considers philosophy and its quest for certainty perverse (*verkehrt*). Here we will discover the way in which Hegel has begun his task by taking seriously the claims to certainty made by individuals in the unreflective, natural, everyday attitude. Hegel begins dialectically in the traditional way, rather than by contentiously confronting common sense. We will come to understand through this analysis of Hegel's beginning just how he took up the quest for certainty in a uniquely dialogical manner despite the apparent monological character of the *Phenomenology*. For the dialectic can be reconstructed to work as a dialogue between the thematics of the natural attitude and the praxical presuppositions which lie buried in that attitude and in the praxis carried out. What is demonstrated—again in a classical dialectical manner—is that the putative presuppositions are not adequate to the real world experienced in natural, everyday experience. We will also uncover here in Chapter Two the concrete way in which interest structures our every contact with the world and with ourselves.

Once the true nature of the natural attitude has been uncovered and its praxical presuppositions and interest-bound structures have been revealed, we can turn to the reconstruction and analysis of the *Phenomenology*. In Chapters Three through Ten I trace Hegel's quest for certainty from its beginnings in the acceptance of a simple, unreflective natural attitude which rejects philosophy and its claims, to a point at which that natural attitude finds itself in agreement with the claims of absolute idealism. This journey will take us through successive layers of praxical presuppositions, each of which in turn proves inadequate to the actual experiences of the natural attitude, until we arrive at the absolute standpoint and access to those presuppositions which are adequate to the natural experience. Throughout this "review" of the *Phenomenology*, the only intention will be to reconstruct what Hegel accomplished. My goal is to show to what degree the *Phenomenology* succeeds in its task.

In the final chapter, I will look back over the journey to the absolute standpoint and will argue that one very important presupposition of the natural attitude itself has been left unexamined, a presupposition which will be shown to be illegitimate and which will invalidate the whole notion of a quest for certainty as Hegel and the tradition had conceived it. It will be argued not that this failure entails a simple rejection of Hegel and the tradition, but rather that it gives us a clue to a direction to be taken by philosophy, a direction which has already emerged in several post-Hegelian philosophies. The result, then, is not simply a critique of Hegel and the tradition, or a call to the end of philosophy, but the establishment of a foundation for post-Hegelian philosophy. In the end the present work is meant to be as much a look at our own philosophical condition as it is a critical appraisal of the past.

A remark is required concerning the extensive critical notes. My text has been written so that it can be read without any reference to the notes, although an important side of my project will be lost if the notes are ignored. For they do not expand on points made in the text, but rather are concerned with reflections on the tradition of secondary literature. I have never read a work on Hegel, small or large, from which I have learned nothing. My reflections are meant to present both criticism of other views and an acknowledgment of insights I have gained from them. The notes thus serve as an ongoing dialogue with others who have attempted to grapple with Hegel's philosophy. In this dialogue, I have for the most part concentrated on works written between 1950 and 1980, although there are a few from earlier years and a few more recent than 1980. The upper limit is there, not because nothing of import was written after 1980, but because one must stop at some point and write a final text. All translations in the notes, unless otherwise stated, are my own.

This book has been a long-term project. If compared to the first "version" written some 15 years ago, it would be almost unrecognizable in its present form. I hope this now-published version is the best of my attempts. In such a long-term project, acknowledgements are due to many. My notes serve in part such a purpose. In addition to that, I thank Richard L. Doll and Robert V. Graybill for their help in my philosophical beginnings. I will be forever in debt to John M. Anderson and Henry W. Johnstone, Jr., who were first my undergraduate teachers and then later my colleagues. I wish also to thank my colleagues Alphonso Lingis and Carl Vaught for their friendship and for constantly reminding me that there is life after Hegel. The Hegel Society of America has been the source of friends, the source of constant education, and a sounding board for my ideas. My thanks are also due to Thomas Magner and his support through the various research funds of The Pennsylvania State University; to Cordelia Swinton and the librarians and staff of Pattee Library who made the long hours in the library over the years much easier and much more pleasant than they might have been in other circumstances; to Claire Davies who typed the original text for this final version; and to Bill Eastman and his editorial staff for their help and patience.

Finally there are four to whom my special thanks is due. John E. Smith has, over the years, been an important source of moral and intellectual support. John McDermott has been both a friend and a faithful believer in what I was doing, even though it would be difficult to find a more committed anti-Hegelian. In terms of the present book, Quentin Lauer has been of great value in advice and support he has given me and, as editor of the series, has seen me through some difficult times. I am also deeply indebted to George Kline, who read with the greatest care and critical insight the penultimate version of the present book. We have philosophical disagreements, and I did not always incorporate fully his suggestions, but the text is better for the care he gave it. The deficiencies, of course, are wholly mine. Finally it is to "the Hegel widow," my wife, that I dedicate this book.

I have written this book in the hope that not only Hegel specialists, but also fellow philosophers who know something about Hegel and have gone on in their own way in philosophy, might share my insights into Hegel.

I
The Phenomenology And The Quest For Certainty

ONE OF THE RECURRING themes in the literature on Hegel is the question of the proper interpretation of his *Phenomenology of Spirit* of 1807.[1] The problems of interpretation encompass questions about theme and method, both of which I shall address in the present chapter. I shall attempt to show that, whatever else the *Phenomenology* may present us with, at the heart of Hegel's own conception of his task was the endeavor to make a proper beginning for a comprehensive philosophical system. Hegel conceived of this proper beginning as constituted by a quest for certainty of a particular kind, a quest in which he was to seek warranty for truth-claims made in his philosophical system. That is, if one is to offer a systematic account of the ultimate nature of reality—and this was Hegel's main task— then one must first show one's indubitable right to make truth-claims of an ultimate sort or, in more traditional terms, one must first show that one has access to that domain in which such ultimate truths are found. The problem is to establish warranty for one's certainty of access, rather than merely professing such certainty.

This is fundamentally a problem of beginning; for if a philosopher is to articulate basic truths about reality, he cannot rely for verification on anything more basic than these truths. This means that at the very moment he begins, some sort of warranty for truth-claims must already have been established. Otherwise claims made about reality will either be groundless or be something to be taken on faith, and neither of these is acceptable. One might of course deny either that there is access to such a domain of truth, or that such a domain exists; but to make either of these assertions of denial is to maintain access to a basic truth about reality, and one must still therefore pursue a preliminary quest for certainty. Anyone who knows the history of philosophy will recognize that the vision of such a task for philosophy was an ancient one; but in Hegel's unique solution to the thematic and methodological problems involved in its undertaking he altered radically the traditional notions about this basic quest for certainty.[2]

It is of course true that for Hegel, as for many others, the warranty or validity of claims made within a philosophical system depends upon criteria internal to that system and cannot depend upon external sources.[3] But this response to the question of warranty assumes answers to a host of other questions. Why is external proof of a system illicit? By what right can this claim for proper criteria within the system be made? What internal criteria are proper and why are they proper? How are we to settle counter-claims by others who have developed different criteria? In short, what gives one philosopher the unique right to claim his criteria valid for all?

One answer, popular especially since the Renaissance, is that method is the only way to truth and that this is to be shown from within the system itself. In Hegel's case this method is that of dialectic, and implies a need to agree with the often made claim that the real beginning of Hegel's system is in the *Science of Logic*. But the question remains: Where are we to find proof that "the proof that dialectic is the only way to truth is to be shown from within the system itself" is itself a valid claim? If one must simply resolve to begin, or to begin with a leap of faith, then one is beginning in a way unacceptable to Hegel and others in the tradition.⁴

It is precisely these difficulties and this problem—the problem of giving a non-question-begging proof for the warranty of one's truth-claims—that moves Hegel to the realization that a *Phenomenology of Spirit* is required in order to begin philosophy.⁵ The *Phenomenology* is a quest for certainty which is to establish certainty by introducing and showing warranty for claims to be made within the system which is to follow. This is not only made clear in the *Phenomenology* itself, but is reiterated much later in the mature system.⁶ As late as Hegel's revisions to the *Science of Logic* in 1831, he insists that the

> concept of pure science and its deduction is . . . presupposed in the present work [i.e., in the *Science of Logic*] in so far as the *Phenomenology of Spirit* is nothing other than the deduction of it (*WdL*, I, 30; *SL*, 49).

He further explains that this entails that the concept of science and its validity claims

> cannot be justified in any other way than by this emergence in consciousness [which is demonstrated in the *Phenomenology*], all the forms of which are resolved into this concept [of science] as into their truth (*WdL*, I, 29; *SL*, 48).

What his discussion of the relationship between the *Phenomenology* and the rest of the system amounts to is a clear and unequivocal view of the *Phenomenology* as a "deduction" or justification of the *standpoint* assumed in the system and from which claims to truth could be warranted. It is here, therefore, that Hegel attempts to show what absolute idealism is and that it is *the* standpoint from which we can, with *already demonstrated* warranty, articulate the ultimate truth about ultimate reality.⁷

That this is the nature of the *Phenomenology of Spirit* of 1807, and just how the quest for certainty is constituted so as to avoid question-begging, must now be shown in more detail. But if the more detailed case can be made, then several theses about the *Phenomenology* and about Hegel's system lose their validity; for it follows that the *Phenomenology* is not a substitute for the systematic articulation of truth found in Hegel's system of philosophical sciences, nor is it an early, youthful, or "existential" version of that system.[8] It is, rather, a work which has a task that is separate from, yet absolutely necessary for, the system of philosophical sciences. It is *separate from* the system because the problem of demonstrating that one has a right to explicate truth is radically different from the problem of actually carrying out that explication of truth. On the other hand, it is *necessary for* and thus intrinsic to the task of a systematic explication of reality because without such a demonstration, one's claims about reality are all simply professions or mere asseverations of certainty, equal but not demonstrably superior to the claims made by others. Without the demonstration that one way of articulating the truth is the only authentic way, we are left with a relativism of opinion; and if we were not to separate that demonstration of warranty from the actual articulation of the truth, we would be embarking on a systematic articulation of reality before showing our right to do so. A brief look at the tradition behind Hegel will further clarify the problem and will introduce a more detailed discussion of Hegel's vision of the quest for certainty.

Early in the historical-philosophical dialogue,[9] the task of demonstrating warranty was sometimes articulated in mythical or mystical terms. Parmenides in his Proem tells of a journey which took him far from the paths of men and, through several legitimating episodes, into the presence of the goddess of truth. Pythagoras and the Pythagoreans claimed the need for a purification in order to be able to grasp the truth. In a more rational, discursive vein, Plato presents to us Socrates and his interlocutors in a quest for certainty which explicitly demands that one show one's right to make claims about reality. But the literary and mythical still remain, for the allegory of the cave in the *Republic* is a most pointed literary device for the preliminary quest for certainty which must be undertaken before achieving a warranted standpoint. For later classical and Christian thinkers, on the other hand, the task of originally achieving warranty had simply to be given up (as in the case of radical skepticism), or else required faith in God (*credo ut intelligam* in its many different versions).

But it was in the modern period, when "first philosophy" became epistemology or needed to be epistemologically grounded, that a full and explicit attention was given this logically first task of philosophy.[10] The

Cartesian meditation and systematic account of the search for a single truth which was in principle indubitable, a task which had to be complete before any credence could be given metaphysical claims; the Lockean suspension of discussion until the limits of reason could be determined; the Spinozist emendation of the understanding and perfection of the second and third kinds of knowledge; the Humean treatise which ended by showing the failure of philosophical thought in its quest for certainty; the Kantian critique of reason: all exemplify the methodological centrality of this quest for certainty as a separate question, a separate task, but one which was necessary. And all demonstrated the difficulty encountered in undertaking the project. Thus, Hegel's theme in the *Phenomenology* finds itself squarely in the historical-philosophical dialogue of the West. It is one more attempt to do what it had been clear had to be done, if warranty were to be established for truth claims concerning the ultimate nature of reality.

It was precisely the difficulties previously experienced in the tradition which finally moved Hegel to break off his early attempts at a system and to begin his system with a *Phenomenology of Spirit* meant to capture the elusive warranty for validity claims in philosophy.[11] Convinced that he lived at the beginning of a new epoch,[12] he set out to accomplish what he thought Kant and the tradition had failed to do: to establish warranty for a certain idealistic claim and to show that other philosophical claims as well as the claims of the natural, non-reflective attitude of our ordinary consciousness were inadequate to the task of reaching the truth about reality.

Several specific difficulties and demands emerge even from this sketchy and merely suggestive discussion of the quest for certainty. First, although it may be granted that it is necessary for a proper beginning for philosophy, the quest for certainty must itself begin somewhere. How is this to be accomplished without in turn begging the question by assuming a direction to be taken in the quest? Does not one already assume something philosophical and thus some particular position merely by insisting on beginning a quest for certainty? Second, it has already become evident that there are and have been many versions of this quest. How is one to begin this quest again without begging the question with those who have engaged in it before? How does one legitimately establish the need within the historical-philosophical dialogue for yet one more attempt? Third, it is not merely the philosophical tradition which is problematic here, but also common sense and the natural, unreflective attitude which sees no need for philosophy and its undertakings and in fact considers philosophy perverse. How is one to begin the quest for certainty without arousing legitimate protests from the natural attitude which, after all, is being told implicitly or explicitly that it does not have warranted certainty about reality?

Three demands must be met in order to satisfy these difficulties, and Hegel is very much aware of all three. He shows this when he undertakes to begin the *Phenomenology of Spirit*, itself an introduction to philosophy, with (1) a preface, (2) an introduction, and (3) a first chapter titled "Sense-certainty." In these three sections he attempts to overcome the three vicious circles involved in the three questions raised in the paragraph above: he mediates and thereby justifies his own beginning in this quest for certainty through (1) a grasp of his own place in the tradition, (2) a grasp of the conditions which must be fulfilled in order not to violate the legitimate claims of the natural attitude to have access to reality all by itself, and (3) a proper beginning to the quest which starts from the natural attitude in its most pure and unreflective form, that form which Hegel calls "sense-certainty." He also develops a method which alone will enable him to avoid all three forms of question-begging.

In the remainder of this chapter the precise nature of this mediated beginning and mediating method will be discussed in order to expose the uniqueness of the *Phenomenology of Spirit* as a quest for certainty, and to demonstrate the non-question-begging grounds of its claimed self-validation.

Two themes which appear in the Preface and Introduction to the *Phenomenology* together mediate Hegel's entry into his quest for certainty. One is the theme of his relationship to the historical-philosophical dialogue (including, as well, his relationship to the contributions of his own contemporaries); the second is the theme of his relationship to the natural attitude of ordinary everyday consciousness. It is important to recognize these themes as central to Hegel's task and as his means of furnishing a *mediated* beginning for his own quest for certainty; for Hegel is not claiming, as did Descartes and others, that he is making a new beginning in philosophy, a fresh start. Rather, he understands himself as in continuity with both the philosophical tradition and the natural attitude of ordinary, non-reflective consciousness.

On the one hand, Hegel uses the Preface and Introduction to bring into focus the theme of the quest by means of a discussion of the tradition and its results for the present (1805) philosophical climate.[13] This discussion specifies the "space" or "place" from which he himself philosophizes. His is not a simple historical discussion, however, for if it were, it would be "external" to the real work of mediating his own beginning, i.e., it would be merely an indication of the boundaries of his thought, merely a statement of what his own position is not. Rather, Hegel attempts through a discussion of the antecedents and of the contemporary matrix of philosophical thought to display and clarify the way in which the beginning proper of his quest in the *Phenomenology* is not only related in some way to other philosophical thought, but actually grows out of that previous thinking and out of the thought of his own time.[14]

Second, this Preface and Introduction also articulate the way in which the second theme, that of the relationship between the natural attitude and philosophy, is connected with the first and thus with the beginning of the *Phenomenology* as growing out of the tradition.[15] This delicate but firm connection was reflected upon years later when Hegel discussed the relation between the *Logic* and the *Phenomenology* in the 1831 Preface to the Second Edition of the *Logic*. There he argued that

> the need to occupy oneself with pure thought presupposes that the human spirit must already have travelled a long road; it is . . . the need of a condition free from needs, of abstraction from the material of intuition, imagination, and so on, of the concrete interests of desire, instinct, will, in which material the determinations of thought are veiled and hidden. In the silent regions of thought which has come to itself and communes only with itself, the interests which move the lives of races and individuals are hushed (*WdL*, 12; *SL*, 34).

Most simply put, Hegel's theme here is to focus on the relationship between the natural and manifold interests of the attitude present as one pursues one's everyday tasks and, on the other hand, the interests of philosophical reflection exemplified as the philosopher pursues the questions of philosophy and the ultimate ground for the intelligibility of "reality." In the former set of interests we are concerned with various objects and events thematized by us out of the totality of what-is. These are the concerns upon which we consciously focus and which are for us objectively and independently in the world, or are given in our thoughts and feelings concerning our relation to that world. Our concern is with situations which form our immediate world and with which we must cope. On the other hand, although philosophers often begin with reflection on such interests as these, they usually seem to move on to a set of interests which stand in stark contrast with the former. These are the philosophical interests in which those of everyday life seem to be silent, as Hegel puts it: still there, but quiet, not actively shaping the activity of the philosopher.[16]

This second theme, which is struck time and again in the Preface, generates Hegel's unique response to the need for a quest for certainty. In the tradition as well as in Hegel's own time, there existed a state of alienation between the everyday concerns of human beings, on the one hand, and philosophy, on the other. As Hegel phrased it, philosophy seemed to be the esoteric possession of a few individuals (*PhG*, 16-17; *PhS*, 7). And this separation of the two seemed not to be a matter of accident, but rather a state of affairs called for by philosophy. One of the claims made by philosophers was that one had to leave behind the concerns of the everyday and the interests of these finite activities in order to enter into the domain of truth, the home of philosophy. Or, if one pursued a more "empiricist" tack and gave credence to the everyday, one seemed to be denied access to a pure philosophical domain. From the "releasement" of the Pythagoreans and the ascent of Parmenides to the domain of truth, onwards to the intellectual love of God in Spinoza; from the ascent of Plato's prisoner out of the cave, to the domain of the absolute accessible through aesthetic or intellectual intuition: this alienation of philosophy from the natural attitude of our natural consciousness of the world constituted the constant character of philosophy. Not only in these obvious cases, but as well in Descartes who had to retire to the quiet of the country to still the moral and political concerns which would interfere with his meditations, and in Locke, Hume, and Kant who demanded that we hold or suspend judgments until we find the limitations of human judgment through philosophical reflection, the opposition and alienation remained. The interests and concerns of our everyday lives is with things and events which are finite and concrete and immediate; the interests and concerns of the philosopher are abstracted from this, an "absolute" or "idea" or "psychological constitution" which supposedly underlies and makes intelligible those ordinary concerns and interests but which nevertheless is, or at least seems, quite inaccessible to the natural attitude. Thus, in the tradition, if one wished to participate in philosophy, one had to adjust to and somehow intuit or otherwise grasp the general standpoint of philosophy. And whether this was accomplished in some immediate way or through the mediation of grace or some act of belief, the separation from the standpoint of the natural attitude was just as decisive.

The task of justifying one's claims, then, came to be identified with the task of justifying a turn away from the natural attitude: the unconditioned which was sought, but not always to be found, was simply not accessible to the natural attitude which had always to concern itself with conditioned or finite events and objects. From "the Good" of Plato, to the God of the Christians, the epistemological turn of Descartes and the British empiricists, and the transcendental turn of Kant, that unconditioned was the vital center of philosophical interest. It was to serve both as a justification for the separation from the everyday and as a self-warranty for the validity claims of philosophy.

Hegel took exception to the way in which this quest for certainty had been carried out in the tradition.[17] In his reflections on the tradition he not only objected to the separation of the natural attitude from philosophy, but also went on to articulate in a positive way two demands which had to be met if philosophy were actually to justify its claims. The following text, focusing on the relationship between philosophy and the natural attitude, both situates Hegel in the tradition and among his contemporaries, and specifies his own task as it is to be differentiated from that of the traditional quest for certainty.

> Science on its part requires that self-consciousness should have raised itself into [the pure domain in which philosophy thinks] in order to be able to live—and [actually] to live—with science and in science. Conversely, the individual has the right to demand that science should at least provide him with the ladder to this standpoint, *should show him this standpoint within himself.** His right is based on his absolute independence, which he is conscious of possessing in every phase of his knowledge; for in each one, whether recognized by science or not, and whatever the content may be, the individual is the absolute form, i.e., he is the *immediate certainty* of himself and, if this expression be preferred, he is therefore unconditioned *being*. . . . Let science be in its own self what it may, relatively to immediate self-consciousness it presents itself in an inverted [or perverted, *verkehrte*] posture; or, because this [natural] self-consciousness has the principle of its actual existence in the certainty of itself, science appears to it not to be actual, since [natural] self-consciousness exists on its own account outside of science. *Science must therefore unite this element [of self-certainty] with [science] itself,** or rather show that and how this element belongs to it (*PhG*, 25–26; *PhS*, 14–15. *Italics added).

Essentially two demands are made here which characterize the quest of the *Phenomenology* as different from and yet rooted in the tradition. On the one hand, Hegel rejects the traditional form of the quest for certainty, i.e., the separation of philosophical from natural consciousness, on the grounds that natural consciousness has its own rights which cannot be violated. In one's everyday activities one has, in principle if not always in fact, self-certainty, certainty that one has access to reality and that one's interests and daily projects either succeed or fail in an ultimate context of that reality. In view of this, philosophy has no *prima facie* right to claim that natural certainty is unjustified or misplaced or, on the other hand, that the claims of philosophy are justified and validated against those of the natural attitude.[18] In an immediate confrontation of the two attitudes where their respectively claimed rights are asserted, each is simply perverse (*verkehrt*) in the eyes of the other. And yet, on the other hand, Hegel is also convinced that philosophy not only has *its* rights, but also that it has progressed in the course of the historical-philosophical dialogue to a point at which it can claim legitimately to be scientific knowledge and need no longer be merely a love of or quest for this state of *epistēmē*. The brilliance and uniqueness of his position in respect to the task of justifying this claim of philosophy is shown in the two new demands which he has made in respect to the *Phenomenology*, demands which are to satisfy the claims of both the natural attitude *and* the philosophical, and at the same time to establish the legitimacy of the absolute standpoint of absolute idealism.

On the one hand, the *Phenomenology* must show that the absolute standpoint claimed by absolute idealism lies *within* the natural attitude itself; on the other hand, it is to be shown that the natural, and ultimately self-justifying certainty *which belongs originally to the natural attitude* belongs in the same way to the philosophical. That is to say, the experience which occurs in the course of the *Phenomenology* is to establish the *unity* of the experience of the natural attitude with the experience instantiated within the absolute standpoint of absolute idealism. Contrary to the difference and separation established by the tradition, Hegel sets himself the task of bringing about a unity. This does not mean that the natural attitude is to be absorbed by or reduced to the philosophical. Rather, it is the absolute standpoint which is to be shown as *implicit within the natural attitude itself*. What is actually at stake is the attempt to remove the mutual alienation of natural consciousness and philosophy—the mutual sense of perversity and inversion each has for the other—and the demonstration of the actual, living, experienced relationship between philosophical reflection and the natural attitude.[19] Neither the transcendence of rationalism nor the retreat of a skeptical empiricism is to be encountered here.

Thus, one does not leave the natural attitude behind in order to pursue philosophy; according to this first demand, one is to philosophize from the heart of that natural attitude itself. Nor is the philosophical quest defeated by the demands and criteria of the natural attitude. In this way the second demand, the demand that it be shown that natural certainty belongs to philosophy, is also satisfied.[20] In fact, as implicit in or presupposed by the natural attitude, the absolute standpoint will be the fullest actualization of that natural certainty which belongs to our everyday interests, an actualization that will *certify* the natural certainty and the everyday, ordinary interests "which move the lives of individuals and whole races of men." The quest for certainty in philosophy will serve to ground natural certainty, not to deny its value.

In dealing with this theme of the relationship between philosophy and natural consciousness Hegel thus mediates his own beginning in the quest for certainty.[21] By demanding that the claims of the natural attitude concerning its certainty be satisfied, his reflection here in the Preface both connects itself to the natural, non-reflective, non-philosophical interests we have in the world, and situates his thought in respect to the tradition in a critical manner. He does not offer an external reflection on the differences between his own and other thought, or between philosophy and the natural attitude, but rather articulates a concern which links all three together: absolute idealism, the tradition of philosophy, and the interests of the natural attitude are all united in the quest for certainty.[22]

This total mediation of the quest for certainty and its beginnings thus resolves one of the most troublesome questions about Hegel's philosophy. It has traditionally been argued that the beginning of the *Phenomenology* (and thus the beginning of the system, however we interpret this) presupposes the absolute idea and the stance of absolute knowledge.[23] And there is *prima facie* evidence that the beginning of the system does presuppose the end and thus that the system is circular. In addition to explicit statements by Hegel, the circularity seems unavoidable in a systemic way once one asks why and how the dialectic of the *Phenomenology* advances through the various stages of the work. Either the "we" of the *Phenomenology* or else some historical nexus is the bearer of the advance; and an individual in a particular mode of the natural standpoint remains relatively ignorant of the continuity of his own epistemic framework with preceding and succeeding frameworks. To the latter, the *Phenomenology* appears as internally discontinuous; to either of the former there is continuity because of the pre-emptive assumption of the absolute standpoint. So the usual argument goes.

The problem with this is that, if the view is correct, the system is circular in a vicious way and the quest for certainty begs the question; for Hegel would assume the absolute standpoint from the beginning, thus acquiring a prescience in respect to the "elevation" of natural consciousness to philosophical consciousness. If this were the case, then the *Phenomenology* would be "rigged," and Hegel would therefore not have fulfilled the two demands of the quest we have just reviewed; for he would not have respected the "rights" of natural consciousness, rights which he himself has declared inviolable.[24] But these rights must be respected if he is indeed to demonstrate to the satisfaction of an individual in the natural attitude with an *initial* hostility to philosophical claims (1) that the certainty of the natural attitude is present in the absolute standpoint and (2) that the categories of the absolute idea as comprehended from the absolute standpoint are implicit in even the most naive mode of the natural attitude.

If we look at the way in which Hegel formulates his task and mediates his beginning with a reflection on the natural attitude and the historical-philosophical dialogue, the problem of vicious circularity is solved. To begin with, Hegel understands himself to be addressing problems which the tradition has generated. I have already noted above that by 'historical-philosophical dialogue' I do not refer to some well-ordered, systematic account of philosophy from an historical viewpoint, but rather to a concern with that history as something which happened on the face of the earth, the event of philosophy itself in which Hegel as a young philosopher imaginatively participated. Hegel philosophizes on the basis of his own intellectual intercourse with the tradition, on the basis of his understanding of the problems of the tradition and of its failures and successes in dealing with these problems. The problems of the tradition in turn, as we shall see below, were generated by problems in the natural, unreflective attitude.

Now there is no doubt that the *problem* of the absolute standpoint, of a standpoint or vantage point or state of consciousness from which ultimate truth about reality could be acquired, had been a problem for philosophy from the very beginning. The obverse of the tension between the natural and philosophical attitudes is the problem of attempting to establish this standpoint for philosophy. This is indeed the essence of the quest for certainty and, as I have already argued, Parmenides' access to the goddess, the entry of Plato's prisoner into the sunlight, Augustine's relationship with God, Descartes' indubitable first principle, the "sound foundation" sought by Hume and Kant, all speak to this problem. Nor can it be doubted or denied that the fundamental content, once one achieved such a standpoint, was to be taken to be something which eventually had come to be called "the idea" or "the absolute idea."

The point is that what is presupposed by Hegel at the beginning of the *Phenomenology* is not the absolute standpoint and absolute idea as an epistemological position and metaphysical unity; what is presupposed is the *problem* of the absolute standpoint and the *problem* of the absolute idea. These problems are not Hegel's invention, furthermore, but have been inherited by him from the tradition in which he self-consciously stood.

Now there is a world of difference between assuming an answer to a problem before one begins, and then allowing that *answer* to shape one's thought *a priori* and, on the other hand, deliberately assuming some problem as central to the work of thought and allowing that *problem* to shape the work *a priori*. The former involves one in a vicious circle; the latter does not. And there is not a single thinker, philosophical or other, who does not begin with the assumption of a problem which structures his work; for without such an assumption of a problem, the thought would have no structure at all, but would consist only in random reflections.[25]

Hegel's discussions in the Preface and Introduction (1) of his contemporaries, (2) of the natural attitude and its view of philosophy as existing in a *verkehrte Welt*, and (3) of the various methodologies employed by philosophers—especially that method which seeks to emulate mathematics and its external procedures—all point to his effort to situate us in the *problem* proper to the *Phenomenology*. The quest for certainty is thus not made out of whole cloth by Hegel, but situates itself in the natural attitude and in the quest for certainty. The Preface and Introduction do not so much offer us a negative critique of these matters, as they present a critical discussion of the way in which the problems arose for the tradition and now arise for Hegel.

We can now bring to completion this present discussion of the theme of the *Phenomenology* as it is given us through the mediation of the Preface and Introduction to that work. The theme is the quest for certainty or for the absolute standpoint. This theme is taken up as a problem, and by means of a discussion of how this problem emerges from the philosophical tradition and from the natural attitude and its antagonism toward philosophical thought, Hegel offers us a mediated beginning to the *Phenomenology* and his own quest for certainty. Second, given the problems of the absolute standpoint and of the absolute idea, the *Phenomenology* itself is then to give us mediated access to the system of philosophical sciences which will professedly articulate the absolute idea both in an abstract form in the *Science of Logic* and in concrete form in the *Sciences of Nature* and the *Sciences of Spirit*.

In his discussion of this in the Preface and Introduction Hegel not only begins philosophy without begging the question, but also introduces us to certain demands which are to be placed on the *Phenomenology* proper in order successfully to gain access truth in the traditional absolute sense of that term.[26] (1) We are to take up the two problems as we have inherited them from Kant and the tradition. Kant and his contemporaries stand as the "last speakers" or "last participants" in the historical-philosophical dialogue, and therefore stand as those to whose contributions we are to respond. This means, of course, that we must also respond in such a way as to take into account what led up to Kant and German idealism and thus, as Socrates would say from time to time in the dialogues, "remember what was said before".[27]

(2) If the ancient problem is successfully to be resolved, we must show (a) that the natural certainty which belongs to the natural, unreflective attitude of our everyday consciousness of the world also belongs, and in

a fully warranted manner, to one in the absolute standpoint; and (b) that the absolute standpoint and its content—the absolute idea in its fully explicit development—is implicit in the natural attitude and gives the latter its ground. Thus, the *Phenomenology* does not begin in an intellectual or historical vacuum, but is a philosophical response to the tradition and has certain well-defined responsibilities to the natural attitude and therefore to common sense and the everydayness of our experience. That is to say, Hegel's thoughtful participation in philosophy and its problems is presupposed as the mediation for the beginning of the quest for certainty of the *Phenomenology* proper, as is also his concern for the satisfaction of the demands of ordinary reason and experience as they are found in the natural attitude. *Mutatis mutandis*, our own participation in that same tradition and with those same concerns for the everyday is also presupposed as a minimal condition if we are to enter authentically into Hegel's thought.[28] Our beginning is with the tradition and in the natural attitude, not with some theory or presupposition of Hegel's own invention.

(3) The *Phenomenology of Spirit* does not involve us in a vicious circle. There is a circularity involved only in so far as we have a pre-understanding of the problem to be thematized in this work and in the system as a whole. But this sort of circularity is one which issues every time some well-defined problem sets the parameters for what sort of answer or explanation is to count as satisfactory. If we are to condemn this kind of circularity, then we condemn all inquiry which begins with a question or problem thematized as the problem to be solved or the question to be answered.

If we now turn to the beginning of the *Phenomenology* proper we shall see more concretely how this thematized problem takes form when structured by the two demands discussed earlier. The beginning of the *Phenomenology* proper is focused upon a natural attitude called by Hegel "sense-certainty." This form of the natural attitude is the most unreflective of all modes, an attitude which takes certainty to be, in principle if not in fact, always achievable: one need not in principle seek certainty because one is always already at the standpoint from which absolute contact with reality is acquired.[29] Sense-certainty is a mode of experience or an attitude which counts sense experience, i.e. the immediate and pure experience of life, to be fully warranted in terms of certainty. This is not to say that in this attitude it is assumed that in fact we are always certain or that our certainty is always in fact warranted; it is rather to assume that in principle we have real and adequate contact with reality which, with care, will suffice to establish warranted certainty. Hegel begins, then, with an examination of the kind of natural attitude which is furthest removed from the reflective and critical attitude in which a philosopher finds himself. In this way, as we shall see in our discussion of dialectic and in the analysis of sense-certainty in the next chapter, Hegel begins in a classically dialectical manner by accepting *as putatively valid* the claims implicit in this naive attitude of sense-certainty. This procedure follows the demands of the Preface and Introduction which we have just analysed, demands based on the claim that common sense and the natural attitude have certain claims to self-certainty and about our access to reality which must be taken into account if the *Phenomenology* is to avoid a question-begging procedure and the alienation which had resulted previously in the tradition. Hence, instead of placing the everyday, natural attitude *against* philosophy as had been common since the pre-Socratics, Hegel begins with an *acceptance* of its claims. Yet he also has in common with the tradition, as we have seen, a focus upon this most natural of all attitudes as something which must be addressed critically. Both acceptance and criticism must inform this encounter with this first attitude.[30]

A preliminary reflection will show why this beginning point is correct, whatever form the confrontation takes. The first and most obvious reason is simply the fact that sense-certainty is the way in which we indeed do live out most of our conscious life. This natural attitude in its most unreflective state and structured for the most part by habit dominates our everyday practical lives, where access to reality is simply taken for granted. In the unreflectiveness of this attitude there is no *conscious* distinction between self and world, nor between physical facts and events and institutional facts and events within that world. The world or reality, as Hegel puts it in the opening passages of the section, is there in all its breadth and depth and is there for the taking. But more precisely, one does not even actively take it; the "taking" just happens. Consciousness is just that: the full content of whatever is present is the natural and unreflected thematic of our experience. Thematization is automatic, and there is no self explicitly present, no intentionality, no distance; only "this" and "that." The claim to certainty and to the possession of reality and meaning is so immediate and all-pervasive in sense-certainty that the claim itself is usually not worth thematizing, not worth mentioning. Therefore, in principle, certainty is taken for granted; and when *in fact* that certainty is shaken—whenever one turns out to be wrong about something and becomes aware of error—it is usually not certainty of access to reality that is brought into question and made thematic, but only the present, factual instance. A mistake does not imply for sense-certainty that there may be a problem with certainty in principle, and a consequent need for a quest for certainty; there is only recognition that in some one instance one *happens* to be wrong. This is precisely the natural certainty to which the individual has a natural right and which Hegel had already defended in the Preface.

However, this first and most obvious reason for beginning with sense-certainty—namely that it is the natural attitude in its most fundamental and ubiquitous form and that it harbors within it that natural certainty which is a natural right—is not by itself a sufficient justification for beginning here. If we were to look to other forms of the natural attitude, be it some form structured by desire in which the self is central or some form of purposive, rational activity in which reason itself or the concrete content of some science is thematized, the same certainty would be discovered, albeit as present in a more reflective way. But this qualification about "reflectiveness" is a clue to the second reason for beginning with sense-certainty rather than with another form of the natural attitude. In any other mode of the natural attitude, certainty has become to some degree problematic, not only in fact, but in principle. In the total naivete of sense-certainty, on the one hand, access to reality, truth, and meaning is supposedly had without reservation, without limitations of any sort. In any other mode, on the other hand, it is recognized that somehow there are limitations to the absoluteness of this certainty. In conscious and deliberate perceptual acts, for instance, one assumes access only to that which is perceivable; in understanding something non-material, only to that which is intelligible in abstraction from physical reality. In purposefully rational activities such as scientific investigations, one realizes that there are certain procedures to be followed if warranty is to be granted to one's findings and that without these prescriptive parameters, there is serious doubt about what is supposedly discovered or formulated. All of these modes of the natural attitude presuppose that some form of a quest for certainty has already been undertaken in order to establish warranty to some degree.

Thus, there is always in the above examples some degree of reflection mixed with the unreflective natural act of facing one's project in the world, while the naive realism of sense-certainty is completely unreflective in its approach to the world.[31] This situation makes it the only defensible beginning given the project which Hegel has taken on; for in that unreflectiveness and immediacy of certainty and in its implicit claim that there is no need for a quest for certainty through some sort of reflection (i.e., in its claim that certainty is not problematic), there is a rejection of the whole of the philosophical project of self-reflection and *proof* for certainty- and validity-claims of all sorts. This unreflective, immediate attitude therefore confronts any discussions which assume that certainty is in principle problematic as discussions by philosophers who live in a private, *verkehrte Welt*, and assesses such discussions with a contempt fitting the presence of such absurdity and perverseness.

In light of this, both Hegel and the tradition understood that if philosophy were not simply to be another unreflective perspective on things, it would be necessary somehow to deal with and differentiate itself from this naive attitude. But Hegel, as we have seen, demanded more; for if philosophy were not to be dogmatic and question-begging, if it were to proceed with a reason and a rhetoric concerned with truth and demonstration, then one must *first* show that certainty is in principle problematic, and thus that the themes of philosophy as well as its methodology and its quest for certainty are not absurd, perverse, or idle. In Platonic/Socratic terms, knowledge that one does not know must precede the possibility of positive knowledge; certainty that one is uncertain must precede the possibility of the establishment of true certainty. If something resists this initial movement—as sense-certainty does *par excellence*—and if what resists is fundamental to the human condition itself—as sense-certainty is—then it must be shown to one in that basic attitude that certainty *is* problematic. In other words, if one does not begin by *demonstrating* in a discussion with this form of the natural attitude that the philosophical problem is a real human problem (and not merely a figment of the philosopher's imagination), then philosophy has violated its own principles of reason and demonstration; for the philosopher has begun by assuming, against the counter-assumptions of the natural attitude, that certainty and the absolute standpoint are problematic.[32]

The basic reason for beginning with sense-certainty, then, is that by doing so one first demonstrates, before attempting to resolve the problem of certainty and truth, that the question of access to truth and the need for a quest for certainty are legitimate and objectively establishable problems; and secondly that the natural attitude of sense-certainty is connected with the philosophical quest for certainty. The only thing assumed is that an individual in the attitude of sense-certainty is willing to become reflective to the extent that he becomes aware of the nature of his attitude toward reality. For the firm convictions of the natural attitude in its unreflective state must be encountered on their own terms, and only subsequently can philosophical reflection be justified on grounds recognized as valid by one in the natural attitude. That is to say, Hegel's quest is grounded in the need to begin by establishing as a legitimate *human* concern the problem of the absolute standpoint and the absolute idea which he has inherited from the tradition. He presents himself and philosophy with the task of first showing to ordinary consciousness that the concerns of philosophy are not simply intellectual exercises for "useless" philosophers, but of direct relevance and importance to the very natural certainty on which everyday consciousness implicitly depends.[33]

This "second" beginning of the *Phenomenology* thus fixes from the start a framework in which the demands articulated in the Preface and

Introduction can be satisfied.[34] Because the initial appeal is made to the certainty of sense-certainty, it is this certainty and not that of the philosopher which will bring about the dialectical progress of the quest for certainty.[35] If the program of the *Phenomenology* is successful, then that natural certainty will be found at the end to reside in the absolute standpoint. Second, since we have begun with the natural attitude in its most unreflective state, and since that natural certainty will be put at stake and will furnish the nexus for argument, we shall in effect be intent on the task of grounding that certainty and thus of showing that the absolute standpoint is to be found within the natural attitude itself. This commencement in sense-certainty is therefore neither arbitrary nor accidental. The philosopher escapes entrapment in a vicious circle by accepting dialectically the claims of sense-certainty and by building on these claims. And by affirming along with sense-certainty the attitude which is most removed from the focus of philosophy, one begins by bringing the problem of certainty out of its deepest recesses in the human condition.[36]

A closer analysis of the section on sense-certainty therefore becomes necessary if we are clearly to understand how Hegel attempted to accomplish his dual task. But before entering into that, it will be useful to look more closely at the question of the nature of dialectic as it appears in the *Phenomenology*. For the remainder of this chapter, I shall offer a preliminary analysis of this dialectic and of the way in which it operates on the two levels of concern, i.e., that of natural certainty and the natural attitude, and that of the quest for certainty and the problem of the absolute standpoint.

The dialectic of the *Phenomenology* is difficult to grasp unless one has first understood the general theme of the work and the way the work begins.[37] The reason for this lies in the nature of dialectic itself. From the time dialectic began to play a part in philosophy, it was not seen simply as a method to be applied externally to some content or other. Rather, it was to have a basis in reality itself or in that aspect of reality which was being addressed. Thus, to understand dialectic as a mode of reasoning which is separate from its subject-matter and which exists primarily in the mind of the thinker, has always been considered by its philosophical adherents as a false view. Dialectic is, on the contrary, the "way" of the subject-matter itself. It is not Socrates who refutes an opinion or who makes doubtful the certainty with which an opinion is first expressed. The opinion, when examined for its sense, meaning, and truth, shows itself to involve contradiction, inconsistency, or absurdity; and the professed certainty with which one began slowly deteriorates as the examination proceeds. The "gift" offered the Prisoner when he is released from his chains in Plato's cave is a freedom and ability to interrogate the reality he has heretofore taken for granted, and to inspect the opinions which he and his fellow prisoners previously held to be true. The dialectic is not brought externally to the opinions and appearances; it occurs within them and reveals itself to our inspection. As often as Socrates is accused of making the better appear the worse and the worse the better, or of being a Proteus and confusing the issue, he responds by insisting that he has not moved or changed or manipulated, but that the opinions themselves are the unstable element and give the lie to themselves. No more than an actual midwife determines the degree of health and beauty of the child, does the Socratic midwife determine the degree of fecundity and truth belonging to an opinion. Both only bring their "charge" into the world to be seen and judged by all.[38]

Thus, if dialectic belongs in this way not to the thinker as a tool, but is what emerges in the process of inspection, then what is thematized makes all the difference. One does not begin positivistically with the positing of definitions, postulates, methodological dicta, etc., and then apply them to various subject-matters, but begins, rather, where the subject-matter itself begins. In the case of Platonic dialectic this usually meant that one began with some opinion offered to Socrates. In so far as what is thematized in Hegel is different—and in so far as within the Hegelian corpus the thematic varies or is transformed—the dialectic will also be different. We are now in a positon, therefore, in which we want to understand the dialectic in order further to throw light on the overall theme; while it is through a pre-understanding of the theme of a quest for certainty that we are able to begin to explicate the dialectic.

But problems seem to appear at the very beginning of an attempt to penetrate the dialectic as the movement of the subject-matter itself. I have argued thus far that the theme of the *Phenomenology* involves us with the problem of unifying two modes of human experience, that of natural, unreflective consciousness and that of philosophical consciousness. This unification, for reasons already given, is to be accomplished in such a way that the natural, unreflective attitude will be revealed as carrying within itself, in tacit form, the kinds of elements which make up philosophical reflection. It has become clear that if this is to be accomplished without begging the question, then one must begin dialectically, i.e., with an *acceptance* of the standpoint of the natural attitude.[39] If, however, that standpoint is characterized primarily by its non-reflectiveness, then how can one ever progress beyond it? In the natural attitude one thematizes objects, events, other persons, one's own feelings, etc., but never the standpoint itself from which these thematizations proceed; this is what constitutes its non-reflectiveness. But the standpoint within which we confront the objects, events, etc. is just that in which the philosopher is interested. How, then, can a beginning be made without violating the natural attitude and thereby aborting the task of the *Phenomenology*? This was the question which Hegel faced initially; and his resolution of the problem is perhaps the most unique aspect of his philosophy.

Hegel's resolution of this problem concerning the difference between the natural attitude and philosophy consists in beginning not with the actual, explicit content of the natural attitude alone, but with both this content and a description of the standpoint of the natural attitude as that standpoint emerges by a first reflection upon the natural attitude itself.[40] He begins, then, by thematizing both levels focused upon by the demand he placed upon himself in the Preface: the level of the standpoint of the natural attitude itself, and the level of what is thematized from within that standpoint. If we examine the relationship between the two thematics *as that relationship appears in the natural attitude itself*, we shall see how this can be done without violating the precept that we take the natural attitude of sense-certainty seriously. An examination of a representative activity will illuminate this relationship.

When one is looking for a book, thinking out a problem in mathematics, taking part in a political activity, participating in religious worship, or doing any one of the countless things one does in one's life, one focuses upon the relevant objects, events, or feelings. This is the natural thematization of the natural attitude. On the other hand, one simply and tacitly presupposes the standpoint from within which one thinks or acts. In most cases the presupposition involved here remains wholly unthematized; but it is nevertheless there as a presupposition, and can be elicited from one in the natural attitude if the occasion arises. For example, if I were looking for a certain book, I would be thematizing the many objects which come under my gaze as I carry out my search. I also would carry with me the anticipation that the book for which I am looking will in time appear as one of the objects. In such a situation there are different sorts of presuppositions at work which govern my rejection of many objects as not being the right object and my expectation that I will find the right book which I will then accept. On the one hand, there are existential or circumstantial presuppositions underlying my actions. I am presupposing that this is the room, or possibly the room, in which the book is to be found. I am presupposing that I know what it will look like when I see it, that my vision is adequate for the search, etc. If I did not presuppose at least these conditions, my search would make no sense. But there are further sorts of presuppositions. First, there are epistemic presuppositions: that vision will be adequate to finding the book; that when I think I see the book I will in fact be seeing it as it lies there in the room; that I could verify it as the proper book by opening it and reading certain passages; etc. In short, I would probably presuppose a simple realist position on perception, and a very simple theory of verification based on that theory of perception. Second, there are ontological presuppositions: that the book is a physical object accessible to my senses; that as a physical object it has certain ontological relations to other physical objects in the room; and so on. Such epistemic and ontological presuppositions are also required if my activity is to make sense and have any hope of consummation.

That I would actually be presupposing such things could be made clear if someone asked me what I was doing. So, for example, if asked what I was doing and why I was looking in this room, I would respond with the relevant statements justifying my search, statements which would make explicit what I thought that I was presupposing as circumstantial conditions governing my search. Questioned in another manner, I would respond with statements uncovering my epistemic and ontological presuppositions. Or, in another situation in which I finally give up looking for the book, I might say that I thought it was in this room, or that I'm sure it's not there because if it were I would have seen it, etc. In each of these cases what would be elicited would not be something which I had just made up for the first time, but something which actually reflected what I was previously presupposing and what I now thematize as having presupposed.

The importance of the presence of such presuppositions within the natural attitude is that the presuppositions putatively define the circumstantial, epistemic, and ontological *standpoint* from within which I focus on objects as I search the room for the book. The same would be true for any activity, whether it be a perceptual activity such as I have just discussed or some other, more complex activity. The standpoint from within which I worship my God, argue for my political candidate, or work in mathematics is *internally constituted* in terms of form or structure by just those presuppositions which are present in the activity itself. I therefore always have some standpoint and can be brought to think about that standpoint once I thematize the presuppositions as I think they exist in my activities. In addition, the standpoint, except for certain of the circumstantial presuppositions, would be identical in many other situations in which I was dealing with material objects or, *mutatis mutandis* religious, political, or intellectual activities.

The relationship between the two thematics—that of the objects and events focused upon by the natural attitude in its unreflective way and that of the standpoints involved in the above which are focused upon by the philosopher—as these actually exist in the natural, unreflective attitude is precisely the relationship which exists between a set of presuppositions and a set of activities which involve these presuppositions. Since philosophers are usually interested in general cases rather than specific cases, the circumstantial or existential presuppositions which constitute a standpoint are usually of little or no importance; one concentrates on the epistemic and ontological presuppositions. But these latter sorts of presupposition are no less involved in unreflective activities than are the circumstantial. Because these are all presuppositions of my activities, rather than being only linguistic or semantic presuppositions of some kind, I shall refer to them as '*praxical presuppositions*'.

The consequence of the presence of such presuppositions is that if one were to concentrate on these two thematics as related to each other in the presupposition relation, one could simultaneously deal with both without violating the rights of the natural attitude. In short, one would have a way of dealing with the subject-matter of the *Phenomenology*— a quest for warranted certainty concerning standpoint—by accepting both the world as thematized by someone unreflectively in the natural attitude *and* a putatively presupposed attitude or standpoint from within which that world is thematized, i.e. the standpoint which is of interest to the philosopher. The two thematics would then not merely confront each other as originating at two different sources, but would be related in terms of their content in the form of the presupposition relation. Sense-certainty could then be taken with complete seriousness, and yet transcend its ordinary posture.

Such a treatment of the relationship between the two thematics constitutes, I think, the foundation for the dialectic of the *Phenomenology*. We shall explore more fully in the following chapters the way in which the relationship between our everyday concerns of the natural attitude are involved with their epistemic and ontological presuppositions, and the way in which Hegel used this relationship for the completion of the quest for certainty concerning the systematic claims of his own system. But before engaging that substantive task, it will be useful first to discuss more fully the nature and logic of the presupposition relation and the way in which it is at its basis itself a dialectical relation.

Philosophical discussions of the past two decades have now made sufficiently clear for the purposes of our present discussion the nature of the presupposition relation.[41] There are, to be sure, disagreements on detail and variations in interpretation, but not to the extent that would damage the use to which that logic will be put here. I will call upon only what seem now to be non-controversial aspects of this relation, beginning with an intuitive definition of the relation followed by some examples, and then by an analysis of the relation in respect to its dialectical qualities.

I understand a presupposition or presupposition set (P) to be related to the states of affairs (S) which presuppose it in such a way that P contains or refers to a set of conditions or circumstances (C) which make the alternative meanings or possibilities belonging to S intelligible and relevant in respect both to linguistic claims made about S and to the appropriateness of specifiable activities found in S. A common example concerning meaning and truth-value claims will help clarify what is meant here.

The most common sort of situation referred to in the literature on the presupposition relation is one in which truth-value claims are in question in such a way that the presupposition relation becomes evident. For instance, let us say that the remark is made of some real person, Charles, that his children are intelligent. If this remark is both meaningful and relevant, and in this case could possibly be assigned a truth-value, then there must be a presupposition set in force which would contain as one of its elements the condition that Charles has children. If such a presupposition set were in force, then it would be possible to assign the appropriate truth-value; if not, then it would not be possible and there would exist a truth-value gap. However, on the other hand, this same presupposition that Charles has children would also have to be in force for another person relevantly to claim of the same Charles that his children were not intelligent. Therefore, both a situation and its opposite necessitate the same presupposition as an element of their respective presupposition sets. Thus, in general, if P is the presupposition and S the statement or situation that Charles' children are intelligent, while not-S is the statement or situation that Charles' children are not intelligent, then if P is in force, S *may* be the case or not-S *may* be the case. But if P is not in force, then neither S nor not-S could possibly be the case and there would be a truth-value gap in respect to S. Both S and not-S necessitate P among whose elements is C.

Several things need to be noted here. First, whether we are discussing statements referring to a situation or we are discussing the situation itself, the presuppositions necessitated are such that they have as their ultimate referent a set of circumstances or conditions which constitute the presupposition set. That is to say, we are referring not simply to statements or propositions which are about states of affairs in the world, but to those states of affairs which must be presupposed if the situation S (or not-S) is to be relevantly meaningful and have a truth-value or some other appropriate value. Presuppositions are not simply a linguistic concern. It is the actual presence in the world of Charles' children which is necessitated as presupposition in order for the children to be, or to be relevantly claimed to be, intelligent or not intelligent.

Second, there is a difference between a presupposition being in force as necessitated, and one's belief that that presupposition is in force. If someone believes (or would believe upon reflection if asked) that a certain presupposition is in force, then that belief is itself either true or false. It is true if the circumstances to which the belief refers actually exist, not true if the circumstances to which the belief refers do not actually exist. So, for instance, if each of the persons discussing whether or not Charles' children are intelligent were actually to believe that Charles has children, but the truth were that he did not, then assignation of the presupposition would be unwarranted and the discussion would have no relevant meaningfulness. But if the children did exist, then the presupposition would be warranted and the discussion meaningful in a relevant way. Every presupposition held as a belief or possible belief is *merely putative* until it is established that the belief is either warranted or unwarranted. Thus, the putative presupposition may or may not be warranted. On the other hand, whether or not a set of presuppositions are held by anyone as putative presuppositions, those presuppositions are in force in the states of affairs which necessitate them.

It will be central to what follows now in the discussion of praxical presuppositions and their relation to the dialectic of the *Phenomenology* that we keep in mind this difference between putative presuppositions and presuppositions actually in force. If P is warranted, then either S or not-S is possibly the case. If either S or not-S is possibly the case, then P must be warranted. If P is putatively presupposed, then whether or not it is a warranted presupposition depends upon whether or not S or not-S is possibly the case. If the possibility (in a real and not simply logical sense) of S or not-S is a fact, then the P putatively presupposed must be such that S or not-S remain real possibilities. If they do not remain real possibilities under the putative presupposition of P, then the presupposition of P is not warranted.

The reason why the difference between putative presuppositions and presuppositions actually in force is central to our discussion is that there is in the logic of presuppositions a *normative dimension* which will actually be the motor of the dialectic. If we return now to the matter of praxical presuppositions or presuppositions which make our activities and our world relevantly meaningful, we will see that praxical presuppositions both prescribe certain possible worlds and proscribe other possible worlds, and that possible worlds when delineated prescribe that there be certain presuppositions in force and that there not be other presuppositions in force. If we take the set of possible worlds which we experience to be the real world, then certain presuppositions are necessitated and others proscribed. In this way we have a way of testing the warranty for any given putative presupposition or presupposition set. If the set is warranted and in force, then the real world we know in the natural, unreflective attitude of the everyday will remain possible. If the assumption of the putative presupposition set makes the real world and its manifold distinctions impossible, then the putative presupposition set is not warranted and must be discarded or altered in some way so as to find the proper presupposition set for the real world and the situations in it which we experience.

Consequently, a praxical presupposition set can now be understood as a set of conditions necessitated by the existence of the real (as opposed to the merely logical) possibility of a specifiable set of alternative states of affairs, possible worlds, or meanings involved in praxis. One can say that praxical presuppositions belong to praxis, as semantic presuppositions belong to sentences or statements. Individuals involved in various instances of praxis can be said to hold tacit beliefs about these presuppositions which can at times be made explicit. The belief, tacit or otherwise, putatively refers to the praxical presuppositions in force, and may either be warranted or unwarranted. If warranted, then the presuppositions putatively in force are actually in force; if unwarranted, then the presuppositions putatively in force are not actually in force. Because praxis is always constituted as the involvement of an actor with the world, the praxical presupposition set in force can be said to belong to the relationship which exists between the relata, e.g., between subject and object, actor and environment, thinker and what is thought, speaker and what is said. As constituent of these relationships, these presuppositions therefore transcend both respective relata in the sense that the presuppositions define the relationship between the relata. And it is in this sense alone that the presuppositions can be said to be transcendent. Praxical presuppositions underlie the relata as a foundation and can be said therefore to form the *a priori* synthetic unity of the constituents of experience. They therefore exist as the heart of the transcendental dimension of praxis, and as such define the literal standpoint within which one knows, experiences, and acts. They constitute the "geography" of the terrain across which one speaks or moves in action. They are in some sense pregiven for every individual, like language itself a storehouse of potential meaning. In another sense, however, they are highly individual: the general and individual sense of the existence of these sets is analogous to the linguistic distinction between *langue* and *parole*. Praxical presuppositions, and more precisely the set which is in force in any given praxis, are what grant appropriateness and intelligibility to that praxis.

We now have a sufficient notion of the relationship to see how it plays a part in the dialectic of Hegel's *Phenomenology of Spirit*. The logic of presuppositions enters dialectic by means of the normative nature of the presupposition relation. Two of the characteristics are especially relevant: (a) the presupposition set prescribes certain alternative situations as appropriate and proscribes others as inappropriate in the ways already discussed; (b) if the alternative situations are taken as determinative, i.e., as really and truly appropriate in the ways discussed, and if a specified putative presupposition set is articulated in relation to the alternative situations, then by the nature of the presupposition relation one can distinguish between a merely putative presupposition set and the actually required presupposition set.

The first point (a) is relatively self-evident from what has already been said; for the presupposition set functions as the determinant of the set of possible situations appropriate and intelligible, as well as of the set of possible situations that are proscribed as inappropriate and unintelligible in a relevant sense. Thus, if Charles does not have children, then in no circumstances can any individuals be identified as Charles' intelligent children or as Charles' unintelligent children; while, if he in fact has children, then there are circumstances in which individuals might be identified either as Charles' intelligent children or Charles' unintelligent children.

Second, (b), it might be the case that we take the situation in question as definitive or as unquestionably real and legitimate. In this case—and this is precisely how Hegel begins—we can distinguish among merely putative presuppositions related to the possibility of these situations those which would have to be in force if the situations were real, and those which could not be in force or which would not constitute an adequate set if the situations are taken as real. Since these presuppositions constitute the actual standpoint from within which we act and think, we can thus distinguish merely putative from actual standpoints. And since we are taking the situations to be definitive, we can actually decide which set of presuppositions is necessitated and thus which is the actual standpoint from which the situation is accessible. For instance, if a scientist were to make certain discoveries and then were also to claim that nothing but simple perception was presupposed in order to make these discoveries possible, we could then examine the discoveries and the activities of the scientist in order to determine whether or not the presupposition of perception alone would constitute a standpoint making the discoveries possible. If we could show that certain elements of the discovery and activity could not be assigned to perception as their source—for instance, some mathematical elements—then we would have shown his putative presupposition set to be inadequate or unwarranted, and that it must either be augmented or be abandoned completely.

We can now turn directly back to the concern of the *Phenomenology*. The dual thematic of that work involves nothing other than these two levels we have just examined in the presupposition relation. What is thematized in the natural attitude in its unreflective state are the situations we take as referents in real experience—the objects of knowledge, the goals of action, the surroundings involved in that goal, in general, the experienced — while what is thematized in the search for the absolute standpoint by the philosopher and presupposed by the natural attitude itself is the *standpoint* of the natural attitude. As to the latter, that standpoint involves contextual, epistemic, and ontological presuppositions which define the standpoint as a particular praxis; for the standpoint is the way of relating to what is thematized in that attitude. The standpoint is the relationship between experiencer and experienced, actor and environment, speaker and what is addressed, knower and what is known or what is knowable; and that relationship is, as we have seen, constituted by the praxical presuppositions which are actually in force in the situation.

If the situations are taken as definitive—i.e., if we assume that what is claimed in the natural attitude to be experienced, known, done, etc., actually exists as claimed—and if we can elicit from the natural attitude a presupposition set putatively in force, then the set can be tested for adequacy.[42] The presupposition relation thus articulates the interplay between what is thematized by one in the natural attitude and, on the other hand, what remains unthematized—the standpoint—but is thematized by philosophy. If the set which putatively characterizes the standpoint is adequate or fully represents the set necessitated for the intelligibility and appropriateness of our experience, knowledge, and action in the natural attitude, then we will have discovered, within the natural attitude itself, the absolute standpoint, i.e., *the* standpoint which gives us access to the world known and acted in. If the proffered set does not, on the other hand, it will be necessary to continue in our search for an adequate presupposition set which will give warranty for our claims of certainty of access to reality. By a careful reflection on precisely how the putative set has failed to grant us access to the standpoint from which we actually experience and know what we do, i.e., by reflection on what Hegel calls "the determinate negation," we shall be able to present a new putative set which will (1) have as part of it the claim that it compensates for the determinate lack or failure of the previous set, and (2) have within it what is now taken to be an adequate account of the noetic and ontological presuppositions required by the praxis taken to be definitive. There is here, then, a "dialogue" between the two levels.[43]

The critical dialectic of the *Phenomenology* can thus be characterized in the following way, abstracting for the moment from the detailed differences which will arise as the subject-matter develops. It consists of an analysis of a series of putative praxical presupposition sets, taken in relation to the situations for which they supposedly furnish the ground. The dialectical examination consists in discovering whether or not those situations *would be* what they *actually are if* indeed the putative set were the actually warranted set in force. If truth-value gaps, contradictions, inappropriatenesses and anomalies of various sorts occur within the situations where they should not, then the putative set is not adequate and is not the required set for those real circumstances which constitute our actual experience, knowledge, and action. Our formulation of the set must then be altered until a set is found which gives us the standpoint which grounds the possibility of the meanings and possible worlds which actually make up our experience.[44]

In the course of the *Phenomenology* there will be a variety of forms which the presupposition relation takes on; but the general description given here will hold. After the initial confrontation with the natural attitude in sense-certainty, in which it is demonstrated to the natural attitude that certainty is in principle a problem, praxical presuppositions will be generally characterized successively under four definitions of '*interest*'.[45] In the section on consciousness, interest is understood as *intentionality*, and the world in which we are interested as the world intended. The general presupposition is that by means of various capacities we have, the intended world reveals itself to our intentionality. But we will be led to the recognition of the general inadequacy of this notion of interest and of the presupposition sets that would constitute it, and turn to the definition of interest as *desire*. In the section on self-consciousness, the praxical presuppositions are taken as structuring an egocentric world. At this point it is maintained that we are partly conscious of the presuppositions in force as we develop "philosophies of life" through which we forcefully shape the world and reality in general to our desires. In this section the general attempt is made, in various ways, to claim that the absolute standpoint is to be found in our own self-consciousness and in the desires which determine our interests in the world.

The failure of this attempt to understand our circumstances as grounded totally in our self-consciousness will have led the natural attitude, originally unreflective in sense-certainty, to understand itself as deliberately and purposefully interacting with the world. It will have been led toward the thematization of its own standpoint and therefore to a position closer to the philosophical standpoint itself. In the following section on reason, both the "we" of the *Phenomenology* and the individual originally in the natural attitude observe how all individuals in the natural attitude are governed by explicitly recognized purposes which are deliberately presupposed and which in turn presuppose a world appropriate to such purposes. We come here to observe how interest as *purpose* actually demonstrates not only the standpoint of the natural attitude, but also the unity of that attitude with reality. The series of observations of rational activity on the part of human beings leads us to the fourth definition of interest, interest as *reflection*. In the long section on spirit the individual in the natural attitude discovers how in the tradition which has led up to his own real, historical world, praxical presuppositions were not abstractly transcendental or merely instinctive as presupposed in reason, but were actually embodied in the institutional facts of the world. Interest, or our standpoint and connection with and within reality, is now seen to be actually reflective. Our actual standpoint is concretized in historical, socio-cultural arrangements whereby we explicitly place before ourselves the presuppositions which grant the possibility of our circumstances as we know them. Our thematizations presuppose or take place within the socio-cultural formation which is publicly recognized as the standpoint of reality. But that standpoint is not simply a *prius*; for it is only through our activities that the institutional facts have existence. We are thus both creator of and participant in the standpoint which underlies and makes possible the praxis which constitutes reality. The ultimate form of such reflective interest is philosophy, in which the search for the ultimate presuppositions is conducted in the various forms which philosophy takes. Hegel claims, in the chapter on absolute knowledge, that our reflection on spirit has led us to this standpoint from which the ultimate presuppositions of our experience, knowledge, and action can be articulated. The actual proof that this is the case will be found in the system of philosophical sciences which follows from the *Phenomenology*.

This relatively abstract account of the course of the *Phenomenology* and its dialectic is necessarily lacking just because we have had to abstract from the actual subject-matter. In the next chapters we shall turn to the actual course of the project and more adequately investigate Hegel's claims to bring together the natural attitude and philosophy, and to furnish thereby a resolution to the quest for certainty and a proof of the validity-claims of absolute idealism.[46]

II

Sense-Certainty and Philosophy

THE OPENING DISCUSSION of sense-certainty is unique in terms of the dialectic of the remainder of the work.[1] We are concerned with a purely unreflective mode of experience, a certainty which trusts sensibility (in an undefined sense of 'sensibility') implicity and absolutely. What is said or thought or known or done is so in a purely immediate, unreflective manner. There is simply "what is going on," the pure facts, simple life. There is absolutely no conscious discrimination between different modes of experience. Things are there, events occur, the world is there, just as it is; and I think about it or know it or talk about it or experience it in the most unproblematic way. Knowledge and experience in general have the simplicity of G. E. Moore's view of the world in his proof of the existence of the external world, only it is more simple yet; for Moore's proof arose from the awareness of a problem with experience, while this unreflective, natural attitude is aware of no such problem. This is the mode of experience which is most difficult from the reflective experience of the philosopher, for the quest for certainty is literally of no concern to sense-certainty.[2]

As I discussed briefly in the last chapter, we begin with this mode of experience because it is unique, because it offers us the chance to show that the problems of philosophy form a legitimate problematic. What we are to begin with are the noetic-ontological praxical presuppositions which would be claimed for and by this most naive and trusting state of experience. To begin with, then, we are focusing not only on what is actually thematized in such an experience—the immediate objects and events which are the concern of an individual in this natural attitude—but also on the putative presuppositions of this experience. The "object" which is *our* object is not the object *of* such experience, but that experience itself, "immediate knowledge itself, a knowledge of the immediate or of what simply *is*"(*PhG*, 79; *PhS*, 58).[3] What then follows in the text and begins the dialectics is a description of how knowledge or knowing would be described in this unreflective mode of experience, if that description were to be elicited from one in the attitude of sense-certainty. And the description is an approximate articulation of the putative noetic-ontological presuppositioins of sense-certainty. The quest for certainty begins by taking up, not a description given by a philosopher, but one which could be elicited from a common-sense attitude which implicitly denied the need for a quest for certainty.

This set takes several forms, the first of which maintains that there is no distinction between one experience and another: experiences are indiscriminately just experience. In addition, truth and certainty are just there, and there is no distinction to be made between them. Nor is there to be presupposed any distinctive relation between I who know and the things which I know. Experience is simply what it is.[4]

This set represents the tyranny of sense-certainty, a complete refusal to be reflective; for what is involved thus far brooks no distinction between certainty and truth, between myself and what I know, or between instances of knowing.[5] This set would be implicit in a response, on the part of one in this attitude, to a question, "How do you know?", "What do you mean?", or "How can you be certain?", in which one is given the blank stare or the answer, "What is *your* problem, what kind of a question is that? I know, that's all."

But Hegel then points out that

> when we look carefully at this *pure being* which constitutes the essence of this certainty, and which this certainty pronounces [in its response] to be its truth, we see that much more is involved (*PhG*, 80; *PhS*, 59).

This is one of the most critical points in the whole of the *Phenomenology*; for it introduces a movement from simple and tacit acceptance of a presupposition set which allows for no distinctions between certainty and truth or between knower and known—in short, permits no interrogation of the *professed* warranty for the presupposition set—to a presupposition set which entangles naive consciousness in some distinctions which will open up the possibility of error and therefore a question of warranty for claims made. It will be necessary, therefore, to go into some detail at this point.[6]

What is thematized at the opening of this chapter is the most naive, common sense set of presuppositions.

> Because of its concrete content, sense-certainty immediately appears as the *richest* kind of knowledge, indeed a knowledge of infinite wealth for which no bounds can be found, either when we *reach out* into space and time in which it is dispersed, or when we take a bit of this wealth, and by division *enter into* it. Moreover, sense-certainty appears to be the *truest* knowledge; for it has not yet omitted anything from the object, but has the object before it in its perfect entirety (*PhG*, 79; *PhS*, 58).

Truth is completely accessible, both intensionally and extensionally. What is said here is of course not directly and immediately thematized by one in the natural attitude; it is what is supposed to be praxically presupposed by the natural attitude in the thematization of objects and events in the world.

At this point in the analysis we break off and, it would seem, begin a critique of this set of presuppositions. The sentence which follows the above description is: "But, in the event, this very *certainty* proves itself to be the most abstract and poorest *truth*" (*PhG*, 79; *PhS*, 58). What then follows, however, does not really constitute a critique; rather we are given an extension and reformulation of the presupposition set first offered for the natural attitude, an extension which would arise from the most simple sort of questioning addressed to anyone who had already, through interrogation, given the above description of the presuppositions of the natural attitude. What follows in the analysis points to a series of presuppositions which indicate that experience and knowledge have to do with particulars only. This presupposition is fundamental to the whole naive natural attitude, whatever its form. Again, we can make this clear by imagining what the response would be to certain questions. If asked, for instance, "How do you know that the table is there before you?", the answer would follow: "There it is; I know because it is there!" What is referred to here is the pure *thereness* of *it*, sheer presence of a particular, "pure being." The presupposition implicit in this answer is that particulars constitute reality. What is also indicated in such an answer is that *I* am certain, immediately certain; there is no process of thought, reasoning, or investigation presupposed, simply "I", confronting a particular, knowing it with simple certainty.[7]

The description given of this presupposition set is strikingly authentic when we remember that we are confronting one in the naive natural attitude who finds no real sense in philosophical questions such as "How do you know that the table is there?", or "How do you know that this is the book you were looking for?". The natural response is disbelief that anyone could ask such questions; and it is just this disbelief which reveals the presupposition set which is articulated now.

> I, *this* particular I, am certain of *this* particular thing, not because I, *qua* consciousness, in knowing it have developed myself or thought about it in various ways; and also not because *the thing* of which I am certain, in virtue of a host of distinct qualities, would be in its own self a rich complex of connections, or related in various ways to other things. Neither of these has anything to do with the truth of sense-certainty; here neither I nor the thing has the significance of a complex

process of mediation; the "I" does not have the significance of a manifold imagining or thinking; nor does the "thing" signify something that has a host of qualities. On the contrary, the thing *is*, and it *is*, merely because it *is*. It *is*; this is the essential point for sense-knowledge, and this pure *being*, or this simple immediacy, constitutes its *truth*. Similarly, certainty as a *connection* is an *immediate* pure connection: consciousness is "I", nothing more, a pure "This"; the singular consciousness knows a pure "This," or the single item (*PhG*, 79-80; *PhS*, 58-59).

Far from being a criticism or a view anathematic to the presuppositions of the natural attitude, this passage represents an eloquent attempt to articulate those presuppositions. It is the denial of any complexus such as a philosopher might suggest. Not only is it the case that whatever is is simply a particular and that I am also a particular, simple and immediate; it is also the case that what I say is true, is true simply because it *is* true. The "it *is*" refers us not only to the simplicity and immediate existence of a particular which I know with certainty, but also to the simple and immediate presence of truth and of the certainty that I have that truth. This constitutes the central element of the praxical presupposition set implicit in any instance of sense-certainty.[8]

Before continuing on to the first dialectical critique, it will be useful to look more closely at this initial situation; for there are some elements of this beginning analysis which are not made very explicit by Hegel, but which must be seen in order to understand the origin and force of the dialectic of the whole work as it is grounded in this beginning.

First, there is the fact that Hegel has insisted that our

approach to the object must . . . be *immediate* or *receptive*; we must alter nothing in the object as it presents itself. In *ap*prehending it, we must refrain from trying to *com*prehend it (*PhG*, 79; *PhS*, 58).[9]

This demand seems to present a difficulty which calls into question the legitimacy of Hegel's actual procedure here. Does he not attempt comprehension? How does the knowing, as opposed to what is thematized by an actual knower, present itself in any immediate way? If we are to get at the knowing itself or to experience as such, then we are certainly not going to have access by looking at or by experiencing what one in the natural attitude himself is experiencing. And is not this latter what is authentically immediate? If the individual is looking for a book, then sees it lying on the table, it is not the experience he is experiencing, not his stance or attitude, but the book itself. And yet we here thematize the attitude, the presuppositions which supposedly structure that attitude.

How can we say that that stance or those presuppositions present themselves to us immediately so that we merely apprehend? Is it not, at best, through the *mediation* of a questioning or of an imaginary questioning that we can have access to such a phenomenon as the knowing or the experiential stance?[10]

The answer to this series of questions as a whole must be a definite "Yes." But the presence of such mediation is not what Hegel has warned us against in his insistence on immediacy of apprehension, and does not betray the promise not to attempt comprehension at first. To be sure, reflection on my part is necessary if I am to question one in the natural attitude about his praxical presuppositions. This is true because *my* thematic in the *Phenomenology* concerns not only what one knows, but also the very act of knowing. The issue here can be clarified by reference to Plato's procedure in his Socratic dialogues. One could say that the *dialogical* constitution of the dialectics of Plato is superior to the constitution of Hegel's dialectics in at least one respect: by separating the questioner and the one questioned in the dialogical situation, Plato thereby distinguishes the element of pure immediacy or unreflectedness from the element of reflection and the desire to attend to what is not thematized in the immediate experience of the natural attitude. Plato thus preserves the purity of the unreflected and allows us actually to experience the movement from unreflectedness to reflection as Socrates and his interlocutors pursue their conversation. In the Hegelian case, on the other hand, the *monological* structure—at best an imagined dialogue between one in the unreflective attitude and the philosopher who critically examines the unreflective attitude—blurs the distinction between the two and necessitates a degree of care and augmentation on the part of the reader or hearer which is not present in the explicitly dialogical dialectic of Plato.

But the difference is clearly there in Hegel as well; for otherwise one could not explain the two radically different kinds of expression or thought attributed to sense-certainty (e.g., on the one hand the unreflective "Here is my house," and on the other hand the reflective "I, *this* particular I, am certain of *this* particular thing, not because I, *qua* consciousness, in knowing it have developed myself or thought about it in various ways").[11] Of course there is, ironically, a different danger in reading Plato, namely the lack of an awareness on the part of the reader of the significance of the fact that it is a dialogue which constitutes the dialectical unraveling of the truth, and that the truth therefore is not to be found only in what Socrates himself says, but in the exchange which constitutes the dialogue as a whole.

We must understand, then, that the *appearance* of knowing in its basic attitudinal structure can come only from a pre-determination on the part of the "we" of the *Phenomenology* to elicit it from the natural attitude.[12]

We do not initially thematize only what is known or experienced. As I have already argued in the last chapter, we must have already been immersed in the historical-philosophical dialogue and have the sense of the problematic of philosophy. The absolute standpoint and absolute idea must already be thematized *as a problem*. But these presuppositions which putatively constitute the natural attitude must be made to appear not only to us, but also to the phenomenal consciousness which is our object, and in such a way that the latter apprehends them as *implicit in his own knowledge and experience of the world*.[13] Thus, the authenticity of the presuppositions is of primary importance to this beginning. What is said to appear as the putative presupposition set must be a reasonable approximation to the kind of response one would receive in an actual interrogation of someone in the natural attitude who would still resist reflection.

These considerations can lead us to see to what the immediacy refers which Hegel invokes as necessary to our approach. He claims that we must limit ourselves to apprehension and restrain ourselves from trying to comprehend sense-certainty on our own, i.e., on philosophical terms. That is to say, what is required are not our own theories designed to explicate what first appears—an undialectical approach which would involve us in a comprehension from our own theoretical viewpoint and thus beg the question with the natural attitude—but an examination of what appears in the natural attitude *on its own terms*. Whatever explanation or analysis is to appear in this "dialogue" must originate in the natural attitude as the individual slowly reveals deeper and deeper levels of presupposition and hence of self-reflection. This is the remarkable strategy of Hegel which we can see more clearly now that we engage sense-certainty; for once the natural attitude turns upon itself in response to a dialectical prodding, it undergoes—at first against its own will so to speak—an investigation in which it will begin to comprehend itself and, in doing so, reveal to us that self-comprehension. This comprehension is *only facilitated* by us, and must actually be given through the dialectic itself.[14] This is the part that immediacy plays in the very first movement of the *Phenomenology*.

This understanding of immediacy also permits us to see more fully what was sketched in the last chapter concerning the nature of the dialectic in the *Phenomenology*. From the viewpoint of the "we," this originally given set is only putatively the adequate set; for we already accept the idea of a quest for certainty. The presupposition set *claimed* to be in force is not automatically warranted through the claim alone, but is either adequate or inadequate, i.e., either is or is not the authentic set. Whether the putative set elicited is adequate or not remains to be seen when the next level, the so-called negative or dialectical component, emerges. However, from the standpoint of the natural attitude of sense-certainty, the answer given is the unproblematic, final answer.

Implicit in this is a further distinction which must be clear if we are not to misconstrue Hegel. The *Phenomenology* aims at a knowledge of knowing. This means that what is at issue is not whether or not there is knowledge in the natural attitude, but rather whether or not the putative presupposition set for this knowledge is the actual set which grounds and makes possible the actual experiences of the natural attitude. The question concerns what *we* thematize in the *Phenomenology* and what is naturally in force as presupposition in the natural attitude, not whether what is supposedly experienced in the natural attitude itself is known or knowable. If someone in the natural attitude finds an object and says, "Here is the book I was looking for," our question is not whether or not he experiences the book he is actually looking for rather than some other object, nor whether or not he really experiences the book. It is not that sort of skepticism which motivates Hegel's enquiries here. Our concern is with the problem of what in fact is the adequate noetic-ontological presupposition set which makes possible these circumstances. The world claimed in the natural attitude is accepted by Hegel as real; what is in question is the imputed presuppositions underlying the knowledge of this world.[15]

Thus, when we take up the negative moment, the moment of questioning concerning the putative set, the statements and bits of knowledge claimed by the natural attitude are to be accepted as authentic. It will be by demonstrating the failure of the putative presupposition set to account for the possibility of knowing what is known—i.e., the trees and houses in the world—and of saying what is said, that Hegel will claim to demonstrate that the imputed set is not authentic.[16] As clearly as Kant or any empiricist takes what we know and what we experience to be authentic, so also does Hegel. The point is the traditional one, alive since the pre-Socratics, that I do not know what it means to know and to experience these things that I know and experience. This second point is further clarified by noting a third aspect of Hegel's analysis which is not made explicit by him at this stage in the *Phenomenology*.

The third point is that what is claimed thus far must be held to be adequate for the purposes of making distinctions made in the world which constitutes our actual experience. This means, then, that when the presuppositions are articulated, so also are the utterances, thoughts, and actions which play a typical role in the actual experience in the natural attitude. If, for instance, in the natural attitude one is able to distinguish immediately between various particular things, then the presupposition set must be so constituted as to make such distinctions both relevantly possible and appropriate. If it does, then in so far the set is adequate; if it does not allow for this, then the set as it is given is not adequate.

This third point leads to a fourth and final clarification which indicates the peculiar kind of force which dialectic has. This point will also reinforce the claim of a dialectician that it is not a mere external method imposed upon a content, but belongs to the content itself. Dialectic is always a circular affair, but does not have the character of a vicious circle. We have already seen that in Hegel's dialectic there is both an immediate element and an element which forces the immediacy into self-mediation. That is, the immediate, the situation which explicitly belongs to the natural attitude (e.g., "Here is a tree") forms the beginning of any proper inquiry. Such a situation is immediate in the sense that it is totally unreflective in respect to the grounds and processes of thematization of the tree and the statement that it stands here. Then, by imaginary or actual questioning, the person in the natural attitude is forced to become reflective, and his own imputation of the praxical presupposition set emerges. This is the element which forces the *self*-mediation of the immediate experience or knowledge. For what is in turn used to test the adequacy of the putative presupposition set is just this statement, and other statements like it, which *should* remain relevantly meaningful *if* the presupposition set is adequate. No standard is brought in from the outside in order to mediate. The claim of the putative set is that it makes possible the relevant intelligibility of these statements, situations, or actions which belong to our common experience; and the test of the claim is to see if it indeed *would* make possible such intelligibility.

In this way the individual in the natural attitude is forced to test his own pronouncements on the validity criteria for his statements. Thus, if this first set is found to be inauthentic, it is because it cannot live up to its own claims concerning the grounding of common experience. That from which the set was derived—the immediate experience of the natural attitude—is in turn the test for the warranty of the set. The philosopher, the "we" of the *Phenomenology*, is therefore actually no more than a Socratic midwife, and Hegel remains faithful to his pledge to permit only apprehension to rule our progress.[17]

If we keep these four points about the dialectic as it functions in this quest for certainty in mind, then the remainder of the opening exposition and critique of this first presupposition set, and the way that we are subsequently led to entertain a second putative set, will fall in place.

After articulating the putative presupposition set for the natural attitude, Hegel finds a lack in what has been given thus far. He indicates, as I have already discussed, that when we look more closely we find more involved than what has been thus far admitted. We find that the putative set involves distinctions between (a) experience or knowledge as such and instances (*Beispiele*) of either, and (b) the "I" and the "This" or the subject and the object. This "careful look," a substitute for further questioning in dialogue, reveals that it would also be claimed by the natural attitude in sense-certainty that there is a difference important to note between knower and known or between subject and object. This would be discovered simply by questioning whether or not one is ever certain—even absolutely certain—but later finds oneself to have been wrong. Anyone in the natural attitude would admit to this experience. Consequently, the original claim to an identity of certainty and truth, to a pure immediacy in this respect, is here amended. Although it is still claimed that knowledge is immediate and simple, it is also held that we do presuppose that certainty and truth, in fact if not in principle, are not always both identical in reference. But if this is admitted, it must also be claimed that a distinction is necessarily in force between the locus of certainty—the "I"—and the locus of truth—the "This." What is true is objectively and independently true; what I am certain of may or may not be true. Other elements of the set then emerge. The object as object not only always is whatever it is, it also exists independently of whether it is known by anyone. On the other hand, the possibility of knowledge depends upon the existence and the essence of the object and thus is not independent of the object. The presupposition set now emerges more fully as identical to the philosophical theory of naive realism.

The presence in the set of this distinction between knowledge of an object and the object in itself marks the first major development in the relationship between the natural and the philosophical attitude;[18] for it is now admitted by the natural attitude that certainty and truth are distinct. This will eventually lead us to see that, starting from the natural standpoint itself, certainty will become *in principle* problematic.

The second new distinction, that between essence and example or instance, is also critical to the formation of the presupposition set and to the course of the *Phenomenology*. As the distinction presupposed between subject and object implicates us in an ambiguity of difference and identity between the two elements and thus in a problematic gap between the two which concerns whatever functions they involve, so also the distinction between experience or knowledge in general, stripped of all contextual, purposive, intentional, and other details and thus the essence, and on the other hand specific instances of experience and knowledge, also imposes an identity-difference element. One has now to admit on a "horizontal" level that there is both a unity and a discontinuity of experience. Instances of knowledge follow one another and differ in specifiable ways and thus are separated from each other. At the same time they are all simply parts of "my" experience and are thus continuous and form an identity.

It is on the basis of these two distinctions which are added to the original set, and which will continue into further sets, that the space-time problems which now enter will occur. The indexical distinctions "now/then," "here/there," "this/that," and "I" (uttered at different times by different persons and at different times by the same person) range over both the instances of experience and the essence of experience. The indexical nature of experience also becomes a problem in terms of the subject-object distinction as it is presupposed in the sets now given from the natural attitude. How this is we shall see in the further examination of this set and the subsequent sets of sense-certainty.

A presupposition set has been evoked, then, and it is one which we can loosely identify as naive realism, both epistemologically and ontologically. The major elements of the set are that what exists are particulars which stand in an immediate and simple relationship to each other, without mediation through each other or through universals; that these particulars also stand in an immediate relationship to the knower, although there is a possible discrepancy between certainty and truth; that, on the other hand, certainty is to be warranted by the thing appearing for the knower, and thus that certainty and truth are in principle identical; that there are many particulars, but that this has no bearing on knowledge; that the subject or knower plays no active role in knowledge and experience, but is only passive and receptive, and thus depends wholly upon the object for truth. The question now is: If we were to limit experience and knowledge to appropriateness criteria determined solely by this presupposition set, would we have the actual knowledge and experience that we have in the natural attitude? Does our sense-certainty itself validate this imputed presupposition set? An answer to this question takes us to the second moment of the dialectic, the comparison between appropriateness as it is actually given in experience and, on the other hand, as it would have to be given according to the proffered presupposition set.

In what now follows in the next few paragraphs of Hegel's text, it is shown that ordinary statements about particulars as explicitly thematized in the space-time continuum of the natural attitude would make no relevant sense under such restrictions. I could not distinguish between this and that, here and there, now and then. The very particulars which supposedly make up the "truth" of reality and which are easily grasped in the natural attitude without the least bit of reflection or trouble, become elusive when I restrict myself to experience as it would be constituted by a presupposition set such as has been articulated. What are in fact relevantly appropriate and intelligible statements in ordinary experience become inappropriate and unintelligible when under the constitutive rule of the presupposition set which characterizes naive realism. It is not that we cannot be certain and know that trees and houses are before us, or be certain and know what time of day it is; on the contrary, we can, and this is just the point. What we *can* know, and *do* know with certainty in the *natural attitude, could not* be known and *would not* be known *if* the actual noetic-ontological presupposition set *were what it has been claimed to be* in this first examination. Instead of the particulars which we in reality have in the natural attitude, we would now have only abstract universals such as "now" and "tree." Therefore it is the putative praxical presupposition set which is wrong and not warranted, not the experience and knowledge we actually have.[19]

With this the *Phenomenology* has properly begun; for the quest for certainty is made a necessity for the natural attitude itself. This inadequacy of the putative presuppositional ground claimed for and by the natural attitude stands in stark opposition to the natural certainty that belongs to knowledge and experience in the natural attitude. It also stands in opposition to the warranty for that certainty which is taken for granted by the unreflective natural attitude. What is to drive the phenomenological analysis and the quest for certainty, then, is not simply a philosophical eros for the truth, but also the natural certainty of the natural attitude which is now faced with its own uncertainty generated by an examination of its own supposed presupposition set. At this moment there is an initial unification of the certainty of the natural attitude with the philosophical quest for certainty of the tradition and of Hegel; for what must be discovered is the true and warranted presupposition set in force which justifies and warrants the natural certainty implicit in the natural attitude.[20]

If certainty is to be warranted, then we must articulate a new set of presuppositions which will give us the situations and possible worlds we actually experience. The question is, how do we go about finding it once the naturally elicited set is shown not to be adequate? In this question we have the first explicit agreement between the philosophical and the non-philosophical. This naturally evoked unity between philosophy and the natural attitude breaks down the initially given suspicion which exists between the two attitudes, the suspicion of each that the other is perverse (*verkehrt*). In the progress of the *Phenomenology* this unity of the two will become more and more explicit precisely because the work has begun with a dialectical acceptance of the terms of the natural attitude itself in regard to its own certainty. This is what makes this work radically different from one oriented toward skepticism; for with the latter, the initial task is to throw doubt upon the claims of the natural attitude, thereby alienating from itself the natural attitude.[21] In the case of Hegel, however, it is through the natural attitude itself that the positivistic attitude of ordinary consciousness is to be subverted. The original putative presuppositions which we have just analyzed have come to subvert themselves. At the same time, then, dialectic is implicitly recognized by the natural attitude as legitimate. This experienced failure of the presupposition set initially proffered by the natural attitude is the key to all further progress.

This initial subversion of the natural attitude—to make it reflect upon its own putative presuppositions—alone makes possible the move to the third moment of the initial dialetic. What is necessary at this point in the analysis of sense-certainty is a clear grasp of the reasons why the realist presupposition set failed to make possible the kind of experiences and knowledge of which one has natural certainty in the natural attitude. For at this point both the natural attitude and philosophical reflection must thematize what is never made thematic for the natural attitude in a stance of sense-certainty. This occurs in the form of a comparison between the original claims for the presupposition set and the result of attempting to limit reality to what it would be if the realist set were adequate.

> When we compare the *relation* in which knowing and the object first came on the scene, with the *relation* in which they now stand in this result, we find that it is reversed (*PhG*, 82-83; *PhS* 61; italics added).

What constitutes the beginning of the third moment of the dialectic here is a comparison between the initial claims for the adequate presupposition set (the relation between knowing and the object, between what is thematized in the presupposition set and what is thematized in the natural attitude), and what must be a corrected set in view of the results. When we assumed that what was actually presupposed was the realist doctrine that certainty has its locus in the sheer presence of particular objects which merely give themselves to the passive subject, the sheer presence of those particulars eluded us. What was lacking and what would fix this or that particular, it can be seen, is to take account of what "I meant" in looking for the book, pointing out this house, etc. Certainty must be somehow located in the actual intentions of the knower. Thus, we in fact must presuppose that one's intentions or meaning locates the particular as a particular. The subject or knower is accordingly not to be understood as simply passive. In fact this analysis posits that we are to locate certainty and its warranty wholly in the subject's intentions.[22]

Thus, we have now to articulate another putative set, one which we can contrast with the first and which I would call a "native idealist" set. The crux of this set is that certainty becomes warranted through the intentions of the "I," i.e., in what I mean when I say, "This book is the one I have been looking for." After articulating this set, Hegel then says that we must look "to see what experience shows us about its reality in the 'I' "(PhG, 83; PhS, 61).

The examination then proceeds as it did in the case of the realist set. Statements, experiences, and bits of knowledge and action which are appropriate and relevant in the natural attitude, are taken up as the test for the authenticity of this naive idealist set. And it is likewise discovered that under this new set of putative praxical presuppositions the appropriateness of the statements, experiences, and actions of the ordinary natural attitude vanishes: distinctions between particulars which can in actual experience be made would not be possible *if* this idealist set were the authentic set. Nor could the 'I' which denotes me at different times or which refers to different persons be clearly identified. Yet in fact experience gives us no such trouble. Again, then, the inference is made that therefore this set must be unwarranted, and we are moved to find the correct set in terms of what, upon reflection, is seen to be determinately lacking in the naive idealist presupposition set as it has been articulated here.

Before continuing with the third and last set considered under the rubric of sense-certainty, we must be clear about what has happened now as a result of the examination of the idealist presuppositions. What was introduced as a result of the first complete dialectical movement was a tension between experience as given in the natural attitude and the imputed warranty for that experience which was to lie in the presuppositions elicited from the natural attitude. The relation between the two levels was at first one of non-tension or matter-of-fact acceptance on the side of the participant in the natural attitude, and one of tension on the part of the philosophical interlocutor. In contrast, at the end of the first movement (naive realism) and the beginning of the second (naive idealism), the difference between the natural and the philosophical altered in such a way that the non-tension of the natural attitude became a tension of the sort one has when a "mistake" has been discovered in something claimed in a factual manner. The presence of the "mistake" in this case led the natural attitude participant to thematize the presupposition set which seemed to be necessary in order to correct this "mistake." However, this was done in such a way that the presupposition set still had no primary importance in the order of things. The natural world thematized in the natural attitude still retained primacy, and the articulation of the presuppositions was intended simply in order to bring it into accord with the world of particulars of the natural attitude. The articulation of the idealist set was presented, from the viewpoint of the natural attitude, only because the natural certainty had been called into question as a result of the failure of the first, realist presupposition set. And thus our focus was still upon that natural certainty and the set of situations which represent the experience and knowledge taken to be complete and real in the natural attitude of sense-certainty.

But this second set is not something simply elicited from the natural attitude as was the first; it is presumed to be in force as a result of the "refutation" of the first set. Thus, what emerged at that point also owed its presence to the philosophical, reflective attitude. The idealist set began not as something to be taken simply as naturally presupposed, but as something which has been thematized as *presupposed*, something which would be *recognized* by the natural attitude as its presupposition set. The claim in the first set is that it *is* presupposed in experience. The claim for the second set is that it *must be* presupposed if experience is to be validated. This "must be" arises not from the direct conviction of the natural attitude, but rather from that natural conviction now combined with two other conscious assumptions: (1) that the certainty claimed by the natural attitude is warranted, *in spite of* the lack found in the originally articulated realist set, and (2) that the lack found in the first set *can now be removed by reflection on that presupposition set* and its replacement with another set designed to remedy in a determinate way the failure of the first set. Thus, there is now an acceptance of the dialectic on the part of the natural attitude which was not present there to begin with. That is to say, as a result of the shared interest in certainty, natural consciousness already begins here to enter as a result and is not simply immediate. That subsequent presupposition sets come from the previous examination and thus from both the natural and the philosophical attitudes rather than from only the former, is not a violation of dialectic, but a result of the shared interest in established certainty.[23]

The interplay between the presupposition set and the circumstances it is supposed to ground, in each movement subsequent to the first, is never the same as that occurring in the first dialectics. In the original, naive realist set, the presuppositions were what would be elicited from the natural attitude itself, the philosophical being responsible only for the eliciting due to its interest in the quest for certainty. In subsequent movements the interplay is such that the presupposition set is the result of the creative, reflective "speculation" of the "interlocutors"; for each of the subsequent sets are constructed in order to remove the faults which have been discovered in prior sets, each of which has been imputed to be the correct set. This new structure of speculative reflection is a result of the shared interest in the quest arising from the original failure to warrant immediate certainty on the part of the natural attitude. That the

Sense-certainty and Philosophy 43

subsequent presuppositions arise out of the previous examination and thus from both the natural and the philosophical attitudes rather than from only the former, is not a violation of the restrictions Hegel has placed upon the activity of the philosophical "we." The restrictions remain, but now under the rubric of an interest in the *quest* for certainty shared by both natural and philosophical consciousness. This new situation of sharing allows us now to make even more clear Hegel's solution to the circularity problem which we discussed earlier.

The circularity was seen to arise from the fact that Hegel was taking up the problem of the absolute standpoint as developed in the course of the historical-philosophical dialogue of the tradition. I argued that it was not the case that Hegel was assuming for himself the absolute standpoint to begin with—not assuming an already given solution to the problem of the absolute standpoint—but was thematizing all of his subject-matter within the parameters of the *question* or *problem* of the absolute standpoint. I also argued that the problem had its sources in the natural attitude itself; for it was determined as the problem of knowing what it is that we do when we know in the natural attitude. Thus, both dimensions were present in philosophy: what is in fact thematized and intelligible in the various possible worlds of our experience, and what is thematized when the reflective question arises. I argued further that this was what lay at the basis of the two demands made by Hegel, namely that it must be demonstrated (a) that the natural certainty which belongs to the natural attitude is warranted in the absolute standpoint, and (b) that the absolute standpoint and the "content" it embraces (i.e., the absolute idea in its fully explicit development) is implicit in that same unreflective natural attitude and is the ground for its certainty. The demand of philosophy to articulate in a warranted and convincing manner the nature of the absolute standpoint and absolute idea arises initially, as we have seen, from a failed demand which the natural attitude makes upon itself.[24]

The dialectic of sense-certainty, even to the brief extent we have explored it, gives us therefore a concretization of this program. (a) The statements and circumstances which originally give rise to the search for the noetic and ontological praxical presuppositions belong to and are recognized as intelligible by a person in the natural attitude. (b) A set of presuppositions is "elicited" from the natural attitude which is also acceptable. (c) An examination of the consequences of the imputed set being taken as the actual set in force in the natural standpoint has shown that if it were the actual set, then a set of possible worlds would be thematized which are incompatible with the actual worlds of our experience. (d) This leaves us with the conclusion that the proffered set is not the proper and adequate set and that such a set must now be found if natural certainty is to be warranted. The philosophical project and the interest of the natural standpoint will come to an end when and only when the worlds acknowledged in the natural attitude are grounded in a presupposition set properly articulated, i.e., when the set of worlds made possible is the same set recognized in the everyday natural attitude.[25]

For all of their dissimilarity, then, the natural and philosophical standpoints have in common that desire for certainty which originally provokes the philosophical project itself and which subsequently separates it off from the natural attitude. This is why we shall constantly be told that what is "in itself," i.e., *an sich* or in reference to itself, and what is "for us" is the same, but is not yet "for itself" in the sense of being explicitly thematized and articulated for the natural standpoint. In itself, the natural attitude is always at the stage at which the philosophical reflection stands; for it has been brought there, out of its own resources and guided by its own sense of the range of the set of worlds possible in experience. But for itself or consciously it is not aware of what it is in itself.[26]

It is clear, then, that both the problematic nature of knowledge and experience and, on the other hand, the thematized worlds of the natural standpoint, are taken up together at the beginning of the *Phenomenology* and soon reveal a common theme. Hegel can consistently assume that both the problem as thematized in the philosophical tradition and also the worlds thematized by the natural standpoint are valid. The circle is not vicious because both the reflective and the unreflective are accepted by Hegel from the beginning. Furthermore, because of the constant return to various modes of the natural attitude, we are not moving away from the natural standpoint to a philosophical one which excludes or places the former in an inferior mode; rather, we are constantly moving *within* the natural attitude to its roots in the absolute standpoint. We do not leave the cave of Plato's prisoners, but rather remain to interrogate over and over again the professed certainty of the natural standpoint. This allegiance to the natural attitude is what both saves us from a vicious circle and gives efficacy to the dialectic. Unfortunately, as we shall see at the end of my analysis, this faithfulness to the natural attitude is precisely the problem with Hegel's thought.

As we continue with an examination of the naive idealist presupposition set, we discover that to presuppose that the intentions of the individual give us a locus for truth and a warranty for our certainty does not give us a set of worlds which are consistent with the worlds we have in fact in the natural attitude. Upon reflection it is shown that what this set lacks is just the opposite of what was lacking in the realist set; for we now lack a stable locus in the world by which to identify the "I" which intends that world. I can only stipulate what *I* mean or intend by

Sense-certainty and Philosophy

reference to a thing itself which, therefore, must be presupposed to contribute to the truth of my statements and the meaningfulness of my actions.

At this point the dialectic moves in a way different again from the move from the realist to the idealist position. It is not even, strictly speaking, the same *kind* of move. But this is just the nature of dialectic; for it is a method determined by the content itself, and not a constant which is external to the content. On the one hand, this move, like the move from realism to idealism does not issue from an examination of the putative presuppositions of the natural attitude as naturally elicited. The new presupposition formulation arises from reflection on the difficulties just shown in the examination of the idealist set. But, unlike the second move, neither does the new set originate simply from the philosophical result; for it is now also recognized that there is at least one move which is *a priori* closed to it: a move to posit naive realism. This latter is impossible because it is just that set whose failure led to the idealist set which has, in turn, also failed. First, then, to suggest a return to the realist set would be to suggest an eternal oscillation between the two positions, a move which would defeat the grounding of certainty which is the project of the quest for certainty. But secondly, what is suggested by the determinate failure of the idealist set is just the objective referential nature which is at the core of the realist set. At this point in the dialectic, then, the search for a new presupposition set within the natural attitude involves us in a reflection on the immediate form which the thematized problematic has taken as well as on the *already* reflected and mediated form.[27] What we are led to is a literal synthesis of both forms. The result is something which includes both realism and idealism as they have appeared thus far and which also transforms the nature of each in the synthesis.

> Sense-certainty thus comes to know by experience that its essence is neither in the object nor in the "I", and that its immediacy is neither an immediacy of the one nor of the other; for in both, what I *mean* is rather something unessential, and the object and the "I" are universals in which the "Now" and "Here" and "I" which I *mean* do not have a continuing being, or *are* not. Thus we reach the stage where we have to posit the *whole* of sense-certainty itself as its *essence*, and no longer only one of its moments, as happened in the two cases where first the object confronting the "I", and then the "I" were supposed to be its reality. Thus, it is only sense-certainty as a *whole* which stands firm within itself as *immediacy* and by so doing excludes from itself all the opposition which has hitherto obtained (*PhG*, 84; *PhS*, 62).

An examination of the set which is now described reveals again a failure. And this failure is critical to the course of the *Phenomenology* in a way yet again different from the preceding two failures; for here we have exhausted the possibilities for any presupposition set which would contain the presupposition that reality is constituted by nothing but simple particulars which are immediately in relation to each other and to a knower. At this point the *paradox of sense-certainty* is made explicit: by presupposing that only particulars exist or constitute existence—a presupposition common to the three possibilities for sense-certainty—we lose precisely our ability to deal in an immediate way with particulars in the natural standpoint. Under the presupposition of simple particulars as the sole constituents of the world, particularity continues to disappear into empty and abstract universality. Since these three presupposition sets exhaust the possibilities for sense-certainty or for unreflective natural consciousness, and since the lack common to all three is this lack of particulars contrary to actual experience, there must be something in our *authentic* natural presupposition set which goes beyond particularity and yet which makes our apprehension of particulars possible.[28]

The reflection in the text which now occurs is rather brief, but adequate. What is now to be presupposed by the natural attitude is not pure immediacy or simple particulars, but a mediation between subject and object such that the subject is particular precisely as various states of awareness determined as a function of different objects, while the object is a particular precisely as various properties or items in a collection which is intended as a function of a particular subject. For the knower to intend something presupposes a "this-here-now" among many; on the other hand, for there to be a "this-here-now" among many presupposes an intentionality of the subject which fixes the one among the many others. In other terms, what is presupposed is not pure immediacy but (1) an indexicality of intention stabilized by a content given by the independent object in terms of discrete properties which are perceptual universals, and (2) a giveness of this content stabilized by the indexical nature of the knower. This mutual stabilization of knower and known, of experiencer and experienced, is a strict mutual stabilization; each is, in experience, only through the other. This is why the three presupposition sets failed; in each of them immediacy or total independence of particulars was presupposed; dependency and mediation now seem to constitute the truth.

We have now brought to reflection, on the part of an individual in the natural standpoint, the *standpoint* of the natural attitude as such. Reflection on the natural attitude has fully thematized the totality of experience as a standpoint always present in our natural, unreflective experience of objects and events in the world, a totality only unreflectively, non-thematically present to the natural attitude at the very beginning of the *Phenomenology*. No longer can either the world or consciousness be the object of primary concern; the relation between them—a relation which, of course, includes the relata—is now what is thematized by both the natural and the philosophical attitudes. The natural attitude is thus now fully aware of itself as an attitude, as a standpoint within which what is experienced and known is thematized.

This sets the general tone for the remainder of the *Phenomenology*.[29] We shall next explore the general thesis, in the form of another putative presupposition, that our sense-certainty or immediate sense of and contact with the world presupposes "perception," and that that means attention paid not only to particulars but also to the perceptual universals which constitute and mediate the particulars. This is a move acceptable to the natural attitude since sensibility is still preserved at the heart of the presupposition sets proffered for our examination, and since there is a "natural" presumption that sensibility always plays a part in experience and thus that perception is a ubiquitous power. When this presupposition fails of itself to ground the possible worlds of sense-certainty, we will then go on to examine our power of "understanding" as it is distinguishable from that of perception. The claim of the natural attitude there will be that not only does sense-certainty presuppose perception, but perception in turn presupposes understanding or a power of grasping pure intelligibles. The claim will be that an analysis of the standpoint of understanding will give us the presuppositional foundation for the certainty and warranty sought by both the natural and the philosophical consciousness.

In the new analysis arising from sense-certainty, we proceed with a "necessity" determined by the failures of our previous attempts; yet we shall also have to proceed in such a way that each new set so derived is also "reasonable" and revelatory to the natural attitude which still deigns to follow us reflectively. Thus, although the natural attitude is in one sense left behind because we are no longer primarily oriented around the particularistic attitude without which the natural standpoint is not natural in its immediate sense of naturalness, in another way, the natural attitude remains at the heart of the inquiry.[30] Its natural certainty together with the quest for certainty it now shares with philosophy is what gives the work its eros. And it is the natural attitude of sense-certainty, transformed into a natural attitude aware of itself, which is subsequently the focus of our attention. Beginning with perception we are no longer inquiring directly into the grounds for the possibility of the circumstances of our experience as thematized in the natural attitude, but rather indirectly into these grounds by means of an inquiry into the grounds of the natural attitude as a standpoint. The first new thesis is that perception is the presupposition for sense-certainty. Thus, it is now the "doing" of knowing in the natural standpoint, and not the "what" of that knowing which is directly our touchstone. We have now explicitly as our object in the *Phenomenology* that relationship itself, the attitude of the natural standpoint. The various possible worlds which belong authentically to it will become only *exemplary* of the attitude, rather than being the focus of our testing of the putative presupposition sets.

Two final remarks are in order concerning this relationship between the natural attitude and the *Phenomenology* as a whole. The first concerns a hidden content on the side of the "philosophical participant," the second the identity of the natural and the philosophical and the ultimate primacy of the natural for Hegel. I have already touched on both points, but they need reinforcing.

As the *Phenomenology* proceeds through the examination of various modes of consciousness, self-consciousness, reason, and spirit, the guiding force which moves us from the analysis of the determinate negation of one putative set of the natural attitude to the positing of the next is not simply the notion that the new set makes up for the deficiency of the preceding set. It is true that, on a natural level and immediately as concerns the *Phenomenology*, this is the case; and it must be the case if the work is to show natural consciousness that the absolute standpoint is implicit in the natural standpoint. But this series of "new" presupposition sets is not simply the creation of Hegel or something accidentally garnered for the task at hand. Each new set has its roots also in the philosophical tradition out of which Hegel's thought arises. Each of the new presupposition sets, in whole or in part, have already been examined as "theories" earlier in the history of philosophy. In assessing the nature of the determinate negation, Hegel—and we—are therefore also calling upon the fund of reflection created in the historical-philosophical dialogue. Each new set is chosen not only on the grounds that it putatively will resolve the problem of the moment, but also because previously in the history of philosophy the same problem which has arisen specifically at this point in the *Phenomenology* also arose as a problem and was resolved, or supposedly resolved, by an earlier contribution to the dialogue. This is the way in which the new sets are chosen.[31]

There is a dual requirement, then. (1) The presupposition set must resolve the failure which has occurred at this juncture and must be reasonable and acceptable to the natural standpoint as its own presupposition. (2) The set must be derived from some prior attempt in philosophy to solve just this problem which has now arisen in the course of the

Sense-certainty and Philosophy 49

Phenomenology. Thus, in assessing the nature of the determinate negation and positing a new set, Hegel is also reviewing and criticizing the theories of his predecessors in terms of the adequacy of their positions as articulations of the absolute standpoint. The education of the individual and the recalling of the education (*Bildungsprozess*) of the tradition are brought together into one systematic whole. However, the course of this systematic review and critique is determined, not by the actual course of that history, but by the requirements of the *Phenomenology* and its quest for certainty.

The total significance of this primacy of the natural attitude and its desire for certainty will become apparent only later. But at this point one thing can already be noted. It is no accident that there is this contiguity of the two projects; for by the very nature of the philosophical project itself, as Hegel sees it, the project of the individual quest for certainty and the project of the philosophical tradition are related to each other in the fashion I have already noted, namely in a circular way. The whole of the historical-philosophical dialogue has been motivated by the natural certainty of the natural attitude, its failure upon reflection to warrant this certainty, and the philosophical quest for certainty which followed in the effort to find warranty for that certainty. Philosophy begins in wonder, but that wonder itself is mediated by the revealed lack of correspondence between professed and warranted claims to knowledge made by natural, unreflective consciousness. The philosopher's theories serve adequately as putative presupposition sets simply because that is what they have always been: attempts to give the grounds for the possibility of the possible worlds that we in fact experience and know. The *Phenomenology* therefore has as its focus the humanistic roots of philosophy and the progress of the self-consciousness of the "world-spirit" or humanity searching through philosophy to bring humanity into perfect freedom through knowledge of the grounds of knowledge.

The first point, then, is that conversance with the history of philosophy is assumed in the *Phenomenology*, but a conversance that does not disconnect us from a primary reliance on the natural attitude.[32] Far from suggesting the radical difference ordinarily perceived between philosophy and the non-philosophical, our present explication of the tradition itself suggests an alliance; and this alliance is at the basis of my second remark. The natural and the philosophical are in one very important sense already identical, since the philosophical is only an extension of the natural standpoint such that human beings attempt in philosophy to gain self-reflective warranty for their natural, unreflective claims of certainty and access to reality. This means, then, that *ultimately* the natural attitude is primary in respect to the philosophical.[33] As we proceed now to assess Hegel's attempt to achieve the absolute standpoint, the anchor will always be the natural certainty of the natural standpoint, the "original" of any idea of certainty. The *problem* of the absolute standpoint as a theme is derivative from the *asseveration* of warranted certainty which underlies the natural standpoint itself. It is not philosophy which originates the notion of absoluteness, totality, totalization, and the quest for certainty; it is the natural standpoint itself. What traditional philosophy attempts to achieve is the warranted certainty of access to that single reality *implicitly* presupposed in the natural actions and experience of an individual in the natural attitude.

III

Interest as Intentionality

IN THE FIRST two chapters I have discussed the nature and rationale of the *Phenomenology* and the way in which the dialectic is to bring together the natural and the philosophical standpoints in a mutual quest for certainty. We can now turn to a more detailed discussion of the *Phenomenology of Spirit* and begin an analysis of how the task is accomplished by Hegel. In this Chapter I shall first discuss how "interest" is a unifying force in human experience and briefly review the way in which Hegel's quest for certainty is carried out in terms of it. Then I shall turn to interest as it first appears—interest as intentionality—and Hegel's analysis of consciousness as putative absolute standpoint.

Put in the briefest and most general way in terms of presupposition, Hegel claims to show in the *Phenomenology* that consciousness, which is at first presupposed by the natural attitude to be sufficient for complete access to reality, in fact presupposes self-consciousness; that self-consciousness, in turn, is inadequate as an absolute standpoint because it itself presupposes consciousness as well as another level of interest, reason; and, finally, that reason is also inadequate as the absolute standpoint because it presupposes spirit. This last stage of the analysis is further divided, and it is shown that spirit in various socio-political forms itself presupposes religion which in turn presupposes absolute knowledge. In this chain of general presuppositions we will have forged the link between the natural attitude as it begins in sense-certainty and philosophy as absolute idealism. But before turning for a closer look at this chain of presuppositions, two preliminary points need emphasis in order to avoid misunderstandings.

Both points have already been mentioned. The first is that Hegel is not denying that our knowledge, experience, and actions are a function of our natural attitude of consciousness and our natural certainty. His is not the claim that only philosophical knowledge grants an authentic relation to reality, leaving other modes of experience, knowledge, and action to a domain of illusion or "mere appearance".[1] On the contrary, as we have already seen, far from denying what is thematized and known in the natural attitude, Hegel is rather attempting to uncover a set of praxical presuppositions adequate to authenticate the possible worlds of that experience noetically and ontologically and consummate the quest for certainty. With each successive move from consciousness through absolute knowledge, we discover sets of conditions and levels of presupposition necessitated by their respective predecessors and thus by the natural attitude if the latter is to have the intelligibility it actually seems to have.

The second point is but a reiteration of what was discussed at the end of Chapter Two. *Our* touchstone is now not simply the world as it is in the natural attitude; rather it is the natural attitude itself as it has now come to be thematized in the discussion of sense-certainty. This important point is stressed by Hegel in the very first paragraph of the chapter on perception.

> Immediate certainty does not take over the truth, for its truth is the universal, whereas certainty wants to apprehend the This. Perception, on the other hand, takes what is present to it as a universal . . . . That principle [of the universal] has arisen for us, and therefore the way we take in perception is no longer something that just happens to us like sense-certainty; on the contrary, it is logically necessitated (*PhG*, 89; *PhS*, 67).

Our object is sense-certainty as an attitude and, Hegel adds, must be developed "from the result that has been reached [by us]" (*PhG*, 90; *PhS*, 67). Sense-certainty remains with things and events as they happen to occur; the quest for certainty proceeds from its own result, from what has been thematized *for us*.

With these two points in mind, I shall now turn to a discussion of "interest" which will enable us to review the dialectical progress of the work with a unity of content clearly in focus.[2] Then, for the remainder of this Chapter, I will offer an analysis of the first major level of interest, that which is manifested in what Hegel calls "consciousness."

There are several possible ways to bring together the content of the *Phenomenology* once the dialectic has been clarified.[3] But the one which seems to me to be the richest and most complete is to unite the content in terms of the various relations which are evidenced between interest on the one hand, and our knowledge, experience, and action on the other. Hegel gives us some evidence of the appropriateness of such a link when, in a text I have already cited, he characterizes the relationship between the domain of the *Logic* and other human concerns.

> As a matter of fact, the need to occupy oneself with pure thought presupposes that the human spirit must already have travelled a long road; it is . . . the need of a condition free from needs, of abstraction from the material of intuition,

imagination, and so on, of the concrete interests of desire, instinct, will, in which material the determinations of thought are veiled and hidden. In the silent regions of thought which has come to itself and communes only with itself, the interests which move the lives of races and individuals are hushed (*WdL*, I, 12; *SL*, 34).

The "long road travelled" is not only that of our civilization, but also the way traversed in the *Phenomenology*, a point Hegel stresses also in the Preface to the *Phenomenology*. It is a way along which the interests of ordinary knowledge and action, of desire, and of the various rational activities of human beings dominate our awareness. "Interest" refers us to that link between subject and object, knower and known, actor and environment, in which the praxical presuppositions in force at any given moment lie buried. Interest constitutes the framework within which the presupposition set is to be found; this presupposition set, in turn, defines the mode of interest in which we act within and think about the world. The quest for certainty is a quest to comprehend the basic possibility of *having* interest in the world, in *being* an interested party in such a way as to legitimately engage the world. The notion of interest, and the presence of interest in the structure of human experience, forms a nexus for the tension between the two respective thematizations which are at first in conflict, but which are to be synthesized as a result of this work.

In sense-certainty our interest has its world of simple particulars as the possible worlds to which attention is to be given. But in this respect, and from the perspective of the philosophical quest for certainty in an absolute standpoint, these worlds are worlds in which we are unfree, caught up in the bondage of an interest structure which we do not comprehend in itself. Hegel calls upon Aristotle (and, indeed, he could have called upon practically any of the philosophers of the tradition) to support his point.

> "In so many respects," says Aristotle . . . , "the nature of man is in bondage; but this science, which is not studied for its utility, is the only absolutely free science and seems therefore to be a more than human possession" (*WdL*, I, 12; *SL*, 34).[4]

The *Phenomenology*, then, can be understood as a process of freeing ourselves from the bondage of varied interests which prohibit our attending to the absolute standpoint itself: it introduces us to the freedom found in the thematization of the categories of the *Logic*, which latter will be introduced as the ultimate presuppositions of the worlds of our experience, knowledge, and action, the determinations of thought which lie buried in ordinary experience. The quest for certainty understood in this way is the attempt to free ourselves from our bondage in the world and for the ground of our true freedom in comprehension of our place in the world.

Each of the various main stages of consciousness, self-consciousness, reason, and spirit can be characterized in terms of the form in which an interest is taken in things and events. I shall first simply note the four forms before beginning an analysis of the first, that of consciousness.

In all modes of consciousness, interest takes the form of *intentionality*.[5] Consciousness is always consciousness *of* something, and that something is presupposed as beyond or transcendent to consciousness itself. Consciousness is presupposed as the correlate of that intended world, a world which is ontologically and noetically separate from and independent of consciousness. But consciousness is also presupposed as united to that world through interest as intentionality. These most general presuppositions structure the remainder of the presuppositions which constitute interest as intentionality or consciousness.

The second form of interest, found in what Hegel refers to as "self-consciousness," is desire.[6] The presupposed correlate of desire is something desired and thus something which, while independent of the desire just as the intended object is independent of intentionality, is nevertheless defined in its meaning and import by desire. Whereas interest as intentionality takes up that in which it is interested as something purely objective to the individual, interest as desire takes up its objects as its own, as objects in a world which is "*my* world," as objects in a world defined by "*my* desires." The "subjective" orientation of the latter is in contrast to the "objective" orientation of the former. Consciousness loses itself in the world intended by it; self-consciousness attempts constantly to bring the world within its own orbit. That world is in fact the "life" which belongs to the individual, life as the life lived and as that world which must be dealt with. Interest as desire does not simply focus on the world as something of interest, but also attempts to dominate that world as something desired and desirable.

At the third level, that of reason, interest takes the form of *purpose*,[7] and the correlate is the world presupposed as a world appropriate (in principle) to the purposes of the individuals in it. Interest as purpose involves a concern with objects and events as independent of our interest, thus preserving the essence of consciousness and intentionality; but, on the other hand, one actively engages that world as appropriate, thus also preserving the essence of self-consciousness and desire. One's purposes are not simply desires, for the interest orientation involves an *a priori* acceptance of the possibility of a *factual inappropriateness* of one's purposes of the moment. Whether or not one's purposes find an appropriate world is determined by the circumstances, by the world. For this reason, one's interest is such that one risks putting one's purposes into action in a world which is only possibly receptive to them. However, on the other hand, one's purposes are not simply intentions; for the orientation of purposive action involves a predisposition toward the world, i.e., not a mere receptiveness to the world, but an attempt to have it in accordance with one's interests. In interest as purpose we shall be able to understand concretely how reason is the presuppositional unity of consciousness and self-consciousness because purpose is the presuppositional unity of intentionality and desire. Intentionality and desire are only abstractions when not considered as "moments" of purpose.

Finally, at the level of "spirit" interest takes the form of *reflection*.[8] It is at this stage that Hegel will be able to make important analyses of the kind of things presuppositions themselves are, and will be able to give an account of their ontological status, not only in terms of whether or not they exist, but also in terms of their type or mode of existence. At the first level of spirit the correlate of interest as reflection is a world of customs, institutions, and artifacts created by and through the interests of individuals, and within which are constituted a series of self-understandings of the praxical presuppositions which structure the possible worlds of our actual experiences.[9] The grounds for our certainty come to be understood as embedded and embodied in the rules and structures of the socio-historical institutions as the latter structure the possible worlds of our experience. Interest is reflection precisely because the activities of individuals occur within institutional frameworks which are themselves creations of the individuals whose activities are embraced within the institutions.

At a second level of spirit, that of religion, the correlate for reflection is a being which transcends the particularity of sets of created institutions. This being grounds both human beings and their worlds. The "object" is a positive given which stands as unconditioned principle of totality outside of the objective form of spirit. Accordingly, it is declared to be absolute spirit.

Lastly, in philosophy interest takes the form of reflection such that the correlate is neither created institutions nor a given, transcendent deity, but reflection itself, i.e., the very domain through which the self-understanding of the *Phenomenology* and of the philosophical tradition which preceded it has been accomplished. The end result of this interest as reflection is the power, finally achieved after centuries of philosophical work, to contemplate the basic, presuppositionless presuppositions which form the logico-metaphysical system of absolute idealism. To stand in this domain with interest in the form of philosophical reflection, is to be able to reveal the self-referential and other-referential categorial structure which grounds both the certainty found in the natural attitude and the finite interests of consciousness (intentionality), self-consciousness (desire), reason (purpose), and spirit itself (reflection). It is to stand in a domain in which the interests of reflection which still referred to something other than the pure ground itself—i.e., society, the divine—no longer draw us, but are themselves now silent in the presence of their ground. It is not interest in general which is relegated to silence, but only those "interests which move the lives of races and individuals."

This journey through four general levels of interest is a journey which both transcends and preserves the natural attitude's own conception of its interest frameworks. On the one hand, neither intentionality, desire, nor transcendental, ahistorical purpose form the most basic interest framework and praxical presupposition set which is to yield warranting of our natural certainty. Each successive presupposes its successor, and all presuppose interest as reflection as a way to the ground. In other terms and as stated above, consciousness presupposes self-consciousness, which in turn presupposes reason, and all presuppose concrete historical spirit. Any act of intentionality presupposes a relation to the world as desire; and act of desire presupposes a relation to the world in the form of purposive action; anypurposive act presupposes a historical nexus which is spirit and which determines the extent and limits of meaningful action, experience,and knowledge. Therein lies the ground of our natural certainty. But, on the other hand, there *are* situations structured as intentionality or desire or purpose. Hegel's point, made in the context of the problem of the quest for certainty, is that the trustworthiness of the certainty found in any of these situations is dependent in the last instance on spirit and interest as reflection. One can be certain in the mode of intentionality, but only if one is firmly grounded within the real context of the real world constituted as spirit. And the same is true, *mutatis mutandis*, for the other modes in which interest occurs. Moved by interests not explicitly structured by the quest for certainty, one proceeds with only a professed or partially warranted certainty; but once the need for the quest for certainty and for explicit knowledge of the grounds of the possibility of our actual certainty is aroused as it has been in the discussion centering around sense-certainty, then the implicit and accepting grounds for naive, natural certainty are rejected and the search is on.

The process of the *Phenomenology* thus involves us, as we already argued in the first chapter, only in the context of a quest for certainty. It is not indicative of any "natural development" of individuals or of the species. Hegel's task does not present us with a philosophical anthropology in that sense; it only reveals to us the journey undertaken to ground our certainty. Let us now turn to the first of these levels of interest and see in a more detailed way the progress through these forms of interest.

The dominant presupposition in the mode of consciousness in general is that there is consciousness and, on the other hand, a world which is related to but also transcendent to consciousness.[10] This presupposition, which we have already noted in the analysis of sense-certainty, is shared also by the modes of consciousness which Hegel calls "perception" and "understanding." All three are typifications of the natural attitude as such when it is governed by interest as intentionality. Consciousness and the world are to be separate, but joined together in some way by intentionality.

This presupposition of separation and of radical difference in kind between consciousness and the world is accompanied by another presupposition, viz., that the truth concerning what-is has its locus in those objects and events which transcend consciousness. There is a positivism to all attitudes of consciousness and thus to all interests formed in terms of intentionality.[11] Consciousness is always oriented toward the world and thus accepts that world as ultimate and fixed. The quest for certainty in these terms, then, is a quest to bring one's knowledge or consciousness of things into a state of adequacy vis-à-vis the given. Knowledge is the adequacy of consciousness to things or to the intended world.

As a consequence of these common presuppositions of intentionality, totality is always totality in terms of the positive objectivity, always in terms of the world independent of consciousness. Totalization, on the other hand, is something radically different from totality; for the totality always exists already, always exists to be presented to consciousness as a positivity. There is no process which belongs to the side of truth, for truth according to this view rests in the positive totality already formed and existent. Totalization, on the other hand, is a process which takes place on the side of consciousness, the attempt to bring that given totality into the awareness of the conscious individual. These presuppositions about totality and totalization give us more precisely the nature of the separation between self and world which defines the standpoint of consciousness.[12] Together with the other presuppositions mentioned above, they form the general framework of presuppositions which classify interest as intentionality.

Hegel's analysis of this mode of interest takes him through the dialectical examination of sense-certainty, perception, and understanding. In sense-certainty, as we have already seen, the object and locus of truth is to be the totality of being as particulars; in the presuppositional analysis of perception, the truth is to be in the totality of perceptual objects constituted as particulars through the mediation of sensible universals; and in the presupposition that understanding is the ground for our certainty, truth is to be found in the totality of intelligible universals which are unified into a presupposed unconditioned universal present in one form or another to the mind. Whatever the specific nature of the presuppositions in the set, however, "what is true for consciousness is something other than itself" (*PhG*, 133; *PhS*, 104).

I have already traced the presuppositions putatively at the basis of the natural attitude for unreflective sense-certainty, and have discussed how we are forced dialectically to recognize that universals as well as particulars must be presupposed. The perceptual world is taken now as presupposed as a world of manifold differences, a world of particulars which are what they are because they have specific universals, qualities, or "properties."[13] Perception and the perceptual world is now to be presupposed as the world intended by the individual in the natural attitude of sense-certainty.

> The wealth of sense-knowledge belongs to perception, not to immediate certainty, for which it was only the source of instances; for only perception contains negation, that is, difference or manifoldness, within its own essence (*PhG*, 90; *PhS*, 67).

This is not only a result for us, but also would "make sense" to one in the natural attitude. The "thing" intended is "the thing with many properties," the act of intending is itself an act which searches among and discriminates between the many different particulars *by means of* these sense universals or properties. If one looks for a book with a red cover, one quickly passes over every book of a different color and searches the titles only of those books with red covers. Thus, the presupposition set articulated at the beginning of the section on perception is there in order to resolve the difficulties and the determination reached in the presupposition sets of naive sense-certainty; but it is also a set which can easily be refined from, and tested in terms of, the actual worlds of experience within the natural standpoint. The certainty we have, it is claimed, is rooted in perception and in the perceptual world intended in our interest in the world.

Since this relationship between the phenomenological analysis and the natural attitude will reappear again and again for some time in the *Phenomenology*, it might be well to make clear again why there is the discrepancy between the origin of the presupposition set and the testing of this set through actual experience or the possible worlds of the natural attitude in question. Whenever one is acting under the supposed general presuppositions of consciousness, the ability to become functionally aware of one's own nature and activity is very limited; for intentionality as interest involves a surrender to the world intended and thus an inability to focus on the standpoint of interest itself. As we proceed through the presupposition sets of consciousness some reflective awareness will accrue to the natural attitude; but this occurs only because the consequences of the critical analysis of the putative presuppositions are slowly clarified and held together by the philosophical reflection in which we are involved. The natural attitude does not begin with, but must develop its capacity to be autonomous in the quest for certainty.

Having given the general putative presuppositions of intentionality, consciousness, and perception, Hegel now turns to additional noetic-ontological praxical presuppositions putatively constitutive for perceptual, intentional experience. They are six in number in respect to the objective side of this experience: (1) the particular is a thing of many properties, which properties are sensuous universals shared by other particulars and therefore abstractable from things themselves; (2) the "this" intended is sensuously given as a whole through the complexus of properties, also sensual, which make it up; (3) each property or quality is distinguishable from each other property or quality; (4) each property in a thing is indifferent to each other property, i.e. the properties interpenetrate in the particular thing; (5) the thing itself is a medium or receptacle for these properties and thus exists only in respect to the properties as their medium; (6) the thing itself is a single unit which is identical with itself and thus excludes all other things from being identical with it.

Consciousness, on the other hand, is presupposed putatively as "percipient in so far as this thing is its object" (*PhG*, 92; *PhS*, 70).

There is also presupposed a criterion of truth and certainty. On the one hand, consciousness

> has only to *take* [the thing], to confine itself to a pure apprehension of it, and what is thus yielded up is the true (*PhG*, 92-93; *PhS*, 70).

Truth thus lies in the object according to this view of the actual presuppositions of intentional consciousness, and truth is defined as self-identity, as the possession of the thing in perception in the simple totality which it is as an objective thing.[14] But the individual who is thus conscious also putatively presupposes that one can be in error, that mistakes can occur in this simple apprehension of the thing (*PhG*, 93; *PhS*, 70). This presupposition of the possibility of deception manifests itself whenever one looks at something carefully or is challenged by another person concerning one's perceptual judgments. This presupposition of the possibility of error is rooted in the general presupposition of consciousness that the totality (the self-identity of what-is) belongs to the objective world and truth, while totalization (the process of perceiving a diversity and of putting it together) belongs to subjective consciousness and mere belief. The thesis buried in the natural attitude, then, is that we will find our ground for certainty in *correct* perception.

This set of presuppositions is of importance in the progress toward self-awareness and warranted certainty, and in the confluence of the natural and the philosophical attitudes. Consciousness is now explicitly aware of demands made by its presuppositions, although it may not be aware of the presuppositions themselves: it is aware of the demand, for example, that it correct its perceptual judgments to bring them into line with the given. This degree of self-awareness represents a small, but significant advance beyond the totally unthinking, unreflective intentionality found in the naive certainty of sense-certainty. This awareness now allows Hegel to defer to ordinary perceiving consciousness in order to test the adequacy of the presupposition set just articulated as the ground for certainty.[15] The first task is to test the general presupposition that perceiving is a passive act in which the totalization occurs in a manner congruent with the totality presumed given. It becomes clear that this presupposition will not give us the possible worlds which are there in experience; for a passive consciousness which takes the thing as one and in simple unity comes immediately and in various ways into contradiction in its attempt to totalize the various aspects and thus the multiplicity of the single thing or event (*PhG*, 93-94; *PhS*, 70-71).[16]

There is then constructed a second putative set which holds that the above noted aspects of the thing are reflected into consciousness in such a way that the thing as it is in itself and the thing as it is for consciousness are not necessarily the same.

> Thus it becomes quite definite for consciousness how its perceiving is essentially constituted, viz. that it is not a simple pure apprehension, but *in its apprehension* is at the same time *reflected out of the true and into itself* (*PhG*, 94; *PhS*, 71).

It is presupposed that something "happens" to the thing as it becomes an object for consciousness. The distinction now presupposed and before us is not a distinction between object and consciousness or simply between subject and object, but between the object as it is in itself and the object as it is for us.[17] What is putatively presupposed is that the activity of consciousness, no longer a simple passivity, has some contribution to make to the constitution of the way the thing is known and experienced. This presupposition is made explicit in doctrines of primary and secondary qualities, as well as in subjective, transcendental idealism. It is also evidenced in the experience of the natural attitude when any attempt is made to differentiate one's own perspective and biases and subjective conditions from the things and events themselves. Any recognition of a difference, such as an admission, after error, of "Well, it seemed to be so to me," is a reflection of this presupposition that the thing as it is in itself is not necessarily the same as it is once I perceive it. What is also to be presupposed now is that the source of error lies in those subjective conditions responsible for difference between object in itself and object as it is for me.

> The behavior of consciousness which we have now to consider is thus so constituted that consciousness no longer merely perceives, but is also conscious of its reflection into itself, and separates this from simple apprehension proper (*PhG*, 95; *PhS*, 72).

With this move there is an even higher degree of self-awareness on the part of the natural attitude. Even the plain statement, "That's how it seemed to me," is an implicit turn inward, an implicit move to intentionality itself and thus away from the world as purely objective to consciousness.[18]

On the basis of this general presupposition set concerning the difference in object and the source of error, Hegel now reviews several possible presupposition sets in which the distinction between object in itself and object for us is made. These sets involve some of the most common epistemological claims found in the modern period of philosophy, and reflect various attitudes of perspectivalism and relativism found in the natural attitude when it is confronted with disagreements in its own perceptions or with the perceptions of other individuals. In general they involve the separation of the various characteristics of the object from each other, one time making consciousness the sheer manifold and the thing in itself the medium which holds them in unity, at other times making the thing in itself the locus of the manifold and consciousness or the thing for us as the locus of unity. But it is discovered that in every case we would be unable to account for the possibility of the possible worlds of perceptual consciousness and for our recognition of and correction of error. These sets fail generally because if all of the characteristics of the object do not belong to the thing itself, then the real thing itself will not be what is known and thus no certainty about the world would be warranted. That is to say, if some of the aspects of the things and events perceived belonged only to our consciousness of them, then the thing in itself would not be a thing-with-many-properties, which is the original presupposition and the true nature of experience. On the other hand, if all of the characteristics of the object are not equally authentic in the object as it is for us, then no hope of correspondence between what is known and what-is would be possible. What is demonstrated here, then, is that it is impossible to have in force a presupposition that the characteristics of the object are divided between these two sides of the object, and still define the possible worlds of perceptual experience so that certainty can be warranted. Either truth-value gaps or contradictions appear where they should not, according to the natural standpoint; or possible worlds inconsistent with the possible worlds of natural perceptual consciousness are the result.[19]

There is one last set to be examined prior to passing on to the next major presupposition set. In this set it is again presupposed that all of the aspects of the perceptual thing belong to the thing itself, thus resolving the difficulty involved in the presupposition of a "sharing" between the thing in itself and the thing for us. However, a new dualism is proposed, viz., that we must presuppose that the thing itself has two aspects, one being its independence and relation purely to itself, and the other being its dependency and its relation to other things. In other words, Hegel here examines what amounts to the philosophical doctrine of external relations. But this set also fails; for although there may be two *perspectives*, externally compared by a consciousness and from which something can be experienced, the thing itself is nevertheless one, an unconditioned totality. However we may distinguish the thing, it is still *the* thing which has the distinctions or which relates in "two ways"; and if we cannot show that we can grasp the thing in its unity, claims to certainty about it cannot be warranted.

What is revealed in this analysis is that the intentionality of consciousness, even at the level of perception, presupposes an unconditioned, absolute universal, a conceptual or intelligible substratum of some sort which underlies and gives unity to all perceptual universals and to the perceptually accessible events in the world. Without this non-perspectival, unconditioned universal, certainty would always be only "subjective" and would never demonstrably be in accord with "objective" truth. If this additional kind of unity is not presupposed, the quest for certainty cannot be consummated, and that result would run counter to the natural certainty of the natural attitude.[20] This involves us, then, in an instance closely related to the presuppositions of perception, with the "*je ne sais quoi*" of a John Locke.[21] It is that which is not accessible to perception alone, but which must nevertheless be presupposed as a substantial unity which holds together the thing of perception and the various things which compose events and the interaction of things. Whether one is discussing a single, particular thing or event, or a collection of such things and events in the synthetic whole of a single experience, the presupposition that perceptual universals and particulars by themselves are adequate to ground this experience fails to prove itself by the test of experience. With this realization of the determinate lack in *any* presupposition set which is limited to perception alone, "consciousness here for the first time truly enters the realm of the understanding" (*PhG*, 100; *PhS*, 77).[22]

Hegel now attempts to show that this revelation of an underlying, presupposed realm of intelligibility separable from perception but yet intimately related to it, is also seemingly recognized in the very behavior of one in the natural attitude. He demonstrates to natural consciousness that it itself presupposes a domain of the intelligible, even while professing to presuppose only a domain of perceptual universals and sensuously given things. He calls the common endeavor to cope with the sorts of problems we have evidenced in this section of the *Phenomenology* the "perceptual understanding" of "healthy common sense" (*gesunde Menschenverstand*). But this understanding, he argues, is a sophistry; for in one's defense of the presupposition of the purely perceptual one employs a set of non-perceptual, non-sensuous, intelligible distinctions such as "thing-in-itself," or "this relation to that." When confronted with an error, for instance, the individual makes distinctions about perspectives and something called "properties," neither of which are in themselves sense qualities or properties.

A "perspective" itself is not perceivable; and although distinct properties are perceivable, "property as such" is not. And the criticism holds even if one claims to know such things only by a process of "abstraction"; for that operation itself cannot be perceptually grounded. More importantly, the distinctions between thing in itself and thing as it is for us, between existence and form, and many other such distinctions which are common to ordinary discussion are not perceptual, are not explicable in purely perceptual terms. If we are to warrant our certainty, we must make such terms and their referents transparent; for their present opacity, on the presupposition of the perceptual alone, leaves the domain to which they belong unaccounted for.

Interest as intentionality must thus be somewhat refined. It has been shown in the analysis, through confrontation with the natural attitude itself, that an understanding must be presupposed which transcends what is possible in purely perceptual terms; but there still exists a discrepancy between the natural and the philosophical attitudes since we, of the *Phe-*

nomenology, must again take up the advance and leave perceptual understanding as such behind. We must step into the place on consciousness in order to advance the work (*PhG*, 103; *PhS*, 80). The "data" are all there for the natural attitude, but it fails to use the information because of the presupposition that the perceptual world is the substantial, real world, while thoughts belong only to consciousness. We see here, then, the major hindrance to a self-reflective intentional consciousness. When interest is in the form of intentionality, the presuppositions which underlie experience and knowledge can be uncovered and brought to the attention of consciousness; but, on the other hand, the progress from one set of presuppositions to the next can have no necessity since that would implicate a self-consciousness which is here in effect denied.[23]

Hegel now considers a set of putative presuppositions about the nature of this unconditioned, intelligible universal which was found to be necessitated in the discussion of perception.[24] The lack found there was that connection between things and events, as well as connections between the various aspects or properties of any given thing or event, are given in an unconditioned totality. At this point the natural attitude has been thrown into confusion; for it cannot give an account of how its world and distinct events within it hold together while at the same time presenting a manifold. In addition the natural attitude is confronted with the fact that it makes distinctions between the autonomous, singular thing and on the other hand its dependency and intimate connections with other things and its vulnerability to change due to the effects of other things or events upon it. There is identity over time, and yet often there is also radical change. The perspectivalism of perceptual claims has failed to account for this internal unconditionedness which remains one with an external conditionedness. If confronted with the many puzzles which arise from this situation, all that the natural attitude at this stage can do is to claim that there is an overarching unconditionedness, that the world does hold together and make sense as a whole. There is a horizontal unity of experience which ensures that things can be known as they are in reality. There is presupposed, then, an unconditioned, non-sensuous universal for the purpose of referring to this ultimate unity.

But there is also another unity presupposed, or rather another dimension of the unity. What has also failed in the presupposition that perception alone gives us a standpoint of certainty, is the attempt to articulate the overarching unity between oneself and the world. Such a unity must be presupposed if we are to claim to have contact with the real world; but at the same time we must preserve the difference between self and world which is evidenced in the possibility of error in knowledge and failure in action. One in the natural attitude presupposes both that he is part of the world and in unity with it, and also that he is separate from it; and this unity and difference or separation are themselves contained within an unconditioned unity of the subject-object relationship.[25]

Hegel now represents this dual unity by means of the exemplary concept of 'force'. Borrowing largely from Leibniz,[26] but reflecting a general philosophical thesis, force represents what is presupposed for the possibility of our experience.[27] But while it is evident that such a concept as force has been present in one form or another in most philosophical theories—and has been present for just the purposes it has arisen here—can we really say that it would be acceptable to one in the natural attitude? A good case can be made for its acceptance by the natural attitude if we remember that what is transpiring here is the complicity of the natural attitude in a quest for certainty. The ordinary perceptual stand has been challenged and doubt has been thrown on the possibility of successfully warranting natural certainty. Ever since the unreflective position of sense-certainty has been overthrown, there has been a slowly developing self-awareness that there is an attitude or standpoint to be accounted for if we are to give warranty for our certainty. With the critique of perception as the absolute standpoint, the self-awareness which natural consciousness has developed to this point is, as I said, in a state of confusion. In the attempt to understand things and events and our relation to them, one has been plunged into the relative uncertainty of a domain demanding true reflection on our presuppositions; for the naivete of sense-certainty is now almost completely effaced. What should have amounted to simply clarifying descriptions on the level of natural, perceptual consciousness are now taken to be difficult puzzles to be solved by an appeal to the use of one's understanding of the non-sensuous relations which are obviously there.

Thus, the articulation of the various presuppositions involved in such an understanding arises out of the quest for certainty and the crisis of this stage to which we have come. Challenged in such a crisis and intent on warranting its natural certainty, one would clearly respond with an appeal to the unity of unity and difference which is presupposed every time one differentiates between objects or events which latter are nevertheless bound together in a unity. And one appeals to the non-sensuous unity of self and world in making any claim to know with certainty. Seen in the light of the quest for certainty, then, an unconditioned universal is taken as the ground for the possibility of our experience of the particulars which constitute experience. As we now examine the various forms this understanding and its world are claimed to have, we shall see more clearly just how the presupposition set would manifest itself for one in the natural attitude.

In its general configuration, force as the unconditioned universal has two moments or aspects to it. It is presupposed that force is something in itself, the substance which holds together the manifoldness of objects and events. It is the power of things and events to interact, and the power to be held together internally. Second, it is presupposed that in addition to this pure power or *potency* of things and events to be themselves and to interact with other things, force is also the expression of itself, the actual phenomena of the perceptual world, the *activity* of holding together and interaction. The first aspect is substance as metaphysical substance, the second is physical substance. The unity of these two aspects of force is a whole, something transcendent both to perceptual consciousness and to consciousness of the potency of force.

This general form of the presupposition about force is now augmented in several ways to produce different specific sets designed to articulate the possibility of having certainty. Hegel begins with the most simple and straightforward account.[28] The claim now to be tested is that in experience we have the presence of substances, i.e., things or events, which are there perceptually for us to understand. The cup or the chair itself, or the meeting of political opponents, is simply present as substantial, as a substance. The way in which what is there holds together the many properties which it evidences—the colors, textures, sounds, movements—is also simple and immediate. In other terms, the thing or event is simply itself and is understood in terms of itself and its properties. The cup *is* the color and texture and weight; the political meeting *is* its sounds and the movements of its participants. On the other hand, the different colors and textures, sounds and weights are the many ways in which its being what it is is manifested or expressed; and the elements of the event as interacting elements are simply the ways in which the event shows itself. The natural attitude is again defended as having simple, direct access to reality.

But with these presuppositions in force, we would be no better off than we were with the presuppositions of perception when taken by themselves. For we have simply transposed the perceptual aspects of oneness and manyness to the level of the intelligible. The unconditioned remains a *"je ne sais quoi,"* and therefore has reality only as thought, only as something which I claim to know is there, which I claim to experience. Our recognition of the two moments of simple togetherness (force in itself) and diversity of elements (the expression of force) have not been accounted for in terms of their unity. Force as this unconditioned unity of the two aspects of unity and diversity has not itself been shown possible by the presupposition set. The problems which the presupposition of perceptual consciousness have as the ground for our certainty have only been repeated, copied. All that one really presupposes here is that the two aspects are *somehow* united. All that we really have is the concept of force, and not the unconditioned unity of the two aspects of force as substance. The

> moments of its actuality, their substances and their movement, collapse unresistingly into an undifferentiated unity, a unity which is not force driven back into itself (for this is itself only such a moment), but is its *concept qua concept* (*PhG*, 110; *PhS*, 86).

In other terms, what has been found to be lacking here is objective force as the unity of oneness and manyness. The absolute unconditioned universal is neither the oneness of things and events which is present in the natural attitude, nor the manyness of the elements and properties found there. It is the unity of these two substantial aspects. It is not something capturable as substance, but rather is an "essence," something accessible only to the power of the understanding alone and not substantial in any way. This is what Hegel means by calling force "concept." The concept (*der Begriff*) is, literally, the holding together of the various aspects of the object, or the various members of a class of objects.[29] The concept of force is neither force as oneness nor force as manifold expression, but the unity of these two substantial elements of force.

In this rather dense section on the understanding we have been brought to an awareness of the necessity for a presupposition that such a concept is operative in experience, not as a substance captured by the "vision" of the understanding, but as essence. Concept is in the former sense only "thought"; for at this stage all that one can say is that we can think the unity.

Hegel now reviews what has occurred thus far in the examination of the presuppositions of understanding. He calls the unconditioned as we first took it up, presupposed as substance, the "first universal," and the unconditioned as essence, as it is now posited, as the "second universal" (*PhG*, 110; *PhS*, 86). The claim at first was that it must be presupposed as substance, immediately accessible to consciousness as understanding. The thing, event, was a substance in the world directly available to cognition through a combination of sense and understanding. But it has been shown that under this presupposition all we can really get are the moments of force, namely its expression and its existence as a potential for expression. We have the actuality and potentiality of force, but not the unity of potentiality and actuality. If we were to remain at this point, our quest for certainty would have failed; for we have failed to reach that level of unity of potentiality and actuality which would guarantee our claims to certainty about that unity we actually experience. Understanding is constrained therefore to realize that force as such, as the unconditioned universal—the unifier of objects intended by conscious, intentional interest—is an object which must remain unknown for *any* sensibly conditioned knowledge. Somehow, then, the lack experienced in this presupposition set must be remedied by the presupposition of some access to reality *independently* of sensibility.

Hegel now introduces a new set of putative presuppositions concerning this unconditioned universal.

> This true essence of things has now the character of not being immediately for consciousness; on the contrary, consciousness has a mediated relation to the inner being and, as the understanding, *looks through this mediating play of forces into the true background of things*. The middle term which unites the two extremes, the understanding and the inner world, is the developed *being* of force which, for the understanding itself, is henceforth only a vanishing (*PhG*, 110; *PhS*, 86-87).

The substantial nature of objective reality is not denied here; for the two elements, unity and diversity in terms both of content and form, are retained as available to sense experience. Hegel denotes them here as the *being* of force, its being there for consciousness. But to this is added another domain, that of the essence of force which is to be presupposed now as lying *behind* that being, a domain accessible to the understanding alone through its encounters with the being of force and its expression in sensible appearances.[30]

At this point perception still maintains a degree of primacy; for the essence behind the appearances is something supposedly comprehended by "looking through" the perceptible world.[31] A distinction, however, has been introduced between perception and understanding; for not everything that is real is substantial or available directly to perception or directly to understanding. Our access to the intelligible is to be presupposed as possible through the mediation of the sensible. But there is also now a third aspect introduced, or perhaps we should say that it is reintroduced: consciousness as understanding. Since a pure immediacy of the unconditioned has proved not to be the ground of the possibility of our professed certainty, *the activity of understanding itself as a penetration of the world of substantial appearance* becomes an important moment of the presuppositions of experience. Consciousness as understanding is no longer to be taken as passive in respect to the world. The things toward which intentionality has directed us now are to play a mediating role, a role serving to unite a faculty of the conscious individual—his understanding—with a realm "behind" appearances—the essence of the reality which appears.

The importance of this introduction of consciousness as an active element—somehow independent of the given reality of the world intended in perceptual consciousness—will become clear subsequently; but it can be remarked here that what has been introduced is a recognition of the necessity for consciousness to reflect on itself *as an activity*.[32] Interest as intentionality at first directed us solely toward things in the world; and so long as intentionality had this other-directed function, the naturalness of the natural attitude—its naivete and immersion in the world—remained intact. Even when putative presuppositions of perception allowed for the difference between the object in itself and the object for us, this remained true; for "our" contribution, i.e. the contribution of the person viewing the object, was to count merely as the source of possible error. Now, on the contrary, those things thematized in the natural standpoint, those "others" to which we direct ourselves, are presupposed as playing only a mediating role in the transaction between consciousness and the essence behind appearances.

The presupposition of this positive role for the understanding is clear if we look to the response from one in the natural attitude when confronted with the puzzles we now have, and when confronted with any problem which demands that one do more than just passively perceive. Caught in the web of the quest for certainty at this stage, or pausing to ponder any difficult problem, one would respond to a question about what one is doing with the answer, "I'm trying to understand what is going on here," or "I want to be really certain, so I must get to the bottom of this." If asked what the problem is, i.e., why the answer to the problem or the evidence of the certainty is not simply forthcoming, the response would be something to the effect that there is more to it than meets the eye or simply that we must try to find better evidence than has appeared thus far. Allusion to "trying" and "wanting" and "a lack in the appearances as they present themselves," all presuppose a positive role for consciousness in its functions as perception and understanding. This, then, is the beginning of a move to recognize that consciousness presupposes self-consciousness, i.e., that in being conscious or directed in terms of interest as intentionality, I presuppose that I am also self-conscious or directed in terms of a desire which reflects back upon my *interest* as *my* interest and not simply upon interests as defined by the objective world intended.[33] The quest for certainty on the part of the natural attitude is about to become a deliberate, self-conscious quest which will later enable it fully to reflect on what it is involved with in the *Phenomenology*.

The new form of consciousness presupposed here is therefore one which imputes a difference between itself and the world of appearances, since as itself it is not only perceptual consciousness defined in terms of perceptual objects, but is also understanding. Furthermore, within that objective world there is imputed a difference between appearances and the essence of those appearances, the latter which belongs to a realm different from the sensuous realm of things. This is a new "geography"; the

> "being" [of force] is ... called *appearance*; for we call *being* that is directly and in its own self a *non-being* a surface show; it is appearance, a *totality* of show. This *totality*, as totality or as a *universal*, is what constitutes the inner [of things], the play of forces as a reflection [of the play within itself, i.e., within the totality of the inner]. In [the totality or inner] the things of perception are expressly present for consciousness as they are in themselves, viz. as moments which immediately and without rest or stay turn into their opposite, the one immediately into the universal, the essential immediately into the unessential, and vice versa. This play of forces is consequently the developed negative; but its truth is the positive, viz. the *universal*, the object that, *in itself*, possesses being. The *being* of this object [i.e., of the intelligible object for the understanding, the totality], for consciousness is mediated by the movement of *appearance*, in which the *being of perception* and the sensuously [given object] in general has a merely negative significance . . . . This inner is, therefore, for consciousness an extreme over against it; but it is for consciousness the true, since in the inner, as the in-itself, it possesses at the same time the certainty of itself, or the moment of its being-for-self (*PhG*, 110-11; *PhS*, 87).

We have now a presupposition set which articulates a realm of objective, non-sensuous entities. The inner world to which the understanding or intelligence has access is a supersensible world of the unconditioned totality, an absolute ground for the world of appearances which in themselves appear as being, but which in reality are *only* appearances. The perceptual world is to be presupposed as lacking independent reality. It is a domain presupposed as secondary and one which derives its being through participation in the essentially true and actual supersensible world (*PhG*, 111; *PhS*, 87-88). The understanding, on the other hand, is consciousness as it actively penetrates into this true world through the world of appearances. The full object of our phenomenological analysis is now the relationship between (a) consciousness as understanding, (b) appearances in the sensible world which we have through perception, and (c) essences in the supersensible world (*PhG*, 111-12; *PhS*, 88).

One can see here that we have a general presupposition set which is an extensive refinement of the natural attitude as it was finally conceived in sense-certainty. At the end of the analysis of sense-certainty that attitude itself as the relation of consciousness and the world of objects became the nexus of experience which was to be shown to be possible by further analysis of consciousness, thus showing us the grounds for our professed certainty. We already understood there the mediated relationship that had to be present between myself and the object if certainty as professed in sense-certainty were to be warranted. At the present stage of the examination of the standpoint of consciousness, we have returned explicitly to the mediating relation between consciousness and world. On the one hand the essences of the supersensible world are presupposed as the ground of possibility for the world of appearances thematized in the natural attitude of sense-certainty. On the other hand that world of appearances mediates our access to the ground supposed in the supersensible world. Finally, perception now has a mediating function in respect to consciousness as understanding, while the understanding penetrates to the supposed ground which is to explicate and make intelligible the world accessible to perception and the natural attitude of sense-certainty.[34]

At this stage of the *Phenomenology*, then, the quest for certainty is again concentrating on that relation between self and world which was maintained at the end of the discussion of sense-certainty. The joint search for warranty for natural certainty has, to be sure, led us rather far from the naive presuppositions first put forth by the natural attitude; but our journey from that beginning has been given continuity by means of a constant probing of the series of presuppositions offered for natural consciousness in order to satisfy its demand for warranted certainty. When the presupposition that perceptual consciousness alone could warrant our certainty failed to produce the possibility of the natural world we all know and act in, we made a natural turn to our ability to comprehend things in terms of non-sensuous universals and concepts and to several trial presuppositions about the nature of those universals as they are taken to exist objectively in the world. Some supersensible component to the world is and must be presupposed whenever we address ourselves to thought or action. If we are to have certainty that we can say "Here is a tree," or "Today is Wednesday," or that we can act in the space-time constituted by these two, then we must show access to that unity which makes real thought and action possible.

We now turn to examine several putative presupposition sets formed around the general presupposition of a supersensible world beyond the sensible. These sets are both elements of philosophical theories which have been put forward in the historical-philosophical dialogue and also elements of noetic-ontological presupposition sets which could be elicited from one in the natural attitude who had come this far with us. In the first set, the supersensible is taken to be beyond consciousness in such a way that consciousness fails to find its certainty about the world. Under this set, the inner being or essence of things is taken as unknowable because "this inner world is determined here as the *beyond* of consciousness"(*PhG*, 112; *PhS*, 88). There is thus an assumption of the impossibility of access for knowledge; there is only access in the sense that one is aware that the domain of the inner is there and perhaps can be "thought" in Kant's sense, but cannot be known. But such a presupposition set effectively denies the very possibility of warranted certainty; for if, by presupposition, the supersensible is the locus of truth and warranty for certainty—the unconditioned universal—and if we have no access to it, "then nothing would be left to us but to stop at the world of appearance, i.e., to perceive something as true which we know is not true" (*PhG*, 112; *PhS*, 88). We might *imagine* what is there in the inner world, but these imaginings would be pure reveries produced by consciousness itself. This, too, would fail to give us access to truth, and therefore would contradict that certainty of the natural attitude which is always to be accepted by us in this quest for certainty.

Here, then, it is not so much that the presupposition set would generate a set of possible worlds inconsistent with the possible worlds of our actual experience; rather the natural certainty which attaches to those possible worlds of our actual experience would be flatly declared as unwarranted certainty, since if access to truth is denied, then certainty can never be warranted.

The determinate lack or negation which arises from this presupposition set is caused by presupposing that the supersensible is something which is purely transcendent with respect to consciousness; for it is that presupposition which necessitates that consciousness would have no access to the unconditioned. This presupposition is now replaced by one in which a connection between consciousness and the supersensible world is proposed. This proposal is derived from the recognition that this inner world has come to our attention by reflection on the problems given us by the perceptual world. In other words, we make this move by reflection upon the process in the *Phenomenology* by means of which we have come to the present impasse. The inner world or supersensible which is to be presupposed and investigated

> *comes from* the world of appearance which has mediated it; in other words, appearance is its essence and, in fact, its filling. The supersensible is the sensuous and the perceived posited as it is *in truth*; but the *truth* of the sensuous and the perceived is to be *appearance*. The supersensible is therefore *appearance qua appearance* (*PhG*, 113; *PhS*, 89).

This distinction between appearance as appearance and, on the other hand, the appearances of what appears, is critical to the analysis at this point, and will lay the foundation for the introduction of "law" as the essence of reality.[35] The distinction is this. The play of forces, or the various manifest things and events thematized in the natural attitude of perceptual sense-certainty, appear and disappear or come into being and perish. But appearance itself—or what one might call the givenness of reality as a world, the characteristic of there-always-already-being appearances of one sort or another—neither appears nor disappears, neither comes into being nor perishes. We always presuppose *as given already* the *world of appearances* as the framework in which what appears appears. If I look for a friend, I presuppose and anticipate that he will appear in that world of appearances—in appearance as appearance—which is that same world which now exists as I look for him and do not see him. Appearance as appearance is the "truth" of appearances or the actual play of forces just because it is the ground of the possibility of there being appearances at all. This is not a mystification through reification, but a simple phenomenological acceptance of the nature of the framework of experience as that framework is actually given in experience. Appearance as appearance is simply the framework of givenness within which the given appears, and is something readily acceptable to the natural attitude; for it is simply that totality which contains all the richness and depth of experience which was at first presupposed in sense-certainty.

The significance of this is that we now are to presuppose access to the supersensible *through* the sensible. The play of forces, i.e., particular things and events of experience as they interact, are thematized on the background of appearance as appearance, which latter is not itself thematized for perceptual consciousness; but it is also the case that it is through the mediation of this play of forces that appearance as appearance or the supersensible can be made explicit as a presupposition. The play of forces or appearances thus has a double significance: on the one hand, the forces have a negative significance in themselves, since we want warranty for certainty and since that warranty can come only from a knowledge of the unconditioned universal which is the inner of appearances; but appearances also have a positive significance as the mediating agency for the inner (*PhG*, 113-14; *PhS*, 89-90). The inner itself also has a double significance. On the one hand it is "outside" or "beyond" the understanding which attempts to grasp it, while at the same time it is the unconditioned universal, the absolute flux of differences of all sorts in appearance which are brought together into a simple universal unity. This unity is to be presupposed as "the law of force," the presupposition that in the intelligible realm there is a universality which brings order to the changes in appearance (*PhG*, 114-15; *PhS*, 90-91).

What is presupposed as content here, in contrast to the former presupposition of the supersensible as an empty form or receptacle, is a domain of law.[36] Law is taken as the

> *stable* image of unstable appearance . . . . The *supersensible* world is an inert *realm of laws* which, though beyond the perceived world—for this exhibits law only through incessant change—is equally *present* in it and is its direct tranquil image (*PhG*, 114-15; *PhS*, 90-91).

Two examples will show what Hegel is claiming here concerning the presupposition sets now formulated. Let us say that the understanding in its natural attitude of consciousness thematizes things or events in a way which involves their motions and the various forces they exhibit. Through observation and reflective understanding, a law emerges which is expressed as "f = ma." What we have here is the presupposition of this law as a stable image of unstable appearances. First of all, "f = ma" remains true through many different appearances of many different things and events on many different occasions. With all of the variations of things and events and their respective interactions, the same law remains true: force is equal to the product of mass and acceleration. In order to work with this and to understand the world on the basis of this and other formulae, one putatively presupposes a stability behind things—a kingdom or realm of law—which grants intelligibility in a warranted way to the many changes and differences in perceptual experience. Secondly, "f = ma" involves us, in itself, with a relation between different elements or aspects of reality. Force, mass, and acceleration are three different "elements" brought together into a relation of identity or sameness without effacing the differences between them. An equation is a framework in which differences are united in some specific configuration or, to say the same thing, in which a unity of elements contains as its essence difference within it. It is the identity of identity and difference. This supposedly grounds our certainty about specific appearances.

A second example would be the taking up with certainty of things in the world. We saw in the analysis of perception that even in perceiving a simple object we presupposed intelligible relations which were not accessible to sensibility and yet which were somehow given with experience. Described in purely perceptual terms under the presupposition sets putatively assigned experience at that earlier stage, we were left with an "unknown and unknowable" which somehow constituted the unity of a thing or event. Under the present putative presuppositions of experience we presuppose that understanding has access to a domain of laws such that the unity demanded but missing before is now to be given, and thus certainty of objects to be justified.

Therefore, there is to be presupposed a realm of law accessible to our understanding which, through the mediation of the changing realm of appearances accessible to sense experience, gives us an unconditioned universality. Understanding is to be taken as the absolute standpoint; the inner of things is to be presupposed as the realm in which warranty for certainty is to be found. If the data of sense experience can be accounted for by these laws, and if the access of the understanding to the laws be warranted, then we will have indeed reached the absolute standpoint and an end to the quest for certainty.

But if we now hold to this presupposition set in a strict manner, we will find that the possible worlds involved are not consistent with the possible worlds of natural experience, even where that experience is the experience of a scientific understanding. Hegel shows this new inadequacy in several ways. First, the presupposition set involves us with a two-worlds thesis; given these two worlds, the supersensible world is not a true and complete image of outer appearances because the former involves pure stability—the law itself without the variations of sensible experience—while the world of outer appearances has in it the constant changes and variation. There is nothing in the presupposition set which can bridge this gap between the stability of lawfulness and the instability and contingency of the actual happening of things and events. The law contains difference within it in terms of the variables and constants represented; but it contains them as abstract. It is thus precisely the variability of content, the contingency which belongs to our experiences for which we have no account. Therefore, under the present presupposition set there would be no connection, but simply a transposition from one level to the other. But in the possible worlds of experience and knowledge as we actually have them, there is a connection, i.e., the laws do give us a way not only to comprehend, but also to predict and control appearances. In this respect, then, the presupposition set is inadequate; for our dealings with contingencies would have no degree of certainty according to the presupposition set.

There is also a second major critique of this putative presupposition set. Turning to the domain of law itself, Hegel notes that the concept of law which is presupposed does not coincide with the nature of actually existing laws; for law is supposed to be necessary, while that necessity is not demonstrated in the laws themselves. The law, for instance "f = ma," is to give us a necessity which will account for what happens in experience and yield certainty. We are told that force *is* equal to the product of mass and acceleration. But we are not shown that it is necessary that mass and acceleration come into such a relation with each other, nor that in such a relation it is necessary that they be "equal to" force. Hegel makes the point by using the example of laws of electricity as they were understood in his time. He argues that, given the laws of electricity, all that we can conclude is that electricity *in fact* has certain properties (*PhG*, 116-17; *PhS*, 92-93). This critique, like the first critique, had already essentially been formulated by Hume.[37]

The present presupposition proposal therefore is deficient in two ways: (1) there is an unbridgeable gap between the world of the supersensible and that of the sensible, even though this gap is somehow bridged in our actual experience and must be if certainty is to be warranted; (2) the very necessity in the laws, which should be there, is not demonstrated. If we now inquire into this double lack, we find that it occurs because the understanding itself has been left out of consideration in the presupposition set. Addressing himself to the second failure of the set, Hegel reflects that the understanding

> *has* the concept of this *implicit difference* just because the law is, on the one hand, the inner, *implicit* being, but is, at the same time, inwardly differentiated. That this difference is thus an *inner* difference follows from the fact that the law is a *simple* force or is the *concept* of the difference, and is therefore a difference belonging to the *concept*. But this inner difference still falls, to begin with, only within the understanding, and is not yet posited *in the thing itself*. It is, therefore, only its *own* necessity that is asserted by the understanding; the difference, then, is posited by the understanding in such a way that, at the same time, it is expressly stated that the difference is not a *difference belonging to the thing itself*. This necessity, which is merely verbal, is thus a recital of the moments constituting the cycle of the necessity (*PhG*, 118-19; *PhS*, 94).

We here make a Kantian move in our presupposition set.[38] The lack of necessity in the domain of law in itself is nothing other than what was discovered by Hume and capitalized upon by Kant: from an "objectivist" point of view, no necessity can be discovered in the laws of appearance. The presupposition set is to give us necessary connections; the best it can do is to give us a factual report of constant conjunction. This is reflected in the natural attitude's attempts to escape having to make absolute truth claims by reverting to relativism as well as by its recognition, implicit in its natural "pragmatism," that somehow we and our interests have something to do with how we operate in the world.

The new set, however, is to change this. What we have, in reality, is not simple force as the inner of things, nor a set of laws objectively constituting a unity in reality in any "realist" sense, but *explanation, clarification*, the verbalization of the unity of unity and difference. Explanation is *our* work, the work of the understanding in the natural attitude itself. In explanation we go through a recital of the elements of the phenomenon which are united in a relation to each other within the simple unity of the phenomenon. We combine in the realm of explanation the expression of force which belonged to the realm of appearances, together with force itself as the inner of things.[39] Understanding itself becomes the unconditioned unity, grounding the way in which appearances are present in appearance as appearance. The necessity which is to be found there must be presupposed as a necessity which belongs to the understanding itself as explanation.

Kant's position of the *First Critique* is essentially the presupposition set which Hegel finds adequate at the level of interest as intentionality. The principles of the understanding and the transcendental unity of apperception make possible the possible worlds of knowledge and experience as we actually have them, and link our certainty to truth. However, Hegel pushes Kant's analysis to a point beyond that which Kant thought proper.[40] First, in the discussion of "the inverted world" Hegel shows that what must be presupposed is not a distinction between the "in-itself" and the "for-us" as two worlds, or even as two ontologically or epistemologically separable worlds. Rather, the in-itselfness of the world is an aspect of experience which belongs to appearance itself. Kant's thing-in-itself is just the aspect of givenness which belongs to appearance as appearance as distinct from the appearances which appear in that appearance. The opposition of "inner and outer, of appearance and the supersensible, as of two different kinds of actuality, we no longer find here" (*PhG*, 123; *PhS*, 98). The reality we presuppose is therefore an inverted or perverse world only to those who would insist on the pre-Kantian presuppositions about the radical difference between two worlds of reality and appearance or who would take positively the notion of a thing-in-itself as inaccessible to experience.[41]

We now see that

> we must eliminate the sensuous idea of fixing the differences in a different sustaining element; and this absolute concept of the difference must be represented and understood purely as inner difference, a repulsion of the selfsame, as selfsame, from itself, and likeness of the unlike as unlike. We have to think pure change, or *think opposition within the opposition itself, or contradiction* (*PhG*, 124; *PhS*, 98-99).

We must presuppose an identity-in-difference in the unity between the world of appearances and the supersensible world, as well as between the world of experience and the world in itself. The supersensible or intelligible is the essence of the sensible and thus different from it; but it is the essence as within the sensible and thus is the same as it. On the other hand, the world in itself is just the unity of appearance as appearance which we discovered is the presupposition at the basis of the givenness of appearances. It is not some world in itself, but the world which actually appears as the matrix of the appearings of things and events. The differences between the world of appearance and the world "behind" appearances are taken up in the unity of understanding as the capacity for explanation. The difference between conscious explanation and this unity of appearance is itself a difference which is at the same time no difference. What is presupposed is in fact the unity of experience, not only horizontally as constituted by the principles of the understanding, but vertically as well. What is to be presupposed is not a subject on one side and an object on the other; rather what is to be presupposed is the unity of experience as experiencing *and* the experienced, an identity of experience such that *within experience* as this totality of subject and object, of experiencing and the experienced, this distinction between knower and known occurs. This is what Hegel calls the infinity of experience; for experience as such is limited under such a presupposition by nothing but itself.[42]

This position does not constitute an indefensible idealism. The key to this presupposition set is a reflection on what occurs in the act of explanation in which we find these laws of the appearances. In the act of explanation, as it occurs in the natural attitude, the individual presents to himself the world as it appears to him and, on the basis of the constitution of consciousness, comes to understand that world as something intelligible. In Hegel's words, the

> reason why "explaining" affords so much self-satisfaction is just because in it consciousness is, so to speak, communing directly with itself, enjoying only itself; although it seems to be busy with something else, it is in fact occupied only with itself (*PhG*, 127; *PhS*, 101).

The world presented is the world constituted by the principles of the understanding under the limitations of sensibility. The explanation afforded in this case is a unification of appearances as they are given in experience thus constituted. There are, of course, many difficulties associated with this presupposition set; and it is this which will lead us to investigate a whole new level of presuppositions, namely presuppositions united by the claim that self-consciousness and not consciousness is the locus of the absolute standpoint. But these difficulties do not change the initial truth to be found in this final presupposition set of consciousness as the putative absolute standpoint.

It is in this sense that consciousness can be said to have itself as object, and in this sense that consciousness is an infinity. This is nothing more or less than the position arrived at in sense-certainty; for the final presupposition set of sense-certainty maintained that it was neither in the subject nor in the object alone that the ground of the possibility of the possible worlds of experience and knowledge was to be found. Now, under this "Kantian" set as amended by Hegel, we have spelled out the constitution of that unity of self and world, of knower and known. And in doing so, we have been led to a wholly new level of presupposition; for what has been shown is that consciousness presupposes self-consciousness. The meaning of this will be explored in the next chapter; but the origin of it in the dialectical analysis can be discussed now in a final review of what has occurred in this first general level of presupposition, the presupposition of interest as intentionality as the nexus of the absolute standpoint.[43]

The genesis of this new level of presupposition derives from the discovery that, with the turn to explanation and the presupposition set which issued from reflection upon it, consciousness has been turned to itself as the source of certainty, as the absolute standpoint. Hitherto, attention has focused mainly on reality as objective or as transcendent with respect to consciousness, rather than on consciousness itself. The latter has been defined prior to this for the most part in terms of the objective reality to which it was to have access. Thus, perceptual consciousness was just that consciousness which had access to the perceptual reality; and understanding consciousness was, on the "pre-Kantian view," just that consciousness which would have access to the *mundus intelligibilis*. Now, however, consciousness has turned to itself as something which constitutes reality in terms of intelligibility, rather than as something constituted by reality or as a *tabula rasa* of one sort or another. This turn toward itself signifies the overcoming of the thesis of consciousness in general, the thesis of the simple separation of consciousness and the world from each other.

In terms of the natural certainty of the natural attitude, the very activity of explanation presupposes that there is a pre-established unity between our understanding and the world such that the inner essence of things and events which appear to us and need explanation, and the terms in which we express that inner essence in law and explanation, are each indistinguishable from the other in form and content.[44] And yet in explanation a distinction is made between (1) my intellectual activity, (2) the appearances which are to be explained, and (3) the realm of laws and explanations which give us the ground of appearances. Thus, although a separation between thought and things and their inner essence is presupposed, it is also presupposed that there is no distinction between them, no separation, but a unity. It is this contradiction—which other presuppositions in effect sought to avoid—that must be accepted and which will be taken up as a contradiction and be made intelligible *if* we take interest to be desire, rather than intentionality.

The natural attitude has thus been shown that if its quest for certainty is to be completed by demonstrating that the kind of world it is naturally certain of can be shown to exist with warranted certainty, then one must presuppose not the simple separation of consciousness and world and then try to find a unity; rather one must first presuppose a unity of self and world which subsequently is found to contain within it a difference which fixes the separation of self and world from within the fundamental unity. To spell out this presuppositional demand will require the whole of the analysis of "self-consciousness"; but the requirement has been shown and the natural attitude is now prepared by the *Phenomenology* to look at itself. This means that there will now be present a degree of self-awareness on the part of the natural attitude which will bring it closer to the standpoint of philosophy, and yet which will remain "natural." When it is presupposed that interest is not intentionality, but is desire, and that self-consciousness is the absolute standpoint, then the individual in the natural attitude can recognize a reflexiveness which is of a kind with philosophical reflection and quite different from the directedness-toward-the-other which marks intentionality. This recognition, then, on the part of the natural attitude is crucial to the progress to be made in revealing to the natural attitude that the absolute standpoint is within it; for it has now turned reflectively to itself.[45]

IV
Interest As Desire

HEGEL'S FIRST TASK in the chapter on self-consciousness is to redefine the interests which move us in our everyday affairs.

> In the previous modes of certainty what is true for consciousness is something other than itself . . . . But now there has arisen what did not emerge in these previous relationships, viz. a certainty which is identical with its truth; for the certainty is to itself its own object, and consciousness is to itself the truth (*PhG*, 133; *PhS*, 104).[1]

On the presupposition that consciousness furnishes the absolute standpoint, interests were constituted as an intentionality which somehow enabled one to receive a world given from without. On the presupposition that self-consciousness furnishes the standpoint, the interests are not *simply* interests in a world, but rather in a world which constitutes and is constituted as my *life*.[2] The world is not simply presupposed as there for me, separate from me, but *also* as simultaneously a part and the milieu of my life as I serially live it. The world now is life, and life is the arena in which my interests are located and toward which my interests direct me. Life is made by me in the process of my living my life, and thus is a function of my interests and the activities which come from them. But life is also accepted as always *there* already, and as the arena of possibilities given me for the living of that life. Thus, the first great change in presupposition is from that of an external world which is noetically and ontologically separate from me, to that of a life which retains the characteristic of that separate world, but which also has as one of its characteristics its dependence upon me as its constitutor. On the presupposition of self-consciousness, if I am to warrant my certainty of access to reality it will be in terms of my interest not simply in a world separate from me, but rather in the world as my life.

A second major change in presupposition is on the side of interest itself. Interest is not only intentionality or an orientation outward toward what is other, but also an interest in hegemony over that which is other. Such an interest is called, in general, "*desire*".[3] Desire is always interest in something other than itself and thus invokes the separation and difference from the object or thing desired; but it is always also that in terms of which the thing desired is defined. The thing desired is not only defined by interest, and thus noetically constituted, but it also appears as the focus of attention and thus is explicitly in experience on the grounds that it is something of interest, something desired. Thus, desire governs the way things are and appear, but yet is also dependent upon the other as something which must be present in order to be desired. In contrast to interest as intentionality, the interests which move us are now to be presupposed as basically desires for objects desired.[4]

It is this complexus of desire and life which marks the general presuppositional structure of self-consciousness. And when we hold that desire is the fundamental form of interest, we also presuppose a new definition of certainty and truth: there is warranted certainty and access to truth, i.e., an adequation of thought and action to things, when and only when desire is satisfied; for every desire brings with it a determination of the range and meaning of things and events which will count for satisfaction and thus for adequation.[5]

The quest for certainty present in the discussion of consciousness has therefore not been laid aside in order that we discuss the nature of social life or something else of the sort. The focus of the quest in the discussion of the presupposition of self-consciousness as the absolute standpoint is now, as Hegel wrote in the first paragraph of the chapter, the striving which is the striving for certainty itself. Warranty is to come from the satisfaction of desires in a world which is the arena of life for the desiring individual. If in this discussion of self-consciousness and interest as desire it can be established that proof of access to reality is ultimately established on the grounds of self-consciousness alone, then we will have reached the goal of our quest, warranty for claims that we have an absolute, unconditioned standpoint. The lack which was found at the end of our discussion of consciousness presupposed as the putative absolute standpoint is to be remedied by the presupposition that my natural certainty is grounded in the desire-life relationship which structures my everyday activities.

This means, then, that the world which was merely presupposed as a given positivity for intentionality and consciousness is no longer that; for as the correlate of a nexus of desire-satisfaction, that world is already circumscribed. It is presupposed as the world in which desires are to be satisfied and thereby where certainty of access is to be warranted. That is to say, the world is *not* just *a* world, but *my* world, the arena of my activities oriented around my interests as desires. The world is putatively presupposed not simply as a totality of positivity, but now as a totality of negativity, of otherness, of mere possibilities which change with the changes of desire.

There are three senses of 'life' in use here, and all three must constantly be kept in mind.[6] First, there is life in the most general sense, an objective sense through which I refer to the totality of the world as when I say, "That is life" or "Life is full of surprises." Here we presuppose a totality which transcends any individual. Second, life refers to the specific life of the individual, "my life," a life lived within life in general and presupposed as distinguished from it. It is presupposed, then, that there is life in general, the universal life of the planet, and life in particular, the specific life which is my own as opposed to the lives of others and to life in general. The difference between these two will be one of the major difficulties found in the general presupposition set of self-consciousness when it is held up as the absolute standpoint. And to these two meanings of the term 'life' is added a third, viz., life as the actual activity of living, the serial, diachronic living which constitutes my life as a whole and as a particular and limited totality within the totality of life in general.

This analysis of 'life' makes it even more clear that life as the correlate of self-consciousness qua desire is radically different from "world" as the correlate of conscious intentionality.[7] It is also clearly not a reference to the biological as such or to a "lower" form of being than consciousness. In life as the object of interest, then, there is no simple positivity of the given; rather, there is a reciprocal mediation coursing through all three meanings of the term. Life in general or the universal is in *its* constitution presupposed as the nexus of the individual, particular lives of individual human beings, and is thus a manifold of particulars. Each particular life, on the other hand, is presupposed as the serial living of a particular life, and thus again is a manifold of particulars. This means, in turn, that the universal itself is also given as mediated by the individual, serial living. But, secondly, the living of the individual only occurs within the particular life itself which, in turn, is only something within life in general. Therefore, each of the three aspects of life mediates and is mediated by the other two.[8]

However, there is yet another way in which the presupposition of this desire-life complexus is differentiated from the intentionality-world matrix of which it is now putatively the ground: the very living of life which is fundamental to life as a particular positivity presupposes a "center" for that life, namely desire.[9] Life, then, immediately presupposes and is presupposed by that of which it is a correlate: self-consciousness as desire. The objects intended in the world under the presupposition of intentionality were, to be sure, intimately connected with the intentional activity of the individual; but that connection was not one such that intentionality was itself an aspect of the object intended. In the case of life, on the other hand, one of its constituent elements or meanings—living—is precisely desire or interest over against the world in which interest is taken.

It is clear, then, that the presupposition of simple separation which characterized consciousness is no longer present in the same form. In its place is an equivocal and ambiguous relation, which we saw in its beginnings in our analysis of 'explanation'.[10] An individual with a desire has an object or event different from himself as the object of desire. In so far there is to be presupposed separation both epistemologically and ontologically. Yet that event or object exists in experience and is defined only in terms of desire itself. In so far, the object or event *is* only as desired and therefore is presupposed in an epistemological and ontological *unity* with the desire of the individual. This analysis of the desire-life complexus is not the result of a careless use of language by Hegel. The ambiguity cannot be removed by focusing on one side rather than another without destroying the veracity of the analysis. *If* interest is desire, and *if* the correlate of desire is the world as life, and *if* life is constituted in part as the living of life—and all three of these conditions seem to be true to our experience—then it follows that it is true both that life is independent of desire *and* that life is dependent upon desire.

This is not to lessen the importance of the separation of the object of desire from the desire.[11] If there were not a presupposition of the independence of objects and events desired, then they would simply be identical to the desire itself and thus could not be desired. But experience shows us that they are not simply identical. Therefore, life itself must be presupposed as having an independence as the arena of possibilities for desire, the arena for the activity of our interests as desires. This ambiguity cannot be effaced without destroying the possibility of a proper description of the presuppositions of self-conscious activity. On the other hand, as we have seen above, one aspect of this ambiguity—the necessary inclusion of living as a serial event within life—entails that life itself is the ground of intelligibility and possibility only so far as it has a focus, a center which is nothing other than the individual, self-conscious desire of the person living that life. Therefore, life presupposes the independence of desire from it in order to be the arena of desire, and yet presupposes the dependency of desire upon life for an arena of possibility. The desiring individual presupposes the independent arena of life in order to make its own life, and yet presupposes life as dependent upon desire. This ambiguity represents the true state of the presupposition set, and must be retained throughout the dialectical analysis of that set.

Here, then, the totality and the totalizing process are not separated as in the presuppositions of consciousness. They are understood rather to collapse into the mediation which constitutes self-consciousness as the absolute standpoint. As a presupposition for consciousness and thus for the possible worlds of the natural attitude in general, self-consciousness is putatively to remedy the lack which occurred there in articulating the connection presupposed between self and world; for both self (in the mode of desire) and world (in the form of life) are to contain within themselves that connection.[12] Desire *is* the center of life; life *is* the arena of desire. World as life is internally self-mediated by desires; desire is internally self-mediated by the living of life. But what of the main question of the *Phenomenology*, namely whether or not we have reached the unconditioned standpoint, the set of praxical presuppositions which will warrant the natural certainty of access to reality? It may be that consciousness presupposes self-consciousness for its possibility and ground. But does self-consciousness ground itself? Is this desire-life complexus the fundamental nexus of warranted certainty and truth?[13]

As sense-certainty and the problem of particulars set the problem for consciousness as the putative ultimate ground, these internal mediations of desire and life are to set the problem of self-consciousness. When, in a natural, unreflective mode of being, I desire something, it would seem at first that what we have described above, and that alone, constitutes a proper noetic-ontological presupposition set. Something appears to me which is desired, and I pursue it to my satisfaction. Or something appears to me which is undesireable and I either ignore it or attempt to destroy it or change it in some way which will make it desireable. My life, and life in general, is simply such a series of existential activities. Life is a series of desires and satisfactions.

However, under this presupposition set alone our actual experience would not be generated.[14] In experience the independence of life shows itself as at times recalcitrant, a resistance to desires and a refusal to be defined in terms of my desires. But if life were presupposed, however ambiguously, in terms of simple desire, then this stubbornness of the world would be inexplicable.[15] Furthermore, since experience shows that satisfactions are often denied, we would be denied certainty and our quest for certainty would fail; for warranted certainty is presupposed as defined by the satisfaction of desire. Finally, life would be nothing but a meaningless series of desire-satisfaction episodes; for the only result of the satisfaction of one desire is the appearance of another. But this also is not always the case in life, although it sometimes might be; for again it is clear that life somehow has the power to negate the desiring individual, a power of negation at least equal in magnitude to that of the individual who negates the world—or who at least attempts to do so—by holding it up for his own consumption.[16] Life as desire-satisfaction would in the end therefore necessitate the collapse of experience into an enclosed, solipsistic whole and, as a consequence, there would be no way actually to distinguish *my* desires and life from the desires and lives of others, and thus no way to distinguish my life and world from life and world in general.[17] But, again, the possible worlds of our experience are such that these distinctions are easily made and solipsism is *naturally* repugnant to the natural attitude. Our existence is neither an unending series of desire-satisfaction and a groundless, meaningless Sisyphean existence, nor a monolithic, solipsistic whole. These determinate failures of the original presupposition set of self-consciousness are what is taken up in the remainder of the analysis of self-consciousness.

In the section of the chapter titled "The Independence and Dependence of Self-consciousness" an attempt is made to articulate and test putative presuppositions which are to resolve these difficulties.[18] However, Hegel's use of the metaphor "master-slave" and "lordship and bondage" has misguided many into interpreting the problem of this section, and of self-consciousness generally, as something radically different from what was explored in the section on "consciousness."[19] But the problem set here, as I have already argued, is not a socio-historical theme; it is a new stage in the quest for certainty in which self-consciousness is to be presupposed as the putative absolute standpoint for access to reality. The social and historical can only arise later, when spirit as such is investigated in terms of its presuppositional role in our access to reality.[20] The terms 'master' and 'slave' or 'lordship' and 'bondage' only refer to the two aspects of self-consciousness which have already been discussed at the opening of the section on self-consciousness: respectively the independence and dependence of self-consciousness. What is discovered in the process of the present analysis is not that some individuals are masters and some in bondage, but that each and every self-conscious individual both has mastery over life and is thus independent of it, and yet is in bondage to life and thus dependent upon it. There is an ambiguity of mastery and bondage which represents in a striking way the ambiguity of independence and dependence already evidenced by our analysis of desire and life as the putative constituents of self-consciousness.[21]

The inquiry into self-consciousness and its constitution at the presuppositional level involves, then, the thematization of the fact that in interest as desire there is both an independence in respect to things in the world and other self-conscious individuals who are a part of that life, and yet, necessarily, a dependency upon life and the other individuals in it. This duality or ambiguity has been presupposed in order to accommodate the failure discovered in the first analysis of self-consciousness, namely that desire and the world would seem to collapse into one another. Two questions lack an answer: (1) how my desires are uniquely mine and not some other individual's, and (2) how I am kept separate from the simple process of desire-satisfaction in terms of which I would be in an identity with the things desired.[22] If the quest for certainty is to succeed, it is clear from experience itself that I must show warranty for the way I clearly and easily distinguish my desires as mine, and for the way I stand opposed to the things desired in the relationship of myself to my desires. Life has an independence from me in which not all of my desires are granted satisfaction; yet in that independence it is still the case that I can identify with that life and have certainty of access to it. The question of this section is: what is presupposed so that this is the case and so that my certainty is linked to my desires?

Such an independence on the side of life presupposes that some aspect of life has the power of negating or resisting me, of making me something other than that simple, desiring being. Beings which are not conscious or self-conscious cannot do this. They can offer resistance, and this is an important aspect of them; but that does not give them the power to change me. If I change because of such resistance, that is a function of my self, not of things. But other self-conscious individuals can bring about change; for what is true of the nature of self-consciousness is true for all self-conscious individuals. As an integral part of my life, other self-conscious individuals in fact appear as objects for me. Therefore, there is something given in experience which appears within the arena of life as part of that life, and yet which also can be identified with the presuppositions which are imputed to me as self-conscious. Hegel now explores three sets of putative presuppositions built around the presupposition of this power of other self-conscious individuals who appear *as object for* a desiring self-consciousness. For the sake of exposition I will call these three sets, respectively, the "master-master" set, the "master-slave" set, and the "slave-master" set.

In the first set the warranted certainty for experience, knowledge, and action is characterized as grounded solely in the presupposition of the mastery or independence of every self-consciousness.[23] The claim is that it is presupposed for experience that each self-consciousness holds everything and every other self-consciousness as simply "the other," as something determined by desire, something to be consumed, used, an object which will bring satisfaction and certainty by being a dependent object. In this case self-consciousness$_1$ would experience self-consciousness$_2$ as a desired object to be subjected to the desires of self-consciousness$_1$. The same is true of self-consciousness$_2$ who has for his object self-consciousness$_1$. However, this set is easily seen to be radically lacking; for under such a presupposition each of us would experience ourselves not simply as a self-consciousness with desires of our own, but also as something reduced to an object desired by an other, a self stripped of its innermost nature. We would no longer be the center of our lives, a desire around which all else is to be oriented and certainty to be established.

Furthermore, satisfaction of desire on both sides would be frustrated since the other would simply refuse to be subjected, but would insist upon being the center of life; for the presupposition is simply that *each is master* over life. That one life which we all share would become then something other than what it is in fact; for each would deny the other the right to that life as its own arena for desire, and thus the world would refuse each person's claims to certainty.

This is the famous "struggle to the death" of which much has been made.[24] But if the significance for the quest for certainty is to be correctly understood, 'death' must be understood in context. It is something opposed to life only in the sense in which the latter term operates in this text. Life, as we have seen, is not a biological phenomenon *simpliciter*, but the arena for action for a desiring self-consciousness, the world as a place of the possibility of the satisfaction of desire. Death, accordingly, is nothing more or less than the loss of *life in this sense*, the loss of the world as such an arena.[25] Life, in the context of the discussion of self-consciousness as the fundamental presupposition for the possibility of my warranted access to reality, is not some mere physical domain, and therefore neither is death. The death of self-consciousness is the removal of the correlate upon which it depends, the effacement of the world as *my* world. Death is the disappearance of the possibility of certainty. Under the hegemony of the "master-master" presupposition set, that effacement of each other would be total and there would be no possibility of self-consciousness and therefore no possibility of certainty. Thus, Hegel can say that self-consciousness comes to realize that life is as important to it as is self-consciousness or desire. In other words, each of us needs a world as the arena of life in order for our desires to have any object. The presupposition that each self-consciousness itself presupposes only mastery or independence is a presupposition that would make self-consciousness itself impossible and along with it the certainty it is held to harbor.

If self-consciousness is to be the ground for the warranty for our natural certainty, i.e., is to be the absolute standpoint, then the other self-consciousness which is for us must also presuppose itself as dependent upon us, as in bondage and not as master. For only in this way can other self-consciousnesses, as an element of life, be dependent upon the determining self-consciousness and thus be the locus in life from which recognition and warranting of certainty will come. This lack, recognized as inherent in the first presupposition set, leads us to the second, the "master-slave" set.[26] We shall be able to offer some concrete examples of what was at stake in this first set if we look briefly at the second set and its structure, and then turn to some concrete examples for comparison of the two sets.

In the second putative set the presupposition is that self-consciousness$_1$ is characterized by independence or mastery, while self-consciousness$_2$, *who exists as an object for self-consciousness$_1$*, is characterized as dependent upon or in bondage to self-consciousness$_1$. Thus, self-consciousness$_2$ also recognizes self-consciousness$_1$ as independent, as master, as the center of life, while at the same time recognizing himself as the object of that desire as dependent upon the other, as part of the life of self-consciousness$_1$. There is agreement on the part of self-consciousness$_1$, who presupposes himself as independent, and the other, self-consciousness$_2$, who presupposes himself as simply a part of that life, one of the possibilities for desire and its satisfaction. Each, then, faithfully mirrors each other's view of himself, and what is the center of life as desire and what is only a dependent part of that life are consistently depicted in the presuppositions of each self-consciousness. In addition, the things and events, i.e., the material conditions involved in the world which is there for self-consciousness$_1$, are presupposed by both as merely a part of the life of self-consciousness$_1$.

Here, then, we do not have the lack discovered in the first set; for each recognizes the other for that which the other takes himself to be, and with the appropriate response grants certainty of access to life. They do not "leave each other free only indifferently, like things," without "reciprocally [giving] and [receiving] one another back from each other consciously" (*PhG*, 144; *PhS*, 113–14); rather, each recognizes the other, each serves to complement the other. Self-consciousness$_2$ appears alongside other elements of the life of self-consciousness$_1$ and recognizes the latter as the center of life. Now let us take some examples in order to make the comparison between these first two sets and clarify the real concern of this famous section of the *Phenomenology*.

What is at stake here is not only masters and slaves, but any and all pairs of relations constituting human relationships.[27] If I am a master, but confront in my life as a self-consciousness none over whom I am master, then I cannot be master. Someone must take the role of slave and recognize that role in my life if I am to have mastery over life as a master and thus gain certainty. But the examples of this structure of self-consciousness are legion. If I am a buyer of goods, but confront only other buyers in my life then I cannot be a buyer; for a buyer needs a seller in order to be a buyer. On the other hand, as a seller I can be a seller only if there are buyers. A life full of other teachers and without students would make it impossible to be recognized as or to be a teacher. Lovers and those who are beloved, doctors and patients, interlocutors in a conversation—all stand in the same relationship of independence and dependence, of mastery and bondage. Each member of the respective pairs presupposes that life is such that the other member is there, and is there to be defined by one's desire to buy or teach or love or converse. Furthermore, neither member of the pair can exclusively be identified as master or slave, as independent or dependent; life is oriented around the seller for the seller and around the buyer for the buyer, and each is, on the other hand, a part of the life of the other. This is a universal condition and has significance far beyond any treatment of master-slave societies.

The point is clear: if reality were constituted as it would have to be under the master-master set, we would have no certainty and no experience of the world as our life since only the mastery or independence of desire would be presupposed; however, under the master-slave set there is presupposed both a self-centeredness of desire in a self-consciousness and also a world for that self-conscious individual in which there is another self-consciousness who recognizes the first as the center of desire and who serves as an object of that desire. Life itself, then, would be what it in fact is. Consequently, self-consciousness as the putative absolute standpoint here is constituted by the presupposition that in life there are others who will recognize and thereby identify my desires as *my* desires and will acknowledge the life constituted by those desires as *my* life. Through the office of the other self-consciousness who is for me, who is part of the life which is mine, my self-consciousness as the center of that life is identified and my certainty warranted. In the seller-buyer relationship, from the perspective of the self-consciousness who is the seller, the buyer who appears recognizes himself as a buyer serving the desires of the seller and the seller as the center for life. This mirrors the presuppositional attitude of the seller himself. At the same time, from the side of the buyer, the seller appears and is presupposed as recognizing the buyer as the center of desire and himself as serving that desire. And this mirrors the view the buyer has of himself.

It would seem, then, that with the presupposition of self-consciousness as the absolute standpoint, structured by the presupposition set of independence and dependence as we now have it, we have arrived at the goal of our quest for certainty. The natural certainty of the natural attitude is shown to be warranted since the other selves who in part constitute the life of the individual not only are structures of self-consciousness which recognize and cooperate with one's desires, thus warranting those desires as in accord with reality, but also structurally locate the source of truth in the desire which is centered in the unique self which one is thus recognized as being. Warranted certainty is identified as the recognition and satisfaction of desire, and desire with its correlate life is the true mode of interest which connects us with ultimate reality. Truth and warranted certainty here have to do not with a static, spectatorial relationship with reality, but rather with an activity of truth-making. The former interest taken as intentionality is now seen to be possible only on the presupposition of first having circumscribed the world desired as a life which belongs to oneself.

However, although there would be mutual recognition on the side of each and thus the desire of the independent self-consciousness is recognized as *his* desire by another self-consciousness who is an object for the first self-consciousness, the presupposition set is still inadequate. This *need* for the other self-consciousness to recognize me as the desiring center of my life and to certify my certainty indicates that I, as an independent self-consciousness, must also presuppose myself as dependent.[28] The student not only constitutes life for the teacher as teacher, and the teacher for the student, but for that reason the teacher is dependent upon the student and the student upon the teacher. The presuppositions in force cannot simply be that the self-conscious individual is the desiring center of his life and is recognized as such to be independent as that center; in addition, and in contradiction to this, that desiring center must also be presupposed as dependent upon the others in life who alone can recognize him and thus baptize his life as his. Self-consciousness$_1$ is both independent of and dependent upon self-consciousness$_2$.

The analysis of self-consciousness as putative absolute standpoint thus far has yielded both a positive and a negative result. On the one hand, it has been shown that we must presuppose recognition forthcoming from others who are objects in our lives in order that we be the center of our lives, in order that we be able to distinguish our desires from those of others.[29] The other who is for me recognizes my certainty by responding to my desire in an appropriate way. An important part of the problem of self-identity, and thus an important aspect of the problem of certainty, has been resolved; for my certainty of access to reality as a self-consciousness rests upon my presupposing that reality as constituted in accordance with my desires in such a way that the positing is validated by that reality itself. Thus, that reality, through other self-consciousnesses, posits itself as a reality in accordance with my desires. But there is also a negative side; for it has also been shown that in that very gain of certainty of self I must presuppose myself as dependent upon the other who is for me, dependent upon that life which is to recognize me and grant me the mastery in which certainty can be found. The master, in order to be master, must be presupposed as in bondage or dependent upon the life which authorizes him that mastery.

This lack brings up the necessity for the consideration of the third putative presupposition set which is *complementary* to the second.[30] The analysis of the "slave-master" relationship is an analysis of the nature of self-consciousness in so far as it is dependent upon another for its centeredness and its certainty. It is therefore an analysis from the perspective of "the other" for a self-consciousness, an analysis which will show the nature of that dependency which is presuppositionally required for the independence or mastery, required both as belonging to the other who "serves" and to the master who is dependent upon that service.

The other, as we have already seen, is presupposed as recognizing himself in a way commensurate with the recognition of the consciousness for whom he exists and whose life he constitutes. The other is presupposed as functioning in accordance with my desires, molding things and his own desires in accordance with my wishes. The student who is for the teacher works over the texts desired by the teacher; the teacher, on the other hand, who is for the student, explicates the texts desired by the student. The seller who is for a buyer procures and offers for sale that which is desired by the buyer; the buyer who is object for the seller brings his needs which will satisfy the seller's desire to sell. One conversant listens to a speaker and responds in a way appropriate to the desires of the speaker to have a conversant. This dependency is recognized on both sides precisely on the presupposition of independence and dependence, and thus life and desire can properly be constituted.[31]

But again, as in the case of the "master-slave" set, there is a reversal. In the case of mastery, mastery presupposed a dependence upon the self-willed dependency of another. Now, in the case of bondage or dependency, the dependency becomes a mastery. The very making of the world for the sake of the other presupposes the dependent self-consciousness as the creator of a world, as the creator and former of life.[32] The dependent other forms and shapes and acts in the world desired by the "master" in such a way that that world takes on the meaning and form which gives certainty of access to the "master." The very dependency of mastery or desire upon the other to form and shape the world makes the latter the master of that world as its creator. The students constitute the life of the teacher, the teacher that of the students. The buyer constitutes the world for the seller, the seller for the buyer. Meaning and intelligibility actually come to the world and life through the office of those who are dependent upon our desires for such a world. Self-consciousness, presupposed as dependency or bondage within a life-system of another self-consciousness, becomes mastery in that world.[33]

But the presupposition is still not complete; for at the same time that one, as part of another's life, is presupposed and presupposes himself as "master" in the way just discussed, there is also presupposed the fragility of participation in life, the risk and danger of being for another.[34] One's mastery as a constitutor of the life-world of another is still nevertheless an existence presupposed as an element of that other life-world. The seller or teacher, as constitutors of the life-worlds of the buyer or the student, is dependent upon the desire for such a life-world and thus must feel the fragility of life, the constant threat of "uselessness" and thus of death in the sense appropriate to the present thesis on self-consciousness as the putative absolute standpoint. If the world no longer needs me as I am, then I can no longer be a shaper of that world. I would become superfluous and sink into the meaninglessness of solipsism. The fragility which must be presupposed here only reflects in bondage the fragility of mastery as a desiring self.

What has occurred here is the demonstration that self-consciousness is constituted presuppositionally both as an independence from life in the sense that life belongs to self-consciousness, and, on the other hand, as a dependency upon that life. It has also been shown that other self-conscious individuals must be presupposed to hold an important position in that life, namely to have the power of creation and recognition which gives identity to the self-consciousness in its drive for the mastery or independence which warrants certainty of access to reality. What is involved here is an extremely rich and complex picture of the human condition which we must now pass over as Hegel does; for our task is to follow him through his proof for the validity of the claims of absolute idealism.[35]

A determinate lack again appears. The truth of what has been discovered in this analysis is that every individual as a self-consciousness must be presupposed as simultaneously both dependent and independent. But that analysis thus far does not give us the ground for the unity of these two characteristics. At best, what one has here is something analogous to the results of the analysis of perceptual consciousness taken as the basis for knowledge: a kind of oscillation and thus a deception which occurs in the ambivalence resulting from the co-presence of these two characteristics. It is claimed, in effect, that from one perspective self-consciousness is independent, but from another is dependent. From one perspective others in my life are dependent upon me, from another perspective they are independent of me and I am dependent upon them. But the unconditioned ground of these two perspectives is not given and thus self-consciousness lacks the totality which would be required were it to be the absolute standpoint.[36] That is to say, our presupposition set has not shown the unity of independence and dependence in each individual which would make him a whole and thus grant warranty to his professed certainty. It is this lack which moves us on to the three sets of presuppositions which are now considered under the title of "the freedom of self-consciousness."

We are in the presence of self-consciousness in a new shape, a consciousness which, as the infinitude of consciousness or as its own pure movement, is aware of itself as essential being, a being which *thinks* or is a free self-consciousness (*PhG*, 151; *PhS*, 120).

The move here is among the most important in the *Phenomenology*.[37] In a manner analogous to that in which the analysis of explanation in understanding led us to the realization of the necessity to presuppose self-consciousness as underlying consciousness, this analysis of the independence and dependence leads us to the presupposition of the freedom peculiar to self-consciousness and will subsequently lead us to the necessity of presupposing reason as underlying self-consciousness. Three points are important to note here: the motivation for this move, the origin of it in praxis itself rather than in thought, and finally the radical change brought about in the natural attitude and the *Phenomenology*.

The actual motivation for this move is found in the prior presupposition that one can shape a world into a meaningful life, thus gaining certainty for oneself, but also shape it for another, thus granting certainty to the other as well. That is to say, the shaping is not just for one's own desires, but also for a desire which transcends one's own, i.e., for the desires of another. The work, the labor itself which is done in shaping the world for another, is intelligible or makes sense both to the one in bondage and to the master, and is the living transformation of the pure possible worlds of experience into an actual life of satisfaction. When the student responds to the teacher, the seller to the buyer, one conversant to another, this labor is in evidence. But the shape that life takes as a meaningful whole is a result of *thought*, of *thinking* which is intimately connected to the meaningful forms which are given to the world in our lives.[38] Our self-conscious interactions oriented in our self-certainty presuppose a power of thought to shape the world in a way which, when carried into action, is intelligible not only to the one who shapes it in response to the other, but to that other as well. If this were not true, then our shaping of a world would not make sense to others and thus *no* recognition of us would be forthcoming. The *subjective* thoughts of the individual self-consciousness are therefore responsible somehow for the human world which is the shared life of all; life is what it is made by us, and what it is made is a function of a subjective thinking which transcends its apparent particularity or subjectivity and becomes *universal as intersubjective*. Thinking must be presupposed as transcending the particularity of both independent will and dependency upon others because (a) it encompasses many particulars over time, particulars which are contingently there in self-consciousness, (b) it forms the basis for comprehending the relationship between the desires of another and one's response to those desires, and (c) it forms the basis of the relationship between the multiplicity of self-conscious individuals and, on the other hand, things and events in life which are worked upon in response to desire. Thinking, which apparently has a subjective origin in the service of another, must be presupposed as always already intersubjective and thus as unconditioned: subjective thought must be presupposed to be conditioned by it. All response taken to be a response adequate to establish certainty presupposes this ground of thought as intersubjective universality.

We must be concerned, then, not merely with the presupposition of interest as individual desire with its correlate of life; for this leaves us only with the mutual conditionedness of the independence and dependence of self-consciousness. What we presuppose is in fact an intersubjectively grounded form of self-consciousness which, through thinking, not only desires and is satisfied by a world which it understands through thinking, but which also exists in a world which is made, formed, and given intelligibility in material form through thinking. Thinking not only comprehends, as previously; it is also actively present in the creation of a world (*PhG*, 152; *PhS*, 120).[39]

It is important, secondly, to note the origin of this new presupposition about thought; for it reveals something about Hegel's philosophy which will appear later in different forms and which contradicts the usual view of Hegel as a pure, idealistic (in the sense of mentalistic) thinker. The present presupposition of the centrality of thinking to our knowledge and action comes from a reflection on the praxis of the individual who shapes the world, from a reflection on action and on the material relations which exist between individuals in so far as these constitute self-consciousness and our consequent access to reality. The argument here has been that thinking must be presupposed as the unconditioned universal unity of self-consciousness; and in so far it appears to be mentalistic. But the reasons for concluding this come not from a reflection on pure thought or even on empirical thinking, but from a reflection on the problem of material desires, material actions, and the actual material production of a world.[40] The world of action and interaction which constitutes actual experience revealed as inadequate the presuppositional framework thus far posited. The "freedom" of self-consciousness which first appears here, appears as an ability to create and shape a world on the basis of one's own thoughts in response to the desires and actions of another. In thinking there is freedom because in thinking I unite the limiting conditions of both independence and dependence. The new presupposition does not efface the dialectics of dependence and independence; rather the praxical presupposition of thinking as freedom serves to make possible the tension between the two.[41]

Consequently, Hegel now turns to three forms in which this presupposition of freedom as thought has appeared. The three are recognizable "philosophies of life," for each involves a self-conscious, deliberate effort to freely act in full cognizance of the fundamental nature of the self and of the problem of certainty.[42] Self-consciousness, in other words, is presupposed here as the absolute standpoint, as the ground of access to reality, in such a way that the presuppositions themselves are thematized by natural consciousness in the very activities themselves. We have here, then, forms of life in which the natural attitude comes to an elementary, yet significant position of standing in a philosophical or reflective attitude in an attempt to have self-warranty for its natural certainty. Here we have the first attempt of the natural attitude to reflexively grasp itself in its own actions.[43]

This leads us to the third point which must be clear before discussing the forms taken up under the heading of the freedom of self-consciousness. The very nature of presuppositions themselves changes at this point. Previously they have been buried within the thought and actions of the natural attitude and had to be uncovered by the phenomenological "we" as we progressed through the work. Now we are presented—and this "we" now includes one in the natural attitude who has been carried along in this quest for certainty—with the phenomenon of explicit thematization by the natural attitude both of the things and events on which we focus in the world and of the attitude itself within which we focus on those things and events. The philosopher, engaged from the beginning in a quest to uncover these presuppositions for the natural attitude itself so that the latter could come to grasp the absolute standpoint within its own naive attitude toward the world, has now come to a point in the "dialogue" in which he can present the individual in the natural attitude with an example of ways in which the natural attitude itself raises tacit presuppositions to full self-awareness. Consequently, it will no longer be necessary to lay out the presuppositions for the natural attitude and then test them for adequacy against the world and life as we actually experience it; now an individual in the natural attitude, together with the philosopher, can begin to observe his own possibility as a self-consciousness, i.e., to thematize and become aware of the adequacies and inadequacies of different forms within which individuals attempt to be free as self-aware self-consciousnesses. And the objective, for both the forms of self-consciousness being observed and the self-conscious individual observing the life-forms, is to demonstrate warranty for certainty with self-consciousness as the absolute standpoint given unconditioned access to reality.

The changed form of presuppositions themselves, now being explicitly thematized in praxis so that one deliberately takes up things and events in one attitude or another, further articulates the motivation and origin of this move in the *Phenomenology*. The intersubjective nature of thought and its origin in the praxis and living of life itself show us the way in which thought is the unity of self-consciousness as both dependent and independent and thus the way in which thought transcends either pole of the ambiguity of self-consciousness. My projection of my desires on life does not create that thinking which links me to others whose own desires are the object of my desire; nor is that thinking created in the recognitive response of others in my life to my desires. Thinking in this form is in some way a prius to both constituting poles of self-consciousness. When this is grasped in our quest for certainty, the drive for that quest points us in the direction of an attempt to capture and control the very power of thinking in which the ground of the unity of self-consciousness seems now to reside. And as self-consciousness, with the capacity for self-awareness, I have the wherewithal to make the move. When consciousness with its outward orientation toward the things and events was presupposed as the absolute standpoint, no such move was possible, although it is now clear just how important was the move to self-consciousness through a realization of the power of explanation. However, as a self-consciousness that move toward self-control is not only possible, but is mandated; for it is the very nature of desire—albeit in the ambiguity of dependence and independence—to exert mastery over the complete circuit of selfhood which has been revealed in the self-other relations constituting self-consciousness itself. In other words, the freedom of self-consciousness is and has been the ultimate goal of the quest for certainty under the presupposition of self-consciousness. The deficiencies which had appeared in the presuppositions of consciousness—the gap between self and world as intended, and the inability under the presuppositions of consciousness to present the ground of the possibility for our certainty of access to the world—now appear to be removable. To be in control of the praxical presuppositions which are in force in our access to the world—in control in the sense of being fully aware of them and acting deliberately in accord with them—is putatively to finally ground our access to that reality in self-consciousness itself. The governing presupposition of all these forms of presupposition in the freedom of self-consciousness is that to deliberately act in accordance with the necessary praxical presupposition set—and to be fully aware of this act—is to have warranted certainty of access to reality. The full significance of this will become clear as we proceed to observe the attempts of self-consciousness to be free, and the subsequent failure of the attempt and the appearance of the necessity for a new presupposition concerning reason as absolute standpoint.

The first set examined by Hegel is articulated as the presuppositions made explicit in the tenets of stoicism and in life of the stoic.[44] This is not to say that we are limited only to philosophers who have been called "stoics"; rather, their philosophical position reflects the presuppositions which can be taken to govern, in a deliberate way, the lives of individuals in the natural attitude. Stoicism articulates the presupposition of freedom as a purity of thought which stands indifferently above all particulars, all things, and by its power determines what is essential and what is unessential, what matters and what does not.

> Its principle is that consciousness is a being that *thinks*, and that consciousness holds something to be essentially important, or true and good only in so far as it *thinks* it to be such (*PhG*, 152; *PhS*, 121).

This, in turn, entails that the "freedom of self-consciousness is *indifferent* to natural existence and has therefore *let this [natural existence] equally go free*" (*PhG*, 153–54; *PhS*, 121–22). The presupposition here is that thought can free one from the conditionedness of the complications of life. This is not to say that, as in a presupposition of "pure mastery," there are no contingencies and there is no dependency; for stoicism recognizes these and the whole complexus of independence and dependence. It is precisely the point of stoicism that independence and dependence are to be recognized, *but are to be treated indifferently*.[45]

> This consciousness . . . has a negative attitude towards the lord and bondsman relationship. As lord it does not have its truth in the bondsman, nor as bondsman is its truth in the lord's will and in his service; on the contrary, whether on the throne or in chains, in the utter dependence of its individual existence, its aim is to be free, and to maintain that lifeless indifference which steadfastly withdraws from the bustle of existence, alike from being active as passive, into the simple essentiality of thought (*PhG*, 153; *PhS*, 121).

Whatever the forms of mastery or bondage, of independence or dependence, what will happen will happen. Thought permits me to stand above contingencies while at the same time being immersed in them. The power of thought as intersubjective does not simply unite me, as earlier, with others in action; it now also is presupposed as granting warranted certainty because I *accept* with full self-awareness both dependence and independence and find certainty in my recognition of the outcome of all actions as being fated by this relationship of dependence and independence.

It is easy to see here that the "contempt" for the vagaries of life reveals a determinate lack in this form of the freedom of self-consciousness; for there is no real freedom here, precisely because of the refusal to deal with the contingencies and realities of life as a series of oppositions. This stoical set comprises only an abstract concept of freedom, and thus one acts only abstractly. This conceptualization and ideology

> as an abstraction cuts itself off from the multiplicity of things, and thus has no content *in its own self* but one that is *given* to it (*PhG*, 154; *PhS*, 122).

That is to say, by letting natural existence and its differences "go free," one presupposes the unreality of that existence in so far as it is not a function of self-consciousness's thinking and shaping activities. There is only inexplicable and thus unintelligible givenness through fate: *certainty* of access to reality is effectively denied here. Thus, the presuppositional framework articulated in stoicism, and the deliberate actions performed on the basis of them, do not ground the possibility of the possible worlds which actually constitute experience; for because of the indifference to all particularity, all worlds are equally possible.[46]

The determinate negation or lack here, therefore, is the absence of an accounting for the radical difference and opposition which constitutes particularity and which gives us the worlds of our actual experience. The presuppositions articulated by *skepticism* are an attempt to repair this lack, while still maintaining the hegemony of self-consciousness and its universal powers to shape and make intelligible a world and life upon which one depends.[47] The presupposition here is that thought has the power not only to shape and mold reality and to hold it together in a totality, but that it can deal with each particular in a way that demonstrates its mastery and certainty in respect to the *specific* reality we have. Natural existence is not let go to be "free," as in stoicism, but is presupposed as actively within the domain of self-consciousness's powers. In the set articulated in skepticism, the previously missing dependency is reflected in the presupposition, self-consciously acted upon, that one ought to take each and every moment of life as it presents itself, and then show one's mastery over it by means of one's own thoughtful criticisms of the given. On the other hand, independence is reflected in that very activity of negating through criticism the moments of life to which, however, self-consciousness is constantly subjected as something independently given. All of the aspects and differences of life are not only recognized and taken up into self-consciousness in this reflective attitude, but they are made its own by being thought *as differences* which are real and in themselves. The freedom which is evidenced in skepticism is not one which ignores difference, but one which sets out to master difference by accepting and criticizing it. Through this determinate mastery, certainty is to be warranted.

But there is a determinate lack here also. In the analysis of this presupposition set there appear two forms of self-consciousness. The one form is that of an unchangeable, abiding, persistent self which endures, untouched, through all changes in content and form. It is the self which is certain and which is "responsible" for the work which the individual does in shaping life through its critique. It is the self of self-consciousness which is presupposed as persisting throughout all change and which is therefore at the heart of its freedom. The other self is the changeable, ephemeral, intermittent self which is directly conscious of the contingencies and differences within life itself, and which changes in content as skeptical consciousness serially brings life within its purview. It is the self which confronts that of which we are to *become* certain. Correspondingly, there are two forms of life presupposed: life in general or the continuity of the parts of life, and the manifold and changing content of life.[48]

The lack here is precisely the absence of the unity of the two selves and of the two worlds; for both life and self, and each respectively in the two forms of the changeable and the unchangeable, must be presupposed as within a single unity, a single totality which holds within itself the differences. Skepticism vacillates between the two, both in respect to itself and in respect to the life which it critically takes up. What is missing in the presuppositions self-consciously held by the skeptic is the unity of certainty and that which is to become certain, i.e., the unity of the unchangeable and the changeable. If the presuppositions are to be thematized in the deliberate actions of the individual, the unity as well as the difference must be faced. In the attitude of the skeptic, the unity remains an unconscious, unthematized element, and thus the freedom is incomplete. Professed access to certainty and truth is not warranted.

> This consciousness is therefore the unconscious, thoughtless rambling which passes back and forth from the one extreme of self-identical self-consciousness to the other extreme of the contingent consciousness that is both bewildered and bewildering. It does not itself bring these two thoughts of itself together. At one time it recognizes that its freedom lies in rising above all the confusion and contingency of existence, and at another time equally admits to a relapse into occupying itself with what is unessential (*PhG*, 157; *PhS*, 125).

The point is that in the actual worlds of our experience, knowledge, and action, the contingent and the permanent coincide. The unchangeable and changeable self-consciousness—the "I think" and identity which persistently constitute experience, and the serial thinking which surfaces in the variable content embraced by self-consciousness—both must be thought together in the unity of self-consciousness itself *if* self-consciousness is to be the unconditioned presupposition, the absolute standpoint in which certainty is to be found.[49] In other terms, the possibility of the unity of transcendental and empirical self-consciousness must be grounded in a self-conscious way; whatever is the ground for the natural certainty which is present in the thoughtful pursuit of our daily tasks in life and in interaction with others must constitute a totality consisting of both the permanence and the transience of our lives. If the universality or unchangeableness and the particularity or changeableness cannot be *shown* to be in the unity of self-consciousness and cannot be deliberately *acted* upon, then that natural certainty of the natural attitude cannot be shown to be warranted. And in all of this, we are of course involved also with the respective correlates of life.

The introduction of the third and most complex form of presupposition set articulated around the notion of the freedom of self-consciousness arises on the basis of this general critique of the failure of skepticism. It is the set which Hegel calls "unhappy consciousness," and in which we take up the distinction between changeable and unchangeable and articulate a position which putatively brings them together in the required unity.[50]

The unity is to be brought about by deliberately presupposing self-consciousness as a contradiction.

> In stoicism, self-consciousness is the simple freedom of itself. In scepticism, this freedom becomes a reality, negates the other side of determinate existence, but really duplicates *itself*, and now knows itself to be a duality. Consequently the duplication which formerly was divided between two individuals, the lord and the bondsman, is now lodged in one. The duplication of self-consciousness within itself, which is essential in the concept of spirit, is thus here before us, but not yet in its unity: the *unhappy consciousness* is the consciousness of self as a dual-natured, merely contradictory being (*PhG*, 158; *PhS*, 126).

In order to understand this new form of self-consciousness, it is necessary always to remember that we are here discussing a self-conscious individual, i.e., an individual conscious of life and the world in such a way that the life-world is defined in terms of the attitude of the individual self-consciousness. We have seen in the discussion of the independence and dependence of self-consciousness that we must presuppose an independence and dependence on both sides of the relationship which constitutes self-consciousness; but it is nevertheless also the case that the unity of self and other is to be self-consciousness itself. This means that the presence of the changeable consciousness implicates immediately the presence of life as a changeable series. Likewise, the presence of unchangeable consciousness immediately implicates the presence of life as unchangeable, eternal, persisting unity or arena for self-conscious desire. And self-consciousness itself is to be the ultimate unity of this duality of changeable and unchangeable if the presupposition that self-consciousness is the absolute standpoint is to be authenticated. The striving of the changeable consciousness toward unity with the unchangeable, and the movement of the latter to encompass the former is therefore at the same time to be the unification of life as serial and discrete with life as a synchronic and already unified totality.[51] What must be presupposed, then, is a movement of totalization toward totality and of totality as self-constituted totalization.

First, this ambiguity is approached by unhappy consciousness by taking upon itself the attitude of the changeable consciousness. One deliberately lives in a stance of finitude, ephemerality, division, diremption from within one's own unity. One stands self-consciously in alienation. The reason for this is that unhappy consciousness is constituted such that each of the aspects of self-consciousness is present to the individual as different from the others. One lives in the recognized tension of the unchangeable-changeable consciousness. The self as unchangeable is aware of itself both as itself and as changeable, while as changeable it is aware of itself as both a striving toward unity with itself and already being that unity.

> The unhappy consciousness itself *is* the gazing of one self-consciousness into another, and itself *is* both, and the unity of both is also its essential nature (*PhG*, 159; *PhS*, 126).

Thus, there is a degree of self-awareness here of which even skeptical self-consciousness was incapable, in spite of its determination to be free in the face of the multiplicity of life and its contingencies. This self-awareness involves a true struggle. There is alienation from the self from within the self.[52] One's unity with oneself in one's own life—the unity of life, the ground of its intelligibility and even of its possibility—is precisely what escapes one. In unhappy consciousness we have finally an explicit, *natural* awareness of the *problem* of the absolute standpoint. What is at stake for this "free" self-consciousness is to *make a reality of* that totality which is presupposed as the unchangeable consciousness and life, and not have it as a merely *presupposed* or taken-for-granted totality. The stoic attempted this act of de-alienation with his indifference to the changeable; the skeptic attempted it by taking up for his own those differences, and doing so with a disregard for the actual totality which he confronts and which he is, necessarily, in his act of confrontation. The unhappy consciousness faces alienation *as* alienation and struggles to unite desire and life in an all-encompassing infinitude of self-consciousness which will bring about autonomy and freedom in the course of one's life.[53]

Before exploring the ways in which this unity is attempted, a remark must be made about the religious dimension of this section. It is not only to serve as exemplary, but must also be seen in a deep and real connection with this particular stance and presupposition set of self-consciousness. There is no better example of this unhappy consciousness and its transcendence than the life and conversion of St. Augustine. However, this connection is not to be such as to overpower the real nature of the problem for the *Phenomenology* at this point, viz. to articulate this most complete form in which the natural attitude as self-consciousness attempts to make itself the absolute standpoint as a self-totalizing totality. This, and not the religious point *per se*, is what is to be worked out.[54]

The general stance of such a self-conscious individual involves us with the presupposition that in our unhappiness we are the changeable consciousness, a consciousness aware of its own alienation from itself as a unity. The individual understands himself as caught up in the vicissitudes of life, yet striving to come to be in unity with that unchangeable, persistent consciousness which is the identity of the self as a totality and with the unity of life. Secondly, this unity in both of its sides is presupposed as a unity which itself in some way already encompasses one as a finite consciousness. With this tension and ambiguity (if not outright contradiction) as a guide, the individual first consciously takes his project to be the freeing of himself from his changeable nature, i.e., to become simply the self as a whole in an existential identity with life as a whole.[55] It is the wish and drive to free oneself from one's identity as finite and changeable and to unite oneself with totality and unchangeableness. I wish to be at peace with myself and with life as the stoic strove to be and, at the same time, I realize that I cannot simply be indifferent to my changing self and to the multiplicities and entanglements of the world (*PhG*, 158–59; *PhS*, 126).

Hegel stresses in a series of paragraphs the totally contradictory nature of the presupposition set which is thematized here by the natural attitude itself (*PhG*, 159–62; *PhS*, 126–30). First, no such unity can be achieved at the cost of simply leaving behind the changeable consciousness and life as a series of changes; for if this were done, the unity would be empty, a pure form, a unity without anything unified. Such a victory would be a "pyrrhic victory." Second, both the changeable and unchangeable must be preserved as moments of self-consciousness as desire-life. One cannot put the changeable on one side and the unchangeable on the other; for this would deny the very structure of self-consciousness which is presupposed for the whole of the movement and without which it could not be proven that self-consciousness is the absolute standpoint. Whatever the final state of this attitude of self-consciousness, the unchangeable must remain an embodied "I," a self which has a life-world which has both independence and dependence in relation to the self. These factors represent the problem involved in the forms which unhappy consciousness takes.

There are three forms, each of which becomes progressively more aware of the nature of self-consciousness itself, and yields a more detailed analysis of the complexity of this self which is to be the absolute standpoint. Thus, a closer look at this examination will prove necessary for us. The first form is that in which the finite individual takes himself to be an embodied unity of pure consciousness which stands toward the life-world as a totality. As a pure consciousness, the individual *thinks* the unity of the life-world, the unity of the manifold of particulars. Thus, nature and the observed world are *known as* a unity brought about by what amounts to a transcendental unity, the unity of the ego and nonego as the unity of the ego. What we have here is a "Kantian" sense of unity, a sense reformulated by German romanticism and Fichte.

But to be in and toward the life-world in this way, i.e., as a pure consciousness, is still to be separated from it. The world is still a beyond, and the individual is still only a "relating" to the unchangeable such that self-consciousness itself is not the relating but stands in relation as one of the relata. This form of unhappy consciousness is one which defines the life-world as an in-itself to be grasped by the in-itselfness of pure, transcendental consciousness. The actual, finite, changeable consciousness therefore of necessity finds that totality which it is seeking for the sake of self-certainty to be elusive to thought. As in Kant, the ultimate connection is simply unknowable; or, as in Fichte, it is simply posited.

The striving for unity has not been consummated; but the unhappy consciousness is now self-aware, and in reflecting on this state of affairs in which it finds itself it can realize that this thinking is only *"eine Andacht,"* an attitude of devotion or, literally, "a thinking upon" (*PhG,* 163–64; *PhS,* 131–32). Thus, what the actual stance and its thematized presuppositions amount to in terms of certainty and warranty is only feeling, a thinking-toward but not a thinking-in the actual unchangeable or unconditional itself.

> Where that "other" is sought, it cannot be found, for it is supposed to be just a *beyond*, something that can *not* be found (*PhG,* 164; *PhS,* 131).

This form of consciousness, therefore, inevitably turns romantically to itself in self-feeling, in a feeling of the striving and hopelessness of the task of achieving unity through self-consciousness between the finite and the infinite, the changeable and the unchangeable.

If self-consciousness were to remain in the attitude of pure consciousness, where feeling or a "sense of things" marked its only access to the absolute, then the quest for certainty would fail.[56] But if this self-feeling comes to involve an awareness of the character of that feeling and a reflection on the reasons or presuppositions on the basis of which it has arisen, then there is a new form of unhappy consciousness. When the attention of this self-conscious individual is directed upon the feeling itself—the relation it actually has to the unachieved objective—then its attention has moved from "the beyond" as it is in itself, to the actual relation between self and world. Feeling, at this point, constitutes the link and thus the real totality of self-world.[57] In this way, the "object" of the pure feeling which is experienced is not the unchangeable beyond in itself, but the unhappiness of the unhappy consciousness. In feeling the failure and in experiencing the beyondness of the unchangeable, the unhappy consciousness is forced to experience itself as an unhappy consciousness.

> Thus, [unhappy consciousness] comes forward here as self-feeling, or as an actual consciousness existing on its own account (*PhG*, 165; *PhS*, 132).

The pure consciousness presupposed at first has been transformed into an actual consciousness. One now presupposes that it is this actual, feeling consciousness, conscious of itself, which is the self-consciousness that will bring the ground and unity of the changeable and the unchangeable. The failure of the first thematically held presupposition set of unhappy consciousness thus brings, in self-awareness of its own thematic, the second form.[58]

This new form brings the unhappy consciousness to the self-awareness of its own individuality as a striving, desiring, embodied consciousness. The individual now understands himself not as pure consciousness, but as a real, finite individual approaching the world through desire and work:

> *The return of the feeling heart into itself* is to be taken to mean that it has an *actual* existence as an *individual*. It . . . has felt the object of its pure feeling and this object is itself (*PhG*, 164–65; *PhS*, 132).

Its own desire and work form a response to the feeling consciousness which has emerged from the unhappy consciousness which took itself only as pure or transcendental thought.

It is important to note here that it is *feeling* and not thought which brings us from "pure" consciousness to actual consciousness, and which orients the unhappy consciousness toward itself as a real totality which works on the world. This real totality is self-conceived as a desiring which gets immediately translated into work and into actual, material commerce with the material life-world. As an unhappy consciousness reflects on his own self-feeling, what is actually discovered is that the individual who is striving for this unity with the unchangeable self and unchangeable life-world is really an individual who desires and who works in relation to the actual world, the here and now, not the beyond. Certainty is now to be warranted not through a pure thought of a pure consciousness, but through desire-directed work.[59]

> In this return into self there comes to view its second relationship, that of desire and work in which consciousness finds confirmation of that inner certainty of itself which we know it has attained, by overcoming and enjoying the existence alien to it, viz. existence in the form of independent things (*PhG*, 165; *PhS*, 132).

The forming-activity, the thoughtful labor which was earlier discovered as the key to freedom of self-consciousness in its independence and dependence, again comes to the fore. By objectifying oneself through work directed by desire and informed by the thinking which permits the forming of the world, self-consciousness as unhappy consciousness actively presupposes itself as achieving certainty of access to reality.

But this certainty is marred and thus self-consciousness again finds itself lacking as an ultimate ground in itself; for the

> unhappy consciousness merely *finds* itself *desiring* and *working*; it is not aware that to find itself active in this way implies that it is in fact certain of itself, and that its feeling of the alien existence is this self-feeling. Since it is not explicitly aware of this certainty, its inner life really remains a still incomplete self-certainty; that confirmation which it would receive through work and enjoyment is therefore equally incomplete; in other words, it must itself set at nought this confirmation, but only confirmation of what it is *for* itself, viz., of its dividedness (*PhG*, 165; *PhS*, 132).

That is to say, the real activities of the individual self-consciousness as he strives for oneness through desire and work is merely a fact, merely there. In neither the desiring nor the working are to be found the ground for desire or work, their *raison d'être*. There is a *givenness* of individual desires and work in and through which the actual finite conscious individual pursues his own realization; but that is all. In other words, under the restrictions of self-consciousness as the absolute standpoint, one simply finds oneself where one is, doing what one is doing, achieving the unifications with the life-world and in the life-world that one is achieving. In spite of the certainty which comes from such success as there is in completing the work desired, the ultimate ground cannot be attributed to self-consciousness alone; for there is always simply the givenness of desire and work. When this state of affairs is fully thematized by unhappy consciousness it finds that its own capacities and powers—those by means of which it pursues its own realization and unity—are merely a "gift from an alien source, which the unchangeable makes over to consciousness to make use of" (*PhG*, 166; *PhS*, 133).

What has occurred here is the following. The self-feeling of the first level of unhappy consciousness led to the thematization of the presupposition of work and desire as the locus of unification with the life-world and with the unchangeable character of both self and world. But in the pursuit of these activities, the unhappy consciousness has again lost sight of its own unchangeableness or that which persists through the various and changing desires and labors. The unchangeable as the unity of the life-world itself looms on the horizon of consciousness as a "sanctified world" which "surrenders or gives itself" to the finite individual for his own enjoyment and work.[60] Life in general is recognized as the source of the capacities and powers which are appropriate to the life-world and which enable the individual in his finitude to work on that world. So the unchangeable totality of the life-world is an actuality, but only as the source of all else. The life-world is divided within itself as creator and creation, as an encompassing and as a world of definite things and tasks. On the other hand, consciousness is itself divided in the same way. The active, working individual faces his life-world with the latter as a passive reality, and proceeds to work on it and deliberately to make his life. But, on the other hand, both the power of activity and the passiveness of the realities of the life-world on which the individual works are *givens*, and their source is simply the unity of all, the unchangeable beyond, the ultimate creative power, the unknown basis for all reality. The working, striving self-consciousness and the life-world "just happen" to fit each other. The opacity of this fit means that self-consciousness has not yet reached its own self-grounding.

Already sketched here is the presupposition that interest is not merely desire, but *purpose*, and that the true orientation of one within the world is through purposive actions directed towards objects within a life-world which is appropriate for those purposes. This is the new framework, the presupposition structure of *reason* which will be seen as necessitated if self-conscious activity, interest as desire, is to be possible. But in the form articulated here—simply the apparent pre-established harmony or our talents and capacities with the life-world in which our desires are to be satisfied—we are still denied access to the absolute standpoint. That our desires "fit" the world generally, and that the world fits our desires generally, *should* be a confirmation of self-certainty; it *should* signify that there is warranty for claims of access to reality. But we do not reach such a warranty because there is still necessarily the opposition between finite and infinite, between the changeable and the unchangeable, an opposition which *cannot* be given up without also surrendering the autonomy of self-consciousness. For a unity of self-consciousness which effaced the difference contained in these oppositions would deny self-consciousness as the ground of its own unity: there is no self-consciousness without this difference within itself.

The consequence at this point is critical; for it shows that any act of thematization, any specific grasp of an object or event, any particular act, must of necessity be the work of a finite consciousness. This is the central insight of the unhappy consciousness and of this section in the *Phenomenology* which deals with the attempt to found warranted certainty in self-consciousness itself: any act must of necessity be finite and thus cannot encompass itself and in this way infinitize itself; and so long as this is true, the individual can be neither self-governing (autonomous) nor absolute.[61]

Kant was right, then, in arguing that the ground can be *thought*, but not be known, at least as long as self-consciousness is taken to be the ground.[62] Thus, this form of unhappy consciousness fails and brings us back to the original problematic.

> Instead, therefore, of returning from its activity back into itself, and having obtained confirmation of its self-certainty, consciousness really reflects this activity back into the other extreme, which is thus exhibited as a pure universal, as the absolute power from which the activity started in all directions, and which is the essence both of the self-dividing extremes as they at first appeared, and of their interchanging relationship itself (*PhG*, 166; *PhS*, 134).

In introducing the third and final form of unhappy consciousness, Hegel reviews the first two and shows the relationship of the three to each other. We moved from inner feeling with no real actualization in the first, to the second form which involved actualization through work and the objectification of the self in general.

> Returned from this external activity, however, consciousness has *experienced* itself as actual and effective, or knows that it is in truth in and for itself. But here, now, is where the enemy

is met with in his most characteristic form (*PhG*, 168; *PhS*, 135).

This "enemy" is oneself, encountered in the struggle to achieve unity with the unchangeable, with that unknown source of the "fit" with reality. In giving thanks for the gift of itself and of the talents with which to work on the world, the individual elevates the unchangeable to the status of a supreme and ultimate foundation and thereby denigrates his own actions as something only "in the service" of the unchangeable. However, it is just these actions, on the other hand, which are sanctified through active relation to the unchangeable. But this latter aspect is at first repressed as a presupposition, and the humility of service is stressed. Because the individual is in the service of "the other,"

> consciousness takes its own *reality* to be *immediately a nothingness*, its actual doing thus becomes a doing of nothing, its enjoyment a feeling of its wretchedness (*PhG*, 168; *PhS*, 135).

This is the utter humility and worthlessness which is felt by the unhappy consciousness. But this self-awareness becomes an obsession; for the finite acts of the individual cannot be eliminated and thus one must always attend to them.

The paradigm for this form of self-consciousness is the ascetic who must continually punish his finite self in order to free himself for the infinite.[63] In more ordinary terms, this is the general lack of feeling of self-worth brought about by the full realization of one's finitude. But there is an irony here, and it is this which leads us as well as the unhappy consciousness to see the true nature of self-consciousness and its foundations in reason. It is just through the striving for one's unity with the unchangeable that the finite takes on this character of worthlessness. Thus, without the infinite power of the unchangeable, the finite would not be a wretched thing. But, on the other hand, the striving and work have their origin or possibility in the infinite and therefore are themselves sanctified by it. Furthermore, it is just that finitude and the finite entrapment of the individual which truly reveals the glory of the unchangeable. Finitude and changeableness are, therefore, the mediated relationship which one has with the unchangeable. Our very awareness of unity with the unchangeable is due to the actions which seem to proscribe that awareness.

At this point Hegel argues that this shows that the mediated relationship with reality necessarily eludes us so long as we insist on self-consciousness as the absolute standpoint.[64] No finite act can capture the infinite; no single act of the self can capture the self as a whole. Likewise, no part of the whole can embody the whole; the totality of reality remains simply a presupposition. Finally, the link between self and world, which would have to be established by articulating what we have failed to articulate concerning the relationship between the changeable and the unchangeable in both of their respective dimensions, cannot be established on the basis of self-consciousness alone. Rather there is here a "syllogism," as Hegel calls it—*ein Schluss*, literally a connection, a shutting up or closing off—through which the elements of self-consciousness are united in their difference.[65] That syllogism remains presupposed and cannot be made explicit by self-consciousness for itself; for the middle term or the connecting link between the finite and the infinite, the changeable and the unchangeable, cannot be made articulate.

The thematization of this failure to connect is accomplished by natural self-consciousness itself. It is no longer necessary for the philosopher to lead the natural attitude; for self-consciousness is now self-aware, has thematized its own presuppositions and seeks to act explicitly on the basis of them. Thus, it is self-consciousness which is led to introduce *reason* as the mediator of the elements articulated in self-consciousness. Reason becomes the new ground which is to be presupposed as the locus of warranty for claims to certainty of knowledge concerning reality. As I shall argue below, it matters not here whether the reason we surrender to is the reason found in nature and in our relation to it, or that found in God and in our relation to the divine. The point is that anyone who comes to this position through unhappy consciousness—and when engaged in the quest for certainty—will either make the surrender or deny the position of an absolute standpoint and give up the quest for certainty. Either outcome is possible. Rightly or wrongly, the *Phenomenology* takes the prior way and reflects the move both possible to the natural attitude and historically taken by most individuals. The full meaning and significance of this move from self-consciousness to reason will be explored fully only in the next chapter.[66]

Hegel's argument here is essentially that we have now come to a point in the *Phenomenology* at which the natural attitude has become explicitly aware of itself as founded upon a set of noetic and ontological presuppositions which, if true and complete, would fail to give us reality as we have it in experience. Under the presupposition sets of consciousness this self-awareness did not occur, since there the major presupposition was that the truth and unity of our being was to be found "objectively," in the world of objects. Then, at the close of that section, the natural attitude turned toward itself *as an attitude toward reality*. The whole of the section on self-consciousness has been an exploration of this turn toward the subject-object relation itself, in the guise of interest understood as desire. The search for the ground of certainty and the absolute standpoint in self-consciousness itself has in turn led to the realization that, although our experience and action is grounded in a presupposition of unity or of an unconditioned absolute, *access* to the nature of that unconditioned and to the way in which the unity is effected is prohibited so long as it is presupposed that this access is possible through individual, desiring, finite self-consciousness itself.

This major segment of the *Phenomenology* ends, then, with the following results. We have learned how and why our conscious acts and our experience belong to us: it is through the recognition of ourselves, our acts, and our experiences by others who appear to us as part of that life-world we call our own. Thereby we have certainty *that* the conscious acts mean what they mean, and *that* they belong uniquely to our life-world with ourselves at its center. But this certainty is still not warranted in any absolute sense; for recognition is conditional and our attempts to bring into unity the changeable and unchangeable consciousness, as well as the changeable and unchangeable life-world, have all failed so long as the effort to bring the unconditioned unity to explicitness is presupposed to rest on self-consciousness itself. Desire cannot bring unity, no matter how refined that desire has become.[67] But although the absolute standpoint seemingly eludes the finite, deliberate acts of the individual, yet it has been found that it is precisely there in the finite act that the absolute standpoint has its point of contact with the individual in his quest for certainty. The individual who has become aware of the presupposition of self-consciousness cannot himself be the ground of his own self-consciousness and certainty; but he does have the certainty that his life is *his* life, that at the same time he participates in that life with others, and that his actions have efficacy in that life. Certain of all of this, the individual must simply surrender to the facticity of that certainty, i.e., give himself up to the activities as grounded. Whether, as in Augustine, this means surrender to God and to God's will (as opposed to his own willfulness, concupiscence, his own desiring), or it means surrender to universal reason in some natural or other sense, the move is the same: a conscious resolve to act on the *instinct* that an ultimate *reason* grounds the possibility of the unity of the changeable and the unchangeable.[68]

The determinate failure of self-consciousness to ground itself indicates upon reflection by selfconsciousness, that (1) both intentionality and desire, and (2) both the intended world and the life-world, are constitutive of that experience. Second, all four of these elements lie together in a unity which is the ground of the possibility of them and of the experience, knowledge, and action they constitute. Hegel argues that the natural, self-conscious individual acts intuitively on what is to be called "the instinct of reason." That is to say, the individual, certain of himself and yet failing to self-consciously ground that certainty, proceeds instinctively to act with the deliberate presupposition of that overall unity. In effect, the individual recognizes the presuppositional nature of his experience, knowledge, and action, accepts this, and proceeds to act purposively in the lifeworld.[69] Whether this instinct takes the form of reliance upon a revealed doctrine of received wisdom, i.e., acceptance of the presupposed unity through a positive religion, or the form of reliance upon the unity of nature as a whole, reason in divine or natural form is the presupposed unity of self and world as well as of the manifoldness of self and world respectively. But this involves us with a new form of interest, to which we must now turn in the next chapter.

V

Interest As Purpose: Observation

OUR QUEST FOR CERTAINTY has brought us in a sense back to the beginning; for the attempt to ground certainty in self-consciousness—an attempt radically different from the naivete of sense-certainty—has ended in a surrender to the facticity of certainty. But the certainty at this point is not simply a blind faith. On the side of the rational activities we are now to observe, there is at first a simple acceptance or as Hegel will say an instinct of reason. But this instinctual action also has some degree of consciousness behind it; for the rational observer or actor *purposively* carries out his observations and activities with an awareness of certain constraints, principles, and problems involving certainty. On the part of the "we" of the *Phenomenology*, which now includes those in the natural attitude who have been transformed by the experiences of the *Phenomenology* thus far, there is also an explicit awareness that the instinct of reason and rational activity we see at work has arisen for us on the basis of the failure of the previous attempts to ground certainty in consciousness or in self-consciousness. Thus, one in the natural attitude who, in sense-certainty, had to be pulled out of the simplicity of the natural attitude in order to examine its own putative grounds, now prepares to experience this new form of interest—interest as purpose—with a full awareness of the problem of the quest for certainty.[1] Because of these differences both on the level of the "we" and on the level of the rational activities about to be phenomenologically examined, there is also a new form of the dialectic. Before turning to the course of the new quest for certainty, we should become clear about all of these changes.

The failure of desire to constitute warranted access to the absolute standpoint has demanded that interest be defined in another way. The choice of "purpose" and its correlate of "appropriate world" is not arbitrary, but rests both upon a reflection on our prior failure to identify interest in an adequate way, and upon an awareness that in the philosophical tradition it is reason as purposive activity in an appropriate world which had been held to be the adequate solution to the problem of the absolute standpoint once self-consciousness had shown itself to fail the task.[2] Essentially, the argument for this new form of interest is the following. The interest found in the forms of intentionality and desire in fact presuppose that the world and life are appropriate for those interests to be carried through; otherwise, neither intentionality nor desire would make sense. Purpose combines the outward, passive orientation of intentionality and at the same time the inward, active orientation of desire. Purpose presupposes both a world separate from and external to the individual, which is only intended as appropriate to the purposes of the moment, and at the same time a life-world which is constituted by and is the arena of the purposes of the individual. Contrary to the presupposition of consciousness and intentionality, therefore, I am *not simply* drawn to a world outside me by chance, but rather am drawn to it with certain desires concerning it. My thinking and conscious action direct my activities, and thus I have transformed that intended world which simply presents itself into one which has become life, the arena for my actions.[3]

Such purposive action, however, does not efface the hegemony of that world, does not merely transform it or attempt to transform it into my private world or into a life meant simply to satisfy my desires. For instance, when I act with purpose in scientific inquiry or in social and political praxis, I act accepting a presupposition of the otherness and of the problematic nature of that world. The world is also therefore presupposed as independent of me and of my purposes, just as it was for intentionality and the straightforward stance of consciousness.[4] The occurrence of error or of failure, while it may sadden or disappoint me, does not utterly paralyze or alienate me, or leave me indifferent to the world; for I also presuppose the possible, momentary inappropriateness of the world in respect to those specific purposes.[5] Yet, acting with purpose, I still presuppose appropriateness; I do not just manipulate the world and others in a blind and willful manner. Purpose makes no sense without the presupposition of an appropriate world; and yet, in accepting failure as a possibility, I presuppose that it is the world and life, and not my desires, which determine their own appropriateness to my purposes.[6]

This unity of intentionality and desire and their respective correlates into one totality designates just what traditionally has been called "reason."[7] In this new synthesis, to act with purpose necessitates the presupposition of a world which is *in principle* appropriate to that purpose; but such appropriateness can emerge only when possible worlds are thematized through purposive action. Thus, reason is presupposed; i.e., I presuppose that there is *a* rational structure which links my purposes to the world and to the life in which they are to be manifested, and which links the latter to my purposes.

These presuppositions of the rational individual and the rational universe reflect the way in which we have gone beyond the presuppositions of both consciousness and self-consciousness as putative absolute standpoints. And yet they are grounded in an important discovery which occurred in the analysis of the presuppositions of self-consciousness; for there we found that thought belonged not primarily and originally to each individual, nor was it only accidentally applicable to that world of life which concerned all individuals. Thought and language transcended the individuals as "atoms" and were fundamentally intersubjective, while at the same time it was through the thoughtful and linguistic activities of the individuals in their relations to each other that thought and language had efficacy. It was precisely the natural, self-conscious attempt to master this intersubjectivity of thought through various philosophies of life—stoicism, skepticism, unhappy consciousness—that we were led to see the impossibility of an ultimate ground for certainty in self-consciousness and the necessity for a surrender to reason. But now we shall see that that surrender was not as radical as it might have seemed; for structurally and functionally reason is identical to thought. What we have done, then, is to accept the peculiar transcendence involved in the presupposition of reason as a nexus for interaction and hence as putative ground for warranted certainty.

Thus, in these presuppositions of reason and rational activity, there is a putative absolute standpoint which transcends both subject and object, both consciousness and its world, and both self-consciousness and its life, and yet which is to be taken as the *immanent* ground of them all. Reason is neither only purpose or something in the rational individual, nor only appropriateness of the world or an external structure; it is the living, dialectical relationship between them. Reason belongs neither to the individual thinker or actor alone, nor to the world in itself; it is the relation between them in which both participate.[8] Or, put in another way, there is now presupposed a shared hegemony between subjectivity and objectivity rather than a domination of either over the other. The scientist conducts his researches and the individual citizen undertakes various social and political actions with "the instinct of reason," i.e., with a *tempered*, presupposed certainty that he can act efficaciously in carrying out his purposes because the possible worlds of experience are in harmony with these purposes. Reason is to be found in the activities themselves, but they also presuppose reason. Yet each rational individual also proceeds with the instinct that all is not immediate harmony, that appropriateness and inappropriateness are not to be decided by the fiat of an individual but, rather, by that set of possible worlds which constitutes and will constitute his experience. No one invents rational activities; they arise in the very processes of interaction between individuals and between individuals and the world of things and events.

When purpose and appropriateness are presupposed as the ground of the interest structures of intentionality and desire, and stand as the putative ground warranting certainty, then the opposition disappears between totalization and totality or between the always-already-fixed and the process of becoming. For it is now presupposed that totality is not something fixed eternally in a world which transcends empirical consciousness and something opposed by the struggle toward totalization in consciousness itself; nor is it presupposed that the need for an act of totalization is only the result of the incompleteness of desire and satisfaction in facing life. Totality, rather, is presupposed as constituted in the very process of totalization. Purposive conscious activity *finds itself* in the world as appropriate or inappropriate; that world, in turn, *is reflected* only in the purposive activities of the conscious individual. For to call something appropriate is meaningful only in terms of some purpose; and to have purposes is meaningful only in terms of possible appropriateness.⁹ This dialectic of purpose and appropriateness and of totalization and totality is explicitly reflected upon now when we realize through recollection that self-consciousness

> is all reality, not merely *for itself* but also *in itself*, only through *becoming* this reality, or rather through *demonstrating* itself to be such. It demonstrates itself to be this *along the path* in which first, in the dialectical movement of "meaning," perceiving, and understanding, otherness as *intrinsic being* vanishes. Then in the movement through the independence of consciousness in lordship and bondage, through the conception of freedom, through the liberation that comes from skepticism and the struggle for absolute liberation by the consciousness divided against itself, otherness, in so far as it is only *for consciousness*, vanishes for *consciousness itself*. There appeared two aspects, one after the other; one in which the essence or the true had for consciousness the determinateness of *being*, the other in which it had the determinateness of being only *for consciousness*. But the two reduced themselves to a single truth, viz. that what *is*, or the in-itself, only *is* in so far as it is *for* consciousness, and what is *for* consciousness is also *in itself* or has *intrinsic* being (*PhG*, 176–77; *PhS*, 140–41).¹⁰

This recollection (*Erinnerung*) of the *Phenomenology* up to this point indicates how reason satisfies and grounds the claims of both intentionality and desire: totality belongs as much to being-for-consciousness as it does to being-in-itself; totalization is as much a process of being-in-itself as it is one of being-for-consciousness. Reason as purpose in an appropriate world and as an appropriate world for purpose is the presupposed unity, a unity, however, which does not give us a simple block universe, but is shot through with ambiguity.

In addition to this change in the character of the presuppositions of the nature of interest, there is also change in the dialectic of the phenomenological analysis.[11] Reason as instinctive, as a presupposition *accepted as* a presupposition, is a ground in which both totality and totalization are brought together. In this togetherness the unity of the self and the world are also presupposed such that the processes involved in having and carrying out a purpose are no longer in opposition to the fixedness of a world in which, somehow, truth is already established. Both process and the stability of essence are properties of both the rational individual and the reality within which he acts. This move to the presupposition of reason, then, frees us from an examination of certainty amidst the "busyness" of consciousness and self-consciousness, both dedicated to establishing themselves; for the individual is now understood to comprehend himself as dealing with experience and its possible worlds in a way in which he seems most often to do so: he proceeds in his activities with a deliberately presupposed certainty and stability. In a sense, as we have already seen, we are back to the "unconsciousness" of sense-certainty; for we now proceed with the presupposition of the *instinct* of reason, not with a deliberate consciousness of its presence.[12] That is to say, we simply presuppose the unity of purpose and appropriateness. And yet we are not in that naive attitude again; for there is awareness of presupposition as presupposition, an awareness that we do presuppose reason as a unity. In a manner of speaking, the rational individual we now examine is aware of his unawareness, he accepts the presuppositional nature of his activities. This awareness of unawareness thereby transcends the simple attitude of sense-certainty in its pure state.[13]

We are introduced to the change in the process of the dialectic by means of a preliminary examination of the question of whether or not with this simple presupposition of reason we have reached the end of our search. We begin with an examination of philosophical idealism, a position which contains the claim that reason is all reality and thus that self-consciousness is simple consciousness of being all reality.[14] By comparing the claims of this philosophical position with the successes of actual rational activity, we will see (1) that this philosophical position, as articulated at this point, is inadequate to the truth and does not really reflect the position of reason, and (2) that our task henceforth in the *Phenomenology* will be to allow rational activity itself, through paradigm cases, to show us the way to the absolute standpoint. First I shall examine the analysis of philosophical idealism, and then the comparison of it with real rational activity. This will then introduce the new phenomenological methodology which is markedly different from that employed thus far.

The fact that we have arrived in our quest for certainty at a position which not only presupposes a ground for consciousness and self-consciousness, but also accepts its presupposition as a presupposition, suggests that we have now the capability to articulate the absolute standpoint and the way in which it gives us access to reality. This is why the section on reason begins with a discussion of a philosophical position which appears to articulate all of the characteristics of the natural attitude as we have come to understand it. The "certainty of being all reality" which is reflected in the instinctive rational activities suggests that there is in principle a certainty of having all reality within one's grasp. The individual has freed himself to work in and with the world in a positive manner, in contrast to his earlier "concern" for himself and his rights to certainty which we have seen manifested in the attitudes of consciousness and self-consciousness (*PhG*, 175–76; *PhS*, 139–40). The general view of any philosophical idealism in one way or another makes explicit these claims contained in the instinct of reason.[15] This, in turn, reflects the ordinary certainty of sense-certainty and, supposedly, shows the unity of philosophy and the natural attitude which we have been seeking.

But if we reflect on the theories, we find that they do not express the absolute standpoint, and in fact do not even adequately express the actual standpoint of rational beings as they act purposively in the world. These idealisms are, of course, not the absolute idealism of Hegel, but the various forms of subjective idealism (ranging from Locke and Berkeley through Kant and Fichte); and the lack which is shown to belong to them, when considered as the explicit expression of the presuppositional attitude of instinctively rational activity, is that each of them in its own way admits to a "remainder" over and above the rational. All such idealisms always admit to an *absolute*, unconditioned otherness of things in themselves in contradiction to the claim of active reason that it embraces all reality and hence that otherness is only *relative*.

> This idealism is involved in this contradiction because it asserts the *abstract concept* of reason to be the true; consequently, reality directly comes to be for it a reality that is just as much *not* that of reason, while reason is at the same time supposed to be all reality. This reason remains a restless searching and in its very searching declares that the satisfaction of *finding* is a sheer impossibility (*PhG*, 181–82; *PhS*, 145).

The "impossibility" is found in a contradiction internal to all such idealist positions in philosophy: there is always posited, simultaneously with the claim of access to reality, a "somewhat" which is called by different names—extraneous impulse, empirical or sensuous entity, thing-in-itself—but which is always something real and yet beyond the capacity of reason to grasp. That is to say, such philosophical idealism in the end proves the impossibility of itself and thus the invalidity of the presuppositional frameworks of reason which it pretends to articulate. We have, therefore, a self-destructive idealism.[16]

Our justification for this initial rejection of such an idealism will now be reinforced by showing that the actual work of reason, i.e., of a rational individual, demonstrates a "true" idealism which does not inconsistently posit a completeness *and* a thing-in-itself which remains outside the bounds of reason. That is to say, unlike the asseverations of the philosophical idealism, the idealism of the instinct of reason as it is in actual operation is itself a driving force which impels the community of rational individuals to articulate the certainty and instinct through their own practices, i.e., to *prove* themselves as rational by actually capturing reality through rational activity (*PhG*, 181–82; *PhS*, 145). Here, then, the actual phenomenon of rational activity comes to the fore *for us*, as well as *for itself*, as a test of its own instincts. Through the display of rational activities of various sorts, both the "we" of the *Phenomenology* and one in the natural attitude of rational activity are able to observe *how* reason is and shows itself both to be the absolute standpoint and to be precisely within the natural attitude in one of the forms in which it pursues rational activities. Thus, we of the *Phenomenology* are now freed simply to look on, to watch human beings in the natural attitude of reason prove reason as the absolute standpoint. The natural attitude is now itself to demonstrate the thesis that reason is the absolute standpoint, the standpoint which gives us warranted access to actuality.

This move to reason, then, has finally placed the natural attitude in a position of which it can be self-aware and in which it takes *as its own task* the proof of reason's ultimacy and the establishment of certainty. This proving of itself removes from the "we" of the *Phenomenology* all further need to "step into the place of the concept" of the natural attitude and work out the presuppositions. Natural, rational *activity* (not theory) will work out its own presuppositions which are given in the actual deeds of the rational individuals as they confront their world in praxis. Therefore, the task is finally the same both for the "we" of the *Phenomenology* and for the natural attitude: to examine whether reason shows *itself* to be the absolute standpoint, i.e., the guarantee for the possibility of the possible worlds of experience, knowledge, and action, the absolute warranty for certainty.[18]

Rational, human activity is the hallmark of human action in its most universal sense (*PhG*, 183; *PhS*, 145–46). We experience the world and act upon and within that world not as an abstract, intended object, nor as a mere object of desire, but as a world to which we belong, as a world appropriate to our purposes. The *Phenomenology* now presents us with an "epic" in which is portrayed the quest actually to appropriate the world and to actualize the mere instinctive certainty of that unity of purpose and appropriateness.[19] In the end we shall see that reason, unlike consciousness and self-consciousness, is found by both the rational actor and ourselves as an adequate locus for the absolute standpoint. But in the quest for certainty in the *Phenomenology* we will nevertheless be forced to a different and "higher" level of reason, viz. reason, not as some pure, transcendental capacity, but as embedded in socio-political and cultural formations which themselves undergo a change through time in the form of history. This realization will move us on to the presupposition of spirit as the absolute standpoint and the domain of the absolute idea.

This first section of the discussion of reason as putative absolute standpoint is thus not a digression nor a mere polemic. It serves an important function in our quest for certainty because it establishes the new form taken by our inquiry. On the one hand, the natural attitude itself is now intent on thematizing both the immediate events and objects with which it is concerned and the attitude structure within which it works. One sets out to validate claims of truth and of certainty about that truth by proceeding methodically and rationally to make sense of reality and to comprehend it. Proof that reason is an absolute standpoint and grants warranted access to reality is to come through a process of actually carrying out one's projects on the basis of reason. It is not enough to claim that reason governs the world nor simply to proceed on the basis of a theory that reason so governs; reason must prove itself in action. On the other hand, we who are involved in the quest for certainty have grounds for rejecting a proclaimed end to that quest; for it is clear that any idealism which does not successfully encompass all of reality—and none of them has—is a betrayal of the claims of idealism itself. What we must do is observe the pragmatic proof of this new putative presupposition set as we observe reason proving itself. Thus, the phenomenal and the phenomenological self-consciousness—the natural and the philosophical attitudes—have come closer to each other; for both are conscious of the quest and now proceed in harmony in the attempt to complete the quest. The quest for certainty—albeit in still slightly different ways—is as much a concern for natural, rational activity as it is for fully reflexive philosophical activity.

The first analysis of reason in the process of self-discovery occurs in three stages. The first stage is that of scientific work, ranging from the work of the natural sciences, through the sciences of logic, psychology, physiognomy, and phrenology. This stage Hegel calls "reason observing." The second stage, called "the actualization of rational self-consciousness through its own activity," is constituted by the activity of individuals, not merely observing the world from various perspectives, but deliberately setting forth ideologies which are to guide their lives and to shape the world in accordance with reason. The third stage is called "individuality which takes itself to be real in and for itself." Here we are presented with the activities of individuals, not merely as individuals attempting purposefully to shape the world, but as social individuals in an already established society, fulfilling their own and others' needs, and trying to devise or to find a theoretical basis on which to make and test the laws of that society and of that existence. In these three stages we move from pure theoretical activity in various sciences to rational praxis which involves not only a *theoria* but also the actual shaping and production of world. We see first the nature of communal scientific inquiries, then of individual ideological praxis, and finally of communal praxis grounded upon and shaping reason.[20] In all three stages we are concerned as before with our quest for certainty and not with a philosophical anthropology, history of science, or philosophy of spirit.

In the first stage we find that reason attempts to show warranty for its certainty through observation, classification, and theory construction. The project is to "find" the nature of what-is by means of purposefully approaching reality with preset questions and theoretical projects. If reality can be found in this way, then the success of the discovery will validate the instinct of reason, namely that it has access to reality. This stage demonstrates to us and to the rational individual himself, however, that reason is not an absolute standpoint merely to be discovered and participated in by "seeing," but rather will be met with only by means of the constructive activities of the observer himself. That is to say, we are presented with the fact that the theoretical work is *work*, i.e., activity on the part of the individuals. With this realization, we are led to the second stage, that of purposive individual activity not as mere observation, but as an attempt deliberately to make the world conform to our purposive frameworks. The claim here is that the degree to which the world conforms is the degree to which certainty is warranted. This stage leads us to the realization that just as reason is not something found through observation, neither is it something only made. Rather it is both found and made, both given as already existing as a framework, and also constructed through the determinate acts of a community of individuals. Thus we turn to the third stage, that of existence in a community of individuals where the standpoint is both already given and in the process of being constructed. But this last putative form of reason as ground of certainty is precisely *spirit*, the final ground of certainty to be examined in the *Phenomenology*.[21]

In each of these three stages, the rational activity itself is more and more reflected in the object and content of that activity, until we are forced to recognize in communal, rational praxis a *given* ground for the rational activity which is both reflected in and constituted by the rational activity itself. In "reason observing" we find the connections of things, which connections make the world an appropriate world for the purposive activities carried out in that world. But we lack any adequate account of the actual connection between interest as purpose and the world appropriate to that interest. In "the actualization of rational self-consciousness through its own activity" reason is presented as attempting forcefully to forge the link between interest and world through various ideological moves. But such forcefulness shows itself to be counter-productive since, as we have already seen in the examination of self-consciousness, it is the world which declares itself appropriate for our deeds, not the actor himself. Thus, at the third level of reason we take up the world as it is, i.e., as a community of individuals acting in concert and with an already established set of social and natural relations. Consequently, reason deals with itself as both constitutive of and constituted by individuals, while society is also both constitutive of and constituted by individuals. Purpose and appropriateness are here synthesized in such a way that neither holds hegemony over the other but, rather, exists in symbiotic relationship with the other. There is here a joining of the subjective and the objective, of self and world, which finally overcomes the separation of the two which, from the beginning of our analysis, has plagued our efforts to achieve the absolute standpoint and warranty for our certainty.[22] Let us turn now to a closer examination of the phenomenological analysis of reason.

We begin our analysis of the instinctive activity of reason with an exploration of the activities comprising the various positive sciences.[23] In these sciences an attempt is made through observation to arrive at a warranted certainty concerning the form and content of reality. The general presupposition is that a rational structure, and therefore reason, is to be found in the world in the form of the ordering and various laws of reality. The rational individual comes to that world, in whatever form that world is thematized by him, and seeks reason in it. This observational activity is explored in six of its forms: observation of (1) nature in general (physics, chemistry), (2) organic nature (biology), (3) logic (as a purely formal inquiry into the forms of thought), (4) psychology (as an inquiry into active consciousness in so far as it shapes and is shaped by its world), (5) physiognomy, and (6) phrenology. In all of these observational modes of rational activity, reason through purposive observation is seen by us to find a world appropriate to that kind of observation and thus to find reason itself in the form of an objective reality. This is the sense in which reason here presents itself to itself in the form of being, i.e., rational thought and observation find a rational reality.

Here we have revealed in a concrete way the difference in the dialectic. Because the presupposition of reason as the absolute standpoint and warranty for certainty involves us no longer with the centrality of individuals as individuals in the quest for certainty, but rather with their conscious, albeit instinctive participation in a transcendent reason of the sort we have described above, the presupposition relation undergoes a significant modification. Already in the analysis of the freedom of self-consciousness there occurred on the part of the natural attitude a thematization of the presupposition relation. Consequently, it was possible for the phenomenal consciousness to test its own standpoint for its adequacy as absolute. With the turn to reason this state of affairs is intensified and advanced; for vis-à-vis the quest for certainty there is present in rational activity, as part of its project, a concern to validate its own claims for access to reality. Therefore, insofar as an absolute and exhaustive access to reality fails to show itself, reason on the part of the rational individual will see the access as partial and, insofar as it is possible, will take steps to remedy the lack. In other words, the comparison between claims and results no longer has to be made by us but is part of the project of the rational actor himself. The logic of the presupposition relation is thus established as actively engaged in the world itself.[24]

In the first and most universal and abstract science the rational observer observes nature in general, nature as simply a collection of entities. Purposive observation finds them suspended in a system of concepts and laws which demonstrate their relations in various ways. Sometimes the relations are explored in simply descriptive or taxonomic ways, at other times as lawful relations between things thus classified. In the latter case we become involved with "abstract matters" or variables involved in "pure laws," e.g., variables such as force, heat, velocity, distance. In these observations and in the laws discovered through them we find a network of rational systems and thus a world appropriate to the exploration of such systems by a rational individual.

But we also discover that the rational observer does not find any internal necessity in such a system of laws.[25] For this reason, physics and other such sciences do not demonstrate the actual existence of reason as warranted, even in the world taken as something in itself and independent of the observer. Because the necessity is lacking, all that we have is, at best, some "operational" or quasi-nominalist view of reality, an access to reality which *can* ground the possible worlds thematized in our other experiences, but which does not evidence of itself any unconditioned warranty for this grounding. The theories and laws turn out to be *a* way of seeing the world, *a* framework which might ground the thematic world of non-scientific experience, and therefore something *conditioned* by (a) the observer approaching the world in this way, and (b) the facticity of the presence of the variables or matters and their relations to each other.[26] If, however, we are to claim that reason itself has demonstrated itself to be the absolute standpoint, then such conditional grounding will not suffice.

When nature is observed from the perspective of biology and its related sciences, however, there promises to be an internal necessity evidenced in the way in which organisms relate to their environment and to themselves.[27] Here we find both some degree of necessity to the laws discovered, and a reflection of the internal relation which must exist between purpose and appropriateness if we are to achieve the absolute ground through reason.

But here, also, when the system of life sciences as a whole is examined, i.e., when we look at life on the most universal plane, there is still discovered no reason which establishes why the relations are as they are. And even if evolutionary theory had been available, that necessity would still be lacking; for there would still be no reason why natural selection should be rational, only the fact that it is rational. Furthermore, the system of species of living things does not evidence in itself why it should be as it is and not otherwise. The fact that creation is what it is may be discovered in all of its detail; but not the why of it. Therefore the "mystery of being" hangs over all the findings of the rational observer in these life sciences.[28]

This is not to say that the rational observer does not find rationality in the world, and to that degree establish some right to claim certainty; for he does, and this is just the advance we find here over the observation of nature as inorganic. The very relationship which exists between an organism and its environment is structured precisely by purpose, and thus the reality observed in part establishes its appropriateness for purposive rational observation just by containing purpose as a central characteristic. We have here a structural analogy between the activity of observation and the object being observed. The human activity is thus reflected in some degree in the reality it observes.[29] But the sort of purpose which can be discovered in the framework of the life sciences still falls short of the purpose which drives the rational activity of the human observer. The reason of the rational observer still does not find itself in any complete way in the world. What is lacking is that the purposes found can only be described as found, as existing, and cannot be described from the perspective of their ultimate origination. On the supposition that life as rational is the ultimate level of reality—that life as the ultimate level can be its own reason and thus the absolute standpoint—we fail to find such a standpoint. In other terms, life does not ground itself and consequently the laws and relations and structures which constitute life are not an articulation of an unconditioned, absolute standpoint. Biology does not give us ultimate knowledge of the ultimate.[30] Nor does biology make that claim for itself.

At this point Hegel is led to introduce logic under a quasi-nominalist argument.[31] Given the well-ordered system of things, and yet the lack of a self-establishing ground for that system, reason now is held to presuppose that the form of things gains its necessity from the laws of thought which are imposed on the material observed. That is to say, reason turns to an observation of itself as rational observation in order to find the basic reason which will ground itself and its observed world. The laws of thought, however, are conceived of as just that, laws of thought only and something "outside" of the reality to which they are applied. All general reflections on methodology *as* methodology are embraced by the analysis we have here made of the logic, so long as methodology is seen as removed from the content examined through it.

Such a view presents reason with a schism between material reality and formal thought, a schism which would make it impossible to claim warranty for certainty. On the one hand, since these laws of thought are outside of reality, "they have no reality," and thus "they lack truth."

> They are indeed not supposed to be the *entire* truth, but still *formal* truth. But what is purely formal without any reality is a mere figment of thought, or pure abstraction without that internal division which would be nothing else but the content. On the other hand, however, since they are laws of pure thought, and pure thought is intrinsically universal, and therefore a knowledge which immediately contains being, and therein all reality, these laws are absolute concepts, and are inseparably the essential principles both of form and of things (*PhG*, 222; *PhS*, 180).

Because of the contradictory claim found in such a view of formal logic—on the one hand merely conventionalist, on the other hand claiming a real validity in respect to its use in reality—reason itself demands that the relation between thought and things be articulated. The instinct of reason demands that we find a science wherein this relation is observed and articulated, promising thereby to give a ground. Such a science is psychology, and thus reason is led to psychologism in respect to the laws of thought.[32]

At this point the quest of reason for intelligibility and certainty through observation comes for the first time into contact with what is to develop as spirit, i.e., the relation between human beings and their reality. From the observation of nature in itself as the general object and putative foundation for absolute warranty, through the mediation of the observation of organic nature with its system of internal relations between living things and their environments, to the observation of pure thought in logic, we have come to find rational activity observing rational activity. Implicitly, human activity has all along been its own object, first abstractly considered as simply physical, then as living, and then as a thinking thing in the study of logic. Now rational observation takes for its observation its own activity which includes observation itself.

> Psychology contains the collection of laws in accordance with which spirit relates itself in various ways to the various modes of its actuality as an *otherness already given* (PhG, 223; PhS, 182).

The project of reason in the science of psychology is to show the necessary structure which grounds the relationship individuals have with the world, i.e., to show how and why consciousness is affected by the world and the world by consciousness. Its project is the observation and comprehension of the standpoint itself within which experience, knowledge and action occur. We here, then, see the phenomenal form of being we are observing turn for its own examination on that being itself. Psychology observes precisely the relationship between self and world which is also *our* object.[33]

Reason indeed does find itself in this relationship as studied by psychology; it finds itself in the explicit exploration of purposes and of criteria of appropriateness and inappropriateness which are present in human activity. But what is found is that we are a "stimulus-response" organism, and laws of adaptation can be developed in accordance with this deterministic framework. On the one hand, there is a positive advance here; for psychology articulates a relationship which is both formal and material, and reason itself overcomes the lack it found in its logical investigations. But at the same time there is a problem discovered which suggests that stimulus-response determinism is deficient in respect to a full articulation of reason at work in the world and thus in respect to the absolute standpoint. The world of the individual

> has at once an ambiguous meaning: it is the actual state of the world as it is in and for itself, and it is the world of the individual; it is the latter either in so far as the individual has merely coalesced with that world, has let it, just as it is, enter

Interest as Purpose: Observation 127

into him, behaving towards it as a merely formal consciousness; or, on the other hand, it is the world of the individual, in the sense that the actual world as given has been *transformed* by the individual (*PhG*, 226; *PhS*, 184).

That is to say, on the one hand the world is simply a given and is what it is, the source of stimuli to which we respond. But that aspect of the world, taken in itself, is no longer of interest to psychology since we are now concentrating not on a nature which is in itself, but rather on the relationship between that world and the *conscious* individual. The individual is not simply part of that world, but a set of purposes and purposive activities set over against that world. Thus, in consideration of this, two views can be taken of the world as it is related to purposive activity: either it *simply* shapes consciousness or consciousness shapes it *as well*.[34] In psychological theory neither case can be ultimately established as against the other. Put in other terms, the question of freedom has arisen: Does the individual have some freedom, some causal efficacy of his own, or is the individual simply caught up in a strict, natural necessity? And if there is freedom, to what extent does it exist and how is it to be shown to be an aspect of the rational? This ambiguity ultimately causes science to search in another way for the rationality which it possesses and finds in the world.[35]

Here we see clearly the way in which the problem of freedom and necessity occurs in a psychological investigation when we do not simply and dogmatically close off the question of freedom:

> The individual either *allows* free play to the stream of the actual world flowing in upon it, or else breaks it off and transforms it. The result of this, however, is that "psychological necessity" becomes an empty phrase, so empty that there exists the absolute possibility that what is supposed to have had this influence could just as well not have had it (*PhG*, 226–27; *PhS*, 184–85).

The result is that the doctrine of voluntarism as easily interprets the phenomena constituting the relationship between the conscious individual and the world as does the doctrine which finds the determinant in the effect the world has on the individual. These opposite doctrines leave psychology in a state of internal struggle which cannot be resolved and which thus force the instinct of reason to look elsewhere for its own implicit ground of warranty.

This result, which would seem to leave psychology with little or no rational power, is to be taken in a positive manner, however. What has come out of the study of psychology and the resultant opposition of voluntarism and behaviorism is a new notion of individuality and law, and of the rationality of reason itself. This result was studied, however ineptly, in physiognomy and phrenology.[36] We need not reflect at length over the detailed character of these two "sciences," but rather only at that at which they were aiming. What we find in these pursuits is another sign of the ways in which the rational human being has attempted to find the world as his own, to come to be absolutely at home in the world with a completely warranted certainty. These two "sciences" sought to determine the relation between the individual and the world. In the views of physiognomy and phrenology, the *dualism* of psychology, both behavioristic and voluntaristic, has shown itself to be within its own parameters contradictory. In behaviorism there is hegemony of world, in voluntarism hegemony of consciousness. What these two new disciplines realize and what places them just for this reason above psychology, is the transcendence of the dualism and its either/or choice. The transcendence of this limitation occurs because one recognizes the *duality* of individuality itself and of the world itself. In the dual*ism* of psychology both individual and world are something in themselves, the former a set of faculties or tendencies, the latter a set of circumstances. In the dual*ity* theory of physiognomy and phrenology—and we would say today in much of our own modern psychology and social-psychology—individuality is itself defined as the *interaction between* the individual and his world. On the other hand, the world itself is defined as the interaction between the individual and the world, a duplication of individuality, but now as a mirror image. It is this view, and especially the definition of individuality, which characterizes these sciences.

Thus, "individuality has now become the object for observation, or the object to which observation now turns" (*PhG*, 227; *PhS*, 185). In our examination of physiognomy we first turn to the foundationalist claims of physiognomy.

> In physiognomy . . . spirit is supposed to be known in its *own* outer aspect, as a being which is the utterance [*Sprache*] of spirit—the visible invisibility of its essence (*PhG*, 238; *PhS*, 195).

Individuality manifests itself as self-mediating, as the expression of the inner reality and faculties through its own physical, outer appearance. The appearance which is explored by physiognomy is "the actual utterance" which links or mediates the individual in his inner essence with the world. What we see here, then, is a position which goes well beyond any mere superstition about the nature of the human profile, however much that may have actually characterized the real practitioners of this science. In fact, this science involves at its core the concept of spirit and of the real activity of individuals purposively acting in the world.[37]

For this reason, the sections on physiognomy and phrenology will mark the transition from the spectatorial shape of rational activity to the non-spectatorial, non-observational, active "proof" which rational beings give themselves of their access to the absolute standpoint.[38] It forms the pivot which moves us from rationality as observation of the world to rationality as construction of the world. It was simply a fact of Hegel's time that these two sciences formed the basis for his reflection on this move; our own, modern social sciences form that basis for us today.[39] But because of the point being made about these attempts to fathom reason's own ground, we shall have to pay attention to some of the details of the examination. If one wishes, one can simply forget the sciences to which these thoughts are attributed, and concentrate on the content alone.

The science begins with a focus on the significance of the real, concrete individual who has two aspects to his individuality.

> The individual exists in and for himself; he is *for himself* or
> is a free activity; but he has also an *intrinsic* being or has an
> *original* determinate being of his own—a determinateness
> which is in principle the same as what psychology thought to
> find outside of him (*PhG*, 227; *PhS*, 185).

In other words, where psychology sought to find laws grounded in the circumstantial, external causes of the individual's behavior, i.e., in the circumstances which were to be found in the world in itself and which affected the nature of the individual, in its place that basis is now to be sought and found in the "original nature" or character of the individual himself. The original nature of the individual is fixed in the outward manifestation of spirit, i.e. in the physical body of the individual. That nature is the character caught in the characteristics of the body. The science of physiognomy has as its project to catalogue and deliver the laws of these appearances and of the characteristics which were not formed by the consciousness of the individual but are his *given*, just as previously the external world and its stimuli were treated as a given by psychology.

In this new science, however, we are not as one-sided as in the science of psychology; for there now appears a *duality of the given itself* which is to be accounted for.

> But since the individual is at the same time only what he has
> done, his body is also the expression of himself which he has
> himself *produced*; it is at the same time a *sign*, which has not
> remained an *immediate* fact, but something through which

the individual only makes known what he really is, when he sets his original nature to work (*PhG*, 227–28; *PhS*, 185–86).

That is to say, that external appearance is supposed to show what the individual does. And the most important aspect of this fact is the notion that the individual is not just a set of capacities or possibilities, but the actuality of what he does. The individual is not defined by what he would want to do or ought to do, or merely has the potential to do; he is supposed to be what he does, what he has done, what he will do. In physiognomy, then, we find further developed the germ of the notion of the centrality of action to human experience and knowledge, of action as informed by and as informing thought. Whether we remain with an individual *per se* or take the individual to be "a general human shape, or at least the general character of a climate, a continent, a people," this science brings into unity with reason the praxis of the individual and of individuals in general. Thus, the givenness of some conditions (i.e., the original nature of the individual) is brought into synthesis with the productiveness of individual action (i.e., the use to which the individual puts his original nature) to form the reality of the connection between self and world.[40]

The criticism which arises against this science leaves intact its central insight into the connection between individual and world as centered in the embodied, practical individual. The criticism is to the effect that physiognomy itself concentrates on the inner being which is *expressed* by the outer being or body as a capacity, as the mere possibility for certain types of behavior. That is to say, physiognomy "reads" the inner nature of the individual from observations of its outer appearance, and leaves the actual deeds themselves, i.e., the actual world which was to be explained, as a mere domain of possibilities. In physiognomic research, "it is not the murderer, the thief, who is to be recognized, but merely the *capacity to be one*" (*PhG*, 235; *PhS*, 192), and capacity, of course, does not reflect actuality. Whether or not one who has the capacity to murder actually does murder, is consequently left to the unknown and unknowable. Thus, if the individual is what he does, then this mere discovery of capacities does not get to the real being of the individual. Nor does it bring us to a knowledge of a set of individuals and the rational ground of their being. This science, then, for all of its "structural" insights, misses the chance to observe reason as present in real activity and in a self-grounding form which would give warranty for our certainty of access to reality.

"The *true being* of a man is rather his deed": it is *praxis* which shows us the truth and which establishes reason in the world as a living actuality

(PhG, 236; PhS, 193–94). The mere intentions or capacities of the individual do not establish actual events, but only possible events. The possible is infinitely *determinable*, and thus the mere guesses of the observing reason in physiognomy do not manifest the rationality of the actual.[41]

The bulk of the discussion of phrenology constitutes Hegel's attempt to show in the best possible light this other science which claims to be rational observation of the rational. Although the attempt by this science also fails, nevertheless, as in the examination of physiognomy, there are now some further important truths uncovered. As in physiognomy it was held that the deed itself is to be the actuality, here the attempt to make spirit into an actual thing in the world reveals a rational structure which nominally justifies our excursion into such a strange science as phrenology. The truth comes ironically from the criticism of phrenology, a criticism which appears at first as a rather simple argument.[42] The upshot of our observation of phrenology is that

> as rain is indifferent to circumstances like these [e.g., that a woman has just hung out her wash or that it is the day on which a family eats pork], so too, from the standpoint of observation, a *particular* determinateness of spirit is indifferent to a *particular* formation of the skull (PhG, 245; PhS, 202).

The critical phrase is "so too, from the standpoint of observation." What this rather ordinary criticism of phrenology amounts to is more than one would expect; for we are shown that *observation itself* discovers this irrelevance and failure as it tries to bring together into a single concept and on the basis of verification the claims of phrenological observation. The presuppositions posited by phrenology as present in the actual structure of reality do not make possible and actual the worlds of our experience and knowledge. The point is that mere being, the mere existence of something (such as the skull bone with its configurations), is not the determinant of the actual existence of the thing in its essence, character, and reality. Phrenological observations hence call out an observation, from the depths of the "raw instinct or self-conscious reason itself," that

> *being* as such is not the truth of spirit at all. Just as the disposition is itself an *original being*, which has no part in the activity of spirit, just such a being is the bone on *its* side. What merely *is*, without any spiritual activity is, for consciousness, a thing, and, far from being the essence of consciousness, is rather its opposite; and consciousness is only *actual* to itself through the negation and abolition of such a being (PhG, 248–49; PhS, 205).

Phrenological observations are indeed based upon the instinct of reason to find itself literally *in* the world; but it is found here in a form which,

> having attained to a glimpse of the cognitive process, has grasped it unintelligently in a way that takes the outer to be an expression of the inner (*PhG*, 249; *PhS*, 205–06).

The true glimpse referred to here is the realization that spirit cannot be a mere potentiality as in physiognomy, nor "world-centered" as in behavioristic psychology. The raw, original instinct of reason retains this glimpse, and it is from the perspective of this instinct that the *Phenomenology* advances to the next major stage in which reason no longer tries to find itself through observational activity, but attempts to make itself and its world through overt actions designed to shape the world.

Hidden in the at times fantastic discussion of the science of phrenology is a critical comprehension which, we see, belongs to rational observation itself. At the point at which spirit—the relation between self and world—has been conceived of as an inert thing in the world—the skull bone—the self-conscious, rational observer has forced upon him two antithetical aspects of his own rational activity. On the one hand, he is confronted with "the individuality that is conscious of itself" (*PhG*, 249–50; *PhS*, 206). This form of self-consciousness refers both to the individual who is making the observations (e.g., the phrenologist) and also to the individual who is being observed by him. Both are involved in *purposive attempts* to find themselves and their ground in the actual world and both are therefore markedly different from that inert skullbone.[43] On the other hand, the observer and the observed are confronted with "the abstraction of externality that has become wholly a *thing*—that inner being of spirit grasped as a fixed non-spiritual being, opposed to just such [an inner spiritual] being" (*PhG*, 249–50; *PhS*, 206). At this extreme point of identification of the purely physical and singular with self-conscious spirit, observational reason, still borne by the instinct of reason, comes to a degree of self-awareness through the disparity of results indicated in this antithetical conception.[44]

When the rational observer reflects upon what it is that he is doing, as well as reflecting upon the purposive activities of the individuals being observed, he finds the following: reason, through observation, finds itself in the world and achieves certainty only by directing itself toward spirit as it first did when in psychology it attended to purposive acts oriented around the individual and his world. Reason on neither side of self or world is inert, and is in a concrete form only in the domain of praxis in and toward the world. Actions have the only complete form which reveal to observation a living reason which actually inhabits the world. Spirit in some way *is*, i.e., objectively exists as a reality and not as mere possibility or abstraction. But the course of inquiry into the sciences of physiognomy and phrenology has reduced that being of spirit discovered in psychology into the being of a spiritless thing, into the skull-bone of a rational being. This reduction denies two things which for observational reason are now clearly true. The first is that from the time of the introduction of spirit in psychological studies, it is clear that deeds, i.e., the living, conscious, material relation with the world and within the world, are the locus of concrete reason and constitute the true objective existence of reason. The second is that the very consciousness of the rational observer is itself a denial of the *mere* physical being of spirit.[45]

The second point is critical; for here a question is asked by the rational observer which concerns his own activity and its instincts: What about the observer himself in respect to his observations? Can the rational activity of the observer, who finds reason in such a form, itself be accounted for by the theory it unfolds? The answer is that such a physicalistic theory, and indeed any physicalistic theory, cannot explain the possibility of the existence of the theory itself as a result of rational activity. Nor can it explicate and ground the source of the theory, i.e., the real, living, conscious rational inquirer. The rational observer is left out of his own universe. We thus conclude that if

> such a consciousness does not reflect on itself, the intermediate position, or middle term, which it occupies is an unhappy void, since what should fill and fulfill it has been turned into a fixed extreme. Thus it is that this final stage of reason in its observational role is its worst; and that is why its reversal becomes a necessity (*PhG*, 250; *PhS*, 206).

The point is rather subtly put and needs some explication. The following, I hope, will make sense of the matter.[46]

The problem is that reason, as the activity of examining and explaining that world which surrounds the rational observer, has run the gamut of observable loci which might make sense of things. But in none of these domains observed has the rational observer found the rationality which would fully warrant his instinctive sense that reality is a totality of rationality. Thus, neither we nor the natural observer have found the absolute ground of warranted certainty. In the final position, phrenology, we have come to the realization that a physicalistic theory cannot account for the very activity which has generated this theory and which enables the rational observer, in this case the phrenologist, to observe and make sense of reality. This dictates a "reversal" (*Umkehrung*) of rational consciousness.[47]

The exact reasons for this reversal by rational consciousness itself arise from a reflective "survey of the series of relations considered so far which constitute the content and object of observation" (*PhG*, 250; *PhS*, 206).[48] We find that in

> their first form, i.e., in the observation of the relations of inorganic nature, sensuous being is already lost to view; the moments of the relations present themselves as pure abstractions and as simple concepts which should be firmly tied to the existence of things, an existence, however, which gets lost, so that the moment demonstrates itself to be a pure movement and a universal . . . (*PhG*, 251–52; *PhS*, 208).

That is to say, as soon as classification and laws appeared, the physical thing itself as a simple entity ceased to be the ground of rational totality. What took its place were the relations between things, not as individual things, but as classes or types of things. Both as relations and as classes or types which are related, we come to comprehend reason in terms of universals, leaving the concrete particulars simply to fill in as a content whose only significance is that they can function as subsumed under a class and within a relation. We could conclude here, then, that certainty of access to reality is not to be found in particulars or groups of particulars, but in the relations which constitute their interactions.

But an irony occurred in the process. When rational observation first moves from simple particulars to universal classes and relations, it is moved from things to thought. This is why logic and psychology were important; for they promised to locate the basis for this thought. But we were then subsequently moved from that thought back to a concern with a concrete particular, the skull-bone. Thus, in phrenology, what was

> ruled out by the very first observation of inorganic nature, viz. the idea that the concept ought to be present in the form of a thing, is reinstated by this last form of observation in such a way that it turns the reality of spirit itself into a thing or, expressing it the other way round, gives to lifeless being the significance of spirit (*PhG*, 251–52; *PhS*, 208).

What exactly is wrong with this? At first it seems that nothing is wrong. From the beginning of the examination of reason and of rational activity we have known that reason is searching for its own warranty by searching for reason in objective reality. In this sense, finding the locus of rationality in a thing is in keeping with this search. What *is* wrong, however, is the physicalistic interpretation of what is to be meant by "thing." Spirit does exist, *it is*, but is in a non-physicalistic sense "a thing." The true interpretation of "thing" will come only from an observation of reason which keeps its eye on the original turn to the self in psychology, a turn which marked out the active/passive relation between self and world as the locus of rationality. Objectivity was there distinguished not as the world, but as the relation between self and world, as the domain constituted in that relationship between thought and things.

Put in other terms, spirit's existence as a "thing" is to be found in the form of actions, not in the pure physicalistic form to which phrenology has led us.[49] Physiognomy and phrenology were right in turning us to the concrete individual human being and in attempting to find the ultimate ground and unity of the certainty of reason in the purposive activity of an individual. But these sciences were wrong in interpreting the individual in physicalistic terms; for such an interpretation reverses the whole direction of rational inquiry, returning us immediately back to the first position in physics, to a point before classification and laws emerged from observation. The physicalistic interpretation is unwarranted on the part of the observer, a reification which essentially denies the possibility of such an act of reification. When the rational observer himself comes to the realization that his own theory cannot account for itself as a *theory*, he is led to this reversal, a reversal in which the relation of self to world again becomes the center of attention.

This is what justifies us in our conclusion that

> what is a thing is self-consciousness; the thing is, therefore, the unity of the "I" and being—the *category*. . . . The category, which is the *immediate* unity of *being* and *self*, must pass through both forms, and it is precisely for consciousness *qua* observer that the category presents itself in the form of being (PhG, 252–53; PhS, 208–09).

To say that "the category" is the immediate unity of "I" and being is to say that reason finds through its own observational activity that the activity itself is structured as the unifying activity. What is meant here by 'category' is just the literal meaning of that term, a meaning which has been too often overlooked. To categorize is to accuse, and to accuse is to bring together into a focus certain things in a certain way. A category is what Kant correctly defined as a *"unifying act*," an activity in which things are unified in one way rather than in another way. The category is thus only a form of "concept" or "*Begriff*," a grasp of things, a holding together.[50]

It has been discovered here that the self-conscious activity of rational, purposive activity in a world presupposed as appropriate to that activity is *itself* the category, the unifying act. The act of being interested in things in a specific way, an act which characterizes the essence of the rational observer and the essence of the self-world relation, is the immediate category, the immediate, spontaneous form of unification, the basis of all other unifications. To conceptualize things, to grasp them in inquiry and in the generation of laws is just to categorize things. If we are to find the locus of warranty for claims of certainty of access to reality, we must turn to the locus of that claimed access, that relation to reality which has here been described as "the category." The activity of categorizing, and not a simple "receptacle" for items, is the true focal point. The totality within which all of the particular acts of categorizing takes place is just the activity of rational beings. Thus, as Kant had already seen, the individual is *the* category, and we consequently have here a reversal of reification: the category is in truth the act of categorizing, the judgment is the act of judging, a reversal which Kant himself had begun with his characterization of judgment and category as act.[51]

Reason has thus demonstrated to us and to itself through its own activities of observation, what was simply the dogmatic assertion of subjective idealism as a philosophical position and at first only instinctive for active reason: conscious, rational activity finds itself *in* reality through its observation *of* reality.[52] On the one hand, purposive deliberate, structured observations *find* a world appropriate to rational observation when an appropriately structured world is articulated through the sciences. Reason even finds itself, as spirit, within the general structures. On the other hand, however, spirit is not just one rational structure among others; it is the one which reflects most completely the nature of the rational, viz. to be self-contained, purposive *activity*. Reason therefore discovers through observation that this presupposition of interest as purposes carried out in an appropriate world is what actually structures both itself and the world. This, in turn, causes reason to see itself not as pure observational, spectatorial activity, but as active insertion of itself in the world. Reason is rational *activity*.[53]

VI

Interest As Purpose: Action

WE HAVE FOLLOWED the instinct of reason in so far as it is conceived of simply as purposive observation. But in the process of pursuing the presupposition that observation will reveal to us the ground for certainty, we have come to realize that rational activity on the part of individuals is not simply spectatorial, but active as well. With this realization, we turn to reason as purposive activity of another sort, i.e., to the activities of an individual who is self-conscious of his own purposes as informing his own activities. The individual here presupposes that rationality not only finds and comprehends, but *also* shapes and makes reality what it is. The rational individual does not simply accept what happens to be given, even in his spectatorial observations of the world; for those observations are structured by his own questions, and therefore what will count as appropriate answers from the world is in part shaped by his own activity of observation. What we now turn to in our quest for certainty is simply an extension of this insight that the individual realizes himself and his certainty through his own rational activity. We now observe typical ways in which individuals attempt to actualize the instinct of reason by making the world their own through purposive action.[1]

We begin with the attempts of the individual himself to form and comprehend the world as rational by means of actions and transactions deliberately oriented in some specific ideological direction. The reason we begin here is that the result of our analysis of reason-observing was the revelation that the individual—the concrete, acting individual—is defined by his acts in such a way that he is what he does. The consequence of this for the quest for certainty is that it is necessary now to continue to explore purposive, rational activity as it is centered on the actually existing person. If the locus of warranty for certainty cannot be given in and for the individual actor, then there cannot be certainty for the praxis concerning whose access to reality the individual has a natural certainty. If, on the other hand, we can discover that locus, we are well on our way to the warranty we seek.

The first form we explore is that of egotistical hedonism. We are here following a pattern which we followed before; for we take up first the most simple and direct form of the general form we are to explore and examine. We are engaged now in a study of the possibility of self-directed, ideologically oriented purposive activity being the ground for warranty of certainty, and the most direct form of this is that form in which purposive activity comes closest to desire, i.e., to the orientation of action being determined by what the individual wants for himself. But in this first form, the individual is seen to come to realize that in the very act of *purposive* mastery and independence—as opposed to simple desire for mastery and independence—and in the subsequent satisfaction of the pleasures which form his purposive activities, those ends or purposes must take account of consequences which confront him in the independent reality in which he acts.[2] This is an insight, on the part of the natural attitude, into the importance of the conflict between the pleasure principle and the reality principle.[3]

In the end, the reality principle must win out. The appropriate world both furnishes conditions for the pleasures and the seeking of those pleasures, and is the totality which "absorbs" the independent individual as a factor of itself. That is to say, the individual objectifies himself in his pleasure seeking, and thus becomes himself a fact in the world. He is this individual who is recognized by others and who thus, in the self-conscious, purposive existence of others, finds reason not only as his purposes in the world, but as the purposes of others as the latter intersect *factically* with his own pleasure-seeking activities. The individual realizes that

> it is not as *this particular* individual that it becomes an object to itself, but rather as the *unity* of itself and the other self-consciousness, hence as an individual that is only a moment, or a *universal* (*PhG*, 263; *PhS*, 218).

What we have here is mastery and independence structured not as desire, but rather as purpose and rationality. Thus, the individual *immediately* recognizes himself as the unity of himself and others in the wake of his actions. Pleasure, as *the* way to actualize the self in a rational manner, as *the* way to yield warranty for our certainty, confronts necessity or the opposed reality of the existing relations between individuals. The rational self-consciousness realizes that not only independence, but also membership in the totality of acts is also his essence. One who tries to make a world through the pursuit of pleasure confronts in turn the consequences of that world-formation as something made, and yet also as a given reality with which one *must* cope. And the "must" derives not from some purely independent given, but precisely from that given which has its formal origin in the acting individual. The hedonistic individual finds himself caught up in a web of necessity formed by his own acts.[4]

> The final moment of its existence is the thought of the loss of itself in necessity, or the thought of itself as a being that is

absolutely *alien* to it. However, self-consciousness has *in itself* survived this loss; for this necessity or pure universality is *its own* essence. This reflection of consciousness into itself, the knowledge that necessity is *itself*, is a new form of consciousness (*PhG,* 266; *PhS,* 221).

Activity structured as egotistical hedonism reveals to itself in a negative manner that the individual is dependent upon the world that he himself has formed and thus does not find himself there as a *simple* individual. But in a positive way the individual comes to recognize that there is structuredness in realization through such activities, i.e., that activity is not fantasy, but involves a self-made connection with things and with others.[5] The first form of the rational individual confronting the world as active spirit gives way, then, to a second and even more egotistical position, the attitude which is called "the law of the heart and the frenzy of self-conceit." The exact nature of this position is somewhat problematic, and centers on the question of the nature of feeling or sentiment, as it is involved here. But whatever the issue might be, it must always be remembered that this position, like that of hedonism, represents an attempt by reason to place and then find itself in the world.[6]

Taken by itself, this attitude involves the attempt of the individual to make the world in accordance with his own feelings, his own sense of things. It is the position of a rebellion against the necessity which is counter to one's own pleasure; it is the position of the individualistic, romantic rebel. On the one hand, the individual recognizes necessity or the link with the world and with others which conditions the consequences of the pursuit of the pleasure principle. This gives us a possible ground for warranting our professed certainty; for our purposes are thus linked to the necessity of what-is. On the other hand, the individual now sets out to regulate that necessity in accordance with his own purposes. The simple, hedonistic individual wanted to ignore that necessity; the conceited rebel intends to shape that necessity to conform to the law of his individual heart. The individual attempts to absorb necessity into his own orbit, thus warranting claims of certainty.

Here we see, in spite of the self-centeredness of the attitude, the interests of the individual recognized by himself as part of the interdependence which occurs in relations between individuals.[7] The individual understands himself to have within himself the law which is to be legislated for the world. For each individual in this attitude, the world is to be made in "my" image, but as a world. All necessity which contradicts the law of the heart is to be abolished. This is the purposive, self-conscious attitude of the anarchistic rebel who is not a simple hedonist but who is, on the contrary, an individual revolutionary with firm conviction of the rightness of his "law." In this conviction he acts to impose this law on the world for the sake of all individuals, for humanity.[8] With this imposition the individual will have consciously and "rationally" created the ground of access to certainty.

However, as the hedonist met a necessity in the form of alien relations and consequences, this zealot meets with a necessity which is essentially ironic. For if and when this law is realized as the world's law, it is no longer a law of the heart, no longer centered in the individual, but now has independent being over against the individual. This newly shaped reality is now a universal power which governs even the individual who has sought to realize it. He has found his rationality realized in the world and thus can legitimately claim access to that reality; but now it is not his, not the certainty of the individual as posited through individual purposive activity, but the rationality of the world which confronts him in the well-organized way of things in the world. Necessity has simply played "musical chairs" with the individual.[9]

Again, then, there is both a negative and a positive result in terms of the rational quest for certainty we are here following. The negative result is that the individual loses himself in a reality created by himself, a reality that now, anew, confronts and absorbs him. He has been alienated by his own success and the grounds for his claims to certainty have been alienated as well. The law of the heart is now perverted into a law of the world, which has its own ontologically independent status. The logic of the presupposition relation rejects this form of grounding because what was to be the eternal source under one's own control is something quite different. But the positive consequence of this experience is that the self, in its active actualization, comes to understand that it always does and always will confront a given order. This given order consists in established laws, which

> are defended against the law of an individual, because they are not an unconscious, empty, and dead necessity, but a spiritual universality and substance, in which those in whom this spiritual substance has its actuality live as individuals, and are conscious of themselves. . . . Since it is precisely in this that the reality and power of public order consist, the latter thus appears as the self-identical essence alive in everyone, and individuality appears as its form (*PhG*, 272–73; *PhS*, 227).

The law of the world, that necessity which the deliberate assumption of the presuppositions of the law of the heart were to overcome, is alive, albeit as the work of individuals who have formed it and who now live in terms of it; for in forming it they give it a life of its own which then absorbs them in their own activities. However, it is a life, and not just a dead necessity: it is itself the objectification of the human individuals who both have created it and must live in accordance with its dictates. This is an early insight into the social complexity of spirit as we shall soon come to understand it.[10] As a matter of fact, what we see here is that, since the law of the world is always the creation of individuals who then must live in accordance with it, that original law which the rebel sought to reform in line with his own desires was itself the formation of other individuals. The reality is always the reality formed by individuals.

But under the present mode of rational activity this established order, the transfigured law of the heart, is simply perverse; for it now contradicts the law of the heart for which law is to be something which is to be rooted in the individual and not in the universal. Furthermore, because it is now to be the established law of "the law of all hearts," it is really only

> a universal resistance and struggle of all against one another, in which each claims validity for his own individuality, but at the same time does not succeed in his efforts, because each meets with the same resistance from the others, and is nullified by their reciprocal resistance. What seems to be public *order*, then, is this universal state of war, in which each wrests what he can for himself, executes justice on the individuality of others and establishes his own, which is equally nullified through the action of the others (*PhG*, 273; *PhS*, 227).

If, that is to say, the law of the heart as the right to objectify one's own version of necessity is to be universalized (as it must be if it is the truth), then it is really nothing but a war of all against all in which one cannot rightfully deny the right of another to realize the law of his own heart. Out of this potential anarchy, in a bad sense of that term, is realized "the way of the world," or the way things are in the world. This is the actuality of the world as realized through the purposive actions of such individuals. Rather than the unitary, peaceful, harmonious world to be created through the law of the heart, we have formed the right to destructive anarchy. This principle, then, cannot be the principle or ideologized presupposition on the basis of which all of reality comes to be known as rational and as warranting in an absolute sense the instinct of reason as the absolute standpoint; for in such legalized anarchy we find the denial of warranted certainty.[11]

From the infantile life in accordance with the pleasure principle, through the childish life in accordance with the law of the heart, we are now turned to the adolescent life of the virtuous individual, a third form of rational, ideological activity in which the individual sees himself as excelling in virtue and as bound to expose the goodness which underlies the evil, selfish anarchy of the way of the world.[12] As an alternative to this ontogenetic metaphor for the progressus, one might also substitute a phylogenetic-political metaphor reflecting the background and basis for the social-contract structure which had governed modern, liberal theory and government. At any rate, the view now taken is that since rampant individuality is what causes the war of all against all, the individual must give up his individuality and make selfless law the essence of rational activity. The virtuous individual deliberately sets out to make reality rational, and thus warrant his certainty by eliminating individuality as it has been produced by hedonism and by revolutionary fervor. In their place is put the sacrificing individual who turns away from the way of the world and attempts to bring forth the hidden essence which underlies that world.

But what is discovered here is that this virture, unlike the virtue of the ancients which was not individual in this "atomistic" sense, is an ungrounded abstraction, something which has nothing at all to do with the reality which is to be rational and thus to warrant certainty claims.[13] There is nothing hidden beneath the way of the world which can be brought forth by the individual: there is neither divine nor natural ground hidden behind the appearances. The only reality which can warrant rationality and access to reality must be found in that world itself, not in something transcending it. The virtuous individual tries to oppose the way of the world without confronting it, without participating in it. He refuses to participate in it because then he would be a part of that very anarchy he is opposing. But one cannot change the way of the world from the outside or through observations; there is no place of safety in virtue, by means of which the individual would remain unsullied by the struggle. Being, including the being of that world and our relationship to it, is constituted precisely through individuality, through the interaction of individuals who act in an arena, a world, to whose construction as an appropriate world they have contributed. Reality, on the present presupposition, is only made and only becomes rational through the interaction of individuals; therefore, virtue can accomplish nothing without sacrificing itself through action in the world. What is discovered is that the concrete interaction of individuals is the very essence of this world in which purpose and appropriateness structure existence. If certainty is to be grounded through individual actions, these latter must in turn be grounded in the interactions of all with all.[14]

With the failure to reach the realization of rationality through activity structured by either pleasure, egotistical reformation of the world, or pure, virtuous action which avoids contact with the real course of the world, we are made to focus on purposive action which is deliberately and consciously an activity carried out in the context of an already formed, on-going, existing society. We have our certainty, and in fact can claim that certainty only in our intercourse within an historically real society. This form of rational action is called "individuality which takes itself to be real in and for itself." It involves us with the ideological attitude that certainty is ours not simply by making the world in our own image, whatever that image might be, but rather by participating in a world already made through past interactions of individuals, a world which will continue to be sustained and reformed through present and future interactions.

> Self-consciousness has now grasped the concept of itself which, to begin with, was only *our* concept of it, viz. that in its certainty of itself it is all reality; and end and essence are for it henceforth the spontaneous interfusion of the universal—of gifts and capacities—and individuality (*PhG*, 283; *PhS*, 236).[15]

First of all, it must be noted that in the midst of this clearly political discussion, the quest for certainty—the overall project of the *Phenomenology*—is still at the center of our concern. We see that the individual, with explicit and no longer simply implicit certainty of himself, undertakes his tasks in a world that is *his* society. He is now certain of himself because he fits the world, because his purposes make him at home in the world in so far as they are purposes recognized by himself and by others in the society.[16] We now deliberately take up the presupposition that I am a "we," that I and others in society mutually recognize our respective purposes as valid purposes just because we have all undergone the process of enculturation which brings the purposes—or at least attempts to bring them—to us as our world. We are brought up to be at home in the world. The individual is now caught up in his own, self-centered actions, presuppositionally accepting the world not as something opposed to him, but as his proper arena explicitly given to him by his society. Action circumscribes the whole being of the individual, as well as the being of the world: his ends fit the reality which is given, and the reality is right for his ends and purposes. In action both individual and world are known and brought together in the *effective category*, i.e., in the living totality which is itself in the process of totalization.[17] The *in*effectiveness of the individual as category is now transcended, as is the elusiveness of certainty; for while it is the individual who acts according to his purposes, and thus who unifies the world, in turn it is the society as category which grounds the individual as category. Furthermore, the talents and capacities developed during enculturation are for that reason fitting and accepted as "natural"; for they are the talents and capacities sought by and declared appropriate to that world. In his certainty the individual accepts the world in which he lives as a natural part of his individuality, and

> the material of [his] life efforts and the aim of action lie in the action itself. Action [*das Tun*] has, therefore, the appearance of the movement of a circle which moves freely within itself in a void, which, unimpeded, now expands, now contracts, and is perfectly content to operate in and with its own self. The element in which individuality sets forth its shape has the significance solely of putting on the shape of individuality; it is the daylight in which consciousness wants to display itself. Action alters nothing and opposes nothing. It is the pure form of a transition from a state of not being seen to one of being seen, and the content which is brought out into the daylight and displayed, is nothing else but what this action already is in itself. It is *implicit*: this is its form as a unity in *thought*; and it is actual—this is its form as an *existent* unity (*PhG*, 284–85; *PhS*, 237).

In this poetic and revealing passage Hegel articulates the underlying presuppositional structure of a full life in society, so far as such a life is to be built on the atomistic individualism which has been seen to develop in this section. As idyllic as it might be, it represents the consciously undertaken fundamental presuppositions of rational life in such a rational society.[18] The capacities and talents which form the individual's actions are such that they are not only his, but are also appropriate to and belong in the world in which he acts. His purposes, ends, and means are also shared with others in that world.[19] The action encompasses both individual and world in a unity, in the effective, existing category.

But in this unity there is also the distinction between the end to be accomplished and, on the other hand, reality or the world within which it is to be accomplished. At this point Hegel gives us his clearest account of action in the form of self-objectification and the resultant alienation. From this also comes a picture of the fragility of certainty. In praxis the individual comes to a self-consciousness not only of the full ambiguity of his concept of himself, but also the ambiguity of his reality as a self-consciousness in his own self-transcendence as spirit.[20]

The whole project of the section on reason has been to observe the ways in which an individual in the natural attitude, accepting the presupposition of interest as purposive activity in an appropriate world, and beginning with the mere unconscious instinct of reason, comes in the process to prove through his own activities that he acts with the certainty of being all reality. As I pointed out in the beginning of the last chapter, it is no longer the phenomenological "we" who must raise consciousness through its different levels: in rational activity this happens to the self-conscious actor himself. At the present point in the analysis of reason we have come to a kind of completion of this task; for we now display the natural way in which an individual acts with certainty in his own culture and society. His science as well as his other activities always occurs in such a context. Here, in a society into which the individual has been enculturated, the natural praxis of the individual brings to his awareness the rational structure of his own consciousness and of the world in and toward which he acts. He also naturally presupposes—and realizes that he presupposes—the unity of himself and the world as he carries out his activities in interaction with others in society. Here we have not that activity of the individual which we examined under the heading of "Self-consciousness," where the presupposition was that self-consciousness itself was the basis for access to reality and certainty. For we now presuppose reason as that foundation. We enter, therefore, into a truly social world and have definitively left behind the presupposition that the self and other are united simply in and by self-consciousness itself.[21]

The individual in his activities manifests the presupposition that things make sense (or, in moments of confusion, that they ought to make sense), that his pursuit of his life makes sense to himself and to others and brings about the good of both. This is the *manifest* presupposition of true social life. The individual appears spontaneously to bring about his own development and the development of the society in which he acts. In this action spirit comes to be as the true form of consciousness and self-consciousness because of the way in which the individual and his society are joined with each other in the respective development of each. For the individual who is acting, neither his actions as actions nor the society as society are thematized; there is, rather, complete immersion of self in society and of society in self. The thematization of that relationship comes only upon certain kinds of reflection which we shall turn to in the next chapters. But in the real, immediate, practical activities of society what is thematized is only "the affair itself" (*die Sache selbst*), the purposive action in which one is involved.

> The individual, therefore, knowing that in his actual world he can find nothing else but its unity with himself, or only the certainty of himself in the truth of that world, *can experience only joy in himself* (PhG, 290; PhS, 242).[22]

One aspect of this state of being, then, is the unity which is both presupposed and experienced. But the actual experience of this activity in a societal context brings out not only this unity in unreflective immediacy, but also a disunity and alienation which results from action because of the multiplicity of individuals who constitute society. In his real, historical, immediate existence, the individual *is* spirit, but is spirit in the concreteness of historical existence, not as some abstraction of a theory of atomistic individualism.[23] Each individual recognizes others through the *concrete* objectification of the self which occurs in all actions. One speaks or acts and is thus *identified* as the speaker of certain words or as actor in a certain context and at a certain time. *One becomes a fact in the world*, and one's identity as defined by both the originator of the action and others affected is tied up in that activity and all the consequences that follow from it. My activity has become a fact in the world which presents me not only to myself, but to others as well. These others, however, have their own activity, their own immediate immersion, their own identity, needs, purposes, etc. For them, the facticity which I become through my activity and with which I am now identified, must be interpreted in terms of the purposes *of each of them*.[24]

My meaning and the meaning and significance of the activity through which I become a fact and in terms of which I become identified are, therefore, not defined by the singular intention, desire, or purpose which oriented me in the action. Nor is the efficacy of the activity, the effect on others and on society, simply as I define it. Rather my meaning and the significance of the activity are defined *also* by the multiplicity of selves affected by the activity. And their reaction, or the return of my act into myself—the response which my act evokes from my world—is thus a matter determined by that world "in itself" and not simply by me. The individual who acts, then, is not the only subject. Nor are the other individuals affected subjects in any serial or merely juxtaposed fashion. The "affair itself" (*die Sache selbst*) is the subject; for the totality of meaning and thus the locus of certainty is a result not just of juxtaposition or an external addition of partial meanings or particular meanings derived from particular individuals. The sum, in respect to that response, is greater than the parts, and it is this sum itself which constitutes the meaning of the act and thus of the fact and my access to the fact. Furthermore, since my own interpretation of the act and of myself in accordance with my intended purposes is also an element in the total meaning, this totality of meaning is not just the world as opposed to me, but is the self-world relation itself. This is the concrete, real meaning of "spirit" which will be developed further. There is here no mysticism concerning spirit, but simply the real fact of a pluralistically constituted totality comprised of myself and my world.

My rational activity within society, then, is not simply a predicate that can be applied to me; rather, in the immediate and mediated unity— in the pure spontaneity of the whole affair which collects within itself all individuals and their relations *without effacing the singularity of each and yet without allowing them an independent reality in any strict sense of the term*—that whole activity is *the subject*, the focus, that to which predicates are to apply (*PhG*, 300–301; *PhS*, 251–52).[25]

This means that when the individual acts with the presupposition of himself at the center of activity and as subject, he actually presupposes this totality as subject. The world in which I act is not just a substance objective to me, although it is that as the milieu of my actions; that world is also the world constituted by the interaction of individuals and is thus "permeated with individuality." To call spirit subject is, therefore, not reification or anthropomorphizing but the straightforward recognition of the nature of that world and my own nature as subject. I have real, concrete existence only in terms of my activities in the world, and my acts in the world exist only as part of that world. The world is both being or objective reality, and also the essence or what sustains that being as objective reality. Through the multiple and multi-faceted objectifications which comprise the world as the effective reality for me, it is truly a living thing, something with a life of its own, a subject.

Thus, the affair or state of affairs in which I am immersed in my purposive activities proceeds to develop on its own, and the individuals who identify themselves through participation in it occur for each other and for themselves as mere moments or aspects of the state of affairs. A real sense of participation is a sense of being a part. In this respect, we are all "swept along" in the course of things. At the same time, each individual carries out his own purposes, responds and acts in his own way, and immediately keeps alive the mediating fluidity of the state of affairs. While the state of affairs still revolves around my purposes, that very revolution reveals the state of affairs as something in itself, spiritual substance of which I am only a part. Every interactional activity is the evolution of a confluence of meanings, and it is therefore only there that the individual can find his ground for certainty.

At this stage we have come to a new realization about the nature of praxical presuppositions and their connection with the quest for certainty. These presuppositions are now seen to be not something abstract, unconscious, or merely linguistic, but have become subjective in the sense that they are embedded in the social matrix and thus in spirit itself. When we have our actual, everyday rational activities before us in the natural attitude as in this section of the *Phenomenology*, then the real existence of praxical presuppositions, i.e. their existence as the "cement" which holds together our societal activities of all sorts—both public and private—is at the threshold of thematization by the natural attitude. For this reason, there has been another advance made in the progress of the convergence of the natural and the philosophical attitudes. As we of the

Phenomenology have before us the problem of the establishment of certainty, those in the natural attitude of participation in society actively pursue, critique, and articulate the living presuppositions of their societies in their own quest for certainty. When the complete thematization occurs at the end of the present chapter, we have entered into a consideration of spirit itself.[26]

Praxical presuppositions are thus now themselves existentially presupposed not as abstractly transcendental, but as socio-historically transcendental.[27] They are presupposed as giving totality to the real world, i.e., to the world as lived, not as abstracted, and as such are presupposed as the ground for certainty. The presuppositions exist in the world in the form of customs, habits, institutional arrangements, expectations shared by the members of the community, etc. I can have certainty precisely to the extent that I participate in the world in accordance with these presuppositions. The acceptance of being a part of a rational, meaningful whole—of a whole which does not simply stand outside of them, but which includes each of them as a constitutive part—has transformed the ontological status of praxical presuppositions from something merely implicit in the thought and action of individuals into a mode of being which in some respects can be called "more real" than the being of the individuals themselves as singular beings. The presuppositions are what link the individuals to each other, they are the actual structural constituents of spirit. They constitute "the way things are, the way things are done," and as such are determinative of the individual and his activities.

This is *not* to say that the individual is absorbed into this spirit, taken up into a whole in which he disappears. This is only the caricature of Hegel's thought which has persisted for too long. Rather it is to say that the very presuppositions of the individuals, those which give them warranted certainty of access to reality in the form of rational praxis in a rational world, are structurally determinative. These actions exist only as carried through the actions of the individuals in the same way that a language lives in and through its use by human beings. But at the same time the individuals exist in their reality only as participants in these institutionalized presuppositions. The possible worlds of actuality are just those which are institutionally determinable. There is also on this side of the discussion an analogy with language; for it is only as participants in a language that speech can be actualized in a meaningful manner.

Thus far, all of this is only immediate for the natural attitude: purposive activities are carried out within the confines of what we now recognize as existing spirit. Yet there is another aspect to the situation, an aspect which arises just because there are conflicts among the purposes of different individuals and a continuing pluralism within the unity of spirit which threatens the trustworthiness of our claims to certainty. In the presence of these conflicts, and in an attempt to stabilize the certainty which each of us desires, judgments of "good" and "bad" are formed and various actions are considered either right actions or wrong actions. These judgments are a *fact* of reality, and this *fact* about the state of affairs calls forth a set of activities from individuals which cause them to become *reflective* about their participation. This will introduce us to the final and highest form of interest, that of *interest as reflection*. The normative element of human existence is thus taken to be itself simply a factical moment of reality which arises out of the conflict of unity and plurality which constitutes spirit in this form and which cannot ever be effaced. An examination of this final element of interest as purpose will carry us over to the last major stage of our quest for certainty, that of "spirit".[28]

In its most immediate form, reason—the awareness which individuals now have of this spiritual substance *as thematized*—attempts to take as truth and rightness something supposedly simply existing in the state of affairs. We are to judge "good" and "bad" on a natural basis grounded in the presupposition that reason itself *gives* us the law:

> Sound reason knows immediately what is right and good. Just as it knows the law immediately, so too the law is valid for it immediately, and it says directly: "this is right and good"—and, moreover, this particular law. The laws are *determinate*; the law is the affair itself filled with a significant content (*PhG*, 302; *PhS*, 253).

That is to say, the institutionalized praxical presuppositions which determine with certainty what is to be done are also presupposed as the determinants of what is right and good.[29] We give the laws immediately to ourselves because we are both the originators of those institutional arrangements and are to act in accordance with the prescriptions which arise therefrom.

But we have already seen conflicts emerge from the differences between individuals, and thus an "ought" can arise which is in opposition to this communal reality. Because of the pluralism, there is no simple, natural determination of the right and the good in terms of the mere facticity of what exists. What exists, although it is spiritual substance and the subject, is nevertheless a matter of contingency and perspective and thus all simple necessity for such right and good is missing.

Nor can reason act merely as a test for right laws or for what might be considered a justified law; for as a test it can only use the law of noncontradiction. The result of this is an ethic which is formal because it takes up whatever the content of the constituted reality is as the basis for testing rightness and goodness. The vacuity of this formalism is realized when it is seen that one can admit anything as right which can be consistently defined within the presuppositional framework of a particular state of affairs. With this confrontation with relativism in the attempt to use universal reason to test laws for their moral validity, we come up against the need to specify some principle of stability in the midst of the tension between the pluralism of autonomous individuals and a monism of the spiritual substance which is society; for without such a specification, our quest for certainty will fail.[30]

A review of what has occurred up to now will throw light on the move from reason as a transcendental constituent to the acceptance of it as historically grounded in actual societies. Part of this move has already been made in the recognition that the interaction of individuals creates the very matrix within which the individuals must act.[31]

Rational activity comes to be reflective activity because of the inherent conflict which is part of its nature in the concrete social form into which we have watched it develop. The rational individual has come to thematize his own activities and their matrices because he is motivated by the quest for certainty and completeness. The institutionalized praxical presuppositions, conceived of within the framework of interest as purpose, are to be taken as the point of access to reality, i.e., as the way I have my world and my certainty. If I comprehend these networks of presuppositions, I can then comprehend and vindicate my professed and natural certainty and the purposes in terms of which that certainty arises and needs vindication. I must become reflective now just because the possibility of conflict brings into question the absoluteness of the purposes and the presuppositional networks in terms of which they can be understood as rational and acted upon with certainty. But the first attempts at reflection or at a comprehension of the ground of reason failed to yield the desired results; for whether we understand reason and the rational individual as the giver or as the tester of laws, the validity of the laws remains abstract and eludes our grasp. Hegel shows this clearly in the following example.

> Suppose the question is: Ought it to be an absolute law that there should be property? . . . Property, simply as such does not contradict itself; it is an *isolated* determinateness, or is posited as merely self-identical. Non-property, the non-ownership of things, or a common ownership of goods, is just as little self-contradictory. That something belongs to nobody, or to the first-comer who takes possession of it, or to all together, to each according to his need or in equal portions— that is a *simple* determinateness, a *formal* thought, like its opposite, property (*PhG*, 307; *PhS*, 257–58).

The problem, then, with this first attempt to comprehend reality as a system of laws to be given by reason or tested by reason lay in the abstractness of the reason. If reason is taken as something which transcends the actual historical matrix—the real substance or social whole which is now recognized as a subject—then, contrary to the reflective intention to achieve a universal grasp of things in order to ground certainty, the individual discovers his own findings to be in conflict with those of others. The unity of self and world appears in an actual social context in which individuals are ends in themselves, and yet are bound up inextricably with other individuals and immersed in a social matrix which is ultimately utilitarian in nature. On the one hand, each individual is an end in himself, employing talents and capacities appropriate to the world in which he acts, and in that action constituting that very world. On the other hand, there is the logical demand that all ends in themselves are equal, and thus that a single end in itself comes into conflict with other ends. Each individual is an end in himself and also a means for others. Thus, no formal criterion for finding or judging the validity of various individual activities can remain without contradiction in such a situation; for the individual defines the end (or else is not an end in himself), and yet must be judged concerning that end (or else the others are not each an end in himself).[32]

With the realization of this, we are led to see how interest comes to exist in a new form, that of *interest as reflection*. In the attempt on the part of the natural attitude to fathom the complex ground of certainty which his rational, purposive activity has revealed, the individual is brought face to face with himself as an element of that very world which his autonomous acts constitute and which, in turn, forms the basis for those acts. The world is no longer simply something opposed to the individual as it was for the observer or for the single actor against the world. Nor is that world any longer simply a state of affairs in which the individual is inextricably entangled with others. In all rational activities in which we are governed by the presuppositions of reason as purpose-appropriateness, the world is in truth an "ethical" or *sittliche* substance, a being which is in and for itself or is a self-contained, fully explicit unity. This world is still something which is "there" for consciousness, but it is objective to consciousness only as its ground and its home. In our quest for certainty—and in the quest of the natural attitude in social life—we have become aware of this mode of reflective being, and have seen reflective attempts to comprehend those presuppositions which have been institutionalized through the rational activities of human beings. The individual, aware of the dialectical unity of his presuppositions and that set of worlds which constitute his actual world, comes to thematize the unity in an attempt to establish warranty for his claim to rational access to the world. When the natural attitude reaches this stage of self-awareness, then the individual reflectively posits and objectifies the question of the ultimate ground of his own unity with that world. The individual has at last, in the natural attitude, become completely reflective in respect to his own ground; his interest is in that ground itself and not only in the various experiences which are grounded in that ground.[33]

This reflectiveness is what raises the instinctive certainty of reality to articulated truth.

> Reason is spirit when its certainty of being all reality has been raised to truth, and it is conscious of itself as its own world, and of the world as itself (*PhG*, 313; *PhS*, 263).

That is to say, the individual, both as an individual and collectively with other individuals in society, comes to reflect upon the meaning and justification of his individual and collective existence. He does this by thematizing the ground or basis, i.e., the praxical presuppositions, upon which the activities of his everyday life in society are grounded. The interest on which we now focus is not in this or that task, but in the presupposed meaning and justification of such tasks: warranty for our certainty in the pursuit of such tasks is to be found in the overall ground for their meaningfulness. *Mere* certainty, in which presuppositions remain presuppositions, is now raised to truth, in which the presuppositions are thematized and explicitly maintained in the communal life of the individuals, i.e., in the institutional facts which both hold together and are held together by the individuals who participate in those institutions.[34] As we have already seen, the presuppositions are not merely in some unconscious, individual mode of being, but in the institutions, mores, and ways of doing things which are objectively embedded in the society. Scientists, for example, do not pursue their work in a given society as atomistic individuals, but within a community of scientists which is institutionalized in one way or another. What we have, therefore, is not merely purposive, rational activity, but such activity as reflectively grounded in the institutions of the society.

On the basis of this fact of our lives, and the fact that we can and do in the range of the natural attitude reflect upon this fact, we are now able to define spirit. Spirit

> is the *self* of actual consciousness to which [spirit] stands opposed, or rather which [spirit] opposes to itself as an objective, actual *world*, but a world which has completely lost the meaning for the self of something alien to it, just as the self has completely lost the meaning of a being-for-self separated from the world, whether dependent on it or not. Spirit, being

> the *substance* and the universal, self-identical, and abiding essence, is the unmoved solid *ground* and *starting-point* for the action of all, and it is their purpose and goal, the in-itself of every self-consciousness expressed in thought. This substance is equally the universal *work* produced by the action of all and each as their unity and identity, for it is the *being-for-self*, the self, action (*PhG*, 314; *PhS*, 263–64).

Spirit is the complete interpenetration of a self and his world, the repository for all presupposition sets on the basis of which we can have certainty of access to reality and certainty in our actions themselves. It is the absolute standpoint which both transcends the individual as individual, and yet is also really only the concretely taken individual in his real activities. Spirit is both immanent in the individual and transcendent to the individual. It is both myself as a real actor—and not as some abstracted self, atomistically facing the world in a series of external relations which supposedly do not define me—*and also* is that world which I face as an actor. Put in other terms, spirit is simply the real, lived world within which I am both participant and constituent, which I sometimes unthematically and unconsciously participate in and constitute, but which I and my fellow beings sometimes also thematize and thus reflectively take an interest in.

The *Phenomenology* now turns to its last task, which is to exhibit for us and for the natural attitude itself the history of its own objective, worldly thematizations of the absolute standpoint. This history is that of the modes in which objective existence has been given as the fundamental, underlying noetic and ontological presupposition sets, i.e., the self-understandings which various epochs of our civilization have posited in an attempt explicitly to stand in the absolute standpoint. We deal now no longer with mere forms or shapes (*Gestalten*) of consciousness, but with forms of thematized worlds. These latter are

> distinguished from the previous ones by the fact that they are real spirit, authentic and true actualities, and instead of being merely shapes of consciousness, are shapes of a world (*PhG*, 315; *PhS*, 265).

This history or "gallery" of *Gestalten* must be now traversed in the *Phenomenology* because if the individual is to comprehend from the absolute standpoint his own world, his own spirit, in order to warrant his claims to certainty, then he must understand the genesis of this spirit. If he is to comprehend that spiritual world which is, for instance, the Europe of 1805, then he must understand how it has developed; for that genesis is what has given spirit its present form. But before we turn to an examination of spirit itself, several things should be noted by way of summarizing what has been discovered thus far in this quest for certainty.

(1) Hegel has shown why and how self-consciousness and consciousness, taken as internal to and belonging to absolutely distinct individuals, can effectively operate in and toward the world in spite of the fact that they do not furnish us an absolute standpoint. Whether under the happenstance of intentionality or in the deliberateness of desire, our interests are in reality *purposively* structured. Intentionality and desire presuppose purpose as ground, and the presence of intended objects as intended and of desired objects as desired, presuppose as ground a world appropriate to our purposes. There is a transcendental unity which grounds our consciousness and self-consciousness, but which is neither psychological nor ontological in a pre-Kantian sense; rather it is an actively taken up domain of presuppositions by which we are held in our intercourse with the world. Thus, desire and intentionality, taken as purely subjective, are governed *a priori* by a set of praxical presuppositions in terms of which the intended can be there appropriately for the intention and the desired for the desire.

At this point, then, the nature of praxical presuppositions should become clear. What they are far surpasses the notion of 'pragmatic presuppositions' to which they are related, as well as the unconscious propositional forms which we first saw them to be under the theses of consciousness. If we here understand the thematization occurring in the *Phenomenology* as a thematization of praxical presuppositions in their relation to our possible experience and knowledge, rather than as a thematization of consciousness in some form or other, then the true nature of spirit becomes more evident. Thus, where spirit is often only vaguely comprehended as a supra-individual consciousness—a conceptualization which raises legitimate questions about the possible meaning of 'consciousness' when it is not the consciousness of an individual—we, in contrast, can now see that it is only a matter of comprehending that the presuppositions of concrete human activity are to be transferred from their putative existence in some unconsciousness or superhuman consciousness to where they actually are, namely in the body of customs, laws, institutions which structure a particular social formation. There is nothing here either mystical or spiritual in a pejorative sense of those terms.[35]

(2) The introduction of the presupposition sets of reason contains a critique of all psychological and all positivistic epistemologies (and their respective ontologies). This critique first developed when self-consciousness failed to give us a standpoint which could ground self-consciousness itself and thus give us an absolute standpoint for warranted certainty.

Neither an account of individual experience nor an account of what all individual experience has in common will suffice. On the contrary, the "surrender" to reason and its instinct is required so that there can be a unity of thought and being which is given *a priori* and yet makes possible the synthetic judgments and temporal experience which constitute knowledge and action as thematized in the natural attitude. Thus, there is a proof here that all psychological, positivistic, or abstract epistemologies must fail; for epistemology, and thus the quest for certainty, must be centered in a socio-cultural reality.[36]

(3) An account of reason as transcendental has in turn also failed to give an absolute standpoint; for the grounds of experience, knowledge, and action still lie in such an account at the unconscious level of experience. As we saw in the examination of the capacity for law-giving and for the warranting of laws given, when such a transcendental ground is thematized in the natural attitude it is in the end abstract and purely formal, lacking any and all content which is its own. The abstractness causes this attempt finally to fail because any and all content are permitted to the status of law so long as the content is not self-contradictory. Hence we are faced with a sheer relativism and no standpoint from which to judge with certainty.

(4) The natural attitude has been at this point transformed to the extent that it has become reflective in relation to its own standpoint and thus converges even more with the phenomenological reflection of the *Phenomenology*. Indeed, we shall see in the end that the *Phenomenology of Spirit* itself is a manifestation of interest as reflection which stands in a line continuous with the historical reflections of spirit which we are about to take up. The move to the examination of the history and development of spirit is a move in which the interest of the natural attitude is shown to have historically functioned as reflection at the point at which, in each period, the fundamental praxical presuppositions of the society were formulated and thus thematized in an objective manner and made the common property of all in that society.

(5) The turn to spirit is a turn away from the modern transcendental tendency of philosophy and toward historical existence. In the transcendental turn our reflection deteriorated into a formalism, eminently reflected finally in the formalism of Kant's philosophy. The formalism is also present in thought based on a mathematical method when that thought is applied to actual social existence. The possibility of the possible worlds degenerates into a purely formal, logical possibility; but these are not the possible worlds in natural experience.[37] The latter are possible in terms of real, and not merely formal possibility. There are concrete conditions, circumstances, etc., which govern what is thematized, and

which allow for far more restricted possible worlds than a merely formal criterion would allow. It is this presence of real possibility as a governing force—this necessity for the unity of the real world and my purposes—that causes the particular reflective grounding of the absolute standpoint to demand a concrete historical basis. In other words, the possible worlds in actuality never emerge and are never thematized solely from the world of all possible worlds, but rather from possible worlds derivative alone from this actual reality which I confront and within which I exist.

Hegel puts this point most eloquently in a passage in his *Lectures on the History of Philosophy*.

> The particular form of a philosophy is . . . contemporaneous with a particular constitution of the people amongst whom it makes its appearances, and their institutions and forms of government, their morality, their social life and the capabilities, customs and enjoyments of the same. . . . Spirit in each case has elaborated and expanded in the whole domain of its manifold nature the principle of the particular stage of self-consciousness to which it has attained. Thus the spirit of a people in its richness is an organization and, like a cathedral is divided into numerous vaults, passages, pillars, and vestibules, all of which have proceeded out of one whole and are directed to one end.[38]

That is to say, the whole, rich expanse and depth of reality—of that reality which sense-certainty took to be its own in a purely immediate way—is in truth not immediate, but grounded in and mediated through the single spirit of a people or a socio-cultural whole which exists not in some pure transcendental domain, but in the very pores of the world itself. It is *a priori*, not from all eternity, but in respect to a given time in history. The universality is a concrete universality: concrete in the sense that it subsists institutionally in the day-to-day affairs of the people, universal in the sense that it holds within itself the unity of all particulars. It is concretely universal in the sense that it is inseparable from the particular individuals and holds for all possible historical experience. And philosophy, whatever form it takes, has its existence alongside all of the other institutions and activities of a people.

(6) The final point to be made here is that all human activity in any form which is intelligible and which is open to certainty presupposes a specific form of social being, i.e., knowledge, experience, and action embedded in and constitutive of mores, customs, and institutions both social and political as well as generally cultural. The individual in pursuing his tasks finds intelligibility, purposiveness, and certainty already grounded in principle and intersubjectively through a particular, specific institu-

tional framework which itself has been objectively and historically instantiated. There is a "pre-understanding" which makes the "work" one does what it is rather than just random activity without established meaning. This pre-understanding is the ground and starting point of all activity and sustains that activity as something intersubjective. But at the same time, this pre-understanding, both as institutionalized in rules, mores, customs, etc., and as borne by the acting individual, is not only the constitutor of the intelligibility of that action; for it is itself affirmed and sustained in the very actions themselves and at times is even changed in accordance with demands internal to the instantiated circumstances themselves. Thus, the individual who acts within such a framework of intelligibility and in relation to others affirms and sustains and is literally the bearer of the praxical presuppositions; and he is so by doing that very work, by performing those activities. There is here no collapse of the individual into some all-consuming whole called spirit; for the individual is himself the bearer of that spirit.[39]

This whole complexus of the relationship between the individual and his world is *spirit*. It both transcends the individual and all individuals as presupposition of their activities—as what informs their praxis—and yet also is only embodied in each and every acting individual. Spirit is embodied, concrete presupposition, and is now to be taken as the ground of our access to reality. This is why interest at this new level is reflection rather than purpose and why the correlate is not just *an* appropriate world, but *the actual world which is appropriate*, a world not just as a place where appropriateness might appear, but one in which it actually does appear in a determinate way. The claim regarding spirit, therefore, is that whenever we act and however we explicitly experience and understand our actions, there is at the basis of our professed certainty a self-understanding which is pre-understood and which concerns what it means "to be," both in general and in a specifically appropriate way. It is a self-understanding which is embedded both in the institutional facts of the world, and in the awareness of that world which is in each individual as he acts in and through these institutions. This self-understanding or reflection is functionally transcendental, but has none of the abstractness and formalism which accrues to formal-transcendental categories, principles, ideas, etc. The possible worlds thematized by individuals have their ground in the actual world and in the actual individuals, and also in the actual relations between individuals and between individuals and the world. What is thematized at this level of reflection by the individual in the natural attitude is the life-blood and affirmation and institutionalization of his own self-understanding: the self-understanding is reflected in the very actions for which the self-understanding is presupposition. This circularity is the ground for warranting certainty.

If we reflect for a moment on the nature of this circularity, the new view of these presuppositions we have come to will be brought into final focus. What we have seen is that the presuppositions which constitute the actual standpoint within which we have our natural certainty are not in the unconscious or abstractly existing in some other form, but are embedded in the specific society in which we find ourselves. What it means to have a standpoint with warranted certainty of access to reality is that we have that standpoint in accordance with the self-understanding of being-in-the-real-world which belongs to our specific civilization. To have warranted certainty, according to this view, is to stand in reality in just the way determined as the authentic way in one's culture. This is the basis and justification of all conservatism, so long as we mean by 'conservatism' conformity to mores, be those mores ones of change—or even revolution—or ones of preservation of the status quo. In a society whose self-understanding is progress and change, one is "in touch with reality" so long as one participates in society in conformity with that self-understanding. On the other hand, in a society whose self-understanding is traditionalism and the absence of change, one who strives for progress and change is "out of touch with reality." On a more specific level, if one pursues an occupation or other specific goal which is "anointed" by the society, then one has warranted claims to certainty concerning reality; if one does not pursue such an occupation or specific goal, then one has no warranty for one's claims about reality.

This state of affairs reveals something of importance concerning the relation of praxical presuppositions to that which presupposes them. Where the presuppositions are warranted, not only is a set of alternatives made possible as alternatives, but it is also the case that those presuppositions are literally embedded in the activities which actualize one or the other of the justified alternatives. That is to say, a Euthyphro can say to Socrates, in answer to the question of what piety is, that his acts give one the meaning of piety. Socrates' response to the effect that he wants a general definition, not a specific instance, misses Euthyphro's point; for Euthyphro knows, or claims to know, that his own actions are an instantiation of the presuppositions present in society. Thus, if one has in one's possession the authentic set of praxical presuppositions as they are present in one's society, then one's very actions will be the bearers of those presuppositions, i.e. the living presence of the presuppositions as they are present in the self-understanding of the society. There is here an absolutely mediated immediacy, an identity constituted by the reciprocity of activity which constitutes spirit; for spirit is nothing other than the transactions of a social matrix built on a given pre-understanding of what it means to interact and transact. On the other hand, if one does not have the authentic set in one's possession, then one's actions have no real, historical meaning and no warranty for certainty claims; for there is no self-mediating identity relation between the praxical presuppositions in force and one's actions. Now we finally see the significance of the difference between merely putative presuppositions and the actual praxical presuppositions in force: to be merely putative is not only to be wrong or unwarrantable, but to have no *real* embodiment at all; to be in force is not only to be the right set, but in addition to have embodiment in those individuals who actually constitute the lived-world through their own living.

We also now see further the significance of the necessity of a move to a consideration of the history of spirit as the history of the reflections on that self-understanding. If we were to remain at the level of abstractness to which ahistorical reason restricts us, then an anarchy of pre-understandings would remain: if one cannot refer to specific institutionalizations of the presuppositions, then one has no determinative criteria by which to decide whether or not a given presupposition set is in force. In the absence of the real historical situation, one lacks any proper authority, in the strict sense of that term; i.e., one is not authorized, one has no legitimacy, for one is not in fact in contact with concrete reality, but rather with a reality abstracted from the real conditions of existence.

The consequence of all this is the following. On the grounds that we have now discovered in our quest for certainty that the absolute standpoint can be neither consciousness, self-consciousness, nor reason in any abstractly cosmological or transcendental sense of the term, there is no longer any ground for a dialectical relationship between individual, putative praxical presupposition sets and the presupposition sets actually in force. Our quest will no longer be directed by comparisons between claims about presuppositions and the instantiatable alternatives which constitute our possible worlds. Instead, since the absolute standpoint is reason as spirit, we must look at the culturally embodied presupposition sets in force in the history of our civilization and come to our own self-understanding of what those presuppositions are. Our project is no longer to test putative presuppositions, but to become reflexively aware of the actually instantiated presuppositions.

Put in terms of our original formulation of the logic of presuppositions, we now have this result. The nature of the relationship between presuppositions and what presupposes them was such that a presupposition set (P) is related to a state of affairs or statement (S) which presupposes it in such a way that P contains or refers to a set of conditions or circumstances (C) which make the alternative meanings or possibilities belonging to S intelligible and relevant in respect both to linguistic claims made about S and to the appropriateness of specifiable activities found in S. Our quest for certainty has now shown us that the states of affairs S and the presuppositions P are authentically related only in the way that constituting activities are related to the society constituted by them and only in the way that constituted activities are related to the society which constitutes them. That is to say, S and P are in the relationship we have discovered to be spirit. With spirit as our necessary standpoint, any state of affairs that exists must have its meaning and intelligibility as a constituent of a specific historical form of spirit. We can have no warranty for claims of certainty of access to reality except when the claims are grounded in that reality. The original attitude of sense-certainty was therefore correct in so far as it appealed to objective reality. The only difference is that, if our analysis has been correct thus far—i.e., if our own quest for certainty is warranted—then reality is spirit. Thus, all claims must be settled by an appeal to spirit as historically concrete. No claim can have warranty outside of spirit because there are no grounds outside of that reality. My right to claim *natural* certainty can only be justified if it is *natural qua embedded in nature*, and this means if it is *natural qua embedded in my actual historical reality*. Since spirit does not simply transcend the individuals who constitute it, but is both constituted by them and constitutes their ground, it follows that a comparison of individual claims with spirit is simply a comparison of spirit with itself.

Thus, our procedure or the dialectic of the new standpoint of spirit will differ from our previous dialectic. Instead of comparing the putative certainty with actual certainty, the actual grounds of certainty will be compared to themselves for adequacy to themselves. If a form of historical spirit has a self-understanding adequate to its own condition as spirit, it will furnish an absolute, unconditioned standpoint for the warranting of certainty. In other terms, if the ideological formation of a socio-cultural whole is adequate to the totality of functions and functioning of that socio-cultural whole, then it will have authentically grasped its own praxical presuppositions and consequently given them visibility for the testing of certainty claims which occur within the socio-cultural whole. But if, on the grounds of that ideological formation, contradictions, value-gaps, or other anomalies occur which are not supposed to occur in the terms of the ideology itself, then the ideology is inadequate to its own claims or, in still other terms, the ideology is distorting reality. Spirit will either show itself to be adequate to itself, or it will not. If and when it does, we will have ended our quest for certainty; until it does, the quest will of necessity continue.

Further discussion in the abstract will not be fruitful. With these thoughts in mind, we can now turn to the actual historical development of spirit and discover in a concrete way just how our quest will proceed. There will be three levels of reflection: (a) that of spirit as the institutional framework and mores of socio-cultural wholes in which are deposited the fundamental praxical presuppositions of that society; (b) that of religion, a mode in which explicit attention is paid to that fundamental bond which exists between all possible societies and forms of objective spirit, a standpoint in which the individual participates in human life *sub specie aeternitatis*; and (c) that of philosophy or absolute knowledge in which the fundamental categorial bond is itself thematized and the individual and his world are totally bound up together in a common whole. In the next chapter we will begin an analysis of the first forms of spirit.

VII
Interest As Reflection: True Spirit

As we have now seen, it is the complex nature of spirit to be both the substance or the institutionalized world I face, and also the subject or individual who faces that world in my tasks and rational projects. Spirit as the presupposition of interest as reflection is formally the presupposition that my *world* is given, there, formative for me, and that, nevertheless, it is *my* world, the arena for my own accomplishments and the accomplishments of others.

> As *substance*, spirit is unshaken righteous self-identity; but as *being-for-self* it is a fragmented being, self-sacrificing and benevolent, in which each accomplishes his own work, rends asunder the universal being, and takes from it his own share. This resolving of the essence into individuals is precisely the *moment* of the action and the self of all; it is the movement and soul of substance and the resultant universal being. Just because it is a being that is resolved in the self, it is not a dead essence, but is *actual* and *alive* (PhG, 439; PhS, 264).[1]

This dual nature at the level of spirit is, on the one hand, the reason why it is more adequate as an ultimate standpoint than abstract reason; but, on the other hand, it is the problematic which causes spirit to have a history and a development.

Spirit is more adequate than is abstract, formal reason as presupposition ground for our certainty because it is, in the first place, no longer only formal.[2] This formality, as we saw, had several specific defects. On the one hand purpose, which was taken to be an end in itself for an end-in-itself (the individual), comes into self-contradiction when there are two or more ends in themselves whose purposes exclude each other as final. On the side of interest alone, therefore, there is an inadequacy since either nothing is legitimate or everything is legitimate and all hope of certainty for our claims disappears. On the other hand, the world is presupposed as being appropriate in general for the purposes of individuals. But "appropriate in general" is abstractly appropriate, and in the face of the contradiction between conflicting purposes, that abstract appropriateness becomes meaningless. When presupposition remains at the level of such reason and is only formally transcendental, this contradiction and conflict negate the possibility of an absolute standpoint and warranted certainty. Spirit, to the contrary, is just this existence-in-tension of many individual purposes and the one substance in which they are to be realized.

The move to spirit is in a limited way analogous to the move from skepticism to unhappy consciousness. Skepticism contained within itself a blindness to the fact of its own pyrrhic victory over the particulars since it itself was both particular and universal, both ephemeral and abiding, both conditioned and unconditioned. Unhappy consciousness, on the other hand, presupposed precisely this tension between the unchangeable and the changeable. Now, in spirit, we do not have an individual attempt to live the tension, but rather a socio-cultural sense and acceptance of the tension and contradiction. Spirit is both the unshaken righteous self-identity of substance and the fragmented and fragmenting, changing activity of being-for-self and individuality.

This analogy is very limited, however, because it must be seen in the context of a subtle but important change which has occurred in this move to spirit as the ground of certainty. The change has an important historical dimension, for when we move from the abstract to the concrete, from reason to spirit, we have in effect a repudiation of the modern philosophical quest for certainty, the attempt to ground certainty in consciousness or self-consciousness. In this turn to spirit and in particular to the spirit of the Greeks, we have a rejection of the modern epistemological orientation in the quest for certainty, and a return to the ancient attempt to deal with that standpoint on the basis of the socio-political reality. The first part of the *Phenomenology*, therefore, can be seen as a "refutation" or *Aufheben* of the modern attempt. In this context skepticism, which in one form or another was the means by which the epistemological quest proceeded, is rejected, and in its place the concrete ambiguity of our being in and toward the world is accepted.[3]

What causes spirit to have a history,[4] on the other hand—to be itself a process of development, i.e., a *Bildungsprozess* on the level of universal history which is to be reflectively comprehended by the individual in his own *Bildungsprozess*—is that at first, with the Greeks, this tension and contradiction are recognized as abiding within the unity of "ethicality" or *Sittlichkeit*. In this first form of our history, there is a self-awareness of the duality of spirit as substance and as individuals within that substance.[5] This takes the form of a self-awareness of the ethical world and, on the other hand, of ethical action. The polis is the unity of these. However, as we shall see below, this unity or the absolute belonging-together of these two elements is never realized in a way that would grant us the absolute standpoint for the sake of the warranting of our certainty. The ethical order [*Sittlichkeit*] lacks the wherewithal to make ultimate sense of the opposition, i.e., is unable to show how the world which is the unity of the polis and its individuals can be the unity of substance and action as a reality. The whole of the development of spirit is the development of this problematic. We have seen that to comprehend our own world and certainty we must comprehend its genesis. This genesis, Hegel believed, began with the formulation of the problem by the Greeks and could be traced to his own nineteenth-century Europe.

A "heady" journey; but when we have completed it and have comprehended this development of objective spirit and its confluence in the nineteenth-century European world, we will have re-collected our world as both substance and our own individuality. We will have comprehended our own ground for certainty; for the ultimate presuppositions of our own lives will have been comprehended as generated and embodied in the institutional facts of our world.[6]

The sections which form this main part of the *Phenomenology* are among the richest and most interesting not only in the *Phenomenology*, but in Hegel's corpus as a whole. But for the purposes of the present project, it will be necessary to restrict discussion almost to the point of missing the life of these sections. I shall discuss each section only to the degree necessary to show the ways in which interest as reflection embodied the presupposition sets which have constituted our historical experience as a totality of real, possible worlds, the worlds to which we claim certainty of access.

We begin with an account of the "Greeks".[7] Through an analysis of the polis as a life-world and an analysis of their poetry—poetry which was a conscious and deliberate objectification of the presuppositions of their existence—we are shown that a distinction was from the beginning assumed to exist between substance (the ethical world) and subject (the individuals acting in that world: ethical action). What is important to understand here is that the plays themselves and not the polis as such constitute the objectivity of objective or true spirit for the Greeks. Spirit is truly alive and reflective not in the polis as such, but in the poetry and other artistic creations which constitute the self-presentation of the polis within and to itself. It is in the interest as reflection—reflection here in the form of the reflected world-view or fundamental praxical presuppositions articulated in the art works—that spirit exists. The Greeks presented to themselves the fundamental ground of meaning for existence and in this way objectified for themselves the ground for warranting their claims of certainty of access to reality. In our own quest for certainty here in the *Phenomenology* we are presented with the first instance of that quest as it was articulated by the Greeks. We now become aware of both the form and the content of interest as reflection—the content being the versions of ultimate reality presented in the art works, the form being that of self-objectified spirit. Thus, what follows in these sections of the *Phenomenology* is not a mere interesting history of our spirit, but a presentation of the quest for certainty as it has evolved.[8]

The presuppositions of their ground for existence and meaning were classified by the Greeks in two ways: the constitution of the ethical world and the constitution of ethical action. On the one hand, in the ethical world there was recognition and acceptance of two orders or laws, one divine and demanding one set of possible worlds, the other human and demanding a different set which had the possibility of excluding the worlds demanded by the first set.[9] The two sets had features in common; but at times, bound in the one, single order of life in the polis, the two sets were in contradiction. It was this tension at the basis of their existence that Aeschylus, Sophocles, Euripides and the others thematized in their plays. The divine order or law presupposed as its major orientation blood ties, the family, nature, and unity in a line of ancestors. The world was to be intelligible and to grant certainty not in terms of particular deeds done, but ultimately in our membership and participation and, eventually, in our death and the subsequent universal membership in the family as an ancestor. As such, one was not primarily a citizen, but a member of the family. The other world, on the other hand, had an order and law which presupposed orientation in and toward the world in terms of the polis: citizenship, the carrying out of deeds for the sake of the polis, and a life of individual honor and accomplishment.

The problem here was that the Greeks understood their spirit as encompassing both of these laws and thus that each and every individual was to exist in accordance with both of these presupposition sets. In plays such as *Antigone*, the Greeks evidence a self-awareness of this, their fundamental standpoint. The tension and contradiction could be seen from two perspectives, albeit perspectives which in the end had to be one as united in the polis. The first way in which it was conceived was as a dynamic structure of the ethical world as substance, i.e., not as action of individuals, but as the substance within which they acted. Hence, the substance was to be one realm, one unity: the

> ethical realm is in this way in its enduring existence an immaculate world, a world unsullied by any internal dissension. Similarly, its process is a tranquil transition of one of its powers into the other, in such a way that each preserves and brings forth the other (*PhG*, 330; *PhS*, 278).[10]

This overarching presupposition of unity is evidenced not only in the reflection that the polis is one, but even more concretely and reflexively embodied in the conservative view of the chorus in the plays to which Hegel directs us. It is explicitly recognized time and again that the only certainty we can have is the limited certainty which issues from this abiding tension.

That "enduring existence" and "immaculate world" with its limited certainty is disturbed, however, as soon as we look at it from the perspective of action.[11] The divine and human law are assigned, respectively, to women and to men. And they are assigned "by nature." When one or the other acts as an actual self, it "disturbs the peaceful organization and movement of the ethical world." What in the ethical world as pure substance

> appears as order and harmony of its two essences, each of
> which authenticates and completes the other, becomes
> through the deed a transition of opposites in which each
> proves itself to be the non-reality, rather than the authentica-
> tion, of itself and the other. It becomes the negative move-
> ment, or the eternal necessity, of a dreadful fate which engulfs
> in the abyss of its single nature divine and human law alike,
> as well as the two self-consciousnesses in which these powers
> have their existence . . . (PhG, 331; PhS, 279).

The powers which constitute the ethical world as substance actually have their respective existences only in women and men, and "the union of man and woman constitutes the active middle term of the whole and the element which sunders itself into these extremes of divine and human law" (PhG, 330; PhS, 278). There is total reflection in spirit: the existence of concrete individuals is that which bears the essence of the ethical world as unquestionable natural duty and thus natural certainty in action; the essence of the polis or of the real ethical substance is that which bears the existence of these concrete individuals as both constituted and constituting.[12] This is why as we now consider action in the polis, we are considering "the absolute being-for-self of the purely individual self-consciousness" (PhG, 331; PhS, 279). The individual self-consciousness is absolute because as individual and in union with its opposite, it both constitutes the ethical world and is constituted by it: it is its own ground of certainty as the bearer of spirit. The individual self-consciousness is being-for-self because the presuppositions of certainty are no longer submerged in an unconsciousness or in an instinct, but rather in a self-conscious individual who acts without caprice and yet without question: "the essence of ethical life is for this consciousness immediate, unwavering, without contradiction" (PhG, 331; PhS, 279). In the great tragedy of Antigone and Creon, where neither is wrong but yet both are right, we have the Greek view of the basic condition of humanity, self-consciously reflected in both the author and the spectators of this play. These plays themselves are a part of the very polis whose presuppositions they take up, an active yet reflective objectification of the explicit self-consciousness of the Greeks about their own presuppositions. This poetry is their form of objective spirit. As in the play, so too in life. Self-conscious, active individuals have simultaneously thematized their specific duty *and* the presuppositions which warrant the claim of validity for this specific duty. There is a concrete, historical, double thematization, respectively, of oneself as oneself and of oneself as one of a people.[13] And it is through performance of the respective duties that the individuals have warranted access to reality. Thus, the presuppositions are not something which stand over against the action in this case, nor need they be dredged up from some hidden source or from the unconscious; for they are public, present on the stage for all to know. The absolute right of the individual

> is, therefore, that when it acts in accordance with ethical law, it shall find in this actualization nothing else but the fulfillment of this law itself, and the deed shall manifest only ethical action. . . . Consequently, the absolute right of the ethical consciousness is that the deed, the *shape* in which it *actualizes* itself shall be nothing else but what it *knows* (PhG, 332–33; PhS, 280–81).

But this absoluteness is ironical. The individual, acting in accordance with one's law, presupposes that one both embodies and is embodied in the essence or the substance, i.e., in the polis as the ethical world. While respective individuals are portrayed as acting in accordance with and as the embodiment of their own law—the divine or the human—there is also present in that essence the opposite law, the law of the other, against which they sometimes must act. This double reflection of duty entails, therefore, a reflection of its opposite duty as well. Action in accordance with one's natural law in the polis is action against the other natural law of the polis. There is therefore duty and, as well, guilt in every such action (PhG, 334; PhS, 282).[14]

The identity and the difference which are presupposed as constituting the individual in relation to his or her world is absolutized here as contradiction. The individual, self-conscious of identity of self with world, in that very self-consciousness is differentiated from that world and becomes aware of the difference. Both the identity and the difference are lived by the individual. The individual is and is not this particular individual who acts and is guilty: one is the guilty individual because one does act; one is not the guilty individual because it is in the terms of the thematized duty itself that an opposite duty, one arising from "the other law," is immediately entailed. Certainty is thus called radically into question; for the accomplished deed is the removal of the opposition between the knowing self and the actuality confronting [the self]. The doer cannot deny the crime or guilt: the significance of the deed is that what was unmoved has been set in motion, and that what was locked up in mere possibility has been brought out into the open, hence to link together the unconscious and the conscious, non-being with being (*PhG*, 336; *PhS*, 283).

And if the individual ever forgets or protests, the chorus as the unity of the polis is there to speak for the ethical substance.

The remainder of the details in this discussion, some of the most insightful in Hegel's writings, cannot detain us any longer here. The articulation of this earliest and most immediate form of interest as reflection—as the artistically objectified embodiment of individual action in spiritual substance and of the latter in individual action—can now be made more clear. In spirit we have reached a first level of absoluteness or that beyond which one cannot and need not go in the quest for certainty. We see in the Greeks a first attainment to absoluteness through art, and specifically through their poetry. Through this medium the individual or the subject is a subject-object, and the socio-political and cultural world or the object is also subject-object. The individual man or woman is an Athenian, a Theban, etc. As such, he or she in the *hexeis* of his or her life immediately embodies the polis itself. Thebes is my *world* and *my* world; for in my individual actions I act immediately as the substance of the polis. Self-conscious of my *hexeis* and acts as those which reflect and are reflected in the polis, I am a being-for-self, a subjective subject-object. But, since I find my ground and actions and reflection in that polis itself to which I am inextricably bound, and at the same time find an affirmation of that life and a dependency upon that life, the polis itself is my unity with it and thus an in-itself which is also a for-itself, an objective subject-object. And for both the individual and the polis this unity of the subjective subject-object and the objective subject-object is embodied in the public, sacred festivals in which the poets objectify and bring to unity this reflection. These art works of the Greeks are the ultimate form of immediate, true spirit. In these works which are themselves actions within the polis, not only are the individual acts and their presuppositions brought to objectivity for the spectacle or the seeing; they are also brought to objectivity as an absolute act of self-consciousness, both in respect to their creation and to their viewing. That is to say, the art works themselves are both an element of culture and an embodiment of that culture as a whole: the polis is self-conscious through them.[15]

With this first excursion into spirit proper, we can now look back on the significance of what has occurred thus far in the *Phenomenology* and its quest for certainty. In the examination of consciousness as a possible absolute ground for experience, it was necessary for the phenomenological "we" to dig out the presuppositions and to trace the progress of the dialectic between the natural attitude and its putative presupposition sets. At the end of the discussion of self-consciousness as absolute standpoint, the natural attitude was shown that it itself could and did thematize its own presupposition sets and act deliberately upon them. But, because of the insufficiency of self-consciousness as absolute, unconditioned ground, this came to a determinate negation such that it became necessary again for the phenomenological "we" to proceed with its thematization of the presupposition set. However, this move to reason did not entail a simple return to the opposition of the two levels; for with the basic presupposition that purpose and appropriateness structure interest and "contain" the presupposition sets, natural consciousness set out upon its own way of discovering through exemplary acts of its own the insufficiency of abstract reason as the unity of consciousness and self-consciousness. But in the end, a world, i.e., a cultural totality, stood opposed to reason's structure and laws, making them relative to historical conditions and not absolute.

Now, in the sections on spirit, the thematizations of the individual in his quest for certainty are of a kind which portray to natural consciousness a succession of real, historical forms in which natural consciousness itself has not only thematized particulars—both objects and projects—but as well the actual and fundamental embodiments of its own presuppositions. In the form of spirit, natural consciousness becomes self-aware of the reason which it has and which it is. The natural consciousness is now in the process of becoming aware that its existence is the category, not as an abstract, transcendental unity of thought and being, but as that unity which is historically lived through in one's societal existence. We can now realize the abstractness not only of sense-certainty and the alleged purity of its world of particulars, but of the other stages as well. They are only abstracted moments of spirit itself.

> This isolating of those moments *presupposes* spirit itself and subsists therein; in other words, the isolation exists only in spirit which is a concrete existence.... Spirit, then, is consciousness in general which embraces sense-certainty, perception, and the understanding, in so far as in its self-analysis spirit holds fast to the moment of being an objectively existent actuality to itself, and ignores the fact that this actuality is its own being-for-self. If, on the contrary, it holds fast to

the other moment of the analysis, viz. that its object is its own *being-for-self*, then it is self-consciousness. But as immediate consciousness of the being that is *in and for itself*, as unity of consciousness and self-consciousness, spirit is consciousness that *has reason*; it is consciousness which, as the word "has" indicates, has the object in a shape which is *implicitly* determined by reason or by the value of the category, but in such a way that it does not as yet have for consciousness the value of the category. Spirit is that consciousness which we were considering immediately prior to the present stage. Finally, when this reason which spirit *has* is intuited by spirit as reason that *exists*, or as reason that is *actual* in spirit and is its world, then spirit exists in its truth; it *is* spirit, the *ethical* essence that has an *actual* existence (*PhG*, 314–15; *PhS*, 264–65).

Thus, none of the acts of intentionality or desire ever occurs in a pure condition founded by consciousness or self-consciousness (and their respective correlates) alone. And every act of intending or pursuit of a desire, no matter how casual or intense, always occurs as an act by a real individual in a specific historico-cultural context. It can be considered as *essentially* an act of perception, for instance, only by abstracting from the concrete conditions and circumstances within which it occurs. Furthermore, no scientific research or other rational, purposive act occurs outside of an historico-cultural context which it presupposes. The purposive pursuits of rational human beings are a result of their enculturation into the society as a whole and into the community which embraces the specific type of activity in particular. On the other hand, the pursuit of the purposive activity affirms (or denies) these various presuppositions and in so doing carries out thematizations which validate or invalidate them. No purposive, and thus no conative or intentional activities or institutions, are real and concrete divorced from a culture.

The stages of spirit we are to traverse, then, are stages in the development of our civilization and thus in the development of individuals in that civilization. In this development the intelligible totality of what-is will be observed to be consciously, deliberately sought after in one form or another. The life of spirit is itself a quest for certainty. In so far as the absoluteness of our standpoint eludes us in each of these stages, there will be operative a determinate lack in respect to the "creation" of our home in the world. But each epoch will come to a more complete self-realization of its condition than the preceding epochs.

One more clarification must be made before continuing with the progress of spirit. In the last passage quoted above, we saw that, if considered only on the basis of transcendental reason, reason is the possession of the individual who is in truth spirit, but that such an individual only "*has reason*: it is consciousness which, as the word 'has' indicates, has the object in a shape which is *implicitly* determined by reason or by the value of the category, but in such a way that it does not as yet have for consciousness the value of the category" (*PhG*, 315; *PhS*, 265). When it does come to have the value of the category for itself, then we have true spirit and the real, concrete progression of forms in history. Hegel is here attributing to spirit, to that complexus of society and its individuals, the character of *being* the category.[16] This term 'category' has arisen before in the text, but as yet little has been said about it. At this point, where there seems to be a "category mistake" in the use of this term, it is important to become clear about the legitimacy of Hegel's use of the term in this way. In addition to clearing up a difficulty with Hegel's thought in respect to the term itself, clarity about the term will also afford a perfect opportunity to explicate in just what the "absoluteness" of "absolute idealism" consists.

Since Aristotle the term 'category' has had at least two distinct denotations, with a difference in connotation emerging from the two different references.[17] It appears in both a verbal and a substantive form. The verb '*katēgorein*' refers one to the *act of predication or judgment* in terms of which we indicate the belonging-together of a universal term (the sentential predicate) and an individual or general term (the sentential subject)—in which case we have reference solely to a linguistic entity, a sentence—or we indicate the belonging-together of a universal as a property of a thing (referred to through the predicate term) and a concrete individual or general (referred to through the subject term which names the individual or general)—in which case we refer to something in the world *by means of* the statement. In the first type of predication act, we do not transcend the sentence in which the judgment is embodied. In the second, we do transcend the sentence in an act of judgment (*katēgorein*) about the world. This verbal function was of primary concern for Aristotle, but was effectively placed aside because of a fascination with the other function of the term as a substantive.

The noun '*katēgoria*' denotes any one of the several forms or modes in which predications can occur. Aristotle generated his famous set of categories (*katēgoriai*) by reflection on the way in which a thing may be said to be, and it was with these that both Aristotle and his successors for the most part concerned themselves. Taken in this way, each category is a genus or class under which other sub-classes can be understood to be thematized. The Aristotelian doctrine of categories is too familiar for me to presume the need to discuss it further, except to point out that way in which it connects with what is often taken to be a different sense of 'category' in the philosophy of Kant.

Even in Aristotle, when there is an *act* of predication which is not simply sentential, i.e., which refers beyond the sentence itself in which the judgment is expressed, there is contained a unity of thinking and being, of the judge and his world, or, in modern terms, of subject and object. This unity of thinking and being is effected precisely because the subject makes the "accusation" or judgment about the world through the utterance of the statement, *and* there is a claim and possibility of validation of the claim that the predication is appropriate from the side of the object. That is to say, the individual speaker claims that what he says is true of the world or of the object referred to through the sentential subject term. In the *act* of judgment there is a unity of thought and being brought about which implicitly claims objective validity on the grounds that the judgment is only reflecting the actual state of affairs in reality or in the object. To categorize or predicate is thus to hold together whatis in such a way that what is held together putatively in thought, in the judgment as an entity, is actually held together in reality, in being. If we forget that *kategoriai* as substantives are *only* classifications of ways in which judging acts legitimately operate and instead treat them as entities of some sort, then we will be left, as has been most of the tradition, with a hopeless enigma concerning the relation between thought and being. But if we remember that even in Aristotle, who perhaps himself subsequently forgot this, the *kategoriai* are only classes of acts of *kategorein* by means of which properties can be said to belong to things, then from the beginning there is a subject-object which is constituted in the very act of judgment.

Evidently, when Kant claimed that his and Aristotle's tasks were the same in essence, he understood something like this. For a category, for Kant, is a "function" or "unifying act" which underlies and gives possibility to the "function" or "unifying act" of judgment in terms of which synthetic as well as analytic judgments are made. The analytic/synthetic distinction in Kant, however it came later to be understood by philosophers, represents a clear distinction between the two kinds of *kategorein* in Aristotle. An analytic judgment for Kant is an act in which a sentential predicate is said to belong to a sentential subject as a necessary aspect of the *meaning* of that subject *term*. A synthetic judgment, on the other hand, is an act of judgment in which objects of experience are claimed themselves to be unified in a certain way. The synthetic judgment involves reference to "the world," is an accusation concerning the way things are in experience; the analytic judgment refers only to meanings in a sentence or in words. A synthetic judgment transcends its sentential form, an analytic judgment does not. The synthetic judgment, be it *a priori* or *a posteriori*, is an act of the individual consciousness in which there is unity with the world and not simply with self. The twelve categories are the twelve fundamental ways in which, according to Kant, unity is *a priori* given to judgments which themselves order experience and hold together what-is in certain ways.

"*The* category" names, then, that general act of holding together which is accomplished through the several categories, i.e., *kategorein*: in Kant, the transcendental unity; in Fichte, the absolute ego; in Hegel, spirit. The *various* categories are various ways in which judgments (*Urteilen*, fundamental divisions) are made; *the* category is this act of judgment itself as a universal activity embedded in the concrete individual.

If this is understood, then it is clear and indisputable that the natural attitude always and everywhere presupposes that the category is operative, effective, actual (*wirklich*); for otherwise one's thematizations and judgments arising from them would make no sense, and what one said and did and thought would not have that relation to reality which is presupposed in its very words, thoughts, and deeds. The question all along has been, then: What is the category? In what form does the category really exist? What is the ultimate, absolute bond and ground within which or across which my experience is an on-going, intelligible affair?

What we have come to understand thus far is that consciousness, be it transcendental or empirical, is not the category; for there is always a given which itself eludes the category if the latter is understood to be limited to consciousness. Nor is self-consciousness the category; for self-consciousness contains not only the moment of consciousness and thus its lack (as we found in unhappy consciousness), but also cannot be sufficiently self-reflexive to be the category. Nor, finally, is reason the category when it is taken in a pure transcendental or epistemological manner; for the abstractness of reason is too formal for the concreteness of the historically appearing content. The category as absolute, unifying act can only be spirit, the activity which both constitutes itself as a world through its thematizations and activities, and is constituted by that world through its embodiment of the presupposition structure of that world. The category is the subjective-objective or absolute subject-object.

It is in this that absolute idealism consists.[18] The idealism to which our quest for certainty is leading us is not that of an ideal constitution of the physical in the sense of mentalistic claims, be the ideal objective and ontological or subjective and epistemological. This idealism of Hegel is as much opposed to subjective and objective or transcendental idealism as it is opposed to realism. Absolute idealism denotes the internal mediation of the immediate, that complex relationship between individual and world which we are beginning to uncover at this point in the *Phenomenology*. The absoluteness of this idealism denotes not some crude notion of "everything that is" in any sense of extension alone, but rather the totalization of the possibility of intensional or essential meaning of that which can constitute the extension of reality and its objects and events. This absolute subject-object, in whatever form it finally comes to exist, has as its essential characteristic that it is that beyond which one need not and cannot go when in search for the *intelligibility* of what-is. The actual unity we have with our world, and thus the ground for warranting our certainty claims, is to be sought in the category, in the absolute subject-object, in the most fundamental unity we have with that world. *That there is* such a unity is never a legitimate question, even for the most naive natural attitude. The question is not whether the category as absolute subject-object exists, but only *what it is*. However odd this claim might seem it is justified; for in effect we are saying that it is not a question of whether or not there is a unity with the world, but only what the unity is. As I have just argued above, every form of thought and action which claims to be talking about the world or to be acting in the world with some efficacy must in fact presuppose such a unity. This is why Hegel can claim elsewhere that every philosophy is an idealism, the only question being one of how adequate or consistent the idealism is.[19] The movement from implicit to explicit thematization of the category, then, is what has been undertaken in the *Phenomenology*. Once we have the real, concrete, historical nature of the category (*kategorein*) before us, we have access to the absolute; for that *is* the absolute standpoint which is always within the natural attitude and which is thus our warranty for certainty.

If we return now to our observation of the attempt of the Greeks to bring themselves to the category, we can see both their success and their failure. The determinate failure of the Greek spirit was its inability to capture and overcome the schism or disunity which appears in both sides of spirit, in the individual and in the polis, as the individual acts in accordance with the presuppositional framework. This inability was recognized by the Greeks in the plays in the way they recognized and represented the absolute subject-object. The absolute subject-object was reflectively understood as self-contradictory and thus, in terms of intelligibility, ineffable. In the eyes of the chorus (i.e., from the putative absolute standpoint within this objective representation of spirit) this ineffability took the form of destiny or fate (*moira, Schicksal*) (*PhG*, 337; *PhS*, 285).[20] The destiny or fate referred to is that of the polis itself, both as substance and as the acting individuals who constitute it, and is rooted in the natural mode of the two laws. Each individual has the immediate relationship to his or her law, a law which nature has itself determined and thus which guarantees certainty of access to nature. At the same time, in following this law the individual acts with certainty within a substance, the polis, which is a mediation of the two laws, albeit one which is immediate or by fiat, namely the *Sittlichkeit* which contains as its elements both laws and both modes of activity respectively associated with the laws. The tension between, on the one hand, the simple immediacy and absoluteness of each of the laws as presupposition for warranted action and, on the other hand, the mediation and relativity of each as presupposition for the polis itself, is not resolved or taken up into a harmonious unity. The outcome is rather the positing and recognition of *moira* and the concomitant phenomenon of *nemesis*. Moira, as a personification of this force, is not one with the other deities of Greek life, but stands above them as final and ineffable; for even Zeus cannot contravene the decrees of Moira. There is, then, in this first historical form of spirit a recognition of the ineffable and unintelligible as the foundation of spirit itself. Moira as the absolute subject-object eludes us and thus we can have no access to the absolute standpoint or certainty except for the knowledge that we cannot.[21]

This recognition has a twofold effect, one which relates to the unity of the ethical world and the claim of certainty, the other to the multiplicity of ethical action and the denial of certainty. With the reflection on the ultimately ineffable, natural aspect—*moira*—the determinateness of the polis and the laws vanishes or is absorbed into the indeterminateness of fate or destiny:

> with the vanishing of this determinateness—which in the form of a real existence is a limitation, but equally the negative element in general and the self of the individuality—the life of spirit and this substance, which is self-conscious in everyone, is lost. The substance emerges as a formal universality in them, no longer dwelling in them as a living spirit; on the contrary, the simple compactness of their individuality has been shattered into a multitude of separate atoms (*PhG*, 342; *PhS*, 289).

Moira is the simple formality of *che sarà sarà*, in which every individual takes his "lot" in life (his *moira* in the original sense of the word); on the other hand, each individual is simply that, a one, a singular which is taken up formally into the natural, or, really, supernatural totality of a cosmos which cannot be understood in its final determinations. Not only is divine law "from all time" as Antigone insists, but the tension of both laws itself derives from ineluctable destiny.

The result here is that the absolute subject-object as *Sittlichkeit* is absolute only defectively; for at the base of its presupposition structure is the unknowable Moira which can only be named, but which cannot be subject. In the end, then, the absolute subject-object is actually only an objective subject-object; for the subjective, the self-consciousness of the acting individual, is actually "lost." But if it is lost, then the certainty which is to belong to one's acts is also lost; for the adequacy of each natural law is effectively denied. This is not to say that certainty is lost in a formal transcendental framework, and thus that we have a reversion to the position of pure reason; on the contrary, this is a real, historically existing spirit which is self-conscious of its own lack. Its self-consciousness, in the form of reduction to blind destiny, is actually present in the fact that *moira* is reified into Moira, i.e., in the recognition that blind destiny is incomplete as an absolute self-consciousness. This first form of spirit, then, contains within itself its own immanent critique, and there is no need for a phenomenological "we" to measure it by the latter's standards.[22] The Greeks, in their own poetry and social fabric, have measured themselves by positing and recognizing destiny.[23]

What is lost here in terms of warranted certainty on the side of the subjective subject-object highlights the difficulty of realizing just how individuals are but moments of spirit, and yet are real individuals who are not simply effaced in the process of their participation in spirit. A comparison with our difficulties in the presuppositions of self-consciousness as absolute standpoint and warranty for certainty might help clarify this matter. In the attempt to make self-consciousness the absolute standpoint, we found that in its immediate form self-consciousness is structured as the simple desire for life, while life is the arena for desire and has its own independence over against the desiring, independent self-consciousness. This led us to the realization of the independence and dependence of self-consciousness and the centrality of recognition to our quest for certainty. This structure of recognition in the midst of the ambiguity of independence and dependence on the subjective side as well as on the objective side gave us the basis for the examination of self-consciousness in three forms of the deliberate attempt to be the absolute standpoint, namely stoicism, skepticism, and unhappy consciousness. What we found was the necessity for a surrender to a pre-constituted yet continuously dynamic unity of self and world which would remedy the lack of certainty found in the attempts to independently ground ourselves and our certainty through self-consciousness alone. In other words, when we examined the attempt of the subject itself to ground certainty—albeit as self-consciousness rather than as simple consciousness—we discovered the loss on the side of subjectivity due to its inability to explicitly lay the ground for unity and thus for certainty.

In this first form of spirit, on the other hand, we find the ambiguity of independence and dependence taken up and revealed through the living spirit. Our discovery of this living spirit has been the outcome of our inquiry into reason as the unity of self and world which was to repair the defects due to subjectivity in the thesis of self-consciousness. In the everyday actions of the individuals we now see that they act, independently, with the certainty of being right in their action, and they do so because their proper law decrees that they act rightly. But they have here also been forced to recognize and portray their dependency on an absolute other, on *moira* or destiny. In this form of objective spirit, to be sure, we do not have the relatively simple form of one self-consciousness existing for another, since the self-conscious individuals are and recognize themselves as moments of the ethical order as such.[24] But again it is on the side of subjectivity that the link is broken; for in the pursuit of one's law one necessarily breaks off intelligible contact with that law itself as the consequences of action flow into the ineffability of Moira.

This loss and the consequent abandonment of the individual to his or her own destiny reflects the constant risk of the effacement of individuality. In the real world, where we act with a certainty based on our law, that certainty seems to be violated. We seem to be simply taken up as one more element in the cosmic drama. In the end, as we shall see, it is the collapse into ineffability, the submerging of the individual in the consequences of his own acts, and the attempt to give this process intelligibility and thus to rescue ourselves from the uncertainty of our own, self-made destiny, which move the real quest for certainty that structures the genesis of our own substance in civilization. The problem is one of making real to ourselves just how we are both individuals and elements of the cosmic drama. The problem is that of the coming-to-self-awareness of spirit. Thus, what this first analysis of spirit shows us is that the quest for certainty has been taken on historically not in single self-consciousnesses, but collectively in spirit itself. In other words, society not only finds a vehicle for the purposes of objectification of its own praxical presuppositions, but as a result also obtains a self-criticism of those presuppositions.

The otherness which causes dependence of spirit to arise is consequently different from the otherness which caused it in self-consciousness; for destiny is itself an aspect of that objective spirit, an aspect which at one and the same time is a bona fide element because it is presupposition, and yet not such an element because of its ineffability. Destiny is both a proper part of spirit and not a proper part. And as a reflection of this, Antigone and Creon act out their respective "roles" while each recognizes the ambiguity of those roles. That is to say, the Greek, although he fully recognizes this ambiguity, yet does not become frozen and unable to act; he acts out life with immediate certainty. Independence and dependence are both accepted as fully recognized, and one knowingly takes the part to be played among the various *moirai* of the cosmos. There is no self-deception, no bad faith, but acceptance of participation in the whole such that one both determines and is determined by that whole.[25]

If this is correct, then we can also expand on brief remarks made above in note 23 on the nature of the connections between the sections of the *Phenomenology*, now that we have discovered spirit. The transitions are not historical in the sense that the Roman society now to be studied was founded consciously on the failure of the Greeks; nor are they simply due to idealistic dialectics in which the stage of the Roman spirit is chosen because it fits the needs of Hegel's theory. Rather, in the context of the project of the *Phenomenology of Spirit*, one in the natural as well as the philosophical attitude who has reached this point in the quest for certainty grasps the critique which was made (in the present case) by the Greeks themselves. On the basis of our awareness of their awareness, and because we ourselves are now aware of what true spirit is, we know that the next form of objective spirit to be turned to is that of the Roman civilization. We know this because our awareness is rooted in an awareness of our own substance and what we have come to know about the history of that substance in a pre-philosophical context. That is to say, having for our own substance our present (1805) civilization, we know that in the actual historical process Rome, and neither China nor India nor some African or Western Hemisphere civilization, next took a formative part in our genesis. None of these latter were of any relevance immediately following the Greeks. What effect they later may have had on our substance is of absolutely no import at this point. We also know, from our own natural sense of ourselves and the enculturation we have had, that with the fall of Rome, Christian Europe itself began its own development. So, the transitions are historical in this sense: if we take the historical and allow ourselves to be led by the spiritual sense we already have in the natural attitude, then we naturally turn to Rome. In addition, since we are guided by the quest for certainty, our turn to Rome will have us focus on the development of that quest.

The next great stage of our spirit, then, reveals an advance over the problem of the ineffability of Moira.[26] The concepts of 'person' and 'formal legality' which characterized the spirit and thus the lived presuppositions of the Romans explicitly introduce into the historical movement of our civilization the first attempt at a resolution of the lack of certainty with which immediate spirit as *Sittlichkeit* is fettered. The legal status of the person under law expresses the presupposition of (1) equality of all as persons and (2) the rights attaching to the independence which this equality gives to each. The absolute subject-object or category is not now presented in an art form as Moira, but rather in codified law as the legal person or the person with rights. The absolute is the law which is for all, and thus the shattering of certainty in the *moirai* of the two Greek laws is avoided.[27]

In the Roman conception of legality and personality, the independence of the individual is recognized to reside in every individual, i.e., it is presupposed that every different individual *is* different, but exists recognized as an individual identical to all other individuals *as a person*. In the codification of law and the consequent institutionalization of the person, a concrete basis *in formal right* is given each individual, regardless of who he is, *so long as he is a citizen*. This proviso is important since, outside of citizenship, one does not exist in the category. Thus, the individual qua person has "independence which has *actual* validity" (*PhG*, 343; *PhS*, 290). But at the same time, this concrete legal existence which gives universal form to a person embodies a negativity; for all "possessions," whether material or non-material, are equally content for the formal legalism of personal rights.

This formalism is the focus of our examination. Because now recognized and codified in public law, the ambiguity of the two laws of the Greeks is avoided; for the different rights are brought together into a unity. But this very universality of the law and of rights is just what is at the same time recognized as the failure of the law to institutionally embody the presuppositions of the people.[28] A radical difference is inserted, not between "natural" individuals as before, but between the form and the "content" in each individual.

> The actual content or the specific character of what is mine—whether it be an external possession, or also the inner riches or poverty of spirit and character—is not contained in this empty form, and does not concern it. The content belongs, therefore, to an autonomous power, which is something different from the formal universal, to a power which is arbitrary and capricious (*PhG*, 344–45; PhS, 292).

The arbitrary and capricious character here referred to could be an emperor, "the titanic self-consciousness that thinks of itself as being an actual living god" (*PhG*, 345; *PhS*, 292–93). But Hegel's point really goes beyond this particular instance to any condition where legal right is taken as the absolute subject-object, as the ultimate presupposition for the intelligibility of what is and our certainty about it. For it is precisely the equality in a legal sense—an equality which must abstract from all individual differences between individuals as unique individuals—which leaves the question of individuality in other matters, e.g., socio-economic or cultural matters, devoid of any determinations toward equality.[29] All have a right to their possessions, including possession of themselves; but *what* their possessions are is not defined in any but formal terms. All also have a right to the protection of their pursuit of the development of their capabilities; but *what* those capabilities are and how they might be developed and, most importantly, of what use they will be to the self and others when developed, are not in any way defined in the formality of law and personhood. Such legal formalism results in abandoning questions of the good to chance; for there is no ground for the qualitatively good content to one's life. Whether the decider of what these goods shall be is an emperor or an "unseen hand," the result is the same: arbitrariness and caprice, or the ubiquitous presence of socio-economic and cultural inequality. Speaking of this lord of the world, but referring equally to any form of hegemony of form over content, Hegel writes that the

> power is not the *union* and *harmony* of spirit in which persons would recognize their own self-consciousness. Rather they exist, as persons, on their own account, and exclude any continuity with others from the rigid unyieldingness of their atomicity. They exist, therefore, in a merely negative relationship, both to one another and to him who is their bond of connection or continuity. . . . Legal personality thus learns rather that it is without any substance . . . (*PhG*, 345–46; *PhS*, 293).

The emperor also senses the emptiness and arbitrariness of this existence and these institutions, and there is on his side an equal loss of substance. A spirit which contains on the one hand the atomicity of individual rights and persons, and on the other hand a purely formal unity in terms of which content or the essence of life for the individual is left open to chance, also then fails to be an absolute subject-object or the concrete category. The quest for certainty again fails and is recognized in the society as failing. Whether in the poetry of a Horace or in the empty practices of bread and circuses and a dissolute emperor, the very presuppositions underlying the activities of the people constitute a concrete unhappy consciousness, an unhappy, self-alienated spirit which realizes the absolute ambiguity which it contains within itself. The turn to the cults and a new religion is only another form of the self-recognition by spirit of its own loss, and a turn toward a new form of spirit as the ground of certainty.

This introduces us, then, to a form of spirit which has developed beyond the simple immediacy of *Sittlichkeit* and personality.[30] In the first form of spirit, custom was of the essence in respect to the certainty of our existence, a unity of two immediately accessible and natural laws which nevertheless came to destruction and lost their binding power in the density of destiny. In the formal atomism of legality and personality, this disappearance into an ineffable beyond seemed for a while stemmed; but in the end this concrete legalism became a merely empty, formal institutional fact which was divorced from the real content of life. This double alienation introduces, through Christianity and the birth of European culture, a spirit which struggles through self-alienation to come to unity in culture (*Bildung*) itself.

VIII
Interest As Reflection: Culture

THE NEW FORM of spirit, ushered in with the rise of Christianity and the decline of Rome, is a form in which spirit is self-alienated.[1] It is a world in which the quest for certainty takes the form of accepting the alienation resulting from one's actions in this world and turning to a beyond in which the alienation is to be removed. But we do not have here a simple replication of the relation between *Sittlichkeit* and Moira, or of the relation between our particular individuality and the formal legalism which defines us as a person. The quest for certainty found in the post-classical period of our civilization is one in which the differences between the uncertainties arising from our actions and the certainty we seek are taken up in a new way.

In this new form of spirit, the world was constituted by two opposing objective structures: culture and faith, this world and the next world, each with its own contribution as a ground for certainty. The presuppositions instantiated here involve a recognition of two worlds, each separate from the other and yet inextricably linked. In the world constituted by culture there is the everyday, present activity of individuals, a unity not so much in terms of formal rights or customs as in terms of collections of overt acts of self-objectification by means of which individuals participate in the world and form the world through that participation. Alienation is seen to be at the heart of this real world. In the world of faith, on the other hand, we have a flight from the real world of culture, and a positing and recognition of a beyond in which the self-objectification and alienation of the "real world" is effaced and the individual is to live in eternal harmony with himself and others. Each world is opposed to the other, the one having to do with the here and now, the other with a beyond. But each is also related to and dependent upon the other; for faith is structured as the consciousness of a beyond where there exists the unity which cannot be found in the present world of culture, while culture and its alienation are the ground and basis for both worldly activity and the need for faith. Alienation and uncertainty thus furnish the recognized ground for a flight to certainty elsewhere, while the certainty which comes from faith is the removal of that alienation and uncertainty.

In culture there arise the institutions of society which focus on the distinction between self and world characterizing modern man and his society and distinguishing it from the unity of *Sittlichkeit* found in the ancient world.² Alienation (*Entfremdung*) of self-consciousness from itself—the objectification of oneself in one's actions—is the hallmark of the world. It is presupposed that in participating in the real world which is here and now one must surrender oneself, i.e., must give of one's labor, personality, and being, in order to take hold of the reality with which one is confronted. On the other hand it is also presupposed that one's institutional life or the real world which confronts the individual is nothing other than the work of the individuals in society. Thus, our alienation of ourselves as we contribute to the effectiveness of society and culture involves only our commitment to ourselves through that which is of our own making. Here the uncertainty of our objectifying actions—the risk in any act—comes together with the certainty of a society made by us and participated in by us.³

The major institution here which constitutes the objectivity of spirit is culture itself (*Bildung*).⁴ In culture is contained the very set of presuppositions which must be in force for the individual as well as for the reality which confronts him *if* he is to have reality in this world, *if* he is to realize himself, *if* the society as a whole is to remain viable, and thus *if* certainty is to be achieved *in concreto*. Our "natural being," our being which in the ancient *Sittlichkeit* was determined by nature, is now not determined by a divinely decreed law of nature, but rather through enculturation as a process in which the naturalness which originally belongs to us is transformed (*PhG*, 351–53; *PhS*, 298–99).

The transformation of our "naturalness" through enculturation is complex. Our presuppositions are, on the one hand, embodied in the institutions of civil society as the basic constitution of things, of "the way things work." These the individual learns through his enculturation and education. They are the recognized presuppositions which are the *sine qua non* for fruitful participation in socio-political life, and thus are the recognized ground of certainty of access to reality. On the other hand, once internalized by the individual, they are held by the individual and underlie his thoughts and actions in his daily intercourse with others in society. The praxical presuppositions as reflected spirit are thus neither mere transcendental entities or thoughts undergirding individual behavior which could be dredged up from his subjectivity, nor simply rules implicit in the institutional facts of the world. As ideological components of both the individual and the institutions, the presuppositions are the fundamental determinants of what constitute meaningful actions or choices in the society. Thus, the ideology does not determine one to some specific set of actions; rather it determines the possible worlds among which choices can be made.⁵

Basic to these presuppositions is the paradoxical set which gives the real possible worlds and the ground for warranty for certainty claims as those in which the individual is both separate from and part of the world; that his actions are both his own and at the same time only functions of the social and political structure of society; that one must both sacrifice oneself for the sake of society and simultaneously realize oneself and complete oneself through action; that the actions are both appropriations of the world by the individual and of the individual by the world. Certainty is ours in this form of spirit *only* by way of our explicit positing and acceptance of the ambiguity of our action and knowledge in respect to certainty. This ambiguity is but the further historical development of the ambiguity we have been tracing, and which has become more and more explicit for the natural attitude.[6] The alternative sets of presuppositions which often appear one-sidedly as *the* correct set in our modern world are here shown to be in truth each a part of the praxis and its presuppositions. The insistence on an either-or in respect to the individual or a society is the stumbling block in the way of an adequate understanding of the grounds of modern life. The attempt to escape contradiction and ambiguity by supposing only one element of the ambiguity as *the* element while discarding the other—i.e., the rights of the individual over society or of society over the individual—is precisely a denial of the presuppositions which structure this form of spirit called 'culture'. There is presupposed both inevitable alienation and at the same time all of the necessary and sufficient conditions for the realization and completion of the individual self. Through my very education and enculturation I acquire the means by which I can realize myself; but those means involve the giving of myself to the whole in social and political activity.[7]

This dialectic of alienation and completion is accompanied by further presuppositions which are embodied as the content of the culture, and which define the possible worlds of the modern individual in terms of two spheres, that of civil society and that of the state, or the sphere of wealth and the sphere of power.[8] Involved with these presuppositions are also those which define "good" and "bad" in respect to the individual and his actions in each of the two spheres. The opposition and contradiction are as ubiquitous here as on the level of presupposition involving the bare relationship of the individual to his world in general. The state and civil society both oppose and undermine each other and, on the other hand, complement each other. In respect to the civil society, each individual is an absolute end in himself, determined by his own desire for satisfaction, in competition with all other individuals. In respect to the state and as a citizen, the individual is to direct himself to the good of the whole instead of to his own selfish good as in civil society. On this level of analysis, each is bad with respect to the others. On the other hand, it is the civil society and its self-interest which is the *raison d'être* of the state and gives the latter its power, while making the overall functioning of the civil society possible. Each, thus, is for the good of the other. And these opposite valuations do not signify simply an ambivalence or undecidability; each opposing valuation as well as the mutual destruction and mutual dependency is absolute and straightforwardly true. It is in terms of the contradictory nature of both the individual in this context and of the substance or world which is the context, that the contradictory activities of alienation and satisfaction take place. Culture and the process of enculturation objectify and internalize this structure of praxis and, in so far as the culture is itself thematized, constitute a profound reflection on the ground of certainty.[9]

The absolute subject-object formed in this spirit of culture makes one well able to be reflective; for the grounding of our quest for certainty in ambiguity and uncertainty—not as a discovered consequence as in *Sittlichkeit*, but from the beginning as a prius—forces reflection. This forced reflection gives rise to a focus on language which was there before implicitly in both the language which constitutes the tragedies and the language which constitutes the codification of the law, but which only now comes explicitly to the surface. For as an element of culture as a whole, and not just one element of it—art or law—language is universally the way in which spirit exists and reflects upon itself.

In a series of paragraphs which virtually inaugurate a completely new theory of language as essentially performative in *all* of its modes, we come to see that in culture language

> has for its content the form itself, the form which language itself is, and is authoritative as *language*. It is the power of speech, as that which performs what has to be performed. For [language] is the real existence of the pure self [*das Dasein des reinen Selbsts*] as self; in speech, self-consciousness, *qua independent separate individuality*, comes as such into existence, so that it exists *for others*. Otherwise, the "I", this pure "I", is nonexistent, is *not there* [*ist sonst nicht da*]; in every other expression it is immersed in a reality, and is in a shape from which it can withdraw itself; it is reflected back into itself from its action, as well as from its physiognomic expression, and dissociates itself from such an imperfect existence, in which there is always at once too much as too little, letting it remain lifeless behind. Language, however, contains it in its purity, it alone expresses the "I", the "I" itself. . . . The "I" that utters itself is *heard* or *perceived*; it is an infection [*Ansteckung*] in which it has immediately passed

into unity with those for whom it is a real existence, and is a universal self-consciousness (*PhG*, 362; *PhS*, 308).

The intricacies of this fecund passage cannot be analyzed here; it is only important for the present task to point out that language, both as language proper and as speech, is the concrete, abiding existence of the "I", that is, of the individual who lives in the grips of the praxical presuppositions of his society. It is the form of objectification which fixes the world as the world that it is, and which both originates from and identifies the individual as unique in that world. Language, and specifically speech, is the "middle term" between one individual and other individuals, between the individual and his tasks and the culture itself as the objectification of spirit. What was before relatively abstract as we found it first in self-consciousness, is now a historical phenomenon: the unity of the world through language, language as the *Dasein des Geistes*. Through language the culture is transmitted to the individual and internalized; through language the individual objectifies himself within that culture by the use of language forms which are institutionally public in that culture. Various kinds of "talk" concretize the presence and commitment of the individual to the appropriate situation. It is in and through language as an activity that the ground of certainty is both fixed and appropriated in the praxical presuppositions embedded in culture. Language is the medium which, as we saw earlier, forms concrete links between individuals as they talk and think their way through their tasks.[10]

But the apex of speech and such "talk" comes when the "truly cultured person" turns reflectively upon the reflection which constitutes culture, focuses on the irony of objectification, alienation, and certainty, and actually articulates and gives existence to the true nature of that presupposition set. The confusion and contradiction of the whole as rooted in the ideology and presuppositions become themselves the object of judgment and talk. Fully immersed in his certainty of access to reality, this person challenges the ground of certainty. Spirit here turns on itself, reflection turns on reflection, and this is once again a form of "true spirit." For in this derisive talk and in these judgments where the confusion of the world and of the existence of culture is unveiled as actually existing, spirit then communes only with itself and holds itself together in a single unity of irony.[11]

> [True spirit] exists in the universal talk and destructive judgment which strips of their significance all those moments which are supposed to count as the true being and as actual members of the whole, and is equally this nihilistic game [*die sich auflösende Spiel*] which it plays with itself. This judging and talking is, therefore,

what is true and invincible, while *it* overpowers everything; it is solely with this alone that one has truly to do with in this actual world (*PhG*, 372; *PhS*, 317).

The not-fully-cultured, "honest consciousness" still claims with professed certainty and in his "uneducated thoughtlessness" [*ungebildete Gedankenlosigkeit*], that all is well with the world, that each aspect (i.e. civil society and state, wealth and power), as well as both individual and society as a whole, must be treated with respect.[12] Still caught up in the ideology, but not aware of the contradiction, he lives the thoughtless life of the hard and fast distinctions of a simple understanding which sees one side, the side appropriate at the moment, as the whole. His certainty is thus rooted in the fully accepted way of life which has become his through enculturation. But the fully cultured individual, caught up in the same ideology, shows the nihilism of the culture in his own nihilistic talk. His ridicule mirrors the true perversion of the culture; culture thus becomes perverse about its own perverseness.

> The content of what spirit says about itself is thus the perversion of every concept and reality, the universal deception of itself and others; and the shamelessness which gives utterance to this deception is just for that reason the greatest truth (*PhG*, 372; *PhS*, 317).

The absolute subject-object or the absolute standpoint now has a degree of concreteness which it has lacked in previous forms. The ironic unity of the world which is brought about both by the world itself and by the individuals who face and act in that world is an absolute; for the moment, there is nothing else. There is a totality only in the irony which is itself both foundation for and product of the totalizing act of the cultured person who talks and who judges his culture as a member of that culture. The totalizing is an aspect of the totality and the totality is the totalizing.[13]

Were culture the sole aspect of modern, alienated spirit, the *Phenomenology* and its quest for warranted certainty would have ended in an irony which, in founding the possible worlds of experience, action, and knowledge, actually destroyed them. But this modern world, arising out of the ancient and harboring within itself Christianity, had simultaneously another aspect, that of faith and pure insight. The duplicity of the world of culture was itself but one aspect of a larger duplicity, that which existed in the tension between self-estranging culture and, on the other hand, faith and insight. The ironical summation to which the cultured person comes is that there is vanity to all things, and thus that certainty is not to be found in culture and its ideology. Alongside and in tension with this self-alienation which finds a perverted certainty in an ironical form, alongside culture and its world and its discussion of the vanity of all things, stands faith and its world beyond, and pure insight and its conceptualization of this world.[14]

The world of faith is a world of "pure" consciousness, the world of an individual who does not act—who is not an "actual" consciousness—but who contemplates and reflects upon a world beyond. This world beyond is presupposed and reflected upon by the individual as the actual essence of the alienated world of culture, the fundament and ground which gives the latter any reality it has, and thus the only possible ground of real certainty. Faith is a "simple consciousness of the positive, or of tranquil self-identity" which "has for its object the inner *essence qua essence*" (PhG, 379; PhS, 324). Pure insight, on the other hand, is a process of consciousness

> which focuses itself in *self*-consciousness, a process which is confronted by and turns itself against consciousness of the positive, and which is confronted by and turns itself against the form of objectivity or of picture-thinking; pure insight's own object is only the *pure "I"* (PhG, 379; PhS, 323–24).

Insight opposes the world with its alienation and vanity as a negativity, as something to be articulated into a whole through pure self-consciousness. This pure insight becomes mature in the Enlightment. In their difference and their identity, both faith and pure insight are forms of spirit, of self-conscious articulation of the praxical presuppositions underlying culture. Both are attempts to give unity and a ground to the actual world which has been reduced through culture to a pure irony. In both, the quest for certainty has come to terms with the ambiguity of certainty/uncertainty, of alienation/satisfaction.

The analyses here are complex, showing the course of self-reflection and cultural instantiation which ends in the Utilitarianism and Deism of the eighteenth century. We come to see how both faith and insight show themselves to be internally contradictory, evidencing this in their mutual misunderstandings of each other in their attacks on each other.[15] They lack also a self-awareness about their actual relationship to the vain, ironic world they seek to explicate and ground. The analyses follow something of the following course.

Faith, on the one hand, involves a flight from this world, presupposing the actual world as simply and truly the vanity of all vanities and a place of uncertainty. No claims of access to reality through culture can be validated. But as this flight, faith is precisely defined only in relation to what it would escape if it could. The essence of this world, the totality which totalizes it, may be "the beyond," but the essence of that beyond is, in turn, this vain world and the necessity to escape it in order to have a totality of intelligibility and the certainty it brings. Moreover, in its attack on insight as simply a part of the vanity of the world, faith itself denounces its own project; for

> the absolute being of faith is essentially not the *abstract* essence that would exist beyond the consciousness of the believer; on the contrary, it is the spirit of the [religious] community, the unity of the abstract essence and self-consciousness. That it be the spirit of the community, this requires as a necessary moment the action of the community. It is this spirit, *only by being produced* by consciousness; or rather, it does *not* exist as the spirit of the community *without* having been produced by consciousness (*PhG*, 391; *PhS*, 335).

The impetus behind faith is to comprehend what-is, to make intelligible and explicit the grounds for the possibility of the world of culture and our warranted certainty of the truth about reality. But as spirit of the community, as what will *for human beings* make sense of the vanity of all things and of the nihilistic irony of culture, it is in and through the self-consciousness of the individuals comprising the community that this being, God, lives. To denounce the quest for certainty belonging to pure insight, not only in terms of specific content but also in terms of the form of a quest, is to denounce therefore the very life of spirit as faith; for faith is itself a quest for certainty rooted in the world of vanity.[16]

This indicates the common origin of both faith and pure insight. Both arise out of the self-alienation which "has existence [*Dasein*] in the world of culture" (*PhG*, 376; *PhS*, 321).[17] The self-alienation which becomes conscious of itself as self-alienation not only generates the problem of subject and object and the problem of knower and known, but as well generates a consciousness of our essence as the beyond (faith) and a *self*-consciousness of essence as both beyond (as Deistic deity) and immanent (the Utility which insight fixes upon). That is to say, the upshot of the alienation of culture is a further alienation of the self from the self in the two attempts, faith and insight, to bring about a solution to the problem of alienation; for however we may turn to the ground of certainty, we never cease to exist in the midst of the uncertainty of culture.[18] Yet in this alienation arising from the alienation of culture there is a kind of resolution which makes both faith and insight a richer form of interest as reflection than is pure culture. Let us now turn to these two movements and observe further the historical progress toward the absolute standpoint.

Faith has three aspects, as does insight. The first aspect is its being a self-sufficient mode of being such that the faithful are able to articulate in an objective fashion the very alienation which is experienced and thus demonstrate their warranted certainty. In this way the faithful transcend the alienation by becoming explicitly aware of it in transcendence.

> In the consciousness of the *believer*, the aspect of *being in and for itself* is its absolute object whose content and determination . . . is nothing else but the actual world raised into the universality of pure consciousness (*PhG*, 380; *PhS*, 324–25).

This first aspect is contained in the doctrine of the trinity: God the Father ("the Good, . . . *the absolute being* that is in and for itself in so far as it is the simple eternal *substance*"), God the Son (the absolute being as it "passes over into *being-for-another*" such that "its self-identity becomes an *actual*, self-*sacrificing* absolute being; it becomes a *self*, but a mortal, perishable self"), and God the Holy Spirit ("the return of this alienated self and of the humiliated substance into their original simplicity; . . . substance represented as spirit") (*PhG*, 380; *PhS*, 324–25). The believer, the man of faith, takes this paradigm of (1) totality, (2) self-alienation of the totality, and (3) return to totality out of self-alienation, as the simple given, as the simple, objective truth which is the essence and ground of certainty for the actual world of culture and the individual's participation in it. The trinitarian doctrine is itself at once a *representation* of alienated spirit and the *promise* of its wholeness. However, the mystery of the happening (*Geschehen*) of the separation and wholeness is taken as immediately there for reflection; it is taken as an eternally true fact, and not as a mere representation. It is believed as a truth presented to the believer rather than as a representation issuing from the believer. The journey of the Godhead itself is the salvation of man and his only ground of certainty.[19]

At one and the same time, the alienation and meaninglessness of the vain, actual world of the here and now is both denigrated and elevated to a sacred mystery; for Jesus dies at the hands of the vain, in the most sacrilegious event of all time, an event which is itself a paradigm for that vanity; and yet He dies as part of the providential plan of the one, supreme, complete substance, God the Father, as He alienates Himself and then through the resurrection elevates this most vain of all acts on the part of the community into the salvation of that very same community. The Holy Spirit, which makes the community a community in the highest sense possible, is the paradigm for the unity which comes out of the diversity and alienation of the world. This is what it means to say that the absolute object of the believer "is nothing else but the actual world raised into the universality of pure consciousness" (*PhG*, 380; *PhS*, 324–25). In this aspect of the absolute subject-object the totality of one's faith is reflected in the doctrine of the trinity itself. The uncertainty itself becomes a moment of the divine and is thus taken up into the ground of certainty.

The second aspect of faith involves the relationship of the individual to the actual world as against his belonging to creation understood from the perspective of the first aspect of faith, that of absolute being:

> the believing consciousness partly has its actuality in the real world of culture, and constitutes the spirit and the existence of that world . . . ;partly, however, the believing consciousness confronts this its own actuality as something worthless, and is the process of overcoming it (*PhG*, 381; *PhS*, 325).

The "unworthiness" of this life is to be overcome by going through life recognizing it as a constant process of overcoming. This second aspect of the beliefs of the believer would seem to mirror the first; but the reflection is imperfect. Although God the Father is reflected in the first in the diremption between the realm of pure consciousness and the reality which is His creation, and the Son is present in the finite struggle to overcome, the moment of the resurrection and the coming of the Holy Spirit seems to be lacking. But we now come to see how even this moment is a part of the second aspect of faith. The religious community as such produces the actual unity for which the individual can only strive; for the religious community is "universal self-consciousness" (*PhG*, 381; *PhS*, 326). Thus, the Holy Spirit is participated in by the individual, although he must himself continue to strive to overcome this world. The paradigm which is immediately present and constantly called upon is thus instantiated in the actual life of the individual, and spirit, as self-reflective interest, would seem to have articulated itself and reflexively reached its ground for certainty.

Finally, there is a third aspect, that of the relationship of faith to pure insight and the consequent "intellectualization" of the mystery of faith. This is still to be clarified and will in the end bring failure to faith as an absolute standpoint. But in order to understand this relation and the complete reflection on reflection which is made by faith, it will first be necessary to look at the view of pure insight in respect to the alienation arising from culture.

Whereas faith is "the tranquil pure *consciousness* of spirit as *essence*," pure insight is "the *self*-consciousness of spirit as essence; it therefore knows essence, not as *essence*, but as absolute *self*" (*PhG*, 382; *PhS*, 326). Where faith transcends this world as a flight to the next world, insight comes to grips with this world as a struggle to make it intelligible in itself and as a rational place accessible here and now to self-conscious reflection and the absolute standpoint. Faith attempts to achieve the absolute standpoint by directing its interest toward an eternal, other-worldly domain which is to remain a mystery; insight is an intellectual struggle with and within the world of culture, the here and now. Insight also has three aspects to it: (1) it is being in and for itself or an immediacy before essence; (2) it is a relationship to the actual world of culture; and (3) it is a relationship to faith.

As immediacy, it is the purpose or goal (*Absicht*)

> of making *pure insight universal*, i.e., of making everything that is actual into a concept and into one and the same concept in every self-consciousness (*PhG*, 382; *PhS*, 327).

The whole, for the man of insight, is to be articulated in terms of universal concepts which belong to everyone and thus which would hold for and be the ground of certainty for everyone. Universal knowledge, not universal mystery, is the nature of the ultimate ground for warranted certainty. In contrast to the trinity of the faithful, the real world is, as a whole, now one concept which is in turn conceptualized in terms of the particulars within that whole, and which, thirdly, is a unity of the particulars and the whole. Through conceptualization, the mystery of the trinity becomes knowledge of concepts, and the quest for certainty becomes discursive.

The second aspect of pure insight articulates the relation of the individual to the actual world of culture in which he finds himself alienated. Pure insight is "the spirit that calls to *every* consciousness: *be for yourselves* what you all are *in yourselves—reasonable*" (*PhG*, 383; *PhS*, 328). Pure insight is not only to make the world of culture intelligible, but it is to bring out in each individual what is common to all individuals: reason. Reason and not mystery and transcendence is the form which spirit takes when interest as reflection takes the form of insight and, eventually, enlightenment (*die Aufklärung*). Fundamental, then, to the whole presuppositional framework of pure insight is the presupposition that both actuality and the individual are united by a reason which can be articulated and grant warranty for certainty.

Pure insight or modern rationality presents itself, then, with two tasks: (1) to bring the irony-infused and alienating culture into a unity as an insight for everyone (and eventually to be made public in an "encyclopedia"), and (2) to attack the superstitions of faith which latter are also an attempt to bring unity to culture and to achieve the absolute standpoint. There is nothing oblique about this attempt to conceptualize reality, as there was in the case of the Greek poets; for here reflection pure and simple is the consciously undertaken form of reflection which is institutionalized. The quest for absolute subject-object and certainty is fully conscious of itself; the enlightened ones, sharing in reason, are to bring to history itself and consequently to all historical persons, the rational, fully accessible account of the ultimate presuppositions for the possibility of the possible worlds of actuality.[20]

This claim to absoluteness rests on the explicit awareness of the presuppositions of culture and its recognition of language as the abiding existence of the self and its world. In this respect, we must renew our discussion of language as we focus on the pretentions to absoluteness which are found in this enlightenment movement:

> we have found that it is not the groups and the specific concepts and individualities that are the essence of this actuality, but that this has its substance and support solely in the spirit which exists *qua* judging and discussing, and that the interest of having a content for this argumentation and chatter alone preserves the whole and the groups into which it is articulated. In this language of insight, its self-consciousness is for it still a being *existing on its own account, this single individual*; but the vanity of the content is at the same time the vanity of the self that knows itself to be vain (*PhG*, 384; *PhS*, 329).

But when insight becomes enlightenment and seeks to overcome the ironic nature of culture, something happens to this individuality, and language becomes universal in a positive manner, i.e., in the form of an encyclopedia. The enlightened ones construct "a collection of the most telling and penetrating versions of all this brilliant talk, the soul that still preserves the whole"; and the

> collection shows to most people a better wit, or to everone at least a more varied wit, than their own, and shows that "knowing better" and "judging" are in general something universal and now universally known. With this, the sole remaining interest is eradicated, and the individual judgment is dissolved into the universal insight (*PhG*, 384–85; *PhS*, 329).

This allegiance to reason and to a complete articulation of the ground of certainty in concepts distinguishes insight and enlightenment from the other form of pure consciousness, faith. But because faith and insight are essentially the same *pure* consciousness, as opposed to actual, concretely acting consciousness caught up in culture, i.e., they are the same quest for certainty meant to overcome the recognized alienation and irony of culture—insight focuses itself in its third aspect in an attack on faith and its mysteries.[21]

The attack of the Enlightenment on faith became an institution of society itself and not just a concern of a few philosophers. The same movement of intellectualism which caused Kant to offer his first *Critique* in order to make room for faith was the high point of spirit as self-consciousness of its own presuppositions. Although there was much misunderstanding on the part of the intellect concerning the real nature of faith and its ethereal object, in the end the positive result of this cultural overcoming of culture had lasting consequences. In the negative sense of its attack on faith, insight is an "infection" (*eine Ansteckung*)

> which does not make itself noticeable beforehand as something opposed to the indifferent element into which it insinuates itself, and therefore cannot be warded off. Only when the infection has become widespread is that consciousness, which unheedingly yielded to its influence, *aware of it* (*PhG*, 387; *PhS*, 331).

When reason and the concept attack the "wisdom" of the faith, faith capitulates; for it cannot really counter this conceptual analysis of the absolute and the attacks against the non-conceptual beliefs, without breaking its own conceptual silence and itself using this same reason and thinking in accordance with the rules of intellectual insight. This is the infection. Faith, on the one hand, wishes to retain a "divine right," reminiscent of the divine law of Antigone; but given the finite, "human right" of reason, this faith, unlike the eternal and silent law of Antigone, cannot withstand the domain of Creon.

The detailed analysis of the attack on faith by reasoned insight need not concern us here.[22] It is the positive side of insight and intellect in this modern world which carries spirit forward as self-recollection and the achievement of warranted certainty. First, in abolishing the faithful's talk of the absolute as superstition, the standpoint of insight is one of empiricism.[23] All determinations are accessible to sense, and through sense to reason. What-is is presupposed as a system of particularities and determinations of limitation. The absolute, on the other hand, is a void, empty of distinctions, something not to be represented in terms of any distinction whatever. Being itself is empty, pure matter, or the supreme being of deism. Matter and the deistic God are the same (*PhG*, 396–97; *PhS*, 340).[24]

Secondly, this involves us with a return to sense-certainty and intentionality. This is not immediate, naive realism, but a reflective realism, realism which is reflectively sure of itself as realism. Here we have the historical, socio-cultural foundation of the instinct of reason, the certainty that all reality is rational and that one has access to it because one is oneself rational. The sensual or sensible and the rational belong to both individual and world. But this is not a one-sided realism; for *human* reality and its ideas are placed in the center of things and thus idealism is also reflectively recognized in terms of the relation of the sensible and conscious individual to reality (*PhG*, 397–98; *PhS*, 340–41). This idealism resides in the conscious and deliberate certainty of self-consciousness as it pursues the intellectual comprehension of everything; the actual world is to be *its* world. On the other hand, the realism resides in the positivity and objectivity of that actual world, the "in-itselfness" of the actual world which is there to be comprehended. And the conscious, enlightened individual himself is also but one among the natural things that are there in the actual world.[25]

The presupposition of the absolute as a void or a pure matter or the deistic God, and of the actual world as particularities which are accessible to sensible, rational consciousness, is brought together in the third aspect of this reflection on culture, "the relation of the individual being to absolute being" (*PhG*, 398ff.; *PhS*, 341ff.). The absolute, on the one hand, is only the mark of the in-itselfness of sensuous beings, their absolute independence and particularity. On the other hand, it is, as in itself, the total absence of relation, pointing to the fact that all particulars are related to each other and therefore existing for one another. This dual characteristic of the relation between the absolute and the particular, individual things is conceptually captured and concretized in the concept of 'usefulness' ('*die Nützlichkeit*'), and the whole of this period of Enlightenment—English, French, and German—is understood as and understood itself as the revelation of *Utilitarianism*. This utilitarianism is not limited to moral matters, narrowly considered, but reaches out to the definition of man himself, of nature, reason, Deity, society, and, in general, constitutes a complete metaphysics.[26]

The comprehensiveness of this utilitarian view as an articulation of the ground for our warranty of certainty is succinctly demonstrated in the claim that

> everything is *useful*. Everything is at the mercy of everything else, now lets itself be used by others and is *for them*, and now, so to speak, stands again on its hind legs, is stand-offish towards the other, is for itself, and uses the other in its turn. From this, we see what is the essence and what is the place of man regarded as a thing that is *conscious* of this relation. As he immediately is, as a natural consciousness *per se*, man is *good*, as an individual he is *absolute* and all else exists for him; and moreover, since the moments have for him, *qua* self-conscious animal, the significance of universality, *everything* exists for his pleasure and delight and, as one who has come from the hand of God, he walks the earth as in a garden planted for him. . . . Just as everything is useful to man, so man is useful too, and his vocation is to make himself a

member of the group, of use for the common good and serviceable to all. The extent to which he looks after his own interests must be matched by the extent to which he serves others, so far as he serves others, so far is he taking care of himself: one hand washes the other. But wherever he finds himself, there he is in his right place; he makes use of others and is himself made use of.

Different things are useful to one another in different ways; but all things are mutually serviceable through their own nature, viz., through being related to the absolute in two ways, the one positive, whereby they exist entirely on their own account, the other negative, whereby they exist for others. The *relation* to absolute being, or religion, is therefore of all useful things the supremely useful; for it is pure utility itself, it is this enduring being of all things, or their *being-in-and-for-themselves*, and it is their downfall, or their *being-for-another* (*PhG*, 399–400; *PhS*, 342–43).

Both the uncertainty of the relations in culture and the certainty of a comprehensive view are brought together here as never before. On the one hand, because everything is useful for everything else we are always at the mercy of the consequences arising from our being used by others and by other things in the universe. Every act of our own makes us a fact in the world and thus part of the universal chain of utility. But on the other hand, we too are users and our certainty of access to reality is to be found in the usefulness of other persons and things. As a matter of fact, even our being useful to others and thus being means for the ends of other elements in the universe testifies to our access to reality; for by being useful we are a part and can claim with certainty our participation in reality. Thus, what was at first the uncertainty which we sought to overcome is now just as much a certainty.

But the power of the utilitarian view does not complete itself in the content of the view; for by being aware of this law of utility we have now also come to self-consciously comprehend our condition and therefore can deliberately act in accordance with our real condition. We can act not only in accordance with it but, to employ a Kantian distinction, we can purposely act for its sake. Knowledge has become power in the sense that we no longer fight against all consequences which would remove our "autonomy," but accept those which are part of the chain of usefulness as at the core of our dignity. Our certainty is now a self-conscious certainty, a certainty of access to reality which overcomes the tension between certainty and uncertainty.

This extended articulation of utilitarianism and the dialectical, universal nature of usefulness shows not only a metaphysics, from which an ethics is to be drawn, but also shows that, in the end, Enlightenment does not so much destroy religion as "do away with the *thoughtless*, or rather *non-conceptual*, separation which is present in faith" (*PhG*, 405–06; *PhS*, 348–49).[27] The flight from actuality which leaves faith with two worlds and thus with an alienation within actuality as great as the cultural alienation it is meant to resolve, is first challenged by enlightenment and insight and then replaced by a utilitarian metaphysics and utilitarian practical philosophy of life. Political theory and activity, capitalist economic theory and activity, and, in fact, all domains of the culture, are permeated by this spirit and hence by the deliberate, self-reflective thematization of experience in terms of utility. Things and reality in general seem now transparent and we have, indeed, the best of all possible worlds. The purposiveness of our actions and the appropriateness of the world for these purposes—so long as they are "natural" purposes—are unified and grounded in utility, a utility which is not opaque, but grasped by human thought and put to work in our real intercourse with the world. Certainty is warranted, reflectively established.[28]

Furthermore, as we have now seen, human beings are not only aware of this schema of utility, but are themselves a part of it. Thus a distinction between the psychological, epistemological, transcendental, and sociohistorical is itself now transcended; for the culture, and the alienation on the basis of which faith and insight arose in the first place, now has as its fundamental structure the presupposition of spirit or human activity as a self-objectification, a giving of oneself in order to complete oneself, i.e. an objectification and return to self such that alienation remains as an aspect or moment of reality. But this alienation is tempered by the total connection of all things through utility. The complex utilitarian relationship between everything, since everything is both an end in itself and a means for another, both maintains alienation (which is first grasped ironically in "high culture") and gives that alienation a *raison d'être*.

Informed by this ideology of utilitarianism, the individual thematizes reflectively his everyday tasks, thus bringing closer the natural attitude and philosophy as phenomenology. The "spiritual" and "material" domains are brought together through the insight of the enlightenment into utility. Held by the presuppositions, and hence grounded idealistically, the actual everyday activities of the individuals in society both reflect and instantiate the presuppositions, thus grounding the presuppositions materialistically. The category is here to be understood, therefore, both materialistically and idealistically; for utility holds together and is held together by the concrete acts of individuals acting with certainty in society and in history. The thematization of immediate actuality and the ground for this thematization in the presupposition sets embedded in modern society mutually ground each other. The individual, certain of himself and of his world, "fits in" with that world and adapts himself to it while adapting it to himself. Certainty and truth, whose coalescence has been the aim of reason from the beginning, at last seem to have an identity in Utility. This "togetherness" of the whole world and of the concrete individual with that world comes to concrete realization historically when "liberty, equality, and fraternity" become the political foundation for a totality ruled by reason and actualizing absolute freedom, i.e., freedom married to necessity.[29]

The high point or ultimate form of spirit as culture and insight comes with the ground laid for the French Revolution and with that revolution itself.[30] In the ideological form of pure insight and its institutionalization in the matrix of society, utility as a metaphysics still exists in the form of an *object for* self-consciousness of pure insight. The socio-political and historical move to realize absolute freedom in actuality—i.e., to give actual, objective, effective existence to the absolute subject-object which we think through utilitarianism—is a move to universalize the actions of all in a *general will* which is not the simple sum of all wills, nor even of the majority, but which is a will in the sense that the actions of individuals as individuals are sublated into a single will which instantiates all of the necessary and sufficient conditions for the actualization of all individuals. This is not a will of compromise or of arbitrariness or combination, but a will which has as its presupposition the *logically* necessary and sufficient conditions for the liberty, equality, and fraternity of all and each.[31] It is the concrete social and political analogue of Kant's moral categorical imperative. Each individual can realize himself in the great schema of utility if and only if he and all others will the general will, and therefore if and only if all are seized by that will itself which both transcends the individual and yet must be willed by him through concrete actions. In this general will, operative and effective in the actual world, *certainty* of self and world as a matrix of utility is brought to *warranted certainty and truth*.

> Spirit thus comes before us as *absolute freedom*. It is self-consciousness which grasps the fact that its certainty of itself is the essence of all the spiritual "masses," or spheres, of the real as well as of the supersensible world, or conversely, that essence and actuality are consciousness's knowledge of *itself*. It is conscious of its pure personality and therein of all spiritual reality, and all reality is solely spiritual; the world is for it simply its own will, and this is a general will. And what is more, this will is not the empty thought of will which consists in silent assent, or assent by a representative, but a real general will, the will of all *individuals* as such. For will is in

itself the consciousness of personality, or of each, and it is as this genuine actual will that it ought to be, as the *self*-conscious essence of each and every personality, so that each, undivided from the whole, always does everything, and what appears as done by the whole is the direct and conscious deed of *each* (*PhG*, 415; *PhS*, 356–57).

The general will and absolute freedom are the ultimate form of the unity of totality and totalization in the socio-political realm, and thus the ultimate form which warranted certainty can achieve in that realm. Totality and totalization constitute a given whole and the process by which this whole is formed and held together. Nothing, it would seem, could be more absolute, more ultimate; for it seems that in the content of the general will lie all of the material and ideal presuppositions required for a competely rational world and thus for a completed rational access to reality. To act in and through the general will is to thematize directly what is necessary and sufficient for a completed rationality, as well as for the thematization of that rationality. Not only are substance (the world) and subject (the individual) identical as "useful," but subjectivity is the subjectivity of a "we" or a fraternity in which equality and perfect freedom maintain. The usefulness and uniqueness of everything and everyone are brought together in the general will: *usefulness and uniqueness*, two thoughts as concepts, *become existent as will*. The concept itself

> comes into existence in such a way that each individual consciousness raises itself out of its allotted sphere, no longer finds its essence and its work in this particular sphere, but grasps itself as the *concept* of will, grasps all spheres as the essence of this will, and therefore can only realize itself in a work which is the work of the whole. In this absolute freedom, therefore, all social groups or classes which are the spiritual spheres into which the whole is articulated are abolished; the individual consciousness that belonged to any such sphere, and willed and fulfilled itself in it, has put aside its limitation; its purpose is the general purpose, its language universal law, its work the universal work (*PhG*, 415–16; *PhS*, 357).[32]

But history itself proves that this mode of interest as reflection is not absolute; for in the French Revolution the attempt to instantiate the general will turned absolute freedom into absolute terror, and turned the realization and certainty of the participating individual into his death.[33] The Declaration of the Rights of Man becomes empty and purely formal simply because there is no longer any world in which to have those rights. The world has become "absolutely in the form of consciousness as a universal will" (*PhG*, 421; *PhS*, 362), and there is not a complete interpenetration of self-consciousness and substance, of individual will and general will. Reality, as conceived and acted upon, is taken to be a fusion of individual and general will; but when steps are taken to govern in accordance with this, the wills of those governing arise again as merely a faction within society, an individual or collective will against other individual or collective wills. The individual does not achieve certainty of self; the general will cannot, on these socio-political grounds alone, be actualized. For there is no standard, no real, historical standard, internal to the concept of utility and general will which can permit it the self-sufficiency it would need in order to be absolute. Freedom and law come into conflict and the Terror is the result.[34]

At this point in the *Phenomenology* we begin the discussion of morality for reasons which will be considered in the next chapter. But before turning to this, it will be helpful to see clearly just what the determinate lack is which causes the failure of culture and enlightenment as the absolute standpoint and, thus, so far as history up to Hegel's time is concerned, causes the rejection of socio-political life in its historically real dimension as the absolute standpoint and basis for warranted certainty.

In order to comprehend the move to morality, it is necessary first to see why the concept of utility and the general will are the highest and most perfect forms which are possible if socio-political-historical reality is taken as the ultimate, as the absolute ground beyond which one need not go for meaning and certainty.[35] Put most simply, it is a view of the absolute standpoint such that not only are the noetic-ontological praxical presuppositions embedded in the institutional facts of the world and held by all who meaningfully participate in that society but, furthermore, the presuppositions are such that individuals, groups, institutions, and even nature itself are totalized into a totality which is *internally* articulate to itself; for the self-consciousness of the individuals are part and parcel of that whole. All elements of reality *in themselves*, i.e., as ends, are unique, and *externally related* to all other elements of reality. On the other hand, all elements of reality are *for another*, i.e., exist as means, and are defined in terms of the needs, purposes, and tendencies of other elements and are thus *internally related* to all other elements of reality. As such, each element is *for itself*, i.e., centered on itself by means of its external and internal relations. Utilitarian theory as a metaphysics therefore reveals a reality free of the one-sidedness of simple atomistic individualism and, as well, of simple organic theory. And since all possible meaning is articulated in the actual interactions of the elements of reality and thereby accessible to individual consciousness, which is itself an element of this reality, the "one for all, and all for one" should make all reality transparent. And to do so is just the aim not only of the phenomenological inquiry on which we have embarked here, but also of natural certainty. Has not the individual now been sufficiently transformed in this phenomenological process and in history in order to find in concrete actuality and his relations to it the absolute standpoint and absolute knowledge? Have we not now found a stance, a real historical attitude, which will give us warranted access to ultimate reality?[36]

If we add to this thought or concept of utility the actual instantiation of the general will, the answer seems irresistibly to be in the affirmative. For the general or universal will is just the state of willing in which the perfection of utility is made a real, active, existing factor in the world. We have here not the individual will based on self-consciousness as ultimate, a will which tends toward fulfillment of goals counter to those of others. We have here the will which makes all things useful, and thus raises each individual to his own highest realization both in terms of his own, unique goals, and in terms of his contributions to the goals of others. Utilitarianism is the ultimate and realized certainty when the general will is operative. Without the general will, utility is merely a desideratum; with the general will it is a concrete reality. It is not enough to answer that *in fact* the general will failed to materialize in the French Revolution and that, to the contrary, the most arbitrary acts followed. For this would not show that in principle such a will must fail, and this must be shown if a true critique is to follow.

But it is precisely this proposed unity of individual and universal consciousness, will, and action which is self-destructive of the utilitarian program and which denies ultimacy to socio-politico-historical being. The individual in fact loses himself in the general will; for nothing positive can be done by the general will, no act can either be proposed or carried out. We do not here have the *difference* which existed between Creon and Antigone, each carrying out his or her allotted law with the reflection of that tension-ridden act in the absolute standpoint of art. Nor do we have the *difference* which existed between the emperor or other power which embodied the law and the persons or citizens who were brought into unity by that power. We have in the utilitarian ideal the destruction of all difference, for the individual will is to be transformed and not simply reflected in the general will. There are three specific difficulties revealed in this destruction, each focused on the opposition between the finitude of the individual, actual self-conscious person who is to will the general will and, on the other hand, the infinitude of the general will itself.[37]

(1) Every act is finite, but the general will is not.

After the various spiritual spheres and the restricted life of the individual have been done away with, as well as his two worlds, all that remains, therefore, is the immanent movement of universal self-consciousness as a reciprocity of a self-consciousness in the form of *universality* and in the form of *personal* consciousness: the universal will goes *into itself* and is a *single, individual* will facing universal law and work. But this *individual* consciousness is no less directly conscious of itself as universal will; it is aware that its object is a law given by that will and a work accomplished by it; therefore, in passing over into action and in creating objectivity, it is doing nothing individual, but carrying out the laws and functions of the state (*PhG*, 416; *PhS*, 358).

Since this general will is founded on the principle of utility, the self-conscious individuals are to find themselves and their certainty in the work they carry out as a general will. But this is not possible, since in order to carry out the general will, that individuality which is to be satisfied, which is finite, must be effaced; for no finite act could accomplish the infinite which is demanded by the general will. Thus, one either attempts to act as the general will, which is in fact now only abstraction, or one attempts to do something particular, which is concrete but not universal. That is to say, to act, one must do *something*; to do something is *not* to do something else; thus, the act remains finite and loses the sought certainty in the ground furnished by an infinte general will.

(2) Not only is the act finite, but the actor is as well.

Before the universal can perform a deed it must concentrate itself into the one of individuality and put at the head an individual self-consciousness; for the universal will is only an *actual* will in a self, which is a one. But thereby all other individuals are excluded from the entirety of this deed and have only a limited share in it, so that the deed would not be a deed of the *actual universal* self-consciousness (*PhG*, 417–18; *PhS*, 359).

From this we must conclude that "just as the individual self-consciousness does not find itself in this *universal work* of absolute freedom *qua* existent substance," referring here to the first problem discussed above, "so little does it find itself in the *deed* proper and *individual* actions of the will of this freedom" (*PhG*, 418; *PhS*, 359).

The French Revolution became, of necessity, a reign of terror just because of this opposition between the finite and the infinite, and thus because of the inevitability of factional dispute and suspicion arising from it. And this factionalism, present in perhaps almost any socio-political situation, is exacerbated in its consequences because of the absolute claims and structure of utilitarianism. As Hegel writes, "*being suspected*, therefore, takes the place, or has the significance and effect of *being guilty*"; for any "break" in the general will is by its very nature a crime. Individual finite goals must be done away with. But again, then, the certainty sought must disappear.

(3) The third problem is the natural resistance of the individual to organicism when the general will and the state are based on the premise of the individuality of the individual and his nature as an end in itself; and it is just this which characterizes utilitarianism as something apart from other forms of organicism. In this respect,

> the supreme reality and the reality which stands in the greatest antithesis to universal freedom, or rather the sole object that will still exist for that freedom, is the freedom and individuality of actual self-consciousness itself. For that universality which does not let itself advance to the reality of an organic articulation, and whose aim is to maintain itself in an unbroken continuity, at the same time creates a distinction within itself, because it is movement or consciousness in general (*PhG*, 418; *PhS*, 359).

The individual is the schizoid who divides himself

> into extremes equally abstract, into a simple, inflexible cold universality, and into the discrete, absolute, hard rigidity and self-willed atomism of actual self-consciousness (*PhG*, 418; *PhS*, 359).

We cannot here escape our finitude which actually and effectively creates the socio-cultural-historical whole to which we address ourselves, or to which we attempt to address ourselves politically in the name of the general will.[38] The strain evidenced in the attempt of modern men to be both citizens (and thus an embodiment of the general will) and productive members of civil society (and thus contributing and receiving in accordance with our talents and needs, but always for ourselves as individual wills) is addressed here with absolute simplicity and at the root: the two are incompatible, so long as the general will is founded on utilitarianism.[39]

Given this lack in the most perfect articulation of a social ethic, historical or socio-political foundations are not absolute, but themselves derivative or dependent upon something else, upon some other domain of being.[40] This is not to say that this domain of spirit is irrelevant to the ground of certainty and intelligibility; for it remains true that meaning is both found and produced within the historical and socio-political matrix, a context which is both itself produced by and in turn supports the actual lives of those individuals for whom we are seeking warranty for certainty of access to reality.[41] All that has been shown is that it, by itself, is not ultimate, not absolute, not independent of some further source of meaning and certainty.

The determinate lack found here in this form of spirit, therefore, is that either the individual in his necessary finitude is lost in the universal or general will, thus losing his meaning and certainty as an individual, or he insists on his individuality against the general will—something which in fact he must do in the end—and thus loses a totality in terms of which certainty could be warranted. What is thus missing is the universality of the finite individual who acts in the socio-historical context. It is for this reason that we turn now to consider another form of spirit, morality, in which the presuppositions are neither embedded in custom (*Sittlichkeit*) or culture (*Bildung*), nor reflectively articulated in art or in the general will; rather, they are embedded and reflectively articulated in moral self-consciousness itself. In the moral view of the world we have a straightforward confrontation between the finitude and the infinitude of reality and out of this confrontation will arise absolute spirit and the final achievement of the absolute standpoint in an absolute subject-object which will provide the ground for certainty.

IX

Interest As Reflection: Morality

CERTAINTY or warranted access to ultimate reality has now been shown to be impossible where the individual orients himself toward the general will as embodied in the institutions of the society. The specific problem was that the general will could not be known and acted upon in such a way that all individuals would in fact be completed through it while participating completely in it. The state showed its failure as *the* totality within which the totalizing was to take place; for the totalizing agent, the individual citizens or representatives are in that circumstance literally cut off from the totality and thus the totality is not truly totality: the individuals stand outside of the putative totality. As such, then, the institutional facts become an ultimate abstraction, a totality which could not be totality because no true totalizing act could take place in or toward it. The universal will became an empty abstraction because it had no actual or effective (*wirkliche*) embodiment through its members. Thus, this present move to the standpoint of morality is not motivated by a need to cope with the presuppositional framework as substance making itself subject or as substance instantiated in the culture, but rather by a need to cope with the failure of culture and enculturation to serve as the ultimate matrix for presuppositions and thus as the unconditioned.[1] Despite the claims consciously made for the warranty for certainty through participation in culture and the general will, the individual found himself cut off from the general will in the very act of participation. The dialectical move to morality, then, is a move in which we leave "the demand to know itself as this specific point in the universal will," and instead come to know "this being which is enclosed within self-consciousness to be essence in its perfection and completeness" (*PhG*, 422; *PhS*, 363). Freedom is now not to be found in the general will as embodied in an institutional framework for a world which is, together with that self-consciousness, spirit. Absolute freedom becomes freedom which is action for the sake of duty legislated by an autonomous but universal will rooted in self-consciousness as spirit. Freedom determines truth.

This characterization of freedom in relation to truth is of some importance in understanding this moral manifestation of spirit as absolute standpoint. With the standpoint of culture and of the general will, one might say that truth determines freedom. Freedom comes through truth,

truth sets us free. The enlightened individuals are a free people; truth determines freedom. It is therefore not really paradoxical under this presupposition set to say that one must force people to be free; for individuals may resist the truth, i.e., they may resist the totality of utility which determines the general will as the absolute. There is a necessity, a necessity of truth, which informs this freedom. Freedom is in this sense action in accordance with necessity. But when, on the contrary, freedom determines truth, the heteronomy involved in forcing individuals to be free is from the beginning disallowed. Truth does not determine or constitute freedom; freedom determines or constitutes truth. What is presupposed in the latter case is freedom, the autonomy of the individual who gives to himself the universal law and acts not only in accordance with it, but also for the sake of it. Freedom is action for the sake of freedom: "for the sake of," i.e., purposively and not accidentally or as determined by forces other than freedom. The "causality of freedom" is immanently a teleological and not an efficient cause. A duty which is given to oneself for the sake of duty is a melding of freedom and necessity such that necessity disappears into freedom.[2]

The progress, then, from the general will as institutionally embodied but impotent in respect to the individual, to the universal will embodied in self-consciousness, is a progress which putatively eliminates the source of the failure of the societal general will to bring an effective totality for the individual and thus one which eliminates the failure actually to articulate an ultimate foundation and give warranted access to the totalizing of the totality. For the heteronomy of the institutionalized general will in respect to the individual is just what caused the alienation of the individual from the general will and invalidated the presupposition that the individual is to be defined as the general will. This is not to say that the general will as institutionalized was presupposed as heteronomous; to the contrary, it was supposed to give autonomy in liberty, equality, and fraternity. But the heteronomy was the dialectical result which led to the failure of this historically actual gestalt, a failure which we have now recalled and observed in the *Phenomenology*.[3]

It soon becomes evident, however, that this new form of spirit is not just another form of interest as reflection; for the object of knowledge is now not merely the life-form itself, but knowledge of this life-form. That is to say, the object is the moral law and the ground of that law which grants a basis for all actions enclosed within a self-consciousness. Here there is no true other, no remainder of a thing-in-itself which must be posited or accepted, and which must be differentiated from the self. Here we are in the realm of the thing-in-itself itself as effective subjectivity and end-in-itself. Here there is not a totality of mutually instrumental beings, but a kingdom of ends-in-themselves which cannot be governed by what is external to them. Knowledge and the certainty that comes with it is self-knowledge in the sense that the totality is *formed* by the knowledge of duty which is formed in the autonomous, free self-consciousness. We have the moral view of the world, the world *of* self-consciousness self-formed in terms of moral significance or what ought to be concerning what-is.[4]

In this moral point of view the world of effective actuality is the object of a dual thematization: (1) that of particulars, projects, events, etc., grounded in one's moral concern for the good and the right, and (2) that of the ground for the good and the right.[5] The self-conscious, spiritual individual thematizes his world as a totality in terms of the totalization made possible on moral grounds. It is this which makes the moral view of the world a high form of spirit and the mediation between pure, "objective" spirit—spirit as socio-political, cultural, and historical—and absolute spirit—spirit as religion and as philosophy. It is the point at which the subject-object is absolutized as subject, i.e., at which, literally, substance has become subject; for the moral *knowledge* of the world and the world as moral *object* is precisely the object or substance of the moral knowledge of that world.[6]

This closure of reflection such that one's object is just one's knowledge of objects (from the moral point of view), brings us to the point at which we can now articulate the experience of totality in respect to certainty, i.e., as something completely explicit in both the natural and the philosophical attitudes. In this move from *Bildung* to *Moralität*, the natural attitude itself experiences its own previous forms of knowing and putative certainty as in fact diremptive and therefore as involving a heteronomy of will even in those cases in which the individual attempted to take a view of things "for himself." That is to say, it quickly becomes apparent that any view other than the moral view as Kant understood it is really only a form of spirit akin to the subject-object as culture, or, if we take the ancient view, as custom or *Sittlichkeit*. What is meant here and what is at stake in the rejection of all other possible "moral" views, can be explained by looking at Kant's argument for the good will as the only thing good without qualification, and his attack on any and all forms of heteronomy of the individual will.[7]

The case against *Sittlichkeit* and the ancient view is clear: one's duties are on that view determined by nature and there arises the inescapable clash of duties whose attempted resolution in the legal concept of person only leads to the instantiation of culture as absolute subject-object. The individual has a certainty of himself and the world; but that certainty reduces to uncertainty. This natural heteronomy is surely destructive of the individual and precludes warranted certainty of access to reality through an absolute standpoint.[8]

The perfection of *Bildung*, on the other hand, introduces a putative subject-object in which all necessary presuppositions are to be contained and articulated in order for intelligibility and warranty of access to reality to be guaranteed. Furthermore, the "natural" origin of this absolute standpoint is now replaced by a standpoint of our own making; for the individual is himself constituted by the process of enculturation, while the world of culture itself is constituted by the individuals who participate in it. The most perfect articulation of this, as we saw, is a socio-historical formation informed by utilitarianism. The "moral" form of utilitarianism is derived from this view of spirit, and gives the individual as an individual his most intimate contact thus far with reality. The individual is at once subject (as one who makes his decisions in terms of utility via the general will) and object (as part of the determination of the general will). Utilitarianism thus combines the most radical form of atomistic individualism (where each individual's good is a determinant of "the good," and where each individual must himself embody the general will) with the most radical form of organicism (where the general will so formed is not a mere majority will, nor even a sum of all individual wills, but rather the will or direction objectively necessary for the fulfillment of all individuals involved). The individual is both an end-in-himself and a means to the ends of others.

However, since according to the spirit so embodied one is equally both end and means, and since hegemony is held by the individual neither as end nor as means, the individual is therefore necessarily torn apart and pulled in both directions. Alienation of the individual is the only possible outcome, whether it be in the form of a reign of terror or in some more "benign" form. Both the objective (society) and the subjective (individual) are forced into schizoid behavior. It is not that no decision can be made, no consistent view of the world held, but that antinomic decisions and views necessarily derive from the utilitarian view. Kant's attack on inclination and on individually determined forms of happiness, on the one hand, and his attack on the determination of right through reflection on consequences, on the other hand, is a two-pronged attack on this central problem of the highest form of culture, utilitarianism, and on its promise of absolute freedom. Both heteronomy and autonomy destroy each other on such a presupposition set, and this is the logic of the absolute terror: neither an order of the whole nor a liberty of the individual can be the unambiguous outcome.[9]

When, on the contrary, the moral point of view forms the absolute subject-object and one acts explicitly on the presuppositions contained in this view, the mutual destruction of autonomy and heteronomy ceases; for the pluralism of atomistic individualism and the means-relation between individuals, as well as the monism of organicism are replaced by the absolutism of duty as autonomously determined in a kingdom of ends which latter is neither monistic nor pluralistic. It offers us a combination in synthesis of the preceding forms of spirit, a combination which transforms each of the previous forms into a new unity of elements. There is immediacy, as in *Sittlichkeit,* but there is no original nature which fixes the individual. There is mediation, as in *Bildung,* faith, and enlightenment, but the alienation of those forms does not appear. In the moral point of view, self-consciousness

> is *immediately present* to itself in its [pure] substance for this is its knowledge, is the intuited pure certainty of itself; and just *this immediacy* which is its own reality, is all reality, for the immediate is *being* itself, and, as pure immediacy purified by absolute negativity, it is *being* in general, or *all* being (*PhG,* 424; *PhS,* 364).

Here we see not only the synthetic transcendence or *Aufgehobensein* of the prior development of spirit, but also an embodiment of the full complexity of the project of warranting certainty. Interest as reflection at this point brings explicitly to self-awareness the three other forms of interest, viz. intentionality, desire, and purpose. The first, which gives us the truth or limits of consciousness as a standpoint, is articulated in the moral presupposition that nature stands there before me, what it is in itself, something to be intended, but indifferent to the concerns of morality and of self-consciousness in general. The moral spirit contains the presupposition that what-is, is as it is, the given state of affairs. The world is other than I, other than my self-conscious desires and my purpose-laden reason. But, second, morality also involves the presupposition of self-consciousness and desire, such that the world is what it is for the desiring self-conscious individual. It is, as life in general, my life, and thus I transcend its indifference. And yet this transcendence does not destroy the indifference of the world to my desires. Third, the world is presupposed as a world appropriate to my actions, a world in which the carrying out of my duty is appropriate. And all three of these moments, as constitutive of the moral attitude itself, are preserved within any and all thoughts and actions committed under the rubric of the moral view. We can now articulate this intermingling and tension of the moral view of the world and lay the ground for the paradoxes of morality which issue from it.[10]

The issue is fully captured in the following passage, which is so central it merits extended citation. As stated above, the world is an otherness, and this

> otherness, because duty constitutes the sole aim and object of consciousness, is, on the one hand, a reality completely without significance for consciousness. But because this consciousness is so completely locked up within itself, it behaves with the perfect freedom and indifference towards this otherness; and therefore the existence of this otherness, on the other hand, is left completely free by self-consciousness, an existence that similarly is related only to itself. The freer self-consciousness becomes, the freer also is the negative object of its consciousness. The object has thus become a complete world within itself with an individuality of its own, a self-subsistent whole of laws peculiar to itself, as well as an independent operation of those laws, and a free realization of them—in general a *nature* whose laws like its actions belong to itself as a being which is indifferent to moral self-consciousness, just as the latter is indifferent to it.
>
> From this determination is developed a moral view of the world which consists in the relation between the absoluteness of morality and the absoluteness of nature. This relation is based, on the one hand, on the complete *indifference* and independence of nature towards moral purposes and activity, and, on the other hand, on the consciousness of duty alone as the essential fact and of nature as completely devoid of independence and essential being. The moral view of the world contains the development of the moments which are present in this relation of such completely conflicting presuppositions (*PhG*, 424–25; *PhS*, 365–66).

The whole of the Kantian analysis of morality is given or implied here: the tension between nature and morality as it re-emerges in the tension between happiness and moral duty; the rejection, for the sake of duty, of the contingencies of that indifferent nature; the incompleteness of absoluteness without the perfection of happiness in harmony with duty; the emergence of happiness on a level which makes of it a gift of grace. In the experience of morality, as well as in philosophical reflection upon it, these presuppositions are taken as presuppositions, as postulates which have become transparent to the individual whose thoughts and actions presuppose them.[11]

On the basis of this, the paradox of morality emerges.

> The harmony of morality and nature—or, since nature comes into account only in so far as consciousness experiences its unity with it—the harmony of morality and happiness, is *thought of* as something that necessarily *is*, i.e., it is *postu-*

lated. For to say that something is *demanded*, means that something is thought of in the form of *being* that is not yet actual—a necessity not of the *concept qua* concept but of *being*. But necessity is at the same time essentially relation based on the concept. The *being* that is demanded, then, is not the imagined being of a contingent consciousness, but is implied in the concept of morality itself, whose true content is the *unity* of the pure and the individual consciousness; it is for the latter to see that this unity be, *for it*, an actuality: in the *content* of the purpose this is happiness, but in its *form*, is existence in general. The existence thus demanded, i.e., the unity of both, is therefore not a wish nor, regarded as purpose, one whose attainment were still uncertain; it is rather a demand of reason, or an immediate certainty and presupposition of reason (*PhG*, 426–27; *PhS*, 367).

This is a valiant attempt on Hegel's part to articulate the dense nature of the *moral* "ought," where the latter involves *not descriptive* rules and laws, but *prescriptive* ones which have the import of the moral. But the problem is that the moral "ought" defies the distinction between description and prescription; for the former term involves a simple fact of being and is categorical, while the latter term is conditional and problematical (e.g., as in a practical "ought"). Rather, we have in the moral "ought" a striving for a unity which proceeds from the known and recognized antithesis of opposition of duty and indifferent nature, or of duty and sensuousness. That is to say, the opposition is experienced and thematized as not merely a thought opposition, but as a lived tension between the descriptive and the prescriptive. The actualization of the harmony of duty and sensuousness, or "ought" and "is," is a

> consummation [which] cannot be attained, but is to be thought merely as an *absolute* task, i.e., one which simply remains a task. Yet at the same time its content has to be thought of as something which simply must *be*, and must not remain a task . . . (*PhG*, 428; *PhS*, 368).

This is the paradox of morality; for the "ought" is to be satisfied and thereby bring about the disappearance of the "mere ought"; but at the same time, in order to be a moral matter and not a mere matter of actualized project and fact, it must remain an "ought".[12]

Moral consciousness itself reflects on this its predicament, and attempts to come to a certainty of itself on the basis of a resolution of the paradox and of the contradictions which constitute the form and content of moral consciousness. But there appears to be no possible resolution, since neither nature or sensuousness (the fact of what-is), nor moral duties (the ought within what-is) can be reduced to the other or be ignored; for in the abolition of either or even in the reduction of one to the other, the tension which gives meaningfulness to morality and distinguishes it from other modes of consciousness and states of affairs would be removed, thus removing the significance of this unique "ought".[13] In the end, the best that can be done in terms of this moral view of the world is to recognize the actual individual as morally imperfect, striving toward perfection, while that perfection or the highest good—the unity of happiness and duty—are realizable only in a supreme being (God) which at times bestows a perfection of sorts on imperfect mortals. Yet even this compromise is a dissemblance or dissolution of the reality of morality; for now either moral perfection is not taken seriously, since it is to reside in actuality only in God, or it is taken seriously, in which case we are led back to the original paradox and the simple truth that such a perfection in the actual world of spirit would only destroy morality itself.

The proffered resolution of this condition arises from a consideration of the fact that in the moral view of the world we have a turn toward the individual and the "subjective." The focus on both levels of thematics is therefore not the only unique feature of this mode of spirit; for now this unification of thematics, the proximate unity of philosophy and the natural attitude, is found in a *knowledge* of duty which is at the same time *praxis* explicitly informed by that knowledge.[14] There is no mere instinct of reason, nor a more explicit, but still partly implicit natural or enculturated and habituated action; rather, there is a deliberate and fully self-conscious praxis which is *antinomical* at its very heart. The individual himself realizes that nothing, not even the presupposition and postulation of a perfect being, can save him from the contradictory nature of himself and his world, a world of which he has become aware, not only in thought, but also in action explicitly informed by this thought. Under this presupposition set constituting the moral view of the world, we must understand our praxis as a "syncretism," a flagrant compromise which "collapses internally" (*PhG*, 442–43; *PhS*, 382). But this collapse generates in self-consciousness itself the totalizing activity of *conscience* (*Gewissen*), a presupposition of totality which brings the antinomies into a resolution by accepting them for precisely what they are.

In this move of the *Phenomenology*, which we see is made by spirit itself in the form of the moral view of the world, we first bring together the antinomies of the moral view of the world. The dependency on a perfect harmony residing within a perfect being who is beyond us is rejected, and the contradictions of the moral point of view are embraced for one's own nature. The individual self-consciousness resolves to act from duty and under the aegis of the moral ought in spite of the paradoxes and however entangled its connotations are; for self-consciousness surmounts the antinomy precisely by grasping it as definitive of the moral relationship it has to what-is. There is no need to postulate a perfect consciousness beyond reality which harmonizes in some inexplicable way the antitheses; moral self-consciousness itself does this by accepting the antinomic nature of morality *as the truth*. The "moral view of the world" as the idea that only a beyond can mysteriously synthesize or resolve the paradox is abandoned for the moral stance of conscience: the center and ground of warranted certainty is the praxis of the individual himself.

> Self-consciousness, *for us* or *in itself*, retreats into itself, and is aware that that being is its own self, in which what is actual is at the same time pure knowing and pure duty. It is itself in its contingency completely valid in its own sight, and knows its immediate individuality to be pure knowing and doing, to be the true reality and harmony (*PhG*, 445; *PhS*, 384).

This conscientious attitude, a new embodiment of spirit, is

> a pure conscience which rejects with scorn such a moral idea of the world; it is in its own self the simple spirit that, certain of itself, acts conscientiously regardless of such ideas, and in this immediacy posseses its truth (*PhG*, 444; *PhS*, 383).[15]

In the stance of conscience, one acts explicitly on the basis of one's duty and one's duties. The conscientious actor gives the content given him a form informed by duty as different from and opposed to what-is as fact, "nature," or sensuousness. The given as already having been formed is transformed in accordance with the dictate of duty, and thereby recognized not as having displaced the naturally given, but as coexisting and in opposition to it. The totality of which we claim certainty contains an opposition in which the individual does not simply or merely resist the given as given, but accepts it and at the same time insists on reforming it in accordance with duty.[16] Not only is there content to spirit which is identical to the *self*-certainty of self-consciousness—a real or actual unity of what was merely *to be* the totality of the general will embodied in the state, and of what was merely *to be* the totality of the moral view which ambiguously existed in the individual and in God; this conscience as immediate knowledge of duty is, in its actions, itself the existence of self-consciousness.

In order to understand this, a further articulation of the presuppositions and structure of spirit as conscience is necessary. In the following passage is contained the most profound, and yet most unstable articulation of the quest for certainty as it is embodied in conscientious action. We find that since the separation of the in-itself and the self has been done away with, a case of moral action is, in the sense-*certainty* of knowing, directly as it is *in itself*, and it is *in itself* only in the way that it is in this knowing. Action *qua* actualization is thus the pure form of will—the simple conversion of a reality that merely *is* into a reality that results from *action*, the conversion of the bare mode of *objective* knowing, [i.e., knowing an object as an object], into one of knowing *reality* as something produced by consciousness. Just as sense-certainty is immediately taken up, or rather, converted, into the in-itself of spirit, so this conversion, too, is simple and unmediated, a transition effected by the pure concept without alteration of the content, the content being determined by the interest of the consciousness knowing it (*PhG*, 447; *PhS*, 385).

Spirit as conscience is not mere thought, not mere structure or form, but action (*das Handeln*) which both does and is aware of doing this action as a way of converting a mere knowledge of reality as given into a knowledge of reality as made by the individual in his actions. Morality thus shows itself to be true spirit and not an abstract, separated knowing of the world; for *morality in its truth as conscience is simultaneously a knowing of the world as given separately from the individual's actions and a knowing of the world as transformed by the individual's own actions and thus as held in the totality of subject-object in an absolute sense*. Furthermore, the totalizing activity of the individual is not separate from the totality as a utility-bound general will, but is identical with the totality itself. And it is in praxis or such deliberate, self-conscious action that the totality and totalizing co-exist. Knowing and acting are not separate in the mode of conscience, but together in the act. On the other hand, the contradictions heretofore evidenced are not absent; for moral spirit, "by retreating into itself, will not become anything different" (*PhG*, 444; *PhS*, 383). Yet there is no deception, no dissemblance, but a living in the heart of the contradiction and paradox, i.e., an action which brings freedom and necessity together in an act. One is committed to duty and acts on duty.[17] Moreover, the praxical presuppositions implicit in this mode of being are themselves thematized in the action of the conscientious individual.

Of even greater significance is the fact that here, in the presupposition set of conscience, sense-certainty, the most simple and in that way most authentic form of the natural attitude, has reappeared. *Conscience marks the unity of sense-certainty*—immediate certainty of the world which is there as immediately given—*with certainty of self*—immediate certainty of self as authentically belonging to and mediating that immediately given world in accordance with duty.[18] Conscience is a mode of being and a mode of knowing in which the individual surpasses the contradictory nature of duty and reality in relation to each other. That is to say, one who acts from conscience acts from the simple conviction of a duty which is not "pure" or abstract duty, separated from the reality which confronts it, but rather is the duty to which the individual is committed and on the basis of which he acts, simultaneously accepting reality for what it is and resolving to change it through his committed action. This duty is actual, effective duty, not pure duty.[19]

Moral self-consciousness which is conscience—and conscience that informs praxis—is an absolute form: a knowing which presupposes immediate access to reality as did the initial sense-certainty, and a knowing which also presupposes that action committed on the basis of this knowing is valid action when informed by duty. The validity-claims of this form of knowing are based upon a totalizing activity which is conscience-directed-praxis. There is no ambiguity for such a knowledge and for such an acting spirit; for the very praxis which is informed by conscience is an immediate verification of one's knowledge of reality. Knowing and acting, theory and practice, are in no way separated, in no way problematic from within this attitude of the individual. In this way, certainty has ceased to be problematic; for conscience, and action directed by conscience, are precisely the presupposition and conscious conviction that certainty is inherent in conscientious action. The very nature of conscience explicitly denies any separation of theory from practice: I do what is right, period. Thus any question of the relationship between theory and practice is effaced; for theory and practice are now identical.[20] This identity is what constitutes the identity of self-certainty and sense-certainty, of certainty of self and certainty of world. This point in the journey of the *Phenomenology of Spirit* is, then, a point at which the individual of the most naive, natural attitude of sense-certainty has been shown that, on the grounds of the initial problem of sense-certainty, there is a reflectively absolute standpoint within him. He in fact not only points to houses and to trees, but builds the former and cuts down the latter, and does so with the conviction—the immediate conviction—that he is right in doing so, that this is the way the world *ought to be*. He both accepts the world immediately and shapes that world in accordance with duty, thus accepting the world also as mediation of self and world. The actions of the conscientious actor are the actualization of his natural certainty.[21]

But to end here would be to end in solipsism; and solipsism shows itself, on the basis of the principle of conscience itself, to be impossible as our ultimate, absolute access to reality. To stop here would be to recognize an absolute insularity of each conscientious actor; but that entails also the recognition of a relativity of conscience; for if each conscience is absolute, then there are as many absolutes as there are consciences, and as many consciences as there are conceptions of duty.[22] Thus, we must now further analyze the presupposition set of conscience and see how conscience, as absolute standpoint, is led out of an apparent solipsism and the consequent relativism of an appeal to an individual conscience alone. This analysis, which reflects only the historical working of spirit itself, brings again to our attention the central position of language as the existence of spirit (*das Dasein des Geistes*), and leads us to absolute spirit as religion.[23]

The analysis begins with the recognition and presupposition on the part of conscientious praxis that one's activities are an aspect of being. Thus, the conscientious act becomes a given both for the actor and for others who also act from conscience and thus in terms of the same principle, the same universal. This leads to an apparent problem; for

> in that this right thing which conscience does is at the same time a *being-for-another*, it seems that a disparity attaches to conscience. The duty that it fulfills is a *specific* content; it is true that this content is the *self* of consciousness, and so consciousness's *knowledge* of itself, its *identity* with itself. But once fulfilled, set in the medium of *being*, this identity is no longer knowing, no longer this process of differentiation in which its differences are at the same time immediately superseded; on the contrary, in *being*, the difference is established as an *enduring* difference, and the action is a *specific* action, not identical with the element of everyone's self-consciousness, and therefore not necessarily acknowledged (*PhG*, 456–57; *PhS*, 394).

That is to say, according to the principle of conscience, conscience is at the basis not only of one's own knowledge and action, but at the basis of all true, adequate, appropriate knowledge and action, the ultimate basis for warranty for claims of access to actuality for anyone. Thus the other individuals, for whom the act of a conscientiously acting individual is a fact of being, a fact to be taken into account and conscientiously responded to, are at one and the same time under the same principle, but have necessarily to make their actions in accordance with their own consciences. In short, there appears to be, within the universality of conscience, a relativity of consciences.

> Both sides, the conscience that acts and the universal consciousness that acknowledges this action as duty [i.e., both the actor as actor under the principle of conscience, and all others who judge and respond to the original act on the basis of the principle of conscience], are equally free from the spec-

ificity of this action. On account of this freedom, their relationship in the common medium of their connection is really a relation of complete disparity, as a result of which the consciousness which is explicitly aware of the action finds itself in a state of complete *uncertainty* about the spirit which does the action and is certain of itself (PhG, 457; PhS, 394).

The kingdom of conscientious actors is a kingdom of ends in themselves for whom being is also given and is to be a matrix for interaction with themselves as ends, rather than as means. The action of the actor who, in his intentions, conscientiously carried out the act, is to the others simply an act, a fact to be taken account of. Thus, a relativity of conscience is recognized as precisely the meaning of the universality of conscience. As in sense-certainty it was discovered that "now" and "here" is a complexus of "nows" and "heres," so too the universality of the principle of conscience and the factical unity of thought, action, and being is found to be a complexus of unities of thought, action, and being. Consciences are in conflict on the basis of their own principle and their own claim to universality.

The individual has all of this for presupposition, but also thematizes this plurality of consciences within the unity of the principle of conscience itself.[24] Each conscience acts conscientiously toward the conscientious acts of others in awareness of the absoluteness of this other in express disjunction. What is important here is not that one act is absorbed into another self through judgment; that sets up only the dialectic of the independence and dependence of self-consciousness. Nor is it important that some act exists which I must engage on my own terms, in terms of my own desires, interests, etc. What is important is that the act is an act of conscience carried out by another conscientious being.

> What is to be valid, and to be recognized as duty, is so only through the knowledge and conviction that it *is* duty, through the knowledge of oneself in the deed. If the deed ceases to have this self within it, it ceases to be that which alone is its essence. Its existence, forsaken by this consciousness, would be an ordinary reality, and the action would appear to us to be the fulfilling on one's pleasure and desire. What ought *to be there* [*Was* da sein *soll*], is here an essentiality solely by its *being known* to be the self-expression of an individuality; and it is this *being known* that is acknowledged by others, and which as such ought to have *existence* [Dasein *haben soll*] (PhG, 457–58; PhS, 395).

This is not knowledge whose interest or stance is in the form of desire and a world of objects and of other desiring beings; it is a knowledge whose interest is in the form of reflection, in the form of an explicit knowledge of the praxical presuppositions which hold the individuals and the world together in a unity or totality of ultimate intelligibility. The point is that the act itself, simply as an act, would not serve to differentiate it as an act of conscience from an act of desire, at least so far as others are concerned with my action. The possible confusion of an act of conscience with an act of desire introduces to us the centrality of language as praxis of a special kind. The act must be identified through speech as an act of conscience, and thereby be placed under special consideration by all others in this community of conscientious actors.[25]

> Here, again, then, we see *language as the existence of spirit* [*Wir sehen hiemit wieder die Sprache als das Dasein des Geistes*]. Language is self-consciousness existing *for others*, self-consciousness which *as such* is immediately *present* and as this self-consciousness is universal. It is the self that separates itself from itself, which as pure "I = I" becomes objective to itself, and which in this objectivity equally preserves itself as *this* self, just as it coalesces directly with other selves and is *their* self-consciousness. It perceives itself just as it is perceived by others, and the perceiving is just this *existence which has become a self* [*das zum Selbst gewordne Dasein*] (*PhG*, 458; *PhS*, 395).

After reminding us of the earlier claims about language as *essentially performative*, and as only derivatively descriptive, emotive, etc., Hegel continues this specification of the authentic existence of moral spirit as conscience rooted in the praxis of language.

> Language . . . emerges as the middle term, mediating between independent and acknowledged self-consciousness; and the *existent self* is immediately universal acknowledgement, an acknowledgement on the part of many, and in this manifoldness a simple acknowledgement. . . . Consciousness declares its *conviction*; it is in this conviction alone that the action is a duty; also it is valid as duty solely through the conviction being *declared*. For universal self-consciousness is free from the specific *action* that merely *is*; what is valid for that self-consciousness is not the *action* as an *existence*, but the *conviction* that it is a duty; and this is made actual in language. To make the deed a reality does not mean here translating its content from the form of *purpose* or *being-for-self* into the form of an *abstract* reality; it means translating it from the form of immediate self-*certainty*, which knows its knowledge or being-for-self to be essential being, into the form of an *assurance* that consciousness is convinced of its duty and, as

conscience, knows *in its own mind* what duty is (*PhG*, 458–59; *PhS*, 396). In calling itself *conscience*, it calls itself pure knowledge of itself and pure willing, i.e., it calls itself a universal knowing and willing which recognizes and acknowledges others, is the same as them—for they are just this pure self-knowing and willing—and which for that reason is also recognized and acknowledged by *them* (*PhG*, 460; *PhS*, 397).

My extensive quoting of Hegel here is justified because of the central position of the passage in respect to the overall project of the *Phenomenology*. This is the place at which the absolute standpoint is first made possible. The point is this: it is only when the act is specified as an act of conscience that it counts as such, that it can be distinguished from the act of a person motivated simply by desire. The interest here is not desire, not the eros for the satisfaction of desire and a consequent determination of the world, including other self-consciousnesses, as objects of desire. Nor is the act itself of any particular significance. Such interest in acts ends in the impossibility of the unhappy consciousness and the irremediable split between infinitude and finitude, between completeness and universality and incompleteness and particularity. In the case of interest as reflection, however, and in particular where reflection takes the form of conscience and conscientious praxis which is articulated and given definite existence in language, the schism inherent in self-consciousness as an ultimate foundation is replaced by a *community*, i.e., by a wholeness and universality. And the essential change is not to be found in the dumb or silent action, but in the action articulated in language. In moral praxis articulated as conscientious, the expressed conviction identifies the act and the actor for what they are: they belong to *me* as committed to responsiblity for an act based on conscience. This utterance brings about a universal recognition of that act as essentially an act of conscience, an act which unites the actor with the community of ends or consciences which must take account, as ends-in-themselves, of the particular act now universalized in conscientious action. *Language here gives us the concrete unity of particular and universal, of individual and community.* Neither individual nor universal are perverted or lost in a reductionism. My utterance of conviction of duty at one and the same time identifies me as responsible in particular, as grounding my responsibility in the universality of conscience, and identifies others as linked to that responsibility and ground. I am I as a member of the community of ends in themselves; but that community is not a general will that stands over against my specific will. Rather, that community is equally grounded in my conviction of the absoluteness of conscience.[26]

This universalization through language and the specificity of each conscientious act together constitute the conflict of universal and particular which now comes to our attention. Moreover, the matters of conscience cannot be considered simply knowledge, but must be considered as actions. Thus, each individual must act and must announce his action as stemming from conscience. This universalizes the action and lays it open to the judgments of other conscientious individuals who must judge it from their own bases in conscience. On the one hand, the act must be recognized as a duty; for to deny this would be to deny conscience as totality and thus pervert one's own judgment. On the other hand, it is only a particular act and can be considered simply as the actor's own judgment of conscience and possibly tied up with his own particular interests. It is notorious that the conscience of one and the conscience of another are not the same and do not necessarily make the same judgments about what is justified conscientiously. And when in disagreement each must, by the very nature of conscience, be judged by the other as wrong and evil. But to do this is to deny the universal validity of conscience and thus the justificatory ground for the conscientious judgment of the act of the other. Each must therefore recognize itself and the other as caught up in this *paradox of evil*: conscience as absolute is relative.[27]

One cannot have it both ways: either one accepts conscience as the universal ground which defines right and gives one access to reality, or one denies it. If one denies it, then we regress to some earlier stand and eventually must end up here again. On the other hand, if one accepts it, then one has this paradox: if conscience is absolute, and individuals who act out of conscience differ in their conscientious judgment over the same matter, then conscience as absolute is relative. But it is not possible to single out only one conscience, or only conscientious individuals who agree with oneself, as proper conscience. Conscience is either a universal ground or it is not; it either gives one access to the absolute standpoint, or it does not.

Reminiscent of the move from unhappy consciousness to reason, there is now a move from moral spirit as conscience to religion. The reflection, both on the part of the natural attitude and on the part of philosophy, is simple and straightforward. In the community of ends, in the community of conscience, we must mutually recognize each other as mutually good and mutually evil, as standing in the absolute standpoint, and yet as finite and limited in that standpoint.[28] Interest as reflection is turned upon itself as a paradox, and in that turning the "word of reconciliation" (*das Wort der Versöhnung*) passes between individuals in this community. There emerges a new totality, a new unity, the absolute standpoint.

> The word of reconciliation is [of itself] the *objectively existent* spirit [*der daseiende Geist*], which beholds the pure knowl-

edge of itself *qua universal* essence, in its opposite, in the pure knowledge of itself *qua* absolutely self-contained and exclusive *individuality*—a reciprocal recognition which is *absolute spirit* (*PhG*, 471; *PhS*, 408).[29]

The community of finite individuals, grounded in conscience but nevertheless finite and only attempting to participate in that universal ground, comes into being by mutual recognition of each other's attempts. The community gains existence and concreteness through language, the word of reconciliation, the recognition of finitude. The religious community is born in the community of conscientious actors and conscientious judges, reflectively oriented toward the absolute standpoint by their quest for that standpoint.[30]

Here there is given a definition of absolute spirit which identifies it, not as some transcendent power or force, but as the interaction of individual, finite human beings in their explicit recognition of their finitude and their bond to each other through interest as reflection. It is important to be very clear about this form of spirit which makes itself manifest to itself as absolute spirit; for given the contradiction and tension and connection to the finitude of our existence, and given this as the emergence of the absolute standpoint as it will now develop, contradiction is not to be removed from the *Logic* and from the system which is to follow from within this absolute standpoint. Whatever course our inquiry might take in the process of the exploration of religion and philosophy, therefore, this rootedness in and identity with the real finite individuals who have been seeking warranty for their professed certainty of access to reality is never to be denied.[31]

There are two sides to the issue: the side of action in conscience and the side of conscientious judgment. The stand of conscience which is not sequestered within itself as silence but which informs the action of the individual and is clearly articulated by him through language, is a stance or mode of being in which both the individual and the world are held together in a unity of knowledge and action, of totality and totalizing process. The individual is certain of himself and of his understanding of the world, and professes that certainty, because he acts from duty, i.e., from a knowledge of what is right and true. But he not only professes that certainty of his knowledge; he gives warranty for it by acting on his knowledge, by objectifying himself, by making himself a fact in the world in terms of his knowledge of that world. The individual demonstrates his warranty for his professed certainty by staking himself on the conscientious actions which he performs. In his act of independence he risks himself completely. But in so doing, he is both object and subject of his knowledge and action, bound up in a unity of his own making, and which he announces to all is a unity of his own making. However, this unity, because conscience has claim to universality, is not simply something of his own making in any merely subjective sense; rather, the claim, staked and risked, is that his conscience is in harmony with the truth of the world. Therefore, from the side of the actor himself, there is a *prima facie* warranty for a claim of access to reality and truth, an access which is self-grounding, itself absolute because the presuppositions of the act are at the same time an explicit aspect of the act, namely the principles given objective existence in language.

But there is for that reason the other side, the side of recognition by other conscientious individuals. In judging the act of the agent, the other individuals must remain true to their consciences and at the same time recognize the universality of the conscientious act and agent which confronts them as well as the authentic individuality of that actor and his act. In this act of recognizing the other in these two ways—a mutual act of recognition and a judgment—the community of conscience is recognized for what it is: a community of finite individuals who act from a conviction of conscience and thus participate in the community which has as its chief characteristic just the universality of conscience.[32] It is important to remember that we are here talking not about theory or ideals of conscience never carried into action; we are talking about a world of active, committed individuals who form and are formed by spirit, and whose knowledge of that formation of and dependency upon spirit is in the form of conscience. It is a world both made by and known by the individuals involved in the knowing and making. Furthermore, the individuals are on the other hand but members of that collectivity of individualized actions, a collectivity which therefore forms the arena, the ground for their actions. There is here the immediate but full intuition of the nature of spirit by spirit itself, i.e., both by the finite individuals who constitute and are constituted by spirit, and by that spirit itself in the form of the ground of conscience recognized by all of the individuals, a ground which both constitutes and is constituted by the individuals. The existence of this spirit in its concrete form is, first of all, religion and the religious community as a self-recognizing community.

What gives absoluteness to this form of spirit—or, rather, what makes this form of spirit the point of appearance of absolute spirit—is the total explicitness of the praxical presuppositions of existence as such. Each of the individuals in the community of conscientious persons is the concept itself precisely because one thematizes reality not only on the basis of the presupposition of conscience, but also directly as that presupposition set itself.[33] The acts of the individual are universalized as conscientious acts in a world immediately accessible to conscience. The act is also individual, i.e., not an act which encompasses the whole of that world, but only an aspect of it. The act is for just that reason a true act of conscience; for it creates an aspect of the world conscientiously formed which is in natural harmony with that world. That is to say, the individual act has the universal for its essence. There is therefore an identity between the individual conscientious act and the infinite universality of conscience.

But this identity of the particular and the universal in the conscientious individual is not an identity in which difference disappears or in which the difference is effaced between the universality of conscience as spirit and the particularity of the constituting and constituted acts. For the very reality of the community of conscience has arisen out of the mutual recognition of finitude, limitedness, and thus of what is called "evil" and "sin." The concepts, embodied as the respective particular individuals acting and judging, are absolutely different from each other precisely because they stand in relation to each other within the element of the pure concept or, in other terms, because each conscience stands within the element of conscience as the community or bond between them. The very continuity and bond between the individuals is constituted and articulated as their discreteness, both in their separation from each other and in their separation from the totality which they constitute and on the grounds of which they are constituted as members of the community.[34]

We have here, then, neither a totality in which the individual is lost, as in the general will of the French Revolution, nor a totality from which he is separated, as in the simple moral point of view. Intelligibility is granted within this new totality such that both the finitude of the individual actions and judgments, and their express unity within the infinitude of conscience as universal presupposition, is comprehended in a tension. This tension does not destroy intelligibility; for it is expressly recognized for what it is: it is neither shunted to a beyond which is never to be reached, nor simply objectified in a will which separates itself from the individual wills. In the recognition of conscience and in the forgiveness of finitude, there is at once a reconciliation of individualities condemned to finite acts, and an acknowledgement of the absoluteness of that finitude in spite of the reconciliation. There is true community in conscience despite the differences, a community which is neither destiny, nor a general will, nor an ideal realization of morality, but rather a commitment to our real, historical, finite being.[35]

In a real sense, now, we have reached the point at which the *Phenomenology of Spirit* has been aiming: to show the individual in the natural attitude (1) that the absolute standpoint is virtually within him, even in his most naive, unreflective mode of being, and (2) that the natural certainty which belongs to this natural, naive attitude toward things is actualized in the absolute standpoint. We have now reached a first approximation to an ultimacy of experience, i.e., to the absolute or ultimate ground of all experience as experience. I argued at the beginning of the present work that Hegel's project differed from the projects of his predecessors in at least one way, namely that he would not attempt to bring one in the natural attitude "out of" or "away from" that attitude, that he would not attempt to cause a rejection of the natural attitude for the sake of a "higher" understanding, but, rather, that he would have as his project this demonstration of the absolute within the very limits of the natural attitude. This meant that transcendence of ordinary experience in the sense of rejecting it, or leaving it behind, or relegating it to a position of confusion or illusion and mere appearance, was itself to be rejected. And yet the resultant knowledge was to be significantly different from that with which the naive natural attitude began.

In reality, we have never left behind the thematizations of the natural attitude; to the contrary, we have experienced an enrichment of them, journeying from the most unreflective, indiscriminate articulations of naive sense-certainty, through various modes of consciousness to self-conscious desire, then through the purposive activity of rational inquiry, and finally to the thematizations of concretely historical persons dwelling within and constituting the institutional-societal frameworks in which their praxical presuppositions were embedded as institutional facts. In the examination of morality we have experienced our finite existence in its profound concern for the question of the meaning of existence, and in its consequent natural quest for certainty.[36]

Religion is the community of conscience which both constitutes and is constituted by the individual consciences in quest of the absolute standpoint and for absolute certainty in community. Religion is the concrete, objective existence of this community as thematized in the natural attitude of the religious person.

> The reconciling *Yea*, in which the two "I's" let go their opposed *existence*, is the *existence* of the "I" which has expanded into a duality, and wherein remains identical with itself, and, in its complete externalization and opposite, possesses the certainty of itself: it is God manifested in the midst of those who know themselves in the form of pure knowledge (*PhG*, 472; *PhS*, 409).

Religion is the complexus of being and knowledge and action which forms the real, as opposed to the ideal unity of conscience, and thus which unites the discrete individuals, discontinuous with each other, and joins them in their actions with the totality of actuality. One who acts in the knowledge given by religion, acts in unity with the totality.

X

Interest As Reflection: Absolute Spirit

OUR REFLECTION on the nature of our existence as a community of conscientious actors permits both us, and the age to which Hegel belonged, to capture the meaning and significance of religion for our quest for certainty.[1] We shall again involve ourselves with an historical reflection, this time not with forms which spirit has taken in various sociopolitical formations, but with those taken in an absolute form and bound up with reflection on the "divine." This recollection of the series of religious forms of spirit as absolute will bring us to a comprehension of absolute spirit in our own day, i.e., in the Europe of Hegel's time, and hence to the end of our quest for certainty. Again, as earlier in the retracing of objective forms of spirit, we shall come to know our own substance by attending to its genesis through history.

But before entering into our analysis of this new mode of interest as reflection, we must undertake a preliminary analysis of religion as a community, and thus distinguish it from earlier appearances of religion in which there was only consciousness *of* absolute being, i.e., appearances of religion entertained as a standpoint conscious of absolute being as an object, rather than conscious of being absolute being itself. We examined, sequentially, the supersensible or inner side of objective existence which was intended by the understanding in its quest to found the absolute standpoint through consciousness alone, then the unhappy consciousness in its struggle to be the unchangeable consciousness with a full grasp of both changeable consciousness and unchangeable consciousness as well as of both changeable and unchangeable being itself; then followed recollections of the underworld and fate found in the spirit of the Greeks, the supersensible beyond of the religion of the enlightenment, and the God of the moral view of the world. In each case, however, we had not reached authentic religion, for absolute being was only an object of consciousness, separate from consciousness, spirit conceived of as object. In the present situation which derives from a self-grasp of conscience by itself and by us, on the other hand, that separation is removed, and we have spirit which is solely object of itself.

However, in each of the former, incomplete cases of religion an attempt was nevertheless made to represent the encompassing, the ultimate ground, the totality of all totalities, and insofar it was religion. But in each case

227

this totality was presupposed as transcendent to the finite life of the individuals, and this transcendence of the infinite in respect to the finite is just what marks the incompleteness, the mere standpoint of consciousness of the absolute rather than of absolute spirit as it is now open to *us* as a result of our realization of the meaning of conscience. In other words, one always previously stood some place other than the absolute and had, for that reason, not achieved the absolute standpoint. The word of reconciliation brought about within a community of conscientious actors, however, and the consequent recognition of community as the infinitude within a realm of the finite, gives us the possibility of comprehending the *immanence of the infinite* in respect to the finite, as well as the *immanence of the finite* in respect to the infinite.[2]

We now realize that spirit recognizes itself in reconciliation as self-constituting, and that religion is the representation of that self-constituting activity which is spirit. Thus, religion is *not only* a reification of relations, a projection of the concrete nature of human existence as spirit; rather it is that *and more*. In mere reification there is falsehood, false consciousness, a transposition of the here and now to another realm, while in spirit as absolute spirit this objectification involves immanence and recognition of our participation in the here and now as part of what is objectified. Spirit comprehends and re-presents spirit: spirit is here self-knowledge. That is to say, the movement which is revealed to conscience as authentic interaction of conscientious individuals in their finitude is now objectified and represented as *divine*. And this representation is, in effect, the positing and recognition of the fundamental praxical presuppositions which structure and make possible the possible worlds thematized in the natural attitude. The divine is the ground and substance in which we all find selfhood; and that selfhood is real only as participating in the divine, just as the conscientious individual is real only as participating in the community of conscientious actors.[3]

But this representation has, so to speak, a price; for it demands that there be a consciousness of this representation as well as a self-consciousness of acting conscientiously in the world as an actor in the community certain of itself and of its community. There again emerges a duality here: *consciousness* of the objective existence of the absolute *as represented*; and *self-consciousness* of oneself as acting in terms of the divine *as represented, but as real and existing in the conscientious acts*. This new division between consciousness (in religion *per se*) and self-consciousness (in that activity which religion represents or in the actual world of everyday thematization) is a phenomenon within absolute spirit or spirit's self-comprehension, a phenomenon of division which as yet has to be overcome if one is to claim with warranty final access to the absolute standpoint. For the unity of the two must overcome the difference implicit in mere representation as opposed to concrete instantiation in the everyday. The divine and the human must be brought together; otherwise mystery still holds some right over comprehension.[4]

In spite of the division still to be overcome, however, this is a significantly different schism between the finite and the infinite than has appeared before in the *Phenomenology*; for now the only thing that one is conscious of is self-consciousness as one's own finite participation in and constitution of the infinite. Consciousness does not now involve the thematization of some object in the world, or even of the presuppositions of existence as objectified in objective spirit; it involves the thematization of thematization itself, the general foundations on the basis of which there is totality and intelligibility *in general*. *The self-certainty of act* and *the sense-certainty of the world in which I act* are now united in a deliberate, explicit quest for absolute certainty of the absolute. The difference between this form of spiritual interest as reflection and previous forms, then, is that what is at issue here is precisely the relationship between the self-consciousness of one's own spiritual activity as the existing reality of actions of finite individuals and, on the other hand, the consciousness of that existing reality as represented. What is at issue is the relationship between the real activity of human beings as on-going and temporal, i.e., the differentiated unity recognized in the community of finite, conscientious individuals—the diachronic—and that unity when focused upon as absoute and as the object of consciousness—the synchronic. Put in still other terms, the stance to which we come in religion is one in which the focus is not simply on the principle of synchrony which constitutes the locus of intelligibility as a totality, but (1) the recognition that there is a principle of synchrony which is precisely the unity of diachrony, and (2) the recognition that the unity of synchrony and diachrony, of being and history, does not efface the diachronous, but is precisely constituted by it. Of course, being and history are not always explicitly the focus: the religions of nature, for instance, have no sense of history, and thus no sense of being as opposed to history. But in so far as history and being can be paradigmatic for diachrony and synchrony, it is proper to see it in this way.[5]

The question of the "evolutionary progress" of religion is a question of the perfection or degree of perfection with which the historical and the ontological, the diachronous and the synchronous, the existential (real spirit) and the absolutely reflective (reflection within and on the divine and its unity with the existential) is accomplished. Since as we now see the existential, historical, real spirit is self-consciously active in its historical community, the criterion of progress in absolute spirit becomes the degree to which self-consciousness as spirit infuses within itself the synchronous or divine, and the mode of spirituality of the divine. The criterion of completeness is one of achieving a unity of the community of self-conscious, conscientious actors with the divine itself. As we move from divinity as Light to the Christian Holy Spirit as element of the trinitarian divinity, we move from a relatively pure immediacy of the spiritual in the divine to a fully mediated spiritual being which is a perfect articulation of the existing spirit (*daseiende Geist*) as a community of conscientious actors grounded in their own being as actors. In the end, full interpenetration of the two dimensions of absolute spirit is accomplished; there is an immanence such that the internal articulation of difference between synchrony and diachrony is fully present and preserved within both the diachronous and the synchronous. The transcendent divine or absolute spirit—transcendent only with respect to the narrow sense of the finitude of each distinct moment of active spirit—will be understood in such a way that it is immanent in the active spirit even in its finitude; the self-transcending of the diachronous and finite active spirit will come to constitute the very infinitude of the absolute, divine spirit.[6] But this can best be understood by turning to the actual recollection and analysis of the progress of absolute spirit through history, a recollection which we now undertake in the *Phenomenology*.

The first group of religions to which we turn are called "religions of nature"; they are not natural religions, but religions which represent the divine through some aspect of nature.[7] In the conception of the divine as "light," we have light as the subject or divine "I" which is the simple "penetration of all thought and all reality" (*PhG*, 483; *PhS*, 419). This divine subject "externalizes itself" in the emanation of the light, diffusing itself by its own power and giving birth to all, while at the same time making it possible for all to be visible, to be seen, to be known. We here catch the essence of much "primitive" religion. Nature in general, the forest, the mountains, the sea, the sun and moon, light—in whatever way appropriate to the people involved—are at one and the same time a clear representation *for* consciousness of the very spirit which they are *in* their reality and their reality and actuality. Here we cut through the *supposed* superstition which western thought and religion often attribute to such representations and now assign to these religions and their divine powers their authentic significance. If one lives in, depends upon, finds subsistence in, and must survive through a forest or jungle, then to call one's divinity by the name for forest or jungle is the most rational, appropriate move conceivable. The totems and other factors of such religions, as we now know, constitute a complete and rational representation of the basic praxical presuppositions which make possible and unite the existence of a people. The forest of a forest people is the subject and substance, the totality of the life-world in which the individuals live out their lives; as such it transcends them, being in existence before and continuing after them, and surpassing any finite possibility of comprehension. But at the same time, the people are participants in the forest, responsible for it and to it, constitutive, together with other beings, of the totality of that forest; as such it is immanent in them, constituted in part by their own self-transcending. Through "light," "plant," and "animal," we trace this most pervasive of all forms of religion, i.e., of reflection as absolute spirit. Whether the one spirit of nature or the many spirits which inhabit nature, the general form is the same.

In the next stage of the religion of nature—religion of the artificer—we see language again appear as the *Dasein* of spirit; for in the hieroglyph—which transforms the representation of nature in its various forms into thought as pictograms in the hieroglyphic writings and inscriptions—and in the sacred buildings and architecture—which transform stone and wood into symbolic monuments and thus into spirit—we find the place in which "spirit meets spirit," in which the artificer meets himself as simultaneously creator and representor of and participant in the holy. But this language of architecture and hieroglyphics is dumb, silent, still not a living speech which would present us with the existence of spirit as it itself is constituted in the word of reconciliation. Nevertheless, it is important that in such religion through architecture and hieroglyphics, thought and being are brought into a unity of sorts. When ritual is combined with this physical form of religion, we come through representative actions to a further and more complete form of religion; for the individuals participating present their own actions as participant in that "divine time" of origins.

From this, it is conceptually a short step to religion in the form of art, the religion of the Greeks.[8] In the statues of the temples and in the temples themselves, we have the conscious creations of the artist as representations of the divine. But in the various forms in which language enters into the religion of the Greeks, we have their most complete mode of absolute spirit. In the myths and stories sung by bards, in the hymns of the cults, there is a beginning to the *self*-presentation of spirit to itself. Secondly, in the "living" work of art, the games, the human body itself is perfected, and there is given

> a work . . . that is equally complete, but not, however, as an intrinsically lifeless, but as a *living*, self. Such a cult is the festival which man celebrates in his own honor, though not yet imparting to that cult the significance of the absolute being. . . . Man thus puts himself in the place of the statue as the

shape that has been raised and fashioned for perfectly free *movement*, just as the statue is perfectly free *repose* (*PhG*, 505; *PhS*, 438).

But even this is only a mediation in the process of the development of religion as art, a development which reaches its zenith in linguistic form in epics, tragedy, and comedy—comedy being, according to Hegel, the highest form; for "actual self-consciousness exhibits itself as the fate of the gods" (*PhG*, 517; *PhS*, 450).[9] The masks of tragedy and the imitations of the bard are gone; the individual actors act in their own personae, without mask, the true nature of things. The self, entangled as a self in existence, is something both actual and respresentative of the universal.

> The self, appearing here in its significance as something actual, plays with the mask which it once put on in order to act its part; but it as quickly breaks out again from this illusory character and stands forth in its own nakedness and ordinariness, which it shows to be not distinct from the genuine self, the actor, or from the spectator (*PhG*, 518; *PhS*, 450).

The poetry which is "comedy" is both representation and not representation, and presents the spectator and the actor with himself in all of his reality and nakedness. This poetry is a *poiēsis* which is reflective of interest, not in an object, but on itself as *poiēsis*.

> Therefore, the fate which up to this point has lacked consciousness and consists in an empty repose and oblivion, and is separated from self-consciousness, this fate is now united with self-consciousness. The *individual self* is the negative power through which and in which the gods, as also their moments, viz. existent nature and the thoughts of their specific characters, vanish. At the same time, the individual self is not the emptiness of this disappearance but, on the contrary, preserves itself in this very nothingness, abides with itself and is the sole actuality. In it, the religion of art is consummated and has completely returned into itself (*PhG*, 520; *PhS*, 452).

Hegel continues in this vein to show the profound meaning of comedy in the context of the Greeks. In the presence of fate, the individual continues on. What is ultimate is this continuity in the face of fate, and thus a certainty of self in the absolute.

> This self-certainty is a state of spiritual well-being and of repose therein, such as is not to be found anywhere outside of this comedy (*PhG*, 520; *PhS*, 453).

Human beings celebrate themselves in their finitude, and in that celebration overcome finitude as something final barring them from the infinite.[10]

In the analysis thus far of religion, on which I have touched only briefly, the main contrast and progress made is the movement from absolute spirit as pure substance, as nature in one form or another and represented as given to human beings, to absolute spirit as subject or represented as presented by humans for humans. In one respect, substance has become subject in so far as substance vanishes, i.e., as in comedy the condition of spirit is simply the condition of man in the universe. In a second way, substance has become subject in so far as the subject is substance, substance is the predicate of the subject, i.e., again as in comedy with the representation of the human condition, the actual individuals surrender themselves by placing themselves before themselves as their own essence. The Greeks humanized religion and divinized man. In the humanization of religion, we have the completion of the movement of the religion of nature such that "substance alienates itself from itself and becomes self-consciousness" (*PhG*, 525; *PhS*, 457); that is to say, in the progress traced here from the religion of light to the hieroglyphics of the religion of the artificer, the Greek religion completes this involvement of the human by humanizing the gods, giving them language and conversation and interaction among themselves and with humans, evolving heroes, and finally creating the representation of the substance in human terms in comedy. In the latter, the divinization of man, "self-consciousness alienates itself from itself and gives itself the nature of a thing, or makes itself a universal self" (*PhG*, 525; *PhS*, 457). The condition of man is presented to him as presentation and representation, and even destiny becomes man's destiny. Destiny, as comedy shows us, is shaped by man himself as he builds his own downfall; and we laugh in order to keep that downfall at a distance and as something universal. We laugh at and not with our own condition.

> The externalization of substance, its growth into self-consciousness, expresses the transition into the opposite, the unconscious transition of *necessity*; in other words, that substance is *in itself* self-consciousness. Conversely, the externalization of self-consciousness expresses this, that it is *in itself* the universal essence, or—since the self is pure being-for-self which in its opposite communes with itself—that it is just because substance is self-consciousness *for the self*, that it is spirit (*PhG*, 525; *PhS*, 457).

The synchronic in its original form—nature, light—has been transposed into the dimension of the diachronic, into the finite life of human beings as represented in Greek art. The diachronic in its original form—the actual self-consciousness and participation in the activities of society—has been transposed into the dimension of the synchronic, this life of man as essentialized and captured in the universality of a "type of situation," a typification of the human condition. The separate divine has come into the human from which it was originally separate as light; the human has risen to the divine and is thus separated from itself. The human condition represented in comedy represents itself to itself self-aware of the representation.

This, together with the breakdown of the pure ethical life of the Greeks and the rise of the Roman world and of the individual as "person," presents the conditions for the production of the third form of religion as absolute spirit—revealed religion.[11] The stoicism and skepticism to which the humanization of the divine and the divinization of the human gave rise historically bring us to an important instantiation of the unhappy consciousness, epitomized I think in the Augustinian struggle against skepticism and manichaeanism.

Christianity is the emergence of the truth of this double movement of the human and the divine, of the capture of the absolute ground which makes possible the community of conscientious selves. The hidden meaning or dimension of the transcendent becomes the appearance of the divine in itself, Jesus as the power of all that is, as a real, living human being who is not a mere representation of the divine, but an actual, living divinity who is at the same time human. Jesus is the self-externalization of the divine, the direct insertion of the separate God into His creation. Thus, the divine being is known as spirit, not as nature or simply as human. "For spirit is the knowledge of oneself in the externalization of oneself; the being that is the movement of retaining its self-identity in its otherness" (*PhG*, 528; *PhS*, 459). That is to say, God as the Father, the omnipotent and perfect ground for all, knows Himself in His own externalization into time, into the diachronous substance which is His own creation. He does not lose Himself in this alienating act; He separates and yet remains with Himself. The divine being thus reveals Himself to Himself and to His creatures (*PhG*, 528–29; *PhS*, 459–60).

We cannot here go into all of the details of Hegel's analysis; but this passage is representative of the complete theory of spirit contained in the Christian religion as Hegel understood it and as he thought it understood itself. What God the Father does, what "the in-itself divine" does, is precisely what humans do in their own spiritual activity, i.e., in their self-conscious participation in the world, in their creation of their own substance through their own activities, in their externalization of themselves and submergence of themselves in that substance, in their knowledge or self-consciousness of this spiritual activity as we have already explored it, and finally in their coming to themselves out of this externalization in their own knowledge of that externalization. Christianity is nothing less than a *perfect representation* of spirit, and thus is the absolute standpoint, the unconditioned grasp of the human condition and its conditions. And this is precisely the conclusion to which Hegel comes at this point: "The divine nature is the same as the human, and it is this unity that is beheld" (*PhG*, 529; *PhS*, 460).[12]

Consciousness of the religions is thus identical with self-consciousness of spiritual activity in the everyday world of the here and now, and this is made explicit in the representation of the Holy Spirit which literally infuses the community of conscientious individuals.[13] It is on this ground, on the ground of the identity of the two and of the adequacy of Christianity, that we now see the foreign (i.e., the merely natural or the merely human) eliminated from the object of reflection. Our interest *as* and *in* reflection has reached itself. We, as self-conscious, as rational, reflective actors in the world, are at home in that world just because we now have an adequate comprehension of that world, a grasp which in the conscious act of interest as reflection represents that world to us completely, as the self-enclosed, self-sustaining world that it is. The representation for consciousness of the trinitarian God who, from the beginning is a consciousness and a self-consciousness based on perfect reason and total reflexivity, is a representation of spirit as a whole, of that very spirit which we have traced through this *Phenomenology*.[14]

But there is still something lacking in terms of an absolute standpoint which will grant warranty to our claims of access to reality, and we now turn to the "criticism" of religion which will introduce "absolute knowing" or philosophy as absolute idealism. As representation of spirit to itself, religion is intuition, a knowing of something which is other than itself; consequently, it is not yet absolute in a totally reflexive sense, i.e., the representation as representation has been given to it, revealed, the representation in terms of the content involves a beyond, a God who is pure spirit and who externalizes himself, etc. But spirit has not come to a complete reflection on reflection itself, i.e., on the connection between itself and its representation, on the ground for the possibility of this representation, this revelation. By its own definition, the ground remains a mystery for religion. Intuition must now become conceptualization and a discursive knowledge. What is in itself for consciousness must become for itself for consciousness.

> [The truth of absolute spirit] is to be not merely the substance or the *in-itself* of the community, nor merely to step

forth out of its inwardness into the objectivity of picture-thinking, but to become an actual self, to reflect itself into itself and to be subject (*PhG*, 532; *PhS*, 463).

It must be noted here that it is being claimed not that the absolute spirit is to become subject, but that the *truth* of absolute spirit is to become an actual self, i.e., a self which is the on-going self of diachrony, of history, the real human being.[15] It is in this sense that the truth of absolute spirit is to be subject. Representation, which functions here as the mode of knowledge for religion, is the middle term between thought and the on-going activities of human beings. As such, representation is important and a necessary condition for conceptual comprehension of the absolute; for the middle term, as Aristotle claimed long ago, is the *cause* which connects the extreme terms. Thus, this development of religion and representation as reflection is the *sine qua non* for philosophy as true and complete conceptual thinking. To be sure, it is only one of the conditions, the others being the development of interest as intentionality, desire, and reason; but since the religious representation contains within itself the reflective representation of the other modes, it is the highest mode of reflection. Further, it is only a *sine qua non*; for what we want in this "syllogism" is to link the minor and major term, actual self-conscious activity and pure, conceptual comprehension which comprehensively reflects self-conscious activity and its ground.[16] Thus, the function of religion, so far as the pursuit of absolute certainty is concerned, is to make itself disappear, or to remain in the end only implicit in the unity of the natural attitude—everyday, self-consciousness—and philosophy—discourse on the categories.[17] This is why religion and its mode of representation are "synthetic"; it makes possible the synthesis of the still separated extremes of immediate self-certainty and sense-certainty and, on the other hand, philosophical thought originally conceived of as the "perversion" of that immediate certainty. If, therefore, we can say that representation is a function of the imagination, which it surely seems to be, then imagination is for Hegel the necessary connection between unreflective and reflective life, between natural consciousness and philosophy. We must now look more closely to see how this important move from religion to philosophy is made.[18]

We comprehend now how religion is the ground for the community of conscientious actors; for it gives form to the community which we are (and at whatever stage of religion we find ourselves), it represents to us that in which we participate, articulated in its most perfect form in Christian form as the divine infused in the human, the Holy Spirit. But in this revealed religion the object, i.e., absolute spirit, "is revealed to it by something alien, and it does not recognize . . . the nature of pure self-consciousness" (PhG, 535; PhS, 466). Yet the representation qua representation is not only adequate, but complete as well. In the representation of the Holy Spirit there is a total interiorization of the divine as represented in the reunification of the Father and the Son in the resurrection. But this inwardization also includes all of us, the community of conscientious actors which is in fact representing this inwardization to itself: God is not only united with Himself, but as well we are united with Him both in the representation and in the act of representation. God dwells within us. This inwardization in and of the representation is the form and act through which representation is itself overcome. The divine, the pure substance, has become human and internal to man, thus collapsing itself as a pure transcendent; and at the same time the power of the transcendent divine remains, for it is represented and lived through on the basis that the transcendent divine being has Himself done this, i.e., united Himself with us. The abstractness of the separate, transcendent divine essence is collapsed and becomes but a moment of the action of living human beings.[19]

Once this inwardization is accomplished and the extreme "being-in-itself" of the Holy Spirit is abolished, so also is the one who has inwardized the divine, i.e., the finite human individual taken as separate from what he represents to himself as the divine. Living in the Holy Spirit, I *am* divine; the divine is just the nature of the Holy Spirit in which I live, the concrete unity of the community of conscientious actors.[20] In terms of reflection via representation, then, both the represented, transcendent being, and the one who objectifies and represents that being, are abolished as real, separate entities. Once interiorized, there is no objectification, no representation, no simple transcendence of what is represented; and once there is no such object, there is no creator of the object, nothing to transcend, nothing to be represented to, nothing for which there is an object of this sort.[21] In other words, imagination, aware of itself as imagination, ceases to be imagination, turns upon itself, and reflects upon its own reflection on the absolute. Then, and only then, is religion united with on-going, actual spirit, finite human activities in community with others. Aware of the true nature of my awareness, I can turn to that awareness itself and seek out its lineaments as they actually or effectively exist in the act of imaginative representation.

Action and reflection reciprocally condition each other. The representation of religion and the divine is created by actual, active spirit itself; for in the community of conscience and in our phenomenological appropriation of that community of conscience, we have become aware of evil and forgiveness, of finitude, and of the common ground which unites us as conscientious actors.[22] Religion is only the attempt to capture this absolute ground of certainty for the sake of certainty. Religion, on the other hand, *is* only through this need for certainty and only through the complete interpenetration of the truth of religion in our everyday, ongoing activities as conscientious actors. Not only the "we" of the *Phenomenology*, but we as individual, finite, moral beings have turned ourselves toward the absolute standpoint. In this relationship we become the concept now in a concrete manner.

> This concept fulfilled itself on one side in the self-assured spirit that *acted*, and on the other, in religion: in religion it won for consciousness the absolute content *as content* or, in the form of *picture-thinking*, the form of otherness for consciousness; on the other hand, in the prior shape *of action* the form is that of the self itself, for it contains the self-assured spirit that *acts*; the self accomplishes the life of absolute spirit (*PhG*, 554; *PhS*, 484).

There is nothing here of the famous, but we must also add merely fictitious mystification in Hegel's analysis.[23] Religion, alive in the actions of conscientious individuals, in fact demystifies itself, demythologizes itself and becomes a living force granting certainty of self and of world in one and the same manner. This is the *concrete concept*.

> Through this movement of action, spirit has come on the scene as a pure universality of knowing, which is self-consciousness, as self-consciousness that is the simple unity of knowing. It is only through action that spirit *is* in such a way that it is *really there*, that is, when it raises its existence into thought and thereby into an absolute *opposition* [*Entgegensetzung*], and returns out of this [*opposition*], in and through [*the opposition*] itself (*PhG*, 555; *PhS*, 485).The complete awareness of the unity of representational thought and action is our ingress into absolute knowing.

The movement from religion as the absolute standpoint to philosophy is the most critical and least specified in the whole of the *Phenomenology of Spirit*.[24] The move is a move from the examination and experience of the imaginative representation of the absolute standpoint—a presentation which is therefore still lacking in absoluteness since the question of the one for whom the representation *is* is still left in mystery—to the examination and experience of the absolute standpoint itself, in complete reflexivity. Hegel writes that one is now prepared to transcend (*hinausgehen*, 'go out', 'leave behind') the separation and difference involved in representational thinking. This is a radical transcendence, not a transcendence in the sense of an *Aufheben*, but in the sense of an *Hinausgehen*.[25] Hegel characterizes this radical transcendence as "a compulsion (*ein Drängen*) on the part of the concept" (*PhG*, 535; *PhS*, 466). Furthermore, it is a compulsion which is only "instinctive." This compulsion is first represented in the doctrines of the revealed religion, but is misunderstood and left in the form of the Holy Spirit. This is why the "we" re-enters at this point in the *Phenomenology* in a position of hegemony: spirit as consciousness in religion knows itself as object, but does not realize that it is only itself that it knows and, rather, represents the self in the form of the representation of the Holy Spirit and the triune God. The step to philosophy is prepared for by religion, but in no way guaranteed. Thus, Hegel must begin by a process of recollection (*Erinnerung*) in which *we* bring together the *Gestalten* "in which the totality of the moments of the object and of the relation of consciousness to [the object] can be indicated only as resolved into its moments" (*PhG*, 550; *PhS*, 480). "[We] have only to recall the earlier shapes of consciousness already encountered" (*PhG*, 550; *PhS*, 480).

This doctrine of recollection is interesting in its contrast to the Platonic doctrine, and some discussion of it will throw light on this last move in the *Phenomenology*.[26] In Plato the doctrine of recollection serves to show that intelligibility is already in some sense implicit as a totality, and that on the basis of this implicitness, there can be intelligibility concerning elements or parts of existence and experience. That which is recalled has its "element of existence" in the domain of the forms, and is in one way or another tied up with an immortality of the soul and its consequent existence prior to this present life. In the *Phenomenology*, on the other hand, the doctrine of recollection serves also to bring intelligibility of the whole into our explicit awareness from something prior. But this prior existence is there on at least two levels which differ from the domain of the forms in Plato.

The first level is the dimension of recollection we have been undergoing in the *Phenomenology* itself, a recollection of the putative praxical presuppositions uncovered in the process of the phenomenological investigation into the possibility of warranting the claims of philosophy as the absolute standpoint. Our examinations have been recollections of what is and is not to be taken as absolute standpoint, and thus of how knowledge, experience, and action are to have their being.[27] This final recollection, on the other hand, is thus a recollection of our recollections.[28] The original of all of this, then, is not some domain removed from time and space and sequestered in the eternal, but rather the actual collection of the spirit of the time found in the actual historical periods which have constituted a diachronous succession to our own time. The first recollection of this collecting has occurred in the chapters of the *Phenomenology of Spirit*. And now a final recollecting is to occur in which those recollections will be collected together one final time in order to reveal the absolute standpoint which is implicit in them. To all those and only to those who have participated in the course of the work and its recollecting, this final recollection in the chapter on absolute knowing will grant access to the absolute standpoint.[29] It is in this sense that Hegel can claim that the *Phenomenology* is the only adequate deduction of absolute idealism. At the same time, since the progress of the recollection has led us from our starting point in the most naive form of the natural standpoint—that common-sense attitude which at first considers something like the absolute standpoint announced as such by philosophy as perverse—this recollection and deduction will have shown that the standpoint is within the natural standpoint itself; for the original collection from which our recollection takes its cue is the actual historical collecting of spirit undertaken by those very individuals who form the peoples and the spirit of our own history.

Thus, the "we" which is involved here is not simply the "we" of the early chapters on consciousness; for there the philosophical and the natural standpoint stood opposed, and the natural standpoint did not itself "see" the connections between the movements, but had to be shown that connection by one in a philosophical standpoint, i.e., by one who already saw the *problem* concerning certainty. But as a result of the dialectical progress of the *Phenomenology*, the individual in the natural standpoint, through the discussion of objective spirit and of religion, has already experienced the objective explication of the absolute standpoint. This exegesis of the meaning of society and religion and of its historical development is absolutely critical for the consummation of the *Phenomenology* and its task of showing natural consciousness how the absolute standpoint is within it and is there with warranted certainty. The "we" is therefore now all those who have traversed the *Phenomenology*.[30]

The second dimension of recollection is therefore crucial. Hegel has argued from the Preface on that the *Phenomenology* was only a recollection of what had already been accomplished in the history of spirit, taking 'history' to denote the actual happening (*Geschehen*) of spirit. The world spirit has already developed to the point at which it now (in 1807) exists and has shaped itself into consciousness of self. This form of spirit constitutes the substance or "world" of each individual. Our task involves again going over that development, but now in a way that is different from the original development of spirit; for

> the content is already the actuality reduced to a possibility, its immediacy overcome, and the embodied shape reduced to ab-

breviated, simple determinations of thought. It is no longer existence in the form of *being-in-itself*—neither still in the original form, nor submerged in existence—but is now the *recollected-in-itself*, ready for conversion into the form of *being-for-self* (PhG, 28; PhS, 17).

In order to understand this passage we must realize that our proximate recollection is a recollection not only in terms interior to the *Phenomenology* itself; the pre-existence involved is a pre-existence in *history* as the happening of spirit. Art, religion, and philosophy have, in each age, originally recollected what was collected in existence, in on-going, natural-attitude experience. The phylogenetic development of our own present world or substance consists not only of a line, but of a line with nodes. The latter are the capturing of the essence of that development *as it developed*. In other terms, the historical-philosophical dialogue and the other forms which spirit takes has already been involved in the process of recollecting spirit through time, and of recollecting each epoch, respectively, for its own time. Our task in the *Phenomenology* is now to recollect that original recollection, to attend to the historical-philosophical dialogue and make our contribution to it in the form of a phenomenology of spirit which brings us finally to warranted access to truth through the absolute standpoint. Our "previous existence" here, then, is the previous existence and development of the present world, the development of the present world through time, and not a removed, eternal domain. In this present world itself is contained the phylogenesis of itself.[31]

The "compulsion" to transcend (*hinausgehen*) the representational thinking of religion and to enter the domain of pure conceptual thinking is thus embodied in this recollection of what has transpired in the *Phenomenology* (and thus, also, in the whole of the history of spirit), a task for which we have been prepared through our penultimate reflection on revealed religion. After completing this recollection and a reflection upon it, Hegel then concludes that we can now see that

> what in religion was *content* or a form for presenting an *other*, is here the *self's* own *act*; the concept requires the *content* to be the *self's* own *act*. For this concept is, as we see, the knowledge of the self's act within itself as all essentiality and all existence, the knowledge of this subject as substance and of the substance as this knowledge of its act. Our *own* act here has been simply to *gather together* the separate moments, each of which in principle exhibits the life of spirit in its entirety, and also to stick to the concept in the form of the concept, the content of which would already have yielded it-

self in those moments and in the form of a *shape of consciousness* (*PhG*, 556; *PhS*, 485).

How is this to be understood? For it is the next sentence of the *Phenomenology* which declares, referring to this "shape of consciousness" which is the result of the gathering together we have just accomplished, that this

> last shape of spirit—the spirit which at the same time gives its complete and true content the form of the self and thereby realizes its concept as remaining in its concept in this realization—this is absolute knowing; it is spirit that knows itself in the shape of spirit, or a *comprehensive knowing*. Truth is not only *in itself* completely identical with certainty, but it also has the shape of self-certainty, or it is in its existence in the form of self-knowledge. . . . As a result, that which is the very essence, viz. the concept, has become the element of existence, or has become the *form of objectivity* for consciousness. Spirit, *manifesting* or *appearing* in consciousness in this element, or what is the same thing, produced in it by consciousness, *is science* [*Wissenschaft*] (*PhG*, 556; *PhS*, 485–86).

That is to say, this shape of consciousness which we have reached in the preceding paragraph is absolute knowing, science. It is here that the final step has been taken in our quest for certainty. But how?

I propose that we must understand what has transpired here in the following way.[32] We must take a very literal and self-reflective reading of the text. What we have just done is to recollect the recollections of the *Phenomenology* which, in turn, are recollections of recollections already accomplished in the historical-philosophical dialogue, which is itself a part of the historical happening of spirit. In this final recollection, we are recollecting only what we ourselves, and through us others before us, have done; our own act of recollection orients us toward our own act of recollection just accomplished in the course of the *Phenomenology*. We are in that way only dealing with ourselves. It is we ourselves who are the object here, not as simple, finite beings submerged unreflectively in existence, but rather as finite reflective beings who have captured that existence and its being; for it is interest, not as intentionality or desire or purpose, but as *reflection* which now orients us. In reflection we have captured our own being as reflective beings who are always implicitly there in the other forms of interest. What this final recollection presents to me as a self is not another, not a form of religion which represents to me the ground of all being; rather, what is presented is my own act, my own phenomenological investigation into reality: "the *self's* own *act*," as Hegel reiterates and stresses. He writes that "our *own* act here has been simply to *gather together* [*versammeln*] the separate moments" of the *Phenomenology,* "and also to stick to [*festhalten*] the concept in the form of the concept" (*PhG,* 556; *PhS,* 485). This recollection is at one and the same time knowledge and action, and the knowledge is knowledge of our knowledge, the action is action directed to itself as a knowing act. However, since the whole of absolute spirit is built upon the realization of the thought-praxis relation to which we first gained access in the analysis of conscience, the action here is not simply thought, but all actions in so far as they are infused with and embody thought. As important as it is to note that the content of absolute knowledge is already there, albeit in different form, in religion, it is just as important to remember that that content *is* the content of absolute knowing or philosophy. Theory cannot be for the sake of theory and divorced from the action which constitutes historical spirit; it is embedded in it as warranty for access to reality.

Thus, Hegel can say at the end of the paragraph cited above that it is one and the same thing to say that spirit appears in consciousness in the element of the concept of that which holds together, or to say that consciousness produces spirit in the element of the concept. Like God, I differentiate myself from myself, both in creation and in that real being which I have reflected upon, and in doing so create a "new" being (the *Phenomenology*); and in this final recollection, I, like the Holy Spirit, bring myself back to myself out of otherness. *As* the concept, or as dwelling in the element or domain of the concept, I am both one and two, and also unity of one and two, which unity depends for its existence on the difference between the one and the two. The difference that remains is the difference represented in religion as that between *natura naturans* and *natura naturata,* as well as that between the Father and the Son. And the difference must be maintained in order to avoid the nothingness of pantheism, while at the same time being a difference which exists within the unity of the concept itself.

I, like God, am at home with myself when I thematize the ground of intelligibility.[33] Only if the *Phenomenology* is taken as *act,* and thus only if and in so far as one commits oneself to the act of experiencing the *Phenomenology* in the sense in which Hegel discusses the experience which belongs to the *Phenomenology* as its own—only if this is the case, can the access to the absolute standpoint be reached and realized. And so, we can now say, not "I, like God," but "God, like me".[34] Only my act, only the act of the *Phenomenology,* makes the absolute standpoint real, explicit. It is there *in time* only when this act has been accomplished, just as the triunity of God is there *in time* only with the resurrection and the establishment of the *ecclesia.* The substance is there prior to this time;

but it is mere substance, world, not recollected in any of the senses of recollection belonging finally to the *Phenomenology.*

Truth, therefore, since truth is the content itself of this knowledge (*PhG*, 556; *PhS*, 485), is not a correspondence between thinking and being, not an adequation of thought to what-is; that is only "correctness" (*die Richtigkeit*). Rather truth is the disclosure or revelation (*Offenbarkeit*) of what makes correspondence correspondence, or of what makes adequation adequation (*PhG*, 557–58; *PhS*, 487).[35] This truth as disclosure, before the final recollection and entrance into the absolute standpoint (which is disclosure as truth itself) is, Hegel claims, "in fact concealment [*Verborgenheit*]" (*PhG*, 557; *PhS*, 487), due to an attention paid to things in their thingness: representation of the substance in religion involves both the last instance of this concealment because of its mode of re-presentation and objectivity, and a disclosure of the absolute ground which is concealed because disclosure is objectified and reified in a divine being.[36]

The step which has been taken, then, is one in which, through interest as reflection, I realize my act as an act which has given me access to the ground of what-is so far as certainty is concerned. In gathering together what has been done, I realize that my own act of pursuing certainty through the *Phenomenology* is the act which has uncovered for me the nature of spirit and thus my own nature. The ground of my act is not something in a form different from me, and not even the Holy Spirit which inhabits me; rather the ground of my act is the act itself.[37] Truth is not something simply given me, nor simply something made; rather it is constituted in that *relating act* by which I *seek* truth. Truth is the disclosure of being which results from my activity of seeking the ultimate intelligibility of what-is, and certainty becomes identical with truth or is the disclosure of being at that point at which I realize what truth is. We shall see what is meant here more clearly if we grapple now with the difficult and obscure formulation which Hegel has made of the relationship between time and the concept, for time is just that mode of concealment within which revelation or disclosure is self-concealing.

> Time is the concept itself that *is there* and which presents itself to consciousness as empty intuition; for this reason spirit necessarily appears in time, and it appears in time just so long as it has not *grasped* its pure concept, i.e., has not annulled time. [Time] is the externally intuited pure self which is *not grasped* by the self, the merely intuited concept. When the concept grasps itself it sets aside its time-form, comprehends intuiting, and is a comprehending and comprehended intuiting (*PhG*, 558; *PhS*, 487).

The concept as concept, the concept as time; truth as disclosure, truth as concealment: being and time. An understanding of these formulations will reveal how we are at this point ushered into the domain in which the interests which drive men in their everyday concerns are hushed and we consequently leave behind time.[38]

The text is very dense and Hegel gives us only a clue to the answer to our problem of comprehending how this last step of the *Phenomenology* is made and of how, as the last step, the original dual task of the *Phenomenology* is completed. It is relatively simple to understand how our culture and social formations grant us some degree of certainty of access to what-is; it is also relatively simple to see how the religions and their representations of the absolute ground of being give us perhaps an even greater degree of certainty of access in so far as we participate in the power manifested in that religion. But here the claim is to absolute access and absolute certainty. For this it must be shown how this absolute standpoint is contained within the natural attitude and how the natural certainty which belongs to the natural attitude also belongs and is finally warranted in the absolute standpoint. It is the "withinness" which is critical here, but which is also difficult to comprehend.

The clue which Hegel gives us is found in his discussion, cited above, of time as it presents itself to consciousness as "empty intuition." What is to be understood here by "empty intuition"? It is really nothing other than the domain of the *adaequatio*, of correspondence itself, that space or "*zwischen*" which is my link to otherness and to others. It is my connection to the world and to the whole of the content of my experience, be it inner or outer experience as the tradition was disposed to say. It is the adequation which hides itself as I hold my interest on what is revealed to me as present for intentionality, desire, purpose, and reflection. In each and every such experience it is the relata, myself and my object, which at one time or another which hold my attention. And they hold my attention across time, in that space-time which is the specious present of my experience, the this-here-now which is always this-here-now, but constantly surpasses itself only to be again "this-here-now." *What* is or is not adequate, *what* is or is not to be adequate holds my interest, moves me in my experiences and action. But the adequation itself, the relation of the relata always thus eludes my interest. In this recollection at the end of the *Phenomenology* I am turned to the act itself, the relating itself, which has all along constituted my quest for certainty.

Thus, on the one hand, in making possible the disclosure of a world which is actual, disclosure conceals itself; for while my interests are what move me in and toward the world, my interest in the correspondence itself is impossible. But as I have now recollected the grounds for the possibility of the intelligibility of that world and of the possible worlds of actual experience, I have turned toward the adequation, the correspondence itself; I have turned to truth as pure disclosure hidden in the form of intuition and interest, and thus in the temporality of all experience. As my interest here now turns to interest itself, the other interests are hushed; for what is now concealed, at least momentarily, are the worlds as such which are revealed by the *adaequatio*. In the natural attitude, that ground across which all is revealed is time as the puncticity of space, time as the this-here-nowness of experience, time as that which gives uniqueness to space and makes it place. The absolute standpoint is the grasp of that ground itself, that which stands within the thematizations and is the "arena" for what is thematized in the natural attitude. Thus we have reached a form in interest which is "comprehending and comprehended intuiting" (*PhG*, 558; *PhS*, 487).[39]

There is an equation here which is fundamental. We can say that is is the same to say that science or the grasp of the ground across which all transpires in experience is a comprehension of the concept, or to say that science is a comprehension of time or temporality. Science involves a comprehension of time as the comprehension of the concealment which is present in the disclosure of beings which are the function of all interests other than that of absolute knowing. On the other hand, science involves a comprehension of the concept as the comprehension of the disclosure of those beings which are the function of our interests in so far as that disclosure is a disclosure concealed in the act of disclosure. In the natural attitude, the concept is time or temporality; in the absolute standpoint the concept is grasped as the concept. Diachrony and synchrony thus come to the same thing, but as different nevertheless: *diachrony is the ground as concealed through what is disclosed; synchrony is the ground as disclosed through the unconcealment of disclosure itself.*[40]

The categorial content which is the development of the categories in the philosophical sciences of logic, nature, and spirit, is thus literally within time as concealed, as implicit praxical presupposition set for those interests which move the lives of human beings. As concealed it is nevertheless what makes possible the intelligibility and the totality of intelligibility which bespeaks our access to what-is as we stand and act in and toward the world. As the disclosure of disclosure we make explicit the categorial content and thus turn to the nature of disclosure itself and the warranty for certainty as professed in the natural attitude. As such, spirit is finally self-conscious spirit, spirit with access to its own ground of access to what-is as whatever it is.

Hegel then goes on to point out again that it is our socio-political and religious *activity* which has prepared us for this possibility of warranted claims of access to reality.[41] Here he reviews again the steps of the *Phenomenology* through which we have been led to the present moment (*PhG*, 559–61; *PhS*, 488–90). Reflection here is manifested as an interest in reflection itself. He then gives one of the clearest summarizing discussions to be found in his works concerning the nature of that spirit which is this time-concept. We have previously engaged spirit both as subjective and as objective.

> Spirit, however, has shown itself to us to be neither merely the withdrawal of self-consciousness into its pure inwardness, nor the mere submergence of self-consciousness into substance, and the non-being of its [moment of] difference; but spirit is this *movement* of the self which empties itself of itself and sinks itself into its substance, and also, as subject, has gone out of that substance into itself, making the substance into an object and a content at the same time as it cancels this difference between objectivity and content. The "I" has neither to cling to itself in the *form* of *self-consciousness* as against the form of substantiality and objectivity, as if it were afraid of the externalization of itself: the power of spirit lies rather in remaining the self-same spirit in its externalization and, as that which is both *in itself* and *for itself*, in making its *being-for-self* no less merely a moment than its in-itself; nor is spirit a *tertium quid* that casts the differences back into the abyss of the absolute and declares that therein they are all the same; on the contrary, knowing is this seeming inactivity which merely contemplates how what is differentiated spontaneously moves in its own self and returns into its unity.
>
> In this knowing, then, spirit has concluded the movement in which it has shaped itself, in so far as this shaping was burdened with the difference of consciousness [i.e., of the latter from its object], a difference now overcome. Spirit has won the pure element of its existence, the concept (*PhG*, 561; *PhS*, 490).

This movement is nothing other than the movement across time as the *Zwischen* which conceals disclosure as disclosure. The concept can now be examined as the categorial framework within which all intelligibility and thus all warranted certainty becomes possible. Not some *tertium quid*, the absolute standpoint which has been reached is the very movement of myself across or within that place which is constituted as my experience and as the intersecting of experience which we have seen developed first as self-consciousness, then as reason, and finally as spirit.[42]

In this last stage of the *Phenomenology*, then, two things are comprehended. The first is that it is our own act, this quest for certainty, which has constituted the *Phenomenology*. The second is that what we need now to seek is the constitutive structure of this act as act, i.e., as a domain of existence (*Dasein*) which underlies the possibility of other domains. First, in the *Science of Logic*, we shall articulate the general categorial structure which underlies all possible experience; then in the various philosophical sciences of nature and spirit we shall articulate special categorial structures which underlie certain domains of possible experience and which are founded upon the general categorial structure disclosed in the *Science of Logic* (*PhG*, 561–64; *PhS*, 490–93). When the general and special categorial structures are articulated, then we shall have the complete anatomy of intelligibility, a categorial map in terms of which our speech, knowledge, experience, and action can all be comprehended as a whole. This comprehension gives final criteria for the warranty of any and all alleged or professed certainty of truth.

Such a move institutes and leaves us with many questions. Has the *Phenomenology* moved with continuity through its various stages so that we have never lost contact with the natural attitude and its certainty? Are there errors or breaks within the *Phenomenology* itself which, even granting the validity of the task as a task, would invalidate the task as carried out? And if we have achieved warranted access to the absolute standpoint, what now is the categorial structure revealed in the philosophical sciences? Are the categories complete? Adequate? Is there a break in the sciences?

Hegel has been criticized on each of these counts and has been found wanting. But I would like now to set aside these and other questions like them, and to accept for the sake of argument that Hegel has accomplished his task as he set out to accomplish it. I have attempted to give a sympathetic reading to the work and to his understanding of the task of establishing warranty for the claims of philosophy to achieve the absolute standpoint. When we have reached in the last chapter of the *Phenomenology* the realization that it is our own work which opens us to the exploration of a categorial structure which explicates and makes intelligible not only all of experience, but also the categorial structure itself, we have completed our "archeological dig" at the site of the natural attitude of common sense certainty and are now ready to explore the ultimate foundations. *If* we have begun fairly with the sense-certainty of the natural attitude, and *if* we have been led, through an investigation of the putative praxical presuppositions which constitute the noetic and ontological structure of interest in its various forms, to the absolute standpoint, then Hegel will have accomplished the perennial task of philosophy: to justify its claims in such a way that even the form of the natural attitude most antagonistic to philosophy must comprehend those claims as fully self-warranting.

XI

The Absolute Standpoint: A Critique

I WOULD ARGUE THAT the conditions posed at the close of the preceding chapter have been satisfied, and that the interpretation I have given Hegel's *Phenomenology* is a faithful and justified reconstruction in terms of the logic of presuppositions.[1] On the one hand, if we adhere rigidly to Hegel's own proposal and characterization of the work—that its *sole* task is to come to know what knowing is, and thus to come to a standpoint in which claims to knowledge can be ultimately and unconditionally warranted—and if we take in a strict way the condition that this be shown to the natural attitude, then we indeed have here a philosophical work which takes up the natural, professed certainty of the natural attitude of sense-certainty and warrants it. On the other hand, we have a work which revolutionized the traditional quest for certainty as it had been conceived; for while in the past the natural and naive common sense was left behind, in Hegel we have a literal plunge to the roots of that natural attitude. Beginning with the natural attitude and its naive and trusting certainty of access to reality, we have traversed that distance which Hegel called also a "journey of despair." That despair has now been left behind as the interests which move us in our everyday concerns are hushed and we calmly survey the domain of absolute knowledge. Our calmness comes from our knowledge that, like Christ, we have died and have left behind the condition of being *solely* concerned with the thematics of the everyday; but we have also come into an eternal domain which is not removed from that everyday in the sense of removal at a distance, but which rather dwells *within* the everyday as, after the resurrection and the descent of the Holy Spirit, we who are finiteexist within the eternal.

The categorial structure to be revealed in the sciences of logic, nature, and spirit are to give us that comprehensive totality, that ultimate structure of intelligibility, which lies within or at the foundation of our natural certainty. The absolute standpoint has been shown to be within the natural attitude, and now natural certainty is to be shown to be grounded in the warranty deriving from philosophical certainty. Thus, we have left behind the natural attitude only in terms of the purely temporal standpoint as the place of natural, finite, human existence. We stand in the absolute as we dwell, religiously, in the Holy Spirit—nothing more, nothing less. How are we to assess this journey? Has it been justified? Are we indeed now in a position to offer a "complete speech," a single, comprehensive grasp of the foundation of all certainty and truth?

The answers to these questions depend upon whether or not we have uncovered, examined, and set straight the praxical presuppositions embedded in the natural attitude itself, i.e., whether we have found the actual ground of our intercourse within the world. In order to be successful in its task, the *Phenomenology* must have brought up for examination the putative presuppositions which underlie in general our access to and activity within the world. This seems to me to be, in addition to being the concern of Hegel, a task proper to philosophy; for whatever may have been wrong with the way in which the quest for certainty has been carried out, that quest to give warranty to our claims is a necessary condition for any legitimate philosophy. Without it, we can have at best aesthetically pleasing discourses on life, but not something which can properly be called philosophical knowledge. If, on the other hand, one is prepared to give up all claims to knowledge, then what Hegel has done, and the quest for certainty in general, is of no interest. But I, for one, am not prepared to give up such claims, and so the quest retains for me a profound significance. If there is to be a critique of Hegel, then, it must be in terms of the actual project of the *Phenomenology*, i.e., it must focus on the question of whether Hegel adequately criticizes the putative praxical presuppositions of the natural attitude and those presuppositions which have arisen on the basis of the criticisms of that attitude in sense-certainty.

Several of the usual critiques of Hegel fail at this point. One I have already discussed, namely the critique of his interest in certainty; for that interest is here assumed to belong to the nature of philosophy itself.[2] Beyond this, the long held criticism that Hegel leaves the individual behind in abstraction or that he has hypostatized the individual has no legitimate ground either; for when we moved from self-consciousness to reason and spirit, we simply took cognizance of the real bond between individuals and between individuals and their respective and common worlds.[3] Spirit is "only" that complexus of place or "common-place" which constitutes the lived world, the actual, living world which is the arena for our lives. The interests which move human beings in their everyday lives are hushed at the end only in the sense and to the extent that we now turn to those categories which bring comprehensive intelligibility to the variety of more limited intelligibilities and interest frameworks which constitute our various activities and modes of thought. The categories which will form the focus of this articulation of the ground of comprehensive intelligibility are no more or less than what John Dewey called "the generic traits of existence".[4] While it is true, then, that we have turned from the everyday

The Absolute Standpoint: A Critique 251

interests, it has only been in order to discover and articulate our interest in those generic traits, and to do this for the sake of warranting claims to knowledge made in those everyday contexts. In fact Hegel will, in the philosophical sciences of nature and spirit, return to the specific or regional ontologies and metaphysics in order to complete in a concrete way his inquiry into the absolute idea. In these latter sciences, in contrast to the science of logic, we return to the basic intelligibility frameworks or comportments within which are found our everyday interests in various domains of thought and action and experience. Thus, our participation in our universe will have become intelligible at its source of intelligibility.[5]

Nor can Hegel's practice of the dialectic and his testing of praxical presuppositions as such be the focus of critique; for with this method of pursuing his goal of gaining access to the absolute or unconditioned standpoint Hegel has discovered, or rather rediscovered, the procedure by which our real, everyday lives are served by and linked to philosophy. As I have argued from the very beginning, the natural attitude is not the focus for skepticism or cursed as something to be left behind, but is what is to guide us and to be in harmony with the philosophical quest for certainty. Philosophy achieves its "presuppositionless" beginning by testing the putative presuppositions of all praxis, and by bringing to consciousness the domain of presuppositions which are the ultimate presuppositions of experience within reality.[6]

However, following the idea that we must adhere to Hegel's own task in a dialogical/dialectical fashion, I think there is one fundamental praxical presupposition—shared by both the natural attitude and philosophy—which has not been examined and which has lain, undiscovered, at the basis of many of the critiques of Hegel which have focused on the problem of the relation of the concrete individual to absolute spirit. In fact, it will be shown not only that this basic presupposition guides and determines the process itself in the *Phenomenology*, i.e., is basic to the movement toward the absolute standpoint and thus absolute spirit, but also that the presupposition is the court of last appeal for the natural attitude itself when its natural certainty is seriously challenged. My strategy will be the following: if we can show that this presupposition is present and warranted, and if there are no others which would be relevant to the level of presupposition examined in the *Phenomenology*, then Hegel will have accomplished his goal of proving warranted access to the absolute standpoint. If, on the other hand, the presupposition is not warranted and its lack of warrant is such that the project of the articulation of the sciences of logic, nature, and spirit is brought into question as a whole, then the absolute standpoint will not have been reached and the whole of the system will be brought into question. My conclusion will be that the latter is the case, and that in discovering this we not only suspend judgment on the system itself, but are led to see a basic error, grounded in the natural attitude itself, which denies validity to the project of articulating the structure of comprehensive intelligibility which supposedly underlies all other, partial intelligibilities. While it may seem at first sight that this projected result affects only the *Phenomenology*, it will in fact affect the system as a whole.

Put in a formula, the presupposition is that *the referents for the principle or ground of totality and for the principle or ground of intelligibility are one and the same.* The presupposition is that intelligibility and totality, in the ultimate sense of each, are grounded in the same locus, and thus that there is such a thing as a comprehensive principle of intelligibility or some common ground on the basis of which particular perspectives, interest frameworks, comportments, and domains of reality are held together as a whole. Put in common sense terms, the presupposition is that the world out there is a whole and makes sense as a whole.[7]

Before discussing this presupposition in terms of the *Phenomenology*, it will be beneficial to clarify in a preliminary way just what is meant here. I shall try to clarify it by showing (1) that and how it lies in the natural attitude itself and is common sense, (2) that it has been shared by the vast majority of philosophers even up to the present time, and (3) that it has indeed served to hold together the movement of the *Phenomenology*.

It might seem at first glance that to attribute this presupposition to the natural attitude—a presupposition about comprehensiveness—is a scandal, indeed that it is the most perverse thesis of all.[8] But what this actually means in common sense terms is not at all bizarre, and a brief reflection on the naive attitude toward the world—and indeed on any more complex natural attitude—will show not only that the presupposition is common sense, but that the philosophical versions of it are actually parasitic on the natural attitude version.

A first point of clarification is this: It is *not* being claimed that one presupposes in the natural attitude that anyone has or can actually articulate the whole as a whole, or has actual, discursive access to the ultimate intelligibility of the whole. Neither omnipresence nor omniscience is being claimed in this presupposition; for what is at stake is not an extensional claim, but a claim about the intensional ground of the extensional reality in which we are interested in the natural attitude. It is simply presupposed that there is a single whole which stands as a whole. We do not presuppose that there are just pieces out there or that there are radical discontinuities; we presuppose that there is a *uni*verse, and that this whole also makes sense as a whole. Everything fits together meaningfully, even though no one may be able to articulate that sense and show the unity based on comprehensive intelligibility. That is to say, it is presupposed that *if there were* a being or force powerful enough to achieve omniscience and omnipresence, then *it would* find that whole and the ultimately consistent intelligibility to the whole within that whole itself. In other words, we presuppose semantic completeness, even though that completeness is not directly accessible to us.[9]

This presupposition is made explicit and becomes objectively clear when, if pressed by the exigencies of a world which seems at times not to make sense or seems not supportive of our natural, purposive projects, we make reference to this single locus of comprehensive intelligibility in terms of God, Nature, or some other ubiquitous force. So, in fact, we presuppose not only on subjunctive grounds that a hypothetical omniscience and omnipresence *would* ground and have access to comprehensive intelligibility, but on indicative grounds that an actual being, force, or domain exists such that there is a ground and access. For natural consciousness God (by whatever name theist or atheist) is that being and Nature is that domain and force wherein lies the comprehensive intelligibility and power which keeps what-is standing as a whole. There is a single referent for the principle of totality and intelligibility, and that referent is God or Nature. Alienation, anxiety about being in general, confusion, skepticism, and other disorienting forms of experience *would not be dysvalues*, as they are for the natural, unreflective attitude, if it were not presupposed in some way or other that *they should not occur*, i.e. these orientations would not be *dis*orienting if it were not presupposed that the whole does in fact stand intelligibly as a whole and thus that the disorientation should not exist.

In terms of certainty, certainty could never become problematic in principle, if it were not presupposed that certainty of access to reality in its fullness should in principle *be* possible. That is to say, if we ask ourselves seriously why disorientation and uncertainty ought to be negative, and ask without the presupposition of comprehensive intelligibility, we find ourselves unable to distinguish in *felt-value* terms between certainty and uncertainty, fruitful orientation and disorientation. There would be a value-gap there where in fact there is no gap in our natural experience, i.e., where the negativity of the one is as obvious as the positivity of the other. As we shall see below, it is in fact with the making explicit of this presupposition that the *Phenomenology of Spirit* begins; for in the original presupposition set of the natural attitude it is maintained that we have access to the wealth of reality in all of its breadth and depth, both extensionally and intensionally, and that no quest for certainty in that sense is necessary.

We can see, then, that when philosophers or theologians appeal to God, Nature, and divine forces, they are not creating esoteric beings, forces, problems, and mysteries, but only reflecting what underlies our common, unreflective experience as a putative praxical presupposition. Philosophy and theology are in that way parasitic on the presuppositions of the natural attitude in that they arise and respond to a need of the natural human attitude. The need for verification of the absolute standpoint is simply the awareness of the assumption that we already have it, i.e., that we do have real and authentic access to reality. Common sense in this way—and philosophy derivatively—simply assumes it is within and is addressing a world which has sense as a whole.

Secondly, the presence of the presupposition of God, Nature, and divine forces, or whatever is functionally identical, does not entail the denial of *relative* difference and discontinuity within what-is and in reference to intelligibility. At the same time that we naturally presuppose comprehensive intelligibility in the way just described, we also recognize that different perspectives, each of them self-consistent and relatively independent, can and do support different and even apparently mutually exclusive senses of reality and of the world as a whole. The way one person successfully sees the world and the way another, in a different way, successfully sees the world; the way one discipline makes sense of things and the way another, in a different way and with different presuppositions and assumptions, makes sense of things, is not thereby characterized as unreal or as a false difference. Nor is the presupposition of comprehensive intelligibility a presupposition that leads to a conclusion that any and all perspectives are valid; for some are ruled out of order precisely by reference to comprehensive intelligibility.

The presupposition of a single referent for totality and intelligibility does not rule out partialness and difference and the simultaneous presupposition and recognition of significant variety and plurality. Rather, it is presupposed that in the last instance the different valid perspectives and their respective intelligibility frameworks are all compatible and part of the whole, irrespective of what appears to us with our limited knowledge. Limited knowledge for the natural attitude does not entail limited access, however; it only entails a limitation to actual knowledge of the whole, taken extensionally or intensionally. Part of the mystery of God and Nature is their capacity to encompass what seem at times to us to be impossible alternatives and copresences in our reality. When it is claimed that "God can understand, even if we cannot," or that "in spite of appearances, there is sense to this situation," this unity of unity and disunity, of continuity and discontinuity is being referred to.

Again, we can see here that the philosophical and theological projects are parasitic on common sense. When philosophers or theologians systematically press toward the ultimate point of unity, or like Hume give this project up and return to the simple instinct or faith in the unity, they are simply attempting to articulate this unity or to demonstrate our limited access to it in its intensional completeness. In the process of the *Phenomenology* there were countless instances of this conflict between differences or perspectives, and the single truth encompassed in a putative absolute standpoint. The whole drive of both the natural and the philosophical quest for certainty was the drive to reach a standpoint *on the whole* which would not simply efface difference—which would not simply generate a night in which all cows were black—but which would allow for and explicate those differences in experience as elements of comprehensive intelligibility. The actual resolution which Hegel found for us stems from the act of reconciliation in the world of conscientious actors and judges, a reconciliation which acknowledged our finitude and its necessitation of perspectivalism. And this was accomplished, and reflected the situation of those who dwell in the communal spirit which generates a religion, along with the insistence that the whole as such and in its ultimate intelligibility escapes that finitude without effacing it. A careful examination of Hegel's system, conducted in light of what we have discovered to be the true nature of the reconciliation which brings us to religion and philosophy, would show clearly that he develops the categories in such a way that this difference within identity is never surmounted, i.e., in such a way that difference is at the heart of intelligibility. What we in fact find is that the only meaningful identity we have is the identity constituted by difference.

Once we see that the referent for ultimate totality and intelligibility is God and Nature, then we also see the strength of the apparent warranty for the presupposition. The natural argument is that to deny that there is a single totality "out there" of which we are a part, and to deny that this single totality in the end makes sense as a whole, would be to deny not only our natural experience—for we experience a continuity of the world in spite of discontinuity, difference, and alienation—but would also be to call into question the sense of the whole. If there is no principle of totality, no force which makes what-is stand as a whole, then there can be no comprehensive intelligibility, nothing which makes sense of different senses; for there would be no whole to which intelligibility could be accorded. On the other hand, if there is no comprehensive intelligibility, no ultimate reason, justification, and sense for the whole as a whole, then we are left with a radical relativism within the whole and thus are led to nihilism. That is to say, to deny either Nature or God or something else as referent for ultimate and comprehensive intelligibility is to make anything and everything possible and true and valuable; for one has removed an *ultimate source of evidence* for truth and value, and is confronted with a sheer multiplicity of worlds and intelligibility frameworks relevant for the "same" world. This problem of nihilism lies deeply rooted in the human condition and in its natural quest for certainty, even when that quest is in terms of particulars.[10] Not only does hopeless disorientation come to the natural attitude, but philosophy and theology are destroyed as well. From the pre-Socratics through Plato, the Christian tradition, modern empiricism and rationalism, and finally Kant and German idealism—irrespective of the final stance taken on the question of our ability to articulate the ultimate nature of this referent; from the courage of Parmenides through the caution of Plato and Aristotle, from the faith of Christian philosophy through the *mitigated* skepticism of empiricism and the trust in reason of the rationalists, from Kant's critical attitude through Hegel's assurances that we can finally know God: philosophy, arising out of the natural attitude, has accepted this putative praxical presupposition of the natural attitude as warranted.

Finally, this presupposition can be seen as the driving force of the *Phenomenology*. We began with the presupposition as sense-certainty made its claim for access to reality in its own natural way. The presupposition, however, was not at that point examined for itself. Rather, the *Phenomenology* pressed on in its quest for certainty, rejecting any presupposition set which could not legitimate the natural certainty of the natural attitude, a certainty based on the claim to have access to reality, i.e., to a reality presupposed as standing there as a whole and making sense as a whole. Thus, so long as the natural attitude and its presupposition of comprehensive intelligibility are taken as the touchstone for adequacy of the authentic presupposition set, this presupposition of a single referent for totality and intelligibility will govern the progress of the quest. The various forms of consciousness which were rejected were rejected as inadequate precisely because they could not give us a standpoint from which we could grasp the comprehensive intelligibility of the world and of our relation to the world. Self-consciousness, on the other hand, gave some degree of access in the freedom of self-consciousness, an access which attempted to bring together the two levels of thematics and to grasp the unity of the unchangeable, persisting consciousness, the changeable, relative consciousnes, and the correlate changeable and unchangeable world. But at the most profound depths of this attempt, the surrender to reason—i.e., to this comprehensive intelligibility as a given—was signalled. Finally, the move to spirit was made on the grounds that only the specificity of an actual lived-world could furnish comprehensiveness. In light of this we can see that, if at any point in the *Phenomenology* something less than a standpoint granting self-warranting comprehensive intelligibility had been acceptable, the whole of the quest in the form it has taken would have ceased; for there was always available to us, even in sense-certainty, some sort of partial, relative, conditioned intelligibility and access to reality. But to have this situation would entail either giving up the natural attitude and its certainty as our guide to adequacy—something Hegel could not do and still satisfy the condition that the natural attitude be given the ladder—or examining the presupposition and finding it unwarranted. Neither of these occurred.

It is clear, I think, that this presupposition of a comprehensive intelligibility is there and shapes both natural and philosophical consciousness. Not only the positive, trusting attitudes of a "rational" person and "rational" philosophy make sense in terms of its necessitation, but also the negative attitudes of relativism, skepticism, and nihilism; for these latter have their present significance only in terms of their *denial* of access to a comprehensive intelligibility. In light of the seriousness of this presupposition, is it possible that it is not warranted?[11] The answer arrived at in the analysis which now follows is that it is not warranted and that it fails to be warranted in a determinate way which directs the quest for certainty in a direction radically different from that heretofore indicated in the tradition. I shall proceed to show this by returning to the beginning of the discussion of sense-certainty and the first appearance of the presupposition, and by conducting a dialectical examination of it for its adequacy to our experience.[12]

This presupposition, as I have already pointed out, emerges at the very beginning of the *Phenomenology* proper. Actually, it is there in the Preface and Introduction, but this is not important; for the actual drive of the *Phenomenology* is to be found not in these self-mediating beginnings of the philosopher, but in the first encounter with the putative praxical presuppositions of the natural attitude. At the beginning of "sense-certainty" Hegel describes the standpoint assumed by sense-certainty as one which,

> because of its concrete content . . . immediately appears as the *richest* kind of knowledge, indeed a knowledge of infinite wealth for which no bounds can be found, either when we *reach out* into space and time in which it is dispersed, or when we take a bit of this wealth, and by division *enter into* it (*PhG*, 79; *PhS*, 58).

In this simple and immediate way, it is presupposed that through consciousness we have access to any and every part of what-is, and that the access is not in principle problematic. As pointed out above, this is not to say that anyone is omniscient or omnipresent, but only that there is at some level of reality a homogeneous, standing whole which in each and every one of its parts yields up a sense which belongs to the whole. The "It is" of which immediate, unreflective knowledge boasts in its putative presupposition set simply reflects this presupposition that the world as I immediately have it is a whole and makes sense as a whole. As we saw in our analysis of sense-certainty in Chapter II, the "It is" refers not only to the referential content, but to the semantic content and to the immediate connection between certainty and truth. The simple fact that one, undifferentiated, immediate stance of natural sense-certainty toward what-is is held to be adequate to explore what-is as it is in itself, necessitates the presupposition of a comprehensive intelligibility located in that world itself.

In Hegel's analysis the presence of this presupposition is ignored in the sense that we are not asked to examine it. In fact, as I have argued above, it is precisely its being continued without examination that determines the further course of the analysis. What is argued, instead, is that the particulars which we know could not be known with certainty and in their specificity if we presuppose that the object alone is the source of certainty and truth. The response from sense-certainty, then, was that we must take account of the "I" and its intentions in order to fix our truths with certainty. This, in fact, was meant all along, it is now claimed by the natural attitude. Thus, for our analysis,

> the certainty is now to be found in the opposite element, viz. in knowing, which previously was the unessential element. Its truth is in the object as *my* object, or in its being *mine*; it is, because *I* know it (*PhG*, 83; *PhS*, 61).

What is of interest here for our examination of the presupposition of the single referent for totality and intelligibility is Hegel's further explication of what this move is to accomplish and thus its justification as a dialectical move. When it was assumed that the single locus was the world and its objects, the Now and Here continuously vanished and we lost that distinctive particularity of which we are certain in our everyday knowledge. That is to say, we lost continuity and totality.[13] With the new move, on the other hand, the

> truth thus lies now in the 'I', in the immediacy of my *seeing, hearing*, and so on; the vanishing of the single Now and Here that we mean is prevented by the fact that *I* hold them fast. 'Now' is day because I see it; 'Here' is a tree for the same reason (*PhG*, 83; *PhS*, 61).

In order to see how this can furnish us with a way to test the warranty for the presupposition about totality and intelligibility, I would like to enrich Hegel's example of sense-certainty. The heart of the purpose of Hegel's opening analysis is to pay attention to the fact that the particulars of the world are constantly changing within experience as I pass from one object to another. But in our daily lives we not only pass from one object to another within the thematics of the natural attitude; we often also pass immediately from one framework of intelligibility or category of comportment to another, and we do this while being presented with the "same" object or situation. For instance, in a day's time I will not only turn from trees to houses or live from day to night, but will also "turn" from giving attention to the trees and houses in the comportment of being a father and husband, to giving attention to these same things in the comportment of being a professor, a religious worshipper, a concerned citizen, etc. In each different category of comportment there is a different set of context-specific, as well as epistemic and ontological praxical presuppositions, presuppositions constitutive of the semantical content of experience. Different semantical contents for the same object not only entail specific variety in respect to the objects themselves, but also a different framework of general intelligibility. In the comportment of being a father, the old tree in front of my house is a beautiful, adventure-laden domain for my tree-climbing son. But as a concerned citizen, I realize that this same tree is a hazard to the public because it obstructs the view of automobile drivers as they approach the intersection at the corner. Moreover, it is a liability for me as a homeowner because its shading characteristics are slowly causing the roof of my house to rot. Thus, the tree does not simply "mean" different things in the specific context, but is an element in different comportments with respectively different value hierarchies, epistemic canons, and even ontological characteristics.[14]

This means that there can appear radical antagonisms and discontinuities between categories of comportment, different intelligibility frameworks, and different elements of experience belonging to the same individual person. What makes sense in one comportment may not make sense in a second one. And yet all the comportments are participated in by the same person, with no radical discontinuity within experience with respect to that experience being a totality. Indeed, it is the presence of the different comportments and semantic contents within the single totality and continuity of one's own experience which make it possible, experientially, for there to be notable tensions and differences between the comportments and between the semantic contents. It is within the totality of experience—whatever the referent for that totality—that I turn from one object to another, from one task to another, from one comportment to another, from one framework of intelligibility to another. The "world" and its specific referential contents can literally change in terms of meaning and intelligibility as I move from one comportment to another, but the totality *qua* totality does not. In fact, the latter remains constant and gives me continuity of "place" within which the conflicts and discontinuities in intelligibility can be experienced.

With the presupposition of a single referent for totality and intelligibility it is only natural at the first sign of a failure in intelligibility to turn away from the natural reference to "the world out there" to another domain in order to obtain a single referent for both. But as a matter of fact, if we take the deficiency in the naive realist position in a very strict way, it is not the referent for totality that seems to have disappeared, but only the world out there as referent for complete and comprehensive intelligibility. The totality has not disappeared; on the contrary, it is precisely because my experience remains a whole that the problem with the semantical and comportmental content occurs. Given the logic of presuppositions, this suggests that the presupposition of the same referent for both totality and intelligibility should be given up; for if totality and intelligibility would actually have the same locus—in this case the object world in reference to itself—then my experiencing of particulars would remain intact in so far as the two parameters are concerned. But what happens is that they do not; rather my experiencing of particulars becomes impossible under the presupposition, while my changes of comportment leave me with ultimate unintelligibility. The latter is true because under the presupposition of identity of referent, with the disappearance of intelligibility, there *should* also be a disappearance of totality and continuity. That is simply not the case. *I* turn or change comportment with respect to the world; and that I do and that I experience both "before" and "after," both "here" and "there," both first comportment and second comportment necessitates the separation of the referents for totality and intelligibility. In fact, the separation of intelligibility and totality from the specific objects is necessitated. For the totality experientially persists through many particulars, as does the intelligibility so long as I remain within a single comportment. Both object and intelligibility can change within a single totality, within a constancy of experience. The comportment and semantical reference change, and thus the framework for intelligibility, but this change occurs within *a* totality. In order to clarify my argument here, I would like to further expand the discussion of the thematics of the natural attitude in order to see how these are related to the praxical presupposition about totality and intelligibility.

The Absolute Standpoint: A Critique 261

The following is meant to be a scenario in which the naive realist standpoint of sense-certainty governs as putative praxical presupposition, and the thematics of sense-certainty are exemplified by a simple, mundane situation. Let us say that on a Saturday afternoon I have set myself the task of repairing a broken lamp. I take up the tools and materials I propose to use, and face the ordinary world of everyday life in the comportment of being a handyman around the house. The first thing to be noted is that this is a specific comportment and framework of intelligibility which differs radically from that in which I stood earlier in the day when I was in the same room studying a philosophical text. But I have "made the change," perhaps even against my inclinations.

The praxical presupposition set which putatively constitutes this new comportment and grants intelligibility to my world and my activities includes, among many other elements, certain epistemic, ontological, and metaphysical presuppositions about my access to reality which have already been discussed in the chapter on sense-certainty. In addition, there are certain autobiographical presuppositions concerning my own mechanical abilities and other aspects of my life, and certain existential or contextual presuppositions about the situation with which I am faced: the lamp is broken and should be fixed by me if possible, and when fixed should be of a certain specifiable form and function; the tools I have at my disposal are sufficient for the job; and so on. In all, there is a very large, but finite set of praxical presuppositions which constitute the comportment of being a handyman around the house.

For the most part, the constituents of the comportment remain at a tacit presuppositional level; but as we have seen in the *Phenomenology*, any of the presuppositions could be made explicit in a natural way if and when I were questioned or questioned myself about what I was doing, how I was doing it, why I thought I could do it, etc. The presuppositions could also surface if and when something about the situation as I thematize it in the natural attitude brought my comportment into question in terms of its adequacy to the situation.

Now, with what has been given already in the scenario, and with the full discussion of praxical presuppositions behind us, a problem with the presupposed identity of referent for totality and intelligibility begins to appear. The situation is one in which I have moved from the comportment of studying a philosophical text to one of attempting to repair a lamp. What makes sense of the world in each case is by far not identical; for each, what the world of experience consists in, and the lexical ordering of values and meanings are very different. And yet, as I turn from one comportment to another, from one intelligibility framework to another, the totality remains constant in spite of the change in intelligibility framework and thus of the context-specific and general praxical presuppositions. As I turn from one to the other, totality remains constant; for the totality of "world" is one which encompasses the two disparate comportments. And as I turn from the thematization of one set of objects—my books, papers, the typewriter, etc.—to the other—the tools, broken lamp, etc.—there is a constancy of totality; for again the totality of "world" is one which encompasses the two different sets of objects. What remains constant in a lived sense of constancy is the totality of my world as *my* world. What also remains constant is some sense of a world out there, a totality which is independent of my experience. What changes are the comportments and the objects.[15]

We can now specify more directly the failure of the simple realist presupposition of the identity of referent for totality and intelligibility. In fact, not an identity, but this *difference* in referents between intelligibility, totality, and objects must be praxically presupposed in my activities. For without that difference the kind of change which is experienced could not be experienced. Furthermore, the praxical presuppositions, except for the autobiographical component, belong to the practice itself, to the comportment itself; they are not really "mine" in any sense of privacy, but are intersubjective, public, shareable with other persons. Given the appropriate change in indexical reference for any autobiographical components, the intelligibility of the world within the comportment of being a handyman around the house is public, objective, something which stands as a way of relating to the world for many different individuals. If a friend, for example, comes to visit me while I am fixing the lamp, he can easily change his original intention of having a purely social visit and the comportment that involves, for the comportment of being a handyman around the house. The autobiographical component would be different, but the general comportment would be the same for my friend as for me. Thus, it is not I who decide on the propriety of the comportment and on what makes the practice intelligible; the criteria come somehow with the situation itself. It is probably therefore more correct to say that one is *held by* a certain praxical presupposition set and that one is *held in* a certain comportment, than to say that one holds the presuppositions and comportment. The comportment is in fact an instance of that element which we have come to recognize as spirit. What lends intelligibility *per se* to my situation and the world is therefore something which, in extension as well as in intension, transcends me and my own possibilities. Whatever the referent for intelligibility, then, it transcends me and my intentionality.[16]

But our scenario and the logic of presuppositions shows that the same is not true for totality. As the first move of the *Phenomenology* shows, and as my own example has also shown, when I turn from one situation to another the continuity and totality remain with the "I" which turns. We do not lose totality at the point as which we change intelligibility. In fact, we change intelligibility on the background of the retention of totality. Therefore, the totality is certainly not the world *qua* intelligible or the world in terms of semantical content; for the latter have changed, while the former has remained the same. Nor is the referent for totality—at least in any concrete experiential sense—the "whole" out there; for *qua* "whole" it transcends me. I do experience totality, but I do not experience the whole universe. Furthermore, that "whole" out there is never thematized, indeed is not thematizable except as a felt possibility; rather it is the objects to which I attend at one time or another and which change through time which constitute the "out there" in concrete terms. The totality, then, has for its concrete referent that "I" who moves through experience and thus through the multiple and multiform changes of object and comportment. If it were warranted to presuppose that intelligibility and totality had the same referent, then as the intelligibility framework changed, so too would the totality. But then there would not be a totality, but only a series of "partial" totalities, a concept which in itself is difficult to grasp.

The primary experiential totality is that source of all indexicality, the "I".[17] All "thises" and "thats," all "heres" and "theres," all "nows" and "thens," and all changes in comportment and intelligibility occur within the totalizing process which is the original location for individual experience and thus for individual certainty, viz., the "I" which an individual experiencer is. That is the ultimate experiential context or ground of totality within experience. Even the changes which autobiographically occur, occur somehow within the primal indexicality of the "I." On the other hand, there is a constancy or totality of givenness *for* this "I," and that is another locus of totality, namely "the world" of which I and my experiences are a part. The only concrete sense of totality in respect to the total universe which transcends both the totality of the "I" and the categories of comportment, is the sense of the givenness of experience, that experience which is not this or that experience, but the experience within which experiences come and go. There is "always already" experience, a continuity of givenness. One totality is thus immanent within the individual, the other transcends the individual, to be experienced only as the givenness of experience as such. On the other hand, the referent for intelligibility is the set of comportments and intelligibility frameworks constituted in praxical presupposition sets. These are neither simply immanent as the totality of "I" nor transcendent as the totality of givenness; they are public, shared, somehow existing as a set of commonplaces in which individuals participate.

It might be argued here that, at the mundane level to which I now direct my attention, it can be conceded that totality and intelligibility lack an identical referent. In fact, it is just some version of that objection to which Hegel refers when he speaks of seeking and entering a domain in which the interests which move us in our everyday lives are hushed. It is argued that so long as I have these interests, and so long as I am "in time"—and time is precisely that totality which is the "I"—to be sure the identity of referent will escape me. On the other hand, in the "higher" domain, where these interests and comportments are hushed, there is to be an identity of referent for totality and intelligibility, and it is this domain which is claimed to give ultimate unity to the partial domains and to the differences experienced. Hegel here follows a very traditional argument which might in its different versions indicate a different name for the referent, but which in the end is functionally identical to Hegel's absolute idea as it is grasped in the stance of absolute knowing. In terms of function, then, if Hegel's metaphysical domain can be shown to be inadequate as a referent for this identity, it will be shown also for analogous cases.

The demonstration is not difficult; for what-is as thematized in the comportment of metaphysical theorizing differs from what-is as thematized in the comportment of being a handyman around the house in no way other than the way we discovered the discontinuity between my studying, on the one hand, and fixing the lamp on the other hand. The sense contained in the praxis of metaphysical contemplation and the sense contained in that of repairing a broken lamp are simply not commensurate. Yet I, or anyone else properly trained, can move from one comportment to another and preserve the totality. Furthermore, one in the metaphysical comportment has in neither sense of 'totality' more totality than one in the more mundane comportment. In terms of intelligibility, precisely in so far as the world is there for and in the comportment of the metaphysical, to that extent it is *not* there for and in the comportment of practical reality. Yet the totality is not lacking in either case, nor is it to be found merely or only in either case. There is, then, nothing unique about metaphysics, nor about religion, history, economics, politics, or any other domain which purportedly would give the key to comprehensive intelligibility. Each is an intelligibility framework, each is "a world" in terms of certain praxical presuppositions; but none is *the* referent for *the* totality of totalities. Such claims for metaphysics and other domains arise only from the presupposition that there must be a single referent for totality and intelligibility, and that this referent must yield a comprehensive intelligibility in terms of which partial intelligibilities have a possibility of sense. Thus, the claims for metaphysics or for some other framework of intelligibility cannot yield a proof of comprehensive intelligibility, but rather erroneously presuppose that such an intelligibility must underlie all partial frameworks.

A well-wrought account of this view which has emerged in the criticism of Hegel's quest for certainty—and of the tradition behind him and after him in so far as that tradition accepts the same presupposition—cannot be given here; for the careful examination of the relationship between the referent for intelligibility and the referent for totality is itself a long and difficult task.[18] I hope that I will be able to pursue this task in the future. The outcome of the inquiry is not clear to me now, but what is clear is that there is not the same referent, and thus that the search for a comprehensive intelligibility in so far as there is a single referent is not justified by experience itself or by an analysis of what experience must presuppose. There are many frameworks of intelligibility and categories of comportment, and they are not necessarily continuous with each other. Many, completely consistent in themselves, exclude others. Furthermore, the frameworks and comportments are spiritually objective, i.e., they are intersubjective, culturally grounded, and public in accessibility, unlike either referent for totality. And the latter are themselves problematic in their difference, for one seems to be experienced directly and immanent to each experiencer's experience, while the other—the givenness—is not experienceable either as totality or as process of totalization. As each of us proceeds within and through and between different frameworks and comportments, there is an experienced, private, subjective totality, that totality which I refer to as my life and which concerned us in the discussions of consciousness and self-consciousness, especially the latter. And yet, despite the privacy, there seems to be the constant intersection of totalities as we somehow "share" experiences and have interests in objects in a communal way. On the other hand, there is a non-experienced, yet felt totality which we loosely call "the world," and within which all that is given for experience is given. It would seem to be a sort of receptacle totality; but all that we are really able to say as this point is that this totality is the referent for the continuity of givenness in experience. Neither of the totalities are intelligible as such, but are surdal: they seem to serve only as a locus for the multiplicity of intelligibility frameworks as we participate in them.

If this is praxically presupposed, rather than a single referent for totality and intelligibility, then the experience of the natural attitude is more adequately grounded. As I turn from one task to another, from one intelligibility framework to another; as I experience the problems of mutual exclusiveness and consequent alienation between different intelligibility frameworks and comportments; as I simultaneously recognize both unity and diversity in experience: I necessitate only a relative referent for intelligibility, namely that referent which I have at any given time, and only the two sorts of referent for totality which have emerged from the present analysis, neither of which is identical with or the basis for the comportment and intelligibility of the world which is present.

Does the spectre of absurdity and meaninglessness return to haunt us, as it has the tradition whenever the single referent came into question in any way? Although a full answer to this question would also take us beyond the limits of a work exploring Hegel's quest for certainty, a preliminary denial is possible here. The imputation of nihilism, like the imputation of the need for a unifying domain and knowledge, arises only on the prior presupposition of the legitimacy of the putative necessitation of a single referent, the putative necessitation of a comprehensive intelligibility for what-is. It is because it is presupposed that there is such a domain—whether accessible to us or not matters not—that the denial of a comprehensive intelligibility seems to imply nihilism arising from relativism. If the domain is not presupposed, then relativism does not necessarily imply nihilism; for there is prima facie nothing wrong with discontinuity of intelligibility frameworks unless one presupposes that there is. In other words, the spectre of nihilism arises from relativism as in the consummation of a self-fulfilling prophecy.

However this may be—and I admit the inadequacy of what I have said in so far as it would be intended as an explanation of the full consequences of denying a single referent for totality and intelligibility—Hegel's quest for certainty does not emerge as a finished account. By Hegel's own standards, namely to bring out all the putative presuppositions of the natural attitude in order to show warranty for claims to an absolute standpoint, he fails in his own task. He has not examined this basic presupposition to the effect that the absolute standpoint or our unconditioned and warranted access to reality is such that there is a single referent for totality and intelligibility. Once it is examined, it is seen to be unwarranted. In its place must be put a presupposition that there are different referents for totality and intelligibility respectively, and that this entails that there is no single underlying intelligibility for all intelligibilities. There is no domain of the philosophical sciences such as Hegel conceived them. Nor is there any domain functionally analogous, which is to serve as ground for intelligibility and as final repository for evidence in all cases. Whatever the absolute standpoint is—and I have in no way denied that there is one, but only that our warranted access to reality does not come via access to a referent for both intelligibility and totality—it is constituted in some other way. But if this is true, then the motor of the *Phenomenology* is removed; for there is no need to go on to seek a single, unifying ground of comprehension.

But this does not mean that the investigation into Hegel's *Phenomenology* as a quest for certainty has been a waste of time. It would not, in my view, have been sufficient simply to begin with sense-certainty and then introduce the critique which has come here at the end. First, the full importance of the presupposition of identity of referent for intelligibility and totality would not have become as clear; for we would not have seen the consequences of being guided to the putative absolute standpoint by the presupposition had we not made the journey. Nor would we have seen the primacy of the natural attitude in that quest for certainty. Second, a real understanding of Hegel and the tradition would have been denied us had we not completed the journey. David Hume, no less than Leibniz and Spinoza, has come to light in the *Phenomenology*. Third, no matter what is discovered as we now set out to follow the consequences of this critique of Hegel, much that is found in the *Phenomenology* is sure to be of help in coming to resolve the problems of philosophy in the future. On the basis of a full conversation with Hegel in his quest for certainty, we shall now be able to continue with the historical-philosophical dialogue in which we share the concerns of Hegel and the tradition. A critique of the tradition is not necessarily a severing of ties with that tradition or a radical departure from it. However strong and seemingly untraditional the claim I make might be, it has its meaning only within the historical-philosophical dialogue itself. We speak only to continue that tradition.

Notes to Chapter I

1 Georg Wilhelm Friedrich Hegel, *Phänomenologie des Geistes* hrsg. von Johannes Hoffmeister (Hamburg: Felix Meiner, 1952), hereafter cited in text and notes as *PhG*. The English translation used and cited is by A. V. Miller, *Phenomenology of Spirit* (Oxford: Clarendon Press, 1977), hereafter cited in text and notes as *PhS*. Minor changes in the translation will from time to time be made without notation. On the history of views of the *Phenomenology*, see Otto Pöggeler [392, 394, 395].

2 This problem is to be found not only in systematic philosophies such as Hegel's, but also in the work of traditional, non-speculative thinkers such as David Hume. Although the outcome of the quest for certainty is radically different in Hume and others, the quest is the same. See my remarks in the Preface above. There are two recent major monographs on this problem as it appears in Hegel. Hans Friedrich Fulda [144] shows clearly the difficulties in defending any place as a beginning point. He argues, however, that an introduction is in some sense always required and that it must be "carried out in a specific discipline which must be the science of consciousness, and yet cannot be a first part of the system and cannot be limited to the formal aspects of consciousness; on the other hand, it has its foundation in a finished system"(12). Karin Schrader-Klebert [443] mounts an impressive analysis and critique of Hegel based on his failure to begin in such a way that in the end, when reaching the goal of science, the beginning still stands within the system (12). I shall, on the whole, be arguing against this conclusion.

For a brief history of this problem, see Jürgen Leopoldsberger [315]. Leopoldsberger stresses that the problem is one of beginning for both natural and philosophical consciousness, a theme I shall take up below. Manfred Baum and Kurt Meist [22] provide an excellent account of the problem of beginning as it relates to philosophy, the natural attitude, *and* concrete praxis. See especially pp. 72-73. See also in this regard Jay William Hudson [228] for a naive, but straightforward and refreshing approach to the problem. Other aspects are taken into account, with varying assessments of Hegel's intentions and success, in Klaus Harlander [180]; Heidegger [207]; Johannes Heinrichs [208]; Howard Kainz [249], 13ff.; Heinz Kimmerle [259]. In Kimmerle, see especially his discussion around pp. 13, 289. For further discussion of my own resolution to the problem, see Flay [132, 134].

3 See, for example, *PhG*, 12; *PhS*, 3; Georg Wilhelm Friedrich Hegel, *Wissenschaft der Logik* (Hamburg: Felix Meiner, 1963), Bd. I, 23, hereafter cited in text and notes as *WdL*. The English translation used and cited is by A. V. Miller, *Science of Logic* (London: George Allen & Unwin, Ltd., and New York: Hemanities Press, 1969), 43, hereafter cited in text and notes as *SL*. This view of Hegel's is discussed widely in the literature. See for instance the works cited in note 2, above, and the discussion of circularity below.

4 This refers us, of course, to Hegel's famous characterization of philosophies which begin with a "shot from a pistol" (*PhG*, 26; *PhS*, 16). V. F. Asmus [13] has an interesting, but as I hope to show wrong, view on this when he claims

that Hegel in fact had a doctrine of intellectual intuition. The only real difference from Schelling, Asmus argues, is not the absence of intuition in Hegel, but the presence in the latter of "the *genesis* of immediate knowledge, the dialectics of *mediation* in the unity of immediacy and mediacy" (49). But this seems to me to be a rather large difference.

5 For an interesting account of this problem in the literature as it bears on the tradition, cf. for example Friedrich Kümmel [283], especially the Introduction where the general problem of the circle is discussed. See also Charles Taylor [495], 98ff.; Charles Andler [11], especially 319–20; Robert B. Pippin [390]; Eugen Fink [126], especially 43–44.

This problem is at the heart of the question of beginning and of the quest for certainty. As such it will be further discussed below. But see the penetrating discussion in Stanley Rosen [421], especially the Preface and Chapter VI. Pierre-Jean Labarrière [291], sees the problem of beginning as necessitating the paradox of having an introduction only in so far as it already contains the system as such (pp. 133–34). Otis Lee [309] discusses the tension between system and method, claiming that for Hegel method or the search for system, and not dogmatic system, is fundamental. Robert L. Perkins [386] focuses on the difficulties of achieving a presuppositionless beginning. Yves Thierry [499] looks at the problem from the perspective of the demands of the *Science of Logic*, as does also Hans Wagner [514].

Friedrich Grimmlinger [170] moves in a direction which I shall take below, namely distinguishing two ways in which a beginning is to be made, subjectively and objectively. For views which explicitly ignore this distinction, see Daniel Guerrière [173]; Donald Kuspit [286]. Kuspit concentrates on the problem as one of establishing the "unnatural attitude which notices the difficulties of self-evidence" (53).

6 For the discussion in the *Phenomenology*, see *PhG*, 31–32, 66ff.; *PhS*, 20–21, 48ff.

7 Even among those who see the *Phenomenology* in this way, it is understood to work in very different ways by different commentators. See for a sample of the variety, Reinhold Aschenberg [12]; Rolf Ahlers [6]; Mitchell Miller [363]; Richard Kroner [275], Bd. 2, 362ff.; Heidegger [207], 4–12; Werner Marx [350], 31–34; Findlay [120], 85–86; Pierre-Jean Labarrière [291], 133–34; Rudolf Haym [193], 233ff.; Nicolai Hartmann [191], Bd. II, especially p. 314; Cassirer [67], Bd. III, 304ff.; Leo Lugarini [334], 20–21; Nicolas Lobkowicz [325], 148ff. My agreements and disagreements with the above will become clear as we proceed.

8 There are several general forms taken by the views I am arguing here against. There is a general Marxist view of the *Phenomenology* which sees it as a work referring to human history. See Lukács [336] for the classical presentation of this. See also Ernst Bloch [43], especially p. 63. It has also been seen as a series of "ideal types" constructed from logical concepts, e.g. by Hermann Schmitz [435], 315–16. Ivan Soll [467], especially 69–73, 150, seems to separate out the proper task of the *Phenomenology*, but then tends also to see it as a work of ethics and epistemology. See also Soll [471].

Such interpretations as these have some relation generally to the "existential"

Hegel found in Maurice Merleau-Ponty [358], and a whole series of variations on the *Phenomenology* as "anthropology." For the latter see for instance Royce [426], 138–40; Hyppolite [238], where it is also described as a *Bildungsroman* (11–12); Kojève [266], where it is claimed that "in spite of what Hegel thought, the *Phenomenology* is a philosophical anthropology" (39) in the form of "a phenomenological description (in the Husserlian sense of the word); its 'object' is man in so far as he is an existential phenomenon" (38); Alexandre Koyré [272], 179; Gustav Mueller [366]; Henri Niel [376].

The "ontological" interpretation, which is in some ways close to what I shall argue, is best found in Heidegger [206], especially p. 58, and in Heidegger [207]. Compare Eugen Fink [127], especially 25–26. The ontogeny/phylogeny interpretations point to an important aspect of the *Phenomenology*, but when stressed too much tend to move also in the anthropological direction and thus to obscure the separation of this work from other parts of the system. See André Cresson and René Serreau [85], especially p. 78; Clark Butler [63]; Jacques D'Hondt [98], especially p. 29; Enzo Paci [381]. Against this ontogeny/phylogeny interpretation, see Werner Marx [350], 31–34.

Johannes Heinrichs [208] has made a strong case for a parallelism between the Jena *Logik* and the *Phenomenology*. For views that in various ways see the *Phenomenology* as an early version of the system, see G. A. Koursanov [270, 271]; L. Bruno Puntel [399], especially 269; Joseph L. Navickas [374], who claims that the *Phenomenology* is "the whole of the Hegelian system . . . from the standpoint of knowledge" (25).

9 What I mean by 'historical-philosophical dialogue' is not the history of philosophy or the philosophical tradition as it stands captured in something like Hegel's own *Lectures on the History of Philosophy*, but the on-going dialogue between philosophers that a systematic treatment attempts to capture. Hegel saw himself as caught up in a long dialogue over time to which we must first listen and then add our own contribution. For more on this see Flay [132, 134].

András Gedö [157] articulates the relation between Hegel and this dialogue nicely when he writes that the historical character of our knowledge does not connote that "one has to do with a no longer existing world," but with a world and a knowledge of that world which has been historically constituted and at the same time contains that history within its present as substance (825–26). He sees, however, an antinomy here concerning the problem of the unchangeability of absolute spirit and the revolutionary character of dialectic, which does not seem to me to follow at all.

The theme of the historical-philosophical dialogue is also taken up in the Hegelian thesis of the oneness of philosophy and the history of philosophy. On this see Ernst Behler [29], especially 186–88. Cassirer [67], III, 285–302, has an interesting discussion of what can be construed as the stage which this dialogue had reached in Hegel's time. W. H. Walsh [517] lays out a clear exposition of the philosophical import of the history of philosophy and the continuity within it but, on the other hand, fails to see the link between the history of philosophy as an historical-philosophical dialogue and the introduction to philosophy necessary in order properly to philosophize. On the other hand, Heinz Kimmerle [257] has clearly shown the development in Hegel of the idea of a historical-philosophical dialogue and the possibility of philosophy having a history occurring together with the development of the idea of a *Phenomenology*. See also Kimmerle [258].

10 *WdL*, 51–52; *SL*, 67–68.

11 The history of Hegel's early development and his break with it in 1804–05 is a complex and important aspect of Hegel's mature philosophy. By far the most complete work in English and perhaps in any language on Hegel's development in the early years is Henry S. Harris [184]. In addition to Harris's own clear and convincing account of Hegel's development, this work contains a quite complete account of other important views on Hegel in his early years. Compare with this especially the influential work of Theodor Haering [178]. Cf. the works of Kimmerele cited in note 9, above, and also Kimmerle [259]; Pöggeler [394], especially 216–17; Marcuse [338], 30–90; Alexandre Koyré [272]; Walter Kaufmann [253], 1–45; Dieter Henrich [212], and the response to this by Eugene Thomas Long [328]; Nicolai Hartmann [191], II, 295–308. André Leonard [314], has an interesting discussion of the importance of Johannes Heinrichs' study of the *Phenomenology* and the Jena *Logic* (see note 2, above), but even if the parallelism is there, the question of the significance of the new form of the *Phenomenology* and its motivation is not responded to, thus leaving the goal of the *Phenomenology* unaddressed. Rüdiger Bubner [59], on the other hand, has a good deal to say about this as he traces the problem of the unity of experience in pre-*Phenomenology* days, centering on the problem of the opposition between unscientific consciousness and science, and the need for philosophy to justify itself in the eyes of the natural attitude. See especially 147ff.

12 *PhG*, 15ff.; *PhS*, 6ff. Cf. Hans Brockard [56], 51–53, and J. C. Horn [224].

13 This discussion of the tradition ties in with a theme to be discussed later, namely that of recollection or *Erinnerung* in respect to the tradition. It is also central to the problem of the relation of the individual to world-spirit. See *PhG*, 24–31; *PhS*, 14–20. The theme has been treated in various ways. It is really the implicit background for the whole treatment of Hegel given by Royce [426]. Walter Schulz [444] discusses how we can see Hegel's metaphysics as in some sense "demanded" by the preceding metaphysics. Judith Shklar [455] takes up these themes by seeing the *Phenomenology* as an elegy—the "kind of reconstruction offered by a funeral oration was now in order: an account of the deeds and works which reveal the meaning and urpose of the life now at an end" (73). But she fails to tie this in with the task of the *Phenomenology* as a whole. Cf. also Cassirer [67], III, 285–305, especially 304–05; Nicolai Hartmann [191], II, 275–89, 322–24; Flay [132, 134].

14 Just what constituted the central focus and its problems has been seen in different ways. For Koyré [272] it is the tradition as such which has broken down (154–55); Marcuse [338], 3–16, focuses on the social and political; Merold Westphal [528] offers an interesting account of philosophical, scientific, and political turmoil, but in an overall context of the religious and "Hegel's allusions to the loss of substantial life and a sense of the divine presence" (27–29). Lauer [305] argues that it is not "to the philosophy of his age that he gives credit for this [breakdown], but to its *religion*" (280). Kroner [275], II, 255–59, discusses

the lost unity of the European spirit and argues that Hegel's primary task was to reconcile the protestant theology with the values of classical antiquity (259). Kimmerle [259] holds that "the need of philosophy" is to bring about a unity from the alienation within life at that time (22–23). See also C. I. Gouliane [162] for a discussion of crisis and philosophy and an attempt to link this with our own time. In the end, I think, one must argue that for Hegel the crisis must be in spirit as such, and that we must reflect on this in the context of Hegel's remarks in the *Lectures on the History of Philosophy* on the relationship within spirit of philosophy, religion, and all forms of objective spirit. See Hegel [202], 73–75, and Hegel [203], Vol I, 53–55.

15 This relationship is highly problematic, and has caused various commentators to miss the nature of the mediation which carries us through the *Phenomenology*. See for instance Evelina Krieger [274] where it is argued that the concrete individual in pure positivity simply contradicts the mediations of reason. This misses the motive power of the quest for certainty which belongs to natural consciousness, and which I will discuss below. Findlay [120] also misses this relation when he holds that "Hegel's view is in principle a *philosophical* way of regarding the world, which depends for its acceptability on conceptual rather than factual considerations, though it can be used to illuminate fact, and though it is more applicable to certain sorts of fact than others" (56). He then continues in a vein which develops the movement of the *Phenomenology* in the direction of a philosophy of "as if" (57). This view of Findlay's is criticized by Aschenberg [12], 245–46, who tries to establish that the phenomenological and natural consciousness do not involve two subjects, but only one in self-reflection, "reflection of the phenomenological consciousness upon itself in the mode of consciousness of natural objectivity" (245–46). Aschenberg thus also misses the connection between the two by removing the real dialogical connection I shall soon demonstrate. For further complexities here, see below my discussion of the difference between assuming the absolute standpoint, on the one hand, and assuming the problem of that standpoint, on the other hand. Finally, Westphal [528] represents yet another view of the relation, characterized as one in which the "we" or the philosophical consciousness "spiritualizes (*begeist*)" the thought of the natural attitude in reference to culture (62–66).

16 This separation of the two consciousnesses must be acknowledged; but one must not go too far. Hyppolite [238] takes the opposition to lead to the view that the road which consciousness follows "is its own itinerary, not that of the philosopher who resolves to doubt," and then is led to discuss what is thematized in the *Phenomenology* as "theories" which natural consciousness has (12–13). Lauer [305] holds that only naive consciousness is necessary as the starting point (42), citing others who agree with him on this. Compare Schrader-Klebert [443] 22–27; Heribert Boeder [48] 157–58; Rüdiger Bubner [59], 147ff.; Aschenberg [12], 243–44. Aschenberg's whole treatment of this, in the context of his discussion of the four concepts of truth operative in the *Phenomenology*, brings out complexities of the opposition which one must attend to, whether one ends by agreeing with Aschenberg or not.

17 J. Rivelaygue [414] touches on the difference between Hegel and the tradition on this point in his discussion of "the phenomenological crisis" and the way in which the question of access to truth appeared to Hegel (especially pp. 330–31). See also Westphal [528] Ia, 1–2, where he articulates the key to the *Phenomenology* and Hegel's "independence from the whole epistemological project as modern philosophy inherited it from Descartes" (2). John Sallis [429] is especially insightful in respect to the opposition and the dialogue between the two (155–56).

18 Several commentators fail to recognize this restriction and Hegel's insistence on and the actual priority of the natural certainty and its rights. A view such as that of Robert Solomon [475] suggests that the "we" operates at a meta-level. Although thus preserving a difference, the driving force and autonomy of the natural attitude would be destroyed if this were the actual relation. On the other hand, to understand the beginning of the *Phenomenology* as abstract also abrogates the rights and power of the natural attitude. See for instance Henry A. Myers [372], 25. Hyppolite's view [238], in spite of his claims for the natural attitude in Hegel, misses the natural drive and rights of that attitude with his talk of theories in natural consciousness and an identification of the beginning with ancient skepticism (77–83). The claim that the absolute standpoint is assumed, as in Heidegger [207], 75–85, also obviously overlooks the rights of the natural attitude.

On the other side, Judith Shklar [457] has an excellent discussion of the inherent certainty and the natural quest for it (see especially p. 6); but she then places too much stress on Hegel's "organizing hand," and denies the Socratic movement in the *Phenomenology* (see pp. 8, 14, 25). Kuno Fischer [129], Bd. I, 299–300 has a good discussion of the natural will to knowledge of natural consciousness. Compare Pierre-Jean Labarrière [287], 30–48. Schrader-Klebert [443] throws an interesting light on natural consciousness with the argument that for Hegel philosophical reflection "cannot deny the right of primogeniture" to the natural consciousness since, claiming to furnish the "'quid juris' of this consciousness as cognition of actuality, it presupposes just the fact of concrete actuality as its point of departure" (69). Cf. also Jay William Hudson [228], 348.

19 As we shall see, the two standpoints begin in an attitude of separation; but as the *Phenomenology* progresses, the standpoints merge. Heidegger [206], 52–53, 102–12 essentially denies the merging. His position here is due to his own peculiar way of articulating the putative assumption of the absolute standpoint from the very beginning (see *Ibid.*, p. 62). G. van Riet [507] makes the same sort of distinction but calls natural consciousness 'intentional' and philosophical consciousness 'reflective'. He denies convergence because, according to him, natural consciousness never comes to know thematically its own subjectivity or intentionality (471–73). But, as we shall see, it comes to know precisely this.

For various views of this convergence, see Jean Ladrière [295], especially 173–75; W. Wieland [532]; 934–35; Ytashaq Klein [261]. For Klein, there is a use of Socratic/Platonic dialogue in a different way than that proposed by Wieland (Klein [261], 373ff., 382–83). See also Jürgen Leopoldsberger [315], 30–37; and Jay William Hudson [228]. There is a very abstract account of the convergence in

Francis Baumli [23], especially p. 227. Reinhold Aschenberg [12], 240ff. has a very complex account of what the convergence is supposed to be. Heinz Kimmerle [259] defends the convergence, but claims that it was necessary only in 1807, and not needed after that; for true philosophizing after the first accomplishment of the *Phenomenology* needed only the free act of thinking (21). Werner Marx [350], 15–25, has a good account of convergence, but I think that it is the inherent quest for certainty and not simply "intelligibility" which joins philosophy and the natural attitude.

20 The co-existence and co-functioning of these two demands is critical not only to an understanding of the *Phenomenology* itself, but also to the comprehension of the nature of the *Logic* and the rest of the system. For example, the question posed by Bubner [60] concerning the legitimate grounding of the assumption that "the theme and task of the *Logic* is to bring the truth of the absolute to articulation [*Aussage*]" (141–42) is answered, I think, by rooting the original motivation in the natural attitude which, in turn, is itself to belong to and to be grounded in the absolute standpoint as internal to itself. The accusation, made by Adorno and others, that Hegel forgets empirical, historical consciousness, can be made only on the grounds that the absolute standpoint is *not* within the real, historical individual. But as we see here in this passage, that internal character is just what is to be shown. On this criticism, see for instance Adorno [3], 28.

The immanence of the absolute standpoint has been argued for in different ways. See G. W. Cunningham [88]: "The standpoint of absolute knowing is involved in every, even the simplest, phase of consciousness; it is implied in every act of knowledge, in every subject-object relation,—which is tantamount to saying that it is coterminous with experience itself"(612). Compare this with W. Wieland [532]. Wieland writes that Hegel holds "that we have always already presupposed an absolute in all our thinking, even in the most trivial form of consciousness, for even the most simple consciousness makes the claim to be in possession of truth" (941). Indeed, among those who claim that the absolute standpoint is presupposed at the beginning, it is often acknowledged that the standpoint is within the natural attitude. On my view, however, this overlooks the distinction between the assumption of the absolute and the assumption of the problem of the absolute. See for example Richard Schacht [430], especially 9–12; Werner Marx [350], 1–5; Heidegger [206], 30; Fackenheim [118]. Fackenheim claims that for "Hegel, the difference between philosophy . . . and the whole remainder of human life (*both* theoretical and practical) is one of standpoint" (17). For a different treatment of the point see Labarrière [291], 136; John Sallis [429], 148–51.

21 Cf. John Sallis's analysis of this self-mediation, Sallis [429]. Guy Besse [36], in arguing for a parallel with *Emile*—between 'le gouverneur' and the author of the *Phenomenology*—skirts the whole issue (see especially 491); Jacques Maritain [342] attempts to settle the issue of mediation by insisting that Hegel begins with an intuition of becoming (41–42). On the self-mediating beginning see also Fulda [144], 18; Emerich Coreth [82], especially 101; Manfred Baum and Kurt Meist [22], especially 44–45, 72–73. The Baum/Meist essay is particularly perceptive on the relation between the beginning of philosophy and concrete praxis.

22 Again, it is important to see that the natural attitude has *as its own characteristic* the quest for certainty and, as we shall see, a presupposition of an absolute standpoint, i.e., in its case a standpoint in terms of which one has, in principle, an unproblematic access to all of reality. This will be fully discussed in Chapter II, below.

Schrader-Klebert [443] begins by recognizing the dual problem of the historical-philosophical dialogue and of the natural attitude, and in the end criticizes Hegel for not resolving the problem of the mediation of finitude and the historical nature of man (94–95). But compare Fackenheim [118], 71, where he wrongly holds that Hegel's view of history only developed later, and thus that the relation between philosophy and the history of philosophy was not on Hegel's mind at this time. For the correct view of this, cf. Heinz Kimmerle [257].

In general, Marxist views of Hegel also miss the real connection here. See for instance Lukács [336], especially 470–71 and the theory of the "three-time traversal of history"; Henri Lefèbvre [310], where Lefèbvre evidences his misunderstanding. "Hegelianism is a dogma: it demands an ascesis, a renouncing of individual experience and problems important to the individual. When the *Phenomenology* describes the anguish of unrealized being, I am touched. But the cosmic adventures of spirit are beyond us. What we really suffer, what obstructs our lives, does not disappear magically—and is not justified—by the efficacy of Hegelianism" (39). This misses not only the connection between the natural and philosophical attitudes in respect to the quest for certainty, but also the true nature of spirit. For another kind of mistake on this, see Cornelio Fabro [117].

My own view finds some support in A. Robert Caponigri [65], although I do not think it necessary to revert, as does Caponigri on p. 14, to the metaphysics of time and the *Encyclopedia* to explain the relation of history to the individual. See also Jean-Louis Viellard Baron [510], where he articulates Hegel's sense of history and the past: "The activity of thought in recollection is . . . the surpassing of immediate existence, it is the interiorisation of the exterior" (152). See also Werner Flach [130].

23 See works cited in note 5. The problem of circularity, which threatens to vitiate the autonomy and efficacy of the *Phenomenology*, is posed in many different contexts, all of which I think are avoided on my interpretation. Rosen [421] argues that the absolute standpoint is presupposed in the sense that Hegel (à la Vergil in his connection with Dante) is our guide (p. 129, but see the whole discussion, pp. 123–30). Such a metaphor is not quite to the point if on the side of philosophy what is presupposed, as I shall argue below, is the *problem* of the absolute standpoint. Bruno Liebrucks [320], VI, p. 9, argues that since the "We" questions and brings into question the subject-object itself, i.e. the consciousness being examined, recognition of this consciousness depends on having achieved the absolute standpoint. But again, if the quest for certainty is shared, and if the natural attitude can come to be aware of its own standpoint, then the achievement of the absolute standpoint at the very beginning of the *Phenomenology* is not required. Hyppolite [238] argues that "Hegel's argument can only be understood here if we already know where it is leading" (96). On my argument, at most one must presuppose recognition of the problem. Heidegger [206] argues on the basis

of the "parousia" and the "being-with-us" of the Absolute (30) that the absolute standpoint must be presupposed. To be sure, one must admit that there is a sense in which it is always already with us, or otherwise the final point of the *Phenomenology*—to show the absolute standpoint within the natural standpoint—would be *a priori* invalidated. But this points only to the implicit presence of the standpoint within the natural attitude, the natural certainty which belongs to the natural attitude, and not any need to presuppose the explicit presence of the standpoint on the part of philosophy. See also on this view Eugen Fink [127], where the absolute and the absolute standpoint are characterized as being at the beginning "an anticipation" (38). On the presupposition, see also Fackenheim [118], 35–37; Jürgen Habermas [176], 10, 12, 23. For some positions closer to my own, see Heinrich Moritz Chalybäus [69], 361–62; G. W. Cunningham [88] 622. For further discussion of my view, see note 25, below.

24 It is a classical criticism of Hegel, made first by Schelling, then repeated by Feuerbach and Kierkegaard and many others since then, that Hegel violates the rights of the natural attitude. Cf. Löwith [331], especially 137–38.

25 For some positions which support me or at least move in my direction on this problem see Lauer [305], 34ff., where a position in my direction is taken against the assumption of the absolute standpoint; Royce [426], 142–43, where Royce argues that the *Phenomenology* "presupposes readers acquainted with the problems of recent idealism"; Werner Flach [130], where philosophy is understood as "the history of problems" and dialectic as the "method of problem-thinking" (450); Puntel [399] where, although leading in quite a different direction, the three senses of presuppositionlessness can be understood as tied together by orientation toward the absolute standpoint as a problem (293–303). See also Werner Marx [350], 23–25, where he cites three conditions necessary for a critique of other standpoints. My insistence on the presupposition of the absolute standpoint as a problem, not as a standpoint, fits all three conditions posited by Marx.

26 This account of mine gives meaning to Hegel's prefatory and introductory remarks without violating his injunction against prefaces and introductions. For on the view just given, neither presents the philosophical view, but rather only situates that view in its natural soil.

27 There are differing accounts of this relation to Kant and to post-Kantian Idealism, all of which have something to teach us. See, for example, Royce [426]; Kroner [275]; Nicolai Hartmann [191]; Ernst Cassirer [67]; Jürgen Leopoldsberger [315]; Miodrag Cekić [68]; Marcuse [338], especially 3–16; Werner Hartkopf [188]; W. H. Werkmeister [525]; Franz Grégoire [169].

28 On the existential demand placed upon us, cf. Walter Kaufmann [253], 115; Merleau-Ponty [358], 1313–14; Jean Wahl [515], 7; Westphal [528], 39.

29 Cf. here Westphal [528] and the discussion of the dogmatic nature of the natural consciousness (pp. 86–87), and Rolf Ahler's [6] discussion of presuppositions, where he argues that we are free of presuppositions only to the degree that we are aware of them, and that to be aware of them is not to abolish them (68).

30 On the other hand, there is a useful comparison to be made, which I will explicitly make below, between this Hegelian focus on the natural attitude and

the similar interlocutory exchanges in Platonic dialogues. Cf. W. Wieland [532], where the complicity of the natural attitude is clearly articulated; Lauer [305], 29; and John Sallis [429], 155.

31 Nevertheless, it is still true that there is implicit in the naive natural attitude the drive to reflection, based upon the natural desire for certainty. See Otis Lee [309], 369, where he argues that there "can be no introduction to philosophy which is not already a beginning *in* philosophy." But, while this alludes to the inherent reflective character of experience, this character, I am arguing, must be made dynamic by connecting that experience to the quest for certainty.

32 Ytashaq Klein [261] focuses nicely upon the discourse character of the *Phenomenology*, but places too much stress on the "ignorance" of the philosophical consciousness. He does the latter in order to avoid the question-begging problem. But philosophical consciousness also has its own interest in the problem of certainty, shares it with natural consciousness, and has no need therefore to suppress it.

33 The necessity for dialogue cannot be overemphasized here. Hinrich Fink-Eitel [128] has made the point well when he argues that the *Phenomenology* is open not only to philosophical alternatives, "but also for a consciousness which is not yet philosophical," and, in fact, that the possibility of philosophy depends upon the possibility of dialogue with nonphilosophical consciousness" (243). He also refers, in the same place, to the Socratic questioning in the *Phenomenology*. See also Ytashaq Klein [261], 372–73.

34 Cf. Sallis [429] for a distinction between the "initiatory" and "second" beginning of the *Phenomenology*.

35 This point has been made before and will play an important role in the discussion in the next chapter below. On the positioning of the natural certainty of the natural attitude see also Pippin [390], 309; Schrader-Klebert [443], 23–28, especially 27–28; Lauer [305], 41–42. Martin De Nys [92] notes the centrality of certainty, but then concentrates his analysis on the sense object. David Lamb [299] moves in the direction I am taking here, but fails to focus on the certainty problem *per se*. Charles Taylor [495] argues that the *Phenomenology* begins and proceeds "purely by taking up the inner logic of our own starting point," and that the work "is above all a work of self-clarification" (124), but also does not see the significance of certainty as a problem (see pp. 140–46). Werner Becker [25] is a good example of the consequences of missing the present point; for he fails to see the consequent mutual engagement of philosophy and the natural attitude, claiming instead that "there is deliberately no philosophical-theoretical claim or pretension connected with the articulation of the stance of sense-certainty" (110). Becker takes the claim to non-interference made by the "we" to mean that there is no locus. But if certainty is seen as central, this in fact becomes a common locus for both philosophy and the natural attitude. This same oversight causes Becker to argue that Hegel forces linguistic expressions on sense-certainty which do not belong there (120). See also Krieger [274] who sees a straightforward opposition between the simple immediate of sense-certainty and the mediation of the articulated critique. On recognition of the single quest for certainty shared by the two, see Fulda [144], 162–71.

36 In addition to the problems cited in the previous note, the centrality and shared concern for certainty, and thus for a quest for certainty, also ameliorate various other difficulties attributed to Hegel. For instance, anthropological approaches of various sorts lose all focus on certainty: see for instance Cassirer [67], III, 327ff. The mistakenly perceived need for the prior establishment of the absolute standpoint, as we have already argued, must also be criticized on the same grounds. See for instance Johannes Heinrichs [208], 54ff., 73, 161–62. Heinrichs is also here forced to resort to appeal to analogy, a logical form incompatible with dialectic. See also Kojève's discussion of method in Kojève [267] 169–259, especially 170–74. Stanley Rosen's insistence on the need for intuition, Stanley Rosen [421], also hinges on failure to see the importance of the quest for certainty as both positive and negative and shared by both the natural attitude and philosophy (see especially 123–30, 268–77).

37 What follows here in my analysis is essentially different from any attempts made thus far to explicate Hegel's dialectic, at least so far as I have been able to tell. For a general history of 'dialectic' see *Historisches Wörterbuch der Philosophie* [216], Bd. II, 163–226.

Attempts have been made to explicate Hegel's dialectic in alliance with as well as against the dialectic of Plato. See Gadamer [147]; Westphal [528], 9–10. Several have seen it in various ways in relation to Kant. See Siegfried Blasche and Oswald Schwemmer [41]; James F. Donaldson [100]; Hans-Joachim Werner [526]; the philosophical exchange between Martin Kalin [251] and Robert J. Dostal [104]; J. Rivelaygue [414].

Others, focusing on the "reality" of the dialectic, have denied that it is a method at all. See for example Kenley R. Dove [105, 106]; Chaim Perelman [385]. Compare the argument against such one-sided positions in Friedrich Grimmlinger [170], 291–92.

For various other views, see *Hegel-Jahrbuch* [204], which is devoted to the question of the dialectic; Robert Heiss [210]; Rugard Otto Gropp [172]; Garaudy [152], especially 14–25; Adorno [3, 4]; Werner Hartkopf [187], which contains an interesting discussion of how and why dialectic goes beyond the formal-logical modes of thought; Nicolai Hartmann [192], on the relation of dialectic to content in terms of the discovery of problems in that content; Reiner Wiehl [531], also on the relation of dialectic to concrete content; Eric Weil [522], and the comments by Findlay [124]; Theodore F. Geraets [158], where reference is mainly to the *Logic*, but of interest to reflections on the *Phenomenology*; Hermann Schmitz [436], especially 75–82ff. where the concept of '*Bedrohung*' is located as the source of dialectic; W. H. Bossart [53]; M. F. Sciacca [446], where dialectic is characterized as a "universal suicide" (*universeller Selbstmord*); Jacob Loewenberg [327] and a distinction between the "comic" and the "histrionic" dialectic; Gustav E. Mueller [365], where the triplicity scheme is attacked, and Philip Merlan [357], where it is defended with some reservations; Taylor [495], especially 131–36, 216ff.; Heidegger [206], 113–22; Jyrki Hilpela [214], where the project is to argue for unique domains for different methodologies, and to ask whether or not there is a domain for dialectic as a method; Georges Marie-Martin Cottier

[84], with a concentration on dialectic as the relation of the finite and the infinite; Findlay [120], 58–59.

38 It is the view in the present work that, because of this, the dialectic cannot be formalized. On the attempt at formalization, see especially Michael Kosok [269]. There has been much discussion of this attempt, but see especially Howard Kainz [249], 31–35, where formalization is defended as a possibility, and Thomas Seebohm [449, 450], where strict limits to formalization are placed in light of the nature of the logic of concepts pervasive at the time. See also P. Trotignon [501].

39 On these grounds alone, Quentin Lauer is correct in his criticism of Kaufmann and Findlay and in his attribution of necessity to the movement of the *Phenomenology*, a movement he characterizes as "the process of self-revelation itself." See Lauer [305], 31–34. This beginning with an acceptance of the standpoint of the natural attitude is a necessary condition for any such process. Cf. also Labarrière [287], 45ff. who takes the autonomy of the natural attitude too far, but who does articulate its importance in the process.

40 For a thorough discussion of this point in relation to the dialectic, see Aschenberg [12], especially 233–40. Compare the view of Puntel [399], 285–308. Hyppolite [238], 21–26, has a good discussion of the dual thematics, and although his language is quite different from mine, it can be interpreted so as to be compatible with my own interpretation.

41 This account of praxical presuppositions has been inspired by reflection on recent work done by logicians and by theoreticians in linguistics on the topic of "pragmatic presuppositions" and their differences from "semantic presuppositions." Of course, the present analysis is my own responsibility, and any difficulties the reader finds with the analysis cannot be attributed to those sources. In fact, in moving to praxis from pragmatics, I have made quite a giant step. What is crucial is that presuppositions of any sort do not work like entailments or assumptions, but serve to lay the ground for the meaningfulness and appropriateness of distinctions of all sorts which arise in experience on the level thematized in the natural attitude. I have already given a brief analysis of the general idea in Flay [138], but since that paper was presented in 1978 my thinking has developed much further.

For the articulation of the general idea which I have come to use in my own way, see Robert C. Stalnaker [481, 482, 483]. The literature on this topic is now quite large. David E. Cooper [80] has a quite good account of the history and early disputes about pragmatic presuppositions, although his linguistic concerns are too narrow for what I do with praxical presuppositions. But the relation with what I argue below will be evident. For a work which is relatively recent, and covers most of the ground of the development to date (as well as offering an interesting analysis), see Gerald Gazdar [156].

Deidre Wilson [537] turns in a psychological direction. B. L. Bunch [61] argues for the necessity of a dispositional account of presupposition, thus throwing some light on my analysis of the "prescriptive" nature of presupposition.

Although the analysis has not been much used outside of the limited use deriving from linguistic concerns, there has been some tendency to apply the analysis in other ways. Trudy Govier [163] carries the analysis into a discussion of Kant's *Critique of Pure Reason*, and in particular the transcendental deduction and the Second Analogy. B. C. Birchall [39], in a general discussion of Habermas, discusses Hegel's critique of knowledge in the *Phenomenology* in terms of presupposition, but limits himself to an analysis of Hegel's dispute with Kant over the way to proceed with critique. See especially 370–71. See note 44, below, for further references to a connection between Hegel and presuppositional logic.

42 Cf. Friedrich Kümmel [283], 177–78, for an argument for the immediate possibility of thematization of the *relation* of the individual to reality. In the *Einleitung*, especially pp. VII-IX, there is an excellent discussion of the problem of knowledge. "The question arises concerning how the essentially open circle of cognition can be thought and also be conceptually and structurally distinguished from a closed correspondence relation. For this it is necessary to be able to bring *the objective relation*, in terms of which cognition orients its objective claims, into the circle structure in such a way that from this the conditions of objectivity can be first of all brought into the open and developed" (VIII, italics mine).

43 Ytashaq Klein [261], 373–77, uses the model of a dialogue and analyses the progress of the *Phenomenology* in terms of repeated demonstrations to natural consciousness that the latter has not said what it meant to say, i.e. in my terms what it in fact praxically presupposes and has expressed in the dialogue wrongly.

44 There have been tentative approaches to this way of understanding what underlies the dialectics of the *Phenomenology*. Solomon [474] explicitly suggests that "pragmatic presupposition" is relevant as the key to how knowledge is self-confirming (282–83), but this is not developed. Michel Corbin [81] argues that the succession of figures in the *Phenomenology* "articulate the totality of their presuppositions and, having done so, show their radical insufficiency," revealing consequently a series of contradictions between "believed and effective truth" (539). But his orientation is not in terms of the logic of presuppositions, and is rather exclusively historical. Lamb [299] comes close to viewing the method of the *Phenomenology* as presupposition critique (see especially p. 287). Bubner [60] discusses the dialectic of the *Logic* in terms of a "discrepancy between claim and result," (141) which tends in the direction I set out here if applied to the logic of presuppositions. Werner Marx [350] tends also strongly in my direction when he discusses "prescriptions" of consciousness. Marx claims that "the standard applied by consciousness contains 'prescriptions' both for knowledge and for the object. Their collective significance for the structure of consciousness is that this consciousness is on the one hand a comparison of form with knowledge (representing), and on the other, a comparison of form with the represented object (content). It is in this fashion that consciousness consists in an act of self-examination" (70). My praxical presuppositions will be seen to concretize this notion of Marx's. In a more limited way, Abigail Rosenthal's discussion of terminal and notional essences also throws light on my analysis. See Rosenthal [424], 205–12: "Terminal essences cover silent assumptions which remain not only unquestionable, but scarcely noticed, and which underlie and channel even the busy problem-solving of progressive cultures" (212). There is something of the nature

of presupposition in the analysis of the *Phenomenology* given by Fink [127], albeit in the "ontological" direction. See especially 48–51 and Fink's idea of a "*Vorentwurf*" which natural consciousness has of the *Ansichsein*, of consciousness as *Entwurf der Seinsgedanken* (54).

45 From the interests which move individuals in their daily lives we will proceed toward an interest in which the former interests are present, but "hushed." Cf. Horn [223] for a fruitful discussion of the way in which rationality exists in life in relation to interest. In a quite different, yet related way, Jürgen Habermas has offered a theory of the relation of interest and knowledge. In the present analysis, "interests" are quite different from what is discussed by Habermas. See Habermas [176], especially the Postscript.

46 Much, in my view, is lost until one sees the place of the logic of presuppositions in the *Phenomenology*. For instance, Werner Becker is correct in claiming that we have to do with "a philosophical construction"; but he does not see that what is constructed are putative praxical presuppositions which are authentically attributable to natural consciousness. See Becker [27], especially 24–26. If I am right, then his critique (and that of others in the same vein), namely that Hegel is reductionist and employs "idealistic-dialectical principles of construction" alien to natural consciousness (137), falls wide of the mark. The same can be said of those who see "jumps" and "philosophical projections" in the *Phenomenology*. Findlay [120] is an obvious case of this; but see also George Seidel [452], especially 161. The praxical presuppositions and the "dialogue" between the philosophical and the natural attitude, remove the occasion for such projections. Also avoided is the need to understand the presuppositions as originating in philosophical methodology; for they are, rather, the putative praxical presuppositions of sense-certainty and other forms of the natural attitude. On this, see Navickas [374], 34ff.

In another direction, the need to appeal to the logic of the *Science of Logic*, or, indeed, the Jena *Logic*, however indirectly, can be circumvented; for the logic of the praxical presupposition structure is what can mobilize the *Phenomenology* and give its own intelligibility to it. Neither a sense of the *Logic* nor an intuition of the whole is necessary or even desirable. Recently Rosen [421] has made a strong case for such necessity and desirability. Finally, if the logic of presuppositions sketched here and worked out in the remainder of this present essay is the logic proper to the *Phenomenology*, then Theunissen's view of dialectic in Theunissen [498], in which dialectic is understood as a power relation of "overreaching" and "appropriation," is radically un-Hegelian. For what is at stake is the warranty for the claims made by human beings in their everyday activities, not the overcoming of these claims. The crisis is a crisis in power, but not of the sort Theunissen paints for us.

Notes to Chapter II

1 The importance of the opening chapter on sense-certainty is widely recognized, and much has been written on it. But its uniqueness is seldom if ever recognized, and many commentators treat it as paradigmatic for the rest of the *Phenomenology*, much as the opening triad in the *Logic* is also treated in this way in respect to the *Logic*. For some of the literature on this, see above, note 35, Chapter I.

Fink [127] acknowledges Hegel's concentration here on the presupposition of the domain of truth as the place of adequation (57–59), but denies that sense-certainty focuses on certainty. His view is that the "expression 'sense-certainty' [*sinnliche Gewissheit*] has nothing to do with the express concept of certainty [*Gewissheit*] in the sense of certitude" (61). Few commentators have been this explicit about the matter, but the view is widespread. On the other hand, many do see the chapter in terms of the beginning of an account of the constitution of consciousness and spirit, rather than as an examination of putative praxical presuppositions. Westphal [528], as a result of this common interpretation, sees sense-certainty as "an unreal abstraction. Our knowledge of the external world does not begin in the rarified atmosphere of pure sensation but in the everyday world of things and their properties" (93). On my interpretation the latter is just Hegel's view.

Many interpretive devices have been employed in the attempt to unlock this chapter of the *Phenomenology*. Lauer [305] works on a comparison between Husserl and Hegel as "two sides of the same coin." See especially pp. 3ff. Wilhelm Purpus [400] presents a classical version of the view that Greek philosophy is the basis of the analysis of sense-certainty. Charles Taylor [496] makes an appeal to transcendental argument and the work of Wittgenstein on private language. See also Taylor [495], pp. 140–46, and Caroline Dudeck [109]. Dudeck also explicitly discusses the notion of 'language games' in her analysis. Lothar Eley [115] uses speech act analysis to explicate sense-certainty. Lukács [335] articulates one of the general Marxist views which takes sense-certainty to be the beginning of the first of three main steps in the *Phenomenology*. See especially pp. 596–97. Gerhard Krüger [277], Bd. I, 285–303, goes in my direction with his analysis. Among the most unhegelian analyses is that of R. I. Sikora [461]. This essay represents what can happen in an analysis of Hegel when one takes a nondialectical view of "truth-testing."

For analyses of the significance of sense-certainty for the whole of the *Phenomenology*, see Heribert Boeder [48] and Reiner Wiehl [530]. This latter work contains a very helpful analysis but, I think, misses the significance of the two levels of thematics.

See also Heinrichs [208], 116–22; W. Wieland [532]; Soll [469]; Kainz [249], 61–64; Hyppolite [238], 80–99; Labarrière [287], 73–76; Judith Shklar [457], 14–26.

2 The relationship between philosophical and non-philosophical consciousness has already been discussed generally. See above, pp. 8ff. and notes 19–21

in Chapter I. Aschenberg [12], 243–44, has a rather radical separation between the philosopher and the natural attitude in his discussion of a "hermeneutical difference." Dudeck [109], p. 106 puts the relationship nicely when she says that sense-certainty "is least open to cultural, intersubjective development, and, consequently, to *Geist* and *Wissenschaft*." However, in my view, Reiner Wiehl [530] goes too far when he claims that philosophy is and remains sophistical for the natural attitude. See below, the discussion of the convergence of the two attitudes. The view argued presently is exactly the opposite of that of Henry A. Myers [372], where he claims that we begin in the *Phenomenology* with the assumption that subjective thought is abstract.

3 But Kenley Dove is also correct in Dove [105] when he argues that *our* "object is at once and inseparably both the object-knowing-subject and the object known-by-the-subject" (618). Eugen Fink [126], although he has an ontological interpretation of the *Phenomenology*, does argue that "the examination [here] is the questioning consideration [*Bedenken*] of the presupposed relation of subjectivity and objectivity. . . . "(43). Then he goes on to claim that "consciousness is . . . not, as we ordinarily use the term, the experiential context of an experiencing [*der Erlebniszusammenhang eines Erlebenden*], it is rather the project [*Entwurf*] of the thought of being [*Seinsgedanken*]"(43). I get some sense from this difficult commentary that there is a vague way in which the *Entwurf* notion functions analogously to my notion of praxical presupposition and interest. See also Fink [127], 48–54.

Compare Labarrière [287], especially p. 74. In fact, the "content" which is indicated in his thesis concerning the self-movement of the content is "just the relation and intercourse between consciousness and its object" (47). See also Charles Taylor [495], pp. 132–36, 216ff. and his discussion of "criterial properties" which allow us to "show that a given conception of the standard is inadequate."

4 Compare Eugen Fink's way of saying this in Fink [127] when he claims that the beginning is made in the "everyday understanding of being, in which we dwell, as it were, blindly and without understanding. Natural consciousness lives in the forgetting of being and gives itself up only to that which it considers the actual and existing" (42). Cunningham [88] also puts the point nicely when he argues that Hegel does not even ask us to assume this standpoint, but rather "merely to place ourselves at the point of view of sensuous consciousness, and to try to discover its implications" (622). Rather than implications, I am arguing for presuppositions in the sense defined. Herbert Hrachovec [227], 189–230, has some interesting reflections on the matter of immediacy, starting with the question of why immediate knowledge is our first object in the light of the Kantian arguments, echoed by Hegel, that all knowledge is mediated.

5 Cf. Heribert Boeder [48], 170, where he discusses the way in which sense-certainty, from the beginning, appears to itself as absolute; and Merold Westphal's discussion of the unexamined presuppositions of natural consciousness in Westphal [528], 86–87.

6 This means, contra Becker, that there *is* a philosophical-theoretical claim attached to the articulation of these presuppositions. See Becker [25], 110. Quen-

tin Lauer [305], in his analysis of the natural attitude, argues that if "consciousness does not reflect on itself, on what it itself contributes to the apprehension of its object, it is condemned to remain caught up in the illusion of a worthless certainty" (12). I would only qualify this by saying that it is not the certainty as such that is worthless, but certainty which has not been properly warranted.

7 Cf. Findlay [120]. One of Findlay's many important contributions to Hegel scholarship was his recognition that the constancy of the "particularity of sense-experience, of the immediately 'given', in which it can discern, or on which it can impose, its various sense-making universals" is a "necessity" which "constitutes the ineliminable element of empiricism in Hegel's philosophy" (44). Compare this with the view represented by Monika Leske [316]. Contrary to what Leske and others think, Hegel is here, and throughout the *Phenomenology*, concerned with the physical and institutional world in its most direct and ordinary sense. The experience of the natural attitude in Hegel's view is more complex than Leske allows. See her critique, especially p. 330.

On the basis of this, two sorts of interpretation are then ruled out. First a view that the initial presuppositions are methodological must be wrong; for these are presuppositions of the natural attitude itself and not of Hegel. On this, see Navickas [374], p. 34, where he argues for methodological presuppositions. On the other hand, (a) given what is thematized by philosophy and put in question, and (b) given the empiricism of Hegel, a view such as that of Ivan Soll is not right. Soll [469] claims that Hegel claims that a particular is not an object of consciousness. But, the contrary is true for Hegel, and the question is, really, how is it possible that we can thematize particulars. See also Soll [467], 99–103.

8 Cf. Gerhard Krüger [277] on the connection between the immediacy of truth and the natural attitude. Cunningham [88], 629–30, explicates this immediacy in the context of a discussion of the basic presupposition of all experience that there is real contact with reality.

9 Heinrichs [208], 113, has a problem with what follows now in my analysis as the "answers" given by one in the natural attitude, and feels that one must say, rather, that the reader answers for the natural attitude since there can be no pure natural consciousness of sense-certainty. In what I now argue, I want to show that the problem Heinrichs sees does not in fact exist, but arises from Heinrichs' view of the *Phenomenology*. For further comments on this problem as it occurs in the literature, see the following footnote.

10 The attack on Hegel concerning this point centers mostly around his introduction of language and the consequent forcing of the naive natural attitude to respond in terms of language. For a general view of the view of Hegel on language and silence from the time of the pre-*Phenomenology* writings, see Guy Debrock [90]. Debrock is mostly interested in the difficulties with language vis-à-vis the articulation of the absolute, but his discussion throws light on the problems of sense-certainty and language as well. Martin DeNys [92] sums up the classical attack by citing Feuerbach's and Löwith's versions of them, and then defends Hegel in the face of them. For Löwith, see Karl Löwith [331], where he also makes the claim that Hegel confuses the actual experience of sense-consciousness with the logic of phenomena and never gets to the former. For other

critiques of Hegel on this point see Jacob Loewenberg [327], 356; Josef Derbolav [93]. Although interesting on the relation of language to action, Derbolav too narrowly conceives language in Hegel when he claims that "Hegel has understood language only as an activity of theoretical intelligence and thus obscured its practical horizon" (78). Werner Becker [25], 120, claims that Hegel unreasonably forces linguistic expression upon sense certainty, forcing the idealistic presupposition that "every determinateness is the product of subjectivity." To the contrary, I shall show that the natural attitude forces *itself* due to its complicity in the quest for certainty.

Many have come to Hegel's defense, and in different ways. Jere Paul Surber [490] argues strongly for the centrality and ubiquitousness of language and thus its naturalness in sense-certainty: "the very *ability to speak a language and reflect upon it* provides the basis upon which we can start on the 'road to Science'. The most elementary form of speaking and reflecting upon the meanings implicit in language provides the framework for that moment with which the *Phenomenology* begins, the moment of 'Sense-certainty'." Ytashaq Klein [261] argues that "there is a possibility of dialogue" with the natural attitude "because man is a thinking being" (379). Theodor Bodhammer [47], especially 19–20, 73–86 takes a position opposed to Derbolav and argues that it is natural to question sense-certainty. There are here also very strong arguments for the presupposition of language from the very beginning. See also Westphal [528], 72–76; Cassirer [67], III, 314–15; Lamb [299].

11 The necessity for Hegel to make reference to both these *kinds* of assertions has generally not been sufficiently noted, missing concrete placement of the two thematics. Aschenberg [12] indicates the two different levels, albeit in a way different from me due to his analysis of the senses of truth. Kenley Dove's discussion of 'experience' and the distinction between appearance of experience and appearance in experience in Dove [105] offers a like contrast.

Among those who miss the significance of the difference there are different tendencies. Hook [220] denies the philosophical in order to preserve the thematic of the natural attitude and thus to defend Hegel against the traditional, mystical-religious interpretations. See especially, p. 246. Findlay [120], 56–57, misses the two levels when he holds that "Hegel's view is in principle a philosophical way of regarding the world, which depends for its acceptability on conceptual rather than factual considerations, though it can be used to illuminate fact, and though it is more applicable to certain sorts of fact than others." This then leads him to a discussion of what Hegel is doing taken on the level of "as-if." But I am arguing that there is not only a casual illumination here: it is the demonstration of the possibility of those facts in a real, not an "as-if" world. As a refinement to my earlier remarks on Krieger [274] in notes 15 and 35 of Chapter I above, the present recognition of the presence of these two levels resolves the difficulties Krieger presents and shows how Hegel recognizes mediation at both the "prereflective" and reflective levels. See also Wiehl [530].

12 The general solution to the problem of the "we" is central to an understanding of the *Phenomenology*. For a survey and discussion of the problem of the "we" see Dove [105], 630–39. My view differs somewhat from Dove's given

our difference on the matter of dialectic. See below, note 32. Although Jan van der Meulen [360] argues against the view held by Heidegger and others that the change [*Umkehr*] in consciousness is not our contribution but belongs to consciousness itself (28–29), I would argue against van der Meulen that our ability to grasp the continuity as continuity does not originate in the "Logos" or pure science, but in our concern for the absolute standpoint as a problem, and in our conversance with the history of philosophy. In this sense, Dove is right in seeing a dialogue between spirit and consciousness. For Heidegger's position, see Heidegger [207], 66ff., and Heidegger [206], 126–27. One further general position should be mentioned, that represented by Solomon [475], where it is held that the "we" operates at a "meta-level." But if this were true, then the link to the natural attitude would be severed.

13 On the involvement on the part of the natural attitude, see W. Wieland [532], 939–40. I must disagree here with Chalybäus [69] and his discussion of the "for us" and "for itself." He is certainly right that the *Phenomenology* has begun with "consciousness placed into the midst of actuality," but wrong that the consciousness placed there in sense-certainty "was the intellect which in itself had already been philosophically trained, and now transported itself back into the beginning of its training, which got into a kind of tension by this making abstraction from itself"(361–62). Such machinations, if I am right, are not necessary. See also above, note 12, Dove's criticisms of Richard Kroner on the "we." The view that the "we" is already at the absolute standpoint leads Kroner away from the possibility of seeing the necessity of the progress of the *Phenomenology*. See Kroner [275], II, 370–72.

14 This self-comprehension is the beginning of convergence. Cf. Fulda [144], 162–71 on the problem of the gradual coming to be of the participation or conscious grasp of what is going on in the *Phenomenology* by the natural attitude. I agree with Fulda on the general direction of the process, and am trying to show here that and how this gradual participation comes about. My difference with him is that I argue that it is accomplished on the basis of the shared quest for certainty, rather than on the basis of a "double ground." On the latter, see especially p. 164. Compare with both our views that of Heidegger [207], 84–85; for Heidegger the "we" lights the way for natural consciousness. See also his discussion of the same in [206], 126–30. His view derives, as I have argued above, from his insistence on the absolute standpoint being presupposed. Compare also Aschenberg [12], 246–47. On the present interpretation one is not led to the "grotesque" consequences alluded to by Aschenberg. For objections to the whole process of joining natural and philosophical consciousness in a natural, unforced way, see Litt [323], 35–40. Litt's view forces Hegel to beg the question with the opposition of the natural attitude. See Bruno Liebrucks critique of Litt in Liebrucks[321], 88.

15 Compare Hinrich Fink-Eitel [128], 251, on the centrality of the "recognition of the validity claims of natural consciousness." Bodhammer [47], in the context of his discussion of language, notes that a "central theme of the presentation in the first chapter of the *Phenomenology of Spirit* is not the immediate linguistic organization of consciousness itself, but rather the experience which the examined

consciousness has when it is shown its own unreflected presuppositions" (73). Charles Taylor [496], 157–60 argues for the "transcendental" nature of Hegel's arguments, and there is justification in this insofar as transcendental arguments also begin from an acceptance of what is given to the natural attitude. But the dialectical nature of Hegel's argument does not allow us to push the resemblance on this point too far. See also on this Pippin [390] and his agreement with Taylor. Pippin's discussion shows how concentration on this resemblance distracts one from attending clearly to the interplay between the two levels of thematics.

In addition, if one grasps this acceptance of the world of the natural attitude, then a view such as that of Adorno [3], 28, loses its grounds; for it is not, as Adorno argues, that Hegel has followed Fichte and hypostatized the abstracted "I" and consequently has forgotten that "the term 'I', whether the pure transcendental or the empirical and immediate, must always signify some consciousness" in particular. Rather, what is at stake is precisely to try to achieve warranty for the claims of such a concrete consciousness.

16 Cf. Westphal [528], 72; Bodhammer [47], 81. See also Ytashaq Klein [261] for an analysis of the dialogical movement in terms of a demonstration to natural consciousness that it has not said what it "meant to say," i.e., in my terms what it in fact praxically presupposes (376–77). That the *Phenomenology* works in this way means that a critique of Hegel as an idealist who can deal with mediation and immediacy only at the level of pure thought and conception, ignoring "material practice," can find no real grounds. This will become an issue latter, especially in respect to the analysis of self-consciousness. For a critique of this sort, see V. F. Asmus [13]. Another general view held by many and articulated by Marcuse [338], 93–94, namely that the confidence of the natural attitude in respect to its ability to perceive the real is undermined by Hegel, is also shown to be false if my analysis is correct. Compare also Soll [469], p. 283.

17 Cf. De Nys [92], p. 465. It is certainly, therefore, not the sort of relationship which exists between Émile and the "tutor." See on this latter Guy Besse [36], 491.

18 For further discussion of the two senses of 'object', see Puntel [399], 287–89. Aschenberg [12] resorts to a concept of 'noema' in order to explicate these two senses of 'object'. But with the present interpretation, this complication is not necessary.

19 It has often been pointed out that in the *Phenomenology* there is no logical entailment in the process. This is of course correct, but with the presupposition logic I have discussed and which is in force here, there is a form of necessitation which does not involve entailment. See for instance Findlay [120], 77ff. Westphal [528] explains that rather "than denying our capacity to refer to individuals, Hegel is asking how it is possible for us to do so" (76). But one must be careful to note that this is not "possibility" in the Kantian sense. Close, but different in many respects, is the view of Solomon [473]. Solomon argues that sense-certainty is "rejected because it does not allow us to speak of what we allegedly know for certain; specifically, it does not allow us to speak of objects" (507). He then continues and puts the stress on philosophical theory rather than on the natural attitude itself: "It is rejected, therefore, because it does not fulfill certain basic

pre-philosophical expectations we have of a philosophical theory—in this case, the very basic expectation that we should be able to express what we know about objects in language" (507). But see further Solomon [474], 282ff.

20 It is clearly the thwarted natural certainty that drives us on. See note 35, Chapter I. Compare Judith Shklar [457], 6. Taylor [495], 140–46 does not see the significance of this section as the place to show that certainty is a problem. Lauer [305] claims that what "Hegel is actually saying . . . is, first, that unless consciousness sees what is necessarily implied in the givenness of its initial object, it is not adequate to that object. . . . " (44) I would substitute 'presupposed' for 'implied'. Ytashaq Klein [261] explains that in part the reason why natural certainty is what drives us on is that in Hegel we have "a Socrates without irony" (382).

21 Cf. Ytashaq Klein [261]. The interpretation given here is in obvious disagreement with that of Klaus Düsing [114]. Düsing claims that Hegel is concerned with the position of ancient skepticism. But I think it is clear that the opening position is not influenced by philosophical history, and even if it is in some sense, the result is not the calling into question of the natural attitude—the goal of classical skepticism—but the attempt to show the legitimate grounds of the natural attitude. For a review of other positions on this point, see Düsing's footnote, pp. 120–21.

22 Compare Werner Marx [350], 78–96 on the role of the phenomenologist in the move to a new position. Marx, I think, is vague on just why the determinate negation leads to a new form here and in general throughout the *Phenomenology*. He gives too much autonomy to the natural consciousness. See also his discussion in [349]. Lamb [299] sees here a move from realism to solipsism. But I think this characterization is too strong. On the other hand, if my analysis is right here, then the accusation that the "we" practices "external reflection" in order to grasp the transitions is ungrounded. On this see Findlay [120], 89. Lauer [305], argues against Becker and others that there is no trickery in this move. I obviously agree with Lauer; for it is sense-certainty's own concern for its certainty which moves the dialectic. See Lauer, pp. 47–48. Kojève [266] claims that the subject is here neglected by Hegel (44). But this is clearly not the case, neither in the turn to the "idealist" set of presuppositions, nor in the next move to the "contextualist" set.

23 Cf. Heribert Boeder [48], 170.

24 See above, Chapter I, the discussion of the problem of circularity, and its proffered solution in terms of the problem of certainty. The present analysis should clarify that solution in concrete terms.

25 Cf. Aschenberg [12] and his distinction between the epistemological and phenomenological senses of truth, especially pp. 221–22.

26 On the difficulties with the "for us" in relation to "for itself" and "in itself" see Pöggeler [395], especially 50–51. My argument throughout is not that Hegel had this view (or any clear view) of what he was doing in the *Phenomenology*, but only that my articulation brings into clear view what is there.

27 I must disagree with Hyppolite here, then, that this move "can be understood only if we already know where it is leading. . . . " Rather, it is intelligible due to reflection on where we have been. See Hyppolite [238], 96.

28 See Dudeck [109] for the view that in order to have particulars we need to admit universals, and her arguments against Ivan Soll and others that Hegel is denying particulars. See pp. 110–11.

29 Lauer's claim that the transition which now takes place is a "model" for the movement of the *Phenomenology* is close, but a bit too strong; for the content must always determine the nature of the dialectic. See Lauer [305], 51.

30 Cf. Boeder [48] for the significance of natural consciousness for the whole of the *Phenomenology*. See also Westphal [528], 87. Werner Marx, [350], 1–5 argues clearly that the natural attitude is not left behind, but rather made transparent to itself. Fackenheim [118] focuses his analysis by claiming that "everything in the end depends on this question: *Can there be a form of nonphilosophic human life which makes the rise to the scientific standpoint on the one hand possible and on the other still necessary, and if so, what justifies Hegel's claim that in the nineteenth century that form of life has become actual?*" (35) To recognize the place of the natural attitude as a result of this first analysis in the *Phenomenology* is to give a positive answer to the first part of his question. For the natural attitude as such is led to religion in the first place (and independently of the *Phenomenology* and its analysis) on the basis of its own quest for certainty.

31 Cf. Ytashaq Klein [261], 376–77 on natural consciousness and philosophical theories. But this does not mean, as Fulda and others argue, that the *Phenomenology* follows an historical sequence, beginning with the Greeks. See Fulda [144], 268–69. Hyppolite [238], 83ff. links the discussion of sense-certainty too closely with the Greeks, using Parmenides, Protagoras, and Plato for the sake of explication. For Marxist interpretations in this respect, see Garaudy [152], 38–44, and other citations in notes 7, 24, and 38 of Chapter I above.

32 This is central to my disagreement with Dove on the matter of the contribution of the "we". See Dove [105] and Flay [134].

33 Compare Aschenberg [12] on the norm as the in-itself. Gerhard Krüger [277], 287–89 defends Hegel on this point about the natural attitude and offers on the basis of it a critique of the traditional ancient and modern project concerning knowledge.

Notes to Chapter III

1 Cf. Findlay [120], 19–21 for criticisms of attempts to connect Hegel with Bradley, McTaggert, and others. See also Findlay [119], especially p. 6.

2 Jürgen Habermas [176] comes to mind immediately in this matter of "interest." See especially the appendix, pp. 301–17. What he describes as his knowledge-constitutive interests are not unrelated to the notion of interest in the present analysis, but do not speak to exactly the same issues. Alphonse de Waelhens [512], in a fruitful comparison between Husserl and Hegel, borders on discussing 'interest' in my sense when he claims that in "perception consciousness reveals itself as an ekstatic interiority, that is to say as an interiority which *is* (and not which *has*) a movement toward what is other than the self" (239). Royce [426] also points in my direction when he centers on the problem of the "correlation" between self and world and the different forms this correlation takes in the *Phenomenology*. "Whatever it is that determines the experience of the self, must also determine not only all of the forms and the relations of the many selves but also the true basis of all the phenomena that appear to us as physical nature" (74). Compare also W. I. Schinkaruk [432]: the object of the *Phenomenology* "is not knowledge in general, but knowing as relation, 'as determinate modes of the relation of object and subject to one another'" (443). The phrase quoted by Schinkaruk is from the *Propaedeutik*. See also J. C. Horn [223] and his use of 'transcendental' in Horn [225], 154.

3 One of the more fascinating ways is that attempted by Martin Heidegger [206, 207]. In the latter, see pp. 69ff. and 115ff. for the discussion of access to the ontological dimension of experience through "absolvent" knowing. Although he makes it clear in *Hegels Phänomenologie des Geistes* that this mode of knowing does not have access to the absolute standpoint in a complete way (p. 71), there is still existent a manipulative aspect in the "letting-be" involved in Heidegger's interpretation. My introduction of 'interest' unites the domain of experience as Heidegger discusses it with what is natural to the natural attitude, i.e., unites what is common to the two thematics. See also the attempt of Eugen Fink [127] to explicate the unity in similar terms.

4 The reference is to Aristotle's *Metaphysics*, 982b. Hegel has been free with the translation, as usual, but he has not distorted the point.

5 Compare Quentin Lauer [305], p. 3, and his comparison between Husserl and Hegel on intentionality. I shall try to show that there is an even more positive relationship. See also Alphonse de Waelhens [512].

6 See below, Chapter 4.

7 See below, Chapters 5 and 6.

8 See below, Chapters 7 through 10.

9 This will be an important aspect of Hegel's analysis; for, contrary to the usual notion that presuppositions remain implicit for the natural attitude, they will be found here to be explicit in the very institutional frameworks within which one moves in the natural attitude.

10 Westphal [528] sees the section on consciousness as embracing "three standpoints": the critique of Theaetetus, with Hegel as Socrates, a retelling of the

history of modern science, and Kant and his Copernican Revolution (60–61). Darrel E. Christensen [75] discusses what I call here the presuppositions of consciousness in general, but within the framework of a discussion of the unconscious. Bruno Liebrucks [320], Bd. 5, has an interesting discussion of the difference between Kant and Hegel on the approach to the question of consciousness and its examination. See especially p. 2. Erhard Albrecht [9] has a good review of works on Hegel and language in respect to the problem of consciousness. See also Findlay [120], 91–95; Judith Shklar [457], 14–26; Milan Sobotka [465]; Heidegger [207], 115–84; Fink [127], 89–156.

11 On the positivism of consciousness see Marcuse [338]. He attempts to characterize the nexus of the chapter on consciousness generally as "a critique of positivism and, even more, of reification" (112).

12 Cf. G. W. Cunningham [88], especially p. 641, on the continuing importance of the difference between subject and object.

13 Charles Taylor [496], 168–82, applies his notion of transcendental argument to the discussion of perception, seeing it as a critique of empiricism in general. Heidegger [207], 115–39 holds the discussion of perception to be a transition from sense-certainty to understanding. See especially pp. 115–20. Fink [127], 89–111, misses the complexity of the movement in perception when he struggles with the question of the transitions between positions. He argues that the transitions occur as a "philosophizing," and that such philosophizing occurs "when the thinking of being is awakened in us, when we participate in the most extreme perplexity and wonder; . . . when we think through the concept of being in which we already blindly move." The connection with the natural attitude is articulated by Fink as the emergence of "philosophical inclinations . . . in natural consciousness as the question concerning being" (91–92). There is some connection between this view and the relation of philosophical theories to praxical presuppositions, but the richness of this latter relation does not come through in Fink. Heinrichs [208], 123–42 interprets the section in light of the categorial analysis of quantity.

See also Labarrière [287], 76–80; Hyppolite [238], 100–17; Sobotka [465], 137–43.

14 Aschenberg [12] 221–22 begins a complex discussion of four conceptions of truth in the *Phenomenology*. Compare Solomon [475], 702–03, who maintains that the section on consciousness constitutes an extended argument against the correspondence theory of truth, "against the idea of 'the facts' as discrete and independent of us" (702–03). According to Solomon correspondence and coherence are combined, and Hegel is a "proto-pragmatist," holding that "belief is never *simply* by virtue of its coherence within our system of beliefs, but by virtue of its coherence *and* correspondence with the facts" (703).

15 Findlay's remark in Findlay [120], 44, about the empiricism of Hegel, nicely reinforces this move involving deference to the natural attitude, although Findlay does not press the point. See also Otis Lee [309], 371.

16 On this first presupposition set about perception, see especially Heidegger [207], 120–24.

17 This is the classical position of the modern period, but as Hyppolite [238]

points out the discussion here has much more to do with Locke than, for instance, with Kant. See pp. 109, 113. M. Meyer [362] misses the realism that is here in this discussion of the two senses of the object and makes Hegel's position into that of a simple subjective idealist. This mistake will turn up again in Meyer's treatment of self-consciousness. Compare here also the analysis of Heidegger [207], 124–27.

18 This articulation of something on the order of "or so it seemed to me" is central to the movement here. Cook [78] has a general view of language in Hegel which throws light on what happens here in the natural attitude. "Through the use of language man transcends his original experience of the world as a collection of independent, unrelated particulars and begins to recognize the fundamental identity between himself and the external world of objects" (120). His whole discussion of language in perception and understanding is penetrating. See also Heidegger [207], 125–26 for an interesting discussion of the relation between givenness in perception and the possibility of error.

19 Cf. Lauer [305], 63–64, where this insight that determinateness in every sense must be on "both sides" of the relation is discussed in comparison with Aristotle.

20 Hyppolite [238] characterizes the move here as proceeding "from *thing* to *relation*, from the thingism of perception to the relativity of understanding" (116). Findlay [120] explains that the "changing aspects of the Thing must have *some* root in its unchanging essence, and this unchanging essense must itself be compared, and therefore *connected*, with external Things" (92). See also Heidegger [207], 127–39. Kainz [249] argues that "the prime analogue here is consciousness, which can only know itself, and thus be for-self, by separating itself from itself in making itself objective—which amounts to becoming 'other than' itself" (141). But this would mean to objectify consciousness in a way impossible to do at this point, and so it seems to me it would not be suitable as an "analogue."

21 Compare Charles Taylor's penetrating discussion of the *aporia* of the *je ne sais quoi* in Taylor [496], 175–78.

22 On the general critique of perception within the framework of the *Phenomenology* see Lauer's formulation of the failure of perception as absolute standpoint, in Lauer [305]: "What has happened is that the 'absolute' validity of perception and the 'absolute' being of the thing for itself have been revealed to be relative and not absolute" (67). Lauer adds a footnote claiming that 'absolute' does not have to mean anything more than 'not relative', but his own discussion in the text shows clearly that it does, i.e., that it means that perception is not the absolute standpoint, that it is not something beyond which we need not go for complete knowledge. On the conditionedness of perception and the transition to the recognition of the unconditioned universal, see also Sobotka [465], 140–43.

In discussing the move to understanding from perception Findlay [120] sees a parallel with Russell's "constructivism" in the latter's *Problems of Philosophy*. In fact Findlay claims that Hegel "even goes a step beyond Russell in asserting the purely constructive, conceptual character of the explanatory entities located behind our sense-data" (95). But here Findlay goes too far, for not even with "explanation" is there this pure constructivism, as will be shown below.

23 What I argue here is quite different from a view such as Heidegger's that we "only understand the transition from perception to understanding if we hold in advance that perception is in place here as a mode of knowledge already in the perspective of absolute knowing; only then is there the necessity of an advance." See Heidegger [207], 138–39.

24 This section on the understanding is notorious, one of the most difficult parts of the *Phenomenology*. See Georges Bataille [21] for an interesting discussion of negativity in Hegel, especially in respect to the subject-object relation as constituted in the understanding. Heidegger [207], 140–84, understands Hegel here in the context of his (Heidegger's) notion of the "onto-theological nature of metaphysics." See especially 140–45. Heinrichs [208], 143–68, interprets understanding in light of the movement in the Jena *Logik* from quantum to infinity, characterizing it as the dialectic of whole and parts. Hyppolite [238], 118–39, uses Leibniz and Kant, not exactly as I shall, but in a similar way.

Westphal [528] discusses reason and understanding together, in spite of the fact that in "the process the realistic attitude of Understanding has been replaced by the idealism of Reason." His defense of this is unsatisfactory to me. See his p. 97. First of all, this conflation radically weakens any legitimate sense of progression in the *Phenomenology* if, as Westphal argues, we are going over essentially the same ground in both places; it especially makes the position of self-consciousness questionable. Secondly, it is not the distinction between realism and idealism which alone is at stake; for there is both realism and idealism in the chapter on the understanding. Thirdly, what we will be doing in the chapter on reason is radically different from what we are doing in the chapter on understanding. In the latter, we are examing putative presuppositions and the processes based upon them in order to discover whether or not consciousness could itself be the absolute standpoint. In the chapter on reason we will be observing observing reason demonstrate through its own praxis that reason, i.e., the unity of consciousness and self-consciousness, is the absolute standpoint, or, rather, the degree to which it is. Neither chapter is simply an examination of science; this thesis of Westphal's weakens his own project of showing the unity of history and epistemology in the *Phenomenology*.

Quentin Lauer [305], 70–89, has a discussion of understanding which also misses to some degree this difference. He tries to define "understanding" as "reason defined by formal logic" (70). As far as it goes this is not wrong, but it is too narrow, both for Hegel and for the tradition. In respect to this and to my comments above on Westphal, see the accounts of 'Verstand' and 'Vernunft' in *Wörterbuch der philosophischen Begriffe* [539], Bd. 3.

See also Labarrière [287], 76–80; Fink [127], 108–56; Sobotka [465], 143ff.; Kainz [249], 69–82.

25 Findlay [120] in his discussion of the understanding seems to miss this "vertical" aspect of the overarching unity.

26 Claude Bruaire [58] defends Leibniz against Hegel's critique here and holds that the *Monadology* is "the perfectly developed contradiction" (118 ff.). In Flay [133] I have more completely articulated the Leibniz paradigm for this section of the *Phenomenology*. Compare the interpretation of Gadamer [146] where Plato

is employed instead of Leibniz. On my view, at this stage of the *Phenomenology* there is no historical strictness, but only exemplifications.

27 For a good discussion of 'force', see Kainz [249] 69–74. Compare Lauer [305], 73–7 and his discussion of force as a concept used by science in Hegel's own time. Heidegger [207] 147–49ff. discusses 'force' in relation to Kant's categories of relation, and characterizes the whole of the section on understanding as pointing to the transition from metaphysics in terms of Kant to metaphysics in terms of German idealism, i.e., the transition "from the finitude of consciousness to the infinitude of spirit" (161). Eugen Fink [127] articulates force as the thinking of "the thing-being of things [*das Dingsein des Dinges*]" (115). On Hegel and force and the modern tradition generally see his *Hegel*, 130ff.

28 Compare the following account with that of Hyppolite [238], 120ff., where he points out that it is "crucial to note that what is now given to consciousness, which has become understanding, is the transition itself—the connection—which previously occurred in it without its knowledge and which was, therefore, external to its moments" (120). This transition he refers to is that movement or relation between oneness and manyness which perceiving consciousness has had to acknowledge, but could not account for.

29 This concept 'concept' will play a large part in what follows, especially with the introduction of 'reason'. For a history of 'concept' from Aristotle to Hegel, cf. Hermann Glockner [159] and *Historisches Wörterbuch der Philosophie* [216], Bd. I, 780–87. See also Lauer [305] who points out that the "concept is not a means employed in order to grasp; it is the very activity of grasping the object" (26); and Kainz [249], 80–81, especially footnote 22 on the concept as subject-object, and its connection with life as infinity. Friedrich Kümmel [283], 187–92, argues that concept in Hegel's sense, as it appears now and later in the discussion of reason, cannot be understood "as a reduction of actuality to the form of the dialectical concept immanent to it, whereby all other modes of its givenness in intuition, representation, belief, etc., are gone beyond and laid aside."

30 Compare Hyppolite [238], 125ff.

31 Hyppolite [238] explains that we do not with this move "return to the prior sensuous world, to perception, for example, or to objective force, but we see this world as it genuinely is—as the movement by which it continuously disappears and negates itself" (126). Westphal [528] notes a link here in the primacy of perception to the preceding analysis of perception. "Having stressed the mediated character of Perception over against the claims of Sense Certainty, Hegel is now stressing the immediate character of Perception in contrast to the mediated and indirect relation of Understanding to its object" (95).

32 Cf. Horn [222] and his argument that in the move to make understanding itself thematic, the inner consciousness experiences only itself.

33 See above, note 22 and my discussion of Findlay's view of this section. His constructivist view is too strong to accurately represent the mere implicitness here.

34 See Hyppolite's interesting discussion in Hyppolite [233], where he links sensibility and intelligibility by means of a discussion of language. "Hegel describes the passage of the sensible to understanding, uncovers the immanence of

the universal in nature. In this dialectic the sensible becomes Logos, language signifies, and thought of the sensible does not remain interior and mute, but is there in language" (27).

35 On this distinction between appearance as appearance and the appearances of what appears, see Gadamer [146], 41–42, and Heidegger [207], 170ff. Kainz [249] makes appearance as appearance the "appearance-of the inner being of force" (76).

36 Cf. Hyppolite [238], 127–32. Lauer [305], 78–80, has a good discussion of the introduction of the domain of law, and on pp. 80ff. has a thorough discussion of law. See Westphal [528], 104–05, and especially footnote 30 on the move from force to law.

37 See Hyppolite [238], 129–32 for a discussion of Hegel's criticism of necessity and law. Horn [222] notes that Hegel here shows the necessity to stand in opposition "to western Platonism," i.e. to any two-world thesis (258).

38 I. Görland [161] claims that Hegel really confronts only Fichte and not Kant, and that the movements from consciousness to self-consciousness to reason cannot be seen as Kant-Fichte-Hegel. See especially 62–63, and below, note 45. See also the view of Fackenheim [118], 16–17, where he comments on the positive relation of Hegel's to Kant's philosophy in respect to pre-Kantian metaphysics; and Werkmeister [525] and the response of Murray Greene [165].

39 Wolfgang Bonsiepen [52] argues that "only from the chapter on Self-consciousness on is an experience of consciousness actually possible." In a sense this is right, and Bonsiepen is also right in locating the place as the beginning of the discussion of the freedom of self-consciousness (Skepticism). But it is also true that the ground for this as for the whole turn to self-consciousness is to be found in this discovery about explanation. Labarrière [287], 86, sees clearly the significance of 'explanation'. See also Cassirer [67], III, 320–21, for an excellent discussion of this phenomenon.

40 See John E. Smith [464], especially 448–50, for a discussion of the thing-in-itself in understanding. Westphal [527], although not citing passages from the *Phenomenology*, claims that Hegel and Kant did not have "a real meeting of the minds," because Hegel did not consider Kant's theism and its relevance to the thing in itself. For Westphal, the thing in itself is "the thing for God's creative intellect." See especially p. 140, and the extended argument, 119–28.

41 Cf. Flay [133] for a more complete account of this movement. Fink [127] also sees the irony at the center of this analysis and notes that it is important that Hegel characterizes it as "a superficial view" (152). Gadamer [146] uses Plato and Aristotle for explication purposes, and gives a rich interpretation of this section. But Gadamer does not grasp the full sense of absurdity, although he does have an interesting discussion of absurdity and satire. See especially pp. 49–52 and footnote 13. Rosen [421], 140–50, has an interesting discussion of the inverted world passage in which he links it to the general structure of the whole section on consciousness and compares it to Plato's project in the allegory of the cave in the *Republic*. "The dialectic of the inverted world is the representation within the *Phenomenology* of the reflection process, albeit not yet understood as absolute reflection in the dual sense of logical circularity and self-consciousness" (150). Compare Greene [166] who also discusses the wider sense of 'inversion' as it is employed throughout the *Phenomenology*.

Solomon [475] makes the suggestion that the inverted world is, in addition to whatever other function it might have in the *Phenomenology*, an argument against a coherence theory of truth *simpliciter* in so far as values are "inverted" or a coherent set of beliefs is turned into its contradictory, but as yet another coherent set of beliefs. But I think that his analysis is off the mark because it misses the irony.

Lauer [305], 84–87, in his discussion of the inverted world, seems to limit considerations to the fact that understanding deals in abstractions and one-sided concepts. But this misses the connection with the Kantian critique of confusing phenomena with noumena.

Sobotka [466] interprets the passage as referring to Schelling's philosophy as opposed to the Newtonian philosophy. See especially pp. 329–30, and his discussion of the same matter in Sobotka [465], 143ff.

See also Kainz [249] 79–80, and Pippin [390].

42 Cunningham [88] shows clearly that reality is here taken as the subject-object relation and not either the subject or the object nor some third transcendent with respect to subject and object. This concept of infinity in Hegel is absolutely central to an understanding of what he is up to. On the difference from Kant, see Seidel [452], 173, where he discusses Kant's limitation to a finite understanding. See also Fink [127], 153–56, 158. Fink argues that this "dialectic does not negate the world of things, it negates the ontological claims made for them." This negation of the "purity" of things is what must be understood if Hegel's analysis from this point on is to be grasped sufficiently. Cf. Kroner [275], II, 402, where he claims that the notion of infinity which is uncovered in the move through 'explanation' and to the law of the supersensible world is the "central concept" of the whole Hegelian philosophy.

'Infinity' is central to the analysis of Hyppolite [238] 132–39, but he says he finds it difficult to understand, and in the end unclear (132). But I think that he simply misses the significance of Hegel's realization that subsequent to what we find in the analysis of 'explanation' in the *Phenomenology*, experience is really limited by nothing but itself and thus is infinite in the traditional sense of that term, with all negativity contained within the subject-object nexus itself.

Lauer [305] seems to limit 'infinity' to comprehensiveness and complexity, "conceptual comprehensiveness." But this misses the ontological relation being indicated in the relation between knower and known and thus the key to the move to consciousness *as* self-consciousness. See pp. 87–88. Yet, on the other hand, Lauer is very clear about the move when he explains why we cannot simply move directly to reason from the analysis of understanding. See pp. 88–89.

43 On the general failure of consciousness as the absolute standpoint, see Westphal [528], 113. Murray Greene [166], 162, discusses how self-consciousness and consciousness are interrelated in Hegel's analysis here. Compare Findlay [120], 94.

Hyppolite [234] also discusses the critique of Kant here. On the move to self-consciousness and the collapse of the Kantian thing-in-itself, see Kainz [249], 81 and especially footnote 24. But I think Kainz is wrong in claiming that consciousness "turns abruptly away at this point from its examination of objective knowledge, and returns to itself. . . . " (82).

Olivier Reboul [403] represents the view that Hegel's critique of Kant is misplaced since Hegel assumes that there is a consciousness of the absolute while Kant sees clearly that reason is purely human and "that nothing authorizes us to transcend the condition of man . . . " (88). But, if my analysis is correct, there is in fact in Hegel no such assumption of the suprahuman in that sense; on the contrary, Hegel has argued for an infinitude which is precisely human.

44 Cf. Schrader-Klebert's discussion in Schrader-Klebert [443], 27–28, of the fact that for the understanding the unity of thought and being is presupposed, but that this unity becomes questionable when pushed far enough, necessitating a move forward.

45 Compare Westphal [528], 125–26, for a discussion of Hegel's difference from Kant on this matter of self-consciousness and its relation to consciousness. Marcuse [338] goes too far in his anthropologizing of the *Phenomenology*, but if allowances are made for its essential epistemological concern, his characterization of the move from consciousness to self-consciousness is helpful. "The world is an estranged and untrue world so long as man does not destroy its dead objectivity and recognize himself and his own life 'behind' the fixed form of things and laws. When he finally wins this *self-consciousness*, he is on his way not only to the truth of himself but also of his world" (112–13).

Hyppolite [238], 143–55, but especially at the beginning of this section, attempts to discuss Hegel's move to self-consciousness via Hegel's understanding of Kant. But Hyppolite's discussion remains rather vague, and at one point the best image he can call up is that what is discovered by the examination of consciousness is that the "world is 'the great mirror' in which consciousness discovers itself" (143). See also Labarrière [287], 76–80.

Notes to Chapter IV

1 It is crucial to insist that the problem of the *Phenomenology* remains constant, not only in the present section of the work, but throughout. This first paragraph of "Self-consciousness" makes the continuity very clear. For a critical review of the ways in which self-consciousness has been interpreted see Otto Pöggeler [396], 231–99. The review is pp. 231–36. See also his remarks, pp. 247–48 on what the *Phenomenology* is not, and especially his view of Kojève. Pöggeler characterizes the general task of the *Phenomenology*, in this particular essay, as "alloting to every mode of knowledge and behavior its place in a connected series and thus 'critically' installing it within its limits" (239).

One of the most influential modern works dealing with the *Phenomenology* and with self-consciousness in particular has been Alexandre Kojève's *Introduction à la lecture de Hegel*, part of which has been translated into English as *Introduction to the Reading of Hegel*. Kojève's influence is unfortunate, for seldom has more violence been done by a commentator to the original. The commentary begins, in its published version, with a section titled "In Place of an Introduction," in the English translation pp. 3–30, in which the radically socio-historical interpretation of the independence/dependence section of the *Phenomenology* is offered as the heart and key of the whole of the *Phenomenology*. This view of Kojève's then forces him to do violence to many sections of the work and to find often a lack of strict transition between sections of the work. The interpretation, however, simply does not work; it might be good Kojève, and might even be correct about reality, but it is not Hegel. Kojève even partially admits this when he says in one of the early lectures, not translated in the English version, that "independently of what Hegel thinks of it, the *Phenomenology* is a philosophical anthropology. His theme is man as human, the real being in history. His method is phenomenological in the modern sense of the word. This anthropology is therefore neither a psychology nor an ontology. It aims to describe the integral 'essence' of man, that is to say, *all* human 'possibilities' (cognitive, affective, active). An epoch, a given culture realizes in act (effectively or actually) only a single 'possibility' "(*Introduction à la lecture de Hegel*, 39). We had better stay, on the contrary, with what Hegel thinks and says if we are to understand Hegel.

For Kojève's lectures on self-consciousness, see "In Place of an Introduction," (11–34 in the original, 3–30 in the English translation), and in the French his early lectures, pp. 49–56, 61–76, neither of which were included in the English translation. For critical discussions of Kojève, see also footnotes 18–21 below. In addition Gadamer [148] has an interesting critique of Kojève. Werner Becker [28] argues against the Kojèvean interpretation and points to the first paragraph of self-consciousness where the knowledge problem is explicitly continued and thus the problem of certainty which motivated the preceding chapter. However, the end of Becker's essay seems to lose sight of this very point which he has made so well. See also Louis Dupré [111].

There are many other views which are not basically Kojèvean in nature, but which ignore the central problem of the *Phenomenology* and stress either an historical or an anthropological or a genetic account of what Hegel is doing.

Findlay [120], 95–103 sees the move to self-consciousness as a passage which "suddenly swings over into the social sphere" (95). He claims that in the move to self-consciousness there is a move "from the epistemological to the practical, social level. Here, as elsewhere, Hegel's transition is in a queer way 'logical', though it shows not a trace of anything that one could call 'rigour'" (96). He completely misses the "epistemological" link given in the first paragraph. See also Koyré [272], especially p. 179.

Royce and Rosen, in different ways, have a genetic account of the chapter on self-consciousness. Royce [426] claims that the *Phenomenology* is a biography or romance which really begins with self-consciousness, and that the "first stage of self-consciousness is represented by the naive individualism of the child or of the savage" (158). Rosen's account is quite different, but still along the lines of seeing what is happening as an account of genesis. His interpretation is to be found in three different places. See Rosen [419, 420, 421]. For instance, in Rosen [419] he argues the following. "The origin of self-consciousness is for Hegel not presented within a political context. The same is true for Plato in the sense that we 'choose' or 'receive' from the gods, prior to incarnation or entrance into political life, the kind of life we will subsequently live" (621). However rich and suggestive this might be, it is inappropriate to the *Phenomenology* since there we are not dealing with the genesis of natural consciousness, but with the development of a proof of warranted access to the absolute standpoint. In all my remarks which follow on Rosen's interesting interpretation of self-consciousness this caveat is in force.

For an anthropological view, see Soll [467] and Taylor [495]. The latter combines the historical with the anthropological. See especially 148–61, and 216ff. Shklar [457] has an historical treatment of the whole of the analysis of self-consciousness.

For various other views which diverge to some degree from a strict "epistemological" account, see the following. Christensen [74] has an interesting but rather fanciful chain of thought, claiming that by "virtue of the rather substantial similarities between psychoanalytic theory and Hegel's phenomenology of mental disease, Freud offers a pedagogically useful point of access to Hegel's theory. Hegel's theory of mental disease, in turn, offers a favorable point of access into his phenomenological method and hence into his thought as a whole" (376). Hyppolite [238], 143–215, discusses a possible connection with Jakob Böhme vis-à-vis the beginning of the discussion of self-consciousness. See p. 148.

Westphal [528] offers up to a point a very clear account of the move to self-consciousness on the grounds of the recognized "incompleteness" of the Kantian analysis. He first cites Dieter Henrich's analysis of the transcendental method in terms of presupposition rather than in terms of entailment, and then argues that Hegel goes beyond Kant with this method of the articulation of presuppositions on the question of the possibility of knowledge. Hegel "claims on the basis of strictly Kantian premises not only that transcendental apperception is only the idea of Self-Consciousness and not actual Self-Consciousness (to which Kant might agree in terms of his own distinction between transcendental and empirical apperception), but also that actual Self-Consciousness first enters the scene as

Notes to Chapter IV

desire" (125). Westphal goes on to explain that Hegel is essentially saying here that not only is consciousness self-consciousness, but also "that it is in desire that Self-Consciousness is first actual. . . . That desire is actual Self-Consciousness in contrast to transcendental apperception means . . . that the moment of empirical reality, *Sein* as genuinely *Anderssein*, is retained in its experience of the object" (126). Thus Westphal sees clearly that to discuss actuality rather than possibility is to treat presuppositions in a different manner, but he does not then return to this insight and use it in an appropriate way.

Heinrichs [208], 169–219, uses the logical category of '*Verhältnis*' for explication of the section on self-consciousness.

See also Solange Mercier-Josa [356]; Labarrière [287], 84–95; Chalybäus [69], 354–59; Dieter Wandschneider [518].

For those who do keep the thematic in perspective, see first of all Ludwig Siep [460] who points out that we are concerned with the "specific problematic of the raising of natural consciousness to the standpoint of absolute knowing. . ." (192). He does not expand on this as I do, but the rejection of "anthropological" and other interpretations is firm. Secondly, see the account of Fink [127], 156–201, who continues his own brand of analysis, but sees "no change of thematic" in the move to this section (165).

2 'Life' is central to the whole of the section on self-consciousness and not only to the first part. It has usually been understood in some direct or indirect biological or physical sense as, for instance, in Jules Vuillemin [511]. In this direction see also Brockard [56] where it is understood as a "model" of the "living organism." See, for instance, p. 159. I think that my argument in the text will show both of these versions to be inadequate. Although too tied up with his anthropological and existential concerns, Hyppolite [230] has nicely traced out the development of Hegel's conception of life and the part it plays in his overall philosophy. Compare his remarks in Hyppolite [238] that the "chapter on self-consciousness begins with a general philosophy of life and living things" (p. 148, footnote). On the other hand, Fink [127], 158–60, has an analysis of life which, given our differences, still moves in the same direction as my analysis.

3 'Desire' as a central concern for Hegel has been less problematic for interpretation than the term 'life'. For a particularly rich description of 'desire' see Fink [127], 168–71.

4 On the contrast between interest as desire and interest as intentionality, cf. Lauer [305]: "'We', then, are beginning to see that any awareness of objects entails an awareness of the self's part in that awareness; consciousness itself is beginning to be aware of itself simply as a sort of center of reference for all its awareness. *What* it is to be this center of reference remains to be seen" (90).

Heidegger [207], 185–96 has a rather long discussion of desire and interest in the context of the difference between the discussion of consciousness and that of self-consciousness. He argues that the move to self-consciousness does not involve us with a claim that with every act of consciousness there is also an act of self-consciousness, but rather that Hegel's claim is that consciousness *is* self-consciousness, that "self-consciousness is the truth of consciousness" (193). In my terms, intentionality is replaced by desire in the sense that desire is that which completes the concept of 'intention', is the truth of intentionality.

Compare, on this matter, Labarrière [287], 84–95.

5 George Kline [263] has a very interesting account of desire as a special case of the interplay between action and passion, an interplay which Kline tries to demonstrate as the general movement of the *Phenomenology*. It helps throw light on the relation between desire and truth.

6 All three senses, as I will articulate them, are important, as is the interrelatedness of the three. Hegel's discussion of the three senses is often problematic for interpretation as, for instance, in Soll [467] 15–16. Soll thinks the movement in self-consciousness to the living thing is obscure. I think that his problem derives from his anthropological treatment of Hegel and his identification of "life" with its biological sense. That is the problem in most interpretations. But see also the discussion of Hyppolite [238] who rightly claims that "life is the medium in which self-consciousness experiences and seeks itself. Life constitutes the first truth of self-consciousness and appears as its other" (161). But his interpretation of 'life' misses the full significance of this—and the broad construction which must be put on life—when he ignores the third element or sense, the living of life and its immediate connection with desire.

7 Like the difference between intentionality and desire, this difference is also important. See Heidegger's discussion of life as a mode of Being and the connection with Aristotle in Heidegger [207], 206–07. See also the essay of Debrock [90], 296ff. For a quite different discussion of 'life' see Lauer [305], 93ff. Lauer's analysis, in my view, misses the significance of life as the correlate of desire, and thus also the significance of death. See p. 106.

8 Compare Kainz [249], 83–85, especially footnote 3. Niel [376], 126–27, seems to recognize only one aspect of life, i.e., life in general, as the multiplicity of lives mediating one another.

9 I have already mentioned Lauer's view in this respect. See above, note 4. On desire as the center of life, see Fink [127], 170–71.

Navickas [374], 88–93, has a good analysis of the reciprocity of desire and life, but he misses the way in which they arise to begin with. He argues simply that "the activity of self-consciousness and the perfection of life are mutually implicative" (91). Compare the version of Hyppolite [236], 27, where he claims of the relation between desire and life that the "supreme end of desire is to rediscover itself in the heart of life, that is to say, to find itself as the unity of universal life or the being-for-itself of this life which scatters itself endlessly through particular living forms."

Debrock [90] notes a certain aspect of ineffability in the relation between desire and life, remarking that "the moment of self-consciousness is first and foremost the moment of silence of existential experience," and arguing that self-consciousness "in its struggle for recognition is completely in the grip of Experience itself. That struggle is an essentially subjective, mute, and silent experience" (298). But see my remarks below, note 38, concerning how this misleads Debrock when he comes to discuss the relation between thought and action.

10 Eugen Fink's analysis in Fink [127] naturally lends itself to a complex understanding of the ambiguity of self-consciousness. See pp. 165–68. See also

the discussion of Heinrichs [208], where he uses the notion of analogy. It is a rich analysis, but I think not a sufficient way of understanding the infinite and the complexity of the subject-object relation; for analogy preserves difference and separation in precisely a way that prevents the necessary ambiguity to emerge in the structure of self-consciousness. 'Ambiguity' ['*Zweideutigkeit*'] is central to Hegel's discussion.

Gadamer [148] captures this ambiguity in a different way. On the one hand, he claims that Hegel conceives 'life' in self-consciousness as in a structural identity of identity and difference, but in identity with self-consciousness. But on the other hand, "more than this structural identity is manifest here. That which is a self-consciousness is itself necessarily life." However, life is grasped as other for self-consciousness because it is "a special kind of life, namely, one which has consciousness and for which, accordingly, the species character of all that lives is 'given'" (59). This comes probably as close as is possible to uniting a biological sense of life with Hegel's sense.

11 Cf. Ludwig Siep [459]. He discusses the importance of separation within self-consciousness in conjunction with the ambiguity of self-consciousness. See especially pp. 390–92. See also Fink [127], p. 162: "Hegel's concept of self-consciousness is linked to the counter-concept of self-alienation."

12 On self-consciousness as the presupposition for consciousness see the remarks of Heidegger in Heidegger [207] that the "transition [*Übergang*] from consciousness to self-consciousness is the return [*Rückgang*]into the essence of consciousness, which latter self-consciousness essentially is, and as this constitutes the inner possibilizing of consciousness, that is, in every single way constitutes that which belongs to consciousness" (194). Compare the account of Murray Greene [166], especially p. 162 where Greene discusses the way in which self-consciousness comes to awareness of the necessity for consciousness and, conversely, consciousness of the necessity of self-consciousness. See also Lauer [305], 91–93 on consciousness and self-consciousness and the complexity of the relation. But what is not made explicit by Lauer is what my use of "interest" in the two different forms makes explicit.

13 Görland [161], 54–56, traces out in a very clear way the problem of self-consciousness in the framework of the problem of the establishment of the absolute standpoint as this is developed earlier in the *Differenzschrift* and in *Glauben und Wissen*. See also Pöggeler, "Hegels Phänomenologie des Selbstbewusstseins," in Pöggeler [396].

14 Debrock [90], pp. 296ff., has an interesting comparison between the failure here at this point in the discussion of self-consciousness and the failure that occurred in the discussion of sense-certainty.

15 Compare Niel [376] who also stresses the importance of preserving realism in self-consciousness regarding the object. "In order that it maintain itself, it will be necessary that the object continue to be posited as object, that is to say, that the world keep the reality which sense-certainty and perception entrusted to it" (126).

16 On the power of negation in life, cf. Labarrière [287], 88–89.

17 Findlay [120] has an interesting parenthetical characterization of the discussion of the confrontation of one self-consciousness by another as an episode belonging to "the Henry Jamesian world where the characters not only see each other, but also see each other seeing each other" (97). This is certainly part of the matter, but misses the necessity of this link to one another as well as a need to argue against the possibility of solipsism.

18 Much has been written on this section of self-consciousness. See the relevant citations above in note 1. See also George Armstrong Kelly [256]; Hyppolite [238], 156–77, but especially 164–77; Heinrichs [208], 179–92.

Rosen [421] calls the dialectic of mastery and bondage "a mythical representation of the historical recognition of the self in its relation with others." Several analyses have tried to establish roots in the history of philosophy. See, for example, Andreas Wildt [534]. The claim is that the analysis here can only be understood in conjunction with Hegel's view of Kant's ethics. H. Mayer [351] attempts to find roots for an anthropological-political interpretation of independence and dependence of self-consciousness in Thomas Münzer, Leibniz, and Diderot and their respective uses of "Herr und Knecht." He then traces consequences of "Hegel's thought" into Brecht and Hofmannsthal, and relies a great deal on Lukács, Marcuse, and Bloch. But even if Mayer is accurate on Münzer, Leibniz, and Diderot, this does not of itself validate such an interpretation in Hegel's case. Nor does the assumption that Marxists have interpreted Hegel rightly.

For an interesting attempt to treat the present section in terms of Freudian sexual analysis, especially that of the Oedipus Complex, see Solange Mercier-Josa [355]. Compare the essay of Christensen [74] where he tries to draw parallels between lordship and bondage and the psychoanalytic notion of transference.

Solomon [476] writes of this section that "the problem is . . . the problem of identifying our own mind" (145). But compare, against this sort of view on the one hand, and the Kojèvèan analysis on the other, the insistence of Lauer that "for Hegel there is no such thing as a disembodied consciousness." See Lauer [305], p. 94.

19 Many have followed or agreed with Kojève. Fackenheim [118] follows Kojève and in some ways is even more radical than the latter in taking the self-consciousness chapter as a piece of anthropology in an historical setting. See pp. 37–44. He does this because of his notion of the task of the book, i.e., to show how in life and history Hegel can demonstrate that the time is right for philosophy as science.

Marcuse [338] has a relatively typical Marxist analysis of self-consciousness and of mastery and bondage, as does also, as might be expected, Lukács [336]. On the latter, see for example pp. 326ff. where Hegel is treated in the context of a discussion of economics and civil society as Hegel conceived of them in his Jena period (at least as he conceived of them in Lukács' view).

Among other misinterpretations, the following are representative. Chalybäus [69] has an interesting exposition of self-consciousness as a form of intuition, but also ties the section too closely with the socio-historical. Recognition is for him the problem of constituting "the Dialectics of the idea of right" which "here makes its appearance in its ultimate foundation" (359). Erhard Lange [300] quickly introduces a social dimension and misses the whole aspect of the quest for certainty.

Wilfred Ver Eecke [509] interprets this move anthropologically. Lordship and bondage is understood as "the necessary means to transcend animal life and reach human freedom" (561). Lakebrink [297] also anthropologizes.

Shklar [455] treats the whole matter in a too historical manner. She claims that "master-slave" is the place where "Hegel traces the path, from classical birth to Christian death, step by step, of the Aristotelian hero-as-philosopher. For it is the autonomy of contemplative man, rather than of the warrior or ruler, that stands in contrast to the enslavement of the producer" (77). See also Shklar [457], Chapter Two.

20 This is perhaps the most important consideration telling against the traditional interpretations of self-consciousness which politicize or make historical in content the concerns of the chapter. Rosen [421] has a strong attack on the socio-historical setting supposed to be here. See also the general remarks by Henri Lauener [303], especially p. 164. Siep [460] puts mastery and bondage in proper perspective and distinguishes it from the later discussions of reason and spirit and the historical-political thesis of Kojève and Strauss. For a specific discussion of Strauss, see below, note 29. Heinrichs and Löwith take a similar stand in distinguishing the discussion of mastery and bondage from the later, explicitly historical sections. See Heinrichs [208], who approaches the socio-political and historical question by arguing that unlike other places in the Hegelian corpus—both before and after the *Phenomenology*—an historical and social interpretation can have no standing because there is at this point in the *Phenomenology* a lack of social conditions necessary for such a discussion, and thus that one could not move in the realms of legal status and society. See pp. 189–91. This lack of discrimination between the *Phenomenology*, with its unique task, and other parts of the corpus may indeed lie at the basis of much of the misinterpretation of the *Phenomenology* generally. The discussion by Löwith is to be found in Löwith [332]. He offers a most direct critique of the interpretation by arguing that one cannot stay with consciousness or self-consciousness, but must understand the ground of what-is to be present only in the "truth of objective reason in the historical forms of spirit." The section on mastery and bondage cannot give us this, since such a truth is not yet present. (208)

The magnitude of the problem of the socio-historical interpretations can be seen in Itshaq Klein [262]. On the one hand, he attacks Kojève's interpretation of mastery and bondage on the grounds that Kojève is forced to reinterpret the totality of the *Phenomenology* in order to make the master-slave interpretation fit. On the other hand, Klein argues, the *Phenomenology* cannot be only an account of the phenomenological development of consciousness, for then "master" and "servant" would only be metaphorically taken. So, we must conclude that there is a double signification of the text, one on the plane of reality (exterior), one within consciousness as such. The real problem, which brings these two planes together according to Klein, is that of the relation between self-consciousness and recognition.

Klein certainly has a point here when he refers us to recognition. But he is forced to bring in what he calls the practical element only on the condition that self-consciousness "is an historical being" (298). In the end, the real problem with Klein and others is that they are taking the *Phenomenology* too exclusively as an anthropology, and are missing the levels of thematics which make the interpretation I am now giving possible and avoid all necessity for speaking of "historical being." Certainly, there is historical being to both the praxical presuppositions and the thematics of the natural attitude, i.e., we are talking about real, historical experiences had by real historical human beings. But in this sense of "the historical," we have been historical from the first moment of sense-certainty and will continue to be through the whole of the *Phenomenology*. But this is quite different from the historical and social as they will appear later in spirit.

Philippe Muller [369] attacks the historical thesis, but replaces it with the claim that we have a psychological analysis. See especially p. 210. On this discussion of the psychological, and on the discussion of the historical in general, see Hyppolite [232]. He claims that "it is not a matter in this chapter of a history, nor of a transcendental psychology, nor even of an analysis of essence. Briefly said, Hegel wished *to found* the historical fact itself" (1277). There is something important here, i.e., the sense of the connection with what follows in the work. Compare this with the remark in Hyppolite [236] that the *"Phenomenology* is the history of human consciousness in its progression to Absolute Knowledge" (23).

21 Kelly [256] was one of the first to offer a sound critique of Kojève's reading and the Marxist reading in general. He moves in the direction I will now take, but still gives Kojève too much by accepting the social reading as "one angle" (195). On the contrary, as has been argued above, the social is not a possibility here. Kainz [249] treats masters and slaves as types of consciousness, but does not go far enough in freeing the figures from a narrow type. Gadamer [148] goes further and suggests expansion of mastery and bondage to other relations than those of master and slave, but the expansion is only slight. In the end he is just as limiting because he claims that "Hegel, in his dialectic, does not describe the wage worker, but principally the farmer and handworker in bondage" (73).

Fink [127] claims that master-slave is "metaphorical," and not to be taken literally; but he does not seem to see that it means just independence and dependence of self-consciousness. See pp. 174ff. Finally, Lauer [305] has a good critique of Kojève and Marxist interpretations of independence and dependence, but he still tends to see what is referred to here as a conflict of two distinct persons, rather than as the structure of self-consciousness as such. See his discussion, pp. 104 and 106ff. He sees master and slave as "types."

22 The second of these points is most often recognized in commentary, but the first is often missed. One who seems to capture both points is Henri Niel [376], where he first describes self-consciousness as a "revelation of human dignity. It is that which permits man to differentiate himself from animals and from the speaking me" (126). Later, he continues, "in defining itself as for itself, self-consciousness posits that the act by which it is constituted is precisely the act by which it is separated and distinguished from the other. The I appears to itself only to the degree that it is limited by the other" (129). George Schrader [441] also singles out this function of the analysis. "Only in the sense that I achieve my own subjectivity through the refusal of the other person's objectification of

Notes to Chapter IV

me does the encounter serve as a condition of my own subjectivity" (29). See also David Rasmussen [401] who, although not writing primarily on Hegel, sees the move to self-consciousness as a move overcoming autonomous rationality and introducing social rationality. His essay is generally supportive of my extended view of the "master-slave" section.

23 Lauer [305] uses children as an example for the struggle for recognition and the risk it involves. See pp. 105–06. Westphal [528] goes in a different, but interesting direction in the matter of this "life and death struggle." For him it is a struggle for love or for the recognition which is a valuing. He identifies love and freedom in a rather vague way, and then writes that "we can say that the unloved life is not worth living" (135).

24 As will be discussed below, the critique of the "master-master" set is usually couched in terms which interpret life and death in reference to the physical and biological. But this is not in keeping with the meaning of 'life' in the *Phenomenology*.

Soll [467] recognizes that this move is made on the grounds of "the need for a witness," but argues that this need is "merely postulated and not justified" (19). I have tried to show that the justification for this move is the failure to obtain self-certainty, and the next claim for the independence and dependence of self-consciousness will putatively make up for this lack.

Fackenheim [118] p. 41, calls up the Faust-motif in respect to the critique of the master-master episode, but also cautions that the allusion to Faust must not be overstated.

25 If I am right, then the mainly biological interpretations of death are wrong. See for example, Hyppolite [238]: "death appears only as a natural fact, not as a spiritual negation" (170); Vuillemin [511]; Fackenheim [118], 40–42; Philibert Secretan [448].

26 This set is widely discussed in the socio-political and anthropological sense. Most of the literature has been already cited in notes above. But see expecially Findlay [120] who holds to the orthodox view that we are discussing masters and slaves in a literal way, but who is also of the opinion that what we have here is a passage into another attitude *simpliciter*. See especially p. 98.

27 Fink [127] goes somewhat in my direction in interpreting the relationship this broadly. See his discussion, pp. 174ff.

28 This recognition that independence requires dependence is central, and has a positive, not a negative significance. Siep [460] writes that "the battle for recognition in the *Phenomenology* is precisely not that which Hobbes took up, but rather the struggle is interpreted by Hegel in an opposed sense: only as negation of self-preservation is the first mode of the self, the certainty of its pure being-for-self, to be realized" (201). The Hobbesian interpretation is too often the interpretation given at this point.

29 Piotr Hoffman [217] argues that mutual recognition is impossible. But he misses the dialectic of independence and dependence which we are here going through. However, the problem of recognition does not, as Hyppolite [238] for instance would have it, arise simply out of the fact that human beings "imperiously desire to be recognized as self-consciousnesses, as something raised above purely animal life," and it is not simply a "passion to be recognized" (169). Such a view

ignores the part played by this section in the overall quest for certainty and in the "deduction" of absolute idealism.

See Mercier-Josa [356] for a discussion of the problem of recognition on the background of Aristotle's distinction between poiesis and praxis: the battle for recognition is neither one nor the other in a simple way (339). See also two essays of Siep [459, 460]. In the latter he compares the state of nature in Hobbes with the struggle for recognition in Hegel and argues against the interpretation given by Leo Strauss. Siep supports his own position with references to the development of this theme in Hegel's earlier Jena writings and before. Compare Itshaq Klein [262].

30 The usual interpretation makes this new position not complementary, but antagonistic or simply other. See for instance the formulation by Ver Eecke [509]. "The passage on 'Lordship and Bondage' lets us see that as labor is the essence of man, the Lord is a figure without a future" (563). As usual, such a view is too historical and is out of place in the project of the *Phenomenology*. But more importantly, the link between the dependence discovered in independence and the discussion of dependence itself is lost on such an analysis.

31 It is important to note that from the beginning of the discussion of self-consciousness there has been a "material" dimension, i.e. things and material and institutional events come "between" the self-consciousnesses and thus count toward the constitution of self-consciousness. This material thrust is often missed in its full significance, which will be discussed below. See for instance Lange [300]. Westphal [528] does see the significance, but see my discussion of his view, below, note 40. Miodrag Cekić [68] also notes the material thrust, but see also below, note 40. Günter Rohrmoser [417], working within a different framework of investigation than mine, has an interesting thesis which puts the materialism of Hegel in highlight. "Hegel's dialectical philosophy wishes to demonstrate that modern reification signifies the condition of the possibility of man being free, and that only in its affirmation and recognition through the self-conscious subject can this subject maintain and preserve himself historically" (17–18).

32 The centrality of work or labor has often been noted, but with various degrees of faithfulness to Hegel's own conception. Some commentators, especially Marxists of various sorts, often stretch the concept. For instance Adorno [3] argues that the *Phenomenology* as a whole and in itself is labor, and thus production, and then makes bad use of analogy. So, p. 34, he claims that the "path of the natural consciousness to the identity of the absolute knowing is itself labor. The relation of spirit to actuality [*Gegebenheit*] appears on the model of a social process, in fact as a process of labor. . . . " To make a connection from this to "labor" as central to Hegel's view is to distort the real place of material activity in Hegel's quest for the ground of certainty and the nature of reality. See in this regard Lukács [336] who also has an extreme view of the importance of "*Werk*" in Hegel, in his chapter titled "Labour and the Problem of Teleology" (338–64). But in spite of the extreme views, there is much of interest in respect to the importance of praxis and materiality in Hegel.

Hyppolite [238] puts the significance of work nicely when he says that not only "does the slave shape himself by shaping things; he also imprints the form of self-consciousness on being" (176). With due alterations to enlarge the scope of this statement, we have a good description of the presupposition set. Compare also Kroner's discussion of the primacy of the practical in Kant and Hegel in Kroner [275], II, 260–61.

Clearly, if our analysis is right, work must be presupposed here within a structure of reciprocity. On this, see Heinrichs [208], 188ff. Heinrichs discusses the whole section in terms of causality, self-causality, and reciprocity.

For more on "work," see infra, pp. 146ff.

33 Thus, we have not simply a matter of the production of products, but also the emergence of subjectivity through objectification of the self. See Mercier-Josa [356] who notes the action of the slave does not exhaust its significance as production (340). See also Rohrmoser [417] who argues, contra the interpretation of Lukács and others on the resolution of alienation, that "the Hegelian dialectic cannot be reduced to the dialectic of social production processes" (102).

34 On the fragility of our existence and the need to risk oneself, compare the physical-historical interpretation of Fackenheim [118], p. 42.

35 Given Hegel's project to validate claims of access to the absolute standpoint, and his lack of interest in a philosophical anthropology or an ontology of experience, his work suffers from the viewpoint of the latter sorts of projects each time he leaves behind a figure of consciousness or self-consciousness. The rich analyses implicit in the *Phenomenology* are never really carried out. See my comments on this issue in note 1 above.

36 Cf. Siep [459] for an excellent overall discussion of the need for grounding of both of the relata in self-consciousness as well as for the relation itself, i.e., the relation to other through self, through the other to the self, and to be the relation itself.

37 Findlay [120] notes quite a different point than I shall argue for here. He sees the move to freedom of self-consciousness as one from a "profound discussion, with its revolutionary social and political implications," i.e., master-slave, "into a quieter philosophico-religious region," which is Stoicism (98). But this misses, I think, the real connection in the process.

38 The connection between thought and language, on the one hand, and action and work, on the other hand, is critical here. Hyppolite [238] misses the connection in relating the analysis of dependence to stoicism. See pp. 172–80, especially 179–80. It is also missed by Debrock [90]. See pp. 299–300. Lauer [305] opposes thinking and work, rather than seeing the positive connection. "The slave's work is for the master, but his thinking is free; the product of the former is for another, of the latter for himself" (113). But if I am right, it is just its being-for-the-master that makes it important for our study of self-consciousness as the putative absolute standpoint.

Although he misses some of the relation between thought and action which I find in Hegel's discussion, Liebrucks [320], V, 97–98, does note the significance of thought to action in a positive way. In spite of our disagreement on the nature and central question of the *Phenomenology*, Soll [471] comes close to my position when he looks at the relation between thinking and acting. See especially p. 5. For further reference, see Bodhammer [47], 94.

39 What I have argued here, with a view to the transition from the section on bondage to that on freedom of self-consciousnes, stops short of the view of Robert N. Beck [24]. Beck does argue that "surely it is more accurate to say, not that the relations among men in civil society are mediated by things, but that they are mediated by conceptions of things as mediary among men" (79). But where he pushes this too far, irrespective of the questionable mention of 'civil society', is in then claiming that the real significance of this is that the slave comes to hold on to an ideal, while the master is at a dead end (79). Compare Heinrichs [208] 193–94. He notes well the comprehension involved in the forming of things, but does not make explicit the whole activity and how thinking is the concrete link through reciprocity.

For a reasonable Marxist analysis of the relation of thought, work, and freedom in Hegel, see Zbigniew Kuderowicz [281], especially p. 1526, and Kuderowicz [282].

40 Cekić [68] discusses the way in which activity and action as well as thinking are of the essence of the concept, but he doesn't get the relation quite right, if I am correct. For instance, in the discussion of lordship and bondage he makes the relation between "slave" and thing an "analog" of the relation between "master and slave" (241–43). But the notion of 'analog' is always too weak when discussing Hegel's philosophy. Sidney Hook [220], on the other hand, in some ways saw the correct relation when he wrote that the "subject-object relation as a formal scheme plays little part in Hegel's thought. It is only as it finds expression in specific forms and on different levels that this relation becomes significant. In the *Phänomenologie* Hegel shows how man discovers the subject-object relation in feeling, action and social duty, before he discovers it in abstract thought" (246).

Compare with my view that of Stanley Rosen [421], pp. 162ff., on the place of work and production as the presupposition for freedom of self-consciousness. "Freedom, in short, is the making of the self in the activity of producing the world. The world is not produced by sheer imagination or mere subjectivity, of course. Hegel is referring to man's appropriation of nature . . . " (163). Westphal [528], while recognizing the importance of the material to self-consciousness, has reservations and thinks it can be carried too far. After citing relevant passages from Marx and Hegel, Westphal writes that "while it is true that for Hegel labor involves creation and not just consumption, Self-Consciousness and not just self-preservation, it is just as clear that the object of labor cannot mediate as complete a mode of Self-Consciousness as another self can. The definitive characteristic of human desire is not labor any more than it is life. It is love. The essential thing is not the postponement of satisfaction but the nature of the satisfaction which recognition involves. Hegel would find Marx's account of his accomplishment one-sided and incomplete" (136). I think that Westphal's critique in a general way is correct; whether or not it is love that is involved is another matter.

41 That the tension between dependence and independence is retained is important, and is often denied. For instance, Fackenheim [118] argues that the "process of slavery results in emancipation from this dependence" (42). But there is not emancipation; rather there is acceptance in the sense I have argued for. If there were emancipation from dependency, then there would be no point to the

stoical attitude or to the skeptical or that of unhappy consciousness. The ambiguity and tension which Hegel claims structures self-consciousness would collapse. This is one of the many places where one must recognize the importance of *difference* for Hegel.

On the other hand, while there is the unity of thought and action, thought and will as Hyppolite says, it does not take the form of an opposition between life or living self-consciousness and thinking self-consciousness as he claims. See Hyppolite [238], 179–80. In both this case and in the sort of case Fackenheim tries to make, the real weakness of the anthropological, existential interpretation comes through, as does the restriction of life to the biological. For the real concreteness of these "philosophies of life" is lost when not placed in the struggle to establish the absolute standpoint.

For a more correct view, compare Kroner [275], II, 266, where he argues for the retention of "life" in thinking as the pulse of that thinking. However, Kroner also has a problem with the proper interpretation of 'life'.

42 These have often been seen as historical figures. See, for example, Wahl [515] who has a very historical (and theological-historical) interpretation of these sections on the freedom of self-consciousness, and is unable to demonstrate a solid connection to what came before and to what will follow. But there is now quite widespread recognition that these positions are not historical in any but an accidental or exemplificatory sense; they are philosophies of life occurring primarily in the mode of the natural attitude. See, for instance, Aschenberg [12], 282–85. In an interesting argument Aschenberg cites Hegel's position from the *Philosophy of History* to the effect that the "*presupposition*, under which the historicizing of the dialectic can alone be possible ... is 'the simple thought of *reason*, that reason rules the world'" (283). There are, of course, more systemic reasons, i.e. reasons systemic to the *Phenomenology* itself; but Aschenberg's insight here is interesting.

Hyppolite [238] gives an interpretation to the forms of freedom, seeing them as "philosophies of life" independent of history in the sense of placing Stoicism, etc., in specific periods. But he misses the way in which, as I will show, the move to stoicism brings more closely together the philosophical and natural attitudes within the *Phenomenology* itself. See p. 179.

43 Compare Bonsiepen [52] where he argues that "an experience of consciousness is actually possible only beginning with the chapter on self-consciousness" (265).

44 On stoicism in general, compare Hyppolite [238], 179–84.

45 Heinrichs [208] notes that stoicism is a "flight into ideality, where actuality is still characterized by bondage" (195). But it is equally true to say that mastery also characterizes actuality here, and that the turn is only against a will to mastery in the former mastery-bondage sense. In this regard see Labarrière [287], who characterizes this position of the freedom of self-consciousness, in contrast to a simple mastery thesis, as "the real equality of the I and its world" (92).

46 The problem, therefore, is that there is an empty formalism. See on this especially Hyppolite [238]. But Hyppolite does not grasp the whole determinate character of the critique, and is led to claim that the "same relation pertains

between stoic self-consciousness and skeptic consciousness as between master and slave" (184). But as we have seen above, just that difference in relation is what must be captured here.

47 On skepticism, see Hyppolite [238], 184–89. See especially his remarks on the meaning of skepticism in history, and his comparison of skepticism with ancient comedy, pp. 185ff.

48 On this first appearance of the two forms of self-consciousness, cf. Heinrichs [208], 196–200, where this is articulated in reference to the form of the structure of judgment.

49 Compare Fink [127] 186ff. on the changeable and the unchangeable as the problem of the unity of self-consciousness.

50 This section, like that on mastery and bondage, has been much discussed in the literature. Hyppolite [238] has a very rich discussion and claims that "Unhappy consciousness is the fundamental theme of the *Phenomenology*" (190). Compare Wahl [515]. Wahl also considers unhappy consciousness as central to the whole of the *Phenomenology*, and grounds his theological interpretation in this position of self-consciousness. "The main concept which here denotes the entry of apologetic theology into history, which itself becomes logic, is that of the unhappy consciousness" (vi). Under this theme, he has an interesting account of various prior themes which are in the background of the discussion of the unhappy consciousness. See pp. 10–118.

Fink [127], 179–201, has a rich characterization of the unhappiness of unhappy consciousness which is in keeping with his overall ontological interpretation of the *Phenomenology*. "The unhappiness, which Hegel discusses here, is neither the unhappiness of a specific factual situation of humanity, nor simply the unhappiness of being human; it is neither an historical situation of existence, nor simply the existential condition or attitude of man" (191). Rather, Fink maintains, the expression 'unhappy' "marks a mode of *legein*, a way of addressing *on*, it designates a mode of understanding Being" (192).

In contrast, Murray Greene [167] treats the unhappy consciousness as the "inherent self-reflectedness of consciousness" (127), and draws out the differences with Nietzsche. See also the comments in this regard of Altizer [10] and Flay [131]. See also, for other views, Christensen [74] where the attempt is made to show the analogy between unhappy consciousness in Hegel and anxiety in Freudian theory; Heinrichs [208], 200–05, for an explication of the problem of the unity of self-consciousness in unhappy consciousness as the structure of the syllogism; Muller [369], 211, for an account of unhappy consciousness as a general analysis of "scission"; Arthur Lessing [317], where Hegel is compared to Kierkegaard (and to "existentialism" generally) on the matter of the crisis in finitude; and Rosen [421], 151–81.

51 Fink [127], 93ff. has an excellent discussion of the complexity of this set of relations, placed in the context of a discussion of the two senses of 'subject', i.e., in relation to predicates and in relation to objects. He manages to make clear in what way in both senses the subject is that which abides. On the other hand, Hyppolite [238] identifies the changeable with consciousness and the unchangeable with the transcendent divine, missing the real complexity. See pp. 199–203.

Compare Heinrichs [208], pp. 210ff., who also misses the point, in spite of the richness of his analysis of self-consciousness in terms of the category of 'syllogism'.

52 The internal nature of this alienation is important to understand, and is what is missed in most interpretations because of an historical understanding of the section on self-consciousness. See the works referred to below in note 53.

53 For a review of interpretations given the term 'alienation', see Dupré [111]. In respect to the distinction between 'alienation' and 'objectification' see Joseph Gauvin [153] where the appearances of each of these terms in the *Phenomenology* is catalogued and analysed. Conrad Boey [49] follows Gauvin on *Entfremdung*, and uses Roman Jakobson's linguistics to articulate the problem of dealing with the relation between alienation and objectification. Compare the discussion of Hyppolite [236], 70–90.

Although most directly relevant for the later section on culture (*Bildung*), the analysis by Mitchell Franklin [141] is of interest, especially pp. 32–33 where he is discussing the concept of alienation in Hegel as differing from the term as it appears in Savigny's defense of feudal alienation. See also Rosen [421], 172–82.

54 What I would consider to be the "over-religicizing" of unhappy consciousness is quite common. To some degree Heinrichs [208] does so, and the consequence is his missing the importance of the unchangeability of consciousness as well as the changeability of "the world," as I noted above, note 51. Hyppolite [238] discusses unhappy consciousness in terms of Jewish and Christian consciousness, causing the problem of the absolute standpoint to disappear from focus. See pp. 190–215. See also Kojève [266], p. 74; Findlay [120], 100–102; and Lauer [305], 117–24. Lukács [336] understands unhappy consciousness as the historical crisis in Christianity which has externalized the individual (i.e., alienated him) in emancipating him from the natural bonds of primitive society and of the classical world. See, for instance, p. 478. Walter Kaufmann [253] has perhaps the most short-sighted view of all when he argues that in the unhappy consciousness section "Hegel evidently wanted to get some ideas about medieval Christianity off his chest. . . . His poetic impulse made the most of this opportunity to visualize and describe a state of mind and a period" (156).

55 On the complexities of such a freeing of oneself, seen in the context of the whole of the project of the *Phenomenology*, see Ahlers [6], especially p. 65.

56 It is here that Hegel makes his remarks about coming upon the open grave. See in this respect Helen Adolf [1] for a discussion of the relation between the "empty grave" section and the quest for the grail. She argues that Hegel could only have had a fleeting knowledge of the story of the grail, but that its structure is to be found, together with the idea of the crusades, in unhappy consciousness. What is important for me is the connection with the much broader problem of the quest for certainty.

57 The structural importance of feeling at this point is too often missed. See, for instance, Findlay [120], 100–01. Without this turn toward the feeling itself, the movement to the next form of unhappy consciousness would not occur in a dialectical fashion.

58 This turn to actual or effective self-consciousness, as opposed to pure consciousness, is what is important. Compare Marcuse [338], 112–13. Following on

his view that the section on consciousness was a critique of positivism, he concludes with the remark that "there is, in the last analysis, no truth that does not *essentially concern* the living subject and that is not the subject's truth." But then Marcuse claims the following turn in Hegel's analysis, which is surely in the right direction, but which anthropologizes and politicizes Hegel's *Phenomenology* in a way which that work cannot support. "The world is an estranged and untrue world so long as man does not . . . recognize himself and his own life 'behind' the fixed form of things and laws. When he finally wins this *self-consciousness*, he is on his way . . . to the truth. . . . And with the recognition goes the doing. He will try to put this truth into action and *make* the world what it *essentially* is, namely, the fulfillment of man's self-consciousness" (113). In addition to the overly political tone of this, it is also too positive; for the presupposition that the world is the fulfillment of man's self-consciousness is just what is in the process of being tested by unhappy consciousness itself and will subsequently be "refuted."

59 Work and action again emerge here as central to the possibility of grounding oneself within life and of finding the absolute standpoint. See above, note 32, and the accompanying text for my earlier discussion of work and action. In addition, see Kuon Boey [51]. Although Boey is mainly interested in a later section of the *Phenomenology*, his discussion is relevant here. Having argued that wherever we discuss self-mediation, "everything is the middle term of everything" (64), he then turns to the question of *das Tun*. "Action shows itself to be the negativity which is no longer exterior to the subject but which is the subject itself as freedom. Action is therefore the movement of the whole itself mediating itself" (66).

60 On this theme of life as a gift from an alien source, compare the interesting view of T. I. Oiserman [379]. Oiserman claims that 'alienation' "played the same role in Hegel's ontology as did the concept of emanation in the systems of the neo-Platonists. With the help of the concept of alienation the gap between such different entities as thinking and being, the knower and the known, knowledge and its subject matter, was bridged in Hegel's epistemology" (40). The particular type of alienation we now have in the recognition of the gift of life and the life world serves, in a dialectical way, to move us on to a positive relation to things through reason.

61 Rolf Ahlers [6], albeit from a perspective different from that of the present interpretation, shows one way in which we can ground such an understanding of the lack in the presupposition about self-consciousness as the absolute standpoint. On this see also Lessing [317] where, although from an anthropological interpretation, he contrasts Kierkegaard and Hegel with Descartes. The former thinkers inherit the Cartesian problem of self-consciousness "upon which both existence and philosophical thought proceed," yet both also "go beyond Descartes in arguing that consciousness fails to establish clear and distinct ideas of its own identity when it turns onto itself through the reflective act" (72). At the present point the lack in self-consciousness is just that.

As usual, Rosen [421] has a rich and suggestive interpretation of a critical juncture in the *Phenomenology*. But I think that the precise problem with self-consciousness is missed. In discussing recognition in the *Phenomenology*, he claims that according "to Hegel, I become radically conscious of myself in another consciousness" (157). In a footnote he clarifies what he means by this. "This is a 'Christian' or 'private' revision of the Greek (Socratic) notion that man finds or understands himself within the *polis*. Cf. Augustine's *Confessions* as well as such post-Hegelian writers as Kierkegaard and Buber" (157). Even leaving aside my problems with his general approach to the *Phenomenology*, the point of the failure of self-consciousness is missed. It is true that I become conscious of myself as myself, thus repairing one of the determinate failures experienced previously in the progress to the absolute standpoint; but it is also true that this consciousness of myself does not give me self-understanding. In fact, not even reason does so. It takes spirit—which includes not only life in the polis as for the Greeks, but the development of life in later societies, a development which, as we shall see, arises just out of the problems of recognition within the polis.

62 See Seidel [452], p. 173 for a discussion of the way in which the investigation of self-consciousness forms a necessary bridge to reason which, lacking in Kant's *Critique of Pure Reason*, caused Kant to limit our knowledge. Compare Elena Panova [382], who claims that Hegel's metaphysics is within the strictures against transcendence laid down by Kant (501). But she then incorrectly sees Hegel's absolute simply as a theory of God, and argues that God's existence is derived, as in Anselm and Descartes, from the concept of God. In whatever sense the absolute may be God or even a theory of God, it is certainly not derived through the ontological argument in any conventional sense.

63 For a perceptive discussion of this paradigm, cf. Fink [127], 199.

64 Fink [127] takes the failure of unhappy consciousness and of self-consciousness in general in a slightly different way. "The unhappiness of consciousness is the failure to unite self and world; self-consciousness cannot be one in its doubled form, because it on the one hand flees and negates the world, and on the other hand, however, depends on it, works upon it, and is bound to it. Self-consciousness is internally ruptured in the opposed compartments of lordship and bondage which latter are nevertheless fundamentally one" (195).

Rosen [421] also sees the centrality of this separation and its connection with the absolute standpoint, claiming that "whenever wisdom is absent, there we find the unhappy consciousness" (152). As we have seen, there is surely incompleteness here, and so the claim can be made that where the unhappy consciousness is, there we will not find wisdom; but I think that Rosen is wrong to expand the sense of the unhappy consciousness beyond its technical sense within the discussion of self-consciousness. Wisdom is absent beyond the stage of unhappy consciousness.

65 On Hegel's use of 'syllogism' here, cf. Heinrichs [208], pp. 200ff., especially footnote 124, pp. 200–01, and the discussion of the third form of unhappy consciousness, pp. 215–19. See also and compare Egenolf Roeder von Diersburg [416] and Kuon Boey's discussion of 'middle term' in Boey [51].

66 For more on this and the move on the part of the natural attitude, see Bonsiepen [52], p. 265, where he discusses the two parts played by the natural attitude and philosophy, respectively, and connects this with the coming to consciousness of the natural attitude in stoicism, skepticism, and unhappy consciousness. Compare also Pippin [390], 309 where, after having argued that

"consciousness must become self-consciousness or face absurdity," he holds that the move within the freedom of self-consciousness effects this self-awareness.

Compare with these a Marxist interpretation of self-awareness in Bloch [43], where it is claimed that the "great concern of the *Phenomenology* is and remains real self-cognition as knowledge of the production of man through his labor and history. . . . When man produces himself with his own objective labor, then the subject must clearly occupy a position of hegemony within the historical-dialectical subject-object-relation" (95). But we have just seen that this self-awareness brings one to surrender the hegemony of the subject, in the sense of an individual grounded in self-consciousness, and the move to the hegemony of reason within a purposive universe. Thus—and this criticism would hold for non-Marxist as well as for Marxist interpretations—self-awareness remains when self-consciousness, and thus the usual interpretation of idealism, has been transcended.

67 If we recognize the thesis of "modern" philosophy to be the search to found philosophy and reality on the basis of an analysis of consciousness, then we can agree with Arthur Lessing [317] that these first sections of the *Phenomenology* show the bankruptcy of the modern attempt to found philosophy. I think, however, that this point is better made at the end of the discussion of reason.

On the general failure to show warranty for the claim of access to the absolute standpoint at this juncture, compare Heidegger [207]: "Self-consciousness cannot authentically take and comprehend itself as that which it already in a certain way understands its own truth to be, as the absolute unchangeable which finds itself, i.e. the truth, neither in the object nor exclusively in the subject of this object, but rather in a higher self which knows itself as the unity of the first self-consciousness and the consciousness of the object, as spirit or—in the preform of spirit—as reason" (202).

See also Hermann Schmitz [436] who, after working out his concept of '*Bedrohung*' or 'threat' on the background of the works of Kleist and Hölderlin, then discusses threat "as the situation of finitude" (68–74) and "as the source of the dialectic" (75–82). His claim is that Hegel shows that the isolation of the individual in his will to be individual brings him face to face with totality as opposed to him and in this way makes visible the threat. Dialectics emerges as the individual, in the face of his terror at the threat, reaches beyond himself to the totality, in a certain way surrendering to the totality and thereby resolving the threat. See especially p. 81.

68 The move to reason is thus necessitated by the realizations we have achieved about the failure of self-consciousness. Contrary to what we have argued here, Navickas [374] maintains that in the move to reason "the subject abruptly assumes a new significance and status" (128). But just the opposite seems to be the case, and there is nothing abrupt; for the surrender has been indicated from within the position of self-consciousness itself. Compare also his whole discussion of subjectivity in Navickas [373]. Garaudy [152], p. 59, also has a view of the transition as radical, but based on his Marxist understanding of self-consciousness.

Fink [127] has a view of the move to reason which, on his general interpretation, is analogous to the one put forth here. He describes the turn to reason as "the turn from ontic consciousness to the 'transcendence of Dasein'" (199). Greene

[166], 164–66, maintains that unhappy consciousness involves an inversion of the subject-object relation, which leads to reason. Shklar [457], 60–75, offers a penetrating analysis of the unity of freedom and necessity in the Greeks, but does not articulate it in such a way that one is led to reason, as in the *Phenomenology*. However, what Shklar says about proceeding with our existence is just what a surrender to reason involves.

69 Compare the view of Pöggeler [396], 292–98, where he articulates self-consciousness as self-becoming as the key to the *Phenomenology*. He argues, in particular, that Hegel "links the question of the possibility and task of philosophy in general with the principle of self-consciousness" (297). On the specific point of the necessity to accept presuppositions, see Ahlers [6], where he argues that true finitude is present only in *not* being presuppositionless, i.e., in having only the absolute for presupposition. Complete liberation from limitations and necessity (for which, Ahlers claims, thinkers of the Frankfurt School in our own century strive) would make true freedom impossible; for then one loses one's finitude and therefore one's freedom (68).

At this point Kojève's analysis is particularly weak. In Kojève [266], he claims a radical, disjointed transition from self-consciousness to reason. He holds that the move depicts "the transformation of self-consciousness into reason, of the unhappy religious man into rational man." He then continues, claiming that this "transformation is equivalent to the negation of all transcendence and therefore of all existential and theoretical dualism. The man of reason is essentially irreligious and atheistic. He lives only in relation to himself, thinks only about himself ('individualism', an essentially a-social, a-political attitude)" (80). This, of course, does not fit at all with any of the sections on reason, but especially not with the sections on practical reason. Kojève himself is forced to contradict himself on this (see, for instance, pp. 80–82). But this is only representative of the generally indefensible position taken by Kojève in his interpretation of Hegel.

Notes to Chapter V

1 Two things are notable concerning this section on reason. The first is that it is probably the least discussed of all the sections, at least in any direct way. In part this is true because it is more often than not thought that Hegel's view of the various sciences was either uninteresting or terribly out of date. This is connected with the second point, namely, that when discussed this section is often treated in conjunction with various sections of the *Encyclopedia*. But this is a mistake; for given the differences in project between the *Phenomenology* and the *Encyclopedia*, such discussion must be undertaken with great care. This section, as we shall see, is pivotal for the general project of the *Phenomenology*. Hegel is in this section not giving a philosophy of nature or anything of the sort, but examining the general thesis that reason, in this form, is adequate to the absolute standpoint.

For a review and critical discussion of the place of reason, see Pöggeler [394]. See also his discussion of the difficulties of the move to reason and the suggestion that it is not without break, in Pöggeler [395], 46–48. On the concept 'reason' and its general history, see the *Wörterbuch der philosophischen Begriffe* [539], Bd. 3, 395–406, the entry on '*Vernunft*'.

Royce [426] holds that the section on reason is a critique of Schelling. See especially pp. 101–14 on the relationship between the self and nature in Schelling. Taylor [495], 161–70 has a rather sketchy analysis of reason, taking the section to consist of partial historical forms which spirit then recapitulates in "the full historical form" (171). Fink [127] has an extended section on reason, pp. 202–352, with his discussion of reason-observing on pp. 202–304. See especially pp. 202–13 for a contrast between Hegel's use of 'reason' and, on the other hand, others' uses in the context of philosophy and the natural attitude. Fink sees Hegel's theory of reason as forming "the parallel to the 'Transcendental Dialectic'" of Kant (206), parallel, but different. As with the other *Gestalten* in the *Phenomenology*, Fink takes reason to be a "specific form of the understanding of being" (207). It is also compared with the identity of thought and being in Parmenides (210). See also Heinrichs [208] 221–64. Heinrichs uses 'proportion' as a category from the Jena *Logik*, and the metaphysics of objectivity from the *Metaphysics*, to explicate the section on reason. The general thesis, according to Heinrichs, is to show the identity of the relations of thought and the relations of being.

See also Arthur Berndtson [31], who gives elements of "a standard conception of reason," and measures Hegel's conception in terms of them. His intentions are not to address the section of the *Phenomenology* alone, but his criteria shed interesting light on Hegel. Other important general discussions of the section in general include Becker [27], 78–115; Labarrière [287], 95–108; Hyppolite [238], 219–318; Findlay [120], 103–15; Kainz [249], 98–133; Kojève [266], 79–96 (none of this material was included in the English translation); Navickas [374], 133–203; and Lauer [305], 125–76.

2 The transition, as I have already noted, is perhaps more problematic here than elsewhere, and in a work in which the question of connections between

sections is always troublesome. See the analysis of Pöggeler [394]. After reviewing the difficulties involved with the structure of the *Phenomenology* in respect to reason, he suggests that the unity achieved at the beginning of reason is only a correctness (*Richtigkeit*) and not yet truth. "Because of that, Hegel leads reason over the road of realization: by the observation of nature and self-consciousness in becoming spirit, reason realizes itself and finally is elevated to absolute knowledge over the route passing through spirit and religion. Hegel thinks that 'pure reason' can be developed only in unity with empirical consciousness, practical consciousness, ethics and religion, with all of history" (226).

Hyppolite [238] rightly stresses the way in which consciousness and self-consciousness are presupposed for the intelligibility of reason. "The impenetrable thing-in-itself and the subjective solitude of the I are both superseded. But these two routes—that of consciousness seeing the phantom of being-in-itself vanish before it, and that of self-consciousness which in the course of its harsh and lengthy formation sees the disappearance of an essence that exists only for it, for it qua specific consciousness—are both prerequisites for the positing of a truth which is both in-itself and for consciousness, a truth such as only idealism can conceive" (228). For me, of course, all of this must be interpreted within the framework of the task of establishing warranty for the claims of absolute idealism, not in the anthropological framework.

I have already noted my disagreement with Westphal [528], where he discusses together both understanding and reason-observing. See Chapter III, note 24, above. The whole sense of progression, and the basis for reason in the problem of positing self-consciousness as the absolute standpoint, is thereby effaced.

Lauer [306], pp. 17–38 has a good account of how reason has emerged as a problem. See also Heinrichs [208], 222–23; Schrader-Klebert [443], 29–37; and Fink [127], 208.

3 Fink [127] somewhat catches this idea of purpose in his argument that Hegel is not here trying to provide a "philosophy of science." See p. 249. See also the essay of Franz Grégoire [168].

4 The otherness found in reason, in spite of the thesis of reason, is absolutely crucial to a correct structuring of reason. See the essay of J. E. Turner [503]. Turner attempts to differentiate Hegel's from other forms of monism and idealism. Compare also the discussion of otherness in the world of reason in Fink [127], p. 213.

5 This most important aspect of rational activity and of the presuppositions underlying reason as articulated by Hegel seems to me obvious, but also is generally overlooked by Hegel's commentators. See for instance Kroner [275] pp. 383–87, who is typical in this respect, in spite of his general thesis of Hegel as "irrationalist."

6 Thus, the ambiguity discovered in self-consciousness has not disappeared, but is transformed and maintained under the presuppositions of reason. In this way Gerhard Krüger's view concerning the ancient and modern attitudes, found in Krüger [277], can be put into focus. Precisely because there is adjudication by the world, and with this a forming of the framework by the purposes of the individual, Hegel indeed brings the ancient and modern views together.

Notes to Chapter V

7 Unfortunately, the whole of *Philosophisches Wörterbuch*, edited by J. Ritter, et al., has not yet been completed, and the entry for 'Vernunft' is missing. But see 'Vernunft' in *Wörterbuch der philosophischen Begriffe [539]*, Bd. 3, 395–401.

8 This kind of transcendence of both subject and object is the most difficult kind to understand, but is the only sort of transcendence which will be found in Hegel. Compare the discussion of Cekić [68], p. 229, where he argues that Hegelian reason is not only epistemological, but ontological as well. Kojève [266] misses the kind of transcendence which functions here. See for instance, p. 80. In fact, he has little to say in any concrete way about reason-observing in general.

9 This discussion of totality and totalization is simply another form of the question of the nature of subject and object under the presupposition of reason, and thus is rooted in ambiguity. Compare Heinrichs [208], 224–45 on the disappearance of the simple opposition between totality and totalization. Much of the cause of the attribution of empty or "block" monism to Hegel comes from a misunderstanding of this point and a failure to see the ambiguity inherent in reason here. See for instance Lobkowicz [325], who attributes a simple kind of perfectionism to Hegel. Lobkowicz claims that Hegel's *Phenomenology* "consists in an ascent to the standpoint from which it becomes obvious that reality is exactly as it ought to be, namely, 'rational'" (148). He then continues, claiming that "instead of either *predicting* that the world will become perfect through and through or trying to *transform* the world in order to make it perfect, Hegel simply *describes* it as perfect" (149). But, as we shall see from this point on and to the end of the *Phenomenology*, the ambiguity in the presupposition of the unity of self and world is not removed.

This reciprocal constitution of purpose and appropriateness is approached by Navickas [374], but never really fixed. In talking about the non-passivity of rational activity he says that "this methodological position is not something that precedes observational activity of reason but something that ensues upon it, or at least emerges simultaneously with it" (137).

On this reciprocal constitution of purpose and appropriate worlds, see Fink [127], 208–09. On the complexities of this mutual constitution compare the analysis of Grégoire [168], especially pp. 253, 262–63. Grégoire argues for the metaphysical realism of Hegel, a position which I think goes too far but which is certainly correct as against any of the usual claims about monistic idealism in respect to Hegel.

10 This summary, in addition to providing a starting point for the discussion of reason, lends support to the interpretation of the section on self-consciousness which I have offered above in Chapter Four. On this also see Fink [127], pp. 208ff. for a discussion of the relation between certainty and truth and what this tells us about reason. See also Kümmel [283], 187–227, for an account of the general sense of first and second negation and how we have been led from consciousness through self-consciousness to reason. In my terms this can be translated into a discussion of the changing "mechanism" of the examination of putative praxical presuppositions.

11 This refers us back to various other forms, already discussed, of the dispute

concerning the unity of the *Phenomenology*, and of the way in which it holds together. In addition to works already cited, see Aschenberg [12], Part V, especially pp. 271ff. For my interpretation, the general difficulties with which Aschenberg deals do not arise. From another perspective, I would argue that the way in which I see the "we" and the natural attitude coming together here resolves Jürgen Habermas's difficulties in Habermas [176] concerning the problem of reflection in Hegel. At this point in the process of the *Phenomenology* the change in method and dialectic bring about a situation in which critique can become self-critique without begging the question.

There is also discussion of this matter in Navickas [374] concerning what is actually occurring here. But his analysis is rather vague, and he talks of a "mutual intimacy of subject and object" (134), and of a process in which "the observing subject may, without relinquishing its self-consciousness, impersonate the 'concrete sensuously-present' mode of existence" (135).

12 Labarrière [287], p. 98, shows both the parallel and the differences between the beginning of consciousness and the beginning of reason. Findlay [120] nicely puts the matter of this "instinct of reason." Reason and rational activity show themselves "in the simple unwavering confidence with which the mind handles what the world lays before it" (103).

13 On this matter of an awareness of unawareness in the instinct of reason, compare Fink [127], 232-33 and his discussion of "a comportment of reason." Hyppolite [238] puts the nature of this instinct in the following way. "As an instinct, it is a presentiment of itself but not a self-knowledge" (235).

14 In addition to his description of Hegel's notion of the instinct of reason, noted above, Findlay [120] also has an excellent discussion of the difference between Hegel's idealism and other varieties. Of the idealism discussed by Hegel in this first part of the section on reason, Findlay writes that such idealism "is merely Scepticism inverted: while the latter rejects all content indifferently, Berkeleyan Idealism indifferently swallows it all. We see from this whole passage how little Hegel's Idealism has of the subjective, productive character commonly associated with the name. Idealism is for him the view that the world may, with great effort and without finality, be intellectually and practically mastered, a view which both permits and entails much that would ordinarily be called realism and materialism" (104). Compare the view of Kojève [266], who argues the point from the view that the discussion of idealism is directed against Fichte, on the grounds that for the latter there is only an ought concerning action, not realized action. See p. 79.

On the idealism section, see also Fink [127], 214–24; Lauer [305], 127–31; Navickas [374], 133–34; Ernst Behler [29], especially 170–71 on the problem of the constitution of reason as absolute, and the way this was left open by Kant, Fichte, and Schelling; and Becker [27] 78–81.

15 On the view that idealism is a release from the concerns of consciousness and self-consciousness, see Labarrière [287], 95–108.

16 On the self-destructive nature of these theories of idealism, see Lauer [305], p. 131, and Hyppolite [238], 226–31. Kainz [249] is rather gentle with the idealism criticized here. "Idealism, as the philosophical insight which has risen

to comprehend the meaning of the first generic category, must beware of becoming arrested at this abstract insight, without going on to comprehend it in the fullness of its concrete applications" (101). Hegel, it seems to me, is more forceful than this; for it is not just a matter of applications of reason. On the other hand, Becker [27] seems completely wrong in his extremist interpretation of Hegel's idealism. See his account, especially p. 88, where he claims that in reason Hegel has only objectivations of the absolute identity of an extreme idealism.

17 On parallels with consciousness and self-consciousness in this matter of the loss of the opening naivete, compare the analysis of Fink [127], 226–27.

18 This further convergence of the "we" and the natural attitude in rational activity is very important for the goal of the *Phenomenology*. But the point, and consequently the progress of the *Phenomenology* toward its goal, seems to have been missed by commentators. See for example the discussion of Becker [27], pp. 78ff., where we find attributed to Hegel here a simple idealism, governed by the demands of an abstract dialectic rather than by that dialectic in the process of the development of the task of the *Phenomenology*.

19 This change in the method and in the relationship of the "we" to the natural attitude has arisen as a result of the surrender to reason and the acceptance through instinct of the unity of self and world. Rational beings show themselves to be rational through their activities. Hyppolite [238] has nicely articulated the project of demonstration involved in reason. "Knowing that it is merely a certainty, it undertakes to acquire truth by putting itself to work and by realizing a knowledge of the world" (232). But he also gives it an historical twist, claiming that the section of "reason corresponds to the development of science from the Renaissance" to Hegel's own time. Concentrating on this historical reference, he misses the real difference in dialectic here which shows the way in which, acting on the instinct of reason and implicitly recognizing itself as doing so, the natural rational individual and the "we" of the *Phenomenology* converge.

Royce [426] also misses the change in method when he briefly characterizes reason as a stage in which "we pass to forms of consciousness which are still individual, but which appear with a highly rational or elaborately categorized world over against them, in which they seek their victory or their task, in terms which are not only individualistic, but also explicitly universal, so that each *Gestalt* seeks what it views as that which all the world is seeking" (159). This fits with Royce's notion of the *Bildungsroman*, but leaves out of sight the real task of the *Phenomenology*.

20 The theme of the place of praxis will emerge again in this section on reason. As in the earlier sections, its position belies the simplistic idealistic theory traditionally ascribed to Hegel. See the lucid comment of Rosen [421]: "for Kant, man acquires significance from the possession of a good will. For Hegel, man is fundamentally what he does" (32). Compare the view of Royce [426] that the idealists, including Hegel, were "pragmatists" in the sense that they "make much of the relation of truth to action, to practice, to the will. Nothing is true, for them, unless therein the sense, the purpose, the meaning of some active process is carried out, expressed, accomplished" (85–86). Those to whom he is referring, of course, are the German idealists.

Compare the discussion of Wilhelm Beyer [37]. "*Work* is recognized by Hegel as the indispensable condition of human existence" (753). Beyer's overall view differs, of course, from mine. In this regard, it is a pity, given the general task of the whole section on reason, and given the introduction of praxis in this section, that Marcuse and others with his sort of view did not pay more attention to the issue. If they had, their view would have had to change. See, for example, Marcuse [338].

21 There is an interesting connection to be made here between Hegel's view of the relation between givenness and making and the convertibility of *verum* and *factum* in Vico. Bloch [43], 58–59, has an interesting discussion of creativity and knowledge in Hegel in relation to Vico. He also discusses their common attack against the mathematical method. Bloch claims that Hegel did not know Vico, and thus is not attributing any historical-genetic connection between the two; rather, we must recognize the structural connection between their respective developments of the theme of the relationship between the true and the made. The connection is also noticed in an indirect way by Taylor [495]. In an otherwise very brief and inadequate discussion of reason-observing Taylor notes that reason-observing, even when it turns to the observation of man in logic and psychology, "fails because of the nature of observing reason itself, which tries to understand man by looking on him as an object, and cannot grasp his nature as a being who also makes himself. Observing reason cannot really cope with the meshing of the given and the self-made in man, . . . but tries to separate these two aspects from each other" (162). Findlay [120] misses the true-made dialectic which arises here and thus, in spite of his remarks about Hegel's idealism, misses most of the movements within the reason section.

22 Rosen [421] has an excellent discussion of the problem of overcoming subject-object dichotomy and why both realist and traditional idealist attempts must fail. See p. 48. See also his general historical account of this problem from the Greeks through Schelling, pp. 50–63. Rosen is discussing the problem here in a general way, but it is significant for the problem as it appears at this point in the *Phenomenology*. Compare W. I. Schinkaruk [432], 444–46, where he argues for the reciprocal grounding of consciousness and self-consciousness in reason, but from quite a different perspective.

Kümmel [283] sees clearly the way we now go beyond the pure idealism section and articulates the nature of the unity of the subjective and objective. "To the insight that the subject cannot be understood and expressed without recourse to the relation to the world, corresponds the thought that one also only has reality in the form of a world opened up by a subject and immersed in its medium. To point to men in the world and to the world in men is to deny the possibility of their derivation from one another, and presupposes their relation as having come to be and having developed. One can neither simply ground the factual relation and overlook the tension of thinking and actuality, nor is it possible to avoid or renounce a relation to the world which is both reflected and at the same time positive" (183–84). This analysis is used by Kümmel to discuss Hegel in a general manner, but is particularly appropriate to the present section on reason.

Heinrichs [208] treats of this joining of the subjective and objective, but in too strong a way. He claims that here in reason there is "anticipation of the thematic of spirit" (249–50). If the instinct of reason is dealt with from within the problem of the *Phenomenology*, then the insights Heinrichs has from the logic and metaphysics, both of the Jena period and later, must be more tempered than in Heinrich's treatment.

This joining of the subjective and objective is given an interesting twist when seen in the light of the claim of Ernst Bloch, among others, that there is a Faust-motif in the *Phenomenology*. See Bloch [42]. Bloch admits that in Hegel's case there is no longer a "Wundermacher" as the subject of the *Phenomenology*, but rather Kant's "Spontaneity of consciousness"; nevertheless "the subject of the *Phenomenology* is from the very beginning a Faust-self . . . " (158). See also the analysis of Kainz [249], pp. 98, 131–33.

23 On the general discussion of reason observing, see Fink [127], 225–82, and Findlay [120], 103–09. For a good commentary on Hegel's view of the various sciences dealing with physical nature, see the critical notes and commentary of M. J. Petry in Hegel [200]. With due caution given to the fact that the project of the *Phenomenology* of 1807 and that of the *Encyclopedia* are quite different, some light can be thrown on Hegel's view of the sciences of his time. Kainz [249], like many others, too easily identifies the subject-matter of this section on the observation of nature with Hegel's *Philosophy of Nature*. See his note, p. 152. This means that those who so identify it also miss the full significance of the critiques for the project of the *Phenomenology*.

There are several other interesting views of this section. Becker [27], 82–101, sees Hegel's discussion of the observation of nature as a critique of empiricism. Hyppolite [238], 232–33, looks into the question of reason as a project of observing nature to see whether the "I" can discover itself in nature alone. See also Lauer [305], p. 132 for a critique of those who see reason observing as a step back to understanding. See also *Ibid.*, 126–27.

24 Thus, transitions from one position to the next are different here in the section on reason; for it is not the case that the presupposition of reason as the absolute standpoint fails, but that the precise form taken by reason at that point is not adequate in the sense of the proper articulation of what reason is. This is another reason why it is crucial to separate reason from understanding for Hegel; for understanding as such *is* inadequate as the absolute standpoint. On this see the discussion of Malcolm Clark [76], 37–38. Cf. *infra*, Chapter III, note 24, and note 2 of the present chapter.

25 This is the central criticism of this position of reason. Cf. Lauer [305], 137–38 for discussion of the necessity of the finding of necessity in the classifications and laws of reason observing.

26 Here the place of concrete purposes and the frameworks that go with them are noted by Hegel. On this, see the analysis of Bodhammer [47], especially pp. 19–20, and his argument that for Hegel the "'natural' and the 'linguistic' world do not simply stand, independently, over against one another" (19). Thus neither do purposes and the world of nature. Compare the position of Derbolav [93], p. 60, against whom Bodhammer argues. Hyppolite [238] makes the point by making a comparison with Schelling. "Schelling thinks nature directly; Hegel thinks

nature through the knowledge of nature—which for him was the philosophy of nature of his time" (244). For his view of the relation between language and the process of description in the observation of nature, see *Ibid.*, p. 237.

27 Hyppolite [238] discusses this section pp. 240–58. For his view of the internality of necessity in organic nature, see *Ibid.*, 245–47. See also Fink [127], 248–82.

28 On the critique of the observation of organic nature, compare the similar analysis given by Kainz [249], 109–10. Fink [127] characterizes this critique as a critique of Schelling's "Identity-thinking, according to which nature is unconscious spirit and spirit is conscious nature" (279). See also Hyppolite [238] on the difference between inner and outer, which comes to the same thing as my discussion of the lack of necessity.

29 On the structural analogy between organic nature as observed and reason itself, compare Kainz [249], p. 105, and Fink [127], pp. 255ff. Fink introduces it with a discussion of the analogy between self-consciousness and organic nature. Hyppolite [238], pp. 246ff. misses this and in general the full significance of the relation between purposiveness in the organic and the purposiveness of reason itself.

30 This whole discussion is interesting in another light, namely that Hegel had previously held life as the absolute.

31 See Lauer's interesting discussion of Hegel's discussion of logic in this section in Lauer [305], pp. 142–44. Fink [127], pp. 283ff. discusses the inevitability of the turn to the knower. Becker [27] does not see the necessity of the move, and claims that Hegel gives no reason for turning to thought and logic (94). Becker's thesis about Hegel's idealism also re-emerges here when he argues that in order to make the move to logic after the observation of nature, Hegel "must have already tacitly accepted the absolute separation of self-consciousness from consciousness of an object which constitutes idealism" (93).

Navickas [374], p. 154, also has problems with the transition to logic and psychology. He characterizes the task here as motivated by the need to reconcile thought and being, which is correct. But what he means by this is quite different from what I think is to be found here. "The subject, instead of simply being a self, must become relationship to self as concrete object. In other words, the authentic subjectivity has to begin its gradual self-realization by assuming the mode of being that is proper to a thing" (155). Navickas then explicitly denies the need to find a ground in logic. "The laws of thought are the essential principles of things in the sense in which the word 'thing' designates all being, except the sensuous. Still, the question as to whether logical laws are ontological is without significance. What is at stake, as Hegel sees the problem, is not the straight affirmation of external reality and its inherently logical nature, but the totality of the thinking process which alone can determine the complete value of these laws" (156–57). In essence, Navickas is here denying the project of the *Phenomenology* as I have been arguing for it.

32 John N. Findlay's remark about the character and critique of logic, and the move to psychology, is pretty far off the mark. He claims that "Hegel would certainly have welcomed the connectedness of modern symbolic calculi, as well

as the semantics which reduces all their principles to a single tautology." See Findlay [120], p. 107. On the contrary, the same lack which Hegel found then occurs today, even more radically. Compare also the discussion of Navickas [374], pp. 158–59. Consistent with his interpretation of the transition to the logic, Navickas sees the relation of logic to psychology in the present transition as a relation of mere parallelism.

33 See Petry's translation of *Hegel's Philosophy of Spirit*, together with his commentaries and notes in Hegel [201]. Again, due caution is needed with respect to the differences in task between the 1807 *Phenomenology* and the *Encyclopedia*. See also Phillipe Muller [369], 214–16 on this section on psychology. Muller refers us to the historical context of Hegel, as well as to studies in the study of personality today. Hegel's discussion and critique of psychology is reviewed from within these parameters. Becker [27] again brings, when discussing Hegel's introduction and analysis of psychology, his critique of Hegel's "idealism" which he has used above. See pp. 95ff. Compare also Navickas [374], 160–63.

34 It is not, as for instance Howard Kainz would have it, that this means we lose necessity or determination; rather, the ambiguity I have here discussed is introduced. See Kainz [249], p. 111.

35 This ambiguity, I think, is generally missed in the literature. See, for example, Fink [127], pp. 294–95. The "freedom/determinism" issue does not come up for Fink, even though he offers a penetrating discussion of the relation between positing and posited and between conditioning and conditioned. As I shall try to show, these latter topics are really at the basis of the ambiguity found in psychological theory as discussed by Hegel.

36 Alasdair MacIntyre [337] has written one of the few essays explicitly dedicated to this part of the *Phenomenology*. He ties the physiognomy and phrenology sections to the contemporary thesis that "there are biochemical or neural states of affairs, processes, and events, the occurrence and the nature of which are the sufficient causes of human actions" (225). He shows that this contemporary position is false by the same arguments as those used by Hegel.

There is also an interesting analysis by Raymond M. Herbenick [213]. Hyppolite [238] writes that what "is in question, in fact, is the relation between spiritual individuality and its most immediate expression, the body" (264). In this way he too recognizes that the import of the discussion is more far-reaching than a mere critique of the two pseudo-sciences. See also Navickas [374], 163–73, and Becker [27], 96–101.

37 One can say at this point that we are involved implicitly with spirit, as Heinrichs has tried to claim for the whole of reason. See my remark in note 22, above.

38 That is to say, the interaction of given truth and made world which arises first in faintest outline in the discussion of 'explanation' in understanding, has slowly developed in explicitness until we now have in some sense a material form of it. See in this regard again the work of Bodhammer [47], especially p. 20. Adapting Bodhammer to the present case, we can say that the world is always already a world mediated by purposes.

39 Alasdair MacIntyre, as noted above in note 36, has shown the parallel with

some of our contemporary sciences and has discussed the relation of truth and construction. There seems to me to be also a parallel with our contemporary discussions of explanation and interpretation, and with the first two knowledge constitutive interests developed by Habermas [176].

40 The centrality of praxis for Hegel again emerges. See Fink [127], 297–301, and the analysis by Herbenick [213]. Hyppolite [238] does not seem to see the importance of the discussion of man being what he does. See pp. 264–71. This has further consequences for Hyppolite's analysis of the transition to active reason. See *Ibid.*, pp. 275–77.

41 On the critique of physiognomy, compare Fink [127], p. 297, and his discussion of Lavater.

42 The positive point which I shall now discuss is most often missed. But see Heinz Krumpel [280], 41–46, where he does see the importance of this critique as the ground for the later consideration of *Sittlichkeit* and for the problem of morality in general.

43 The identity of the project on both sides of observer and observed is crucial here and is, so far as I know, not noticed in commentary on Hegel.

44 Lauer [305] is too hasty in bringing reason to full activity with observation. "What reason, then, *discovers* in observing things are the concepts it itself *produces*. . . . The observation of things has already turned into the observation of the observation of things" (134). But then see his analysis of the self-reflection in reason in the physiognomy-phrenology section, especially pp. 150–52, where this judgment is tempered.

45 The denial of *mere* physical being is not, of course, the denial of physical being as such. See on this my comments in note 18 above on the analysis given by Werner Becker [27].

46 Hegel's critique of physicalism is important as it is given here, both in itself and in relation to the progress of the *Phenomenology* and to the way in which spirit is eventually to be interpreted. Cf. Herbenick [213], especially p. 110, on Hegel's critique of physicalism and of reductionisms in general.

47 It must be noted and stressed here that there is a reversal (*Umkehrung*) and not a transcendence of the *Aufhebung* sort. This presents us with an interesting parallel with the surrender at the end of self-consciousness which first brought us to reason. Findlay [120] misses the nature of this transition and claims that Hegel "laugh[s] at [the] pains" taken by those who would try to find "strict deductive necessity in [his] transitions" (109). As noted above, there is no deductive necessity in the sense that Findlay refers to here, but there is the necessity found in the logic of praxical presuppositions. See also Kainz [249], who notes a reversal, but does not link it to the critique just completed in the text. Rather he sees it as "paradoxical," arriving "as if by a rebound at its highest point" (114).

48 This is the first of several moves in which a "recollection" or "*Erinnerung*" is undertaken for the purposes of making an advance in the *Phenomenology*. Actually, one might argue that there have been many thus far in that each advance rejects a move back to any of the previous positions. I shall have more to say about 'recollection' in Chapter X. Compare also the chart of Kainz [249], p. 55.

49 We have the recognition here of things, not as substances, but as forces and actions. Fink [127] puts the matter very nicely. "Reification is unavoidable when and so long as spirit is thought in the form of something at hand, existing, lying before one. Then, in fact, spirit is a bone" (304). Hence the move to reason acting.

50 The subject of the concept as the "I" will now become a constant focus of concern. In addition to Hermann Glockner [159] see his essay, "Die Ethisch-Politische Persönlichkeit des Philosophen," in Glockner [160], 153–207 for a discussion of the complexity of '*Das Ich*' in connection with the concept. See also Quentin Lauer's discussion of the category as "not pure," in Lauer [305] pp. 129–30, and Schrader-Klebert [443], p. 53. Here Schrader-Klebert has a good discussion of the concept as the "I" at the beginning of reason. See also *Ibid.*, 48–68, especially 59–62 for a further discussion of this, in the broader context of the *speculative Satz*.

51 Compare this view with a view of the same thing, but in the context of a marxist analysis as in Oisermann [380]. "The Hegelian theory of the power of reason is finally (naturally, only if one refers to its rational core) the theory of the objective lawfulness of the appearances of nature and of society, the theory of the freedom which knowledge of this lawfulness and its practical mastery signify" (121).

52 The view expressed by Merleau-Ponty [358] should be re-thought in light of what I have shown thus far about the section on reason. See also Merleau-Ponty [359]. For another "existential" twist to reason, see Gustav Mueller [366]. "The major theme in the middle part of Hegel's book [i.e. in Reason] is the grim and pessimistic critique of the incompetence of man. In principle ('in itself') comprehension understands reality as a beloved and loving, organic whole, in which all individuated forms of life would be known in their contribution to this 'we that is an I'. But, alas! in practice, comprehension (*Vernunft*) fails most miserably. It only 'observes' vague analogies to itself in external teleological relations; or in equally vague interpretations of physical appearance, body types, bone structures as clumsy expressions of soul or life. . . . But this irrevocable failure of comprehensive 'observation' is still a harmless affair compared with all the enormous failures of practical reason" (21). In such a dark view of things, the positive side found at this stage of the quest for certainty is missed completely.

53 Compare Lauer [305], p. 151, on the connection between reason observing and reason acting. See also the brief remarks of Hyppolite [238], 272–80. It is not very clear to me here just what Hyppolite is trying to argue. Navickas [374] claims that we move to active reason simply because we have exhausted the possibilities for observation. This is rather weaker than the case which I think Hegel makes. See Navickas's discussion pp. 171–73 and then the beginning of his analysis on the next section of the text, pp. 174–75. See also Nicolai Hartmann [191], II, where he briefly remarks on this turn to active reason. If we are to find ourselves in reality, Hartmann explains, then we can do so "only in the will and in the act of man. When consciousness grasps this, it abandons the unessential expression [sought in phrenology] and turns directly to the inner. It thereby is immediately admitted into the domain of the active life, the life of action and of its ethos. And here it finds that there is an 'actualization of rational self-consciousness through itself'" (342).

Notes to Chapter VI

1 There is a fairly rich body of commentary on this section on active reason. Hyppolite [238], 273–318 uses the general theme of active reason in modern individualism to explicate the section. One aspect of this is the presence of ambiguity, and this is taken as a theme by both Josiah Royce and Judith Shklar. Royce [426] characterizes the stages of active reason as sharing in common "the explicit recognition that without actively pursuing its ideal in a world of life, in a world of objective fortune, in an organized and social order, the self cannot win its own place, cannot be a self at all. Common to them all is further the fact that the self, despite this recognition, tries to center this acknowledged social world about just that individual man in whom the self, by chance, conceives itself, in each new incarnation, to be embodied" (190). Shklar [457] captures the air of optimism as well as the tragic ambiguity in the attitudes discussed here. "Practical reason does not merely look, it acts, but with the same intuitive certainty as observing reason that there is a world out there that corresponds exactly to its idea of a rational order. There are only a few obstacles to be removed, and a 'rational' society will be achieved. The ego makes a model of social life which it expects to actualize" (98). Then, from a complementary perspective, she explains that such an individual "really only plays a number of variations on a single theme: aloneness. It never makes a move toward recognition. Purposeless self-display and self-rule are all that can be achieved by so dissociated a mind" (101).

This theme is taken up in a very different way by Heinrichs [208], 228–49. Heinrichs uses 'division' (*Einteilung*) from the Jena *Logik* for the purposes of explicatiion. The "essential dialectic" of division is that "every species contains within itself the genus, yet this latter lies outside of it" (230). The general problem and connection with the present section, according to Heinrichs, is that it is the task of division to manifest the unity of identity and difference that *is* the self which we are here attempting to find as active in the world and reflected in what-is. See especially pp. 228–32. Becker [27], 101–05, relates this section closely to the section on self-consciousness, too often ignoring important differences. On this, see especially pp. 101–03.

Kojève and Lukács, on the other hand, take a more strictly historical perspective. Lukács [336], 479–80, characterizes this section on reason as reflecting the development and crises found in the moral and social framework of bourgeois society. Kojève [266] again takes up the thesis that the active, rational person is an atheist and characterizes the positions as "existential idealism" (84–96). The irony of this interpretation is that in large part it misses the real social character of Hegel's discussion, as well as the way Hegel leads us to a consideration of spirit.

See also Taylor [495], 162–70; Nicolai Hartmann [191], II, 342–46; Findlay [120], 109–15; Navickas [374], 174–203; Kainz [249], 116–33; Lauer [305], 151–76; Fink [127], 305–52; and George L. Kline [263].

2 On the section on pleasure and necessity there are several interesting analyses based on historical and literary references. Shklar [457], 102–06 cites not

only parallels with the story of Dr. Faustus, but as well with various forms of historical reference. There is a close commentary with an eye to Faust in Joseph Gauvin [154]. Gauvin also discusses the relation to reason observing and to the unhappy consciousness. Kainz [249] has an interesting commentary pp. 119ff., and a note on 'pleasure' in Hegel in relation to Aristotle and Spinoza. For the latter, see *Ibid.*, p. 156. See also Fink [127], 316–21, and Hyppolite [238], 280–84. Of this section in general Hyppolite characterizes it in the following way. "We experience the fragility of our specificity, which has posed itself for-itself, and we see it shatter against the universal" (283).

3 This is not to suggest that there is anything proto-Freudian here, but only to note the functional parallel. See the comments of Kainz [249], p. 156, on the pleasure-necessity relation in connection with Freud, and the discussion of Becker [27], 103–05 where, in a discussion of the Faust theme, the pleasure/reality theme comes through clearly. See also the reference to Johannes Heinrichs, below, note 4.

4 The concept of 'necessity' is complex, especially in its relation to its traditional opposite, namely 'contingency'. The fullest account is to be found in Dieter Henrich [211] where it is shown that Hegel has a "theory which recognizes absolute contingency" (132). Linking the discussion rather directly with Faust and sexual pleasure, Heinrichs [208] introduces necessity through use of Hegel's pun on '*Gattung*' and '*Begattung*', i.e., on 'genus' and 'copulation'. See paragraph 369 of the *Encyclopedia*. The category which the individual is to be realized as, the fully concrete unity of genus and species, of identity and difference, is "experienced as alien, blind necessity, which is taken as a third in the unwilled consequences of sexual union" (234).

In a different way, Hyppolite [238] argues that here "man sees himself as the plaything of a necssity that is as barren as his specific desire to enjoy was abstract and limited. Man is annihilated by an inexorable mechanism which continuously recurs through various contents which he has not yet thought through" (284). This plays on an important theme, but must be seen from within the conception of necessity which Dieter Henrich has articulated. See also the idea of *Bedrohung* in Hermann Schmitz [436] and the analysis of Findlay [120], where the necessity is to be found in another person. "Each man's pursuit of his own personal fulfillment must necessarily be the Nemesis, the *Schicksal*, of the other person" (110). While probably true, to limit oneself to this gives too external a sense of what Hegel is intending here.

5 The critique of hedonism and the transition to the law of the heart is seen quite differently by Navickas [374]. "What we have before us is a complicated argument whose primary characteristic is that it moves from the pleasure-seeking to fatalistic resignation and from the fatalistic resignation to a kind of sentimentalism" (181). But if we are considering the hedonistic position from the perspective of the problematic of the *Phenomenology*, then the resignation does not come with fatalism, but rather with a more positive move, a move stronger than one to sentimentalism. On the critique of the view that the next position is one of sentimentalism, see note 6, below. Compare Fink [127] on the quandary to which hedonism is led. The individual, he claims, "is for itself as this specific

Notes to Chapter VI

individual and is at the same time also all that which appears to lie out there in relation to it as the material of possible pleasure and gratification" (320). Whether one puts the issue in this way or some other way, the relation between contingency and necessity as articulated by Dieter Henrich [211] must be considered. Henrich argues that through "the construction of the contingent as a moment of subjectivity, of *eidos* itself, Hegel safeguards himself in the presence of the consequences which the literature imputed to him as inescapable" (132). If we apply this to the analysis of pleasure and necessity here, we can say that the problem is that in the mind of the hedonist contingency is supposed to be freed from necessity while, in fact, it itself constitutes necessity and thus confronts the individual with an alienation of his own making because of his inadequate view of this relation.

6 Part of the complexity is brought out in Quentin Lauer's treatment of the section in Lauer [305]. "For Hegel, 'law' is always the work of reason ... and to speak of a 'law of the heart' is equivalent to speaking of a square circle. But since Hegel's concept of reason is a far cry from that of the rationalist, it would be a mistake to think that in reason he finds no place for the heart or that the kind of universal law the heart seeks to establish has no significance as a moment along the path to adequate rationality. The inadequacy, then, of a 'law of the heart' is not that the heart is involved in it, but that the consciousness which is recoiling from individualism should seek a remedy in a sentimental universalism of ethical demand which, because it is sentimental, is ineluctably individualistic. Sentiment is not a framework which can contain the universality proper to reason." Lauer then adds that the "sentimental 'law', like the Kantian 'maxim', is a guide purely for individual behavior," but unlike Kant's, it lacks even a basis in a categorical imperative (158). Compare the position of Fink [127], 321–33. Fink argues that the phrase 'law of the heart' does not refer us to something "sentimental, it is not a matter of placing feeling against reason, but rather a matter of placing individually subjective innerness against inner subjectivity" (322). This way of putting it certainly addresses the issue which arose in the examination of hedonism in terms of opposition between self and world.

Ver Eecke [509] claims that the law of the heart passage "teaches us that the way to integrate oneself into the society is to oppose it" (563). A deeper view of this sort emerges in Shklar [457], 106–14, where she analyses the law of the heart using many literary and historical figures. Shklar describes this attitude as in part "a megalomaniac self-infatuation" which becomes evident "as soon as several hearts stake out their claims for general validity" (108). Here she addresses the pluralism of individual laws. She also nicely links this to the epistemology of the modern period. "Philosophy now denied men certain knowledge. Locke had told them to settle for probability and Kant had rendered certain knowledge of God inaccessible. However, people went right on yearning for certainty. They found it in feeling" (112). Compare with this the analysis of Royce [426], pp. 192ff., who sees the law of the heart as a "longing for a passionate ideal," and quotes some verses of Byron by way of example. Jean Hyppolite also takes up this issue, with an eye to the alienation. Hyppolite [238] claims that the reference here is to Rousseau. See pp. 284–90. See also his discussion of the law of the heart in Hyppolite [237], 64–67, where he claims that here "*the alienation of concrete self-consciousness* reproduces itself" (64). See also the view of Becker [27], 106–08. All of these matters are complex, but must also be understood in the framework of the project of the *Phenomenology*.

7 Navickas [374] notes well the intersubjectivity which arises here, but interprets it as leading to a change from selfishness to "altruistic ideals" (183). But there is no such change here, the project being simply to create a rational world.

8 Becker [27] misses the point of this action when he claims that Hegel is claiming that "proposals to make the world better are always the result of subjective idiosyncracies" (107) and then proceeds to destroy this straw man he made of Hegel. Compare the brief contrast between the hedonist and the romantic reformer made by Findlay [120], p. 111.

9 This irony, found in the attitude of the law of the heart when it is transformed into an active form, is one of the great ironies of the *Phenomenology*. Compare the view of Fink [127], 324–26. Hyppolite and Navickas both have extended analyses of the irony. See Hyppolite [238], 285–89, who devotes the greatest part of his analysis of the law of the heart to a discussion of the irony, and also Navickas [374], 183–84. James L. Marsh [345] explores the attitude of radicalism in respect both to this section and to the succeeding section on virtue and the course of the world. He catches the irony in both positions when he writes that every form of radicalism "validly affirms personal conscience and freedom, idealism, and political participation," but that it does so in a way which reverses the principles which one wants to uphold (196).

10 Cf. Heinrichs [208] who notes that we "will later see that this alienation corresponds logically and temporally with the alienation of self-alienated spirit" (235); and Labarrière [287] who argues that in this section we no longer confront an "empty necessity," but rather "an already living necessity" which is essentially spirit (106).

11 For an extended discussion of the critique of the law of the heart see Fink [127], 328–33. Fink sees the critique of the law of the heart as directed against the "sovereignty principle of Rousseau and the 'general will'" (326), and has an extended discussion of the deceptions involved. But see also Navickas [374], 184–85, who denies a connection with either Rousseau or Hobbes in terms of this critique.

12 Shklar [457], 113–19 discusses this section on virtue and the course of the world, citing as an historical instance "republican virtue" confronting a "Machiavellian politician willing to use whatever weapons are available to serve his ambitions" (115), a view which seems a bit off the mark to me because the virtuous individual is not here such a positive moment of the dialectic. Lauer [305], 160–64 has an insightful account of the struggle of the virtuous individual with the course of the world. See also Hyppolite [238], 290–95; Fink [127], 334–40; and Becker [27], 108–09. The theme of Don Quixote is explored by many commentators.

13 On the difference between this conception of virtue and that of the ancients, see Hyppolite [238], 295; and Navickas [374], 187–88.

14 On the critique of virtue and the course of the world, see Nicolai Hartmann [191], II, 342–46; and Kainz [249], 124. The problem with the position is fairly

transparent and thus has not generated much controversy. Taylor [495] suggests that the section on virtue is reminiscent of the discussion of stoicism. "The peculiar feature of this kind of phase is man's sense of his own unworthiness, his apologizing for his existence, and his attempt to suppress his particularity, and become nothing but universal will." He then characterizes well the positive sense of the critique, arguing that "against the philosophy of self-abnegating virtue, Hegel's is a philosophy of self-realization; becoming the vehicle of the universal is also for man a fulfillment—or at least it will be when he is fully formed" (166). I am not certain of the remarks concerning stoicism, but the positive sense of self-realization is surely right. But see in comparison Becker [27] who, contrary to what is argued by most, sees the dialectic between virtue and the course of the world as only a "construction" of Hegel's idealism (p. 109).

15 On this crucial section of the *Phenomenology* there is a rather extensive literature. Hyppolite [238], 296–318 titles this section of his analysis "Human Works and the Dialectic of Action," a title which captures an important part of the core of the discussion. For an interesting Marxist analysis, see Hermann Ley [319]. See also Lukács [336] who links this section to Hegel's contemporary social world and capitalism (pp. 481ff.). One problem, in my view, is that the interpretation of Hegel's discussion is sometimes too closely linked to intellectual activity as such, at the expense of a broader discussion of the nature of action and the part it plays in the project of the *Phenomenology*. See Kojève [266], pp. 90ff., and Lauer [305], 171. Such a reading gives us no real bridge to the section on spirit. See the rather weak transition to spirit in both of these readings, and especially Lauer's note quoting Findlay's skepticism concerning the rigor of Hegel's procedure.

Heinrichs [208] uses the category of '*Erkennen*' from the Jena *Logik* as paradigm. See pp. 237–49. Compare Hermann Schmitz [437] where '*Erkennen*' is also discussed. On this see pp. 19–20. André Kaan [245] makes reference to the Jena *Metaphysics*. He claims that there is a parallel between the birth of absolute spirit in the Jena system of metaphysics and the occurrence of real individuality in the *Phenomenology*. We are led in both "to discover the limit of individual reason as the place of the union between consciousness and self-consciousness," and to the necessity of embracing reason in history or real history, spirit in the world (48).

Shklar [457] suggests that what we have here is the internalization of the ego as in Fichte, an "original nature" which "bears a strong resemblance to Rousseau's man in the state of nature" (122). "The Fichtean ego is an internalization of Rousseau's isolate" (123). See also Royce [426], 196–201; Fink [127], 340–50; Gary Shapiro [454]; Findlay [120], 112–15; and Becker [27], 109–15.

16 Compare the way in which Kainz [249] notes this convergence of purpose and appropriateness. "The individual consciousness at this point no longer has inner purposes which are in some way at odds with outer reality. For now no inner purpose has significance which is not immediately adapted to outer reality. And it no longer looks upon universality as something opposed to individual realization; but has come to the insight that there is no true individuality which is not universal, no true universality which is not implemented in the activity of

individuals" (125). See also the account of Fink [127], 340–45, where he discusses the meaning of this interpenetration of the individual and the universal.

17 Henry S. Harris [182] includes an excellent discussion of what is involved here in the idea of an effective or actual (*wirkliche*) category. This unity of effectiveness and actuality in the same concept is what is so important for a correct understanding of Hegel. Harris argues, against those who would miss this real meaning of 'actuality' as 'effectiveness', that if the connection between essence and existence were denied, then there would be two consequences unacceptable to Hegel. "First, we should have to admit that the actual world is not completely intelligible; and, secondly, it would be theoretically possible to construct a completely rational system of ideas without even considering whether or not such a system was, or could be, existentially realized—indeed this problem could not legitimately arise for the theorist, since it could never be resolved by purely rational means. Hegel regarded these consequences as irreconcilable either with philosophy or with sound common sense. In his view it simply did not make sense to suggest that the world may not ultimately 'make sense', or to suggest that something could be imagined which does completely 'make sense' and yet is not realized in the world" (114). Harris is right on the mark here, and this matter will be of importance in my last chapter when Hegel's project in the *Phenomenology* is critically examined.

In this matter, Dieter Henrich's analysis [211] of contingency and necessity is again crucial. Hyppolite [238] describes the present structure by noting that the "acting self is simultaneously being and self; *it is the category that has become conscious of itself*" (298). Royce [426], like not a few other commentators, has a rather more narrow view of what is going on here, limiting it to those, such as artists and scholars, who have a "calm love for a definite calling" (197–98). See Hyppolite's criticism of this in Hyppolite [238], 297.

18 Put in still other terms, the presupposition is that society is always already rational in the sense of being a totality in the constant process of totalization, a self-contained containing which sustains itself. See the discussion of Fink [127], pp. 309ff. on the fluidity of society, and the analysis of Hyppolite [238], 278–79.

19 That is to say, capacities, talents, ends, etc. are not the exclusive property of individuals, but ways of being and acting shared by different individuals. The misunderstanding of this point is responsible in part for generating the caricature of Hegel as a "block universe essentialist." But see the analysis of Hyppolite [238], 300–04 where he discusses the relation of talents, etc. to individuals. When coupled with the remark noted in note 20, below, that here existence precedes essence, we see a very balanced view of Hegel which avoids the usual caricature of him as such an essentialist. See also the discussion of Heinrichs [208], 243–44.

20 Again praxis arises as central to Hegel's analysis, this time explicitly recognized in the natural attitude as central to the rational activity of individuals in society. See Navickas [374], 193–97, for an interesting discussion of 'work'. He introduces the discussion with an important distinction between Plato and Hegel which can serve to defuse much misunderstanding about Hegel. He writes

that "we see here the enormous distance that separates Hegel from the rationalistic teleology and the Platonic tradition. Hegel could not conceive of universality as being some ideal 'telos' introduced by reason or imagination; nor could he conceive of it as belonging to the Platonic world of ideas" (193). In the same way, Hyppolite [238] notes that here "there is a primacy of existence over essence" which would by itself remove any Platonic separation of existence and essence (301).

For a good discussion of work (*Werk*), activity in a productive sense (*Handeln*), and deed (*Tat*) together with its verbal form (*tun*), see Lauer [305], pp. 167ff. On praxis generally for Hegel, see the discussion of Nicolai Hartmann [191], II, 342–43, on the nature of praxis as both creative, on-going activity and also ground for that activity. He is addressing the opening passage of active reason, but his analysis is important for the present point.

21 We have here the first true entrance of a social world as explicitly thematized. We will now become concerned with enculturation, objectification, and alienation in a concrete social sense, rather than within self-consciousness. But above all, we shall see the intensification, in the natural attitude, of the ambiguity of the true/made relation. Cf. the argument of Fackenheim [118], pp. 44–45 on the inadequacies of the position of self-consciousness, where it is often maintained that the social world enters into consideration.

22 In this section we are not thematizing spirit itself, but rather thematizing the way in which the natural attitude takes its world, a thematization which will lead us to spirit. What we have here, then, is spirit in its immediacy, i.e., the tasks of the world or, as Hegel refers to it, *die Sache selbst*. Hyppolite [238] sees this section in much the same way. "When we are about to act, the world that offers itself to us as the matter of our action is not in-itself distinct from us. It is already the external revelation of what we are within. It is an objective world only for the individuality that recognizes itself therein. . . . It is our world, and only our world, that we see in it. By our *interest* in this or that aspect of it we discover ourselves in it" (303). And this has just been the project and theme of reason. See also Hermann Schmitz [437] who claims that what is thematized here as *die Sache selbst* is "the interpenetration, the comprehensive whole of various subjective and objective aspects of action; as such there is at the same time universality, the essence of being and of action which is independent of contingent particularities" (32). Compare with this the interesting discussion of Winfried Kaminski [252]. Kaminski understands *die Sache selbst* to be a "synonym for the concept of commodity" (49).

Findlay [120] has a more exclusively negative interpretation of this first description of community and *die Sache selbst*. "In this phase the whole nature of a reasonable individual becomes completely absorbed in carrying out some task or enterprise-on-hand: it is, says Hegel, no longer possible to draw a distinction between the individual's capacities and attitudes, the circumstances that provoke them, the end that the individual aims at, his personal interest in this end, and the means he uses towards its realization. All these things are 'moments' in a single activity, and that activity simply *is* the individual. What emerges as alone solid and permanent is the Task, the Enterprise, the Game, the Cause, the Matter-on-hand itself (*die Sache selbst*), of which these factors are merely vanishing 'moments'. . . . . A man's consciousness achieves honesty of purpose (*Ehrlichkeit*) in so far as he sets himself to get on with the Matter-on-hand, to 'do his bit', 'play the game', to serve 'the cause' . . . *regardless of either failure or success.* The cult of the Matter-on-hand is, therefore, yet another case of . . . self-absorbed high-mindedness. . . . Not only was it the typical vice of German Romanticism, but we may identify it also as the vice of the American business executive, the nineteenth-century empire builder, the disinterestedly frightful Nazi, or the pure practitioner of scholarship or research. (This last was probably most in Hegel's mind.)" (112–13).

See also Becker [27], 112–13; Fink [127], 348–50; Lauer [305], 165; and Kainz [249], 117–18, where he also makes the distinction between thematizing spirit and thematizing the activity of the natural attitude itself as it produces spirit.

23 In what now follows, we have an excellent discussion by Hegel of what the concrete historical acitivity of spirit is in its real, immediate existence. We come to understand that spirit is the individual, I myself, but in the concreteness of my contextual existence and not as some abstraction of a theory of atomistic individualism. Thus, if I am right in the analysis which now follows, Adorno [3] and others are wrong in maintaining that Hegel abstracts from the individual. André Kaan [245] has an excellent account of "the compenetration of the individual and the universal as adequation of work and of the action that produces it" (48). See also Hook [220] on the nature of objective spirit as a confluence of individual acts which result in unintentional praxis. His analysis is quite good, but must be taken outside of his general perspective on Hegel. Furthermore, his criticism of Hegel as a "fossilizer" with a penchant for "system" is shown to be unjustified precisely in this passage which Hook has so well captured. See especially pp. 256–60.

We also find here the basis for Hegel's critique of social contract theory. On this, see Patrick Riley [409]; Norberto Bobbio [46]; and Christopher J. Berry [32]. Fackenheim [118], 45–46, has a very concise analysis of why social contract is inadequate in Hegel's terms. "One cannot take social standards and the social wholes sustained by them as the product of mere sums of individual selves, initially owned wholly privately and only subsequently shared as if by an agreement or contract" (46).

24 Hyppolite [238], 309–10, has an excellent discussion of 'thing' as it appears here and as it appeared earlier in the section on perception. The point is that here, in my objectified and objectifying being, we have the true existence of spirit as a thing. Bringing together the discussion of *die Sache selbst* and this activity of objectification, see Kainz [249], pp. 126–27 and the accompanying notes in the commentary. Kainz calls *die Sache selbst* "Subjective/Objective individuality" and claims that it is here strictly determinate, "a *determinate* subject-object reciprocity, a fluid categorical unity of determinate subjective and objective 'moments'" (127). See also Albert Hofstadter [219]; and Heinrichs [208], 246–47.

25 If this can be properly understood, namely that each individual has no actual, effective reality as an isolated atom, yet is also not effaced as an individual

and as the sole source of all actions, then the true nature of spirit in the philosophy of Hegel can be understood. At the basis of an understanding, the analysis of Henrich [211] is crucial. Fink [127], 305–16 also has a penetrating discussion of what 'actualization' means for a grasp of effective reality as spirit. In a discussion of what is accomplished in a rational activity as it leads us to the level of spirit, Kroner [275] has this to say. "With this stage the level is reached at which Hegel establishes his theory of objective spirit. The individual as such has disappeared into the species or has returned into it, but without surrendering itself. The species lives in the individual, reason is actualized in the naturally determined individuals and becomes conscious of them in this synthesis as spirit" (II, 387). See also Hermann Schmitz [436], and his discussion of this in terms of the crisis evolving from the attempt to express oneself through work, found in Schmitz [437], p. 29; and Navickas [374], 195–97.

26 On the advance made here in thematizing our own activities while pursuing them, see Kainz [249], pp. 130–31. Becker [27] does not seem to me to understand the complexity of the irony and ambiguity contained in this conception. See his whole discussion of the "category" and of the formation of individuality, pp. 110–12. He erroneously claims at one point that the "new stage, i.e. the individuality which takes itself to be real in and for itself, in reality is nothing more than a new *name* for the old negativity: the *unattainability* of the unity of absolute identity and opposition" (110).

27 On this I agree with Rolf Ahlers on the matter of presuppositions. We do not rid ourselves of them, but come to comprehend them as they are in reality. See Ahlers [6], p. 68.

28 This final section contains two parts, a discussion of reason as giver of laws and a discussion of reason as tester of laws. In both cases, reason turns upon itself as found in the world in order to give itself warranty. Navickas [374] characterizes the discussion in these sections as the "convergence of reason, moral concern, individuality, and universality" (198). See his discussion pp. 198–203. See also Fink [127], 350–52; Nicolai Hartmann [191], II, 345; Heinrichs [208], 247–49; Lauer [305], 172–76; and Hyppolite [238], 315–18.

29 On the nature of these laws, see Nicolai Hartmann [191], p. 345, where he describes the laws in the context of the ethical substance to which Hegel next turns.

30 For a rather well-balanced view of Hegel's struggle with Kant at this point, see Taylor [495], 169. The whole issue of Hegel, Kant, and moral theory will be discussed below, Chapter Nine. For the present, we will limit ourselves to only what can be discussed in the context of the present project of reason, leaving the more concrete discussion to the concrete section in spirit. Findlay [120] puts Hegel's critique of reason, both as source and as evaluator of laws, in the following way. "The upshot of these considerations is that Reason, whether considered as laying down or as criticizing laws, can guide us to no positive collective ethical enterprise. As prescribing laws, it is *insolent* in its arbitrary positiveness, while as criticizing laws it is insolent in its detached intellectual negativity" (114).

Shklar [457], 138–41, argues that Hegel was not right about Kant in his critique of reason as tester of laws. On this see also Shklar [456], especially 597–603.

But compare with this the view of Navickas [374], who concludes that in the critique, "Hegel proposes not to correct Kant's categorical imperative, but only to explain the irrelevancy of the principle of contradiction to morality" (202). Hegel's point, in my view, is that whatever the criterion is, it cannot be ahistorical and acultural, while at the same time it must avoid the bad consequences which Kant saw in any simple relativisim.

31 Westphal [528], 138–50, has a very interesting discussion of the ethical life as it arises here, especially concerning the change from the transcendental to the historical. Joachim Ritter [411] has a discussion of the move from reason to ethicality (*Sittlichkeit*). His source and focus is the *Philosophy of Right*, but with appropriate care there is much here which throws light on the present movement in the *Phenomenology*. Marsh [345] sees the transition to spirit accurately, but a bit too simply. "Hegel's alternative to the radical solution is the ethical consciousness" (196). Taylor [495] sees the transition to spirit in quite a different way than I do. He claims that in what has preceded, including that which is discussed in the section on reason, "we are dealing with forms of individual consciousness, even if we deal with men in interaction. . . . But in the chapters which follow, on Spirit and Religion, we are taking spirit as a supra-personal subject, first as the spirit of a people, and then as the self-consciousness of the world-spirit in religion" (167). This rather common view of a "supra-individual" arises, as I have already argued several times, out of a misconception of the task of the *Phenomenology*—reading it as some form of metaphysics or philosophical anthropology—and of the method involved. This whole matter will be further discussed in the next chapters on spirit.

On the transition to spirit, see also Fackenheim [118], 44–50.

32 Thus again, at the end of the discussion of ahistorical reason as the possible absolute standpoint, we are left with ambiguity. The oppositions are not antinomical, but rather of the essence of what-is, and this will remain constant in what follows in the discussion of spirit. This is most often missed. Gustav Mueller [366] interprets the end of reason here as an "enormous failure of practical reason," rather than in terms of the ambiguity which forces us on to spirit, which is practical reason in history. Hofstadter [219] claims that Hegel makes a crucial error in confusing what is mine with what is mine as me in external form: "for the meaning of *mine* something that is closely associated with it, the meaning of *me*, is substituted" (691). This, then, supposedly causes the ambiguity. But Hegel is surely not guilty of this. If this substitution had been made at any point in a positive way, and such an idealism had been fostered by Hegel, then the tension between self and other, and the ambiguity of the self-world relation in all of its richness—both of which are always preserved—would have been destroyed. It is *not* a case of "metonymy," as Hofstadter would have it.

The case for ambiguity can also be made on the basis of the thesis of Kroner [275], II, 267–72, that Hegel is an irrationalist. But see also the criticism of this view by Pantscho Russew [427]. On the matter of the propriety of ambiguity, see also Hermann Schmitz [437].

33 On this convergence of the natural and the philosophical attitudes, compare Heinrichs [208], 239–40 where, in his own terms, he argues that "we have now

arrived at the point at which reflection remains no longer simply operative, but rather is itself thematized" (239–40). It is no longer "the logician," but now also the content itself which is at the level of reflection. In this light, the subsequent discussion by Heinrichs of '*Erkennen*' is very instructive. See pp. 240–43.

34 On the matter of raising certainty to truth, Kainz [249], 129–30, comes close to my view when he discusses the absoluteness of this standpoint and the conclusions to which we are drawn. See especially p. 133 on the matter of the conclusions.

35 Compare Lauer [305], p. 177. Thus, when Lauer refers to spirit vaguely as "a more-than-individual consciousness," and yet explains quite clearly that "*Sittlichkeit* is a general term covering any behavior based on norms provided by the general consciousness of the community," we can identify this "general consciousness" concretely as the body of praxical presuppositions embedded within and embodied in the social formation. They are institutional facts of the most important kind, which no philosopher would wish to deny. See Lauer's discussion, *Ibid.*, 180.

36 Compare Ahlers [6], p. 74. Ahlers is referring us ahead to absolute spirit, but the groundwork for this unity of the absolute, unconditioned and finite temporal existence has been laid here. See also above, pp. 243–45.

37 Again, the point must be stressed, that the natural attitude and the natural world are always the touchstone for truth for Hegel. See the discussion of Schrader-Klebert [443], 69–88, on reason as the self-articulation of a ground which is absolute and yet which does not go beyond the self-awareness of the natural attitude.

38 Hegel [202], 73; [203], I, p. 53.

39 Heinrichs [208] claims that the individual as sole bearer of spirit is already uncovered in the results of the critique of virtue: the "universal has actuality and power only in and as the individual" (237).

Notes to Chapter VII

1 There is an extensive literature on the general concept of 'spirit' and on this whole section of the *Phenomenology*, beginning with "true spirit" and ending with "absolute knowing." For an account of the history of this concept, see *Historisches Wörterbuch der Philosophie* [216], Bd. III, pp. 154–203. The discussion of the meaning of *Geist* from the Greeks through Hegel is to be found pp. 154–99. Nathan Rotenstreich [425] has an historical treatment of the concept in Hegel, maintaining that "there are two main motives which sponsored Hegel to introduce the concept of Mind; the Aristotelian motive on the one hand and the Cartesian motive on the other" (33). The former is the motive to articulate potentiality-actuality, the latter to consider reflection as "an index of itself and of existence" (34). In addition, Shklar [457] has an excellent discussion of spirit, pp. 142–79. She discusses the relation between Montesquieu and Hegel on spirit and modernity. For background on this concept in Hegel's earlier work, see D. Souche-Dagues [477], and Henry S. Harris [184].

For an analysis of the systemic place of this section and the problems surrounding the question of that place, see the position of Pöggeler [394], pp. 222ff. where he argues that the place where spirit confronts itself is spirit, not the *Logic* which follows upon the achievement of absolute knowing.

There are many attempts to explicate the central meaning of this concept as it functions within the *Phenomenology*. Taylor [495] resorts to analogy-language. "The universe is the embodiment of the totality of the 'life-functions' of God, that is, the conditions of his existence. And it is also throughout an expression of God, that is, something posited by God in order to manifest what he is. The universe must therefore be grasped as something analogous to a life-form, hence understood by the Aristotelian-derived category of 'internal teleology'; and be read as something analogous to a text in which God says what he is" (88). On the one hand, I would argue that there is no need here to being in 'God' as a concept, since that is only one way in which spirit manifests itself. I shall have more to say of this later. On the other hand, Taylor does not take his embodiment thesis far enough, nor does he draw sufficiently on his own thesis about expressivism. If spirit involves the imbedding of praxical presuppositions in institutional facts and in the activities which produce and are based on them, then we have here no need for analogy. For Taylor's general account of spirit and its unfolding in the *Phenomenology*, see pp. 171–213.

Solomon [476] holds that 'Geist' is the underlying, unifying principle of consciousness and, at the same time, the underlying rational will "behind all practical reason and action" (148). He uses the notion of "methodological solipsism" to explicate what he means here. There are several clear and insightful discussions of this concept. Westphal [528] treats of the concept and its development in the *Phenomenology* on pp. 121–219. Chapter V contains a good introduction to spirit, but lacks in systematicity. See also his various characterizations of spirit pp. 129–30, and the discussion of history and spirit, p. 154. The latter will be important for Westphal's development of his thesis concerning the relation between time and eternity. Jonathan Robinson [415], pp. 16–18, has a simple and clear discussion of the meaning of 'spirit'. Findlay [120], pp. 39–47, 116–48, gives a many-sided account of the meaning of 'spirit' in terms of the subject-object problem. Kroner [275] discusses spirit in volume II, pp. 387–95. He points out an interesting thematic structure to spirit: in the section on spirit the earlier movement from certainty to truth is reversed as we proceed to the introduction of the discussion of religion. We now proceed from objectivity and truth with the discussion of "true spirit," toward subjectivity and certainty with the section on "morality or spirit certain of itself." See II, p. 388. See also the discussion of John Plamenatz [391], 32–45. He has a simple and straightforward account, but I must disagree with him when he claims that we can still make sense of spirit when we divorce it from dialectics.

See also Becker [27], 116–40; Navickas [374], 207–74; Stephen Crites [87]; Nicolai Hartmann [191], II, 346–62; Lauer [305], 177–269; Esperanze Duran de Seade [113]; Hyppolite [238], 321–606, especially the introduction to spirit pp. 321–33; Labarrière [287], 109–211; Heinrichs [208], 265–526; Kojève [266], 97–443.

2 This claim to move to concreteness from abstractness has generated some problems of interpretation in the literature. Some hold that there is no such gain in concreteness. See, for example, Becker [27], 118–19, where he claims that the abstractness is not really overcome, except as an assertion made by Hegel but without proof. On the other hand, it is often too narrowly interpreted as involving only a move from individuals to the social as such. See, for example, Navickas [374], 207–10. This thesis is quite generally held, but, as I hope to show, too simple to cover what is really involved here.

Hyppolite [238] has a good discussion of the move, but has evidently missed the double thematization which occurred in reason as it stood as giver and tester of laws. See his discussion, pp. 316–18. C. I. Gulian [174] also has an interesting view of the overcoming of the abstract here in spirit, but misses the relation between that overcoming and the problem of the *Phenomenology*.

There are two discussions oriented around parallel structures. Labarrière [287], 109–19 begins to draw out his parallels with consciousness and self-consciousness, and Heinrichs [208] continues his analysis of the parallels with the early Jena systems. Heinrichs claims that "the transition from the treatment of individual consciousness and its objectivity into the thematic of spirit and thus the self becoming object itself of spiritual being corresponds phenomenologically to the transition of the unreflected logic into the metaphysics of Jena" (265).

Aschenberg [12] places this move in the context of the problem of truth. He maintains that the first part of the *Phenomenology* (through reason) is to be understood as a derivation of the fundamental correctness (*Richtigkeit*) in his sense of the epistemological concept of truth. The second part, beginning with the present section on spirit, is the derivation of the fundamental categoriality and the fundamental truth involved therein, in the sense of the categorial concept of truth. That is, reaching the concrete category, which will be discussed below, warranty for the claims of absolute idealism is now to be given in terms of that concrete category. See Aschenberg's discussion, pp. 279–80, 293.Pöggeler [395] discusses the transition in connection with the thought of Kant, Fichte, and

Schelling. See pp. 64ff. Ritter [411] discusses the move from reason to *Sittlichkeit*, mostly in the context of Hegel's concerns in the *Philosophy of Right*. But there is much here that is relevant to the concerns of the *Phenomenology*.

3 In this respect, compare Krüger [277] who sees the move to spirit in terms of the ancient-modern difference, but in my view in a too simple epistemological way. He argues that the move to spirit is a move back to a simple epistemology based on natural thinking and objectivity, and which accepted the law of non-contradiction as absolute. This argument is based on Krüger's earlier discussion of the opposition between the ancients and moderns as the opposition of certainty and truth, the former being fundamental for the moderns, the latter for the ancients. But if, as I suggest, it is a repudiation of the modern way to certainty and a return to the fundamental need to ground knowledge within a discussion of the polis, then, far from being a "natural thinking rooted in the law of non-contradiction," it is rather a move to an objectivity of spirit which acknowledges contradiction and paradox in the tragedies. See especially the discussion of Krüger, pp. 292–303.

4 The problem of history enters in a special way here and, since the old accusations of Rudolf Haym, the reason for an historical treatment of spirit has to be made explicit. Otto Pöggeler tries to deal with this in several places, but see especially Pöggeler [395] where he lays out the thesis that we have the discussion of the history of spirit in order to show "how speculative philosophy in general is possible" (68). Many other factors have been brought into play by others. Litt [322] has an insightful essay on the way in which Hegel's notion of spirit takes us beyond the Enlightenment's sense of 'tradition', and how the concept 'tradition' helps us understand 'spirit'. See also the observations of Hyppolite [232], characterizing the general Hegelian project in terms which indicate the necessary place for the historical. "Hegel wished to *found* the historical fact itself. He looked for the general conditions of human existence, that on the basis of which a human reality is possible as such. Man, as one says today, is always in a certain situation, but this variable situation supposes general conditions which it is important to disentangle, for they will always be more or less implied in the whole human situation as such" (1277). Caponigri [65] employs the distinction between presence as *factum* and presence as *fieri*. He argues that "the condition of the actuality of truth is presence, total presence to itself. And this total presence of truth must be, not the presence of a given, which would but confirm the diremption, but the presence which embraces its own coming to be as its own proper self-generative activity: presence not as *factum*, but as *fieri*, and *fieri* not as the consequence of the agency of another, but as the consequence of its own action, indeed as wholly contained in its own action, never transcending that act, but eternally residing in it. Truth, in this mode of absolute presence to itself, Hegel calls the *Idea*" (6). Ahlers [6] has a very deep analysis of the absolute finitude and historical character of spirit although, as already noted, we do not agree on all points. See especially his discussion, p. 74. In a critical essay, Jean Ladrière [296] argues for a sense of history beyond that of Hegel, but his account of Hegel and the relation of the individual to history is very helpful.

5 Here we have yet another instance of a question of the historical which is

problematic for the interpretation of Hegel: Why begin here with the Greeks? For example, Becker [27], 116–17, claims that there is no reason other than that it fits Hegel's purposes. But, as I shall argue, the needs generated by the quest for certainty which controls our attention to history are not so arbitrary as this. The Greeks, for Hegel and for us, *are* the beginning of our genesis as a civilization, and it is they who first embody the tension that shapes us. For more on this, see my opening discussion also below, note 25. On another version of why it is rational that we begin with the Greek plois, see Hyppolite [238], where he links it to the relation between history and our present substance. See pp. 326–32, especially pp. 330–31.

6 Compare the similar account by Labarrière [287], 116–17. No one has put the matter more simply or clearly than Shklar [457]. "No one can understand the process of knowing unless he is aware of his own place in the cultural whole and of all that the past has contributed to the present. Those who forget the past are not only doomed to repeat old errors, they willfully deny their own character" (6). This view, like all of Hegel's views, did not spring full born from his head. See the discussion of Cassirer [67], who understands this as part of the "problem of objectivity" which Hegel had inherited from Kant, Fichte, and Schelling. See Volume III, p. 327. See also on this Blasche and Schwemmer [41], p. 466, where, following a discussion of Kant's moral philosophy and Hegel's critique of it—a matter we have just gone through at the end of reason, at least in part—they consider the turn to *Sittlichkeit* and its historical dimension in the light of the critique of Kant.

Two French commentators approach the problem, not from the perspective of the history itself, but from that of the present. Dominique Janicaud [243], p. 156, calls our attention to the fact that the first stage of spirit (and it is also true of other stages) is structurally present in any modern political formation, i.e., there is always present as a basis *Sittlichkeit* in its relevant form. Hyppolite [238] looks at the matter in the following way. "Spirit is a 'we': we must begin not with the *cogito* but with the *cogitamus*. Spirit is history: it becomes what it is only through a historical development because each of its moments, in making itself essence, must realize itself as an original world, and because its being is not distinct from the action through which it poses itself. Spirit is knowledge of itself in its history: it is a return to itself through, and by means of, that history, a return such that nothing alien subsists in or for spirit and such that spirit knows itself as what it is and is what it knows itself to be (this being of spirit is nothing but its very action). These are the three fundamental theses of Hegelian idealism" (322–23). See also Hyppolite's general discussion, pp. 331–32. Hyppolite's remarks about the *cogito* also reflect back on the matter of Hegel's rejection of the modern procedure for establishing warranted certainty for knowledge, discussed above in note 3. In this vein see also the citation and discussion of Caponigri, above, note 4. Jere Paul Surber [491] also has a good discussion of the relationship between spirit and time.

7 Several writers have discussed this section in the light of earlier periods of Hegel's thought. See the ever useful work of Henry S. Harris [184]. Janicaud [243], Part I, "La Genèse du theme grec dans l'oeuvre de Hegel" gives an account

Notes to Chapter VII 347

of the development of Hegel's view of the Greeks. See especially p. 16 where he characterizes the strength and importance of this first epoch of spirit in the *Phenomenology*. Westphal [528] looks at Hegel's earlier writings to cull a sense of Hegel's view of the Greeks as a healthy culture, contrasted with the Judeo-Christian culture. See pp. 28–36. E. Wolff [538] offers an account of '*Sittlichkeit*' in Hegel's Tübingen days. Wolff also discusses Hegel's relation to Schiller on this matter. See also E. Staiger [480].

For explication through contrast with the moderns, see the discussion of Greene [164a]. He has a good contrast (albeit using Plato and Aristotle, rather than the poets) with later, modern senses of alienation, throwing light on the nature of this section of the *Phenomenology*. See a more direct contrast with the moderns in Shklar [457], Chapter 2. This is a discussion of Greek spirit in general. See also her discussion of '*Sittlichkeit*' in Shklar [455].

Heinrichs [208], 277–310, uses the category of 'identity' for his articulation of true spirit. Labarrière [287], 120–28 focuses on a parallel with the earlier discussion of sense-certainty and the movement from that to perception, the latter being a parallel with the next section on the self-alienated world of *Bildung*. This underscores the immediacy of spirit at this first stage, and its movement to difference and mediation.

Kojève [266] discusses true spirit pp. 98–107, building his analysis on the pattern of the analysis of the master as he understood this pattern in self-consciousness. Pöggeler [393] holds that tragedy is the central determinant of Hegel's view of the Greeks. In contrast, Livio Sichirollo [458] discusses Hegel's views, but concentrates almost completely on his views of Greek philosophy as given in the *Lectures on the History of Philosophy*. See also Nicolai Hartmann [191], II, 346–62; Navickas [374], 210–20; Crites [87]; Taylor [495], 172–77; Hyppolite [238], 334–64; Lauer [305], 179–90; Findlay [120], 116–19; and Becker [27], 116–20.

8 This point is generally missed, if I read other commentaries correctly. Becker [27] treats the plays as mere examples and claims that the reflection here is due to some pure form of self-consciousness. But we are far beyond such a stage. Hyppolite [238], 335, presents a weaker version of my claim, holding that the ancient tragedies are correspondences to the actual spirit. Janicaud [243] argues that tragedy is, par excellence, the place where the contradictory tension of ethical existence is revealed (177). See his further discussion of this pp. 177–80. Krumpel [280] maintains that "the thoughts about ethicality, right and morality in the *Phenomenology of Spirit* are thoughts of self-consciousness about the social world, about itself in this world" (16). For Lauer [305] myths and the tragedies are only the "means of introducing a distinction" (182). If Greek tragedy is, for Hegel, what I claim, then as the real embodiment of the Greek spirit as re-presented in the *Phenomenology*, it is not simply the case as Charles Taylor [495] would have it, namely that the "vocabulary" for this section "is borrowed from the Greek tragedians" (173).

9 Findlay [120] has a good, straightforward formulation of the divine and human laws which structure ethical substance. "The Human Law is . . . the body of usages and publicly promulgated laws which obtain in the Community, and

which are given authority by its governing elements. The Divine Law or Power, on the other hand, has its obscure roots in elemental family relationships, and, since the Family lies at the foundations of the Community, the Divine or Family Principle underlies all communal life" (117). However, it must be noted that the Human/Divine for Hegel is not determinant in only one way; for the polis and its laws are, after all, the place in which the family exists and carries out its destiny. See also the account of Lauer [305], 180–84, and the close analysis of Heinrichs [208], 280–95.

10 Cf. the discussion of Lauer [305], p. 15, on the terms 'sittlich' and 'Sittlichkeit', and his further discussion pp. 177–80. Heinrichs [208] does not have an adequate discussion of the actual content in this section, but his logical analysis is helpful. See especially his analysis, pp. 292–93, of the "transition of the two laws into one another," and his discussion of the ethical world as calm equilibrium, pp. 293–95. Westphal [528], 138–50, has a close discussion of the section. See also Hyppolite [238], 339–48, and Eric Weil [520]. On the other hand, see E. F. Carritt [66] for a rather shallow view of this section. His essay is an example of what happens when one tries to discuss Hegel while ignoring dialectic and the matter of the genesis of the subject-matter under consideration.

11 On the complexity of ethical action and its relation to ethical substance, see Hyppolite [238], 177–80. Findlay [120], on the other hand, has a rather weak transition to the discussion of ethical action. Findlay is not, in fact, following out his own excellent discussion of the nature of spirit. Heinrichs [208], 296–305 has an analysis which understands the consideration of individuals in action within the substance as a move necessary in order to make explicit the latent contradiction (or law of contradiction) in the identity of substance (or in the law of identity). See also Raymond Pietercil [388] for a review and discussion of the arguments for and against Hegel's interpretation of Antigone and tragedy.

12 Here, again, we have the matter of the reciprocity within spirit and the total reflection. Compare the view of Bloch [43]. "The great concern of the *Phenomenology* is and remains the real self-cognition as knowledge of the production of man through his work and history. That alone is the important, and consequently unelimination subject for Hegel: not as a vapor, but as action, not as spirit, but as the heart of the matter. Since man produces himself with his objective work, for that reason the subject must above all possess a prevalence within the historico-dialectical subject-object-relation" (95). But on the contrary, neither can be given prevalence. Nor is the view of Garaudy [152], concerning the primacy of individual subjectivity, defensible in the face of this mutual reciprocity. Garaudy writes that the subjective is prior to intersubjective social relations in a real society, for Hegel. "Hegel considers . . . this subjectivity of desire as a real origin, as a point of departure, whereas it is a result, a moment of an already long evolution. This inversion is at the source of all idealistic inversion: to take for the beginning what is at the end" (53). But Hegel is beyond either of the alternatives discussed here by Garaudy.

Navickas [374] takes up a position of ambiguity concerning this matter. On the one hand, he claims that for Hegel, spirit "has the peculiar power of inspiring individuals to form social orders and of determining the goals of communal life"

(209). But this suggests not total reflection, but a one-way determinism. On the other hand, he asserts that "Hegel himself would be the last to claim that it is permissible to speak of a spiritual reality without relating it to the concrete social activities through which such a reality can be realized as actual and as concrete by the society-oriented individuals" (209–10).

Several analyses seem to capture well the reciprocity. Hyppolite [238] claims that spirit is "the genuine development of that universality which self-consciousness reached as reason. As spirit, reason has become the we. It is no longer the subjective certainty of discovering itself immediately in being or of posing itself through negating that being; it knows itself as this world, as the world of human history, and, conversely, it knows this world to be the self" (326). See also Litt [322], 314, for an explication of the total interpenetration of individual and world and the way in which that relationship is both abiding and temporal. We should also here keep in mind what Heimo E. M. Hofmeister [218] points out. "It is Hegel who has to be credited with the discovery that man does actualize his freedom not merely morally but *ethico-socially* as well. This insight permitted him to distinguish not only between abstract right and morality but also between both of them and ethical life. Within the ethical life freedom appears neither as mere *thing* nor as mere *intention* (*Gesinnung*), but as concrete human relation and condition of man's social interaction" (144). Perhaps Hoffmeister goes too far in suggesting that Hegel discovered this, but he is right that it is at the heart of the analysis. See also the discussion in Westphal [528], 144–45, concerning the mutual creation of individuals and society.

13 See the discussion of Hegel's concept of a people in Durán de Seade [113], 369–70. The rather blunt statement of Lauer [305] that what "distinguishes 'the ethical' in this context, then, is that it involves sacrificing the *particularity* of individual reason to the generality of communal consciousness" (180) can be misleading, and must be made more subtle by a reading of Lauer's discussion of *Sittlichkeit*, Ibid., pp. 180ff. There, the notion of "identification" with its double thematization of individual and "the people" nicely develops the full intentions of Hegel's analysis.

Carl J. Friedrich [143] has an interesting definition of 'ideology' which casts light on the double thematization here. He writes that "ideologies are sets of ideas related to the existing political and social order and intended either to change it or to defend it" (16). But Hegel's view here would seem to go beyond this sort of notion, and takes ideology to be both the basis and the result of reflection on the human condition, furnishing the cement of the life of individuals within the given society.

14 This, and not a simple judgment of guilt on the part of one of the individuals, is what objectifies the tragedy of the human condition. See the discussion of Antigone and Creon and of Hegel's notion of guilt in tragedy in Salvatore Russo [428]. The complexity of the situation in true spirit is well portrayed: "Pure evil is empty and unfit for dramatic tragedy" (137). Others have used the phrase 'guiltless guilt' to try to capture this. See Kroner [275], II, 389, and Heinrichs [208], 299–301.

15 On Hegel's theory of art generally, see William Desmond [95]. On Hegel's

view of tragedy in particular, see Russo [428], who remarks that for Hegel, in "life as in literature, tragedy signifies that the Spirit is divided, that it is suffering from an inner dissonance due to the conflict of universal and particular" (133). See also P. Szondi [494]; Pietercil [388]; Christos Axelos [17].

16 This "being of reason" is too often reified or made into a wholly intellectualistic notion by commentators. See, for instance, the view of Lobkowicz [325], where he reflects on the relationship which Hegel attributes to will and thought, will being the urge of thought to give itself existence. Lobkowicz interprets this as meaning that will is an activity of spirit in so far as spirit works to make reality conform to thought. "Thus will is the urge resulting from an *ought* of thought" (153). On the basis of this interpretation, he turns Hegel into a "one-sided" thinker, maintaining that for Hegel practice "is for the sake of contemplation" or "for the sake of theory" (153). This might be true in some of the deficient modes of reason presupposed as the absolute standpoint which we have already surpassed, but it certainly does not hold in any of the forms of spirit, where spirit is reason. As a balance, see the discussion of Nicolai Hartmann [191], II, 346–47.

17 On the term 'category' as it developed from the Greeks, see *Historisches Wörterbuch der Philosophie* [216], Bd. 4, pp. 714–76. The discussion relevant for us, through Hegel's employment of the term, will be found pp. 714–36. See also Josef Simon [462]; Achim Hager [179], pp. 220ff.; Klaus Hartmann [190]; and Royce [426], pp. 1–30, especially pp. 23–30.

18 No problem has been more difficult in the attempt to understand Hegel than the problem of the meaning of 'idealism' and of the 'absoluteness' of absolute idealism. But since the 1950's much progress has been made, both in clearing away misconceptions arising from a Platonizing of Hegel, and in coming to an adequate formulation in an authentically Hegelian way. As a representative of the still lingering problem see the discussion of Friedrich Grimmlinger [170]. My main discussion of his essay will come later when I deal with the question of absolute knowing itself, but mention of Grimmlinger's view will be useful here. Grimmlinger notes the ambiguity in Hegel, an ambiguity which I have been trying to discuss in a positive manner, accepting it as Hegel's answer to the question. Grimmlinger takes a negative attitude toward the ambiguity, insisting that Hegel decide on either realist or subjective idealist grounds. "The true chasm in the problematic ambiguity of the absolute concept in Hegel appears connected with the problem of necessity. For the concept, even the absolute concept as continually formed, is a human concept. Whether this is now to necessarily comprehend actuality in true philosophical knowledge, depends upon whether this human concept can be given the necessity by actuality (1) or whether it give, i.e. prescribes, the necessity (2). Hegel has not held apart and distinguished in any clear way these two possibilities" (297). As I have tried to argue, it is Hegel's intention to show, through the discussion of the total reflection within spirit, that precisely this distinction is *aufgehoben*, already at the present stage. On this question of realism and idealism in particular, see Rosen [421], p. 48, where there is a succinct discussion of the problem of overcoming the subject-object distinction and why both realist and idealist attempts must fail. See also Rosen's several extended

discussions of the nature of the absolute in terms of subject-object, beginning p. 42 where the absolute is described as "the formation process of subjects and objects." Pp. 47–63 contain the main discussion of subject-object. See also his account of this problem as it existed historically from the Greeks through Schelling, pp. 50–63. Monika Leske [316] represents the view which reifies Hegel's absolute and misses the subject-object dimension in its dynamic, constitutive presence. See especially the discussion of totality, p. 327.

Hager [179] traces the problem of subject-object through Kant, Fichte, and Schelling to Hegel, pp. 162–285. His discussion of the *Phenomenology* begins on p. 219. Heinrichs [208], with his use of the category '*Erkennen*', is very helpful in understanding this absoluteness. Henri Niel [376] explicates this absolute idealism of subject-object in terms of the historical self-mediation of spirit with itself. See especially the discussion pp. 113–14. Sallis [429], pp. 133–40, analyses the complexity of subject-object. The discussion continues, pp. 140–43, on Hegel's view of the subject-predicate relation and how this relates to the subject-object.

See also Findlay [120] and his discussion of spirit, pp. 44–47, and Grégoire [168], especially pp. 262–63.

19 Hegel's claim that every philosophy is an idealism embraces, of course, more than just this problem of the unity of subject and object as we have it in the *Phenomenology* and the quest for certainty. See his discussion in *WdL*, 145–46; *SL*, 154–56.

20 A basic and most recent work on the question of 'destiny' is that of Dominique Janicaud [243] and will be discussed further below. Taylor [495] argues in the same direction I do when he claims that "*Moira* plays a big role in Greek thought precisely because men have not achieved universal consciousness, and cannot contain within their purview the whole sweep of necessity, which appears thus as something willed from outside" (175–76).

Pierre Bertrand [34] argues for the centrality of 'destiny' for the whole of the dialectic of the real. "The fact is that through action alone man creates reality as produced through his consciousness. All action being imperfection, it is necessary therefore for him to accept the imperfection. . . . Without imperfection, there is no salvation. The tragic is thus the proper atmosphere for all true action . . . " (178). Findlay [120] remarks in relation to Hegel's treatment of fate in the form of moira and nemesis that "Hegel has nothing to learn from modern psychology as to the inexorable, unreasoning, contradictory pressures of the 'Super-Ego'" (118). See also Hyppolite [238], 352–64, and Pietercil [388], 309–10.

21 The striking thing about the Greek spirit, if I am right here in interpreting Hegel, is that there is a unity of silence and comprehension which transcends mere intuition and articulates itself. See the discussion of Pietercil [388], who calls this the "primitive experience of the tragic: not primarily the encounter with an outside obstacle, with an obvious and insurmountable resistance, nor the expiation of a specific wrongdoing, but rather an interior collapse, a fracture deep within, beyond the reach of words, whose unfathomable depths can be measured only by an enigmatic and despairing numinosity" (296). This view explicitly addresses the dynamics of action within the substance which of itself generates moira and nemesis. Moira is no transcendent god or power in any

simple way. This theme is taken up and explicated by Crites [87] by means of a discussion of time as the existence of the concept and the relation of that concept qua time to fate. "Insofar as the meaning of temporal events is not comprehended, time is encountered as fate. Fate is the brute succession of events as such. But events are not merely inflicted on men by the movements of insensible objects. They transpire among men. That is, fate is 'the necessity of the Spirit' itself, an inexorable procession within its own life. Fate, in other words, is *historical* time, the temporality of human intention" (28). I do hold that in some sense there is comprehension by the Greeks insofar as they are able to objectify the human condition in their poetry. But I agree with Crites that this grasp is not that of the absolute subject-object, but only of an objective subject-object. For a thorough discussion of ineffability, see Janicaud [243], pp. 160–61, 237–39.

22 It is important for the process of the *Phenomenology* that there is a critique of itself immanent to Greek spirit and to all stages of spirit, and that the philosophical "we" is no longer called upon to perform or to initiate the task of critique. My argument is, simply, that the objectification in the plays makes them conscious of their own condition and lack. This is often not taken properly. For example, for Royce [426] the Greeks as portrayed by Hegel through the plays are there in "an ideal commonwealth." This "ideal commonwealth lives through an unconsciousness as to what its own inner doubleness of loyalty means" (203). I am trying to defend the view that precisely the creation of the poetry makes them conscious of what it means.

Janicaud [243] has a very complex view of this, which is lacking in part because the project of the *Phenomenology* is not taken up as a guide to interpretation. Rather, he treats this whole thing as a political matter, and regrets that Hegel did not bring together the account in the *Phenomenology* and that contained in the lectures on the philosophy of history. So, once again here we have the question of the nature of historical dialectics in the *Phenomenology* and elsewhere. For Janicaud, "the dialectic of *Sittlichkeit* represents an authentic philosophical effort to grasp from the inside Greek man as *zoon politikon*, without isolating him from the ensemble of the processes of world history." For this reason, Janicaud does not see the immanent critique which is contained in the plays, although he does see a critique in Plato (161). But then see also his account of "art as religion," 199–228, and his discussion of Socrates, pp. 230ff., and the reflections on philosophy in Part III. Yet, when discussing finally the "cunning of destiny," Janicaud moves somewhat in the direction I think Hegel actually took. The distance from and the superiority over men and the gods on the part of moira is the mark of its "absolute exteriority," as well as a sign of "its force. Among all the epithets which qualify destiny one alone is positive and affirmative: that which designates its total power." All the rest are negative. "The Greek spirit is dominated by this absolute negative whose power it experiences and fears; but it can not know that this negative is its own, without losing all that which keeps it alive" (238). Janicaud here sees the "ruse" of destiny in a very complex manner.

23 Findlay [120] understands the critique in an almost opposite manner. "The primitive Ethical Substance therefore destroys itself dialectically through its own inherent conflicts, as by the forceful deeds and knot-cutting choices of strong-

minded individuals. Its authority passes to an order which will take more account of the individual's force and right" (118). For Findlay, it would appear, the individuals and not the hegemony of destiny and ineffability are involved. But, as I argue now, the latter must be the case, especially within the framework of the *Phenomenology* and its project of proving warranty for the claims of absolute idealism.

In contrast, see Heinrichs [208] who sees the success and failure in much the same way as I do, but putting this in terms taken from his understanding of the *Phenomenology* in relation to the Jena *Logic* and *Metaphysics*. He points to the "contradiction of the immediacy of being and the immediacy of reflection which, as latent, constituted the life of the ethical spirit. The identity is completed in the explicit equipositing of both sides, which marks the essence of determining reflection. This means: every immediate determinateness of being is now posited at the same time as determinateness of reflection" (305).

Hyppolite [238] nicely captures the complexity of the success and failure of the Greek spirit. "That . . . an actuality exists, precisely as an alien term, depends on the very fact of acting and is a result of it" (360). Hyppolite then goes on to point out that the content, but not the structure, of human action in historical conditions has changed since the move from reason (359–60). "Although the community can maintain itself only by repressing the spirit of specificity, it simultaneously calls on it as the mainstay of the whole. . . . The fate of the city depends on the very principle that it represses, which is why the ethical order dissolves. Human and divine law lose their individuality in the unity of substance. Substance itself, detached from naturalness, becomes negative and simply destiny, but, simultaneously, the self becomes actually real" (363–64).

The question of the positive aspect which allows us now to go on to the next form of spirit is a difficult question. Taylor [495] for example, finds the breakdown of Greek spirit and the transition to the Roman world "left rather vague in this chapter" (176). The problem is centered on the nature of historical dialectics in the *Phenomenology of Spirit* (as compared with historical dialectics in the philosophy of history or the history of philosophy). See in this regard the discussion of Lauer [305], where he argues that "Hegel is out to give a dialectical not an historical account of the stages of consciousness and of their relationship to each other" (187). When we come to spirit in its concrete historical forms, the problem of the connections is not quite as simple as Lauer would have it. See further my discussion of this, *infra*, p. 278.

24 However, to call human beings "vehicles" of *Geist*, as Taylor [495] does in various places in his discussion of spirit on pp. 76–124, is not good enough; for this puts them in too subordinate a position. In the end Taylor reifies spirit in a way that is unacceptable. Compare his talk of things in the world as "an emanation from *Geist*" (97). Although he modifies his talk of emanation in recognizing that unlike a true emanationist view, what emanates—the finite— "is a condition of the existence of infinite life" (102), he has still brought along too much from traditional views. For a good remedy to this, see the discussion of Westphal [528], 144–45, where he draws the distinction between transcendence in spirit and in traditional theism. It would be well also to refer here again to

the view of Cunningham [88], who deals with the nature of transcendence in Hegel as the transcendence of a "pure" subject into the immanence of a subject-object as intersubjective. See especially p. 627.

Litt [322], p. 312, shows through the notion of tradition that for Hegel the individual is *not only* a function of his relations to others, that relation constituting in concrete terms their common tradition, but as well that that relation is a function of the individuals. In a parallel manner, Findlay [120] has a discussion of the finite and the infinite which also explicates the complexity of the place of the concrete individual in spirit. See also Durán de Seade [113], and Lauer [305], p. 91.

25 The argument is that the ambiguity is concretely recognized in spirit itself. In a discussion of externalization and alienation, Dupré [112] claims that once consciousness knows itself as universal, as in spirit, alienation "occurs when *in spite of this knowledge* consciousness is unable to recognize itself in a particular form which it *knows* to be its own" (220). In the present case, there is added to this the complexity of the tragic dimension; for each knows and recognizes itself in its own form, which is true spirit, but also does not recognize itself in any purity because the other form (the divine or the human, respectively) is also present. This, as I have argued, is what generates the conception and recognition of Moira as a personification.

26 For a discussion of the material on Roman spirit as it appeared in Hegel's earlier works, see Hyppolite [305], 365–69. See also Labarrière [287], 124–28, where parallels with stoicism and skepticism are drawn; Janicaud [243], 237ff., who explores the way in which in Rome, the political takes the place of destiny; Lauer [305], 187–90; and Heinrichs [208], 305–10.

27 Lauer [305] notes that the "'legal status' of the Roman citizen is nearer to 'actual *self*-consciousness' than is the custom-bound status of the Sophoclean tragic figure" (190). On my view this is true because movement has occurred from the natural toward the "made" and thus toward the self-conscious in an explicit way. This movement contributes greatly to the introduction of *Bildung* later. Heinrichs [208] discusses the comparison with stoicism and skepticism in this section. See pp. 307–09. On the aspect of abstractness in the person and in the position of legality, see Hyppolite [238], 370–75.

28 On the failure of law as the absolute subject-object and thus of the Roman spirit, see Hyppolite [238], 371–72. Hyppolite explains that the law and its codification "culminated in a mechanical form of understanding. . . . There is indeed no mediation between the person I am in law and the contingent content that constitutes me in other respects" (372). Taylor [495] also notes the problem with such contingency. "Hence the person experiences, as the sceptical consciousness did, his total dependence on the contingent and mutable, his utter lack of integrity" (178). This must be seen, of course, in tension with the "universality" supposedly given by the law and, overall, in the context of the problematic of the *Phenomenology*. Heinrichs [208] repeats this same theme in logical terms when he writes that the "determination of reflection in the mode of identity could not produce an affirmative solution for the necessary mediation of individual and

universal in spirit. The original harmony of the 'true' or identical spirit must make way progressively for the latent contradiction . . . " (310). Becker [27], 119–20, on the other hand in effect denies that there is any problem here with the law.

Westphal [528] makes the point that the "truth" of the ethical world is a problem, not a solution, and in this way leads us on to explore spirit. "The form of recognition realized in legal personality is thus an intense form of the alienation Hegel seeks to overcome, by no means its solution. Yet this is presented as 'the truth of the ethical world'. Antiquity founders on the problem of the individual and society. Their relation swings violently from the extreme of immediacy to the extreme of reflection, from identity to difference, without being able to find the classical ideal, expressed by Aristotle as the mean, more profoundly by Hegel as the identity of identity and difference, of immediacy and reflection" (159). But it must also be noted here that philosophy, and hence Aristotle, could not be called upon by Hegel to represent spirit for the Greeks. Philosophy was not yet the prime bearer of spirit.

29 This is the case, not only because it happens structurally to fit this later form, but because, in a form which has been *aufgehoben* and thus is preserved in an altered manner, what constitutes the genesis of our substance is present in that substance. Hyppolite [238], 369–70, alludes to this further significance by pointing to the *Philosophy of Right*, a work which articulates our substance at that level of development. Lauer [305], 189–90, does not explicitly make the point about broader significance than merely a reference to the Romans; but what he does say about this abstractness lends itself easily to that wider context.

30 This transition will be discussed further. But see the analysis of Heinrichs [208] who contrasts the move from stoicism and skepticism to unhappy consciousness. Here, the latency of the contradiction, according to Heinrichs, becomes explicitly taken up into the form of society and thus of spirit.

Notes to Chapter VIII

1 This form of spirit, which Hegel calls "self-alienated," has attracted a fair amount of attention. Heinrichs [208], 310–56, uses the category of 'opposition' and its development as the key to the section on self-alienated spirit. Kojève [266], 108–44, claims that we deal here with "pseudo-masters and pseudo-slaves" who are in reality the bourgeoisie or Christian citizens (113). We are led to the Revolution where the pseudo-slaves gain recognition, but do not become masters; for after this there are no longer properly speaking any slaves or masters but the end of history. For Lukács [336] this spirit and its culture (*Bildung*) constitutes the rise of civil society, which is followed by an ideological crisis in the Enlightenment and then a world crisis in the French Revolution. All of this leads us, according to Lukács, only to Hegel's utopian dream of a Germany under the dominion of Napoleon, articulated in the section on morality. See Lukács' discussion of "objective spirit," 485–507. Rosen [421], 183–211, devotes a chapter to the problem of self-alienated spirit and focuses on the Enlightenment.

For other general views, see Becker [27], 120–27; Nicolai Hartmann [191], II, 348–55; Kroner [275], II, 390–92; Navickas [374], 221–40; Westphal [528], 160–73; Taylor [495], 178–88; Hyppolite [238], 376–464; Lauer [305], 190–215; and Findlay [120], 119–26.

2 In the term 'culture' or '*Bildung*' we have a technical term for Hegel, a term which is not to be identified with 'culture' as used by anthropologists. For its richness in meaning, see note 4, below. At the least, it is quite different from true spirit or *Sittlichkeit* in which, properly speaking, no culture in its present sense is to be found. On the difference from true spirit see Lauener [303], who characterizes it as the negation of true spirit. Heinrichs [208], 312, discusses this difference by showing how the present form of spirit as self-alienated and self-alienating culture arises out of the contradiction latent in the identity which characterized true spirit. In a more political vein, the difference according to Kojève [266] is simply that between pagan and Christian versions of master and slave, and Hegel's discussion is there to show us the overcoming of that distinction in both forms by Hegel. Stressing the epistemological dimension, Franco Chiereghin [71] holds that culture in general is "the most complete and perfect expression of the accomplishments of the understanding," which latter arises out of the individuality which itself arose from the loss of ancient unity (463). On the parallels with aspects of true spirit, however, see Labarrière [287], 130–31.

3 Alienation constitutes the complex internal structure of this particular form of concrete spirit and differs from alienation in other spheres of spirit. Gauvin [153] has a survey of this term which we discussed earlier in reference to other sections. The term 'alienation' in its various forms appears most frequently in the discussion of culture. See also his discussion of the relevance of this in relation to the concept of 'objectification'. Robinson [415], 22–26, has an explicit discussion of culture and alienation in the framework of the requisite objectification, and the way in which in order to be one with the substance one must give oneself up to the substance. Hyppolite [238], 385–91, has an extended analysis of this alienation in culture. He looks back to its emergence from true spirit, charac-

terizing culture itself as "the alienation of immediate self, which we have seen emerge from ethical substance and starting with which we must see the reconstitution of that substance ... " (377). See also his further discussion, p. 416. This reconstitution out of alienation is central to the whole movement of the modern period. Taylor [495] also articulates the meaning of alienation in the present context in a contrast with the "at-homeness" of Greek ethicality. "Alienation consists in this, that men no longer try to define themselves as pure thought, that they accept their identification with external social reality, and in this they are once more like the citizens of the city-state; but unlike these, they experience this social reality as other, they do not feel *bei sich* in it" (178). But as we shall see, there is also a way in which an ambiguity resides in this alienation, an ambiguity constituted by the purpose of objectification, namely to be at home in the world. Mitchell Franklin [141] has interesting historical commentary on alienation in *Bildung*. See especially pp. 32–33. See also Franklin [142]. He here traces this concept of 'alienation' forward to Weber and neo-Kantianism, and links it to bureaucracy and its undialectical nature. See especially pp. 97ff. Compare with these the highly political discussion of Kojève [266], 116–32, where he claims that the world of culture is a world of dissatisfaction, a world of vocal but ineffective intellectuals and ideologues (117). Becker [27] argues that "the concept of alienation has its philosophical origin in Hegel's dialectical-idealistic construction," in terms of which, through a "dissembling objectivity" it is again to re-establish its essence, which is identity" (121). But Hegel is not arguing for such an identity, only pointing out that an individual has concrete existence or "*wirkliches Dasein*" through this opposition of identity and difference. For a needed balance to this one-sided interpretation of Becker, see the remarks of Navickas [374] cited below in note 6.

4 We see here that spirit takes on, in its objective aspect, radically different forms. As for the Greeks it was their dramatic poetry and myths, and for the Romans it was law, for the modern Christian-European spirit it is culture itself and the various forms of collective life which grow out of it. The concept '*Bildung*' is itself complex, meaning for Hegel 'culture', 'enculturation', and 'education'. For a history of the concept see '*Bildung*' in *Historisches Wörterbuch der Philosophie* [216], Bd. I, 921–37. On the development of the idea in Hegel's early work, see Henry S. Harris [184], 19–21 and passim. Karlheinz Nusser [377] maintains that in discussing culture and self-alienated spirit "Hegel uses a simile from Schelling's philosophy of nature in order to explain the general structure of culture. As nature consists of the elements and is developed within them and into them, so also culture" with its elements (286). He also argues that, although there are major differences from the mode of alienation in master-slave, "at the same time there is present a positive similarity to the chapter on culture. In master-slave there occurs in relation to individuals—in the figure of the slave—what happens in the chapter on culture as the movement of a world: the objectification in the object as a necessary condition for coming-to-oneself" (282). Although this is true, as I have warned before the dissimilarities deriving from the radical difference between self-consciousness and spirit make the parallel only formal, and only to some extent. Nusser does not seem to me to pay enough attention

Notes to Chapter VIII 359

to this difference and will often, in his further discussion of the Revolution, make reference to master-slave.

On the complexity of '*Bildung*' as culture, enculturation, and the tension within spirit, see Lauer [305], 190–93, and his general discussion on culture. In the same vein, Wim van Dooren [102] discusses this concept under three meanings: 'enculturation', 'education', and 'culture'.

On the involvement of a negative dialectic and the reconstitution of unity, see Chiereghin [71], 463–65. For general discussions, see Hyppolite [238], 377–417; Koen Boey [50]; and Löwith [330].

5 While it is true that *Bildung* is constituted in estrangement, and thus in uncertainty, it is nevertheless the case that it is the embodiment of the praxical presuppositions which are concretely in force and not merely putative. In fact, it is precisely this that makes alienation what it is; for if there were mere external determination, then we would have not the alienation of culture, but a real external, transcendent fate. See the discussion of Hyppolite [238], 378ff. and 384–86. This determination of possible worlds through praxical presuppositions in culture is discussed in a different light by Udo Müllges [368]. The complexities of education, enculturation, culture and action are thoroughly discussed in terms of what Müllges calls "criterial horizons" (*Normenhorizonte*) which bring together a pre-givenness for the individual and an autonomy, but in such a way that we go beyond the notion of autonomy present in the Kantian notion of law-giving.

6 Navickas [374] focuses the ambiguity in terms of the problem of subjectivity which he traces in his work. "The equivocation is that 'culture' in the one sense means the 'development of individuality *qua* universal objective being', while in the other it is not edifying at all, for in conforming itself to cultural standards and rules, consciousness empties 'itself of its own self'. But with this new and deeper awareness of cultural conditions and their transforming influence the inward subject and the cultured subject break apart. Understood in this way the problem of alienation is traceable to the fundamental attitude of the culturally oriented subject. It is when this subject allows himself to be shaped by cultural factors and wants to promote them for the whole social order, and ceases to seek anchorage in his inward self that he begins to experience his truly dramatic predicamènt" (222–23).

On the explicitness of the ambiguity in culture, compare Labarrière [287]. "This world, as *spiritual* essence, is the interpenetration of being and individuality: its being-there is therefore at the same time the work of self-consciousness (of all self-consciousness) and a foreign reality, immediately presented, in which self-consciousness does not recognize itself. It is that which places a double movement on the self: not being able to remain within itself (where it is deprived of substance and of reality), it must definitively surrender to all alienation in that which is alien to it (*Entfremdung*), and win a reality by means of a veritable going-out from the self (*Entäusserung*). The ambiguity of these two imbricated movements give birth on the one hand to pure consciousness (= in giving oneself up to the alien world, consciousness disappears at the same time as the world), and on the other hand to actual, effective consciousness (= the conscious unity of essence and self)" (129). In spite of his claiming at one point that consciousness is not achieved in culture (pp. 389–90), Hyppolite [238] shows nicely how the ambiguity does emerge in the presuppositions of culture. See pp. 391–417. See also Wim van Dooren [102], pp. 164ff. for another account of the ambiguity and alienation constituting the relation of the individual to the society.

7 For a good discussion of this denial of the either-or, see Wim van Dooren [102]. In taking up the question of whether the individual or the substance is prior in *Bildung*, he responds that "there is no answer to such a question because what we have here is a parallel development in which each encompasses and develops the other" (165). Dooren also argues that this means that the individual is not engulfed by society or state, to which I would add that only those who consider atomistic individualism and its abstractions a tenable approach could reproach Hegel in this way. However, what is shown here is that neither the individual *in abstracto* nor the socio-economic or political structure *in abstracto* can be prior.

8 Most commentaries discuss this set of distinctions in a more or less adequate way. See for instance Kojève [266], 122–33, especially 129–33; Wim van Dooren [102], 165–67. Navickas [374], 224–30, thinks that Hegel has a valuable and original contribution in his discussion of the two spheres of civil society and state, and of the factors of wealth and power, but on the other hand criticizes Hegel for restricting himself and his account of the full scope of the cultural problem. True though this might be in terms of an anthropology or general political work, for the purposes of the *Phenomenology* it seems to me that the spheres and factors analysed in fact express the attempt to instantiate the absolute standpoint.

9 The rich dialectics here are quite obvious and provoke little disagreement. See, for example, Nusser [377], 286–88; Heinrichs [208], 319–23. However, Becker [27], 121, mistakes Hegel's intentions here, claiming that Hegel has a "curious theory of value judgments" which runs counter to the normal way in which we speak of good and bad. But it is curious only on the basis of Becker's own curious interpretation of Hegel. Wim van Dooren [102] argues that the choices between wealth and power and good and evil are only apparent (166). This is true only in the special sense that they are so inextricably intertwined that an exclusive choice is impossible. Finally, Hyppolite [238] 395–99, goes too far, as do others, in trying to draw a parallel between noble and base consciousness, on the one hand, and master and slave, respectively, on the other hand. The presuppositions of self-consciousness as the absolute standpoint, and of spirit as the absolute standpoint, are so different as to make an analogy very tenuous.

10 Hegel's notion of language, both in general and in respect to this section of the *Phenomenology* in particular, has come in for closer inspection recently. In my opinion one of the most important reconsiderations of the topic is to be found in Daniel Cook [79]. See especially pp. 79–90. "In the mere act of speaking out, language performs its function of enabling the individual ego to relate itself to its social world, by gaining the recognition and attention of others and thus transcending its own private existence. . . . Language represents the external embodiment (*Dasein*) of ego itself. Individual consciousness finds in the act of

speaking a way of adequately projecting itself into the world" (84–85). See also Cook [77] where the main theses of the later book are laid out, and my review of the book in Flay [135].

Bodhammer [47] offers another general view of language in Hegel according to which language is "a first, immediate and natural mode of appearance or existence for spirit" (239). In respect to culture in particular, see pp. 94ff., where language is discussed as "the immediate existence of spirit as a world" (95). See the review of Bodhammer's book by Simon [463], and the comments by Wim van Dooren [102]. There is also extended discussion of these matters in Liebrucks [320], V, pp. 206ff, on language as the existence of the "I," and on pp. 254ff.on language as the existence of spirit. Among others, see Hyppolite [238], who claims that language "gives the world of culture a spiritual being" (403) and who has an extended discussion pp. 402–17.

Heinrichs [208] also has a good discussion of language. "Language presents the existence of the I developed into universality for others. That the individual can avail himself of this universal medium, into which he objectifies himself and is alienated, this constitutes his intersubjective value and recognition. . . . Language is the existence of self-consciousness as a spiritual form and, conversely, the existence of spirit in egoistic [*selbsticsher*] form. Language is the 'middle' . . . between the individual selves as well as between each individual and the universal as a whole" (324). See further Heinrichs' careful analysis, pp. 324–32, of how this existence gets expressed throughout this whole section and how it corresponds to the "equipositing of identity and difference," which is precisely "the concept of disunion and inner strife [*Das Verhältnis . . . der Gleichsetzung von Identität und Unterschied—eben dies ist der Begriff der Zerrissenheit*]." Kuon Boey [51], 67–69, also discusses language in the perspective of the middle term of culture. See also Boey's discussion in Boey [50], where he argues that "speaking has an omnipresent role in the *Phenomenology of Spirit*" (283), and that in culture in particular "the existence of spirit shows itself wholly in the occurrence of language and speech" whereby the universality and the internal disunion of the "I" is manifested (284).

Heinz Hülsmann [229] discusses the phenomenon in the context of the theory of the sentence or proposition (*Satz*) in Hegel. "The sense of the sentence is contained in each of its moments. But more than that. The sentence contains in each moment both speaker and hearer and therefore social communication as its moment. It contains them in such a way that they are contained at the same time in the absolute movement of spirit as concept. . . . The sentence is the model of an absolute situation. But, of course, the concept of a model is not completely adequate, for sentence and actuality belong together" (79). Malcolm Clark [76] discusses language and the existence of spirit by linking it to the problem of "representation."

Another aspect of this rich language analysis is to be found in Werner Bahner [18], who has a discussion on the social origin and function of language. See also Paul Gamberoni [151] on linguistic structuring of the world. "If there is 'spirit in the world', there is also *eo ipso* 'spirit in language'. And conversely, for spirit, world is always already and only given immediately in linguistic structuring"

(318). Mitchell Franklin [141] offers an interesting commentary on the importance of language as the existence of spirit in respect to law and contract in modern and contemporary contexts. See also Franklin [142], pp. 84–85. Compare the discussions of Labarrière [290], especially pp. 218ff., and Lauener [303].

In this wealth of commentary, there are several negative notes. Löwith [330], with his theological interpretation of Hegel, finds language as the existence of spirit to be a problem since it is only for finite human spirit. This is a problem which does not exist on my interpretation. There seems to be some confusion in Ansgar Klein [260] when he claims on the one hand that language is "only the existence of spirit," and that that means that "language is not historically actual" (249). See his general discussion of language and culture, pp. 247–49. He also claims, in a way which I cannot understand, that "a people is objective *through*, but not *in* its language" (243). Becker [27], 121, argues that Hegel's theory of language is not to be taken seriously, but is only an unconvincing way out of a "calamity" in which he has placed himself due to his idealism; and Findlay [120], p. 121, finds Hegel's stress on language in the section on self-estranged spirit "curious."

11 On the return to "true spirit" in irony—irony and dialectic again in relation to each other—see the analysis of the "language of laceration" in Hyppolite [238], 410–17. Koen Boey [50] underscores the significance of irony and the recognition of vanity: "the gain and advantage of schismatic consciousness consists in the fact that one knows that one has lost all substance in relation to effective objectivity. It knows it as vain, idle, empty reality" (285–86), to which it must be added that this is the reality itself. See also Rosen's discussion of nihilism in connection with culture, in Rosen [421], 193–99. Westphal [528] paradoxically identifies the "cultured and their rebellion" with the proletariat, although he admits that this is off the mark. He even makes reference here to the French Revolution; but we are not yet at the discussion of the Revolution. See especially p. 165.

12 Compare Hyppolite [238], 415–16. "The sparkling language of wit is not merely the language of the tragicomic bohemian; it is the truth of the world of culture—a truth which the naive, nondialectical philosopher cannot understand" (415).

13 Navickas [374] shows well the movement which comes out of this ironic unity of actuality and total reflection. The individual, he writes, is led "to a deeper estrangement, because the inner self can posit himself only by breaking away from the cultivated self. There is for the spiritual subject a chasm into which he is forced to gaze. What is more, he gives up all concern about state power, all interest in economic resources, in order to concentrate on his dramatic predicament" (229–30). The emptiness of this position is also brought out by Nicolai Hartmann [191], II, 350, when he points out that this absolute is here without the aspect of action, i.e., it is "chatter". See also the other side of philosophy as the questioning of culture in Chiereghin [71].

14 For general accounts of faith and insight and their relationship to culture, see Kojève [266], 133–34; Hyppolite [238], 417–47; and Heinrichs [208], 333–50.

15 On the mutual misunderstanding of faith and insight, see Taylor [495], 184. Findlay [120] notes the common misunderstanding, but remarks that it "is, however, only a fact for *us*, the phenomenological reporters and observers: for the man of Insight and the man of Faith it is by no means obviously so" (123). This is, of course, true, but not very relevant at this point. At this stage in the *Phenomenology*, the for-us/for-itself distinction is not relevant when applied to individuals as such or as something separated from culture as the spiritual whole. The question is not whether or not it is visible to this or that individual, but whether or not spirit, in its progress through objective forms, recognizes it. Hegel's answer is that this is recognized in spirit as we have already seen, and that this constitutes the progress to the moral view of the world and the failure of the French Revolution as the absolute standpoint.

16 The point is that faith here in this form misunderstands the meaning of 'transcendence'. On this error, see Hyppolite [238], who writes that "[t]he defect of faith is that it presents itself as a beyond, as a content that is alien to self-consciousness; the truth of rationalism is that it asserts the absolute freedom of the spirit" (430). Becker [27], 122–23, misses this form of the misunderstanding, arguing that faith is mistaken because it does not comprehend that the whole matter of God is simply its own projection. But this is not Hegel's critique here; for he wishes to comprehend the position of faith itself from within the viewpoint of faith. Faith, he claims, defeats itself because of its pure appeal to transcendence in some absolute sense.

17 Rosen [421] articulates the common origin in the instability of culture: "Culture is intrinsically unstable: it leads to solipsism or nihilism on the one hand, and to political revolution on the other" (184). Lauer [305], 199–203, focuses on the origin in their respective views of vanity. See also Findlay [120], 122; Hyppolite [238], 422, 429–30; and Navickas [374], 231.

18 Dupré [112], 220–22, has a good discussion of the double alienation in culture. In this connection also see the discussion of Hyppolite [238], 420–21, concerning the way in which what we have in this section differs from unhappy consciousness as well as from stoical and skeptical consciousness. Koen Boey [50] discusses the double alienation issue in the context of the difference between pure and effective consciousness. See pp. 289–90, as well as his discussion of vanity, p. 290.

19 Hegel's notion of the trinity will be discussed in Chapter Ten. But see for the present Hyppolite [238], 419.

20 Hegel's discussion of the Enlightenment is in many ways the center of this whole section on self-alienated spirit. For an account of the development of Hegel's ideas on the Enlightenment, see Henry S. Harris [184]. Rosen [421] rightly recognizes Hegel's main approach to the Enlightenment as a matter of spiritual activity, and not one of politics. "The contemporary student emphasizes the role of the intellectuals in the Enlightenment as contributing to the emergence of modern liberalism and the democratic state. Hegel, on the contrary, studies the Enlightenment as a religious crisis in which reason repudiates faith through ignorance of its intrinsic identity with what it rejects. The political character of the Enlightenment . . . is not central for Hegel because . . . he sees the activity of

its intellectuals as the last form of spiritual disintegration. . . . Beyond this, however, the political solution of the crisis of nihilism is a *consequence* of spiritual activity, not a cause of that activity. The road to Napoleon is, properly speaking, neither political nor scientific (in the Enlightenment sense of the term), but ethical, cultural, or aesthetic" (183). To which one might add that the political solution shows itself as a failure and as well brings on a crisis in spirit.

In a different, but related vein, see the essay of Peter Christian Ludz [333] for a discussion of this section as "ideology-critique," and the critical discussion of Ludz's view by Kurt Lenk [311]. Nicolai Hartmann [191], II, characterizes the Enlightenment's place here as an account of a movement which "wished to be the great elevation and exaltation of reason, but was a great fiasco of reason" (351). He also then points out that, as such and for Hegel, "spirit on its way to the comprehension of itself also needed the Enlightenment as a constant ferment" (*Ibid*). See also Hyppolite [238], 426–52, where there is an extended discussion of the Enlightenment. He notes that pure insight "turned against faith comes to be called 'the Enlightenment': it is the light that dispels shadows" (425).

Dieter Jähnig [240] has an interesting essay on the Enlightenment and its relation to history and to the *Phenomenology*. He claims that "Hegel takes over the principle of autonomy," which in effect contains the claim that "science . . . has its ground in the moral-practical principle of autonomy." But Jähnig sees in the Enlightenment itself a false interpretation of this principle, corrected by Hegel. His view is that "the Enlightenment confuses authority with tradition, and autonomy with emancipation from the tradition. The self-misunderstanding of the Enlightenment is the view that science is the alternative and the opposite of history" (65). Jähnig is here writing mainly about Hegel's discussion of skepticism and release from authoritarianism as discussed in the Introduction, but it sheds light on the whole problem of culture and the Enlightenment in the present section. Jacques D'Hondt [99] has a critical assessment of Hegel's treatment of the Enlightenment. Becker [27], 123–25, claims that Hegel has a perverse view of the Enlightenment, especially when, because of his idealistic principles, he tries to argue for a common basis between himself and the Enlightenment.

See also Boeder [48], 170–71; Besse [35]; Eduardo Chitas [72]; Heinrichs [208], 337–50; Dubarle [108]; and Taylor [495], 179–84.

21 This view that they are essentially the same pure consciousness is the complement of the view, discussed above in the text and in note 17, that faith and insight have a common origin in the alienation of culture. Findlay [120] puts the point nicely when he writes that the "absolute unity which Religious Faith obscurely thinks, is the same as the absolute unity towards which Rationalistic Insight painstakingly seeks to arrive" (123).

22 See Dubarle [108], pp. 258ff. for a discussion of the struggle and the outcome of the struggle between faith and the Enlightenment, especially in respect to the philosophy of Kant. This will have an important bearing on our discussion in Chapter Nine of the nature of the Kantian God in respect to morality and happiness. Lauer [305] concludes that in the end faith "has the dialectical advantage; dissatisfaction is the key to dialectical advance. Enlightenment cannot attain to its own truth (content), because that is contained in the faith which

Enlightenment has unceremoniously rejected" (209). Given the stage at which we now find ourselves in the *Phenomenology*, what Lauer says of the dialectical advance is true of both the epistemic and the historical dialectic. See also Nicolai Hartmann [191], II, 352–53, who develops this section in terms of inner contradiction; Heinrichs [208], 340–42; and Hyppolite [238], 436–37.

23 Heinrichs [208], 343, discusses this empiricism in the context of the "emptiness" of the Deism of Enlightenment.

24 On the concept of 'matter' here, see Wim van Dooren [103]. But Dooren seems to miss the connection which the concept of 'utility' gives Hegel in respect to the French Revolution and what preceded it. Becker [27] misunderstands the identity of matter and deistic God, holding them to be dialectically related by Hegel as "pure being in and for itself" and "pure thinking," respectively, and holding their identity to be in the fact that each of the sides is "useful" to the other (125). On the identity, see Hyppolite [238], 447–50, and Findlay [120], 124.

25 What I call here 'reflective realism' in the Enlightenment, as opposed to 'naive realism', is in actuality the unity of realism and idealism. Becker [27] has hopelessly idealized the whole affair. See his discussion pp. 125–26. On the reconciliation of realism and idealism, see Wim van Dooren [103] and his discussion of Bloch and Liebrucks on this same topic. The naturalness of all things in this context is underscored by Charles Taylor [495]. "The Enlightenment represents the beginning of the end of alienation in that the realities towards which the piety of alienated consciousness is directed, and to which it tries to conform, are cut down to size. All external reality is objectified, deprived of spiritual significance and seen as a world of sensible material things spread out before a universal scientific consciousness" (179–80).

26 On the completeness of utilitarianism as a metaphysics and an ethics, see Boeder [48], 170–71. He also discusses its culmination in the French Revolution. Compare the contrasting discussion of Wim van Dooren [103], p. 87. See also Hyppolite [238], 445–46, who discusses utility as "the category"; Taylor [495], 181–82; and Besse [35].

27 Navickas [374], 231–37, has a long analysis of the situation existing between enlightenment and religion in which he captures the complexities of this overcoming of separation. Heinrichs [208], 349–50, has a good discussion of how this separation of reason from reality is overcome as well as the distinction present here between pure and actual consciousness. Compare the quite different view of Kojève [266], 108–10, who claims that we have here a discussion of a solipsistic, existential Christian and an individualistic, atheistic intellectual. The passivity and ineffectiveness of both lead to the Revolution and its activities, according to Kojève. See also the analysis of Nusser [377], pp. 288ff.

28 Given this primacy of the practical, there can be seen in modern culture generally and in philosophy in particular, at least as found in this particular movement of the Enlightenment, an ethical concern behind the epistemological and metaphysical. See note 26, above. Heinrichs [208] refers to this unity as "the utilitarian optimism," and notes its production of liberalism (344). Franklin [142] has a good discussion of the moral dimension of the "educational" sense of

'*Bildung*', linking it to the overcoming of alienation (63–65), and then follows this with a discussion of self-determination in a rational person (67). Compare also the discussion of the practical in Wim van Dooren [103], 87.

29 We see here, then, a unity of materialism and idealism, of realism and idealism, and of the true and the made. They are the backbone of the Enlightenment and the true historical form—i.e. the actual form—of total reflection in culture, in terms of theory as well as in terms of practice. These unities are the ground of absolute freedom as the absolute standpoint and thus this utilitarianism has in it the roots of the French Revolution. On the identity of materialism and idealism under utilitarianism, see Hyppolite [238], 447–50. On the other hand, Wim van Dooren [103] essentially denies a synthesis of materialism and idealism here, and argues for what he refers to as a synthesis of heaven and earth. Nusser [377] sees a concrete unity of realism and idealism in the Enlightenment and the French Revolution. "Hegel paints the movement of spirit in the form of the general will of Rousseau and the terror of Robespierre. The unity of this movement is the 'spirit of absolute freedom'. . . . The word 'spirit' is here to be understood as nothing other than . . . a real and ideal reflecting of a whole within itself, which strives for a wider, more encompassing unity" (191). See also the discussion of Rosen [421], 202–11, on the partial negation of nihilism through the Enlightenment. But then compare his discussion, pp. 280ff. on the overcoming of alienation.

On the move from utility to the French Revolution, see Findlay [120]. Findlay maintains that the movement from utility to absolute freedom and terror is tenuous. But he then procees to explain clearly just what the relation is which constitutes the movement, so I find it difficult to understand why it is to be considered so questionable. "The notion of Utility which appears to be no more than an objective relation of one thing to another obviously conceals an implicit relation to the self which sees all things. When this is brought out, the reduction of all things to Utility is the reduction of them all to the unfettered liberty, the pure self-consciousness of the subject" (125). Besse [35] argues that not only is everything useful to everything else in this stage, but that absolute freedom lies hidden in this instrumental conception of reality, a freedom declared in the French Revolution (356). On the other side of the argument Shklar [457] sees an opposition between the Revolution and utility, rather than the consummation I am arguing for. "The turn toward revolution begins when the idea of utility proves less stable than the Enlightenment had thought" (173). She does not connect the proffered unity of the general and particular will as I will. See *Ibid*., pp. 174ff. Yet, Shklar actually seems to be arguing shortly thereafter that the corrosion of utility comes with the Terror or the collapse of the Revolution (175–76). This latter view seems to me to be correct and will be discussed at the end of the present chapter. On this account, see also Nicolai Hartmann [191], II, 354, where he claims that the notion of usefulness becomes a dead idea. Becker [27] claims that, "without question such a deduction of the concept of freedom has nothing at all in common with the actual state of affairs we call human freedom" (126). But Hegel's whole claim to "at-homeness" in utilitarianism and in the concept of freedom seems to be placed in question here, and that notion of being at home in the world seems to me very much linked to what we call 'freedom'.

30 The topic of Hegel and the French Revolution has attracted many commentators. For an account of the development of Hegel's relationship to and ideas about the Revolution, see Henry S. Harris [184]. For well-reasoned arguments against the view that Hegel showed in his approach to the revolution that he was a reactionary, proto-fascist, etc., see Harris's arguments connecting Hegel's development with this question in Harris [185]. For a different view of Hegel's development and of his grasp of the Revolution, see Georg Mende [353].

Jean-Francois Suter [492] makes a comparison with Rousseau and Burke. Although the comparison is not made with a specific reference to what Hegel says in the *Phenomenology*, the analysis by Suter is interesting. He claims, for example, that Burke was simply anti-revolution, while Hegel was not: "Hegel elaborated a *philosophical theory* which bore in mind at the same time the possibility of the revolution and the necessity of maintaining the state. . . . The superiority of Hegel over Burke comes from Hegel's comprehending the positive significance of the revolution, in particular the necessity of re-thinking and of changing the law in order to adapt to social and economic evolution" (324). This may be right in other respects, but taken alone it is too economistic for the problem at the center of the *Phenomenology*. See also Suter's comments on this in Suter [493]. There is a quite different view of this relationship in René Ladreit de Lacharrière [294], a view which links Hegel's perspective on the Revolution to a hostility toward democracy and a view that a real people, acting concretely, presents us with "a frightening spectacle" (115–16). See his extended discussion of Hegel, pp. 114–75.

Joachim Ritter's influential essay, Ritter [413], presents a balanced view of Hegel's relation to the revolution, defending Hegel against Haym's attack and all subsequent accusations that Hegel was a reactionary. His account also deals with the end of history question and the question of the relation of Hegel and the Revolution to the Restoration. Ritter maintains that the Revolution was, for Hegel, the spirit of the time in its concreteness (pp. 43ff., 56–57), and "political restoration is . . . for Hegel the pure antithesis of revolution; without any relation to the historical principle of the present, the restoration pits the past against it, and thereby makes this itself an empty form wich historically has no real content left" (56). To accuse Hegel of a defense of such an abstraction as the Restoration, taken in a simple positive way, is to ignore the historical in Hegel. This defense of Hegel is combined with a careful assessment of the famous end of history thesis and of the relation between the Revolution, its negative outcome, and what followed it. Ritter argues, convincingly to me, that both the revolutionaries and the champions of restoration share the same view of the Revolution and of its marking the end of history and a break with the tradition. On this, see my remarks, below, note 34.

This matter also reveals, according to Ritter, something about Hegel's view of philosophy and its relation to this part of history. Philosophy, for Hegel, "*proves itself to be the settlement of the problem posed by the Revolution that the continuity of world history no longer stands and is broken for it as well as for its restorative opponents. What emerges with the new age and with the revolution is for both the end of former history; the future has no relation to tradition.*

Hegel's theory takes up the problem of this historical discontinuity. ... The romantic restorative dismissal of the new age and its revolution belongs together with the revolutionary emancipation from the historical tradition; they have the same foundation. Both have in common the conviction that 'the ethical world is Godless' . . . ; whereas for the revolutionary theory and its followers the present signifies the end of the old world and the liberation of man from what have become the 'unreal' powers of religion and metaphysics, from the other side this identically recognized end of the historical tradition appears as the elimination of divinity from the world, as the loss of the true, the holy, and the beautiful, as the downfall of the humanness of man himself. *The revolutionary negation of the past and the restorative negation of the present are therefore identical in their presupposition of the historical discontinuity of tradition and future, and this discontinuity thus becomes for Hegel the decisive problem of the age; it goes unresolved in all the tensions and antagonisms of the period.* He takes it up and settles it philosophically, thereby exposing his philosophy itself—almost out of necessity—to dual misinterpretation as a reduction of the religious substance to what is political and historical, and as a reactionary idealistic veiling of the revolutionary liberation of man from theological and metaphysical heaven" (61–62).

This view is opposed by Nusser [377]. Nusser argues that Hegel did not treat the Revolution as the "emancipative process of civil society," to which Hegel said, simply, "Yes." For Nusser, Hegel's response is a "serious No" (277–79). For more discussion of this point, see note 34. On the positive side, Nusser develops his account of Hegel's view of the Revolution by giving a central place to the problem of "master-slave," which latter he takes as the problem of the "presence and development of culture in the individual." There is another view, opposing Ritter, to be found in Jürgen Habermas [177]. Habermas claims to be "amplifying" Ritter's thesis. According to Habermas, "Hegel celebrates the revolution because he fears it; Hegel elevates the revolution to the primary principle of philosophy for the sake of a philosophy which is to overcome the revolution. Hegel's philosophy of revolution is his philosophy *as* the critique of revolution" (121).

More on the end of history question and the question of the new epoch which Hegel saw arising from the problematic of the French Revolution, will be found in Weil [523]. Weil argues that although philosophy can have no preview of the future, it can understand the "problematic, that of the present, this present which resolves and endeavors and which, in its attempt, projects itself into the future" (5). See also Hyppolite [238], 453–60, and Hyppolite [231]. In the latter Hyppolite discusses the "new epoch" character of the revolution and an interesting account of the reconstruction of modern history in the context of recollection. "The Revolution appeared as the prodigous effort of reason to realize itself on earth, to find itself again in its manifestation without this manifestation constituting an alienation of consciousness from itself" (345). Kojève [266] presents his analysis on pp. 141–44. His chief characterization is that the "French Revolution is the attempt to realize, on earth, the Christian ideal" (141).

See also Alfred Stern [486]; Ver Eecke [509]; and Georg Biedermann [38].

31 This connection between Enlightenment and utilitarianism, and the general

will and its connection with the French Revolution is crucial to an understanding of what is occuring here. See Besse [35] who discusses this in terms of Rousseau's opposition to utilitarianism *per se*, but characterizes the opposition as a "corrective" for the "rootlessness" of utilitarianism (360). Heinrichs [208], 350–54 has a good discussion of the relation between the general will and utilitarian theory. See also Taylor [495], 185–86; Irving L. Horowitz [226], especially pp. 14ff.

32 Navickas [374] focuses on this unity of uniqueness and usefulness in Hegel's account of utilitarianism: "No thinker has emphasized more than Hegel the fundamental distinction between the individual and the universal while at the same time asserting their mutual implication and complementarity" (239). Lauer [305] makes the point of this unity in an interesting way. "Consciousness has separated reality from itself and has then related it back to itself as 'useful'. . . . Self-consciousness has become selfishness—and more singular than ever. Even the suprasensible world is significant only as useful. . . . Man is free, not because he determines himself internally, but because he has determined everything else to be for himself. The 'truth' which the Enlightenment ('enlightened self-interest') will bring to self-consciousness is a freedom little better than that which skepticism achieved—with this difference: reality need no longer be negated; it can be used" (210–11). But one must add to this comparison with skepticism that there is another difference, namely that the Enlightenment is an actual form of spirit, while skepticism is only a form under the presupposition of self-consciousness. I think also that Lauer is a bit too heavy in his claim that there is no self-determination here. See the discussion of self-determination here in respect to Kant and the French Revolution in Jähnig [240], p. 68. See also Labarrière [287], 134–35, where this unity is discussed in terms of the unity of finite and infinite; Besse [35], p. 360; and Nusser [377], 291–93.

33 An understanding of the relationship between freedom and terror here is crucial. See, for example, Ritter [413] who argues that, on the one hand, Hegel's "passion for immediate participation and continuation [of and in the Revolution, which he had earlier] begins to recede from approximately 1795 on. The experience of the Terror belongs henceforth to the tableau of the revolution" (45). But, on the other hand, "neither the experience of the Terror nor the critical insight into the Revolution's inability to come to any positive and stable political solutions were able to turn Hegel into its opponent. For him, the positive mastery of the political problems that arose with it in history remained the task before which the age was unconditionally set" (46). See, by comparison, Danko Grlić [171]. He discusses the general problem of how the Revolution is a discontinuity with the past, but misses the positive significance of this. See especially p. 52. It is quite true, as Grlić says, that the "principle of individuality, of independence, separated from the principle of universality is the principle of the terror" (54), but this only brings out for Hegel the need and significance of the next stage or, rather, the developing stage of morality. This, and the whole reason for the occurrence of the absolute terror, is missed by Ladreit de Lacharrière [294] in his discussion of the Revolution and its thrust toward democracy, pp. 114–75. For other views of this relation, see Hyppolite [231]; and Heinrichs [208], p. 354.

34 This is the barest sketch of Hegel's critique of the Revolution, which I will now discuss more fully for the remainder of this chapter. The problem of understanding just what constituted the "failure" of the Revolution has already been discussed above, both in the text and in notes. What is important is that we see both the positive and the negative side of it. Nusser [377] clearly sees the positive side to the Revolution and its failure which carries us on to what follows in the *Phenomenology*. "The Revolution is the final phase of culture, and therefore of self-alienating spirit. The thinking of this step has its presupposition in usefulness; for on the basis of this principle the Enlightenment makes everything into a possession and satisfaction of its own and is actually consciousness. . . . At the same time this principle is its own resolution, it has taken up immediately alienation into itself and has transcended itself [*hebt sich auf*]" (291). This positive aspect takes further form in Nusser's arguments against Habermas' view of Hegel's view of the Revolution. "Contrary to all misunderstandings that Hegel binds the progress finally in philosophical reflection, Hegel has explicitly recognized that every advance—even the socio-political—is possible only under the presupposition of a society with division of labor and institutions which are existing and present. The assertion of Habermas that Hegel contradicts himself because he justifies the revolution and condemns the revolutionaries is to be corrected to read that Hegel saw that the historical-philosophical justification of the Revolution was possible in no other way than through the critique of the revolutionaries; for this critique produces the insight, after the thousand-year long split between state, society, and the individual which was there since the fall of Greek ethicality, that the negation of the concrete universal in the realm of the political *eo ipso* signifies destruction" (296). Thus, on this view of Nusser's Hegel's "No" to the Revolution is a denial which affirms the necessity of the particular, of compromises in politics, and of a rooting in the moral to which Hegel will now turn.

Whatever the merits of any aspect of this many-faceted discussion on the French Revolution by Habermas and others, in the context of the task of the *Phenomenology* the Revolution is without doubt a form of spirit which proved itself, in its failure concretely to instantiate the absolute standpoint, to lack in a determinate way just what it itself claimed itself to be, viz. the absolute standpoint.

Ritter [413], as we have seen above in note 30, holds that the Revolution, its critique, and the restoration belong together for Hegel. "For Hegel, the perennial driving on of the Revolution and the opposing restoration of the old belong together. The abstractness of the Revolution appears in their opposition. It is not two principles, two independent historical worlds, that stand anew opposed to one another after the Revolution. Rather, the restoration is itself the—essentially post-revolutionary—product of the Revolution. The restoration is founded upon the fact that the Revolution, in positing universal freedom in regard to man as man, simultaneously contains the contradiction of excluding from itself the historical substance of human existence and [at the same time] being its negation" (59–60). Compare my discussion, below in the text, of the failure, in principle, of the utilitarian principle.

Ver Eecke [509] follows Ritter in part, arguing that "the dream of a state without alienation for its citizens has shown itself to be impossible. . . . It is that the dream of a state without alienation requires a concept of man that neglects the principle of individuation" (563). Stern [486] stresses the abstractness of the French Revolution, and traces this abstractness to the philosophy of the understanding which governed the Enlightenment. However, he does not note the important part played by utilitarianism. Marcuse [338] holds that "Robespierre's deification of reason as the *Être suprême* is the counterpart to the glorification of reason in Hegel's system" (5). But this can be true only in a most limited way, as Hegel's critique of the Revolution shows. Taylor [495] has yet a different view, pointing to a struggle between the ideal of "radical participatory democracy" and the necessity that not "everything he lives can issue from his will, some things have to be accepted as given, and accepted with the same loyalty and identification as he would give to his own creations" (186). But with spirit in general we are already beyond such oppositions, so this does not characterize the Revolution in particular, but is a mark it shares with all forms of concrete historical spirit.

Suter [493], following out his socio-economic interpretation, claims that Hegel "does not criticize the French Revolution for having proclaimed the principles of freedom and equality, but only for having failed to put them into practice" (56). While Suter is correct that Hegel is not a reactionary, he misses the failure, *in principle* and not just in fact, of that revolution. See my further remarks on this below, note 37. Wildt [534] argues that the central principle of the Revolution, the concrete general will, is the principle of liberalism for Hegel, out of which comes "the constant alternation of government and opposition . . . but by no means universal suspicion and the reign of terror" (269). But everything in Hegel suggests that it does lead to the terror, and for reasons I will discuss in a moment. See also the view of Findlay [120], 125.

35 Royce [426] refers to the position of utilitarianism as described by Hegel here as "wisdom's last social word" (205). Compare the view of Rosen [421], 209–11 on the concept of utility as Hegel understood it. Richard H. S. Tur [502] also focuses on this in his discussion of the general will.

36 Westphal [528] has an interesting discussion of utilitarianism as the absolute standpoint. See p. 169 and his discussion of the link between epistemology and the history of spirit. For my interpretation, however, we are not suddenly returned to the topic of that link here, but have been focusing on it all along. See also Nusser [377] and his general discussion of the Revolution. "The model of actuality which belongs to the Enlightenment can, according to its own presuppositions, be first validated when all goods stand under its hegemony. This experiment is carried out with the French Revolution" (290).

37 Lauer [305] has a good discussion of Hegel's critique of the general will as a failure in principle and not just in some historical instantiation or other. He notes that "Rousseau's 'general will' has been pushed as far as it can go, and it has culminated in the pure abstraction of contentless knowing and willing. . . . The self-determination which is freedom has turned out to be determination without a self" (213). In a discussion of the move to morality from culture, he notes that "without the seriousness of moral consciousness, 'culture' turns out to be an empty game and the cultivated man an empty shell" (193). Both are

important aspects of the whole movement culminating in the French Revolution. For a slightly different perspective, see the discussion of the political in W. B. Gallie [150]. "For Hegel, every political achievement or value is a kind of self-fulfillment—a new achievement of a wholeness within which the individual subject realizes himself as rational; by contrast, the importance of adhering to abstract rules of equity—usually negative or prohibitive in character and applying to oneself (or one's own state) among others *irrespective of who these others may be*—simply does not figure in his scheme of things" (23). Heinrichs strikes yet a different, but equally important note, when he discusses Hegel's critique here as parallel to the necessity to move from contradiction, as Hegel had already understood it at Jena, to ground. See Heinrichs [208], 354–57. See also Heinrichs' discussion of Napoleon, *Ibid.*, pp. 356–57. Consult also Nusser's view in Nusser [377], 292–93.

38 Charles Taylor [495] also sees the problem of finitude and infinitude in conjunction with Hegel's discussion of the Enlightenment and utility theory—"we have a bad infinite" (181)—but thinks that the real problem is that neither before nor in conjunction with the notion of the general will in the French Revolution was there recognition of "a cosmic *Geist*" (182), or "significant reality outside man" (185). However, as I shall argue later, *Geist* never becomes such a transcendent as is suggested here by Taylor.

39 It is for this reason, namely that utilitarianism cannot deal with finitude and infinitude adequately, that Hegel's unity of civil society and the state is neither liberal nor reactionary, but unique. See the account of Hegel's rejection of utilitarianism in Horowitz [226] and Horowitz's view of Hegel's view of freedom. When Grlić [171] argues for the supremacy of the state in Hegel, he misses this most important point. See pp. 55–56 especially. Hook [221] also misconceives Hegel's relation to the principle of utility, arguing for Hegel's acceptance of it. According to Hook, Hegel accepted the "exaltation of the principle of utility, . . . provided we realize that what is useful is not necessarily the pleasurable, that there are long-time uses not always visible to the myopic eyes of the critic who wants quick results, that what appears useless to contemporary eyes may be the necessary condition for the health, virtue, and ultimate happiness of mankind" (43). But even with these "extensions," Hegel's rejection of utility in principle still holds. On the matter of the less "extended" conception of utilitarianism, see the account of Hegel's critique of hedonism and individualism as found in utilitarianism in Gottfried Stiehler [487].

40 Thus, at least from within the problem of the *Phenomenology*, the social and political is not ultimate, although as we saw earlier it is more fundamental for the problem of the *Phenomenology* than is the "epistemological." For further arguments that the social and political are not ultimate in Hegel, see Ritter [413], Appendix III, pp. 100–04. This general point is also argued by Nusser [377], 295–96, and by Rosen [421] pp. 183ff. As we saw above in note 20, what is central according to Rosen is the religious, cultural (in a general sense), and ethical. On the other hand, Grlić [171] argues that Hegel leads us here to statism, totalitarianism, and a place where we must fear not unleashed individuality, but the power which comes from the side of the law-givers themselves, from the power

of the "wholly rational state" (58). As much as this fear may be a reality for us today, it cannot be rooted in Hegel since the state remains derivative of the absolute standpoint from the perspective of the *Phenomenology*.

41 Thus, Hegel's materialism is still present here in the recognition of what comes positively from the attempt of spirit to ground itself in culture. Horowitz [226] sees a paradox emerge from this fact that Hegel gives materialism its due. On the one hand, Hegel realized that "what is important in the evolution of mankind is the concrete conditions of social life (especially in its institutional forms) which give substance to the quest for freedom." But, on the other hand, if "the essence of freedom is the identification of individual reason with universal reason, the true realm of freedom is pure thought. Far from yielding freedom as concrete activity, freedom once more assumed the classic contemplative pose" (9). Horowitz's problem here is that it is not "pure thought" but something else which stands together with the material. This will become clear when we deal in the next chapter with the community of conscientious actors. See also Nusser [377], p. 296, for a complex discussion of the place of materialism in Hegel's view.

Notes to Chapter IX

1 The historical connections for this section are clear for the most part, focusing on Kant and post-Kantian philosophy. Hyppolite [238], 467–90, makes clear the connection between this section and the last, observing that "Rousseau's *general will* becomes Kant's *pure will*; the world of the French Revolution becomes the moral world of German idealism—a transition to a creative subjectivity" (460). Taylor [495], 188–96, pursues the thesis that Kant and Fichte play a part here, but seen within a tension with expressivism. Moltke S. Gram [164] agrees with the focus on Kant, but convincingly argues for it as "a criticism of themes and ideas to be found in the literature of the German *Sturm und Drang* and early German Romanticism" (375). But Gram does not keep in focus the task of the *Phenomenology*. Krumpel [280] discusses Hegel's view of morality and ethicality with a view to showing how morality gives a ground for Marxist thought. Kojève [266], 145–54, characterizes our position here as having arrived "at the end of history" and at the time of the *Phenomenology* itself (145). While this is true, it does not mean what Kojève takes it to mean. This will be discussed further in the next chapter.

Heinrichs [208], 357–407, focuses on the structure of this section, using the category 'ground' as a guide to interpretation. It is, as with his other analogies, very useful, but limited in the way that all such analogies must be limited. See especially his discussion of 'ground', 359–63. Westphal [528], on the other hand, suggests a parallel with self-consciousness. See pp. 173–81.

There is a general discussion of morality in R. Vancourt [506]. This is mostly a discussion of the philosophy of spirit, but is of interest for the *Phenomenology* as well. Robinson [415] concentrates his efforts on this section on morality, but is useful in only a limited way because of the abstract way he approaches the section, i.e., taking up what is discussed here as if it were simply a matter of discussing morality and not an integral part of the quest for certainty. He even admits to a view "which deliberately downplays ... dialectical development" (3). See also the commentary of Emanuel Hirsch [215]. Hirsch thinks that, in the end, Hegel did not really understand the problem of morality and the ethical.

There are also accounts of this section in Becker [27], 127–32; Lauer [305], 213–29; Fackenheim [118], 58–67; Navickas [374], 241–57; Royce [426], 206–09; Findlay [120], 126–31; Labarrière [287], 136–43; Nicolai Hartmann [191], II, 355–58.

2 There is an interesting discussion of the relation of truth and freedom in H. S. Harris [182]. Harris distinguishes between what he calls moral and theoretical rationalism, and claims that Hegel is a moral rationalist, a view which clears up many of the traditionally imagined difficulties in Hegel. Harris claims that "whereas a theoretical rationalist holds that moral freedom is subservience to the rational order of things (which is thought of as already established) a moral rationalist is one who holds that the rational order is one that has to be established by action (which may or may not be moral—it is here that there is room for something resembling theodicy) but which is judged to be rational precisely because it subserves and promotes the development of moral freedom" (118).

Taylor [495] tends in the direction I suggest here concerning the relationship between freedom and truth, but it is difficult to determine just how far he is willing to go; for he claims that what "is on trial in these pages is the Kantian-Fichtean aspiration of radical moral autonomy in its extreme onesided form, where no concessions are made to the aspiration to unity with nature" (189). Compare my view also with that of Hyppolite [238], 467–68, where a different link to Kant is made. "The keystone of the Kantian system is freedom. . . . Self-consciousness is the autonomy of the moral subject which can desire nothing other than itself. 'To will oneself', as universal self: therein lies freedom and morality. Pure will which wills itself is being in general or every being. Kant's critique of classical ontology is designed to prepare for a new ontology, in which being is no longer anything more than the subject that poses itself, an act and not an inert substratum. *Being is freedom*" (468). The discussion of Heinrichs [208] also throws light on the matter; for ground is self-constituting for Hegel, and is precisely what gives us an adequate concept of freedom. For an opposing view, see Werner Marx [350], 99, where he argues that, to the contrary, for Hegel it is truth that makes us free.

3 It is, then, the failure caused by the heteronomy of the institutionalized general will which brings us to the present section and Kant. Robinson [415] misses this when he argues that Hegel is surely not a Kantian here. But the dialectics (which Robinson wants to ignore) make it necessary here to discuss the moral view of the world in a Kantian framework, and precisely because utilitarianism and the political instantiation of it have failed. The attack on heteronomy is the Kantian attack, and is made for Kantian reasons. Ironically, when Robinson continues his discussion, pp. 30ff., he brings up Kant, but is too much concerned with the merely historical to understand the historical in the context of the project of the *Phenomenology*.

An opposite sort of problem emerges in the discussion of Navickas [374] when he claims that, opposed "to the previous modes of spiritual consciousness, which, incidentally, hardly reflect any genuine spiritual content, stands moral consciousness" (241). I hope to have already shown that both the claim of opposition and the denial of spiritual content to the discussion of *Bildung* are wrong. Whatever its faults, heteronomy does not preclude spirituality.

4 On the moral view of the world as a form of knowledge which relates directly to what-is, see Blasche and Schwemmer [41]. In fact, the whole movement for the rehabilitation of practical philosophy, as represented in the volume of which the Blasche/Schwemmer essay forms a part, is of interest on this topic of knowledge and morality. See *Rehabilitierung der praktischen Philosophie* [405].

5 It is important to see that the dual thematizatiion is present here from the beginning. On this, see Ritter [412]. Ritter argues for the world-historical and objective significance of the reformation, and that it was not something which was only an individualizing, subjective, internal affair. In this move to morality, we have not only a discussion of Kant, but of the Reformation as well. The dual thematization is present in socially active, religiously grounded individuals who historically pursue the problem of certainty in the course of their lives.

6 Taylor [495] also focuses on this section as a pivot between objective and

absolute spirit. "In this section on morality, we are making this transition from the spirit of a people or society expressed in their laws and institutions . . . to absolute spirit. We are looking at views of the world in which the individual is—perhaps unwittingly—the vehicle of a larger self-consciousness" (188). The theme of the "larger self-consciousness" will not really enter into the matter, as I shall argue in the next chapter, and it may be a bit out of place to understand the relation between the individual and the complexus of the holy spirit on the model of the former being a vehicle for the latter. Another view is presented by Ahlers [6], especially p. 65. Ahlers's view is tied to that of Michael Theunissen's in Theunissen [497], and presents an interesting alternative to my view. At any rate, there is presented no break between objective, finite human existence and the divine.

7 The significance of Kant here is obvious, and further views will be noted in notes below. See Adrien Peperzak [384] for a good account of Hegel's development. One of the best critiques of Hegel's treatment of Kant is by Reboul [403] in which he centers his discussion on the three postulates and claims that it is not true that Kant's moral theory rests on them; on the contrary, "Kant's moral theory precedes them and authorizes them" (89). Reboul turns to Kant's *Doctrine of Virtue* and argues that it is there that a foundation is given which is not culturally bound, but which "constitutes human nature" across all cultural variations (92). This argument may have some bearing on the critique of Kant given at the end of the section on reason, but it is not relevant here; for Kant is not here criticized by Hegel so much as carried to a proper conclusion in the account of actual conscience, conscientious action, and the basis for religion.

H. S. Harris [183] has an account of early writings in relation to Kant's practical reason: "Hegel's development is the story of how the Kantian *praktische Vernunft* is gradually assimilated to and absorbed in the Greek conception of reason [*phronēsis*] as the self-sufficient virtue" (64). See also the commentaries by Thomas Munson [371] and Warren E. Steinkraus [485]. Steinkraus also has a good critique of Walter Kaufmann's interpretation of Hegel's treatment of Christianity as "vitriolic"—pure hyperbole, stemming supposedly from Hegel's regret that concrete community had vanished from Christianity in his own day.

See also Hofmeister [218] where, although dealing mostly with the accounts in the *Philosophy of Right*, there is light thrown on the meaning of *Moralität* in the *Phenomenology*; Odo Marquard [340]; Fackenheim [118], 58–67; Lauer [305], 213–21; Becker [208], 127–29; Taylor [495], pp. 189ff.; Heinrichs [208], pp. 368ff.; Robert Brandom [54]; Werkmeister [525]; Roland Pelzer [383]; Findlay [120], 126–31.

8 On the comparison with *Sittlichkeit* see Hofmeister [218], pp. 142ff. Hofmeister has a good discussion of the significance of Kant's moral theory in relation to Aristotle and the ancients, and of Hegel's attempt to come back to the concreteness of ethical life without destroying the focus on the individual and freedom which Kant introduced. Hyppolite [238] has a recurring discussion of this relationship. See especially p. 469, but also *passim* in this section on morality. Ritter [411] deals mostly with the distinction in the *Philosophy of Right*, but as usual is helpful in connection with the *Phenomenology*. There is also an interesting

discussion of *Moralität* and *Sittlichkeit*, but from a rather different point of view, in Birchell [40].

9 On the differences with *Bildung*, in addition to those already cited in the last chapter, see Besse [35]. But too much cannot be made of this difference. Robinson [415] writes that the "emergence of morality has been the passage from the substantial spirit of ethical life to spirit which is subject, spirit which knows itself as the centre of its world and is certain of its grasp upon its spiritual characteristics, a spirit which as doer creates its own history" (29). But this misses the negativity which has given rise to morality in terms of the quest for certainty. It is not enough to say merely, as Robinson does, that the "willing becomes interior, for there is nothing left in the external world to which it could attach itself, and it therefore wills that freedom which is its own true nature" (29). We in fact now understand how we have a knowing, active contact with the world and its activities, and are far from such an abstraction as Robinson describes.

10 Not much is written on the relationship between interest in the form we now have it and the earlier forms of interest (intentionality, desire, purpose, and earlier forms of reflection). But see Theunissen [497], especially pp. 429–30, and the various essays found in *Rehabilitierung der praktischen Philosophie* [405].

11 On the nature of these tensions between 'is' and 'ought' see Fackenheim [118], 64–65. Brandom [54] uses an analogy with linguistic usage and behavior to argue for the resolution of the tensions between the 'is' and the 'ought' or, in his terms, determinism and freedom. Heinrichs [208], pp. 374ff. works out the tensions by means of a discussion of the three forms of ground: formal ground, real ground, and completed ground. Taylor [495] refers to the oppositions as a "very unGreek dichotomy which offended the young Hegel ... " (189–90). Birchell [40] gives a good account of the tensions, but comes to a very different conclusion than does Hegel concerning the resolution of the problem.

12 Lauer [305] incorporates into his discussion of the paradox of morality an articulation of the nature of the dialectics of experience. "In the Hegelian dialectic, where contradiction is inescapable, the contradictory terms become 'moments' essentially related to each other and to be synthesized at a higher level. Thus, in the dialectical movement of moral consciousness, 'duty' (*Pflicht*) and 'actuality' (*Wirklichkeit*) are 'moments', indissolubly linked to each other, dependent on each other, engendering contradictions whose resolution will be meaningful only in a higher form of consciousness embracing both duty and its accomplishment" (218). Compare to this Robinson [415], 51–97, who has an extended treatment of the paradox of morality, but takes hypocrisy in a very strong sense, i.e., in a sense bordering on deliberate dissimulation. But this destroys the power of the paradox.

Becker [27] discusses in some detail this paradox of morality, pp. 128–30. But he criticizes Hegel for just that which makes the paradoxes so important: Hegel retains contradiction and paradox in actualized conscientious action. Becker argues that Hegel correctly criticizes Kant and correctly sees the basis of Kant's problem in the latter's view of self-consciousness. Becker then argues that Hegel is not prepared "to draw the correct consequences from this: that the conception of a pure self-consciousness is simply and absolutely false. Rather Hegel again—

in following the principle of dialectical method—transforms this insight into the falsehood of such a representation in turn into a *positive* step of development for the 'absolute concept', 'which merely understands the other-being as such and its absolute opposite as it itself'" (129). It seems to me that Hegel is here in touch with reality, and has not simply forced some dialectical move on us.

See also Nicolai Hartmann [191], II, 355–56; Findlay [120], 127–28; Hyppolite [238], 472–90; Reboul [403], pp. 92ff.; Birchell [40], 411–13.

13 For an interesting discussion of the impossibility of reductionism either way, see Brandom [54]. Brandom argues on the basis of an analogy with language and linguistic usage.

14 On the unity of knowledge and praxis in morality and in moral actions, see Blasche and Schwemmer [41]. After discussing the procedure of Kant's moral philosophy and Hegel's critique of it as accepting without proof certain material norms, they then characterize the move here in the following way: the task is "to test for their justness the norms which are historically accepted and actually obeyed in our situation, i.e. the mores and customs and above all the moral institutions. . . . In this expansion of practical philosophy, in which knowledge concerning the justification of material norms is not to be declared situation-invariant, we see the decisive step beyond Kant" (466). In a different, but related way, it is here that the claim of Liebrucks [320], V, 329, that Hegel is not concerned for the possible as is Kant, but only for actual knowledge and its foundation, can be substantiated. In a very different direction see also the interesting attempt to link Hegel's discussion of the moral view of the world to evolutionary theory in David George Ritchie [410].

15 On conscience, see the article on *Gewissen*, in *Historisches Wörterbuch der Philosophie* [216], Bd. 3, 574–92. Heinrichs [208] has an interesting account of the move to conscience and the complexity of the issue as it is bounded by the paradox of morality. "Already . . . the timidity before the hypocrisy is itself the beginning of conscious moral hypocrisy in the sense of insincerity and dissimulation. For moral consciousness recognizes now its pretended autonomy, its claim to be exclusively the ground, as *conditioned* ('pregiven'): it therefore recognizes the ground as itself grounded, to be sure not by the conditioning other, but by the *unity* of itself with the other which is the true ground" (381). This then leads, as in the *Logic*, to the dialectic of mutual, reciprocal conditioning of all by all. Hyppolite [237], 67–70, has a discussion of conscience in which he describes conscientious actors as being "Jesuitic. We cannot help it. Jesuitism has something eternal, unavoidable by itself" (68), and this is the need both to act and to justify our actions. See also his extended discussion of conscience in Hyppolite [238], 491–528.

See also Michael Despland [96]; Falk Wagner [513]; Lauer [305], 221–29; Hirsch [215].

16 On this co-existence of acceptance and motivation to change, see Nicolai Hartmann [191], II, 356. Hartmann points out that whatever else is involved in this assessment of the paradox of morality, for the purposes of the *Phenomenology* what is important is "that the moral consciousness itself seek a way out of the deadlock, and also finds it" in conscience (356). Lauer [305] puts the issue of

acceptance and conscientious action from the other side. "As Hegel sees it, Kantian morality *needs* a nature which is recalcitrant to it and yet *wants* nature to be in harmony with it" (220).

17 The importance and legitimacy of the retention of contradiction and paradox in the "resolution" to the paradoxes cannot be overstressed and will be discussed further below. Anselm K. Min [364] puts the matter succinctly. "Hegel's task . . . is this: to heal the split *within* both reality and consciousness as well as *between* reality and consciousness as such, and at the same time to locate the necessity, the foundation of religion in the very structural exigency of reality and consciousness" (84–85). I would only add to this that this is what we experience here in our quest for certainty as we observe that quest in the natural attitude. It is not predetermined that religion should be founded, but only that it in fact is. Min then further expands this when he writes that the task is "to conceive the nature of the dialectical movement of subject and object in such a way that it breaks the bounds of individual consciousness *qua* individual without, however, destroying the *unity* of that consciousness within which the movement takes place" (89). This proviso is most important. See also the five conditions which must be fulfilled in order to accomplish this task of preserving contradiction and tension while transcending it in its bare form, pp. 89–93. Heinrichs [305], 381–87, also preserves the real sense of contradiction and paradox through his discussion of the contradictions found in the relationship between conditionedness and unconditionedness.

Fackenheim [118], 65, seems to be arguing just the opposite, if I understand him rightly. I would argue that if one does flee from the discord, then knowledge becomes impossible and the task of the quest must be abandoned—a consequence far from Hegel's intentions.

18 This connection between *Gewissen* and *Gewissheit* is missed by Robinson [415]. Robinson notes, but with little effect on his exposition of Hegel, that "Hegel's discussion of conscience is interwoven with his account of the development of the self towards absolute knowledge; this gives a kind of momentum to his treatment which is often very compelling but may at times leave his reader somewhat breathless from his effort to keep up or create the suspicion that the delicate fabric of experience is being ironed into particular patterns for ulterior motives" (113). I have already commented above, in note 1, that Robinson has divorced his discussion of morality from the context of the *Phenomenology*. Because of this, he does not see the naturalness of the discussion of knowledge at this point. There are no "ulterior" motives, only the interior motive of the *Phenomenology* itself. But see Cook [79] for an excellent discussion of the unity of sense-certainty and self-certainty. "The language of conscience (*Gewissen*) is the language of consciousness certain (*gewiss*) of itself" (93). See also Hyppolite [238], where he argues that in "self-certain spirit" we find "what the whole *Phenomenology* was looking for: the identity of knowledge and the object of knowledge" (467–68). Andler [11] has an excellent discussion of knowledge here, pp. 319–20. It is here that the remark of Pippin [390], that "consciousness must become self-conscious or face absurdity *on its own terms* (or *for-itself*)" (309) finds its final mark. See also Min [364]. It is at such a place as this, with the

unity of knowledge and action, that the critique of V. F. Asmus and others, namely that Hegel's conception of knowledge does not involve praxis, is shown to be unfounded. See for example Asmus [13], 48.

19 Again, the unity of effectiveness and activity in *Wirklichkeit* cannot be overlooked as it often is. Hyppolite [238], 496–505, employs an interesting comparison with the work of Karl Jaspers in order to show the meaning of effective duty as we have it here and as it is to be distinguished from pure duty. Despland [96] does not make enough of the difference between pure and effective duty. He writes that conscientious certainty can be claimed in the sense that one is sincere, or has tried to read his duty (359). But this is not enough to warrant the claim, and that is precisely Hegel's point. By missing this point, Fackenheim [118], 65–66, blurs the difference between conscience and a simple moral view of the world. See also Lauer [305], 218–21, and the intriguing account of this difference in Anthony Wilden [533].

20 There is an excellent attempt in Ahlers [7] to show Hegel's philosophy as one which works toward the unity and not a philosophy which is "resigned to forego all attempts to change the world" (71). See especially the use to which he puts the concept of archeological eschatology. Heinrichs [208], 366–67, shows that the foundation for this unity of theory and practice was already laid in the opening discussion of the moral view of the world. See also the work of Manfred Riedel [407] and the essay "Hegel und Marx. Die Neubestimmung des Verhältnisses von Theorie und Praxis," in Riedel [408], especially pp. 14–15. Riedel's thesis on history is, I think, complementary to this present discussion of moral action.

The relation of theory and praxis here offers evidence against a common view such as that of Henri Lefèbvre [310] to the effect that Hegel has confounded action and the thought of action (31). Here they are surely not confounded, but rather unified. I think that it is also counter to the view of Lobkowicz [325]. Lobkowicz holds that for Hegel practice is for the sake of theory, i.e. that the task is to make reality conform to theory. But Lobkowicz himself realizes that this form of practice goes against the grain in Hegel. Thus, he then adds that when confronting a reality that does not conform to reason, we can either long for such a reality, or take another look and see how it already is rational. He holds that the latter is Hegel's suggestion: "a 'reconcilation' of man with the given world" (154). The whole thrust of the paradox of morality and the contradiction of acceptance and motivation to change is missed by Lobkowicz.

21 See the account of Labarrière [238], 142–43, of the unity of knowledge and effective action as the actualization of natural certainty which comes about in this transformation of the self. In contrast, see Gram [164]. Gram sees "an abrupt swerve in Hegel's argument" at this point, rather than the actualization of natural certainty (381). If Habermas [176] had included a discussion of the critique of Kant which has been given here in respect to *practical* knowledge, then he might have seen the unity of theory and practice. See his first chapter on Hegel.

22 See the discussion of Westphal [528], 176–79, concerning what he calls "the anarchic nature of conscience." Another aspect of the issue is reflected upon

by Lauer [305]: "We may admire someone for always following his conscience; we need not always admire what he does" (224). I think there is something stronger than this at issue, but what Westphal calls our attention to is certainly involved. Heinrichs [208] focuses on the arbitrariness of self-determination and how this relates to the relativism of conscience at this point. See also Hirsch [215], 522–24, for a discussion of Schlegel in relation to this relativism.

23 Language comes again to the fore. Cf. Cook [79], 91–94; Hyppolite [238], 507–12; Hirsch [215], 516–17. Werner Marx [347] is focusing on a more general problem, but throws light on language in conscience. See especially pp. 26ff. Here the thesis of Liebrucks [320] receives further justification in that in concrete conscientious action such as we have here, our existence clearly rests upon language and consciousness as they emerge in mutual recognition within community. Heinrichs [208], pp. 387ff., captures the flux of exchange when he identifies the "spoken word" as "the *coincidentia oppositorum*" in this context. Although there is too much intellectualism in his account of Hegel's theory of language as the *Dasein des Geistes*, see Angel Bankov [20], especially p. 205.

Robinson [415] takes the significance of language in a radically different way than I argue for here. See his discussion, 102–13, and especially his claim that the "dialectic of conscience has gradually developed from a concentration on action to an awareness of the self which speaks about its own conscientiousness. The emphasis is now less on what is to be done than on the assertion of moral integrity" (112). But this is to separate the language from the action, just the opposite of what has in fact happened.

24 What I refer to here as the thematization of the plurality of conscientious actors by one another is usually referred to more abstractly as the universalizing of the individual conscience. I think that the way I describe it is more accurate because it makes clear that the particular individual still remains concretely in place. See the discussion of Nicolai Hartmann [191], II, 357, where it is made clear that the reconciliation does not efface the opposition of individual to individual, but rather puts it at a level proper to reality and to our condition of finitude. There is a need to stress the importance of the recognition of finitude as the truth of conscience as universal.

25 On the identification of the act as a conscientious act, cf. Cook [79], 92.

26 The generation of community here is lost by Werner Becker. See Becker [27], 129–30. But see the view of Westphal [528]. "The mediating process by which community arises out of anarchic individualism, i.e., out of sheer individual conscience, is not that of political reform. It is most adequately described, on Hegel's view, in religious categories, confession and forgiveness" (178). See also Heinrichs [208]: "The true absolute unconditionedness is now reached *in the spirit of the community*" (389).

27 On what I call here "the paradox of evil," see Hyppolite [238], 519–21. "Consciousness of evil is . . . linked to the opposition between finitude in action and the element of mutual recognition between self-consciousnesses which is an immanent demand. I recognize the universal by stating my conviction to others, and I await *judgment*" (520). Charles Taylor [495] also has a good discussion of the paradox of evil, and calls it "the dilemma of purity" (194–95). See also Findlay [120], 129.

28 On this mutual recognition that the infinite is finitude as it emerges here, see Hyppolite [238]. "Absolute spirit is neither abstract infinite spirit which is opposed to finite spirit, nor finite spirit which persists in its finitude and always remains on this side of its other; it is the unity and the opposition of these two I's" (523). See also the discussion of Ahlers [6], especially the beginning, p. 65. There is much in agreement with me here, but we do disagree on whether this is to be interpreted "Christologically" or with a domination of the Holy Spirit. This matter will be further discussed in the next chapter. Cook [79], 91–94, seems to miss this move into community.

But real disagreement comes with a view such as that of Robinson [415]. There is a sort of one-sidedness to his analysis of this move. He argues that Hegel's theory of hypocrisy "is a theory which holds that self-awareness in the moral situation will reveal to the agent that the endeavor to define himself as a moral being has failed" (125). Although this is true as far as it goes, it is necessary to see further that there is a failure to ground certainty in morality, even when we have morality in the form of conscience. This causes Robinson to come close, but still miss the real significance of this move. He argues for a parallel of sorts with the failure of culture: the "Revolution ended in the empty, meaningless death of the Terror; morality has ended in the malicious affirmations of the hypocrite. But all is not lost, for out of the wreckage of the moral point of view the self has learned that in recognition of others as spiritual beings who share the same faults and yet have the same immediate awareness of self there is the possibility of a community based on the reality of spirit" (125). Instead of seeing continuity, Robinson is then led to see a separation between morality and religion.

29 This "word of reconcilation" is central and is the theme now until the end of this section. Peperzak [384] has an excellent account of the early drive toward this goal. The main issue is that tension is not removed, difference is not removed, but preserved. See Falk Wagner [513] for a basic insight into the matter. He argues that in reconciliation, one cannot lay aside "estrangement and contradiction"; rather "reconciliation presupposes as a condition of its possibility estrangement and separation; without alienation no man would have consciousness of reconcilation" (176). He argues that they presuppose each other, both in thought and in action. It is at this point—the point of reconciliation as recognition of finitude—that the best case could be made for Hegel's "irrationalism." But Richard Kroner [275], II, 393–94, who champions this view, has little to say about this extraordinary point of the *Phenomenology*. Compare also, in light of the present passage, the criticisms of Russew [427]. This account of mutual reconciliation presents a good case for the necessity of identifying reason with life and praxis and also the necessity of understanding Hegel's irrationalism as Kroner suggests.

Shklar [457] does not seem to see the full significance of this reconciliation. Yet she has in her account most of the factors which bring us to a fuller sense of knowledge and of the possibility of the move to absolute spirit. She writes that it "is when men fully understand that they are parts of a shared history that they come to see that the subjective 'I' is an incomplete self" (200). And, when the judging ego "finally utters its 'yes' the ego is at last one. That unity is the self-knowledge of the ego. It knows that the tension between conscience and action is permanent, that to be human is to be part of a universal whole, of mankind, but also to be individual and particular" (202). But to say, as Shklar does, that the "*Phenomenology* might well have ended here" (203) is to ignore the main function of the work, namely to give the absolute standpoint as warranted access to absolute truth. For this not only religion, but also philosophy is necessary, i.e., a complete and reflexive articulation of this human condition we have come to know at this point in the *Phenomenology*. Despland [96] fails in another way to see the positive moment which comes out here with recognized forgiveness, and this is why he argues that conscience fails. See also my remarks, above, note 20, concerning the view of Nicholas Lobkowicz.

30 There is rather widespread disagreement on the precise nature of the relation between the reconcilation and religion and the religious community. For another discussion, see Flay [137]. See also Ahlers [7], and Min [364].

Lauer [305] misses the community focus of evil and its forgiveness and thus the real transition to religion (228–29). It is not that religion "gets conscience out of the vacuum in which it floats into a real world where alone spiritual activity and the consciousness of it have meaning" (232), but rather that the community of conscientious actors opens that level of spirit which is religion and which reveals the center of religion. Lauer certainly recognizes this to some degree when he later argues that "the phenomenology of religious consciousness does not begin with an individual experience which only gradually becomes aware of its social implications. As Hegel sees it, religious experience is from the beginning a corporate experience, whether of human society as a whole at a given stage or of a segment of that society which is taken as paradigmatic of a stage in the overall development" (235). That corporateness of which Lauer speaks emerges for us, as well as for the participants, with the community formed by the mutual recognition of finitude and the commitment to conscience. Miller [363], 205–06, also seems to miss the communal nature of this movement. But he rightly notes that "insofar as this man is fully consciousness of the life he lives as *his own*, the structure of consciousness which emerges from the process of 'forgiveness' is more than religious. The new structure is rather that of philosophical self-consciousness or, in Hegel's terminology, 'absolute knowledge'" (204).

Hofmeister [218] concentrates the question of the realization of morality and freedom through conscience on Hegel's view of the relation of morality to the state as described in the *Philosophy of Right*. Insofar, he is right in finding a deficiency in Hegel's results from the perspective of an attempt to unify the finite and the infinite and to show the possibility of a perfected ethical life. But if one looks to the *Phenomenology* and its project, one sees, I think, a resolution to the problem presented in the moral view of the world. Hofmeister concludes that "Hegel's perfect ethical life therefore has to remain in a beyond as does Kant's 'perfect morality'" (158). But this is true only if we refuse the finite-infinite relation as Hegel presents it both here and in the *Logic*, and only if we ignore the continuation of the quest for certainty made possible by the phenomenon of conscience and reciprocal reconciliation. In a similar way, Fackenheim [118] is right about the inwardness of the religion which arises out of the conscientious action, but his historical orientation vis-à-vis the *Phenomenology* causes him to miss the significance for those of us who undertake the project of this work. It is not that "the *moral* self turns *religious*," (66) but that we who have traversed the *Phenomenology* now realize the foundation of all religiosity: our recognition of our finitude.

There is a radical break here posited by Lukács [336] when he comments on this section. He acknowledges that the move to religion is a move in the resolution to the conflict in the moral view of the world, but he considers this an insubstantial matter. After quoting the passage on reconciliation and on the appearance of God, he writes that "Hegel's general philosophical position has always been that the 'objective spirit' must be transcended by 'absolute spirit'. . . . But elsewhere he never fails to give a real description of the social contradictions that can only be resolved in this ultimate synthesis and supersession *before* proceeding to that 'reconciliation'. Here, however, the positive side, the social content of reconciliation, is left vacant and thought leaps *directly and without mediations* from the preparatory stages of social morality straight into the sphere of 'absolute spirit'" (504–05). Lukács concludes that the reconciliation is "wholly utopian." But it is precisely the social character that, for the purposes of the *Phenomenology*, Hegel has appealed to here, albeit on a level deeper than that of any given social formation. There are two other criticisms of Lukács which should be noted here. There is an extended critique in Rohrmoser [417], pp. 102ff. Rohrmoser argues later that religion "is the place of reconciliation, and in it is consummated the transformation of substance into subject" in such a way that "the individual is both preserved and transcended in religion" (113). There is also a critique in Ritter [412], where a case is made precisely for the social and political significance of morality and religion. Ritter cites the story that Hegel toasted, together, the storming of the Bastille and Luther's posting of his theses in Augsburg, and draws from it the important fact "that the connection between religious inner freedom and political freedom is essential for Hegel's philosophy. Almost of necessity, this connection must remain subject to the double contradiction that it does damage as much to the Christian, reformational freedom as to freedom's political and legal concept. Nevertheless, it has a fundamental and universal significance for Hegel: the inner religious and the political dimensions belong together in freedom; freedom loses its basis where they are opposed to and separated from one another" (184–85).

Navickas [374] misses the connection completely. Beginning from a view that "the impression one gets is that Hegel's transition from morality to religion is quite arbitrary and incredibly abrupt" (248), Navickas proceeds to demonstrate that this appearance is the reality. He does this by insisting on the solitude of conscience and sees the reconciliation as a giving up, rather than as a deepening, of conscience. He claims that "with this reciprocal recognition, which opens up a way to mutual approbation in moral matters, the disturbing condition of tension and mistrust falls away" (251). He adds that "the reciprocal recognition of each other as acting conscientiously must be suppressed and revoked once and for all" (253). But, if he is right, then we have here an abdication of dialectic.

Shklar [456] claims that there is no connection between morality and religion (615), but a gaping hole there. "This mutual forgiveness is not an act of Christian love. It is rather a return to the fraternity of those who know that because they are men nothing human is alien to them. The reconciliation of conscience and action, or of the self and the world, is not a religious phenomenon" (613). See also Shklar [457], 199–200.

31 Another way to put the theme here is to say that this communal reconciliation is the incipient form of absolute spirit, and its characteristics, however transformed, will not vanish in the absolute standpoint when that is reached. This does not mean, however, as Fackenheim [118] and others argue, that the *Phenomenology* "moves from beginning to end in the 'circle' of the free self-activity of the Notion," and that because of this, the *Phenomenology* "presupposes the 'science'—Hegelian logic—which explicates the Notion" (69). As I have argued from the beginning, the whole of the *Phenomenology* as well as the "subject-matter" it has been studying comes out of the natural quest for certainty in its confrontation with the philosophical quest for certainty.

If I am right here about the lasting effects of this insight into knowledge and knowing, and the abstractionist view of Hegel is wrong, then a very traditional view, presented by Kierkegaard and others, is also wrong and essentially indefensible. See the penetrating discussion by Perkins [386], where Perkins argues for the correctness of Kierkegaard's position: "the existential must be excluded from logic because the import of the existential results in an illusion of movement and causes logical contradiction. . . . A logical system is for Kierkegaard possible, but it must be free of the existential and contradiction. Logic for Kierkegaard is then coextensive with the principle of identity and is a tool of knowing in its purely formal characteristics. With the exclusion of existence and movement, contradiction is excluded. But with this exclusion the very effort of Hegel is rejected" (484). However, I am arguing now that precisely the situation we have just observed in the *Phenomenology* forms the basis for our entrance into the absolute standpoint. If this is the case, then any logic which is not connected with this standpoint at its very foundations in the existential and contradictory cannot be logic except in an empty, abstract, and inappropriately formal sense. If logic does not take up contradiction and preserve it, it is a past-time, a game, a fantasy. This same criticism, *mutatis mutandis*, would hold for the view of Grimmlinger [170], who holds that a move is grounded at this place in the *Phenomenology* which will eventuate in a move to absolute knowing which is absolutely pure and transcends every sense of experience. But see, for a like criticism, Heinrichs [208], 398–402.

Hegel's position is also misrepresented by Löwith [330], 292–93, who seems to import a Cartesian view and force it on Hegel in order to make the transition to religion without the tension. Löwith claims that at this point the correspondence of man and world needs God as common creator. The separation of human and divine is here thus revealed as in truth non-existent from the beginning, albeit not existent as a simple identity either. I shall argue below that only a clear view of the profound nature of the holy spirit can give us insight into Hegel at this point. Even Falk Wagner [513], in spite of his insight into the nature of reconciliation, interprets this relation between reconciliation and religion as a "reductionist" mistake committed by Hegel when he confuses the reconciliation of man to man with the reconciliation of man and God. He argues that here is only an abstract sense of 'reconciliation' in play here (182–87). But in the holy spirit, the completeness of the absolute standpoint as we shall discover it, there is no such difference.

32 See the account of W. L. La Croix [293]. La Croix describes what occurs in mutual recognition of evil and finitude with the phrase "the two subjects *actualize trans-particularity of spirit*" (112). But his analysis is in the context of trying to understand Hegel's view of evil in general, and not the way it plays a part in the context of the task of the *Phenomenology*.

33 Compare the discussion of the presupposition problem in Ahlers [6], 68.

34 Heinrichs [208] has an excellent discussion of this unity, basing it on Hegel's doctrine of the reciprocal grounding of what-is as both conditioning and conditioned. Applying this to the discussion of the word of reconciliation, he argues that the "*intersubjective reconciliation*, the reciprocal recognition, contains here a spiritual-historical and logical meaning . . . for which we have already been prepared through the earlier discussion of 'talk of the community concerning its spirit'. The long sought-after unity [*Ineinsetzung*] of essential universality and immediate individuality has been reached: the perceived other presents within his individuality at the same time the absolute unity of ground and condition, which however is warranted only in the recognition of him as such a unity which occurs through the other individuals . . . " (399). All conscientious individuals in such a community are both grounded and constitute together with others the ground.

Rosen [421] claims that the "battle of good and evil within the individual prevents him from fulfilling the transcendental or absolute significance of his individuality" (232–33). My present argument and what now follows is an attempt to show that it is precisely the opposite of this which occurs. Taylor [495] seems also to separate the particular and universal here in a way contrary to Hegel's meaning. In so doing, he seems to me to fail to cash in on the real value of his discussion of expressivism; for what we get is not what Taylor claims— the emergence of a "super-consciousness"—but through the present movement and this realization about our own striving for unity, the emergence of our unity with what-is. Taylor is ambiguous on this. At one point he claims that what has happened is that we have overcome the "gap not only between inclination and morality but also between man and God. The community of these consciences is the locus of God's life" (193). This is just what we have; for it is the meaning of the holy spirit in Hegel's interpretation. But Taylor also speaks of "the cosmic *Geist*" (197), and this seems to me to be some sort of Platonizing of Hegel. But see also Taylor's probing discussion of the particular and the universal (194–96).

35 This again stresses that the tension, difference, and contradiction are not removed, but only transformed. See my comments above, note 29, on Falk Wagner's view in Wagner [513]. Wagner has a discussion, pp. 176–77, which ends with the following summary. "The transcendence [*Aufhebung*] into the absolute does not mean that estrangement is laid aside. Rather estrangement remains as a moment of the absolute" (177). A very strong case for the retention of tension is also made by Min [364], 89–93. See also Hyppolite [238], where this recon-

ciliation is described as a sign of optimism, but with the paradox of evil remaining as the basis, albeit in modified form. Hyppolite clarifies this with a comparison with Leibniz. "Hegel's optimism is not that of Leibniz, for whom evil is only a partial point of view which disappears in the heart of the whole. Infinite spirit itself is not without finitude and negativity" (527–28). This difference with the modern tradition, and not only Leibniz, must kept in view. Royce [426] has a somewhat weaker version of this view of reconciliation: "it is not the consciousness of sin but the consciousness of the forgiveness of sin that brings us to the threshold of understanding why and how the true self needs to be expressed, i.e., through a process of the conscious overcoming of the defects of its own stages of embodiment, through a continual conquest over self-estrangements that are meanwhile inevitable, but never final" (209).

On the other side of the question of how to interpret this "transcendence," Kojève [266] argues for the removal of difference and the existence of a state of homogeneity or complete and final satisfaction. If his view were correct, it would mean that a claim was being made here that sin had disappeared along with finitude, and that a state of beatific vision remained. See the critique of Kojève by Rohrmoser [417], 102. Findlay [120], 130, also argues that in religious consciousness these oppositions and limits vanish. See also my remarks on Navickas [374], above in note 30.

36 The individual has thus been shown the absolute standpoint within himself, but only the standpoint; i.e., we must now work out the nature of this standpoint and then, in the *Logic*, come to know what-is from the absolute perspective of this standpoint. On the presence of the absolute standpoint within the individual, see Hyppolite [238], 328–29. Gustav Mueller [366] finds a profound existential significance in this entrance to the absolute standpoint. "The absolute spirit has shown itself already as ruthless critic of all moralisms and their deceptions. The absolute spirit is 'the infinite sorrow', which has chosen individual agents in religious, artictis, and philosophical forms of self-knowledge. It is rooted in the truth that there is no absolute wisdom in this world. Hegel's *Phenomenology* is the philosophy of a latent human-moral crisis which has become actual in the twentieth century" (22). I would disagree with Mueller here only in finding a more positive interpretation of the outcome. Compare the questions asked by Fackenheim [118], 67–73. I think my present interpretation gives a satisfactory answer to all of them.

If I am correct here, then the critique of Schrader-Klebert [443] will not hold as it is made there; for with the complexity of this *Aufhebung*, and the doctrine of the holy spirit which is central for Hegel, one does not have to "become God" in order to dwell in the pure domain of God. The difference is preserved in spite of the identity or, rather, the kind of identity we have here is just an identity within difference and a difference within identity. See *Ibid.*, 94–95.

Notes to Chapter X

1 The general topic of religion has long drawn attention, and in one sense must always be commented upon if one is looking at Hegel in any extended fashion. Among the general works on this section of the *Phenomenology* see Lauer [305], 230–55; Kojève [266], 196–267; Hyppolite [238], 529–70; Taylor [495], 197–213; Navickas [374], 258–74; Kroner [275], 404–14; Becker [27], 132–36; Labarrière [287], 145–83; Corbin [81]; Ahlers [6]; and Raymond Vancourt [505].

Ahlers [7] throws light on the move to religion. For the meaning of religion in and through Hegel's early development, cf. Henry S. Harris [184]. The topic is so central to the development, that it would be fruitless to select any particular sections of Harris' work. Albert Chapelle [70] examines the historical question from the other side, situating Hegel's thought in the history of Christianity as Hegel understood that history. See especially the long section in Vol. 1, "L'histoire chrétienne et l'heure de la pensée," 26–114. This account is interesting as a recapitulation of the whole of the *Phenomenology*, but also in that it underscores the importance of Christianity as Protestant Christianity. This is also in large part the theme of Findlay [120], 131–43. Findlay argues for the centrality of the section on religion, claiming that Hegel's "whole system may in fact be regarded as an attempt to see the Christian mysteries in everything whatever, every natural process, every form of human activity, and every logical transition. If this is the case, it is important to know what interpretation Hegel put upon these mysteries, and upon the whole religious frame of mind of which Christianity was for him the highest expression" (131). These remarks of Findlay's must be understood in the light also of his important contribution to Hegel studies in showing the errors of the traditional Anglo-American interpretations.

Heinrichs [208] in general argues that "this history of religion contains no completely new logical developments, but rather modifies the already traversed logic 'only' by means of fundamentally altered standpoint. This change of standpoint or perspective brings an unexpected or surprising turn to the work which one—at least from the phenomenological standpoint—must decidedly name as the turn which took place in the entrance into the chapter on spirit. . . . Hegel here develops a logic of appearance, which expresses in his own thought a novelty" (409). For a general, but influential view of Hegel from his early years through the late lectures on religion, see Löwith [329]. For a different view, see Lukács [336]. Lukács sees this section and the section on absolute knowledge as constituting the recapture of the ways in which, historically, humanity has attempted to grasp its essence. This is his "third level" of the *Phenomenology*. See especially pp. 507–33.

Language will again play an important role. Cf. Bodhammer [47], 197–218, where discussion is centered on the *Lectures on the Philosophy of Religion*; Cook [79]; and Kenneth L. Schmitz [439]. Schmitz speaks generally of a dialectical discourse which derives from Hegel, but in doing this throws interesting light on the relationship between language and religion in the *Phenomenology*.

Two further writings must be noted. William van Dooren [101] argues forcefully against a purely transcendent God in Hegel. Finally, Fackenheim [118] is in a sense as a whole the discussion of religion. Fackenheim has a central complaint about Hegel, which I shall try to show is wrong. He accuses Hegel of treating religion in general "*as it is already reenacted and transfigured by philosophic thought: [his writings] give no sustained description of religion from the representational—i.e., philosophically unreenacted and untransfigured—standpoint of religion itself*" (117–18). For me, this complaint is unwarranted; for the standpoint is in fact articulated in the presuppositions of the reflective, representational, and *subsequently* criticized from the viewpoint of philosophy as not adequate to the absolute standpoint in terms of form. But it seems clear to me that the presuppositions of the present section of the *Phenomenology* do show us the standpoint itself and thus show how the absolute is manifested in non-philosophic life.

2 Hyppolite [238] characterizes the difference on the basis of what he distills as the "essential problem in this dialectic of religion: the relation between finite consciousness, which portrays to itself the divine or the infinite spirit, and this infinite spirit itself" (533). See also Taylor [495], 198–99, especially on the distinction between the earlier section on "faith" and the present discussion of religion.

3 But this is not to say that the atheism thesis of Kojève and others is correct. Kojève's opposition of theism and atheism misses the whole point of spirit in Christianity as Hegel saw it and as it has been articulated in the *Phenomenology*. See especially Kojève's discussion in Kojève [266], 197–201, 235–39. But the reification thesis is a long-standing one.

Westphal [528] has an excellent critique of projectionist views, especially what he calls the "Durkheimian-Feuerbachian interpretation." See pp. 195ff. See also Georges Van Riet [508]. He argues that Hegel's view of God "does not mean that the idea we have of God is a subjective invention. Nor does it mean that we reach this idea by attributing to God the simple perfections that we find in the finite, and more particularly in man. . . . Man's truth is to be a moment of God, to live the life of God, to be free, to go beyond finitude. Man discovers this truth progressively, to the extent that he effectively achieves his freedom" (13). Along this line, Hyppolite [238], 525–27 argues for the ambiguity of Hegel's "romantic drive" to capture the infinite. The ambiguity puts Hegel between transcendence and immanence, i.e., in alienation. Min [364] 93–96, discusses the existential nature of Hegel's task and makes clear the unfairness of any accusation against Hegel on the matter of reification.

4 Hyppolite [238] puts the remaining problem of the difference between the representation and our actual life in terms of a resolution through "symbol." "Our life in the world and our religious consciousness are distinct; hence our religious consciousness is still imperfect and our life in the world is still without true reconciliation. Our religious consciousness is imperfect because it uses the world in which we live as a sign or a symbol of absolute spirit. It is through the intermediary of this object—which in religion no longer has the character of pure objectivity, of a negation of self-consciousness—that spirit portrays itself to itself. But this object, the actual spirit of history, is simultaneously treated as a *symbol*

Notes to Chapter X

(which does not respect its full rights), and grasped as being inadequate to what *it claims to represent*. We come back to the difference we started from, that between consciousness and self-consciousness. Spirit knows itself as spirit, but consciousness, by means of which spirit represents itself to itself as object, is inadequate to this absolute self-knowledge, and must move forward until this object has become the figure of spirit itself, knowing itself as spirit. This object, as world spirit, actual spirit, is not yet reconciled with its essence, infinite spirit" (538). Compare the view of Fackenheim [118], pp. 163ff. The treatment on this matter is thorough and penetrating.

5 It is therefore not clear that one can make the causal claim made by Kojève [266]. "Religious evolution is only a 'constitutive element' (*Moment*) of real, active historical evolution. And it is this *real* process, the infra-structure, which determines the particular forms of different religions" (218). Even though Kojève adds that "on the other hand, the people are constituted as a homogeneous unity only by the fact of having elaborated a *religion* common to all its members," (219), he is still arguing for the one-way causal relation. The complexity of synchrony/diachrony helps us avoid this mistake in interpreting Hegel.

Cf. Labarrière [287], 145–48, on the relation of diachrony and synchrony in respect to the difference between now and what has happened before in religion. "We pass from a horizontal account to a vertical account" (146). "Religion ... will manifest itself as self-consciousness vis-à-vis the four first sections comprehended together as consciousness of spirit" (148). Compare with this the statement of the "central problem" here as seen by Fackenheim [118]: the central problem is "[t]he problem of the relation between comprehensive system and radical openness ... " (22). Compare also Rolf Ahlers' analysis of the unity of theory and praxis tied to the notion of archeological eschatology as it is reflected at this point in the *Phenomenology*. See Ahlers [7], p. 85. Finally, one could also employ here the discussion of history in Avineri [14], where he argues that history "is ... not a meaningless calendar of senseless events but a hieroglyph of reason, and an adequate philosophical understanding has to look for the keys to its meaning" (65). Given our disagreement about the *Phenomenology*, it is likely that Avineri would reject the borrowing here, but I do find it interesting.

6 Kroner [275] articulates the unity of the two in terms of the "dialectic in the relation of the finite to the infinite [which] rules the history of religion. Finite spirit becomes more and more conscious of its identity with absolute spirit" (II, 403). See the careful and detailed reflections on the ordering of this history in Heinrichs [208], 410–60. Kojève [266] distinguishes it from a history of religion written by an historian, a distinction which is necessary here. "The historian describes a given religion as it appears to those who believe or believed in it. The phenomenologist only describes the *essential* character of this religion. That is to say: he tries to situate it in the totality of the evolution of religion, he wishes to indicate the *role* played by a given religion in this evolution. In other words, he wants to *comprehend* how and why the *general* result of this evolution is the result of an evolution which goes through such and such given steps" (238–39). As necessary as such a distinction is, this would seem to oversimplify the historian's task and surely ignore the place of this history in the task of the *Phenomenology*.

Compare the discussion of Labarrière [287], 148–61, and the discussion of Ahlers [7]. Ahlers again uses the notion of 'archeological eschatology'. "Hegel conceives philosophy as the retracing of its own path to determine in *history* where repression has been overcome, where truth has emerged, and where it has not." Hegel stresses "that the *subjective* spirit, being empowered by the reality of the objective spirit, must participate in the emancipatory historical process already begun. The historicity of the logic of spirit's self-movement is the movement of history itself; it is at the same time the unfolding of absolute spirit, and such an unfolding must be understood as not slighting or eliminating chance and arbitrary occurrence in history but, to the contrary, as empowering it" (88).

Findlay [120] remarks that "the states of mind called 'religious' *do* show some tendency to develop from a stage where they seem merely to be talking of facts comparable to the presence of rats in a barn or of cockroaches in the kitchen, to a stage where they express little beyond a wholly new way of viewing life and experience, and a way which has many of the distinction-overriding features of Hegel's 'Spirit' and 'Idea'" (132–33). In light of Findlay's other comments on religion, this seems a weak and undeserving account.

7 See Hyppolite [238], 544–57; Heinrichs [208]; Findlay [120], 133–35. Labarrière [287], 161–66, demonstrates the parallels with consciousness and self-consciousness, and concludes that in "the religions of nature, spirit . . . contemplates itself in the immediate unity of its self with the existence (being-there) which it invests with its presence" (166).

8 Labarrière [287], 166–74, concentrates on the obvious parallels with ethical substance. Findlay [120] downplays the power of this section by relativizing it as historicist. Noting that we are "living long after the age of Winckelmann, [and thus] will find in this pathos [of Greek religion] little beyond a pathetic fallacy. " He has also just characterized Hegel's view of the Greeks as one which shows us that the Greeks merely chose works of art "to be the vessels chosen by Spirit to enshrine its sorrow and body forth its pathos" (135). This would seem to miss again the progress here, and trivialize the importance of religion.

For accounts which are relatively orthodox in their view of this relatively unproblematic section of Hegel's account of religion, see Heinrichs [208], 433–43; William Fowkes [140]; Janicaud [243], 191–239; Kainz [247]; Hyppolite [238], 547–57; and Lauer [305], 238–44.

9 Findlay [120] has interesting comments on the various forms of art. But he thinks that after the discussion of statuary, architecture, and the cults, "Hegel might have made a wholly natural and easy transition to his Absolute or Revealed Religion . . . " (137). But this would violate the importance of tragedy and comedy, as well as that of the human body as an artwork.

10 Compare the account of comedy (as well as of tragedy) in Kojève [266], 253–55, who describes it simply as atheistic and bourgeois. Also, in Westphal [528] the importance of comedy is only partly recognized when he contrasts the "sacrilege of comedy" with the "miracle of incarnation."

Hyppolite [238] notes the special place of comedy, and sums it up in the following way. "The ethical world has lost its substance, has terminated its movement, and has been completely resolved into the *self certain of itself*. Henceforth it is this certainty which surges forth and which constitutes the essential content of comedy; it is happy consciousness, 'the return of everything universal into self-certainty'. ... The principle that expresses this joy can be stated as follows: 'Self is absolute essence', but this self must discover its inconsistency; when it claims to attain itself, it finds itself alienated from itself. By itself finite, it is *human all too human*. The truth of this absolute self-certainty is that it is the opposite of itself; it claims to be happy consciousness, but it must learn that it is unhappy consciousness, the consciousness for which 'God himself is dead'" (557). The connection between happy and unhappy consciousness here is also noted in the accounts of Heinrichs [208], 441–42, and Kroner [275], II, 410.

John Findlay's attitude toward comedy, noted above, note 9, is explained by him as a sort of religious duplication of the religious accomplishment of the cult. He argues in Findlay [120] that "in the comic form of literature, the individual claims his complete and absolute due: he silences the gnomic wisdom of the Chorus, liquidates the abstract forms of the Gods, and reveals himself, under all high masks and appearances, as the everyday, commonplace, vulgar man, at one with actor and audience alike. He performs, in short, in ironical fashion, the same liquidation of the transcendently divine that is more solemnly carried out in the sacrificial cult" (137).

11 For a view critical of Hegel's view of revelation and revealed religion, see Perkins [387], especially 138–44. I have already voiced my disagreement with Fackenheim [118] on the matter of Hegel's fairness to religion as it is in itself. Compare Fackenheim's account of Hegel's Christianity as it exists without philosophy (pp. 116–59), with Hegel's own account and my analysis of it.

Van Riet [508] offers an exposition of Hegel's view of the Christian religion via a comparison with Thomas, and makes a clear distinction between the God of philosophy and the God of religion in Hegel. There is an inestimable amount to be learned from the reading of Theunissen [497], especially concerning Theunissen's reflection on the unity of "archeology" and "eschatology" in Hegel. Although we obviously disagree on the place of the *Phenomenology* in Hegel's corpus (see p. 80), I am not sure in the end that the views are incompatible. To argue for the religious *nature* of Hegel's *oeuvre* is one thing, and I don't think I would disagree. But to admit that is not to deny the necessity for the function of the *Phenomenology* as I see it. For further discussion on this section, see Flay [137].

In general, see also Chapelle [70], vol. II; Bruaire [57]; Findlay [120], 139–43; Labarrière [287], 174–83; Hyppolite [238], 557–70; Heinrichs [208], 442–60; Lauer [305], 244–55; Rosen [421], 220–28; Westphal [528].

12 Taylor [495] views the special place of Christianity in terms of adequacy in a slightly different way. "These lower religions are distinguished ... from the higher in that they have to have recourse to symbolization. Ultimately God is presented to us in the community of finite spirits; there is no symbolization here, God is rather present and evident" (198).

13 The primacy of the Holy Spirit is crucial to an understanding of Hegel. Many commentators have shown this in different ways. Westphal [528] focuses on the importance of the Holy Spirit in a contrast with Hegel's earlier thought

and his education in the seminary. "Hegel's hostility towards orthodox Christianity has not lessened since the days just following his seminary education. The difference is that now he sees other possibilities in the Christian tradition. . . . These other possibilities lie in the fact that Christianity is not only a religion of the Father and Son, but also of Spirit. It teaches not only incarnation but also community" (192–93). And this community, for Westphal, is of course historical, like the historical incarnation of God in Jesus. This historical character, when properly understood, prevents Christianity from becoming a religion in which incarnation is true just of Jesus "rather than a universal truth about the relation of the human to the divine" (192). This theme of the relation between Christ and Spirit is also taken up by Hyppolite and Fackenheim, each in a different way. Hyppolite [238] writes: "This community is no longer Christ as a specific figure, but the Holy Ghost in which the Incarnation becomes eternal. The Christocentric point of view of the Bible tends to disappear to make place for this universal Christ which is the community" (568). See Hyppolite's whole discussion, *Ibid.*, 562–70. Fackenheim [118], 203–04 has a discussion of the nature of the trinity as it bridges the human and the divine. There is also an earlier discussion, pp. 143–49, in which he explains that "*Christian cult, then, is* one double *activity, uniting the Divine and the human, and the antinomy which lives in this uniting is of the Christian essence. The redemption begun in the Christ is completed in the Holy Spirit*" (146).

Cf. Martin Puder [398] for a view of the Holy Spirit as the unity of the static and the dynamic, and the power of God to surrender completely to "his other" without being in danger of his own destruction. On this, see especially p. 30. Puder also makes it very clear that Hegel's God is not the traditional God of the philosophers, "not the brittle, reserved [*spröde*] God of the ontological proof, whose function is exhausted in the guarantee that my thought yields knowledge" (31). The aspect of tension is also taken up by Taylor [495], 210–11, where he makes clear the necessity to transcend, qua central event, the person of Jesus Christ. "The whole movement then from Incarnation to Pentecost can be taken on one level as reflecting the necessary tension in the unity of God and man between his embodiment in particular beings and his continuing life beyond these beings" (210). Heinrichs [208] has an extended discussion of the self-consciousness of the congregation, 450–52. "Concerning the actuality of this last form of revealed religion, we need not waste many words: it is the German Protestantism of Kant's time, and therefore in Hegel's exposition that of moral spirit" (450), a link again to conscience. But one must also take care about ascribing any orthodoxy to Hegel's view; as he pushed Kant, he is also obviously pushing Protestantism. On the question of Christology, see Yerkes [540].

Two commentators combine an accurate view of this centrality of the Holy Spirit with criticisms of Hegel. Falk Wagner [513] offers a many-sided discussion of this. But, as I have already noted in the notes to Chapter IX, Wagner has both an excellent interpretation of the reconciliation at the basis of this community, but also a short-sighted criticism of Hegel as being reductionist in his lack of a distinction between reconciliation with other human beings and reconciliation with God. The doctrine of the Holy Spirit in fact forces on us an identity of the two reconciliations. On the other hand, Perkins [387], 135–37, notes the trinitarian, as opposed to the "Christocentric" locus of Hegel's views, and then claims that the individual, opposed to the community, has no place in Hegel's philosophy of religion. Although this is true, it can hardly be a criticism of Hegel unless one is able also to criticize what he has heretofore established about the true nature of the individual. Such an individual, opposed to community, has been shown to be an abstraction. Surely, *on any view* spirit—especially the Holy Spirit, even in the form of Christ—is not for the sake of such an abstract individual, but for the sake of concrete mankind. For further discussion of this and of the whole matter of the Holy Spirit as central, see Bodhammer [47], 214–15; Lauer [305], pp. 245ff. and [308], and my discussion of the latter in note 20, below; and Van Riet [508], 81–84.

14 It is in this sense that there is truth here in religion. Westphal [528], 193–94, is very clear on the point that religion *is* self-knowledge "which does not know itself to be that," and calls up a Freudian sense of "projection," duly modified, to explain what is going on here in religion. Hyppolite [238] puts the point proleptically by explaining that the knowledge which the religious community has "in the language of *representation* is the text of which Hegelian philosophy claims to be the authentic translation into the language of *concept*" (561). Compare the discussion of Heinrichs [208], 443–44, on the conditions for revelation which make this knowledge. Heinrichs points out that religion in the form of Christianity does not involve only the unmasking by the actors as in a Greek comedy, but the actual externalization of the divine become human. Heinrichs later sums up this point in the following way: "The faithful as members of the congregation—whose actual spirit is morality certain of itself—stand in fact already in themselves at the standpoint of speculative thinking" (458).

15 Compare Findlay [120] who, if I understand him rightly here, also points in the direction of such a distinction. "Theism in all its forms is an imaginative distortion of final truth. The God outside of us who saves us by His grace, is a misleading pictorial expression for saving forces *intrinsic* to self-conscious Spirit, wherever this may be present" (143). On community and truth, see also Hyppolite [238], who argues that "for the community the truth is not a content that is alien to it; the community is itself this truth, and this truth is its self-knowledge" (564).

16 Cf. the discussion of the "three syllogisms" which characterize the realm of the Father, the Son, and the Holy Spirit, in Heinrichs [208], 454–60.

17 However, if the function of the *Phenomenology* is not kept firmly in mind, this "disappearance" can be overstated. See, for instance, Willem van Dooren [101]. Compare also the view of Findlay [120], who writes that the "ultimate fate of all imaginative religious presentations is therefore to hand over their majesty and authority to self-conscious Spirit, that the latter may be all in all" (143).

See Lauer's account of the positive meaning of this disappearance in Lauer [305]. "Ultimately . . . Christian religious consciousness, in making God present to man, tells man a great deal about himself, but not all. It is all there in what it does tell him, but he is not aware of all that is there. He will not be aware of all that is there, of the diginity which is his as autonomous spirit, until he has plumbed conceptually the representations with which religious consciousness covers the divine Spirit present to it and in it" (254–55). See also Lauer's struggle with the general question of the relationship between religion, theology, and philosophy in Lauer [308], the chapter titled "Philosophy and Theology," and the earlier Lauer [304].

Westphal [528] makes an interesting comparison with Marx's view of "the withering away of the state." Westphal justifies this in part by arguing that "the self-transcendence of religion must in some sense be an historical fact and not simply a philosophical requirement or expectation" (212). From this he gathers that "one can speak here of the withering away of the religious point of view. For just as Marx sees the pre-revolutionary, bourgeois state to be incompatible with truly human society, thus requiring radical transformation in the transition to socialism, so Hegel sees in divine transcendence, traditionally conceived, the last and most strategic stronghold of the philosophy of finitude in human knowledge. Only a radical transformation of that point of view can make the world safe for Absolute Knowledge. . . . Hegel calls this withering away of the religious point of view the 'overcoming of the object of consciousness'" (212).

18 There are a variety of interpretations of this difficult move in the *Phenomenology* which contrast with my own, many of the differences being due to the difference in over-all interpretation of the *Phenomenology*. Grimmlinger [170], 297, sees an ultimate ambiguity in the move; but this is due, I think, mainly to his doubts about the meaning of 'absolute' in the *Phenomenology*. See my earlier remarks in note 18, Chapter VII above. Van Riet [508] claims that the philosophy-religion relation is analogous to the theology-religion relation. "Hegelian philosophy plays practically the same role in relation to the faith of believers that Christian tradition assigns to theology. Now no one dreams of saying that theology 'suppresses' faith; it is rather the expansion of it. In an analogous sense philosophy accomplishes Christianity according to Hegel" (85). There is also contained here a good critique of various Marxist criticisms of Hegel on the topic of religion. There is another critique of such interpretations, centering on that of Kojève, in Albert Chapelle [70], Vol. 1, in the section titled "La verité du christianisme," 149–78. Chapelle captures the problem of the move to philosophy in his own way by centering on the paradoxes concerning the absoluteness of revealed religion. He argues that "to think the truth of Christian consciousness is to affirm the absolute identity of its unique and incommunicable certitude with the truth which the universe communicates" (161). For Kojève's view see Kojève [266]. His view is that this is a move from theism to anthropotheism, or from theology to anthropology. See my remarks below in note 24, concerning this. The transcendence, supposedly there in theism and to which Kojève alludes in making his case, has of course already been "abolished" with the Christian doctrine of the Holy Spirit, thus taking the ground out from under Kojève's interpretation.

Kroner [275] holds that "absolute knowing brings in no alternative to belief or faith; it is a believing, devout knowing—a belief which knows itself, a will which judges itself, a life which thinks itself . . . " (II, 415). See also Fackenheim [118], 160–222; Ahlers [7]; and Miller [363].

19 There is a very deep analysis of absolute finitude and the historical character of the absolute in Ahlers [6] which throws light on this collapse. See especially his arguments, p. 74, on the necessity of finite being. Peter Cornehl [83] argues against this reconciliation. See especially pp. 160–62, "Die Zukunft der Versöhnung—zum Ansatz einer theologischen Hegelkritik." But what seems to me to be missing from Cornehl is the sense of the total significance of the Holy Spirit for Hegel.

Findlay [120] captures well the concreteness of this collapse, arguing that "what Hegel thinks important is not the *Incarnatio Filii Dei*, but the *belief* in such an incarnation: if this incarnation is said to be actual and not imaginary, its actuality is one *in* the believer, rather than in the historical person of Jesus" (139). See also the passage from Fackenheim [118], cited below in note 23.

20 One of the consequences of this is that the view, such as is represented by Ahlers [6], 76–78, must be tempered. There is a priority of absolute spirit to finite spirit, but this absolute spirit is on the order of the whole trinity, united in the Holy Spirit.

Hans Küng [284] has given one of the most penetrating analyses from a Roman Catholic position, concentrating both on the traditional Christology and on Hegel's effect on it. See especially pp. 268–77 on the relation between Christ and the Holy Spirit. "The incarnation of God in this One is only a beginning, can only be a beginning. The dialectical process cannot be arrested here. What became actual in this One must become universal actuality. Not only must the descent of God into the world be testified to, but certainty [of it] here and now. In the Christian religion what is at stake is not only the revelation of the conversion of substance into self-consciousness (historical incarnation), but also the conversion of self-consciousness into substance, and this happens in the self-consciousness of the *church*. It is the church as the community of spirit which has access to the truth of the incarnation of God. Even more: it is the church as the community of spirit which is the result of the incarnation of God. There can be, there must be a church, because the one Christ died and rose from the dead. Thus Hegel could say quite positively that the church is the surviving Christ" (268). This insight into the concreteness of Hegel and of the Holy Spirit for Hegel, does not stop Küng from his "critique," but, on the contrary, makes the latter's "Hegel in der Krisis" a reasonable approach, given Küng's problems with Christology.

Equally importantly, see Lauer [308], especially the chapters "God as Spirit," "The Question of Pantheism," and "Philosophy and Theology." At one point here Lauer brings the issue into sharpest focus: "God reveals himself *to* finite spirit; in a very real sense that is what we *mean* by 'revelation'. But, God also reveals himself *in* finite spirit; the preeminent revelation of God is the human spirit itself, whose essence is to be manifestation of the divine; other than as manifestation of the divine the human spirit essentially *is not*" (156). There is also an excellent formulation of this in Lauer [305]. "God and man are *not* one and the same *being*; they *are* one and the same process" (254). This is an excellent distinction which also clarifies Hegel's defense against accusations that he has simply humanized God and divinized man. See also Lauer [307].

21 Thus, both "subject" and "object" disappear in the form they exist in the

stance of representation. Miller [363] has an excellent account of the nature of the need for overcoming the form of religious consciousness. He argues that although through resurrection and communion God has become human and united himself with the human and then returned to himself as divine, and although through this act of God "man may come to know himself as God, as the whole process of simple unity, self-opposition, and self-conscious reunification," all the same, this is a gift from God and is "reflected by *the form* which Christian consciousness takes: it is a pure thinking of God, representative imagining of Christ, and feeling for the reunification of these opposites in the Resurrection . . . " (198). This amounts, according to Miller, to a contradiction: "subject as religious knower remains opposed to what, through religious knowledge, it knows itself to be. The union of God and man which is accomplished in the object of religious knowing is denied by the subject's mode of knowing" (198). Thus, the *form* must be overcome.

Thus, there must be a corrective, I think, to Findlay's version of this. In Findlay [120], discussing the "final reconciliation of consciousness with self-consciousness" in absolute knowing, he argues that this "reconciliation consists in the realization that every object of which we may be conscious is no more than an 'externalization', a presupposition of our thinking self-consciousness, and a consequent reabsorption of such externality into our subjective life" (144). But there is no subjective life if there is nothing objective in the traditional sense of an absolute separation of subject and object. This problem is reflected earlier in Findlay's pronouncement that the whole of the reflection on the Christian trinity "lives enshrined in the Cartesian *Cogito*" (141). Of all things, it can certainly not be the *Cartesian* subject. On this collapse, see also Westphal [528], pp. 193ff.

22 Hyppolite [238] explains that man, "as the field of . . . opposition [between good and evil] and to the extent he is for himself the consciousness of this contradiction, takes himself as evil and expels the good beyond himself. Thus he poses his *difference* from and his *equality* with God. Spirit knows itself in-itself as absolute, divine as essence, but for-itself as nonabsolute, as being-in-the-world" (566). Thus, action and knowing are in reciprocity. Labarrière [287] puts this reciprocity of action and reflection in another way, but links it to the nature of activity. "Revealed religion . . . is the reconciliation of the religion of nature and the religion of art, that is to say of the substantiality of spirit and of its activity as subject" (175).

23 For the most part, the "mystical" Hegel of earlier times (of interpretation) has pretty well disappeared. Both Findlay and Fackenheim, for example, show clearly the absence of this. Findlay [120] writes of this concreteness of spirit that the "Divine Man who has died is the communal self-consciousness implicit: the community must make His self-consciousness explicitly its own" (142). And Fackenheim [118] explains that the "past divine incursion becomes present reality only if it *lives in* the present community, as well as being the past object of its present representation" (145). Hyppolite [238], 541–44 has an extended discussion on the problems of mysticism and humanism, Eckhardt and Feuerbach. His conclusion: there is ambiguity, but surely neither mysticism nor humanism in the senses referred to.

Westphal [528] deals with the argument against mystification with an appeal to the way in which Hegel argues that both religion and active political life are brought here into the absolute standpoint. Westphal contrasts objective spirit and religion as, respectively, "a sacralizing of the secular" and "a complementary secularizing of the sacred" (216). But so as not to fall into other problems, e.g., atheism, Westphal is also careful to explain what this "exchange" actually means. He compares the general will and the development of autonomy of the will in conscience as community—one element of the move to absolute spirit—to Rousseau: "The emergence of Absolute Knowledge means taking in dead earnest the affirmation of Rousseau's *Discourse on Political Economy*: 'the voice of the people is in fact the voice of God'." This is the sacralizing of the secular. Then Westphal continues: "In a similar way the religious consciousness must incorporate the perspective of Conscience. It must learn that the content which it takes to be basic, the sacred, is the self's own act" (216). This is the secularizing of the sacred. Both are basically the literal doctrine of the Holy Spirit.

24 This movement has already been discussed in part, and further discussion is required. But during this discussion one should keep in mind the various views taken of the section on absolute knowing. The bulk of the analysis in Labarrière [287], 185–263 is on the process of recollection on which I also concentrate below. For a methodical analysis of the section as a whole, see Miller [363]. Miller opens his discussion with the claim that "the arrival of consciousness at the absolute standpoint, the completion of phenomenology, will be the actual recognition by consciousness itself of itself as this process of self-determination—a process which has, as its own culminating moment, precisely the appearance of consciousness to itself as this very self-consciousness of itself as process" (195–96). See also Findlay [120], 144–48. Findlay puts the project of absolute knowledge in the following way. "Since the existence of a 'subject' or 'self' is for [Hegel] nothing beyond the universalizing activity of thought, a self's consciousness of itself is simply the consciousness of this universalizing activity (which is also an *exercise* of this activity), and in this consciousness of self all particular acts of universalization are in some manner summed up: they will be rethought *as* thoughts, or 'given the form of self'. Spirit in being self-conscious will also be conscious of all it has ever thought, but it will be conscious of them *as its own concepts*, and not as alien objects" (145).

Kojève [267] consists mostly of parts of the texts of the late lectures from 1938–1939, devoted to this chapter of the *Phenomenology*. There are also appendices which relate to the same topic or to the topic of method. In this English translation, which I will cite where possible now, the relevant pages for absolute knowledge are pp. 75–168. In the French original, these correspond to pp. 271–443. The whole interpretation by Kojève is faulted at this point, to begin with, by the definition of wisdom he attributes to Hegel. But it is certainly not Hegel's, for it would entail the necessity to be able to deduce one's pen, a position to which Hegel responded negatively in his lifetime. See especially Kojève [267], 75–77. The claim of moral perfection, which Kojève introduces *Ibid.*, p. 78, has also been satisfactorily rejected by Hegel and by us in the realization that in a reconciliation such as occurs in conscience, and which lays the ground completed in religion, sin is in no way abolished; rather we comprehend the reality of sin and of our finitude and lack of perfection. Since the rest of Kojève's interpretation rests on these misunderstandings, it seems to me that it can be rejected in general as inauthentic. It may be good Kojève, but it is not Hegel.

For a good discussion of the difference from Fichte and Schelling, see Hager [179], 219–31. On the place of language here, see Jeanne Delhomme [91]. But, as I have argued earlier, there is no end of history here in any absolute sense. On language, see also Cook [79]. For other views, see Cunningham [88]; Becker [27], 136–40; Dubarle [107]; Lauer [305], 256–69; Heinrichs [208], 469–90; Hyppolite [238], 573–606; Rosen [421], 229–35.

25 But, again, it must be insisted upon that even with this "radical" transcendence, religion is not simply set aside. Compare Willem van Dooren [101]. My quarrel with Fackenheim [118] can be put in the following way in light of this radical transcendence. On the one hand, philosophy does not have an *Aufgehobensein* in respect to religion, since this movement here is not that of an *Aufhebung*. On the other hand, Hegel is, and has been throughout the *Phenomenology*, seeking the absolute standpoint from which to articulate the absolute idea in all its concreteness. With this move to philosophy, philosophy is no substitute for religion or for any other standpoint; it is simply the reaching of a warranted absolute standpoint. This does not have it replace religion, which it cannot. But Fackenheim's argument, pp. 163ff., over the problem of the relationship of religion and philosophy would demand a general hegemony of philosophy in terms of the infinite, etc., something which is not forthcoming. Hegel is simply saying what must be said by religion from its own perspective, namely that religion does not comprehend itself completely, and thus is not the absolute standpoint. But since religion has the content of the absolute standpoint, we cannot have an *Aufhebung* here, but must have, rather, an *Hinausgehen*. Philosophy comprehends both itself and religion. See my remarks above, note 1, in defense of this last point.

26 Viellard Baron [510], on the basis of the part played by recollection here, argues against various negative interpretations of Hegel and relates recollection to Hegel's rejection of the supersensible (154). The tricky relation between inwardizing and capturing the past is looked at by Hermann Schmitz [438]. Schmitz claims that the sense of '*Erinnerung*' as "recollection" of something past is not important for Hegel, but only the sense of making inner, of "altering" the given phenomena. Without denying the importance of the second sense, the first is also surely indispensible, both in the sense of the past of the historical-philosophical dialogue and in the sense of the past of the *Phenomenology*. Jähnig [240] has already been discussed in respect to *Bildung*, but has now much to add in respect to recollection. See his discussion, p. 70, of the way in which, after culture, we make the history of spirit our own through the *Phenomenology*, by setting aside the pastness of the past and making it a "partner" in the present.

Hyppolite [238] brings together the recollection here with the knowledge we are to develop in the *Logic*. Through the consideration of certain previous shapes of consciousness, Hegel begins by showing how the self has experienced itself as *identical with being*. This identity between self and being, which has been revealed concretely through the various alienations of the self and through the characters of being-for-consciousness, is the result of the *Phenomenology*, which culminates in the conception of a science which is simultaneously the science of being and the position of the self in being" (574). See also Bloch [44]; Ahlers [7]; and Labarrière [292], especially p. 97.

27 On this first level of recollection, which we have been undergoing in the *Phenomenology*, compare Kojève [266], 306–20. Kojève takes this as the birth of the wise man from the philosophical evolution of humanity (320). But this would be to deny, in effect, what exists at the second level of recollection, discussed below; for Kojève leaves the latter on its own and not attached to the natural attitude. Compare Findlay [120], who refers at the beginning of his account of this recollection to "the Homeric book of the dead or the Proustian *Temps Retrouvé*." A most important point is made, however, by Labarrière [287]. Labarrière argues that this last section on absolute knowing "is not content to relate some already constituted totalities, but rather constitutes them in their very relations by manifesting the still hidden dynamism which effects their interior unity and relates them to one another" (185). See also Hyppolite [238], 592–95, and Lauer [305], 258–62.

28 Jähnig [240] brings together this final recollection and the original problematic of the unity of natural and philosophical consciousness, and then judges Hegel's "finale" here as a form of nihilism. "The 'estrangement' in terms of which Hegel saw the situation of his own time determined, the contradiction between 'natural' and philosophical-scientific consciousness, between the object-consciousness of society and self-consciousness of philosophy, is designated by Hegel as a reciprocal 'non-self-possession-in-the-other' [*Im-Anderennicht-'sich-selbst-Besitzen'*]. Both sides, the natural as well as the scientific consciousness, must 'unlock' this history in order that the alienation—which would continue to exist without this unlocking—be set aside, the alienation which stands in the way of absolute self-possession" (68). But, Jähnig then goes on to argue, this leads to an "eschatological-teleological nihilism" which demoralizes humanity because the "sacrifice of the human present upon the altar of this final purpose has its ground in a setting aside of actual history" (69). That is, actual history is lost to conceptualized history. This is a very clear statement of this general thesis and criticism on Hegel. I shall respond more directly to it in my final chapter when I take up the question of an overall criticism.

29 While it is true that only those who undergo this recollection at the end of the *Phenomenology* can in truth stand at the absolute standpoint, this is not to agree with Kojève under his interpretation of wisdom and of the result of the *Phenomenology*. What absolute knowledge is, is knowledge of the praxical presuppositions, not knowledge of reality in any other sense. See Kojève's discussion in Kojève [267], 81–85, and my comments in note 24 above.

30 Thus, the "we" here is essentially different, extensionally and intensionally, from the "we" of the beginning of the *Phenomenology*. This is essentially denied by Kojève's interpretation of "who" is involved in the *Phenomenology*. The "we" for Kojève is not extensionally different now from its extension at the beginning, for there has been no progress for the natural attitude. See his discussion of this in Kojève [267], 92–93.

31 This does not support any of the phylogenesis/ontogenesis theses concerning the *Phenomenology*. We are at a quite different level here. Jähnig [240] connects the possibility of this second level of reflection to the relation of spirit and time. Spirit, as man, has the capacity both to reach out into time, to objectify itself and to lose itself in the past and project itself into the "not-yet-future," but can also annul time, i.e., come back out of this objectification, "win itself by internalizing or re-collecting [*er-innert*] the external" (69). But "the final, absolute 'internalization' [*Er-innerung*], the 'comprehending history' . . . is only the final, closing point of a process which exists *from the beginning* in a temporal and historical destruction [*in einer Zeit- und Geschichts-Tilgung*]" (69). Thus, the whole of the process of history has been such a destruction for Jähnig.

See my earlier remarks, above, note 18, on the essay by Grimmlinger [170]. This second level of recollection, which is presupposed for Grimmlinger's first alternative meaning of 'absolute', namely that the absoluteness consists in the internalization through reflection, is what concretizes the internalization involved in Grimmlinger's second alternative. They are not, then, alternatives, but come together to define the absoluteness of absolute knowing as a standpoint. Hyppolite [238], pp. 591ff., seems also to miss the complexity of these two levels of recollection.

32 If I am right in what now follows, there is nothing left which stands outside of a fully mediated immediacy, and thus there is a full comprehension in terms of standpoint. What now follows should be read on the background of (1) the problem inherited by Hegel from Kant, Fichte, and Schelling, and (2) several criticisms of Hegel. On the background of the problem, see Behler [29], who focuses on the problem of the constitution of reason as absolute and the way it was left open by Kant, Fichte, and Schelling. Behler points to the unique contribution made by Hegel in his effort to make concrete the transcendental by means of grasping it in history. See especially his discussion, p. 189, where history is shown not to be secondary or epiphenomenal, but the concretization of reason. Considering the present process of recollection, we then understand the way that the history of philosophy is philosophy.

As for the criticisms of Hegel, if I am right here on the mediation of immediacy, then the criticisms offered by Krieger [274], lose their substance. It is claimed that Hegel simply presupposes the relation of the concept to sheer immediacy, while at the same time denying relevance for this immediacy as such. This Hegel does, according to Krieger, by positing a radical distinction between immediacy and reason. See especially pp. 261–63. If I am right about the two levels of recollection, and the relation to the natural attitude, then we have a fully mediated immediacy in which there is nothing presupposed except what has been made concrete by the *Phenomenology*. The following account should also be considered on the background of the kind of account given by Kojève [266], pp. 310–11ff., concerning the requirements for the unity of consciousness and self-consciousness. My two levels of thematics, now joined in the new "we," make unnecessary the sort of unity of consciousness of the world and consciousness of the self which is Kojève's proposal.

Hyppolite [238] has come to much the same conclusion as I, albeit without

Notes to Chapter X   403

the express recognition of the epistemic dialectics of the *Phenomenology* in terms of the logic of presuppositions. See especially his characterization, p. 574. See also Lauer [305], 254–56.

33 See, for instance, Findlay [120], for the comparison with Thomas and Aristotle. "Hegel is here saying much what Thomas says when he holds that God *seipsum cognoscendo alia omnia cognoscit*, or what Aristotle means when he refuses to differentiate between thinking of this or that ideal form, and thinking of one's thought in so thinking" (145).

34 Findlay [120] points out, correctly, that this is already present in the ground laid by comedy. "The comic consciousness is summed up in the light-hearted proposition: 'I, the self, am the Absolute Essence' but this light-hearted utterance at once permits conversion to the serious statement: 'The Absolute Essence is I, the Self', in which self-consciousness is merely an adjunct, a predicate to something more substantial" (138). However, it must be remembered that, "speculatively," the predicate is not a mere adjunct, but the matter itself.

35 On the difference between this and the "ordinary" adaequatio notion of truth, see Aschenberg [12], especially pp. 223, 232. See also Andler [11] for a discussion of truth understood as "the whole" in the context of the present discussion. This absolute thought is God or the "thought which becomes aware of the universe as the universe establishes it; a thought which becomes aware of the universe as a reality which does not differ from it" (319). The process of the *Phenomenology* and the present notion of truth, according to Andler, has its roots in the fact that "human thought can only imitate by degrees this thought by destroying in its conceptual journey the limits assigned it by its place in the physical, organic, and social world" (320). In my interpretation the limits have always shared the important characteristic of concealing the *adaequatio* as such.

36 This passage about concealment and unconcealment has been largely ignored, but is in my view extremely important in giving us a clue to Hegel's view. Aschenberg [12] throws light on this dialectic by means of his discussion of the difference in intentionality between different modes of knowing. See especially his discussion, p. 257. See also the explanation by Ephrem-Dominique Yon [541]: "Absolute knowledge is not the self-sufficiency of subjectivity transparent to itself, but a return to the being-there which is immediate, a return by means of a position in a new mode of objectivity" (553). What can now be disclosed as the standpoint mediates the original immediacy to the object, a mediation which was concealed before this.

Cf. Miller [363], where he makes this dialectic of concealment/disclosure the "thesis" of the *Phenomenology*. The thesis "is that consciousness, *qua* object-oriented, necessarily transcends itself and, if one permits himself to be consciousness self-consciously, shows itself to be the movement of becoming the concept, that is, of interiorizing the otherness which, regarded naively, appears as the ultimacy of the subject-object separation" (206). See also my comments below, note 38.

In an interesting way Joan Stambaugh [484] both focuses us on this relationship of concealment and disclosure, yet misinterprets it. The basic problem with her interpretation is that she sees the dialectic as something wooden, external, and mechanical, which "enforces" conditions on things. Stambaugh also takes a non-Hegelian, Fichtean interpretation of 'positing'. Then, coming to the problem of time (and citing all of the crucial passages from the chapter on absolute knowing), she argues that it is "precisely the relation of the predetermined structure of dialectic to the structure of time that Hegel cannot explain. That Hegel was aware of this difficulty is evident in his constant polemic against bad infinity (the problem: how are you going to *stop* time, when is the dialectical process *completed*, what prevents it from starting all over again) and in his attempt to relegate time to an inferior sphere, to a mere externality yet to be elevated through dialectic into the higher sphere of the concept and thus overcome its independent character by being incorporated in the concept" (89). It is clear that Hegel would be surprised to hear that *this* is the problem of the bad infinite. Moreover, although Stambaugh quotes Hegel on the existence of the concept and related passages, she does not see the importance of *time* as the *existence* of the concept. Time is not a negation of a negation, for it is the negation of empty space, and thus makes it possible that *space (der Raum)* becomes and concretely exists only as *place (der Ort)*, the latter being that space/time which is reality and which is of such interest to Stambaugh.

37 There is here a final argument against the view of Werner Becker and others to the effect that Hegel imposes "idealistic-dialectical principles." See Becker [27], 137, and Becker [25]. Compare Findlay [120]. "Truth is here not merely implicity equated with certainty, but has the character of certainty of self. It stands there for the Spirit that knows it in the form of a knowledge of self. The truth is the content which in Religion is not as yet equated with certainty. This equation consists therein, that the content has acquired the form of self" (145).

38 The topic of time is crucial, and has evoked many different views. Westphal [528] has perhaps put the matter most straightforwardly in reminding us of the paradigm furnished by the doctrine of the trinity and incarnation. We do not simply rise, or try to rise to eternity out of time; rather, eternity comes into time, transfigures itself, and through that mediating move, we can move to eternity. The parallel with time and the concept is precise. Dealing directly with the question of the annulment of time here, Westphal asks what that could mean in light of the apparent Hegelian doctrine of the emergence of eternity, i.e., the emergence of science in time. "The answer requires our taking note of the fact that Hegel's chief concern with time is not with either duration or succession as such but with the externality of temporal relations. This is particularly clear and close at hand in the critique of *Vorstellungen* in religious knowledge. In this form the unity of human and divine is conceived as a temporal event. In this sense, reconciliation is viewed as a past or future event. . . . Now if the primary significance of time is separation and externality, its abolition would be identical with the reconciliation with which Hegel's narrative culminates. . . . To speak of time's abolition is simply to refer to the socio-religious event in which man is freed from a world in which his ultimate values and joys are always beyond his reach, whether in some past paradise or in some future utopia, and enters the heavenly world (or worldly heaven) in which he is fully at home and fully satisfied" (220). This gives us no form of Platonism, and fits fully with the original claim of philosophy,

namely that we come to a position in which the ordinary interests of human beings are hushed. In the connection with the Holy Spirit, see also Lauer [305], pp. 262ff., on self-consciousness as consciousness of the divine. The paradoxes concerning time which are well developed by Rosen [421], 130–40, derive from an insufficient attention to the phenomenon of the Holy Spirit in Christianity. In a more secular vein, see also Paul C. Rasmussen [402]. On Rasmussen's view, spirit creates its own objectivity out of itself, and this creative molding is what Hegel conceives of as time (97).

Miller [363] discusses time in the context of the "thesis" of the *Phenomenology*, cited above in note 36. Miller cites the passage on time from Hegel ("Time is the pure self in external form, apprehended in intuition, and not grasped and understood by the self") as the place where Hegel "gives a characterization, from the standpoint of absolute knowledge, of the appearance of time insofar as it is grasped from a non-absolute standpoint. The need to become other, or the need which consciousness has of proceeding beyond each of its particular object-oriented shapes, as moments, presents itself to the self—as it exists *qua* one of these shapes—as external" (207–08). This last qualification is important if we are properly to understand Hegel's discussion of time. The contrast with the absolute standpoint is then made explicit by Miller. "From a non-absolute standpoint, spirit exists in time—but from the standpoint of absolute knowledge, time or temporality is only the form of spirit's existence for itself as nonabsolute, the pervasive mode which, as a *proceeding towards* full self-consciousness, it assumes in its own eyes *before* its vision has become fully reflexive" (209). To which I would add, only, that in the absolute standpoint time is correctly understood as the locus of the concept qua intuition.

M. E. Williams [536] deals with the problem in terms of what standing in the absolute standpoint allows us to articulate: the *Science of Logic*. "Spirit overcomes or annuls time when it succeeds in completely structuring time. Then the life of the spirit is that of the eternal present—not the present conceived as the unstable boundary between the two unrealities of past and future—but a present which comprehends and preserves its past and which, because it is complete, contains no *nisus* towards futurity. . . . Reason abides in the concrete and is at home in the world" (161).

J. Ellis McTaggert [352] presents a classical example of the British idealist's crude sense of time in Hegel. He considers it neither in its association with spirit as the *Dasein des Geistes*, nor its explication as the "puncticity" of space in the *Philosophy of Nature*. Findlay [120] has a good critique of these interpretations. "In this passage Hegel is not teaching any doctrine of the 'unreality' of Time, such as is accepted by McTaggert and Bradley, and is widely thought to be Hegelian. On the contrary he is holding that it is only by achieving self-consciousness *through* a temporal process that self-conscious Spirit can *be* at all. Time, so far from being unreal, is the very form of that creative unrest which represents Spirit as it becomes conscious of itself. Hegel certainly says that, in the final insight of philosophy, Time will be expunged or annulled, but this 'annulment' stands for no metaphysical or theological timelessness, but for an annulment *in and for philosophy*. It means that, for the philosopher, concepts are universal and principles true, and that the precise moment at which anyone appropriates them is completely unimportant" (146). See also the critique by Alan B. Brinkley [55]. But there is here also a radically temporalized Hegel, which seems essentially to deny the achievement of the concept.

One of the major, if not the major treatise on the problem of the relation of the concept and time is that of Kojève [267], 100–49. Kojève attempts his explanation by a comparison with Plato, Aristotle, Spinoza, and Kant. His analysis is correct *if* his prior analyses of the transcendence of God in Hegel, of the nature of history and of self-consciousness, of the relation of the finite and the infinite, etc. has been correct; for the discussion of time and the concept is grounded on these prior discussions. But I hope to have shown by now that his analysis is not correct, especially that of the relationship of the finite and the infinite and of Christianity. See below, note 42. See also Koyré [272], especially the essay "Hegel à Jena," 147–89, which originally appeared in print in 1934 in *Revue d'histoire et de philosophie religieuses* and came from Koyré's own earlier lectures at the Collège de France, lectures which preceded those of Kojève. The basis for Kojève is here, especially the extended discussion of time in Hegel, pp. 165–89. Koyré's own critique of Hegel's "compenetration of time and eternity" is based upon an injection of the bad infinite by Koyré. See pp. 188–89. For a critique of Kojève, see John Burbidge [62]. Burbidge centers his discussion on the identification of the existing concept as "empty intuition," appealing to the *Encyclopedia* to clarify what this means. There is also a critique in Klaus Hedwig [194]. Hedwig himself has a complex account of this relationship, characterizing Hegel's procedure as "a dialectical analogy" (148).

Heidegger's misconception of Hegel has also been influential. See Heidegger [206] and *Being and Time*. There are several good critiques of Heidegger. See Surber [491]. Surber combines his critique with a good discussion of spirit and time. See also Howard Trivers [500] for a relatively early critique and sensitive treatment of Hegel's conception of time. Trivers discusses Heidegger's treatment as "purely formal," formal because characterized largely as negation of negation, which we have seen it is not, and as a "fall" into time by spirit. Trivers argues that it is significant that time is *within* spirit: "the truth for Hegel is '*die Innerzeitigkeit der Zeit*' and the '*Innerzeitigkeit des Geistes*' only on the prior basis of the '*Innergeistigkeit der Zeit*'" (167).

Bernhard Lakebrink [298] expresses a view of time in Hegel which makes time and space "according to Hegel only minimal, indeed the most minimal of things [*Entitäten*] in this world, empty receptacles which wait for their filling" (291). And after arguing forcefully that there is not any separation *per se* between the concept and time, Lakebrink alludes to a "traditional Platonic-Christian thought concerning the 'participation' and 'imitation' of the created" (289). Both of these points seem to me to miss the relation of time and the concept and of the content of experience to both. See my general remarks below on the "*Zwischen*" character of both time and the concept.

See also Hyppolite [238], 575–81, 595ff., and Labarrière [288].

39 On the continued importance of the subject-object relation at this point, see Cunningham [88], 641. For another account of the absolute standpoint as

the *adaequatio* itself, see Liebrucks [320], VI/3: "Die Absolute Idee als Entsprechung." At the beginning of his discussion Liebrucks argues this point in light of the claims made for language in the *Phenomenology* and in the *Logic*: "the absolute idea is the correspondence of propositions with actuality in our human experience. It is neither the world within us nor that outside of us, neither phenomenal nor noumenal world, nor is it a God who is enthroned as sovereign beyond both. The absolute idea is language itself, which we could never have discovered or conceived *without* the logical status of correspondence. . . . The absolute idea is the event [*Ereignis*], which is in all existing, real, and conceptual 'events'. The *Logic* of Hegel is the logic of the occurrence of events [*des Ereignisses der Ereignisse*]" (581–82).

40 Labarrière [292], 95–96, discusses synchrony and diachrony in respect to absolute knowing.

41 Praxis again emerges as central. On this, see the discussion of theoretical and practical reconciliation at this point in Heinrichs [208], 473–80. Heinrichs argues in general that "*intersubjective praxis and religious knowing of objectivity together constitute the remaining premises of absolute knowing which are no longer to be transcended, that therefore absolute knowing itself expresses and displays the theory of reconciled praxis*" (478). See also the discussion of Merold Westphal's view, above, note 21.

42 This *Zwischen*, and not some form of objective history as in Kojève, is the focus of time. Kojève [267] writes that the "aim of Hegel's philosophy is to give an account of the fact of History. From this it can be concluded that the Time that he identifies with the Concept is *historical* Time, the Time in which human history unfolds, or better still, the Time that realizes itself (not as the motion of the stars, for example, but) as universal History." To which there is then added a footnote: "Therefore, the identification of Time and the Concept amounts to understanding History as the history of human *Discourse* which reveals Being. And we know that actually, for Hegel, *real* Time—i.e., universal History—is in the final analysis the history of *philosophy*" (133). Here we have, in capsule form, what is wrong with the whole of Kojève's discussion of Hegel. He has reduced the *Phenomenology* to philosophical anthropology, and that is just what the work is not.

There is a brief, but succinct discussion of time in Thomas Munson [370], which tends in the same direction I have articulated here. "Ontologically, the externality of otherness is the root of what we call time, for the thrust of knowledge is an effort on the part of consciousness to assimilate and thus free itself from the alienating others. Hence it is in the act of knowledge that time comes to be. Man, Hegel reminds us, would be like God, knowing good from evil; for his attempt to comprehend the other in its otherness is a drive to burst the bonds of his finitude and thereby abolish time. In contrast to Kant, then, time for Hegel was not a condition for the appearance of objects. Rather, it was the very life or movement to which we refer when we speak of human consciousness" (298). If we remember the definition of spirit *as* this movement itself, Munson has here defined time in terms of spirit as the "*Zwischen*." In a similar vein, Paul C. Rasmussen [402] explains that "Hegel's Absolute Knowledge, which is the annulment of time, is not a power alien to man, but is human consciousness itself" (100). My only reservation here is that it is as spirit, not as simple consciousness, that this power is there. In light of this *Zwischen*, see the discussion of Horn [225], where he discusses the absolute in terms of the "transcendental, i.e. neither the subject nor the object, but the movement from one to the other and from the other to the first is called transcendental" (154).

M. E. Williams [536] uses his analysis of time to articulate the immanence of the absolute. "Hegel's Absolute which annuls time is not a power alien to man but is human consciousness itself. Because human consciousness in its development *is* the capacity to structure time by thought, man is the historical animal and his existence has a meaning more profound than that of bare naive immediacy" (161). This analysis is spoiled only by Williams' concern with the end of history thesis attributed to Hegel. Williams, however, would not champion it if he saw the full significance of his own phrase in the above analysis, namely, "a present which comprehends and preserves *its* past" (italics mine).

This interpretation of time and the concept and its relation to the *Zwischen*, if correct, shows a "compatibility" between Hegel and what Labarrière calls "the Kantian-type representation" of time. Labarrière [287] writes that, given the formulation of time as the concept and as empty intuition, "one suspects that Hegel cannot rest content with this 'representation' of a Kantian sort; for time, for Hegel, far from being an 'empty intuition', is really the form which holds the concept when it shows itself to consciousness, and it subsists so that the concept, at the end of its historical production, has not appeared in its native purity" (226). But, contrary to Labarrière, the kind of "emptiness" time has under my interpretation of Hegel would give it just this power. As usual, Hegel has concretized and pushed to their extremes Kant's transcendental discussions.

Although I cannot agree with the attribution of a "metalanguage" to Hegel at this point, the argument against the *tertium quid* is made well by Dubarle [107], who writes that "to speak *of* the absolute is already to have left the absolute, to have surrendered and to have consented to exterior reflection. The absolute, in truth, is that which *itself speaks* in the doctrine" (29). On the definition of spirit in respect to this sort of intersection which is the *Zwischen*, see Hager [179], 222.

Notes to Chapter XI

1 Throughout the notes, I have already attempted to answer many of the criticisms of Hegel. I consider those to stand, and will for the most part not repeat them. Rather, I will concentrate on only those criticisms which either go in the same direction as mine, or are specifically responded to in terms of my own critique of Hegel.

2 I have commented on this throughout. Many attacks have been made on Hegel by Marxists, Existentialists, and others to the effect that Hegel's quest is unreasonable. But more often than not, his quest has been misunderstood in the direction of being an attempt to know everything. See for example Lefèbvre [310], where Hegel is attacked for making the assumption that one man can know the entire content of human experience. No such assumption was ever made by Hegel.

3 Against the view that the absolute is simply a projection of subjectivity, see Ahlers [6]. Ahlers here also cites others who have answered this critique. For representative works which touch on the question of the individual, see Adorno [3], especially p. 28; Krieger [274]. Contrary to these views, and to the view of Lefèbvre [310], the "cosmic adventures of spirit" are not beyond us, but are what evolve from us and involve us in turn.

4 John Dewey [97], p. 51.

5 This is the proper response to unfair criticisms of Hegel as an idealist. It is now fairly widely recognized that his idealism was not of the usual, mentalistic, subjectivistic, or even objectivist sort. However, this still seems to escape some critics. See for example Asmus [13], especially p. 48; the various writings of Werner Becker. Becker [25] cites a specific cause for the "misguided" idealism, namely the critique of long-standing that Hegel confuses opposition as contradiction with opposition as contrariety, deriving from the idealistic speculations concerning self-consciousness in Fichte and Schelling. However, my response would be that if the presupposition relation is the governing relation, then these logical relations do not play the part which they play in traditional logic.

All of this has been nicely answered by Hyppolite [238], 575, where he argues that we are not led either to intellectualism or to formalism, but to a spiritualization of logic.

6 My interpretation of the dialectic in the *Phenomenology* takes us in yet another direction than that taken by Heinrichs [208], who discusses it in terms of a categorial logic which avoids the extremes of simply making the dialectic logical and on the other hand dismissing logic altogether. See his discussion, *Ibid.*, pp. 515–26. I would say that the present interpretation is in the direction of a categorial hermeneutics.

I must protest Findlay's critique of the "pseudo-method" of dialectics, Findlay [120], 352–53. But Findlay, it must be said again, is very clear that Hegel is an anti-metaphysician and empiricist, and that his idealism is not one which simply transcends the ordinary. See *Ibid.*, 346–54. My only quarrel with him is in his attribution of a strong teleology which corrupts the dialectic. See also Findlay [119, 122].

7 Fink-Eitel [128], 244, discusses Hegel's allegiance to this presupposition. It is also discussed by Leske [316], where the problem of totality is traced from Kant to Hegel. But the problem with her analysis is that (1) she understands Hegel's totality as simply "suprahistorical and pre-existing" (327), missing the subject-object dimension of totality; and (2) that ironically she seems herself to presuppose the identity of referent for totality and intelligibility in her discussion of Marxism.

Henry S. Harris [182] also addresses this issue in a passage already cited, but which is revelatory for the present issue. He argues for the connection between essence and existence on grounds which will also be used to argue for the identity of referent for totality and intelligibility. Denial of the connection between essence and existence would lead to two "unacceptable" consequences. "First, we should have to admit that the actual world is not completely intelligible; and, secondly, it would be theoretically possible to construct a completely rational system of ideas without even considering whether or not such a system was, or could be, existentially realized—indeed this problem could not legitimately arise for the theorist, since it could never be resolved by purely rational means. Hegel regarded these consequences as irreconcilable either with philosophy or with sound common sense. In his view it simply did not make sense to suggest that the world may not ultimately 'make sense', or to suggest that something could be imagined which does completely 'make sense' and yet is not realized in the world" (114). Harris also seems to accept this connection and thus the claim to identity of referent for totality and intelligibility implicit in the first reason attributed to Hegel.

8 See for example the essay of Serge Latouche [301].

9 Compare the discussion of Findlay [125], where he lists seven characteristics which an absolute must have in order to be an absolute. They collectively depend, I think, on the presupposition of comprehensive intelligibility which is the full consequence of presupposing an identity of referent for totality and intelligibility.

10 Jähnig [240] has already been cited on this problem of nihilism. See my remarks, notes 26, 28, Chapter 10 above. He sees nihilism coming from the totalisation in Hegel; I would argue that it comes only with the presupposition of the identity of referent for totality and intelligibility.

11 On the seriousness of the loss of this presupposition, see the very thoughtful essay by Janicaud [242].

12 The general direction which my critique now takes has been taken by others in other ways. For a sampling of this general direction, cf. the following. Fowkes [140] points to a critique of the presupposition of identity of referent for totality and intelligibility, as does Eric Weil [521], and Jan van der Meulen [360], although the issue is not addressed directly. Blasche and Schwemmer [41] go in the direction of my critique in trying to show that Hegel is an extension of the moral philosophy of Kant.

Although my critique will agree with Charles Taylor that the Hegelian ontology is "dead," it will be for different reasons. I have already commented on Taylor's version of Hegel's absolute. See his discussion at the end of Taylor [495]. Werner Marx [350], 98–108, discusses post-Hegelian philosophy in light of Hegel's quest

Notes to Chapter XI   411

for certainty. He introduces a rejection of the quest for the single logos, but not explicitly in terms of a rejection of comprehensive intelligibility as an identity of referent for totality and intelligibility. Rosenthal [424] has an interesting discussion of essences which I alluded to earlier, and these are interesting in light of the categories of comportment I shall discuss below. But it is not at all clear whether she herself still presupposes the identity of referent for intelligibility and totality.

13 The problem of continuity and totality introduces the time problem into this discussion. See the discussion of Brockard [56], 180–84, and the critique of the tension between the temporal and the eternal as it exists in Hegel. One will always have that tension so long as one presupposes the identity of referent.

14 What is introduced now, in addition to our previous sense of 'interest', is the context-specific dimension of interest, a dimension not unimportant to the general comportment. In this regard, compare the attempt of Habermas [176] to bring totality and intelligibility into the unity of the emancipatory interest. Two things save this from being relegated to just another attempt at comprehensive intelligibility: (1) the historical character of the transcendental, and (2) the fact that it is an interest or drive which does not necessitate any particular framework of intelligibility.

15 There is a pluralism here, but it is quite different from that suggested by Myers [372].

16 In respect to these categories of comportment, see Flay [136]. In my preliminary explorations of this question of totality and intelligibility, I have found two philosophers of great interest on the question of these categories. The first is C. I. Lewis who, in Lewis [318], developed a theory of categories which goes far toward addressing them in the way I am doing here. The second is Michel Foucault in his archeological projects. See especially Foucault [139]. I do not necessarily subscribe to either the latter's notion of discursive formations or to Lewis's categories, but find them helpful in thinking through further this notion of categories which has arisen for me out of my critique of Hegel.

17 On this notion of indexicality, something is suggested in this way by Ladrière [296]. He reflects on the relation between what I refer here to as "indexicality" and concrete reality as historical. While it seems clear that he still sees a need for an identity of referent for intelligibility and totality (in the form of a supernatural being), the essay goes far in requiring a disjunction. Alphonse De Waelhens [512] does indicate a difference in his discussion of Husserl's notion of consciousness as existing in the individual. I am not sure that Husserl does escape the notion of identity of referent, however, since he seems to demand some single, final source of "evidence" in the perceptual world.

18 The philosopher who, so far as I know, has most carefully worked out the separation between totality and intelligibility as I have here in this critique is Karl Jaspers, with his distinction between '*Existenz*' and the forms of 'the encompassing'. See Jaspers [244].

Bibliography of Works Cited

1. Adolf, Helen. "G. W. F. Hegel. Die Kreuzzüge und Chretiens Conte del Grael," *Deutsche Vierteljahrsschrift für Literaturwissenschaft und Geistesgeschichte* (Stuttgart), 49 (1975), 32–42.
2. Adorno, Theodor W. "Erfahrungsgehalte der Hegelschen Philosophie," *Archiv für Philosophie*, 9 (1959), 67–89.
3. _____. "Aspekte," in *Drei Studien zu Hegel* (Frankfurt-am-Main: Suhrkamp, 1963), 11–65.
4. _____. "Metacritique of Epistemology," *Telos*, 38 (1978–1979), 77–103.
5. Ahlers, Rolf. "The Absolute as the Beginning of Hegel's Logic," *The Philosophical Forum*, 6 (1974–1975), 288–300.
6. _____. "Endlichkeit und absoluter Geist in Hegels Philosophie," *Zeitschrift für philosophische Forschung*, 29 (1975), 63–80.
7. _____. "The Overcoming of Critical Theory in the Hegelian Unity of Theory and Praxis," *Clio*, 8 (1978), 71–96.
8. Albrecht, Erhard. "Hegel und das Problem von Sprache und Bewusstsein," *Deutsche Zeitschrift für Philosophie*, 18 (1970), 843–60.
9. _____. "Über den Gegensatz von dialektisch-materialistischer und idealistischer Interpretation der Bezeihungen von Sprache und Bewusstsein," *Hegel-Jahrbuch*, (1970), 125–41.
10. Altizer, J. J. "Comment on Murray Greene: Hegel's 'Unhappy Consciousness' and Nietzsche's 'Slave Morality'," in *Hegel and the Philosophy of Religion*, edited by Darrel E. Christensen (The Hague: Martinus Nijhoff, 1970), 147–52.
11. Andler, Charles. "Le fondement du savoir dans la *Phénoménologie de l'Esprit*," *Revue de Métaphysique et de Morale*, 38 (1931), 317–40.
12. Aschenberg, Reinhold. "Der Wahrheitsbegriff in Hegels *Phänomenologie des Geistes*," in Klaus Hartmann, *Die ontologische Option* (Berlin/New York: Walter de Gruyter, 1976), 211–304.
13. Asmus, V. F. "The Problem of Immediate Knowledge in the Philosophy of Hegel," *Soviet Studies in Philosophy*, 1, no. 4 (1962–1963), 44–50.
14. Avineri, Schlomo. *Hegel's Theory of the Modern State* (New York: Cambridge University Press, 1972).
15. _____. "Hegel Revisited," in *Hegel*, edited by Alasdair MacIntyre (Notre Dame/London: University of Notre Dame Press, 1972), 329–48. Essay first published in 1968.
16. _____. "Aspects of Freedom of Writing and Expression in Hegel and Marx," *Social Theory and Practice*, 4 (1977), 273–86.
17. Axelos, Christos. "Zu Hegels Interpretation der Tragödie," *Zeitschrift für philosophische Forschung*, 19 (1965), 655–67.
18. Bahner, Werner. "Sprache, Bewusstsein, Geschichte bei Hegel," *Hegel-Jahrbuch*, (1970), 152–58.
19. Ballard, Edward. "The Philosophy of Merleau-Ponty," in *Studies in Hegel* [Tulane Studies in Philosophy, IX] (The Hague: Martinus Nijhoff, 1960), 165–87.

20. Bankov, Angel. "Hegels Theorie der Beziehung zwischen Denken und Sprache," *Hegel-Jahrbuch*, (1971), 204–18.
21. Bataille, Georges. "Hegel, la mort et le sacrifice," *Deucalion*, no. 5 (1955), 21–43.
22. Baum, Manfred, and Meist, Kurt. "Durch Philosophie Leben Lernen: Hegels Konzeption der Philosophie nach den neu aufgefundenen Jenaer Manuskripten," *Hegel-Studien*, 12 (1977), 43–81.
23. Baumli, Francis. "Hegel's Primary Approach to the Dialectical Methodology—A Reappraisal," *Philosophical Forum*, 7 (1976), 225–36.
24. Beck, Robert N. "Idealism, Marxism and Action," *The Personalist*, 60 (1979), 76–81.
25. Becker, Werner. *Hegels Begriff der Dialektik und das Prinzip des Idealismus* (Stuttgart: Kohlhammer, 1969).
26. _____. *Idealistische und materialistische Dialektik. Das Verhältnis von "Herrschaft und Knechtschaft" bei Hegel und Marx* (Stuttgart/Berlin/Köln/Mainz: Kohlhammer, 1970).
27. _____. *Hegels Phänomenologie des Geistes. Eine Interpretation* (Stuttgart: Kohlhammer, 1971).
28. _____. "Hegels Dialektik von 'Herr und Knecht'," *Hegel-Studien*, Beiheft 11, 429–39.
29. Behler, Ernst. "Die Geschichte des Bewusstseins. Zur Vorgeschichte eines Hegelschen Themas," *Hegel-Studien*, 7 (1972), 169–216.
30. Bergner, Dieter. "Erscheinungsformen und Motive subjektivistischer Hegelkritik," *Hegel-Jahrbuch*, (1975), 520–26.
31. Berndtson, Arthur. "Hegel, Reason and Reality," *Philosophy and Phenomenological Research*, 20 (1959–1960), 38–6.
32. Berry, Christopher J. "From Hume to Hegel: The Case of the Social Contract," *Journal of the History of Ideas*, 38 (1977), 691–703.
33. Berthelot, René. "Thèse: Sur la necessité, la finalité et la liberté chez Hegel. Avec discussions de E. Boutroux, Darlu, Delbos, Drouin," *Bulletin de la Société française de philosophie*, 7, no. 4 (1907).
34. Bertrand, Pierre. "Le sens du tragique et du destin dans la dialectique hégélienne," *Revue de Métaphysique et de Morale*, 47 (1940), 165–86.
35. Besse, Guy. "L'utilité-concept fondamental des 'Lumières'," *Hegel-Jahrbuch*, (1968–1969), 355–71.
36. _____. "De Jean-Jacques Rousseau à Hegel: Premices d'une *Phénoménologie*," *Hegel-Jahrbuch*, (1974), 490–95.
37. Beyer, Wilhelm. "Der Begriff der Praxis bei Hegel," *Deutsche Zeitschrift für Philosophie*, 6 (1958), 749–76.
38. Biedermann, Georg. "Hegel und die Französische Revolution von 1789," *Wissenschaftliche Zeitschrift der Friedrich-Schiller-Universität Jena*, [Gesellschafts- und sprachwissenschaftliche Reihe], 21 (1972), 63–71.
39. Birchall, B. C. "Radicalisation of the Critique of Knowledge: Epistemology Overcome or the Restatement of an Error?", *Man and World*, 10 (1977), 367–81.

40. _____. "Moral Life as the Obstacle to the Development of Ethical Theory," *Inquiry*, 21 (1978), 409–24.
41. Blasche, Siegfried, and Schwemmer, Oswald. "Methode und Dialektik. Vorschläge zu einer methodischen Rekonstruktion Hegelscher Dialektik," in *Rehabilitierung der praktischen Philosophie*, I, herausgegeben von M. Riedel (Freiburg: Rombach, 1972), 457–86.
42. Bloch, Ernst. "Das Faustmotiv der *Phänomenologie des Geistes*," *Hegel-Studien*, 1 (1961), 155–71.
43. _____. *Subjekt-Objekt. Erläuterungen zu Hegel* (Frankfurt-am-Main: Suhrkamp, 1962). First published in 1952.
44. _____. "Hegel und die Anamnesis," *Hegel-Studien*, Beiheft 1 (1964), 167–80.
45. _____. *Über Methode und System bei Hegel* (Frankfurt-am-Main: Suhrkamp 1970).
46. Bobbio, Norberto. "Hegel und die Naturrechtslehre," in *Hegel in der Sicht der neueren Forschung*, herausgegeben von Iring Fetscher (Darmstadt: Wissenschaftliche Buchgesellschaft, 1973), 291–321.
47. Bodhammer, Theodor. *Hegels Deutung der Sprache. Interpretationen zu Hegels Äusserungen über Sprache* (Hamburg: Meiner, 1969).
48. Boeder, Heribert. "Das natürliche Bewusstsein," *Hegel-Studien*, 12 (1977), 157–78.
49. Boey, Conrad. "L'aliénation hégélienne. Un chaînon de l'experience de la conscience et de la *Phénoménologie de l'esprit*," *Archives de Philosophie*, 35 (1972), 87–110.
50. Boey, Koen. "Die Grundlagen der Bildung," *Hegel-Jahrbuch*, (1972), 280–91.
51. Boey, Kuon. "Le moyen terme dans la dialectique hégélienne, *Hegel-Jahrbuch*, (1974), 62–70.
52. Bonsiepen, Wolfgang. "Dialektik und Negativität in der *Phänomenologie des Geistes*," *Hegel-Jahrbuch*, (1974), 263–67.
53. Bossart, W. H. "The Exoteric and the Esoteric in Hegel's Dialectic," *The Personalist*, 58 (1977), 261–76.
54. Brandom, Robert. "Freedom and Constraint by Norms," *American Philosophical Quarterly*, 16 (1979), 187–96.
55. Brinkley, Alan B. "Time in Hegel's *Phenomenology*," in *Studies in Hegel* [Tulane Studies in Philosophy, IX] (The Hague: Martinus Nijhoff, 1960), 3–15.
56. Brockard, Hans. *Subjekt: Versuch zur Ontologie bei Hegel* (München: A. Pustet, 1970).
57. Bruaire, Claude. *Logique et religion chrétienne dans la philosophie de Hegel* (Paris: Éditions de Seuil, 1964).
58. _____. "Leibniz et la critique hégélienne," *Akten des Internationalen Leibniz-Kongresses*, 1966, Bd. 5 [Studia Leibnitiana, Suppl. Vol. 5] (Wiesbaden: F. Steiner, 1971), 116–23.
59. Bubner, Rüdiger. "Problemgeschichte und systematischer Sinn einer *Phänomenologie*," *Hegel-Studien*, 5 (1969), 129–59.

60. _____. "Zur Struktur dialektischer Logik," *Hegel-Jahrbuch*, (1974), 137–43.
61. Bunch, B. L. "Presupposition: An Alternative Approach," *Notre Dame Journal of Formal Logic*," 20 (1979), 341–54.
62. Burbidge, John. "Concept and Time in Hegel," *Dialogue* (Canada), 12 (1973), 403–22.
63. Butler, Clark. "Hegel and Freud: A Comparison," *Philosophy and Phenomenological Research*, 36 (1976), 506–22.
64. Calvez, J.-Y. "L'âge d'or. Essai sur le destin de la 'belle âme' chez Novalis et Hegel," *Études Germaniques*, 9 (1954), 112–27.
65. Caponigri, A. Robert. "The Pilgrimage of Truth through Time: the Conception of the History of Philosophy in G. W. F. Hegel," in *Hegel and the History of Philosophy*, edited by Joseph J. O'Malley, et al. (The Hague: Martinus Nijhoff, 1974), 1–20.
66. Carritt, E. F. "Hegel's 'Sittlichkeit'," *Proceedings of the Aristotelian Society*, 36 (1936), 223–36.
67. Cassirer, Ernst. *Das Erkenntnisproblem in der Philosophie und Wissenschaft der neueren Zeit* (Darmstadt: Wissenschaftliche Buchgesellschaft, 1974). First published 1906–20.
68. Cekić, Miodrag. "Zur Rekonstruktion der hegelschen Erkenntnistheorie," *Hegel-Jahrbuch*, (1971), 225–44.
69. Chalybäus, Heinrich Moritz. *Historical Development of Speculative Philosophy from Kant to Hegel*, translated by Alfred Edersheim (Edinburgh: T. T. Clark, 1854). First published in 1837.
70. Chapelle, Albert. *Hegel et la religion* (Paris: Éditions universitaires, 1964–1967).
71. Chiereghin, Franco. "Der Bildungsbegriff in der Hegelschen Philosophie," *Akten des XIV. internationalen Kongresses für Philosophie (1968)*, IV, 462–66.
72. Chitas, Eduardo. "Hegel et l'Aufklärung," *Hegel-Jahrbuch*, (1971), 112–16.
73. Christensen, Darrel E. "The Theory of Mental Derangement and the Role and Function of Subjectivity in Hegel," *The Personalist*, 49 (1968), 433–52.
74. _____. "Hegel's Phenomenological Analysis and Freud's Psychoanalysis," *International Philosophical Quarterly*, 8 (1968), 356–78.
75. _____. "Phänomenologische Methode bei Hegel und die Theorie des Unbewusstsein," *Wiener Jahrbuch für Philosophie*, 6 (1973), 178–207.
76. Clark, Malcolm. *Logic and System. A Study of the Transition from "Vorstellung" to Thought in the Philosophy of Hegel* (Löwen: Universitaire Werkgemeenschap, 1960).
77. Cook, Daniel J. "Hegel's Theory of Signification and the Origin of the Dialectic," *Akten des XIV. internationalen Kongresses für Philosophie* (1968), V, 603–08.
78. _____. "Sprache und Bewusstsein in Hegels *Phänomenologie des Geistes*," *Hegel-Jahrbuch*, (1970), 117–24.

79. _____. *Language in the Philosophy of Hegel* (The Hague: Mouton, 1973).
80. Cooper, David. *Presuppositions* (The Hague: Mouton, 1974).
81. Corbin, Michel. "Le système et le chemin: de Hegel à Thomas D'Aquin," *Archives de Philosophie*, 39 (1976), 529–66.
82. Coreth, Emerich. "Die Geschichte als Vermittlung bei Hegel," *Philosophisches Jahrbuch*, 78 (1971), 98–110.
83. Cornehl, Peter. *Die Zukunft der Versöhnung* (Göttingen: Vandenhoeck & Ruprecht, 1971).
84. Cottier, Georges Marie-Martin. "Signification de la dialectique chez Hegel," *Revue thomiste*, 69 (1969), 378–411.
85. Cresson, André, and Serreau, René. *Hegel* (Paris: Presses universitaires de France, 1955). First published in 1949.
86. Crites, Stephen. "For the Best Account of What Hegel Thought (or Should Have Thought) the Next Stage of History, After his Own, Would Be Like," *Review of Metaphysics*, 16 (1962–1963), 144–46.
87. _____. "Fate and Historical Existence," *The Monist*, 53 (1969), 14–39.
88. Cunningham, G. W. "The Significance of the Hegelian Conception of Absolute Knowledge," *Philosophical Review*, 17 (1908), 619–42.
89. Damnjanovic, Milan. "Kann die Sprache im System Hegels die Position des Absoluten einnehmen?", *Hegel-Jahrbuch*, (1971), 197–203.
90. Debrock, Guy. "The Silence of Language in Hegel's Dialectic," *Cultural Hermeneutics*, 1 (1973), 285–304.
91. Delhomme, Jeanne. "Le troisième langage," *L'Arc*, 38 (1969), 65–72.
92. De Nys, Martin. "'Sense Certainty' and Universality: Hegel's Entrance into the *Phenomenology*," *International Philosophical Quarterly*, 18 (1978), 445–65.
93. Derbolav, Josef. "Hegel und die Sprache. Ein Beitrag zur Standortbestimmung der Sprachphilosophie im Systemdenken des Deutschen Idealismus," in *Sprache, Schlüssel zur Welt. Festschrift für Leo Weisberger*. Herausgegeben von Helmut Gipper (Düsseldorf: Pädogogischer Verlag Schwann, 1959), 56–86.
94. Derrida, Jacques. "Speech and Writing According to Hegel," *Man and World*, 11 (1978), 107–30.
95. Desmond, William. "Hegel, Art and Imitation," *Clio*, 7 (1978), 303–13.
96. Despland, Michel. "Can Conscience Be Hypocritical? The Contrasting Analyses of Kant and Hegel," *Harvard Theological Review*, 68 (1975), 357–70.
97. Dewey, John. *Experience and Nature* (New York: Dover Publications, 1958). First published in 1925.
98. D'Hondt, Jacques. *Hegel, sa vie, son oeuvre* (Paris: Presses universitaires de France, 1967).
99. _____. "Le Sacré de Voltaire par Hegel," *Revue internationale de philosophie*, 32 (1978), 357–70.
100. Donaldson, James F. "The Origin of Hegel's Dialectic," *Laval théologique et philosophique*, 25 (1969), 115–29.

101. Dooren, Willem van. "Die Bedeutung der Religion in der *Phänomenologie des Geistes*," *Hegel-Studien*, Beiheft 4 (1969), 93–101.
102. Dooren, Wim van. "Der Begriff der Bildung in der *Phänomenologie des Geistes*," *Hegel-Jahrbuch*, (1973), 162–69.
103. _____. "Der Begriff der Materie in Hegels *Phänomenologie des Geistes*," *Hegel-Jahrbuch*, (1976), 84–89.
104. Dostal, Robert J. "The 'A priori' of Experience in Kant and Hegel: A Reply to M. Kalin," *Southern Journal of Philosophy*, 15 (1977), 267–75.
105. Dove, Kenley R. "Hegel's Phenomenological Method," *The Review of Metaphysics*, 23 (1970), 615–41.
106. _____. "Die Epoche der *Phänomenologie des Geistes*," *Hegel-Studien*, Beiheft 11 (1974), 605–21.
107. Dubarle, Pierre-Louis. "L'absolu et le système chez Hegel," *Akten des XIV. internationalen Kongresses für Philosophie* (1968), II, 28–33.
108. _____. "De la foi au savoir selon la *Phénoménologie de l'Esprit*," *Revue des sciences philosophiques et théologiques*, 59 (1975), 3–37, 243–77, 399–425.
109. Dudeck, Caroline. "Hegel on Private Experience," *Philosophy Research Archives*, 3 (1977), 102–12.
110. Dufrenne, Mikel. *The Notion of the A Priori*, translated by Edward S. Casey and Paul Ricoeur (Northwestern University Press, 1966). First published in 1959.
111. Dupré, Louis. "Dialectical Philosophy Before and After Marx," *New Scholasticism*, 46 (1972), 488–511.
112. _____. "Hegel's Concept of Alienation and Marx's Reinterpretation of It," *Hegel-Studien*, 7 (1972), 217–36.
113. Durán de Seade, Esperanza. "State and History in Hegel's Concept of People," *Journal of the History of Ideas*, 40 (1979), 369–84.
114. Düsing, Klaus. "Die Bedeutung des antiken Skeptizismus für Hegels Kritik der sinnlichen Gewissheit," *Hegel-Studien*, 8 (1973), 119–30.
115. Eley, Lothar. "Sinnliche Gewissheit, Sprache und Gesellschaft," *Sprache im technischen Zeitalter*, 43 (1972), 205–14.
116. Escaraffel, F. "Des mouvements parallèles dans la *Phénoménologie de l'Esprit*," *L'Arc*, 38 (1969), 93–105.
117. Fabro, Cornelio. "The Problem of Being and the Destiny of Man," *International Philosophical Quarterly*, 1 (1961), 407–36.
118. Fackenheim, Emil L. *The Religious Dimension in Hegel's Thought* (Bloomington/London: Indiana University Press, 1967).
119. Findlay, John N. "Some Merits of Hegelianism," *Proceedings of the Aristotelian Society*, 56 (1955–1956), 1–24.
120. _____. *Hegel: A Re-examination* (London: George Allen & Unwin; New York: The Macmillan Company, 1958).
121. _____. "Hegel der Realist," *Hegel-Studien*, Beiheft 1 (1964), 141–49.
122. _____. "Hegel's Use of Teleology," *The Monist*, 48 (1964), 1–18.

123. _____. "The Contemporary Relevance of Hegel," in *Hegel: A Collection of Critical Essays*, edited by Alasdair MacIntyre (Notre Dame: University of Notre Dame Press, 1972), 1–20.
124. _____. "Comments on Weil's 'The Hegelian Dialectic'," in *The Legacy of Hegel*, edited by Joseph J. O'Malley, et al. (The Hague: Martinus Nijhoff, 1973), 65–71.
125. _____. "Hegel's Contributions to Absolute-theory," *The Owl of Minerva*, 10 (March, 1979), 6–10.
126. Fink, Eugen. "Hegels Problemformel 'Prüfung der Realität des Erkennens' (in der *Phänomenologie des Geistes*)," *Praxis*, 7 (1971), 39–47.
127. _____. *Hegel* (Frankfurt-am-Main: Vittorio Klostermann, 1977).
128. Fink-Eitel, Hinrich. "Hegels phänomenologische Erkenntnistheorie als Begründung dialektischer Logik," *Philosophisches Jahrbuch*, 85 (1978), 242–58.
129. Fischer, Kuno. *Hegels Leben, Werke und Lehre* (Darmstadt: Wissenschaftliche Buchgesellschaft, 1963). First published 1909–1910.
130. Flach, Werner. "Hegels Auffassung von der Geschichte der Philosophie und die Dialektik," *Hegel-Jahrbuch*, (1974), 444–51.
131. Flay, Joseph C. "Comment on Murray Greene: Hegel's 'Unhappy Consciousness' and Nietzsche's 'Slave Morality'," in *Hegel and the Philosophy of Religion*, edited by Darrel E. Christensen (The Hague: Martinus Nijhoff, 1970), 142–46.
132. _____. "Hegel, Hesiod, and Xenophanes," in *Essays in Metaphysics*, edited by Carl G. Vaught (University Park, Pa.: The Pennsylvania State University Press, 1970), 39–49.
133. _____. "Hegel's 'Inverted World'," *Review of Metaphysics*, 23 (1970), 662–78.
134. _____. "The History of Philosophy and the *Phenomenology of Spirit*," in *Hegel and the History of Philosophy*, edited by Joseph O'Malley, et al. (The Hague: Martinus Nijhoff, 1974), 47–61.
135. _____. "Review of Daniel J. Cook, *Language in the Philosophy of Hegel*," *Studies in Language*, 2 (1978), 116–19.
136. _____. "Categories of Comportment," in *Categories: A Colloquium*, edited by Henry W. Johnstone, Jr. (University Park, Pa.: The Department of Philosophy, The Pennsylvania State University, 1978), 121–41.
137. _____. "Religion and the Absolute Standpoint," *Thought*, 56 (1981), 316–27.
138. _____. "Pragmatic Presuppositions and the Dialectics of Hegel's *Phenomenology*," in *Hegel's Phenomenology of Spirit*, edited by Merold Westphal (New Jersey: Humanities Press; Sussex: Harvester Press, 1982), 15–26.
139. Foucault, Michel. *The Archeology of Knowledge*, translated by A. M. Sheridan Smith (New York/Hagerstown/San Francisco/London: Harper & Row, 1976). First published in 1969.

140. Fowkes, William. "Hegel and the End of Art," *Clio*, 8 (1979), 365–76.
141. Franklin, Mitchell. "Aspects of the History of Theory of Alienated Consciousness," *Philosophy and Phenomenological Research*, 20 (1959–1960), 25–37.
142. _____. "On Hegel's Theory of Alienation and Its Historic Force," in *Studies in Hegel* [Tulane Studies in Philosophy, IX] (The Hague: Martinus Nijhoff, 1960), 50–100.
143. Friedrich, Carl J. "The Power of Negation: Hegel's Dialectic and Totalitarian Ideology," in *A Hegel Symposium*, edited by D. C. Travis (Austin, Texas: Department of Germanic Languages, University of Texas, 1962), 13–35.
144. Fulda, Hans Friedrich. *Das Problem einer Einleitung in Hegels Wissenschaft der Logik* (Frankfurt-am-Main: Klostermann, 1965).
145. _____. "Zur Logik der *Phänomenologie* von 1807," *Hegel-Studien*, Beiheft 3 (1966), 75–101.
146. Gadamer, Hans-Georg. "The Inverted World," in *Hegel's Dialectic: Five Hermeneutical Studies*, translated by P. Christopher Smith (New Haven: Yale University Press, 1976), 35–53. First published in 1964.
147. _____. "Hegel and the Dialectic of the Ancient Philosophers," in *Hegel's Dialectic: Five Hermeneutical Studies*, translated by P. Christopher Smith (New Haven: Yale University Press, 1976), 3–34.
148. _____. "Hegel's Dialectic of Self-consciousness," in *Hegel's Dialectic: Five Hermeneutical Studies*, translated by P. Christopher Smith (New Haven: Yale University Press, 1976), 54–74.
149. _____. "The Idea of Hegel's Logic," in *Hegel's Dialectic: Five Hermeneutical Studies*, translated by P. Christopher Smith (New Haven: Yale University Press, 1976), 75–99.
150. Gallie, W. B. "Kant's View of Reason in Politics," *Philosophy*, 54 (1979), 19–33.
151. Gamberoni, Paul. "Bildung als Sprachproblem," *Hegel-Jahrbuch*, (1972), 313–24.
152. Garaudy, Roger. *La Penseé de Hegel* (Paris: Bordas, 1966).
153. Gauvin, Joseph. "Entfremdung et Entäusserung dans la *Phénoménologie de l'Esprit* de Hegel," *Archives de Philosophie*, 25 (1962), 555–71.
154. _____. "Plaisir et necessité," *Archives de Philosophie*, 28 (1965), 483–509.
155. _____. "Le 'für uns' dans la *Phénoménologie de l'Esprit*," *Archives de Philosophie*, 33 (1970), 829–54.
156. Gazdar, Gerald. *Pragmatics: Implicature, Presupposition, and Logical Form* (New York: Academic Press, 1979).
157. Gedö, András. "Die Einheit von Geschichtlichkeit und Objektivität der Erkenntnis," *Deutsche Zeitschrift für Philosophie*, 18 (1970), 825–42.
158. Geraets, Théodore F. "Dialectique et interrogation," *Archives de Philosophie*, 39 (1976), 269–83.
159. Glockner, Hermann. *Der Begriff in Hegels Philosophie. Versuch einer logischen Einleitung in das metalogische Grundproblem des Hegelianismus* (Tübingen: Mohr, 1924).

Bibliography 421

160. _____. *Beiträge zum Verständnis und zur Kritik Hegels* [*Hegel-Studien*, Beiheft 2], 1965. First published in 1924.
161. Görland, I. *Die Kant Kritik des jungen Hegel* (Frankfurt-am-Main: Klostermann, 1966).
162. Gouliane, C. I. "Crise vécue et philosophie chez Hegel," *Revue philosophique de Louvain*, 24 (1970), 14–30.
163. Govier, Trudy. "Presuppositions, Conditions and Consequences," *Canadian Journal of Philosophy*, 1 (1972), 443–56.
164. Gram, Moltke S. "Moral and Literary Ideals in Hegel's Critique of 'The Moral View of the World'," *Clio*, 7 (1978), 375–402.
164a. Greene, Murray. "Alienation Within a Problematic of Substance and Subject," *Social Research*, 33 (1966), 355–74.
165. _____. "Comment on W. H. Werkmeister: Hegel's *Phenomenology of Mind* as a Development of Kant's Basic Ontology," in *Hegel and the Philosophy of Religion*, edited by Darrel Christensen (The Hague: Martinus Nijhoff, 1970), 111–15.
166. _____. "Hegel's Notion of Inversion," *International Journal of the Philosophy of Religion*," 1 (1970), 161–75.
167. _____. "Hegel's 'Unhappy Consciousness' and Nietzsche's 'Slave Morality'," in *Hegel and the Philosophy of Religion*, edited by Darrel Christensen (The Hague: Martinus Nijhoff, 1970), 125–41.
168. Grégoire, Franz, "Hegel et la primauté respective de la raison et du rationnel," *Revue néoscolastique de philosophie*, 43 (1945), 252–64.
169. _____. "L'attitude hégélienne devant l'existence," *Revue philosophique de Louvain*, 51 (1953), 187–232.
170. Grimmlinger, Friedrich. "Zum Begriff des absoluten Wissens in Hegels *Phänomenologie*," in *Geschichte und System*, herausgegeben von H.-O. Klein und E. Oeser (München/Wien: Oldenbourg, 1972).
171. Grlić, Danko. "Revolution und Terror," *Praxis*, 7 (1971), 49–61.
172. Gropp, Rugard Otto. "Die marxistische dialektische Methode und ihr Gegensatz zur idealistischen Dialektik Hegels," *Deutsche Zeitschrift für Philosophie*," 2 (1954), 69–112, 344–83.
173. Guerrière, Daniel. "With What Does Hegelian Science Begin?", *Review of Metaphysics*, 30 (1977), 462–85.
174. Gulian, C. I. "Hegel und die Fragen der Kulturphilosophie," *Hegel-Jahrbuch*, (1968–1969), 163–72.
175. Guppenberg, Rudolf. "Bewusstsein und Arbeit. Zu G. W. F. Hegels *Phänomenologie des Geistes*," *Zeitschrift für philosophische Forschung*, 26 (1972), 372–88.
176. Habermas, Jürgen. *Knowledge and Human Interests*, translated by Jeremy J. Shapiro (Boston: Beacon Press, 1971). First published in 1968.
177. _____. "Hegel's Critique of the French Revolution," in *Theory and Practice*, translated by John Viertel (Boston: Beacon Press, 1973), 121–41. First published in 1963.
178. Haering, Theodor. *Hegel. Sein Wollen und sein Werk. Eine chronologische Entwicklungsgeschichte der Gedanken und der Sprache Hegels* (Leipzig: Teubner, 1929–1938).

179. Hager, Achim. *Subjektivität und Sein* (Freiberg/München: Verlag Karl Alber, 1974).
180. Harlander, Klaus. *Absolute Subjektivität und kategoriale Anschauung. Eine Untersuchung der Systemstruktur bei Hegel* [Monographien zur philosophischen Forschung, 57] (Meisenheim an Glan: Hain, 1969).
181. Harris, Errol E. "Dialectic and Scientific Method," *Idealistic Studies*, 3 (1973), 1–17.
182. Harris, H. S. "The Legacy of Hegel," *The Monist*, 48 (1964), 112–29.
183. _____. "The Young Hegel and the Postulates of Practical Reason," in *Hegel and the Philosophy of Religion*, edited by Darrel Christensen (The Hague: Martinus Nijhoff, 1970), 61–88.
184. _____. *Hegel's Development: Towards the Sunlight, 1770–1801* (Oxford: Clarendon Press, 1972).
185. _____. "Hegel and the French Revolution," *Clio*, 7 (1978), 5–18.
186. Harris, William Torey. "Hegel Compared with Kant," *Journal of Speculative Philosophy*, 15 (1881), 241–52.
187. Hartkopf, Werner. "Die Dialektik Fichtes als Vorstufe zu Hegels Dialektik," *Zeitschrift für philosophische Forschung*, 21 (1967), 173–207.
188. _____. "Die Anfänge der Dialektik bei Schelling und Hegel," *Zeitschrift für philosophische Forschung*, 30 (1976), 545–66.
189. Hartmann, Klaus, editor. *Die ontologische Option* (Berlin/New York: Walter de Gruyter, 1976).
190. _____. "Hegel: A Non-metaphysical View," in *Hegel*, edited by Alasdair MacIntyre (Notre Dame/London: University of Notre Dame Press, 1972), 101–24.
191. Hartmann, Nicolai. *Die Philosophie des deutschen Idealismus* (Berlin: de Gruyter, 1929).
192. _____. "Hegel et le problème de la dialectique du réel," translated by R.-L. Klee, *Revue de métaphysique et de morale*, 38 (1931), 285–316.
193. Haym, Rudolf. *Hegel und seine Zeit. Vorlesungen über Entstehung und Entwicklung, Wesen und Werth des Hegel'schen Philosophie* (Hildesheim: Georg Olms, 1962). First published in 1857.
194. Hedwig, Klaus. "Hegel: Time and Eternity," *Dialogue*, 9 (1970–1971), 139–53.
195. Hegel, G. W. F. *Phänomenologie des Geistes* (Hamburg: Felix Meiner, 1952). First published in 1807.
196. _____. *Phenomenology of Spirit*, translated by A. V. Miller (Oxford: Clarendon Press, 1977).
197. _____. *Wissenschaft der Logik* (Hamburg: Felix Meiner, 1963). First published in 1812–1813.
198. _____. *Science of Logic*, translated by A. V. Miller (London: George Allen & Unwin, Ltd., and New York: Humanities Press, 1969).
199. _____. *Enzyklopädie der philosophischen Wissenschaften im Grundrisse (1830)* (Hamburg: Felix Meiner, 1959).
200. _____. *Philosophy of Nature*, translated by M. J. Petry (London: George Allen & Unwin, Ltd., and New York: Humanities Press, 1970).

201. _____. *Philosophy of Spirit*, translated by M. J. Petry (Dordrecht/Boston: D. Reidel, 1978).
202. _____. *Vorlesungen über die Geschichte der Philosophie* [Werke in zwanzig Bänden, Bände 18–20] (Frankfurt am Main: Suhrkamp, 1971).
203. _____. *Lectures on the History of Philosophy*, translated by E. S. Haldane and Frances H. Simson (London: Routledge and Kegan Paul; New York: The Humanities Press, 1894–1896).
204. *Hegel-Jahrbuch*, (1974) (Köln: Paul-Rugenstein Verlag, 1975).
205. Heidegger, Martin. "Hegel et les Grecs," translated by Jean Beaufret and Pierre-Paul Sagave, *Cahiers du Sud*, 47 (1958), 355–68.
206. _____. *Hegel's Concept of Experience* (New York: Harper & Row, 1970). First published in 1950.
207. _____. *Hegels Phänomenologie des Geistes* [Gesamtausgabe, II. Abteilung: Vorlesungen 1923–1944, Bd. 32] (Frankfurt am Main: Klostermann, 1980).
208. Heinrichs, Johannes. *Die Logik der Phänomenologie des Geistes* (Bonn: Bouvier Verlag Herbert Grundmann, 1974).
209. Heintel, Erich. "Der Begriff des Menschen und der 'spekulative Satz'," *Hegel-Studien*, 1 (1961), 201–27.
210. Heiss, Robert. *Die Dialektik bei Hegel und Marx* (Bremen: Angelsachsen-Verlag, 1961).
211. Henrich, Dieter. "Hegels Theorie über den Zufall," *Kantstudien*, 50 (1958–1959), 131–48.
212. _____. "Some Historical Presuppositions of Hegel's System," in *Hegel and the Philosophy of Religion*, edited by Darrel E. Christensen (The Hague: Martinus Nijhoff, 1970), 25–43.
213. Herbenick, Raymond M. "Hegel's Concept of Embodiment," *Philosophical Studies* (Ireland), 20 (1972), 109–12.
214. Hilpelä, Jyrki. "The Concept of Methodology and the Possibility of Dialectical Methodology," *Hegel-Jahrbuch*, (1974), 400–03.
215. Hirsch, Emanuel. "Die Beisetzung der Romantiker in Hegels *Phänomenologie*," *Deutsche Vierteljahrsschrift*, 2 (1924), 510–32.
216. *Historisches Wörterbuch der Philosophie*, herausgegeben von Joachim Ritter (Basel & Stuttgart: Schwabe & Co., 1971–).
217. Hoffman, Pietr. "Hegel, Marx and the Other," *Philosophical Forum*, 7 (1976), 211–24.
218. Hofmeister, Heimo E. M. "Moral Autonomy in Kant and Hegel," in *Hegel and the History of Philosophy*, edited by Joseph O'Malley, et al. (The Hague: Martinus Nijhoff, 1974), 141–58.
219. Hofstadter, Albert. "Ownness and Identity: Rethinking Hegel," *Review of Metaphysics*, 28 (1975), 681–97.
220. Hook, Sidney. "The Contemporary Significance of Hegel's Philosophy," *Philosophical Review*, 41 (1932), 237–60.
221. _____. "Hegel and the Perspective of Liberalism," in *A Hegel Symposium*, edited by D. C. Travis (Austin Texas: The Department of Germanic Languages, University of Texas, 1962), 39–62.

222. Horn, J. C. "Hegels 'Wahrheit des Sinnlichen' oder die 'zweite übersinnliche Welt'," *Kant-Studien*, 54 (1963), 252–58.
223. _____. "Hinweise auf eine Theorie sensibler Erfahrung," *Zeitschrift für philosophische Forschung*, 25 (1971), 48–59.
224. _____. "Hegels Denkform—Ende der Neuzeit," *Hegel-Jahrbuch*, (1972), 247–57.
225. _____. "Die absolute Dialektik des Absoluten," *Hegel-Jahrbuch*, (1974), 152–59.
226. Horowitz, Irving, L. "The Concept of Political Freedom: The Hegelian Contribution to Political Sociology," *Journal of Politics*, 28 (1966), 3–28.
227. Hrachovec, Herbert. "Unmittelbarkeit und Vermittlung. Konsequenzen der Wahrheitsfrage in Hegels Philosophie," *Salzburger Jahrbuch für Philosophie*, 17–18 (1973–1974), 189–230.
228. Hudson, Jay William. "Hegel's Conception of an Introduction to Philosophy," *Journal of Philosophy, Psychology, and Scientific Method*, 6 (1909), 345–53.
229. Hülsmann, Heinz. "Der spekulative oder dialektische Satz. Zur Theorie der Sprache bei Hegel," *Salzburger Jahrbuch für Philosophie*, 10–11 (1966–1967), 65–80.
230. Hyppolite, Jean. "Vie et prise de conscience de la vie dans la philosophie hégélienne d'Iéna," *Revue de métaphysique et de morale*, 45 (1938), 45–61.
231. _____. "La signification de la Révolution Française dans la *Phénoménologie* de Hegel," *Revue philosophique de la France et de l'étranger*, 128 (1939), 321–52.
232. _____."Situation de l'homme dans la phénoménologie hégélienne," *Temps moderne*, 2 (1947), 1276–89.
233. _____. *Logique et existence* (Paris: Presses universitaires de France, 1953).
234. _____. "La critique hégélienne de la réflexion kantienne," *Kantstudien*, 45 (1953–1954), 83–95.
235. _____. "Note sur la préface de la Phénoménologie de l'esprit et le thème: l'absolu est sujet," *Hegel-Studien*, Beiheft 4 (1969), 75–80.
236. _____. *Studies on Marx and Hegel*, translated by John O'Neill (New York: Basic Books, 1969).
237. _____. "Hegel's Phenomenology and Psychoanalysis," in *New Studies in Hegel's Philosophy*, edited by Warren Steinkraus (New York: Holt, Rinehart, Winston, 1971), 57–70.
238. _____. *Genesis and Structure of Hegel's Phenomenology of Spirit*, translated by Samuel Cherniak and John Heckman (Evanston: Northwestern University Press, 1974). First published in 1946.
239. Iljin, Iwan. *Die Philosophie Hegels als kontemplative Gotteslehre* (Bern: Verlag A. Francke, 1946).
240. Jähnig, Dieter. "Die Beseitigung der Geschichte durch 'Bildung' und 'Erinnerung'," *Praxis*, 7 (1971), 63–72.

241. James, William. "Hegel and His Method," *Hibbert Journal*, 7 (1908), 63–75.
242. Janicaud, Dominique. "L'ombre de Hegel," *L'Arc*, 38 (1969), 21–28.
243. _____. *Hegel et le destin de la Grèce* (Paris: J. Vrin, 1975).
244. Jaspers, Karl. *Reason and Existenz*, translated by William Earle (New York: The Noonday Press, 1955).
245. Kaan, André. "L'honnêteté et l'imposture dans la société civile," *Hegel-Jahrbuch*, (1971), 45–49.
246. Kainz, Howard. "Hegel's Characterization of Truth in the Preface to his *Phenomenology*," *Philosophy Today*, 13 (1969–1970), 206–13.
247. _____. "Hegel's Theory of Aesthetics in the *Phenomenology*," *Idealistic Studies*, 2 (1972), 81–94.
248. _____. "A Non-Marxian Application of the Hegelian Master-Slave Dialectic to Some Modern Politico-social Developments," *Idealistic Studies*, 3 (1973), 285–302.
249. _____. *Hegel's Phenomenology, Part I: Analysis and Commentary* (University, Alabama: University of Alabama Press, 1976).
250. _____. "What is Living and What is Dead in Hegel, Today?", *The Owl of Minerva*, 10 (1979), 1–5.
251. Kalin, Martin. "Inference and Illusion in Dialectic," *The Southern Journal of Philosophy*, 15 (1977), 253–66.
252. Kaminski, Winfried. "Der Arbeitsprozess als Prozess der Subjektivierung der Substanz," *Hegel-Jahrbuch*, (1977–1978), 46–50.
253. Kaufmann, Walter. *Hegel: Reinterpretation, Texts and Commentary* (New York: Doubleday & Company, 1966). First published 1965.
254. _____. "The Hegel Myth and Its Method," in *Hegel: A Collection of Critical Essays*, edited by Alasdair MacIntyre (Notre Dame: University of Notre Dame Press, 1972), 21–60. Essay first published in 1951.
255. _____. "The Young Hegel and Religion," in *Hegel: A Collection of Critical Essays*, edited by Alasdair MacIntyre (Notre Dame: University of Notre Dame Press, 1972), 61–99.
256. Kelly, George Armstrong. "Notes on Hegel's 'Lordship and Bondage'," in *Hegel: A Collection of Critical Essays*, edited by Alasdair MacIntyre (Notre Dame: The University of Notre Dame Press, 1972), 189–217. Essay first published in 1965.
257. Kimmerle, Heinz. "Notwendige geschichtliche und philosophische Bemerkungen zum Verhältnis von Geschichte und Philosophie bei Hegel," *Hegel-Jahrbuch*, (1968–1969), 135–46.
258. _____. "Zur Entwicklung des Hegelschen Denkens in Jena," *Hegel-Studien*, Beiheft 4 (1969), 33–47.
259. _____. *Das Problem der Abgeschlossenheit des Denkens. Hegels System der Philosophie in den Jahren 1800–1804* [Hegel-Studien, Beiheft 8] (Bonn: Bouvier, 1970).
260. Klein, Ansgar. "Sprache und Geschichte bei Hegel," *Hegel-Jahrbuch*, (1973), 241–51.
261. Klein, Ytashaq. "La *Phénoménologie de l'esprit* et le scepticisme," *Revue philosophique de Louvain*, 69 (1971), 370–96.

262. _____. "Conscience de soi et reconnaissance," *Revue philosophique de Louvain*, 73 (1975), 294–303.
263. Kline, George L. "The Dialectic of Action and Passion in Hegel's *Phenomenology of Spirit*," *Review of Metaphysics*, 23 (1970), 679–89.
264. Knox, T. M. "Hegel's Attitude to Kant's Ethics," *Kantstudien*, 49 (1957–1958), 70–81.
265. Koch, Traugott. *Differenz und Versöhnung. Eine Interpretation G. W. F. Hegels nach seiner Wissenschaft der Logik* (Gütersloh: Gütersloher Verlagshaus, 1967).
266. Kojève, Alexandre. *Introduction à la lecture de Hegel* (Paris: Gallimard, 1947).
267. _____. *Introduction to the Reading of Hegel*, translated by James H. Nichols, Jr. (New York: Basic Books, 1969).
268. _____. "The Idea of Death in the Philosophy of Hegel," *Interpretation*, 3 (1973), 114–56.
269. Kosok, Michael. "The Formalization of Hegel's Dialectical Logic," *Hegel. A Collection of Critical Essays*, edited by Alasdair MacIntyre (Notre Dame/London: University of Notre Dame Press, 1972), 235–87. Essay first published in 1966.
270. Koursanov, G. A. "L'éducation pour la vérité. *Phénoménologie de l'esprit* et la théorie de la vérité de Hegel," *Hegel-Jahrbuch*, (1973), 198–201.
271. _____."La structure de système hégélian," *Revue Philosophique de Louvain*, 69 (1971), 495-524.
272. Koyré, Alexandre. *Études d'histoire de la pensée philosophique* (Paris: Gallimard, 1971).
273. Kremer-Marietti, Angele. *La pensée de Hegel* (Paris: Bordas, 1957).
274. Krieger, Evelina. "Die Grenzen der Vermittlungsmethode bei Hegel," in *Hegel in der Sicht der neueren Forschung* (Darmstadt: Wissenschaftliche Buchgesellschaft, 1973), 255–76. First published in 1962.
275. Kroner, Richard. *Von Kant bis Hegel* (Tübingen: Mohr, 1961). First published in 1921–24.
276. _____. "Hegel heute," *Hegel-Studien*, 1 (1961), 135–53.
277. Krüger, Gerhard. "Die dialektische Erfahrung des natürlichen Bewusstseins bei Hegel," in *Hermeneutik und Dialektik* (Tübingen: Mohr, 1970), I, 285–303.
278. Kruks, Sonia. "Merleau-Ponty, Hegel and the Dialectic," *Journal of the British Society for Phenomenology*, 7 (1976), 96–110.
279. Krumpel, Heinz. "Gesellschaftstheoretische Aspekte der Hegelschen Philosophie," in *Zum Hegelverständnis unserer Zeit* (Berlin: Deutscher Verlag der Wissenschaften, 1972), 305–13.
280. _____. *Zur Moralphilosophie Hegels* (Berlin: VEB Deutscher Verlag der Wissenschaften, 1972).
281. Kuderowicz, Zbigniew. "Der doppelte Sinn des Begriffs Freiheit bei Hegel," *Deutsche Zeitschrift für Philosophie*, 24 (1976), 1525–30.
282. _____. "Dialektik der Freiheit bei Hegel," *Hegel-Jahrbuch*, (1975), 142–50.

283. Kümmel, Friedrich. *Platon und Hegel zur ontologischen Begründung des Zirkels in der Erkenntnis* (Tübingen: Verlag Max Niemeyer, 1968).
284. Küng, Hans. *Menschwerdung Gottes. Eine Einführung in Hegels theologisches Denken als Prolegomena zu einer künftigen Christologie* (Freiburg/Basel/Wien: Herder, 1970).
285. Kursanow, G. A. "Hegels Phänomenologie des Geistes," *Deutsche Zeitschrift für Philosophie*, 10 (1961–1962), 1451–60.
286. Kuspit, Donald. "Hegel and Husserl on the Problem of the Difficulty of Beginning Philosophy," *The Journal of the British Society for Phenomenology*, 2 (1971), 52–57.
287. Labarrière, Pierre-Jean. *Structures et mouvement dialectique dans la Phénoménologie de l'esprit de Hegel* [Analyse et raisons, 13] (Paris: Aubier-Montaigne, 1968).
288. ———. "Le concept hégélien, identité de la mort et de la vie," *Archives de philosophie*, 33 (1970), 579–604.
289. ———. "Histoire et liberté," *Archives de philosophie*, 33 (1970), 701–18.
290. ———. "L'homme et l'absolu," *Archives de philosophie*, 36 (1973), 209–23, 353–71, 569–601.
291. ———. "La *Phénoménologie de l'esprit* comme discours systématique: histoire, religion et science," *Hegel-Studien*, 9 (1974), 131–53.
292. ———. "La sursomption du temps et le vrai sens de l'histoire conçue: comment gérer cet héritage hégélien?", *Revue de métaphysique et de morale*, 84 (1979), 92–100.
293. La Croix, W. L. "Hegel's System and the Necessity and Intelligibility of Evil," *Idealistic Studies*, 1 (1971), 47–64, 102–19.
294. Ladreit de Lacharrière, René. *Études sur la théorie démocratique, Spinoza, Rousseau, Hegel, Marx* (Paris: Payot, 1963).
295. Ladrière, Jean. "Hegel, Husserl, and Reason Today," *Modern Schoolman*, 37 (1959–1960), 171–95.
296. ———. "History and Destiny," *Philosophy Today*, 9 (1965), 3–25.
297. Lakebrink, Bernhard. "Geist und Arbeit im Denken Hegels," *Philosophisches Jahrbuch*, 70 (1962), 98–108.
298. ———. "Hegels Metaphysik der Zeit," *Philosophisches Jahrbuch*, 74 (1966–1967), 284–93.
299. Lamb, David. "Hegel and Wittgenstein on Language and Sense-Certainty," *Clio*, 7 (1978), 285–301.
300. Lange, Erhard. "Die *Phänomenologie des Geistes*—wahre Geburtsstätte und Geheimnis der Hegelschen Philosophie," in *Hegel und Wir*, edited by Erhard Lange (Berlin: VEB Deutscher Verlag der Wissenschaften, 1970), 13–49.
301. Latouche, Serge. "Totalité, totalisation et totalitarisme," *Dialogue* (Canada), 13 (1974), 71–83.
302. Lauener, Henri. *Die Sprache in der Philosophie Hegels mit besonderer Berücksichtigung der Aesthetik* (Bern: Haupt, 1962).
303. ———. "Die Sprache der Zerrissenheit als Dasein des sich entfremdeten Geistes bei Hegel," *Studia philosophica*, 24 (1964), 162–75.

304. Lauer, Quentin, S. J. "Hegel on the Identity of Content in Religion and Philosophy," in *Hegel and the Philosophy of Religion*, edited by Darrel E. Christensen (The Hague: Martinus Nijhoff, 1970), 261–78.
305. _____. *A Reading of Hegel's Phenomenology of Spirit* (New York: Fordham University Press, 1976).
306. _____. *Essays in Hegelian Dialectic* (New York: Fordham University Press, 1977).
307. _____. "Hegel's Pantheism," *Thought*, 54 (1979), 5–23.
308. _____. *Hegel's Concept of God* (Albany: State University of New York Press, 1982).
309. Lee, Otis. "Method and System in Hegel," *Philosophical Review*, 48 (1939), 355–80.
310. Lefèbvre, Henri. *Le matérialisme dialectique* (Paris: Presses universitaires de France, 1962).
311. Lenk, Kurt. "Dialektik und Ideologie. Zum Ideologieproblem in der Philosophie Hegels," *Archiv für Rechts- und Sozialphilosophie*, 49 (1963), 303–18.
312. Léonard, André. "La structure du système hégélian," *Revue philosophique de Louvain*, 69 (1971), 495–524.
313. _____. "Comment lire Hegel? Considérations speculatives et pratiques," *Revue philosophique de Louvain*, 70 (1972), 573–86.
314. _____. "Pour une exégèse renouvelée de la *Phénoménologie de l'esprit* de Hegel à propos d'un ouvrage récent de Johannes Heinrichs," *Revue philosophique de Louvain*, 74 (1976), 572–93.
315. Leopoldsberger, Jürgen. "Anfang und Methode als Grundproblem der systematischen Philosophie: Reinhold, Fichte, Hegel," *Salzburger Jahrbuch für Philosophie*, 12–13 (1968–1969), 7–48.
316. Leske, Monika. "Die Kategorie der Totalität in der Marxistisch-leninistischen Dialektik," *Deutsche Zeitschrift für Philosophie*, 26 (1978), 324–37.
317. Lessing, Arthur. "Hegel and Existentialism: On Unhappiness," *The Personalist*, 49 (1968), 61–77.
318. Lewis, C. I. *Mind and the World Order* (New York: Dover Publications, 1956). First published in 1929.
319. Ley, Hermann. "Zur *Phänomenologie des Geistes* und einer marxistisch-leninistischen Theorie der Handlung," in *Zum Hegelverständnis unserer Zeit* (Berlin: Deutscher Verlag der Wissenschaften, 1972), 269–304.
320. Liebrucks, Bruno. *Sprache und Bewusstsein* (Frankfurt am Main: Akademische Verlagsgesellschaft, 1964–1970).
321. _____. "Zur Theorie des Weltgeistes in Theodor Litts Hegel-buch," in *Erkenntnis und Dialektik* (Den Haag: Nijhoff, 1972), 21–67.
322. Litt, Theodor. "Hegels Begriff des 'Geistes' und das Problem der Tradition," *Studium Generale*, 4 (1951), 311–21.
323. _____. *Hegel. Versuch einer kritischen Erneuerung* (Heidelberg: Quelle & Meyer, 1953).
324. Lobkowicz, Nicholas. "Abstraction and Dialectics," *Review of Metaphysics*, 21 (1968), 468–90.

325. _____. *Theory and Practice: History of a Concept from Aristotle to Marx* (Notre Dame/London: University of Notre Dame Press, 1967).
326. Loewenberg, J. "The Exoteric Approach to Hegel's *Phenomenology*," *Mind*, 43 (1934), 425–45.
327. _____. "The Comedy of Immediacy in Hegel's *Phenomenology*," *Cross Currents*, 6 (1956), 345–57. First published in 1935.
328. Long, Eugene Thomas. "Comment on Dieter Henrich: Some Historical Presuppositions of Hegel's System," in *Hegel and the Philosophy of Religion*, edited by Darrel E. Christensen (The Hague: Martinus Nijhoff, 1970), 50–54.
329. Löwith, Karl. "Hegels Aufhebung der christlichen Religion," *Hegel-Studien*, Beiheft 1 (1964), 193–236.
330. _____. "Hegel und die Sprache," *Die neue Rundschau*, 76 (1965), 278–97.
331. _____. "Mediation and Immediacy in Hegel, Marx and Feuerbach," in *New Studies in Hegel's Philosophy*, edited by Warren E. Steinkraus (New York: Holt, Rinehart and Winston, 1971), 119–41.
332. _____. "Nachwort zu Hegels Einleitung in die *Phänomenologie des Geistes*," in *Aufsätze und Vorträge, 1930–1970* (Stuttgart/Berlin/Köln/Mainz: Kohlhammer Verlag, 1971), 204–10.
333. Ludz, Peter Christian. "Dialektik und Ideologie in der Philosophie Hegels. Ein Beitrag zur Phänomenologie des Ideologischen," *Archiv für Rechts- und Sozialphilosophie*, 47 (1961), 133–46.
334. Lugarini, Leo. "Die Bedeutung des Problems des Ganzen in der Hegelschen Logik," *Hegel-Studien*, Beiheft 18 (1978), 19–36.
335. Lukács, Georg. *Der junge Hegel* (Zürich/Wien: Europa Verlag, 1947).
336. _____. *The Young Hegel*, translated by Rodney Livingstone (London: Merlin Press, 1975).
337. MacIntyre, Alasdair. "Hegel on Faces and Skulls," in *Hegel*, edited by Alasdair MacIntyre (Notre Dame/London: University of Notre Dame Press, 1972), 219–36.
338. Marcuse, Herbert. *Reason and Revolution. Hegel and the Rise of Social Theory* (New York: Beacon Press, 1960). First published in 1940.
339. _____. "On the Problem of the Dialectic," translated by Morton Schoolman and Duncan Smith, *Telos*, 29 (1976), 12–39. First published in 1930–1931.
340. Marguard, Odo. "Hegel und das Sollen. Wilhelm Szilas: zum 75. Geburtstag," *Philosophisches Jahrbuch*, 72 (1964–1965), 103–19.
341. Maritain, Jacques. *Moral Philosophy. An Historical and Critical Survey of the Great Systems* (New York: Charles Scribner's Sons, 1964). First published in 1960.
342. _____. 'Il n'y a pas de savoir sans intuitivité," *Revue thomiste*, 70 (1970), 30–71.
343. Marquet, J. F. "Système et sujet chez Hegel et Schelling," *Revue de métaphysique et de morale*, 73 (1968), 167–83.
344. _____. "Prehistoire et posthistoire," *Revue de métaphysique et de morale*, 84 (1979), 1–12.

345. Marsh, James L. "Political Radicalism: Hegel's Critique and Alternative," *Idealistic Studies*, 4 (1974), 188–99.
346. Maurer, Reinhart Klemens. *Hegel und das Ende der Geschichte* (Freiburg/ München: Verlag Karl Alber, 1980).
347. Marx, Werner. *Absolute Reflexion und Sprache* (Frankfurt am Main: Vittorio Klostermann, 1967).
348. _____. *Heidegger and the Tradition*, translated by Theodore Kisiel and Murray Greene (Evanston: Northwestern University Press, 1971). First published in 1961.
349. _____. "Die Dialektik und die Rolle des Phänomenologen," *Hegel-Jahrbuch*, (1974), 381–87.
350. _____. *Hegel's Phenomenology of Spirit*, translated by Peter Heath (New York: Harper & Row, 1975). First published in 1971.
351. Mayer, H. "Herrschaft und Knechtschaft. Hegels Deutung, ihre literarischen Ursprünge und Folgen," *Jahrbuch der deutschen Schillergesellschaft*, 15 (1971), 251–79.
352. McTaggart, J. Ellis. "Time and the Hegelian Dialectic," *Mind*, NS 2 (1893), 490–504; NS 3 (1894), 190–207.
353. Mende, Georg. "Hegel und die Französische Revolution—die Entwicklung seines philosophischen Denkens in Jena," *Wissenschaftliche Zeitschrift der Friedrich-Schiller-Universität Jena* [Gesellschafts- und Sprachwissenschaftliche Reihe], 21 (1972), 11–24.
354. Mercier-Josa, Solange. "La notion de besoin chez Hegel," *Pensée*, 162 (1972), 74–100.
355. _____. "Dialectique hégélienne et psychoanalyse freudienne," *Hegel-Jahrbuch*, (1975), 544–53.
356. _____. "Après Aristote et Adam Smith, que dit Hegel de l'agir?", *Les études philosophiques*, (1976), 331–50.
357. Merlan, Philip. "Ist die 'These-Antithese-Synthese'-Formel unhegelisch?", *Archiv für die Geschichte der Philosophie*, 53 (1971), 35–40.
358. Merleau-Ponty, Maurice. "L'existentialisme chez Hegel," *Temps modernes*, 1 (1945–1946), 1311–19.
359. _____. "Philosophy and Non-philosophy since Hegel," translated by Hugh J. Silverman, *Telos*, 29 (1976), 43–105.
360. Meulen, Jan van der. *Heidegger und Hegel oder Widerstreit und Widerspruch* [Monographien zur philosophischen Forschung, XIII]. (Meisenheim an Glan: Westkulturverlag Anton Hain, 1953).
361. _____. "Begriff und Realität," *Hegel-Studien*, Beiheft 1 (1964), 131–39.
362. Meyer, M. "Le paradoxe de l'objet chez Kant," *Kantstudien*, 68 (1977), 290–304.
363. Miller, Mitchell. "The Attainment of the Absolute of Hegel's *Phenomenology*," *Graduate Faculty Philosophy Journal*, 7 (1978), 195–219.
364. Min, Anselm. "Hegel on the Foundation of Religion," *International Philosophical Quarterly*, 14 (1974), 79–99.
365. Mueller, Gustav E. "The Hegel Legend of "Thesis-Antithesis-Synthesis," *The Journal of the History of Ideas*, 19 (1958), 411–14.

Bibliography 431

366. _____. "The Interdependence of the *Phenomenology, Logic,* and *Encyclopedia*," in *New Studies in Hegel's Philosophy,* edited by Warren E. Steinkraus (New York: Holt, Reinhart, Winston, 1971), 18–33.
367. Müller, Joachim. "Hegel und die Theorie des Romans," *Wissenschaftliche Zeitschrift der Friedrich-Schiller-Universität Jena* [Gesellschafts- und Sprachwissenschaftliche Reihe], 19 (1970), 637–44.
368. Müllges, Udo. "Hegel als Bildungstheoretiker," *Pädagogische Rundschau,* 26 (1972), 255–69.
369. Muller, Philippe. "Connaissance concrète de l'homme chez Hegel," *Studia philosophica,* 30–31 (1970–1971), 207–24.
370. Munson, Thomas. "Phenomenology and History," *Philosophy Today,* 13 (1969), 296–301.
371. _____. "Comment on H. S. Harris: The Young Hegel and the Postulates of Practical Reason," in *Hegel and the Philosophy of Religion,* edited by Darrel E. Christensen (The Hague: Martinus Nijhoff, 1970), 85–88.
372. Myers, Henry A. *The Spinoza-Hegel Paradox. A Study of the Choice between Traditional Idealism and Systematic Pluralism* (Ithaca: Cornell University Press, 1944).
373. Navickas, Joseph L. "The Hegelian Notion of Subjectivity," *International Philosophical Quarterly,* 8 (1968), 68–93.
374. _____. *Consciousness and Reality: Hegel's Philosophy of Subjectivity* (The Hague: Martinus Nijhoff, 1976).
375. Negt, Oskar. "Zum Problem der Aktualität Hegels," in *Aktualität und Folgen der Philosophie Hegels* (Frankfurt am Main: Suhrkamp Verlag, 1970), 7–16.
376. Niel, Henri. *De la médiation dans la philosophie de Hegel* (Paris: Aubier, 1945).
377. Nusser, Karlheinz. "Die Französische Revolution und Hegels *Phänomenologie des Geistes,*" *Philosophisches Jahrbuch,* 77 (1970), 276–96.
378. Odujew, S. F. "Hegel über die Rolle der Philosophie in der Bildung und Erziehung," *Hegel-Jahrbuch,* (1973), 186–91.
379. Oisermann, T. I. "Man and His Alienation," *Soviet Studies in Philosophy,* 2, no. 3 (1963), 39–44.
380. _____. "Die Hegelsche Philosophie als Lehre über die Macht der Vernunft," *Hegel-Jahrbuch,* (1976), 113–21.
381. Paci, Enzo. "La *Phénoménologie* et l'histoire dans la pensée de Hegel," *Praxis,* (1971), 93–100.
382. Panova, Elena. "The Identity of Logic, Epistemology, and Ontology in Hegel and in Marxism," *Hegel-Jahrbuch,* (1975), 501–05.
383. Pelzer, Roland. "Studien über Hegels ethische Theoreme," *Archiv für Philosophie,* 13 (1964), 3–49.
384. Peperzak, Adrien. *Le jeune Hegel et la vision morale du monde* (La Haye: Nijhoff, 1960).
385. Perelman, Chaim. "Dialektik und Dialog," *Hegel-Jahrbuch,* (1970), 11–21.
386. Perkins, Robert. "Beginning the System: Kierkegaard and Hegel," *Akten des XIV. internationalen Kongresses für Philosophie* (1968), VI, 478–85.

387. _____. "Hegel and the Secularization of Religion," *International Journal of the Philosophy of Religion*, 1 (1970), 130–46.
388. Pietercil, Raymond. "Antigone and Hegel," *International Philosophical Quarterly*, 18 (1978), 289–310.
389. _____. "De la *Phénoménologie de l'esprit* aux *Leçons d'esthétique*," *Revue philosophique de Louvain*, 77 (1979), 5–23.
390. Pippin, Robert B. "Hegel's Phenomenological Criticism," *Man and World*, 8 (1975), 296–314.
391. Plamenatz, John. *Ideology* (New York: Praeger, 1970).
392. Pöggeler, Otto. "Zur Deutung der *Phänomenologie des Geistes*," *Hegel-Studien*, 1 (1961), 255–94.
393. _____. "Hegel und die griechische Tragödie," *Hegel-Studien*, Beiheft 1, (1964), 285–305.
394. _____. "Qu'est-ce que la *Phénoménologie de l'esprit?*", *Archives de Philosophie*, 29 (1966), 189–236.
395. _____. "Die Komposition der *Phänomenologie des Geistes*," *Hegel-Studien*, Beiheft 3 (1966), 27–74.
396. _____. *Hegels Idee einer Phänomenologie des Geistes* (Freiburg/Müchen: Verlag Karl Alber Freiburg, 1973).
397. Popper, Karl. *The Open Society and Its Enemies* (London: Routledge and Kegan Paul, 1945).
398. Puder, Martin. "Hegels Gottesbegriffe," *Neue deutsche Hefte*, 16, Heft 4 (1969), 17–36.
399. Puntel, L. Bruno. *Darstellung, Methode und Struktur. Untersuchungen zur Einheit der systematischen Philosophie G. W. F. Hegels* [Hegel-Studien, Beiheft 10] (Bonn: Bouvier, 1973).
400. Purpus, Wilhelm. *Die Dialektik der sinnlichen Gewissheit bei Hegel* (Nürnberg: Schrag, 1905).
401. Rasmussen, David M. "Between Autonomy and Sociality," *Cultural Hermeneutics*, 1 (1973), 3–45.
402. Rasmussen, Paul E. "The Meaning of Time in Hegel's *Phenomenology of Mind*," *Kinesis*, 4 (1972), 96–105.
403. Reboul, Olivier. "Hegel critique de la morale de Kant," *Revue de métaphysique et de morale*, 80 (1975), 80–100.
404. Reck, Andrew. "Substance, Subject and Dialectic," *Studies in Hegel* [Tulane Studies in Philosophy, IX] (The Hague: Martinus Nijhoff, 1960), 109–33.
405. *Rehabilitierung der praktischen Philosophie*, herausgegeben von M. Riedel (Freiburg: Rombach, 1972).
406. Reiter, Josef. "Die geschichtliche Gegenwart der Sprache," *Hegel-Jahrbuch*, (1970), 142–51.
407. Riedel, Manfred. *Theorie und Praxis im Denken Hegels* (Stuttgart: Kohlhammer, 1965).
408. _____. *System und Geschichte. Studien zum historischen Standort von Hegels Philosophie* (Frankfurt am Main: Suhrkamp Verlag, 1973).
409. Riley, Patrick. "Hegel on Consent and Social-Contract Theory: Does He 'Cancel and Preserve' the Will?", *The Western Political Quarterly*, 26 (1973), 130–61.

410. Ritchie, David George. *Darwin and Hegel* (London: Sonnenschein, 1893).
411. Ritter, Joachim. "Morality and Ethical Life," in *Hegel and the French Revolution*, translated by Richard D. Winfield (London/Cambridge, Mass.: MIT Press, 1982), 151–77. Essay first published in 1966.
412. _____. "Hegel and the Reformation," in *Hegel and the French Revolution*, translated by Richard D. Winfield (London/Cambridge, Mass," MIT Press, 1982), 183–91. Essay first published in 1968.
413. _____. "Hegel and the French Revolution," in *Hegel and the French Revolution*, translated by Richard D. Winfield (London/Cambridge, Mass: MIT Press, 1982), 35–123. Essay first published in 1957.
414. Rivelaygue, J. "La dialectique de Kant à Hegel," *Les études philosophiques*, (1978), 315–32.
415. Robinson, Jonathan. *Duty and Hypocrisy in Hegel's Phenomenology of Mind* (Toronto: University of Toronto Press, 1977).
416. Roeder von Diersburg, Egenolf. "Die Pseudosyllogismen in Hegels *Phänomenologie des Geistes*," *Archiv für Philosophie*, 12 (1963), 46–68.
417. Rohrmoser, Günter. *Subjektivität und Verdinglichung. Theologie und Gesellschaft im Denken des jungen Hegel* (Gütersloh: Gütersloher Verlag, 1961).
418. _____. "Die theologischen Voraussetzungen der Hegelschen Lehre vom Staat," *Hegel-Studien*, Beiheft 1 (1964), 239–45.
419. Rosen, Stanley. "Sōphrosynē and Selbstbewusstsein," *Review of Metaphysics*, 26 (1973), 617–42.
420. _____. "Self-consciousness and Self-knowledge in Plato and Hegel," *Hegel-Studien*, 9 (1974), 109–29.
421. _____. *G. W. F. Hegel. An Introduction to the Science of Wisdom* (New Haven: Yale University Press, 1974).
422. _____. "Hegel and Historicism," *Clio*, 7 (1978), 33–51.
423. Rosenkranz, J. F. K. "Hegel's *Phenomenology of Mind*," translated by G.S. Hall, *Journal of Speculative Philosophy*, 6 (1872), 53–82. First published in 1870.
424. Rosenthal, Abigail. "A Hegelian Key to Hegel's Method," *Journal of the History of Philosophy*, 9 (1971), 205–12.
425. Rotenstreich, Nathan. "Hegel's Concept of Mind," *Revue internationale de philosophie*, 6 (1952), 27–34.
426. Royce, Josiah. *Lectures on Modern Idealism* (New Haven/London: Yale University Press, 1964). First published in 1919.
427. Russew, Pantscho. "Hegel im Schatten des Irrationalismus," *Hegel-Jahrbuch*, (1971), 300–05.
428. Russo, Salvatore, "Hegel's Theory of Tragedy," *Open Court*, 50 (1936), 133–44.
429. Sallis, John. "Hegel's Concept of Presentation," *Hegel-Studien*, 12 (1977), 129–56.
430. Schacht, Richard. "A Commentary on the Preface to Hegel's *Phenomenology of Spirit*," *Philosophical Studies* (U.S.A.), 23 (1972), 1–31.
431. _____. "Hegel on Freedom," in *Hegel*, edited by Alasdair MacIntyre (Notre Dame/London: University of Notre Dame Press, 1972), 289–328.

432. Schinkaruk, W. I. "Die *Phänomenologie des Geistes* und die dialektische Logik bei Hegel," *Hegel-Jahrbuch*, (1975), 441–49.
433. Schmidt, Franz. "Hegels Philosophie der Sprache," *Deutsche Zeitschrift für Philosophie*, 9 (1961), 1479–86.
434. Schmitt, Gerhard. *The Concept of Being in Hegel and Heidegger* (Bonn: Grundmann, 1977).
435. Schmitz, Hermann. "Der Gestaltbegriff in Hegels *Phänomenologie des Geistes* und seine geistesgeschichtliche Bedeutung," in *Gestaltprobleme der Dichtung*, herausgegeben von Richard Alewyn, u. a. (Bonn: H. Bouvier Verlag, 1957), 315–34.
436. _____. *Hegel als Denker der Individualität* [Monographien zur philosophischen Forschung, 20] (Meisenheim an Glan: Hain, 1957).
437. _____. "Die Vorbereitung von Hegels *Phänomenologie des Geistes* in seiner Jenenser Logik," *Zeitschrift für philosophische Forschung*, 14 (1960), 16–39.
438. _____. "Hegels Begriff der Erinnerung," *Archiv für Begriffsgeschichte*, 9 (1964), 37–44.
439. Schmitz, Kenneth. "Embodiment and Situation: Charles Taylor's *Hegel*," *Journal of Philosophy*, 73 (1976), 710–22.
440. _____. "Restitution of Meaning in Religious Speech," *International Journal for the Philosophy of Religion*, 5 (1974), 131–51.
441. Schrader, George A. "Hegel's Contribution to Phenomenology," *The Monist*, 48 (1964), 18–33.
442. _____. "Comment on W. H. Werkmeister: Hegel's *Phenomenology of Mind* as a Development of Kant's Basic Ontology," in *Hegel and the Philosophy of Religion*, edited by Darrel Christensen (The Hague: Martinus Nijhoff, 1970), 116–20.
443. Schrader-Klebert, Karin. *Das Problem des Anfangs in Hegels Philosophie* (Wien/München: Verlag R. Oldenbourg, 1969).
444. Schulz, Walter. "Hegel und das Problem der Aufhebung der Metaphysik," in *M. Heidegger zum 70. Geburtstag. Festschrift von Jean Beaufret* (Pfullingen: Neske, 1959), 67–92.
445. _____. "Das Problem der absoluten Reflexion," in *Einsichten. Gerhard Krüger zum 60. Geburtstag* (Frankfurt am Main: Vittorio Klostermann, 1962), 334–60.
446. Sciacca, M. F. "Unaktuelle Betrachtungen über den Historizismus Hegels," *Wissenschaft und Weltbild*, 24 (1971), 35–42.
447. Scott, Charles E. "Comment on Dieter Henrich: Some Historical Presuppositions of Hegel's System," in *Hegel and the Philosophy of Religion*, edited by Darrel Christensen (The Hague: Martinus Nijhoff, 1970), 45–79.
448. Secretan, Philibert. "Le thème de la mort dans la *Phénoménologie de l'esprit* de Hegel," *Freiburger Zeitschrift fur Philosophie und Theologie*, 23 (1976), 269–85.
449. Seebohm, Thomas. "Das Widerspruchsprinzip in der Kantischen Logik und der Hegelschen Dialektik," *Akten des 4. internationalen Kant-Kongresses (1974)*, II.2.

450. _____. "The Grammar of Hegel's Dialectic," *Hegel-Studien*, 11 (1976), 149–80.
451. _____. "Schelling's 'Kantian' Critique of Hegel's Deduction of Categories," *Clio*, 8 (1979), 237–55.
452. Seidel, George. *Activity and Ground. Fichte, Schelling, Hegel* (New York: Olms, 1976).
453. Shapiro, Gary. "Hegel's Dialectic of Artistic Meaning," *Journal of Aesthetics and Art Criticism*, 35 (1976), 23–35.
454. _____. "Notes on the Animal Kingdom of the Spirit," *Clio*, 8 (1979), 323–38.
455. Shklar, Judith. "Hegel's *Phenomenology*. An Elegy for Hellas," in *Hegel's Political Philosophy*, edited by Zbigniew Pelczynski (Cambridge: Cambridge University Press, 1971), 73–89.
456. _____. "The *Phenomenology*: Beyond Morality," *The Western Political Quarterly*, 27 (1974), 597–623.
457. _____. *Freedom and Independence. A Study of the Political Ideas of Hegel's Phenomenology of Mind* (Cambridge: Cambridge University Press, 1976).
458. Sichirollo, Livio. "Hegel und die Griechische Welt," *Hegel-Studien*, Beiheft 1 (1964), 263–83.
459. Siep, Ludwig. "Zur Dialektik der Anerkennung bei Hegel," *Hegel-Jahrbuch*, (1974), 388–95.
460. _____. "Der Kampf um Anerkennung. Zu Hegels Auseinandersetzung mit Hobbes in den Jenaer Schriften," *Hegel-Studien*, 9 (1974), 155–207.
461. Sikora, R. I. "Foundations without Certainty," *Canadian Journal of Philosophy*, 8 (1978), 227–45.
462. Simon, Josef. "Die Kategorien im 'gewöhnlichen' und im 'spekulativen' Satz. Bemerkungen zu Hegels Wissenschaftsbegriff," *Wiener Jahrbuch für Philosophie*, 3 (1970), 9–37.
463. _____. "'Daseinender' und 'absoluter' Geist," *Zeitschrift für philosophische Forschung*, 25 (1971), 307–15.
464. Smith, John E. "Hegel's Critique of Kant," *Review of Metaphysics*, 26 (1973), 438–60.
465. Sobotka, Milan. "Die Auffassung des Gegenstandes in Hegels *Phänomenologie des Geistes*," *Wiener Jahrbuch für Philosophie*, 8 (1975), 133–53.
466. _____. "Der Weg des Wissens zur Dialektik," *Hegel-Jahrbuch*, (1975), 329–35.
467. Soll, Ivan. *An Introduction to Hegel's Metaphysics* (Chicago: The University of Chicago Press, 1969).
468. _____. "Bildung, Geschichte und Notwendigkeit bei Hegel," *Hegel-Jahrbuch*, (1972), 292–96.
469. _____. "Das Besondere und das Allgemeine in der sinnlichen Gewissheit bei Hegel," *Hegel-Jahrbuch*, (1976), 283–87.
470. _____. "Charles Taylor's *Hegel*," *Journal of Philosophy*, 73 (1976), 697–709.
471. _____. "Denken und Tun," *Hegel-Jahrbuch*, (1977–1978), 51–54.

472. Solomon, Robert C. "Approaching Hegel's *Phenomenology*," *Philosophy Today*, 13 (1969–1970), 115–25.
473. _____. "Hegel and Systematic Philosophy," *The Philosophical Forum*, 2 (1970–1971), 500–10.
474. _____. "Hegel's Epistemology," *American Philosophical Quarterly*, 11 (1974), 277–89.
475. _____. "Truth and Self-Satisfaction," *Review of Metaphysics*, 28 (1975), 698–724.
476. _____. "Hegel's Concept of 'Geist',", in *Hegel*, edited by Alasdair MacIntyre (Notre Dame/London: University of Notre Dame Press, 1972), 125–49. First published in 1970.
477. Souche-Dagues, D. "Note sur la formation de la dialectique hégélienne dans 'Système de la vie éthique'," *Revue de métaphysique et de morale*, 83 (1978), 244–57.
478. _____. "Une exégèse heideggerienne: le temps chez Hegel d'après le §82 de *Sein und Zeit*," *Revue de métaphysique et de morale*, 84 (1979) 101–20.
479. Stack, George. "On the Notion of Dialectics," *Philosophy Today*, 15 (1971), 276–90.
480. Staiger, E. *Der Geist der Liebe und das Schicksal. Schelling, Hegel und Hölderlin* [Wege zur Dichtung, 19] (Leipzig: Huber, 1935).
481. Stalnaker, Robert C. "Pragmatics," *Synthese*, 22 (1970), 272–89.
482. _____. "Presuppositions," *Journal of Philosophical Logic*, 2 (1973), 447–56.
483. _____. "Pragmatic Presuppositions," in *Semantics and Philosophy*, edited by M. Munitz and P. Unger (New York: New York University Press, 1974), 197–213.
484. Stambaugh, Joan. "Time and Dialectic in Hegel and Heidegger," *Research in Phenomenology*, 4 (1974), 87–97.
485. Steinkraus, Warren E. "Comment on H. S. Harris: The Young Hegel and the Postulates of Practical Reason," in *Hegel and the Philosophy of Religion*, edited by Darrel E. Christensen (The Hague: Martinus Nijhoff, 1970), 79–84.
486. Stern, Alfred. "Hegel et les idées de 1789," *Revue philosophique de la France et de l'étranger*, 128 (1939), 353–63.
487. Stiehler, Gottfried. "'Rameaus Neffe' und die *Phänomenologie des Geistes* von Hegel," *Wissenschaftliche Zeitschrift der Humboldt-Universität zu Berlin* [Gesellschafts- und sprachwissenschaftliche Reihe], 13 (1964), 163–67.
488. Stillman, Peter G. "Hegel's Idea of Punishment," *Journal of the History of Philosophy*, 14 (1976), 169–82.
489. Stormer, Gerald D. "Hegel and the Secret of James Hutchinson Stirling," *Idealistic Studies*, 9 (1979), 33–54.
490. Surber, Jere Paul. "Hegel's Speculative Sentence," *Hegel-Studien*, 10 (1975), 212–30.

491. _____. "Heidegger's Critique of Hegel's Notion of Time," *Philosophy and Phenomenological Research*, 39 (1979), 358–77.
492. Suter, Jean-François. "Tradition et révolution," *Hegel-Studien*, Beiheft 1 (1964), 307–25.
493. _____. "Burke, Hegel and the French Revolution," in *Hegel's Political Philosophy*, edited by Zbigniew Pelzynski (Cambridge: Cambridge University Press, 1971), 52–72.
494. Szondi, P. "Zu Hegels Bestimmung des Tragischen," *Archiv für das Studium der neueren Sprachen*, 198 (1961–1962), 22–29.
495. Taylor, Charles. *Hegel* (Cambridge: Cambridge University Press, 1975).
496. _____. "The Opening Arguments of the *Phenomenology*, in *Hegel*, edited by Alasdair MacIntyre (Notre Dame/London: University of Notre Dame Press, 1972), 151–87.
497. Theunissen, Michael. *Hegels Lehre vom absoluten Geist als theologisch-politischer Traktat* (Berlin: de Gruyter, 1970).
498. _____. "Krise der Macht. Thesen zur Theorie des dialektischen Widerspruchs," *Hegel-Jahrbuch*, (1974), 318–29.
499. Thierry, Yves. "Contexte et commencement," *Archives de Philosophie*, 41 (1978), 69–80.
500. Trivers, Howard. "Heidegger's Mis-interpretation of Hegel's Views on Spirit and Time," *Philosophy and Phenomenological Research*, 3 (1942–1943), 162–68.
501. Trotignon, P. "Lire Hegel," *L'Arc*, 38 (1969), 81–92.
502. Tur, Richard H. S. "Anarchy versus Authority: Towards a Democratic Theory of Law," *Archiv für Rechts- und Sozialphilosophie*, 63 (1977), 305–26.
503. Turner, J. E. "The Essentials of Hegel's Spiritual Monism," *The Monist*, 44 (1934), 59–79.
504. Ulrici, H. "Die falsche und die wahre Dialektik," *Zeitschrift für Philosophie und philosophische Kritik*, 19 (1848), 238–74.
505. Vancourt, Raymond. *La pensée religieuse de Hegel* (Paris: Presses universitaires de France, 1965).
506. _____. "État de nature et péché original selon Hegel," *Mélanges de science religieuse*, 26 (1969), 113–44.
507. Van Riet, Georges. "Y a-t-il un chemin vers la vérité? À propos de l'introduction à la *Phénoménologie de l'esprit* de Hegel," *Revue philosophique de Louvain*, 62 (1964), 466–76.
508. _____. "The Problem of God in Hegel," *Philosophy Today*, 2 (1967), 75–105.
509. Ver Eecke, Wilfred. "Hegel's Dialectic Analysis of the French Revolution," *Hegel-Jahrbuch*, (1975), 561–67.
510. Viellard Baron, Jean-Louis. "Hegel, philosophe de la réminiscense," *International Studies in Philosophy*, 8 (1976), 145–66.
511. Vuillemin, Jules. "La mort dans la philosophie de Hegel," *Revue philosophique de la France et de l'étranger*, 137 (1947), 194–202.

512. Waelhens, Alphonse de. "Phénoménologie husserlienne et phénoménologie hégélienne," *Revue philosophique de Louvain*, 52 (1954), 234–49.
513. Wagner, Falk. *Der Gedanke der Persönlichkeit Gottes bei Fichte und Hegel* (Gütersloh: Gütersloher Verlagshaus, G. Mohn, 1971).
514. Wagner, Hans. "Hegels Lehre vom Anfang der Wissenschaft," *Zeitschrift für philosophische Forschung*, 23 (1969), 339–48.
515. Wahl, Jean. *Le malheur de la conscience dans la philosophie de Hegel* (Paris: Presses universitaires de France, 1951). First published in 1911.
516. _____. "À propos de l'introduction à la *Phénoménologie* de Hegel par A. Kojève," *Deucalion*, 5 (1955), 77–99.
517. Walsh, W. H. "Hegel on the History of Philosophy," *History and Theory*, Beiheft 5 (1965), 67–82.
518. Wandschneider, Dieter. "Selbstbewusstsein als sich selbst erfüllender Entwurf," *Zeitschrift für philosophische Forschung*, 33 (1979), 479–520.
519. Webb, Thomas R. "Scepticism and Hegelian Science," *Dialogue*, 16 (1977), 139–62.
520. Weil, Eric. "La morale de Hegel," *Deucalion*, 5 (1955), 101–16.
521. _____. "Hegel et nous," *Hegel-Studien*, Beiheft 4 (1969), 7–15.
522. _____. "The Hegelian Dialectic," in *The Legacy of Hegel*, edited by Joseph O'Malley, et al. (The Hague: Martinus Nijhoff, 1973), 49–64.
523. _____. "Hegel et le concept de la révolution," *Archives de philosophie*, 39 (1976), 3–19.
524. Weinhandl, Ferdinand. "Einige Bemerkungen zur Hegelinterpretation," *Zeitschrift für deutsche Kulturphilosophie*, 7 (1941), 1–11.
525. Werkmeister, W. H. "Hegel's Phenomenology of Mind as a Development of Kant's Basic Ontology," in *Hegel and the Philosophy of Religion*, edited by Darrel E. Christensen (The Hague: Martinus Nijhoff, 1970), 93–110.
526. Werner, Hans-Joachim. "Spekulative und transzendentale Dialektik. Zur Entwicklung des dialektischen Denkens im deutschen Idealismus (Kant-Hegel)," *Philosophisches Jahrbuch*, 81 (1974), 77–87.
527. Westphal, Merold. "In Defense of the Thing In Itself," *Kantstudien*, 59 (1968), 118–41.
528. _____. *History and Truth in Hegel's Phenomenology* (Atlantic Highlands, New Jersey: Humanities Press, 1979).
529. Wetter, Gustav Andreas, S. J. *Die Umkehrung Hegels. Grundzüge und Ursprünge der Sowjetphilosophie* (Köln: Verlag Wissenschaft und Politik, 1963).
530. Wiehl, Reiner. "Über den Sinn der sinnlichen Gewissheit in Hegels *Phänomenologie des Geistes*," *Hegel-Studien*, Beiheft 3 (1966), 103–34.
531. _____. "Phänomenologie und Dialektik," *Hegel-Studien*, Beiheft 11 (1974), 623–34.
532. Wieland, W. "Hegels Dialektik der sinnlichen Gewissheit," in *Orbis Scriptus: Dmitrij Tschižewskij zum 70. Geburtstag*, herausgegeben von Dietrich Gerhardt, u. a. (München: Wilhelm Fink Verlag, 1966), 933–41.
533. Wilden, Anthony. "The Belle Âme: Freud, Lacan, and Hegel," in *The Language of the Self. The Function of Language in Psychoanalysis* (Baltimore: Johns Hopkins Press, 1968), 284–308.

534. Wildt, Andreas. "Hegels Kritik des Jakobinismus," in *Aktualität und Folgen der Philosophie Hegels*, 265–92 (Frankfurt am Main: Suhrkamp Verlag, 1970), 265–92.
535. Williams, M. E. "For the Best Account of What Hegel Thought (or Should Have Thought) the Next Stage of History, After His Own, Would Be Like," *Review of Metaphysics*, 16 (1962–1963), 139–44.
536. _____. "Time in Hegel's Philosophy," *Dialogue*, 9 (1970), 154–67.
537. Wilson, Deidre. *Presuppositions and Non-Truth-Conditional Semantics* (London: Academic Press, 1975).
538. Wolff, E. "Hegel und die griechische Welt," *Antike und Abendland*, 1 (1945), 163–81.
539. *Wörterbuch der philosophischen Begriffe*, Historisch-quellenmässig bearbeitet von Dr. Rudolf Eisler (Berlin: E. S. Mittler & Sohn, 1927–1930).
540. Yerkes, James. *Hegel's Christology* (Albany: State University of New York Press, 1982).
541. Yon, Ephrem-Dominique. "Esthétique de la contemplation et esthétique de la transgression. À propos de passage de la Religion au Savoir Absolu dans la *Phénoménologie de l'esprit* de Hegel," *Revue philosophique de Louvain*, 74 (1976), 549–71.
542. Zarader, M. "La dialectique du crime et du châtiment chez Hegel et Dostoievski," *Revue de métaphysique et de morale*, 81 (1976), 350–75.
543. *Zum Hegelverständnis unserer Zeit. Beiträge marxistisch-leninistischer Hegelforschung*, herausgegeben von Hermann Ley (Berlin: Deutscher Verlag der Wissenschaften, 1972).

Index

Absolute idealism: connection with tradition and the natural attitude, 10, 240-41; nature of, 174-75. *See also* Idealism
Absolute knowledge, 28, 225-56, 235, 243
Absolute spirit, 227-48
Absolute standpoint, 9, 49-50, 102, 115, 170, 188, 217-18, 225-26, 228, 235, 240, 249-67
Action, 237-38. *See also* Praxis
Aeschylus, 166
Alienation, 102-03, 144, 183-205 passim, 210, 233
Ambiguity, 84, 102-03, 116, 126-27, 144, 164, 177, 185
Antigone, 166-79 passim
Appearance, 70, 72-73
Aristotle, 53, 172-75 passim, 256
Art, 169
Asceticism, 109
Augustine, St., 11, 103, 111

Beginning: problem of, 1-2, 4-12, 13-28, 34, 36, 43-44
Berkeley, 118
Bildung, See Culture
Biology, 124-25
Body, 129-33 passim

Category: as effective, 143-44; meaning of, 135-36, 172-75
Certainty, 30, 38-39, 113, 124-25, 185, 207; meaning of quest for, vii-ix, 1-28, 35, 53, 97, 137-38, 178-79, 183-84, 186, 193-94, 225-26, 239-44, 247-48, 249; and truth, *see* Truth and certainty
Christianity, 3, 7, 188-92, 234-38
Civil society, 185-86
Community, 221-26, 228. *See also* Religious community
Conscience, 214-26, 228
Concept, 67, 238, 243-47
Consciousness, 57-80, 170, 228; definition of, 59; presuppositions of, 57-58
Culture (*Bildung*), 183-205, 209-11
Death, 88
Descartes, 4, 7, 11

Desire, 27, 111, 113-16, 171; defined, 54, 81-82; as interest, 81-112
Destiny, 175-79
Dewey, 250
Diachrony, 229-30, 233-34, 246
Dialectic, 17-28, 41-44, 45, 117, 123, 133-34; in Hegel and Plato, 18, 33; necessity of, 23-24, 26-28, 42-43, 48-49, 52, 159-60, 179, 208; self-motivation of, 39, 241-44, 256-57; and sense-certainty, 29, 34-36, 42-44
Duty, 168, 215-26

Enlightenment, the, 189-95 passim
Error, 59-60, 61-62
Essence, 67-68
Ethicality (*Sittlichkeit*), 164-82, 209-11
Euripides, 166
Evil, 222
Experience, 37-38; immediacy of, 31-32; the indexical nature of, 38-39, 259-64 passim; self-mediation of, 36
Exolanation, 77-80
External relations, 62-63

Faith, 183, 188-92
Feeling, 104-06
Fichte, 104, 118
Finitude, 109-10, 202-05, 221-26, 228-29, 242
Force, 65-68, 73-74
Formalism, 125, 155-56; ethical, 148-51; legal, 180-82
Freedom, 53-54, 127-28, 200-05 passim, 207-08; of self-consciousness, 97-112
French Revolution, 199-205

Geist. See Spirit
General will, 199-205 passim, 221
Guilt, 168

Hedonism, 137-39
Hegel: and the philosophical tradition, 3-16 passim, 256
Horace, 181
Hume, vii, 4, 7, 11, 76, 267
Idealism, 78-79, 117-19, 195-96; in Hegel, 174-75; and the natural attitude, 119. *See also*

441

Absolute idealism
Imagination, 236
Individuality, 128-33 passim, 146-47, 178, 203-04, 214-15, 242-44
Infinity, 79, 225, 228-29
Insight: pure, 188-95 passim
Intentionality, 27, 51-80, 113-16, 171, 195-96; and self-awareness, 64, 69
Interest, 27-28, 51-57; and the natural attitude, 56
Intuition, 245-47
Inverted world, 77-79
Irony, 187-88

Judgment: analytic/synthetic distinction, 172-75

Kant, vii, 4, 7, 11, 12, 35, 76-80 passim, 104, 108, 118, 135-36, 172-75 passim, 194, 199, 209-14, 256
Knowledge, 208-09, 214, 217-26, 243; as object of the *Phenomenology*, 29, 32-34

Language, 115, 186-88, 194, 218-26 passim
Law, 73-77, 166-70 passim, 179-82 passim; of the heart, 139-41; nature of, 74
Leibniz, 65, 267
Life, 54, 81, 82-83
Locke, 4, 7, 62, 118
Logic, 125
Lordship and bondage, 86, 89-95

Moira. See Destiny
Moore, G. E., 29
Morality, 201-05 passim, 207-26; as paradox, 212-13

Natural attitude, 4-10, 12, 174; and dialectic, 18-28 passim, 256; and particulars, 31, 38-39; and philosophy, 6-8, 19-28 passim, 29-50, 96-97; and philosophy, their unity, 9, 39, 49, 60-61, 119-20, 126, 155, 202, 225-26, 236, 246-47; and the quest for certainty, 39-40, 46-47, 80, 102-03, 110-11, 120, 137, 150, 152, 160, 170, 174-75, 198-99, 246-48, 250; primacy of, 17, 38-39, 41-42, 44, 47, 49, 51-52, 256
Necessity, 75-77, 127, 138-41, 208
Nihilism, 257, 266

Objectification, 138, 144-48, 178, 187, 233-38; in European civilization, 183-205; among the Greeks, 165-66; among the Romans, 179-82
Operationalism, 123-24
Other, the, 92-93
Ought: origin and nature of the, 149-51, 213

Parmenides, vii, 3, 7, 11, 256
Particulars, 38
Perception, 58-63, 171; primacy of, 68
Person, 179-82 passim
Phenomenology of Spirit, the: and its relationship to the system, 2-3, 6, 240, 248; and the "we," 33-36, 43, 63-64, 96-97, 113, 119, 170, 177, 239-40; project of, 1-13, 56-57, 121, 143, 153, 188, 242-44
Philosophy: and the natural attitude. *See* Natural attitude and philosophy; and religion, 235-44; as spirit, 55-56, 209, 235-48
Phrenology. *See* Physiognomy and phrenology
Physicalism, 133-36
Physiognomy: and phrenology, 128-33
Plato, 3, 7, 11, 17-18, 44, 239, 256. *See also* Dialectic in Hegel and Plato Pleasure. *See* Hedonism
Praxis, 119, 122, 130-33 passim; 143-44, 214, 269. *See also* Action; Thought and praxis
Presuppositions, praxical, 19-24, 123, 147-48, 152, 154, 158-60, 201, 216, 224-25, 228, 246; and the *Phenomenology of Spirit*, 24-28, 48-49, 147-48, 239-41, 250, 251-52
Psychology, 125-28
Purpose: as an interest, 27-28, 54-55, 107-08, 113-16, 171
Pythagoras, 3, 7

Reality principle, 138
Reason, 110-11, 113-61, 170, 172-75; as activity, 136-61; defined, 114-15, 121-23; as instinct, 111-12, 115, 117, 132, 137, 152, 214; as observation, 122-36
Recognition, 86-93, 218-26
Recollection, 116, 134, 227, 239-41
Reconciliation, 222-26
Reflection: as an interest, 28, 149, 151-52, 186
Relativism, 61-62, 76, 124, 150, 217-18
Religion, 103, 226, 236-38; as spirit, 55, 209, 218, 227-38
Religious community, 192. *See also* Community

Schelling, 270
Sciences: physical, 123-25
Self, the: and its connection with the world, 130, 143-53, 163, 169, 174-75, 183-88, 198-99, 216-26, 230, 245-47
Self-awareness, 102-03, 105, 110, 119, 132-33, 152, 164-65, 167-68, 170, 178, 234, 242-44
Self-certainty, 215-18
Self-consciousness, 81-112, 164, 170, 177, 215-18, 228; independence and dependence of, 86-97, 177-79
Self-identity, 86-87, 90-91

Sense-certainty, ix, 13-17, 29-50, 117, 160, 170, 195-96, 215-18; paradox of, 46
Sittlichkeit. See Ethicality
Skepticism, 99-101
Social being: primacy of, 156-57
Society, 144-45
Socrates, vii, 3, 17-18
Sophocles, 166
Spinoza, 4, 7, 267
Spirit (*Geist*), 151-53, 163-267; absoluteness of, 169, 174-75; as interest, 55-56, 164-65; meaning of, 126, 128-29, 134-35, 145-49, 157, 163-64, 171, 228, 234-35, 247; objective, 55, 145, 165-66, 169
State, the, 185-86
Stoicism, 98-99
Substances, 66-68
Syllogism, 110
Synchrony, 229-30, 233-34, 246

Thought, 115; as intersubjective, 94-98 passim, 224-25; and praxis, 95-97 passim, 106, 122, 148, 216-17, 226, 243

Time, 243-47
Truth, 207-08, 215, 236, 244-47; and certainty, 30, 37, 59-60, 90-91, 120, 207, 217-26, 242-44
Understanding, 63-80; as activity, 68-70
Unhappy consciousness, 101-11
Universal: unconditioned, 62-63
Universals: intelligible, 64-65; perceptual, 58-63 passim
Utilitarianism, 196-99, 210-11

Values, 149-52. *See also* Morality
Virtue, 141-42

Work, 94-95, 106-08
World: constitution of, 94-95, 139-54 passim, 163, 183-84

*Only the text has been indexed. The Notes will usually be found to contain the same general topics as the passages to which they are respectively appended.

Index of Authors Cited in Notes

Adolf, Helen, 313
Adorno, Theodor W., 275, 279, 288, 308, 338, 409
Ahlers, Rolf, 270, 277, 313-14, 317, 339, 341, 345, 376, 381, 383-84, 387, 389, 391-92, 396-97, 401, 409
Albrecht, Erhard, 292
Altizer, J. J., 312
Andler, Charles, 270, 380, 403
Aschenberg, Reinhold, 270, 273-74, 280, 284, 286-90, 292, 311, 322, 344, 403
Asmus, V. F., 269-70, 288, 381, 409
Avineri, Schlomo, 391
Axelos, Christos, 350

Bahner, Werner, 361
Bankov, Angel, 382
Bataille, Georges, 294
Baum, Manfred, 269, 275
Baumli, Francis, 275
Beck, Robert N., 310
Becker, Werner, 278, 282, 284, 286, 299, 319, 322-23, 325-28, 331-32, 334-35, 338-39, 344, 346-47, 355, 357-58, 360, 362-66, 375, 377-78, 382, 389, 400, 404, 409
Behler, Ernst, 271, 322, 402
Berndtson, Arthur, 319
Berry, Christopher J., 338
Bertrand, Pierre, 351
Besse, Guy, 275, 288, 364-66, 369, 378
Beyer, Wilhelm, 324
Biedermann, Georg, 368
Birchell, B. C., 281, 378-79
Blasche, Siegfried, 279, 346, 376, 379, 410
Bloch, Ernst, 270, 316, 324-25, 348, 401
Bobbio, Norberto, 338
Bodhammer, Theodor, 286-88, 309, 325, 327, 361, 389, 395
Boeder, Heribert, 273, 283-84, 289-90, 364-65
Boey, Conrad, 313
Boey, Koen, 359, 362
Boey, Kuon, 314-15, 361, 363
Bonsiepen, Wolfgang, 296, 311, 315
Bossart, W. H., 279
Brandom, Robert, 377-79
Brinkley, Alan B., 406
Brockard, Hans, 272, 301, 411

Bruaire, Claude, 294, 393
Bubner, Rudiger, 272-73, 275, 281
Bunch, B. L., 280
Burbidge, John, 406
Butler, Clark, 271

Caponigri, A. Robert, 276, 345
Carritt, E. F., 348
Cassirer, Ernst, 270-72, 277, 279, 286, 296, 346
Cekić, Miodrag, 277, 308, 310, 321
Chalybäus, Heinrich Moritz, 277, 287, 301, 304
Chapelle, Albert, 389, 393, 396
Chiereghin, Franco, 357, 359, 362
Chitas, Eduardo, 364
Christensen, Darrel E., 292, 300, 304, 312
Clark, Malcolm, 325, 361
Cook, Daniel J., 293, 360-61, 380, 382-83, 389, 400
Cooper, David, 280
Corbin, Michel, 281, 389
Coreth, Emerich, 275
Cornehl, Peter, 397
Cottier, Georges Marie-Martin, 279-80
Cresson, André, 271
Crites, Stephen, 344, 347, 352
Cunningham, G. W., 275, 277, 284-85, 292, 297, 354, 400, 406

Delhomme, Jeanne, 400
Debrock, Guy, 285, 302-03, 309
DeNys, Martin, 278, 285, 288
Derbolov, Josef, 286, 325
Desmond, William, 349
Despland, Michel, 379, 381, 384
Dewey, John, 409
D'Hondt, Jacques, 271, 364
Donaldson, James F., 279
Dooren, Willem van, 389, 395, 400
Dooren, Wim van, 359-61, 365-66
Dostal, Robert J., 279
Dove, Kenley R., 279, 284, 286, 290
Dubarle, Pierre-Louis, 364, 400, 408
Dudeck, Caroline, 283-84, 290
Dupré, Louis, 299, 313, 354, 363
Durán de Seade, Esperanza, 344, 349, 354
Düsing, Klaus, 289

445

Eley, Lothar, 283

Fabro, Cornelio, 276
Fackenheim, Emil C., 275-77, 290, 296, 304, 307, 309-10, 337-38, 340, 375, 377-78, 380-81, 384, 386, 388, 390-91, 393-94, 396-98, 400
Findlay, John N., 270, 273, 279-80, 282, 285-86, 288-89, 291-95, 297, 300, 304, 307, 309, 313, 319, 322, 324-25, 327-28, 331-32, 334-35, 337, 339, 344, 347-48, 351-52, 354, 357, 362-66, 371, 375, 377, 379, 382, 388-89, 392-93, 395, 397-99, 401, 403-05, 409-10
Fink, Eugen, 270-71, 277, 282-84, 291-92, 294, 296, 301-03, 306-07, 312, 315-16, 319-23, 325-29, 331-36, 338-39
Fink-Eitel, Hinrich, 278, 287, 410
Fischer, Kuno, 274
Flach, Werner, 276-77
Flay, Joseph C., 269, 271-72, 279, 290, 294, 296, 312, 361, 384, 393, 411
Foucault, Michel, 411
Fowkes, William, 393, 410
Franklin, Mitchell, 313, 358, 362, 365
Friedrich, Carl J., 349
Fulda, Hans Friedrich, 269, 275, 278, 287, 290

Gadamer, Hans-Georg, 279, 294-96, 299, 303, 306
Gallie, W. B., 372
Gamberoni, Paul, 361
Garaudy, Roger, 279, 290, 316, 348
Gauvin, Joseph, 313, 332, 357
Gazdar, Gerald, 280
Gedö, András, 271
Geraets, Theodore F., 279
Glockner, Hermann, 295, 329
Görland, I., 296, 303
Gouliane, C. I., 273
Govier, Trudy, 281
Gram, Moltke, 375, 381
Greene, Murray, 296-97, 303, 312, 316-17, 347
Grégoire, Franz, 277, 320-21, 351
Grimmlinger, Friedrich, 270, 279, 350, 386, 396, 402
Grlić, Danko, 369, 372
Gropp, Rugard Otto, 279
Guerrière, Daniel, 270
Gulian, C. I., 344

Habermas, Jürgen, 277, 282, 291, 322, 328, 368, 381, 411
Haering, Theodor, 272
Hager, Achim, 350-51, 400, 408
Harlander, Klaus, 269

Harris, H. S., 272, 336, 343, 346, 358, 363, 367, 375, 377, 389, 410
Hartkopf, Werner, 277, 279
Hartmann, Klaus, 350
Hartmann, Nicolai, 270, 272, 277, 279, 329, 331, 334, 337, 339, 344, 347, 350, 357, 362, 364-66, 375, 379, 382
Haym, Rudolf, 270
Hedwig, Klaus, 406
Heidegger, Martin, 269-71, 274-76, 279, 287, 291-96, 301-03, 316, 406
Heinrichs, Johannes, 269, 271, 279, 283, 285, 292, 294, 301, 303-05, 309-13, 315, 319-21, 324, 331-32, 334-36, 338-41, 344, 347-49, 351, 353-55, 357, 360-62, 364-65, 368, 372, 375-82, 386-87, 389, 391-95, 400, 407, 409
Heiss, Robert, 279
Henrich, Dieter, 272, 332-33, 335, 339
Herbenick, Raymond M., 327-28
Hilpelä, Jyrki, 279
Hirsch, Emanuel, 375, 379, 382
Hoffman, Pietr, 307
Hofmeister, Heimo E. M., 349, 377, 384
Hofstadter, Albert, 338, 340
Hook, Sidney, 286, 310, 338, 372
Horn, J. C., 272, 282, 291, 295, 408
Horowitz, Irving L., 369, 372-73
Hrachorec, Herbert, 284
Hudson, Jay William, 269, 274
Hülsmann, Heinz, 361
Hyppolite, Jean, 271, 273-74, 276, 280, 283, 289, 290, 292-98, 300-02, 304, 306-09, 311-13, 319-20, 322-23, 325-29, 331-39, 344-49, 351, 353-55, 357, 359-66, 368-69, 375-77, 379-83, 387-90, 392-95, 398, 400-02, 406, 409

Jähnig, Dieter, 364, 369, 400-02, 410
Janicaud, Dominique, 346-47, 351-52, 354, 392, 410
Jaspers, Karl, 411

Kaan, André, 335, 338
Kainz, Howard, 269, 280, 283, 293, 294-97, 302, 306, 319, 322, 325-28, 331-32, 334-35, 338-39, 341, 392
Kalin, Martin, 279
Kaminski, Winfried, 337
Kaufmann, Walter, 272, 277, 313
Kelly, George Armstrong, 304, 306
Kimmerle, Heinz, 269, 271-73, 275-76
Klein, Ansgar, 362
Klein, Ytasaq, 274, 278, 281, 286, 288-90, 395, 308
Kline, George, 302, 331

Index 447

Kojève, Alexandre, 271, 279, 289, 313, 317, 319, 321-22, 331, 335, 344, 347, 357-58, 360, 362, 365, 368, 375, 388-92, 396, 399, 401-02, 406-07
Kosok, Michael, 280
Koursanov, G. A., 271
Koyré, Alexandre, 271-72, 300, 406
Krieger, Evelina, 273, 278, 286, 402, 409
Kroner, Richard, 270, 272, 277, 287, 297, 309, 311, 330, 339-40, 344, 349, 357, 383, 389, 391, 393, 396
Krüger, Gerhard, 283, 285, 290, 330, 345
Krumpel, Heinz, 328, 347, 375
Kuderowicz, Zbigniew, 310
Kümmel, Friedrich, 270, 281, 295, 321, 324
Küng, Hans, 397
Kuspit, Donald, 270

Labarrière, Pierre-Jean, 270, 274-75, 280, 283-84, 292, 294-96, 298, 301, 303, 311, 319, 322, 334, 344, 346-47, 354, 357, 359, 362, 369, 375, 381, 389, 391-93, 398-99, 401, 406-08
LaCroix, W. L., 387
Ladreit de Lacharrière, René, 367, 369
Ladrière, Jean, 274, 345, 411
Lakebrink, Bernhard, 305, 406
Lamb, David, 278, 281, 286, 289
Lange, Erhard, 304, 308
Latouche, Serge, 410
Lauener, Henri, 305, 357, 362
Lauer, Quentin, 272-73, 277-78, 280, 283, 285, 289-91, 293-97, 301-04, 306-07, 309, 313, 319-20, 322, 325-26, 328-29, 331, 333-35, 337-39, 341, 344, 347-49, 353-55, 357, 359, 363-64, 369, 371, 375, 377-79, 381-82, 384, 389, 392-93, 395-97, 400-01, 403, 405
Lee, Otis, 270, 278, 292
Lefèbvre, Henri, 276, 381, 409
Lenk, Kurt, 364
Léonard, André, 272
Leopoldsberger, Jürgen, 269, 274, 277
Leske, Monika, 285, 351, 410
Lessing, Arthur, 312, 314, 316
Lewis, C. I., 411
Ley, Hermann, 335
Liebrucks, Bruno, 276, 287, 292, 309, 361, 379, 382, 407
Litt, Theodor, 287, 345, 349, 354
Lobkowicz, Nicholas, 270, 321, 350, 381
Loewenberg, J., 279, 285
Long, Eugene Thomas, 272
Löwith, Karl, 277, 285, 305, 359, 362, 386, 389
Ludz, Peter Christian, 364
Lugarini, Leo, 270

Lukács, Georg, 270, 276, 283, 304, 313, 331, 335, 357, 385, 389

MacIntyre, Alasdair, 327
Marcuse, Herbert, 272, 277, 288, 292, 298, 304, 313, 324, 371
Maritain, Jacques, 275
Marquard, Odo, 377
Marsh, James L., 334, 340
Marx, Werner, 270-71, 275, 277, 289-90, 376, 382, 410
Mayer, H., 304
McTaggart, J. Ellis, 405
Meist, Kurt, 269, 275
Mende, Georg, 367
Mercier-Josa, Solange, 301, 304, 308-09
Merlan, Philip, 279
Merleau-Ponty, Maurice, 271, 277, 329
Meulen, Jan van der, 287, 410
Meyer, M., 293
Miller, Mitchell, 270, 384, 396, 398-99, 403, 405
Min, Anselm, 380, 384, 387, 390
Mueller, Gustav E., 271, 279, 329, 340, 388
Müllges, Udo, 359
Muller, Philippe, 306, 312, 327
Munson, Thomas, 377, 407
Myers, Henry A., 274, 284, 411

Navickas, Joseph L., 271, 282, 285, 302, 316, 319, 321-22, 326-27, 329, 331-32, 334, 336, 339-40, 344, 347-48, 357-60, 362-63, 365, 369, 375-76, 385, 388-89
Niel, Henri, 271, 302-03, 306
Nusser, Karlheinz, 358, 360, 366, 368-73

Oisermann, T. I., 314, 329

Paci, Enzo, 271
Panova, Elena, 315
Pelzer, Roland, 377
Peperzak, Adrien, 377, 383
Perelman, Chaim, 279
Perkins, Robert, 270, 386, 393, 395
Pietercil, Raymond, 348, 350-51
Pippin, Robert B., 270, 278, 288, 297, 315, 380
Plamenatz, John, 344
Pöggeler, Otto, 269, 272, 289, 299, 303, 317, 319-20, 343-45, 347
Puder, Martin, 394
Puntel, L. Bruno, 271, 277, 280, 288
Purpus, Wilhelm, 283

Rasmussen, David M., 307
Rasmussen, Paul E., 405, 407

Reboul, Olivier, 298, 377, 379
Riedel, Manfred, 381
Riley, Patrick, 338
Ritchie, David George, 379
Ritter, Joachim, 340, 345, 367, 369-70, 372, 376-77, 385
Rivelaygue, J., 274, 279
Robinson, Jonathan, 343, 357, 375-76, 378, 380, 382-83
Roeder von Diersburg, Egenolf, 315
Rohrmoser, Günther, 308-09, 385, 388
Rosen, Stanley, 270, 276, 279, 282, 296, 300, 304-05, 310, 312-15, 323-24, 350, 357, 362-63, 366, 371-72, 387, 393, 400, 404
Rosenthal, Abigail, 281, 411
Rotenstreich, Nathan, 343
Royce, Josiah, 272, 277, 291, 300, 319, 323, 331, 333, 335-36, 350, 352, 371, 375, 388
Russew, Pantscho, 340, 383
Russo, Salvatore, 349-50

Sallis, John, 274-75, 278, 351
Schacht, Richard, 275
Schinkaruk, W. I., 291, 324
Schmitz, Hermann, 270, 279, 316, 332, 335, 337, 339-40, 400
Schmitz, Kenneth, 389
Schrader, George A., 306
Schrader-Klebert, Karin, 269, 273-74, 276, 278, 298, 320, 329, 341, 388
Schulz, Walter, 272
Schwemmer, Oswald, 279, 346, 376, 379, 410
Sciacca, M. F., 279
Secretan, Philibert, 307
Seebohm, Thomas, 280
Seidel, George, 282, 297, 315
Serreau, René, 271
Shapiro, Gary, 335
Shklar, Judith, 272, 274, 283, 289, 292, 300, 305, 317, 331, 333-35, 339, 343, 346-47, 366, 383, 385-86
Sichirollo, Livio, 347
Siep, Ludwig, 301, 303, 307-09
Sikora, R. I., 283
Simon, Josef, 350, 361
Smith, John E., 296
Sobotka, Milan, 292, 293-94, 297
Soll, Ivan, 270, 283, 285, 288, 300, 302, 307, 309
Solomon, Robert C., 274, 281, 286, 288-89, 292, 297, 304, 343
Souche-Dabues, D., 343

Staiger, E., 347
Stalnaker, Robert C., 280
Stambaugh, Joan, 403
Steinkraus, Warren E., 377
Stern, Alfred, 368, 371
Stiehler, Gottfried, 372
Surber, Jere Paul, 286, 346, 406
Suter, Jean-François, 367, 371
Szondi, P., 350

Taylor, Charles, 270, 278-79, 283-84, 288-89, 292-93, 300, 319, 324, 331, 335, 339-40, 343, 347, 351, 353-54, 357-58, 363-65, 369, 371-72, 375-78, 382, 387, 389-90, 393-94, 410
Theunissen, Michael, 282, 377-78, 393
Thierry, Yves, 270
Trivers, Howard, 406
Trotignon, P., 280
Tur, Richard H. S., 371
Turner, J. E., 330

Vancourt, Raymond, 375, 389
Van Riet, Georges, 274, 390, 393, 395-96
Ver Eecke, Wilfred, 305, 308, 333, 368, 370
Viellard Baron, Jean-Louis, 276, 400
Vuillemin, Jules, 301, 307

Waelhens, Alphonse de, 291, 411
Wagner, Falk, 379, 383, 386-87, 394
Wagner, Hans, 270
Wahl, Jean, 277, 311-12
Walsh, W. H., 271
Wandschneider, Dieter, 301
Weil, Eric, 279, 348, 368, 410
Werkmeister, W. H., 277, 296, 377
Werner, Hans-Joachim, 279
Westphal, Merold, 272-74, 277, 279, 283-84, 286, 288, 290-91, 294, 295, 297, 300, 307-08, 310, 320, 340, 343, 347-49, 353, 355, 357, 362, 371, 375, 381-82, 390, 392-93, 395-96, 398-99, 404
Wiehl, Reiner, 279, 283-84, 286
Wieland, W., 274-75, 278, 283, 287
Wilden, Anthony, 381
Wildt, Andreas, 304, 371
Williams, M. E., 405, 408
Wilson, Deidre, 280
Wolff, E., 347

Yerkes, James, 394
Yon, Ephrem-Dominique, 403